CW01212872

The Lancaster Manual

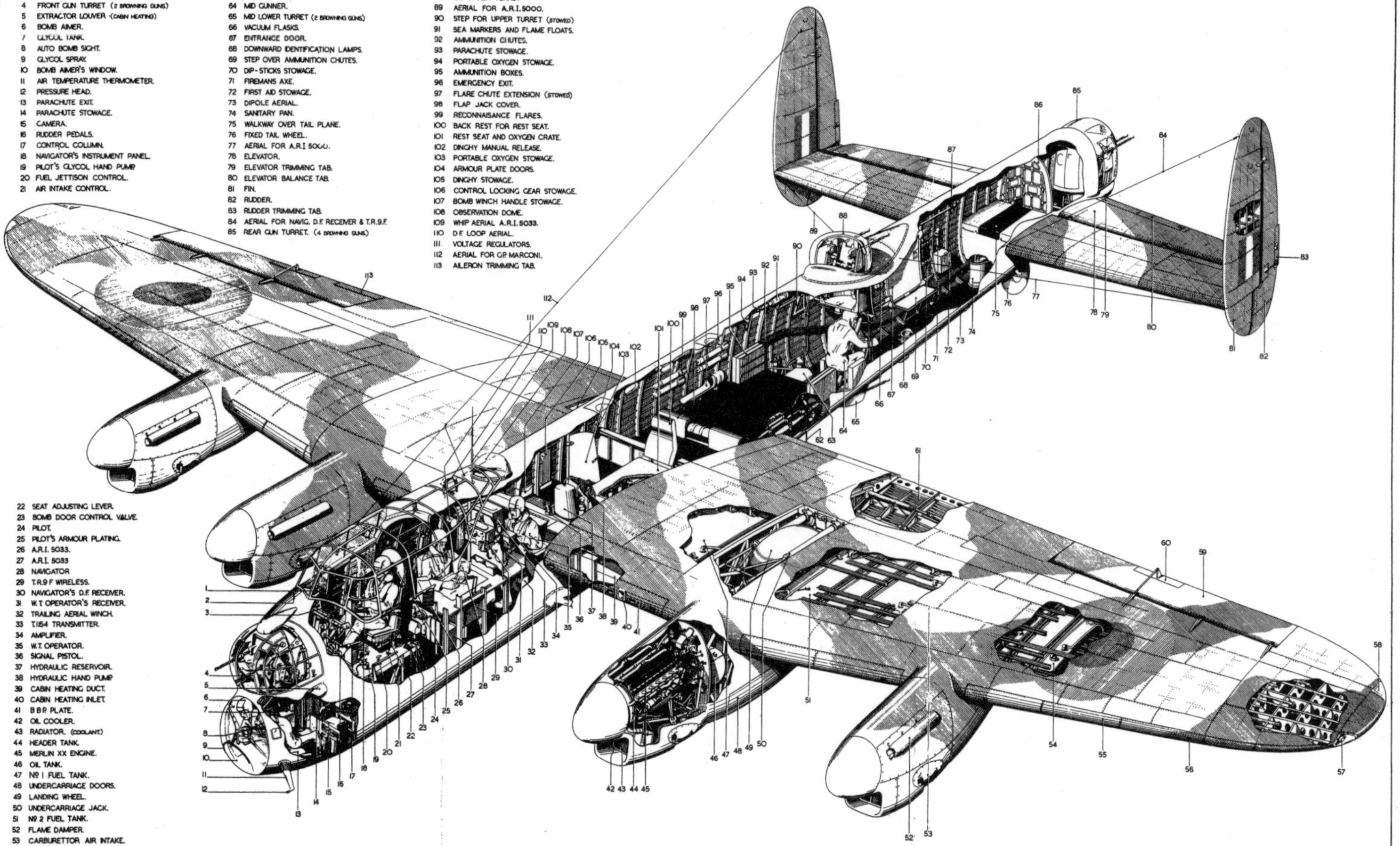

1 SECOND PILOT'S SEAT. (FOLDED)
2 WINDSCREEN GLYCOL SPRAY.
3 ENGINE CONTROL LEVERS.
4 FRONT GUN TURRET (2 BROWNING GUNS)
5 EXTRACTOR LOUVER (CABIN HEATING)
6 BOMB AIMER.
7 GLYCOL TANK.
8 AUTO BOMB SIGHT.
9 GLYCOL SPRAY.
10 BOMB AIMER'S WINDOW.
11 AIR TEMPERATURE THERMOMETER.
12 PRESSURE HEAD.
13 PARACHUTE EXIT.
14 PARACHUTE STOWAGE.
15 CAMERA.
16 RUDDER PEDALS.
17 CONTROL COLUMN.
18 NAVIGATOR'S INSTRUMENT PANEL.
19 PILOT'S GLYCOL HAND PUMP.
20 FUEL JETTISON CONTROL.
21 AIR INTAKE CONTROL.
22 SEAT ADJUSTING LEVER.
23 BOMB DOOR CONTROL VALVE.
24 PILOT.
25 PILOT'S ARMOUR PLATING.
26 A.R.I. 5033.
27 A.R.I. 5033
28 NAVIGATOR
29 T.R.9 F WIRELESS.
30 NAVIGATOR'S D.F. RECEIVER.
31 W.T. OPERATOR'S RECEIVER.
32 TRAILING AERIAL WINCH.
33 T.1154 TRANSMITTER.
34 AMPLIFIER.
35 W.T. OPERATOR.
36 SIGNAL PISTOL.
37 HYDRAULIC RESERVOIR.
38 HYDRAULIC HAND PUMP.
39 CABIN HEATING DUCT.
40 CABIN HEATING INLET.
41 B.B.P. PLATE.
42 OIL COOLER.
43 RADIATOR. (COOLANT)
44 HEADER TANK.
45 MERLIN XX ENGINE.
46 OIL TANK.
47 Nº 1 FUEL TANK.
48 UNDERCARRIAGE DOORS.
49 LANDING WHEEL.
50 UNDERCARRIAGE JACK.
51 Nº 2 FUEL TANK.
52 FLAME DAMPER.
53 CARBURETTOR AIR INTAKE.
54 Nº 3 FUEL TANK.
55 B.B.P. PLATE.
56 B.B. CABLE CUTTER.
57 NAVIGATION LAMP.
58 FORMATION KEEPING LAMPS.
59 AILERON.
60 AILERON BALANCE TAB.
61 FLAPS.
62 WHIP AERIAL (BEAM APPROACH)
63 FLARE CHUTE.
64 MID GUNNER.
65 MID LOWER TURRET (2 BROWNING GUNS)
66 VACUUM FLASKS.
67 ENTRANCE DOOR.
68 DOWNWARD IDENTIFICATION LAMPS.
69 STEP OVER AMMUNITION CHUTES.
70 DIP-STICKS STOWAGE.
71 FIREMANS AXE.
72 FIRST AID STOWAGE.
73 DIPOLE AERIAL.
74 SANITARY PAN.
75 WALKWAY OVER TAIL PLANE.
76 FIXED TAIL WHEEL.
77 AERIAL FOR A.R.I 5000.
78 ELEVATOR.
79 ELEVATOR TRIMMING TAB.
80 ELEVATOR BALANCE TAB.
81 FIN.
82 RUDDER.
83 RUDDER TRIMMING TAB.
84 AERIAL FOR NAVIG. D.F. RECEIVER & T.R.9.F.
85 REAR GUN TURRET. (4 BROWNING GUNS)
86 DRAUGHT PROOF DOORS.
87 ACCESS LADDER.
88 MID UPPER TURRET
89 AERIAL FOR A.R.I.5000.
90 STEP FOR UPPER TURRET (STOWED)
91 SEA MARKERS AND FLAME FLOATS.
92 AMMUNITION CHUTES.
93 PARACHUTE STOWAGE.
94 PORTABLE OXYGEN STOWAGE.
95 AMMUNITION BOXES.
96 EMERGENCY EXIT.
97 FLARE CHUTE EXTENSION (STOWED)
98 FLAP JACK COVER.
99 RECONNAISANCE FLARES.
100 BACK REST FOR REST SEAT.
101 REST SEAT AND OXYGEN CRATE.
102 DINGHY MANUAL RELEASE.
103 PORTABLE OXYGEN STOWAGE.
104 ARMOUR PLATE DOORS.
105 DINGHY STOWAGE.
106 CONTROL LOCKING GEAR STOWAGE.
107 BOMB WINCH HANDLE STOWAGE.
108 OBSERVATION DOME.
109 WHIP AERIAL A.R.I. 5033.
110 D.F. LOOP AERIAL.
111 VOLTAGE REGULATORS.
112 AERIAL FOR G.P. MARCONI.
113 AILERON TRIMMING TAB.

LANCASTER I AEROPLANE

The Lancaster Manual

The Official Air Publication for the Lancaster Mk I and III,
1942–1945

RAF MUSEUM SERIES

General Editor: Dr Michael A Fopp
Director General, RAF Museum, Hendon

Greenhill Books, London
Stackpole Books, Pennsylvania

This edition of *The Lancaster Manual* first published 2003 by
Greenhill Books
Lionel Leventhal Limited
Park House
1 Russell Gardens
London NW11 9NN
and
Stackpole Books
5067 Ritter Road, Mechanicsburg, PA 17055, USA

© Crown Copyright, 1942
Foreword and new photographs © Trustees of the RAF Museum, 2003
This edition © Lionel Leventhal Limited, 2003

The Lancaster Manual is Crown Copyright and published by permission of the Controller of Her Majesty's Stationary Office. The material contained in this publication originally appeared under the Air Publication reference 2062A & C Volume I entitled LANCASTER I AND III AIRCRAFT, MK. I FOUR MERLIN XX POWER PLANTS; MK. III FOUR MERLIN 28 OR 38 POWER PLANTS.

The original Air Publication was produced for official and internal purposes by the Air Ministry.

All rights reserved. No part of this publication may be reproduced, stored in a retrieval system, or transmitted in any form or by any means, electrical, mechanical or otherwise without first seeking the written permission of the publisher.

The quality of the illustrations in the original of this volume falls short of the high standard of reproduction normally expected in modern books; they have of necessity been reproduced to complete this facsimile edition.

British Library Cataloguing in Publication Data

The Lancaster manual: the official publication for the Lancaster Mk I and III, 1942–1945. – (RAF museum series)
1. Lancaster (Bombers) – Handbooks, manuals, etc.
623.7′463′0941′09045

Library of Congress Cataloging-in-Publication Data available
ISBN 1-85367-568-7

Printed and bound in Singapore by Kyodo

Contents

Section 1:	Leading particulars, Introduction, Pilot's controls and equipment	7
Section 2:	Pilots and flight engineer's notes	37
Section 3:	Controls and equipment at crew stations	89
Section 4:	Instructions for ground personnel	101
Section 5:	Removal and assembly operations	245
Section 6:	Electrical and radio installation – Maintenance	283
Section 7:	Design and construction of airframe	399
Section 8:	Engine installation	463
Section 9:	Hydraulic and pneumatic systems	489
Section 10:	Electrical and radio installations – Description	499
Section 11:	Armament and general equipment	513

Foreword

By Dr Michael A Fopp MA PhD FMA FRAeS
Director General, Royal Air Force Museum, Hendon

Arguably one of the most famous bomber aircraft of all time, the Avro Lancaster and its crews played a decisive role in the Second World War.

It is often stated that the Lancaster was developed as a consequence of the failure of the twin-engined Avro Manchester, but in fact proposals for a four-engined Manchester were being made in late 1938 – several months before the first flight of the twin-engined design. The first prototype flew on 9 January 1941 and the Lancaster entered service with No. 44 (Rhodesia) Squadron at Waddington in December that year. Over the next 3 years Lancasters carried out some 156,000 sorties and dropped over 608,000 tons of bombs. By the end of the war Lancasters equipped 57 of Bomber Command's 97 squadrons and no less than ten of the thirty Victoria Crosses awarded to the RAF were for actions in Lancasters.

Lancasters were being prepared to take part in the Far East war as part of the RAF's Tiger Force but the atomic bomb attacks brought a sudden end to hostilities. Bomber Command reduced in size and the new Avro Lincoln began to replace the Lancaster in late 1945. Lancasters took on new roles – photographic reconnaissance and maritime patrol, serving in the Middle East and the Mediterranean – and the RAF's last Lancaster was retired on 15 October 1956, although PA474 continues to fly in Europe with the Battle of Britain Memorial Flight and FM213 in North America with the Canadian Warplane Heritage.

The Museum's Lancaster, R5868, had a remarkable career, completing some 137 operations – although confused entries in some records suggest that the actual total may be 127 – against targets as far-flung as Danzig, Hamburg, Essen, Genoa, Bordeaux and Munich, including 10 attacks on Berlin – "The Big City" as the bomber crews used to call it. Only one other Lancaster completed more sorties. Built by Metropolitan-Vickers in Manchester in 1942, R5868 was delivered to No. 83 Squadron at Scampton on 29th June and became "Q – Queenie". Her first operational sortie was a raid on Wilhelmshaven on the night of 8/9 July, flown by Squadron Leader R L Hilton, 83's B Flight Commander. By mid-August 1942 she had completed 13 sorties and sustained flak damage on a couple of occasions. 83 Squadron became part of the new Path Finder Force, moving to RAF Wyton on 15th August, and three days later R5868 took part in the PFF's first operation – against Flensburg, although haze over the target prevented the crew dropping their load of flares. Over the course of the next year she flew another 54 raids with a variety of crews, attacking targets in Germany, Italy and France.

In September 1943, having completed some 450 flying hours, R5868 was transferred to No. 467 Squadron based at Bottesford, Leicestershire and became "S – Sugar". The kneeling nude figure painted on her nose was replaced by a red devil, thumbing its nose and dancing in flames with the motto 'Devils of the air'. During a raid on Berlin on 26th/27th November "Sugar" was coned by searchlights, and during evasive action hit another Lancaster. The aircraft went into a dive to port, but the pilot Flying Officer Jack Colpus, was able to recover and brought her back to a safe landing in Yorkshire. Repairs included the fitting of a new port outer wing, since about 5 feet had been lost in the collision, and it was to be three months before the aircraft was again ready for operations. Her third operation after returning to service was aborted due to engine problems – her first 'early return' in 85 sorties. Further engine problems occurred in March and the aircraft was overhauled. The red devil was replaced by Goering's statement that "No enemy plane will fly over the Reich territory" and her 100th raid (on Bourg Leopold in Belgium) was celebrated on 12 May 1944.

After supporting the invasion of Normandy and attacking V-1 sites "Sugar" went back to Avro for repairs – increasing numbers of rivets had failed in the wings and the opportunity was also taken to fit new engines, H2S radar and the Rebecca navigation aid. Returning to 467 Squadron in December she continued bombing, making her last operational flight on 23rd April 1945, although thick cloud over the target prevented bombs being dropped. Two days later she made her first flight as part of operation *Exodus* – bringing British Prisoners of War back from Europe. Several more *Exodus* flights were made during April and May. On 16th June 1945 the squadron moved to Metheringham, Lincolnshire to prepare for service with Tiger Force against Japan, but the war ended two months later.

R5868 was transferred to No. 15 Maintenance Unit at Wroughton on 23rd August 1945, for use as an exhibition aircraft. Declared "non-effective" in August 1947, she was transferred to the Air Historical Branch's aircraft collection at Wroughton, moving to Fulbeck for storage in 1958. In April 1959 the Lancaster was moved to her former base at Scampton and was displayed there, initially at the presentation of a standard to No 617 Squadron, and the following year at the station's main gate. At that time she still wore her 467 Squadron markings, but when 83 Squadron returned to Scampton in 1960 her original codes OL-Q were restored.

The RAF Museum was originally allocated Lancaster PA474, which was loaned to 44 Squadron at Waddington by the Ministry of Defence and made airworthy. When the time came for that aircraft to be returned to the Museum and prepared for display at Hendon, R5868 was offered in its place. R5868 was refurbished at RAF Bicester, with work being carried out to combat extensive corrosion in the wings. The move to Hendon was carried out in March 1972, with the aircraft being painted after assembly. Ten years later the Lancaster was moved into the newly constructed Bomber Command Hall where it dominates the entrance – a place of honour for a very special aeroplane.

Section 1:
Leading particulars. Introduction. Pilot's controls and equipment.

*This page amended by A.L. No. 2
March, 1942*
*This page amended by A.L. No. 23
April, 1943*

A.P.2062A & C, Vol. I

LEADING PARTICULARS

Name...	Lancaster I and III
Type ...	Four engine, mid-wing monoplane
Duty ...	Heavy bomber and troop carrier

PRINCIPAL DIMENSIONS

Complete aircraft

Span ...	102 ft. 0 in.
Length, tail up	69 ft. 6 in.
Length, tail down	68 ft. 10 in.
Height, tail up, to top of fins	20 ft. 6 in.
Height, tail down, to top of whip aerial ...	20 ft. 4 in.

Main plane

Aerofoil section, root	N.A.C.A.23018
Chord, at root	16 ft. 0 in.
Chord, at wing tip joint (43 ft. 2·6 in. from centre-line of fuselage)	9 ft. 2·43 in.
Incidence	4°
Dihedral, outer plane, on datum ...	7°
Dihedral, outer plane, on top of rear spar	5° 19′
Aileron span (actual length)	17 ft. 3½ in.
Aileron mean chord...	2 ft. 6 in.

Tail plane

Span ...	33 ft. 0 in.
Mean chord (including elevator) ...	7 ft. 0 in.
Incidence	2° 30′

AREAS

Main plane, including ailerons (gross) ...	1,300·0 sq. ft.
Main plane, including ailerons (net)	1,205·0 sq. ft.
Ailerons, total, including tabs	85·5 sq. ft.
Trimming tabs (two)	1·4 sq. ft.
Balance tabs (two)	2·2 sq. ft.
Flaps, total ...	146·0 sq. ft.
Tail plane, including elevators and tabs ...	237·0 sq. ft.
Elevators, total including tabs	87·5 sq. ft.
Trimming tabs (two)	2·9 sq. ft.
Balance tabs (two)	4·2 sq. ft.
Fins and rudders, total, including tabs	111·4 sq. ft.
Rudders, with tabs	41·2 sq. ft.
Trimming tabs (two)	2·2 sq. ft.

F.S./1

This page amended by A.L. No. 15
July, 1942
This page amended by A.L. No. 23
April, 1943

CONTROL SURFACES—SETTINGS AND RANGES OF MOVEMENT
(Linear dimensions measured on chord of arc of trailing edge)

Ailerons	Up 16°; down 16°
Trimming tabs...	Up 19°; down 19°
Elevators	Up 28°; down 14¾°
Trimming tabs...	Up 6°; down 6°
Trimming tabs linear travel	0·58 in. up and down
Rudders	Inwards 22¾°; outwards 22¼°
Trimming tab	Inwards 22°; outwards 22°
Trimming tab linear travel	1 29/32 in. inwards and outwards
Flaps...	Down 56½°

UNDERCARRIAGE
Main wheel units

Type	Two retractable, single wheel units with twin shock-absorber struts
Track...	23 ft. 9 in.
Shock-absorber struts	Dowty oleo-pneumatic
Air pressure (no load)...	995 lb./sq. in.
Wheels	Dunlop AH.2238 (17·5 in. × 19 in.)
Tyres	Dunlop SK.A.641 (24 in. × 19 in.)
Tyre pressure	43 lb./sq. in.
Brakes	Dunlop pneumatic AH.8039
Working pressure	80 lb./sq. in.

Tail wheel unit

Type	Non-retractable, castoring
Shock-absorber strut	Dowty oleo-pneumatic
Air pressure (no load)...	600–650 lb./sq. in.
Wheel	Dunlop AH.8013 or SK.A.887 (10 in. × 10 in.)
Tyre	Dunlop NX.30 (12·5 in. × 10 in.)
Tyre pressure	54 lb./sq. in.

HYDRAULIC SYSTEM

Fluid	Specification D.T.D.44C Stores Ref. 34A/43–46)
Pressure at which automatic cut-out operates	800 lb./sq. in.
Accumulator inflation pressure	220 lb./sq. in.

ENGINES

Name...	Merlin **XX** (Lancaster I) Merlin **28** or **38** (Lancaster III)
Type	12-cylinder, 60° V-type pressure cooled, two-speed supercharged

This page amended by A.L. No. 20 February, 1943
This page amended by A.L. No. 23 April, 1943

A.P.2062A & C, Vol. I, Leading Particulars

Number	Four
Fuel	See A.P.1464/C.37.W
Oil	See A.P.1464/C.37.W
Coolant	30% ethylene-glycol (D.T.D.344A Stores Ref. 33C/559) and 70% distilled water.

Oil dilution system—

Valve ref.	5U/1567
Voltage	24
Jet ref.	5U/1561
Size of jet	0·089 in. dia.
Fuel pumps	Pulsometer, type FB. Mk. I

Note.—Aircraft not incorporating Mod. No. 539 are fitted with immersed fuel pumps:
Type EP1. Mk. II–17 (No. 1 tanks)
EP1. Mk. II–29 (No. 2 tanks)
EP1. Mk. II– 1 (No. 3 tanks)

PROPELLERS

	(i)	(ii)
Type	de Havilland type No. 5140, variable pitch, hydromatic	Nash Kelvinator type No. A5/138, variable pitch, hydromatic
Control	Constant-speed and feathering	Constant-speed and feathering
Pitch settings	Fine pitch 25° Feathered pitch ... 90°	... ... 22° ... ... 89°
Direction of rotation	Right-hand tractor	Right-hand tractor

TANK CAPACITIES

Main fuel tanks (three port and three starboard)—

No. 1 tanks	580 gals. each
No. 2 tanks	383 gals. each
No. 3 tanks	114 gals. each
Total fuel, port or starboard ...	1,077 gals.
Total fuel in main tanks ...	2,154 gals.

F.S./2

This page amended by A.L. No. 20
February, 1943
This page amended by A.L. No. 23
April, 1943

Overload tanks in bomb cell (one or two may be installed) ... ... 400 gals. each
Oil tanks (two port and two starboard)—
Inboard tanks { oil... ... ... $37\frac{1}{2}$ gals. each
              { air space ... ... $4\frac{1}{2}$ gals each
Outboard tanks { oil... ... ... $37\frac{1}{2}$ gals. each
               { air space ... ... $4\frac{1}{2}$ gals. each

Total oil ... ... 150 gals.

Note.—Aircraft L.7527 to L.7532 inclusive are fitted with four fuel tanks only (two port and two starboard) with the following capacities:—
No. 1 tanks ... ... 580 gals. each
No. 2 tanks ... ... 275 gals. each

Total fuel, port or starboard ... 855 gals.
Total fuel in main tanks ... 1,710 gals.

AIRSPEED INDICATOR PRESSURE HEAD

Position ... ... Port side of fuselage nose
Incidence (in flying position) ... ... 0°
Distance from centre-line of aircraft ... 2 ft. 7·4 in.

This Revised Introduction issued with A.L. No. 23
(Superseding Introduction issued December, 1941)
April, 1943

AIR PUBLICATION 2062A & C
Volume I

INTRODUCTION

1. The Lancaster I and III are all metal mid-wing monoplanes, the former having four Merlin XX and the latter four Merlin 28 or 38 power plants; both have variable-pitch constant-speed propellers. Mk. I and Mk. III aircraft differ only in respect of the power plants and associated services and controls. They are designed and equipped for heavy bomber or troop carrier duties, normally carrying a crew of seven consisting of captain, second pilot, air observer (navigator-air-bomber), two wireless operator-air gunners and two air gunners.

2. The fuselage is constructed of light-alloy and incorporates transverse formers braced with longitudinal stringers, covered with a light-alloy skin. Two longerons carry the cross members of the main floor in which the bomb gear is housed. To facilitate transport the fuselage is divided into four portions, viz.: the front portion, comprising the nose and front centre portions, the intermediate centre portion consisting of the fuselage between the spars and the centre section of the main plane, the rear centre portion, and the rear fuselage which carries the tail unit.

3. The main plane is of the two spar type and consists of two outer planes attached to a centre section which is integral with the fuselage. The outer planes are tapered in plan and elevation and the skin covering is of light-alloy sheet with the exception of the ailerons, which are fabric covered. The leading edge is reinforced for balloon barrage protection, and is fitted with cable cutters. Six fuel tanks are housed in the main plane, one in the centre section on each side of the fuselage, and two in each outer plane. The main wheel units are housed in the inboard engine nacelles at the outer ends of the centre section. The tail plane is of similar construction to the main plane and has fabric-covered elevators and twin metal-covered fins and rudders.

4. The entrance door is on the starboard side of the fuselage just forward of the tail plane. The door opens inwards and an entrance ladder, stowed inside the fuselage above the door, is hooked to the bottom of the door frame when the door is in use.

5. The flying controls are conventional, pendulum type rudder pedals operating the rudders, and a handwheel type control column operating the ailerons and elevators. Tubular push-pull connections are used except for the aileron controls in the fuselage, which consist of chains, tie-rods and cables. Trimming tabs are inset in the trailing edges of the rudders, elevators, and ailerons, and balance tabs are fitted to the elevators and ailerons. Mark IV automatic controls are employed. Hydraulically-operated split-trailing edge flaps extend from the fuselage sides to the ailerons.

6. The undercarriage consists of two retractable main wheel units, one under each inboard engine nacelle, and a fully castoring tail wheel unit which is not retractable. Each main wheel unit is retracted backwards and upwards into the engine nacelle by means of two hydraulic jacks. When retracted the

F.S./1

B (AL23)

units are completely faired in by doors which are interconnected to the shock-absorber struts and automatically closed when the wheel retracts. A compressed air system is installed for lowering the main wheels in an emergency.

7. The four engines, which are equipped with two-speed superchargers, are mounted on nacelle structures built out from the centre and outer plane spars. Fuel is normally supplied to the port and starboard engines from the port and starboard tanks respectively, but when required, the four engines may be fed from one side by means of a balance cock system. The oil tanks are mounted in the engine nacelles behind the fireproof bulkheads. The engines are pressure-cooled and are fitted with constant-speed propellers. The coolant radiator is mounted in a duct underneath the engine and is fitted with a thermostatically-controlled shutter. The outboard engines are protected by armour plate fitted to the bottom of the fireproof bulkhead and to the bottom of the nacelle front former. A single pump mounted on each inboard engine supplies power for the hydraulic operation of the retractable undercarriage units, main plane flaps, bomb door jacks, carburettor air intakes and fuel jettisoning. A single pump mounted on each engine supplies the power for each turret, i.e. front, mid-upper mid-lower and rear. An R.A.E. compressor mounted on the port inboard engine, working at low pressure, operates the automatic controls and a Heywood compressor on the starboard inboard engine, working at high pressure, operates the pneumatic brake and radiator shutter system, and on the Mk. III, the slow-running cut-outs also. Vacuum pumps are mounted on each inboard engine and operate the gyroscopic instruments on the instrument-flying panel. The engines are started electrically from ground accumulators or from the aircraft's own accumulator, and hand-turning gear is provided for maintenance purposes only.

8. The gun armament consists of ·303 in. Browning guns in hydraulically operated turrets, two in the nose turret, two in the mid-upper turret, two in the mid-lower turret and four in the rear turret. Various bomb loads may be carried in the bomb compartment in the lower portion of the fuselage; these include small-bomb containers, mines and bombs from 250 lb. to 4,000 lb. each. The bomb doors, which are hydraulically controlled, must be opened before the bombs can be released.

9. A 24-volt electrical installation is provided, the power being supplied from two 1,500 watt generators, one on each inboard engine. These generators work in conjunction with four 12-volt, 40-Ah. accumulators, interconnected to give a 24-volt, 80-Ah. supply to operate all the services. An electrical services panel and an auxiliary fuse panel on the starboard side of the fuselage just forward of the front spar carry the fuses and charging instruments. The radio equipment consists of a T.R.9F or T.R.1196 set remotely controlled by the pilot, a T.R.1335 set at the navigator's station, and a T.1154–R.1155 set at the wireless operator's station. Beam approach, R.3003 or R.3090, and T.3135/R.3136 equipment is also installed.

10. Hand operated de-icing equipment is installed for the air-bomber's window and the pilot's windscreen.

This Revised Section issued with A.L. No. 23 **AIR PUBLICATION 2062A & C**
(Superseding Section 1 issued with A.L. No. 3) **Volume I**
April, 1943

SECTION 1—CONTROLS AND EQUIPMENT FOR PILOT
AND
GENERAL EMERGENCY EXITS AND EQUIPMENT

LIST OF CONTENTS

	Para.
INTRODUCTION	1
MAIN SERVICES—	
Fuel system	2
Hydraulic system	3
Pneumatic system	4
Electrical system	5
AIRCRAFT CONTROLS—	
Control column and rudder bar	6
Flying control locking gear	7
Automatic controls	8
Suction pump change-over cock	9
Trimming tabs	10
Undercarriage control	11
Undercarriage indicator	12
Flaps control	13
Hydraulic hand pump	14
Emergency operation of main wheel units and flaps	15
Main wheel units safety links	16
Brakes	17
ENGINE CONTROLS—	
Throttle and mixture controls	18
Automatic boost cut-out	19
Propeller controls and feathering switches	20
Two-speed supercharger control	21
Carburettor air intake control	22
Radiator shutters	23
Fuel cock controls	24
Slow-running cut-outs	25
Electric fuel pumps	26
Ignition switches	27
Engine starting	28
Electrical master change-over switch	29
Generator switches	30
Oil dilution system	31
Engine instruments	32
COCKPIT ACCOMMODATION AND EQUIPMENT—	
Seating	33
Entrance door	34
Direct vision window	35
Cockpit heating	36
Oxygen	37

F.S./1

OPERATIONAL EQUIPMENT AND CONTROLS—

	Para.
Camera	38
Glider release	39
Bomb door control	40
Bomb release button	41
Flares	42
Sea marking equipment	43

NAVIGATIONAL, SIGNALLING AND LIGHTING EQUIPMENT—

T.R.9F or T.R.1196	44
Intercommunication	45
Beam approach installation	46
D.F. loop aerial	47
Signal pistol	48
Navigation, identification and recognition lamps	49
Landing lamp control	50

DE-ICING CONTROLS—

Windscreen de-icing control	51
Pressure head heater switch	52

EMERGENCY EQUIPMENT AND CONTROLS—

General	53
Fire extinguishers	54
Parachute and crash exits	55
Dinghy	56
Crash axe and first-aid outfit	57
Fuel jettisoning	58
Bomb jettisoning	59
R.3003 controls	60

LIST OF ILLUSTRATIONS

	Fig.
Instrument panel	1
Lower portion of cockpit	2
Port side of cockpit	3
Air observer's panel	4
General emergency equipment and exits	5
Locking of flying controls	6
Simplified fuel system diagram, E.P.I. pumps	7
Simplified fuel system diagram, Pulsometer pumps	8

SECTION 1—CONTROLS AND EQUIPMENT FOR PILOT
AND
GENERAL EMERGENCY EXITS AND EQUIPMENT

Note.—This Section covers the controls and equipment in the pilot's cockpit and equipment elsewhere in the aircraft, with which the pilot should be acquainted. The layout of the various items is illustrated and annotated in figs. 1 to 4 at the end of the section, each item being given an individual number. Where an item appears in more than one illustration the same reference number is used in each instance.

INTRODUCTION

1. The Lancaster I and III are heavy bombers, the former having four Merlin XX and the latter four Merlin 28 or 38 power plants; both have de Havilland or Nash Kelvinator fully-feathering propellers.

MAIN SERVICES

2. *Fuel system—*
   (i) Three self-sealing tanks are fitted in each wing, numbered 1, 2 and 3 outboard from the fuselage, and of the following capacities:—

Port and starboard No. 1 :	580 gals. each
Port and starboard No. 2 :	383 gals. each
Port and starboard No. 3 :	114 gals. each
	1,077 gals. each side
or	2,154 gals. in all.

   Provision is made on some aircraft for carrying one or two 400 gallon tanks fitted in the bomb cells; these tanks are connected so that their contents may be transferred into either or both No. 1 wing tanks and thence to the engines. When the maximum bomb load is carried, the No. 2 tanks should be filled first, and the remainder of the fuel put in No. 1 tanks.
   Note.—In a few early aircraft two tanks only are fitted in each wing as follows:—

2 inner tanks at 580 gals.	1,160 gals.
2 outer tanks at 275 gals.	550 gals.
Total	1,710 gals.

   (ii) *Fuel system variations between Mk. I and Mk. III aircraft.*—The Merlin 28 or 38 engines of Mk. III aircraft have Stromberg injection-type carburettors fitted with a vapour vent system and electro-pneumatically-operated slow-running cut-out controls, and the fuel pressure at which the warning lamps operate is raised from $+6$ to $+10$ lb./sq. in. Except as required by the starting instructions, it is most important with this carburettor *never* to switch on the fuel tank electric pumps when the master cock is open and the engine stationary,

F.S./1

unless the slow-running cut-off switch is in the IDLE CUT OFF (down) position and the air supply pressure not less than 120 lb./sq. in., otherwise fuel would be sprayed into the supercharger. The carburettor must remain full when the engine is stopped, or much difficulty will be experienced in starting again. The master engine fuel cock must, therefore, remain open until the engine has been stopped by moving the slow-running cut-out switch to the IDLE CUT OFF position.

(iii) The fuel systems in each plane, for port and starboard engines, are identical and entirely independent, but are interconnected by a cross-feed pipe and cock. This cock is normally kept shut. Two tank selector cocks are situated on the observer's panel, but the pilot has the four engine master cocks under his control. (For details of fuel cock controls, *see* para. 24.)

(iv) *Electric fuel pumps.*—Originally immersed pumps were fitted in all tanks; Mod. 594 (temporary) removed the immersed pumps from No. 1 tanks and fitted stack pipes in their places. This Mod. was later replaced by Mod. 512 which replaced the immersed pumps in No. 1 tanks and incorporated a suction by-pass at No. 1 and No. 2 tanks to allow fuel to be drawn from the tanks when the pumps are not in use. No. 3 tank (*see* fuel system diagram, fig. 7) is used to replenish No. 2 tank by switching on No. 3 tank pump. In aircraft incorporating Mod. No. 539 all the immersed pumps are replaced by Pulsometer Mk. I pumps which also have a suction by-pass at No. 1 and No. 2 tanks to allow fuel to be drawn from the tanks when the pumps are not in use. When the 400-gallon tanks are fitted in the bomb cells they each have a Pulsometer Mk. I pump fitted to enable their contents to be transferred to the No. 1 tanks.

(v) *Use of electric fuel pumps.*—The main use of the electric fuel pumps in No. 1 and 2 tanks is to maintain fuel pressure at altitudes of approximately 17,000 ft. and over in temperate climates, but they are also used for priming the carburettors before starting the engines, and at take-off the pumps in the tanks being used should be switched on (but *see* Para. 2 (ii)). This is a precaution against fuel shortage during take-off and is necessary also because if one engine fails during take-off and the electric fuel pump is not on, air may be drawn back into the main fuel system before the master engine cock of the failed engine can be closed, thus causing the failure of the other engine on the same side. (In an emergency, of course, it is permitted to take off without the pumps being switched on, but in this case if an engine fails during take-off, its master fuel cock must be turned off immediately.) The pumps should also be switched on at any time when failure of the fuel pressure is indicated by the warning lamps; and when an emergency renders it necessary to run all engines from one tank, by opening the cross feed cock, the pump for this tank should be switched on. (*See* Pilot's Notes for management of the fuel system.)

3. *Hydraulic system—*
  (i) Four pumps, one on each engine, supply the gun turrets.

Pump on:	*Operates turret*:
Starboard outer engine	Upper mid.
Starboard inner engine	Front
Port inner engine	Lower mid.
Port outer engine	Rear

A.P.2062A & C, Vol. I, Sect. 1

(ii) Two pumps are fitted (one on each inboard engine) and feed the following services:—

  Main wheel units Carburettor air intake shutters
  Flaps Fuel jettisoning
  Bomb doors

4. *Pneumatic system.*—Two compressors are fitted, one on each inboard engine, and feed the following services by means of the air container which is behind the front turret:—

  Wheel brakes Two-speed superchargers (Mod. No. 465)
  Radiator shutters Slow-running cut-outs (Mk. III only)

5. *Electrical system.*—One 24-volt, 1,000-watt generator is fitted on each of the inboard engines. These generators are connected in parallel and feed the following services:—

  Charging accumulators Radio equipment
  Propeller feathering Landing lamps control
  Flap and main wheel Engine starting
   indicators Dinghy inflation
  Pressure head heating All the usual lighting and other services
  Immersed fuel pumps

 Note.—On later aircraft the power of these generators is increased to 1,500 watt each.

AIRCRAFT CONTROLS

6. *Control column and rudder bar.*—The handwheel control column is conventional in operation. A bomb-release button (36) is incorporated on the handwheel. The rudders are operated by pendulum pedals (28). Each footrest is independently adjustable by lifting it up and moving it over the spring-loaded ratchet mechanism provided on each arm of the pedal.

7. *Flying control locking gear.*—This gear (*see* fig. 6) is stowed on the starboard side of the fuselage just aft of the wireless operator's seat and consists of:—

(i) A strut fastened to the top of the pilot's seat and to a bracket on the control column.

(ii) A strut inserted at one end into the port cockpit rail, and fitted by two screwed hooks to prevent it rotating.

(iii) A T-tube with the transverse member inserted in the hollow footrest of each rudder pedal and the other end attached to the bracket on the control column.

8. *Automatic control.*—Mk. IV automatic controls are fitted, the master switch (64) being on the pilot's auxiliary panel. For operation, *see* A.P.2095/16.

9. *Suction pump change-over cock.*—A suction pump is mounted on each inboard engine, and the change-over cock (15) is on the right side of the instrument panel.

F.S./2

10. *Trimming tabs.*—The aileron (52), elevator (53) and rudder (56) trimming tabs are controlled by handwheels on the right of the pilot's seat; these wheels operate in the natural sense. Indicators are provided beside the handwheels to show the position of the tabs.

11. *Undercarriage control.*—The lever (54) controlling the hydraulic operation of the undercarriage is on the right of the pilot's seat aft of the trimming tabs mechanism and has two positions only. To retract the undercarriage the lever is pulled up. A spring-loaded safety bolt (55) must be held aside before the lever can be raised, but automatically engages when the undercarriage is lowered. A warning horn is also provided, but only works in conjunction with the throttle levers of the inboard engines. The tail wheel unit is fixed.

12. *Undercarriage indicator.*—This instrument (37) is mounted on the left-hand side of the instrument panel and operates as follows:—

    Locked DOWN   ...   ...   two green lights
    Unlocked   ...   ...   two red lights
    Locked UP   ...   ...   no lights

The lights can be dimmed for night use by rotating the knob at the centre of the indicator. A change-over switch is provided below the indicator switch (4) to bring into operation an auxiliary set of green lamps in the event of failure of the primary set. An additional set of red lamps is wired in parallel and light with the primary set. The indicator switch is fitted beside the main ignition switches; a bar attached to the switch knob prevents the ignition being switched ON until the indicator is switched ON.

13. *Flaps control.*—The push-pull handle (51) controlling the hydraulic operation of the flaps is also on the right of the pilot's seat in front of the tab controls. To lower the flaps, the handle is pushed down until the indicator (38) on the left side of the instrument panel shows the required setting, when the handle should be returned to the neutral position, which is indicated by a spring-loaded catch. The flaps are raised by pulling the handle up; the handle should afterwards be returned to the neutral position. The flaps indicator is controlled by a switch (39) mounted immediately above it.

14. *Hydraulic hand pump.*—In the event of failure of the engine-driven hydraulic pumps, the hydraulic system can be operated by means of a hand pump situated on the port side of the fuselage, just aft of the front spar.

15. *Emergency operation of main wheel units and flaps.*—If the hydraulic system fails, the undercarriage and flaps can be lowered by compressed air. The control consists either of a cock just aft of the front spar on the starboard side, or of a knob just forward of the air observer's instrument panel. When the emergency control is operated the undercarriage is lowered irrespective of the position of the normal control lever, and compressed air is admitted to the flaps control valve. <u>After</u> the undercarriage is lowered, the flaps may be lowered by operating the flaps control, which admits the air pressure to the flap jack. The flaps can be raised again, but this should only be done in extreme emergency, as there may not be sufficient air pressure to lower them again; also in raising the flaps by this method, <u>extreme care must be taken to raise them slowly, by stages.</u>

16. *Main wheel units safety links.*—Two red-coloured jury **struts are provided** for fixing into the main wheel units frames when the aircraft is on the ground. These struts prevent the wheels from being accidentally retracted.

A.P.2062A & C, Vol. I, Sect. 1

17. *Brakes.*—The pneumatic brakes lever with parking catch is on the pilot's handwheel. Differential control is provided by the rudder pedals, and a triple pressure gauge (20) is fitted on the right side of the instrument panel.

ENGINE CONTROLS

18. *Throttle and mixture controls.*—There are four throttle levers (26) and, in Mk. I aircraft not incorporating Mod. No. 630, a single mixture control (25) mounted in the centre of the cockpit below the instrument panel. There is an interlocking arrangement between the throttles and mixture lever whereby the latter, if in WEAK, is automatically returned to NORMAL if the throttles are closed. A friction adjuster (49) is fitted on the side of the quadrant.

19. *Automatic boost cut-out.*—This lever (29) is on the extreme left of the control quadrant, and is pulled down to operate the control. The lever is locked in either position by a spring catch.

20. *Propeller controls and feathering switches.*—Four propeller speed control levers (27) are fitted below the throttles. To increase the engine speed the levers are moved upward. Four push-buttons (17) on the right side of the pilot's instrument panel are used for feathering the propellers. To feather a propeller the appropriate button should be pressed and finger removed; the switch will return to normal after the propeller has feathered. To unfeather the propeller the knob on the panel should be pressed and held until the propeller rotates at 1,500 r.p.m.

21. *Two-speed supercharger control.*—In aircraft incorporating Mod. No. 465 the superchargers are controlled by electro-pneumatic rams which are operated by a double switch, near the centre of the instrument panel. A warning lamp shows if the switch is moved to the F.S. (down) position when the main wheels are lowered. On aircraft retaining the manual control the lever is on the right side of the starboard master fuel cocks. With the lever in the UP position FULL (S) gear is engaged.

22. *Carburettor air intake control.*—These shutters are hydraulically operated. On early aircraft the control lever is mounted on the floor below the navigator's table and behind the radio set. On later aircraft the control is brought forward and upward to the port side of the pilot's floor. The positions of the control lever are:—

AFT for COLD air
FORWARD for HOT air

23. *Radiator shutters.*—These are pneumatically operated, the control being entirely automatic, by means of an electrical thermostat.

24. *Fuel cock controls.*—The pilot controls the four master cocks from levers (23) on either side of the control pedestal. The controls (83) for the tank selector cocks are situated at the observer's panel, and the cross-feed cock is mounted on the floor just forward of the front spar, with the control handle visible through the front spar cover. When the 400-gallon tanks are fitted in the bomb cells they each have an ON–OFF cock situated behind the front spar in the middle of the fuselage.

F.S./3

20

25. *Slow-running cut-outs—*
  (i) *Mk. I aircraft.*—These are interconnected with the pilot's master engine cocks, and are operated when the cocks are closed.
  (ii) *Mk. III aircraft.*—The cut-outs are operated by electro-pneumatic rams, four switches on the instrument panel just above the engine starter buttons controlling the individual engines. These switches each have two positions, the top one being the engine RUNNING position and the bottom one the IDLE CUT OFF position (for starting and stopping).

26. *Electric fuel pumps.*—One pump is fitted in each tank and the controlling switches (84) are on the observer's panel.

27. *Ignition switches.*—Eight ignition switches (6) are fitted at the top centre of the instrument panel and may be operated individually, or in unison by means of a bridge plate.

28. *Engine starting.*—An induction priming pump is mounted in each inboard nacelle and serves both the inboard and outboard engines. Carburettor priming is effected by switching on the electric pumps in the selected tanks. The engine starter buttons (10) and the booster coil switch (9) are mounted on the right-hand side of the pilot's instrument panel.

29. *Electrical master change-over switch.*—This GROUND/FLIGHT switch is fitted on the starboard side of the fuselage just aft of the front spar, and is for isolating the aircraft batteries when the outside accumulators are connected, or when the aircraft is not in use.

30. *Generator switches.*—On early aircraft generator switches are on the electrical panel on the starboard side of the fuselage and should be on during flight. On later aircraft these switches are not fitted.

31. *Oil dilution system.*—The push-buttons (72) for the oil dilution valves are mounted on the observer's panel (for times of operation, *see* Sect. 4, Chap. 2.)

32. *Engine instruments.*—Four boost gauges (7) and below them four engine-speed indicators (8) are mounted at the centre of the pilot's instrument panel. The following indicators are mounted on the observer's instrument panel:—

  Oil pressure (75)   Fuel pressure warning lamps (71)
  Oil temperature (77)   Fuel contents gauges (79)
  Coolant outlet temperature (78)

  Note.—The fuel pressure warning lamps and fuel contents gauges are controlled by a switch fitted below them; this switch (81) should always be left on in flight.

COCKPIT ACCOMMODATION AND EQUIPMENT

33. *Seating—*
  (i) The pilot's seat is provided with hinged armrests (57) and is adjustable for height by a lever (63) on the left-hand side; the safety harness is released by a lever (50) on the right armrest. Armour plate is fitted to the back of the seat, including a hinged panel behind the pilot's head.

A.P.2062A & C, Vol. I, Sect. 1

(ii) The second pilot's seat is on the starboard side of the cockpit. The backrest is a strap of canvas webbing, and a tubular footrest is mounted beneath the pilot's floor. When not in use the backrest is released from the attachment to the first pilot's seat and the end dropped between the formers which carry the second pilot's seat. The seat is then folded up against the fuselage starboard side, and secured by a strap to the cockpit rail. The footrest is slid under the pilot's floor.

34. *Entrance door.*—This is on the starboard side of the fuselage forward of the tail plane. It is provided with a short detachable ladder which is stowed in the fuselage nearby.

35. *Direct vision window.*—On each side of the windscreen there are hinged windows which may be opened for direct vision if the windscreen is obscured. If the window frame is frozen, gradual unscrewing of the release knob will force the window inwards thus breaking the ice.

36. *Cockpit heating.*—The admission of hot air into the cabin is controlled by a knob on each side of the fuselage just forward of the front spar; to introduce hot air turn knob counter-clockwise. Two adjustable extractor louvres are provided in the fuselage nose.

37. *Oxygen.*—The pilot's flexible oxygen pipe is secured by spring clips to the port cockpit rail. The economiser is located below the rear end of the pilot's floor together with the second pilot's economiser and flexible pipe. A regulator (16) which controls the supply throughout the aircraft is fitted on the right of the instrument panel. A portable oxygen bottle for the pilot is stowed on the lower starboard side of the cockpit.

OPERATIONAL EQUIPMENT AND CONTROLS

38. *Camera.*—A push-button control for the F.24 camera in the nose, is mounted on the starboard cockpit rail.

39. *Glider release.*—A handle just forward of the flaps control operates the glider release mechanism when the latter is installed.

40. *Bomb door control.*—The bomb doors are opened hydraulically by pushing down the lever (67) on the left of the pilot's seat. The bomb release system is inoperative until the doors begin to open.

> *Note.*—As fifteen minutes of pumping is necessary to open the bomb doors by hand pump, it is recommended that the bomb doors should be opened by the pilot before the engines are switched off, if it is subsequently required to "bomb up".

41. *Bomb release button.*—The pilot may release, by means of the button (36) on the handwheel, single bombs or sticks of bombs fuzed, selected and set by the air bomber.

42. *Flares.*—Eight reconnaissance flares are fitted in the fuselage, aft of the rear spar, five on the starboard side, and three on the port side.

43. *Sea marking equipment.*—Six holders are provided on the fuselage, at the flare station (three on the port side and three on the starboard) for carrying sea markers or flame-floats.

F.S./4

NAVIGATIONAL, SIGNALLING AND LIGHTING EQUIPMENT

44. *T.R.9F or T.R.1196.*—In aircraft fitted with a T.R.9F installation the remote control is on the canopy struture above the pilot and the NORMAL/SPECIAL switch on the pilot's auxiliary panel on the port side. The set is under the navigator's table. In aircraft incorporating Mod. No. 612 a T.R.1196 set is on the port side just aft of the rear spar. The pilot's control unit is on the auxiliary panel, and a "press to transmit" push-button on the control handwheel. The pilot's microphone telephone socket (58) is on the front edge of his seat.

45. *Intercommunication.*—The pilot's call light and push-button (44) are on the auxiliary panel on the port side of the cockpit. The panel also carries a mixer box (59) by which he may switch to intercommunication only, intercommunication and beam approach together, or beam approach only.

46. *Beam approach installation.*—The beam approach control unit (60) is on the auxiliary panel on the port side of the cockpit, and the visual indicator is on the main instrument panel.

47. *D.F. loop aerial.*—A visual indicator is provided above the instrument panel for use in conjunction with the D.F. loop aerial.

48. *Signal pistol.*—This is stowed on the top of the front spar, and an upward firing position is provided in the roof just forward of the front spar; the cartridges are stowed in spring clips on the starboard side near the firing position.

49. *Navigation, identification and recognition lamps.*—The pilot's instrument panel is fitted with two signalling switch-boxes. The left-hand box (30) is for the air-to-air recognition lamps, and the left switch only is used. The right-hand box (21) controls the upward and downward identification lamps, separately or together. There are three downward lamps and by means of the switches (31) above the left-hand box, the required colour, red, green or clear, may be selected. The electrical panel on the starboard side forward of the front spar carries the selector switches for the recognition lamps, enabling the colour red, green or yellow to be selected, and the headlamp switch which also provides for the headlamp to be put in circuit with the downward identification lamps. The navigation lamps switch (66) is mounted on the pilot's auxiliary panel on the port side of the cockpit.

50. *Landing lamp control.*—Two switches (3) at the top centre of the instrument panel control the landing lamps, one switch per lamp. With the switches at UP the lamps are retracted and switched off, at INTER they are switched on and moved electrically to mid-position giving a dipped beam, and at DOWN they are in their lowest position and give a normal beam.

DE-ICING CONTROLS

51. *Windscreen de-icing control.*—A spray for de-icing fluid can be directed over the windscreen by operating a hand pump, mounted in the forward end of the pilot's floor, on the left-hand side.

52. *Pressure head heater switch.*—The switch (76) is at the top right-hand corner of the observer's panel.

A.P.2062A & C, Vol. I, Sect. 1

EMERGENCY EQUIPMENT AND CONTROLS

53. *General.*—The emergency equipment and exits are illustrated in fig. 5.

54. *Fire extinguishers.*—The automatic fire extinguishers mounted one in each nacelle may also be operated by the pilot from push-buttons (19) on the right of the instrument panel. Six hand fire extinguishers are provided, of which one (68) for the pilot is mounted on the port cockpit rail.

55. *Parachute and crash exits.*—Parachute exists may be made from the hatch in the floor of the nose or from the main entrance door. The pilot's parachute is stowed immediately behind his seat on a panel at the end of the navigator's table. The hatch in the nose is released by means of the handle at the centre, lifted inwards and jettisoned through the hole. Three "push-out" type emergency exits are fitted in the roof of the fuselage, one in the canopy above the pilot, one just forward of the rear spar, and one above the rear end of the main floor. These should not be used as parachute exits.

56. *Dinghy.*—A type J dinghy stowed in the starboard plane may be inflated and released in any of three ways:—
   (i) By pulling the release cord running inside the fuselage along the roof aft of the rear spar.
   (ii) From outside by means of the loop on the starboard side adjacent to the leading edge of the tail plane.
   (iii) Automatically by an immersion switch. A special emergency pack is supplied with the aircraft; it is carried in the dinghy compartment stowed on top of the dinghy to which it is attached by means of a lanyard. In addition to this pack, standard emergency packs Type 4 and Type 7 are stowed on the starboard side of the fuselage, just aft of the rear spar. The contents of these three packs are given in the current Appendix A for the aircraft.

57. *Crash axe and first-aid outfit.*—These items are stowed on the starboard side aft of the entrance door.

58. *Fuel jettisoning.*—The contents of both No. 1 fuel tanks may be jettisoned by lifting and turning anti-clockwise the hydraulic control handle on the left of the pilot's seat. The flaps should be lowered 15 deg. and speed reduced to 150 m.p.h. I.A.S. before jettisoning. If the flaps will not lower by the hydraulic system, do not attempt to lower them by the compressed air system, as this will also cause the undercarriage to lower.

59. *Bomb jettisoning.*—The complete bomb load (excluding bomb containers) may be jettisoned after the bomb doors have been opened, by means of the jettison handle (14) fitted on the right side of the instrument panel; if bomb containers are carried they should be jettisoned first by the bomb container jettison switch (13) fitted to the left of the bomb jettison handle.

60. *R.3003 controls.*—The pilot's master switch (12) and two push-switches (11) for emergency destruction are on the main instrument panel. These two push-buttons (11) also destroy the T.R.1335 set if fitted.

F.S./5

INSTRUMENT PANEL

Key to Fig. 1

1. Instrument flying panel.
2. D.F. indicator.
3. Landing lamps switches.
4. Undercarriage indicator switch.
5. D.R. repeater compass.
6. Ignition switches (eight).
7. Boost gauges (four).
8. Engine speed indicators (four).
9. Boost coil switch.
10. Engine starting push buttons (four).
11. R.3003 emergency switches.
12. R.3003 master switch.
13. Bomb containers jettison switch.
14. Bomb jettison control.
15. Suction pump change-over cock.
16. Oxygen regulator.
17. Propeller feathering switches (four).
18. Air temperature gauge.
19. Fire extinguisher push buttons (four).
20. Brake triple pressure gauge.
21. Signalling switch box (identification lamps).
22. Two-speed supercharger control.
23. Fuel cock controls (four).
24. Steering indicator.
25. Mixture lever.
26. Throttle levers (four).
27. Propeller speed controls (four).
28. Rudder pedal.
29. Boost control cut-out.
30. Signalling switch box (recognition lamps).
31. Downward identification lamp selector switches.
32. D.R. compass switches.
33. D.R. compass deviation card holder.
34. Automatic controls—speed and steering levers.
35. P.4. compass deviation card holder.
36. Bomb release button.
37. Undercarriage indicator.
38. Flaps indicator.
39. Flaps indicator switch.
40. Beam approach visual indicator.
41. A.S.I. correction card holder.
42. Watch holder.

A.P.2062A, VOL.I & P.N. SECT.I.

INSTRUMENT PANEL

FIG. 1

A.P.2062A., VOL.I & P.N. SECT. I.

FIG. 2

LOWER PORTION OF COCKPIT

A.P.2062A Vol.1 and P.N. Sect.1

Key to fig. 2.

LOWER PORTION OF COCKPIT.

25. Mixture lever.
26. Throttle levers. (four)
27. Propeller speed controls. (four)
29. Boost control cut-out.
43. Automatic controls - attitude control.
44. Intercommunication call light.
45. Automatic controls - cock control.
46. Automatic controls - pressure gauge.
47. Automatic controls - clutch control.
48. P.4 magnetic compass.
49. Friction adjusters.
50. Pilot's harness release lever.
51. Flaps control.
52. Aileron trimming tab control.
53. Elevator trimming tab control.
54. Undercarriage control.
55. Undercarriage control safety bolt.
56. Rudder trimming tab control.
57. Folding arm rest.
58. Pilot's mic./tel. socket.
59. Mixer box.
60. Beam approach control unit.

F.S/10.

Key to fig. 3.

PORT SIDE OF COCKPIT.

43.	Automatic controls - attitude control.
44.	Intercommunication call light.
45.	Automatic controls - cock control.
46.	Automatic controls - pressure gauge.
47.	Automatic controls - clutch control.
58.	Pilot's mic./tel. socket.
59.	Mixer box.
60.	Beam approach control unit.
61.	Oxygen connection.
63.	Seat operating lever.
64.	Automatic controls - master switch.
65.	T.R.9 switch.
66.	Navigation lamps switch.
67.	Bomb doors control.
68.	Hand fire extinguisher.

A.P.2062A., VOL I & P.N. SECT.I.

FIG. 3 PORT SIDE OF COCKPIT FIG. 3

30

FIG. 4

AIR OBSERVER'S PANEL

FIG. 4

A.P.2062A Vol.1 and P.N. Sect.1

Key to fig. 4.

AIR OBSERVER'S PANEL.

70. Knob for operation of emergency hydraulic system.
    <u>Note</u>. On later aeroplanes this control is moved aft of the front spar.
71. Fuel pressure indicators.
72. Oil dilution push-button switches.
73. Ammeter test socket.
74. Panel light.
75. Oil pressure gauges. (four)
76. Pressure head heater switch.
77. Oil temperature gauges. (four)
78. Coolant outlet temperature gauges. (four)
79. Fuel contents gauges. (six)
80. Test socket.
81. Switch to control fuel contents gauges and fuel pressure indicators.
82. Engine Limitations data plate.
83. Fuel tanks selector cocks.
84. Immersed fuel pump switches.

F.S/12.

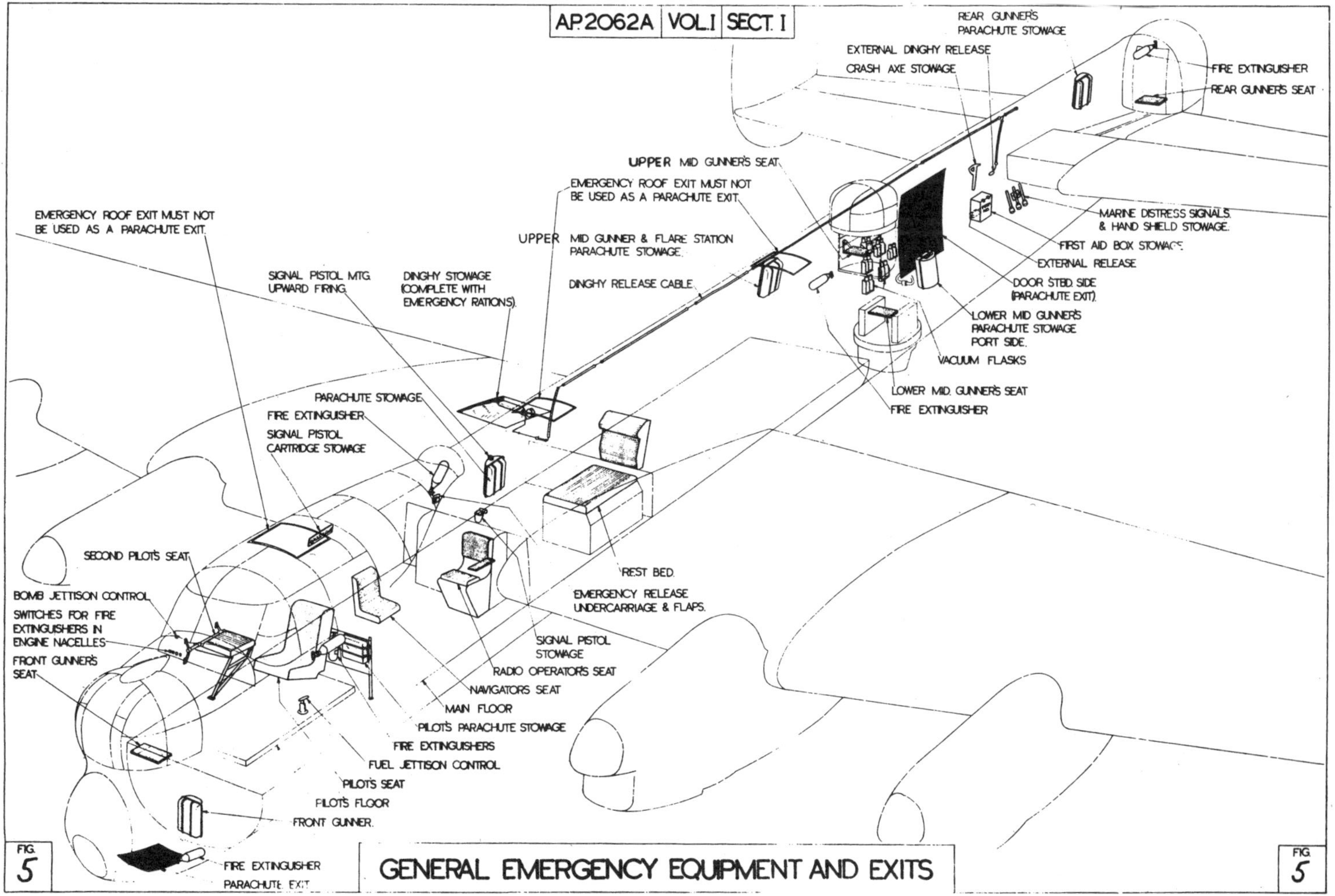

GENERAL EMERGENCY EQUIPMENT AND EXITS

AP.2062A | VOL.I | SECT.I

FIG 5

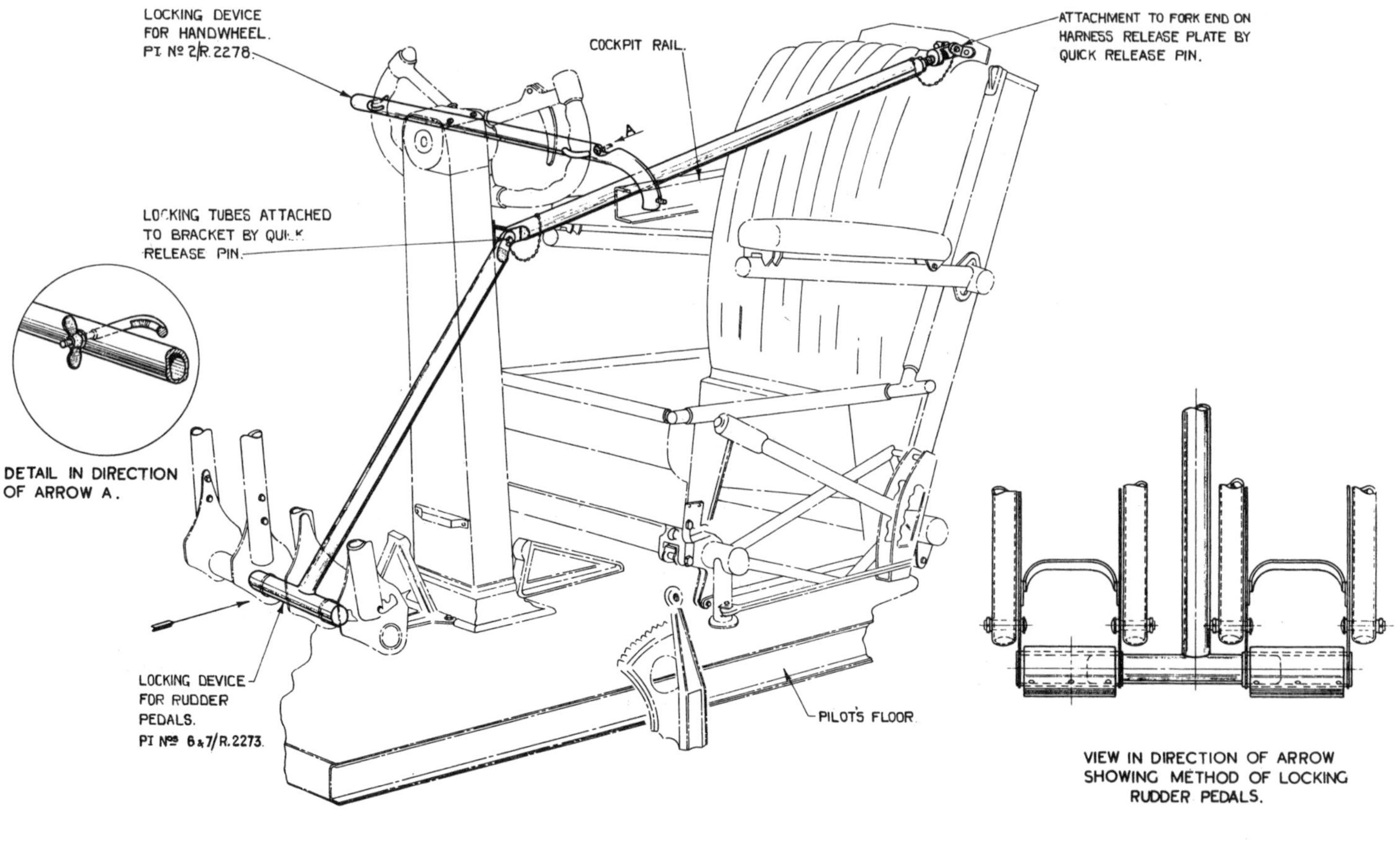

AP. 2062 A | VOL.I | SECT.I

FIG. 6

LOCKING OF FLYING CONTROLS.

ATTACHMENT TO FORK END ON HARNESS RELEASE PLATE BY QUICK RELEASE PIN.

VIEW IN DIRECTION OF ARROW SHOWING METHOD OF LOCKING RUDDER PEDALS.

COCKPIT RAIL

PILOT'S FLOOR

LOCKING DEVICE FOR HANDWHEEL. PT Nº 2/R.2278.

LOCKING TUBES ATTACHED TO BRACKET BY QUICK RELEASE PIN.

DETAIL IN DIRECTION OF ARROW A.

LOCKING DEVICE FOR RUDDER PEDALS. PT Nº 6&7/R.2273

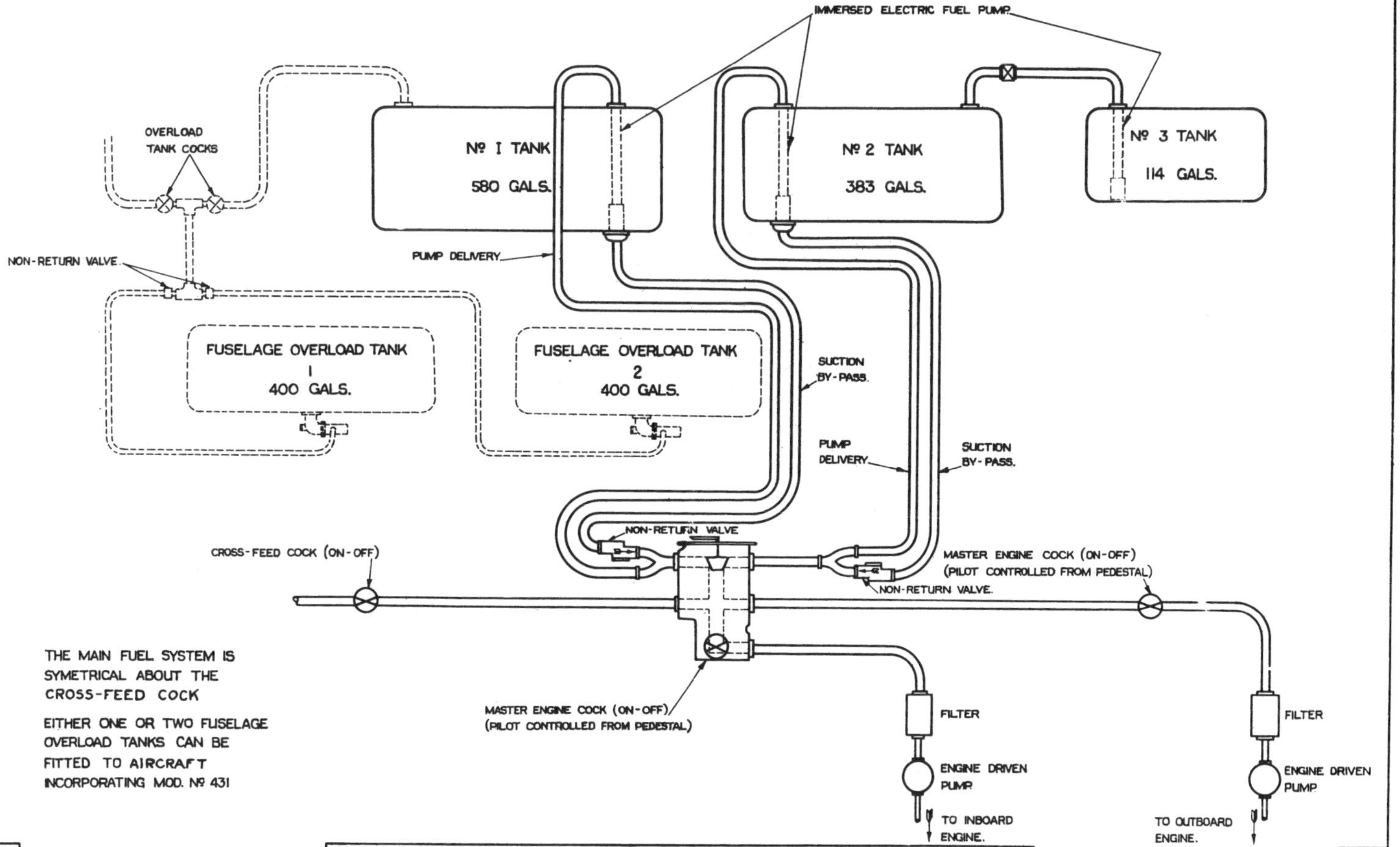

THE MAIN FUEL SYSTEM IS SYMETRICAL ABOUT THE CROSS-FEED COCK

EITHER ONE OR TWO FUSELAGE OVERLOAD TANKS CAN BE FITTED TO AIRCRAFT INCORPORATING MOD. Nº 431

FIG. 7

SIMPLIFIED FUEL SYSTEM DIAGRAM. E.P.I. PUMPS

FIG. 7

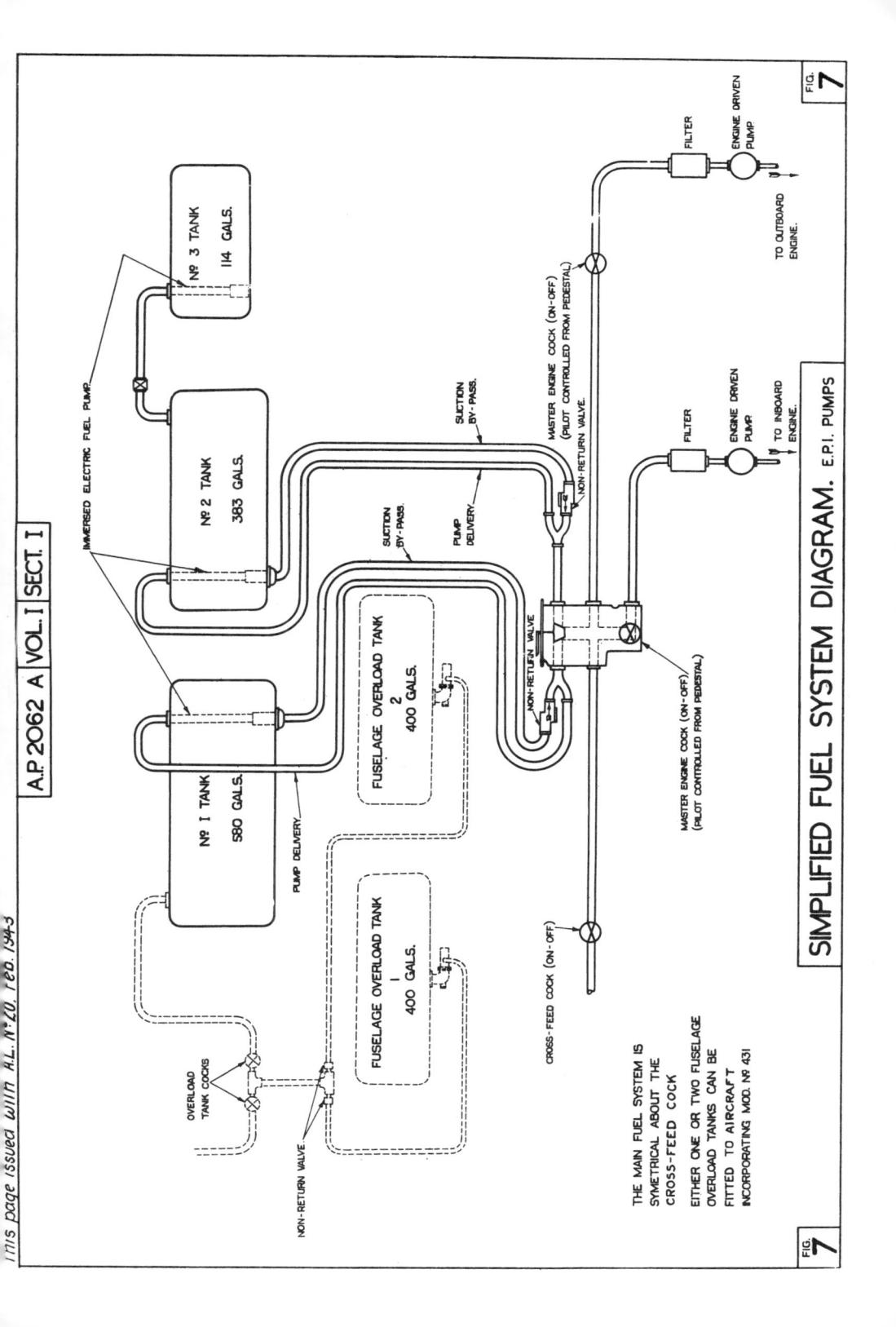

This page issued with A.L. Nº 20, Feb. 1943

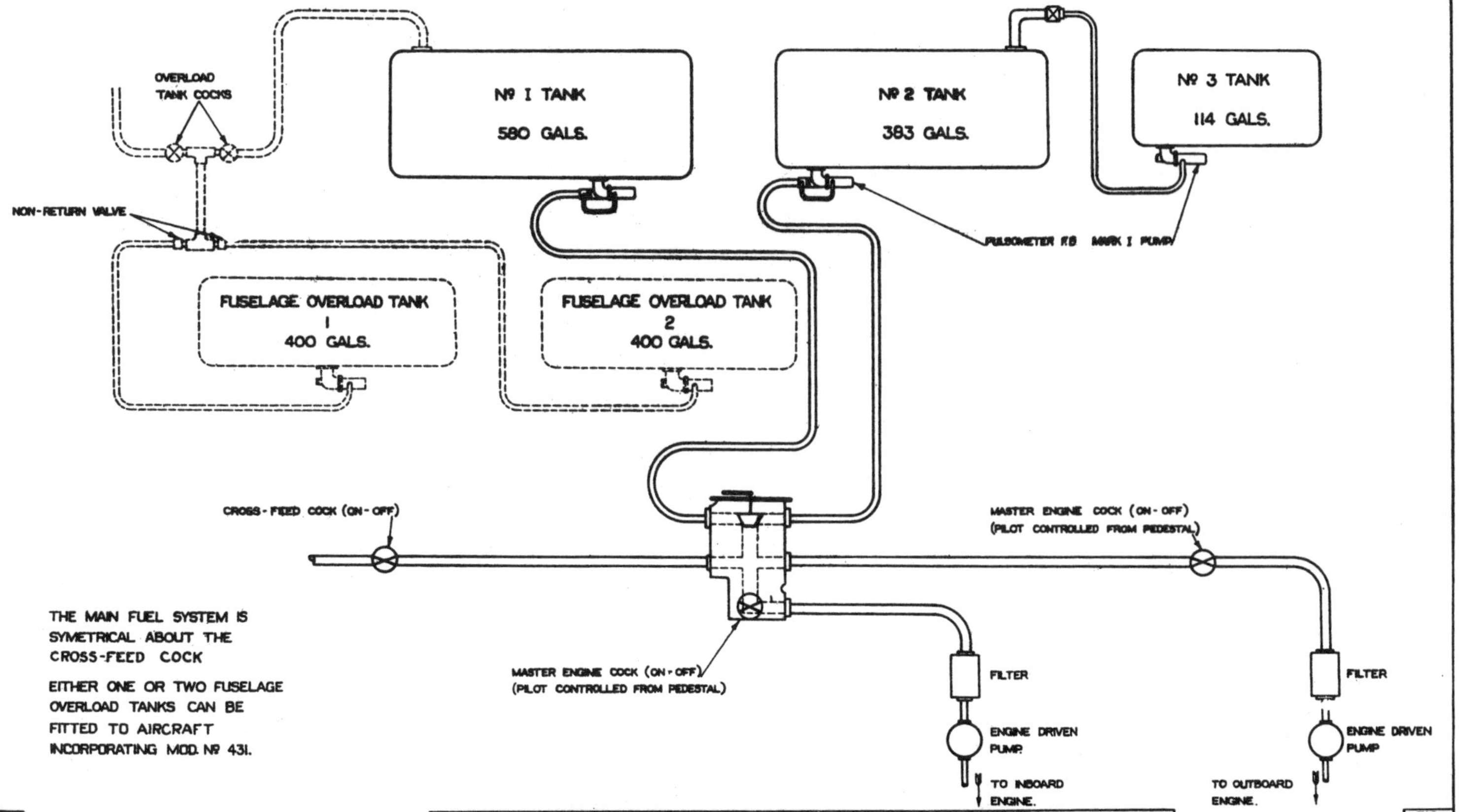

THE MAIN FUEL SYSTEM IS SYMETRICAL ABOUT THE CROSS-FEED COCK

EITHER ONE OR TWO FUSELAGE OVERLOAD TANKS CAN BE FITTED TO AIRCRAFT INCORPORATING MOD. Nº 431.

FIG. 8

SIMPLIFIED FUEL SYSTEM DIAGRAM. PULSOMETER PUMPS.

FIG. 8

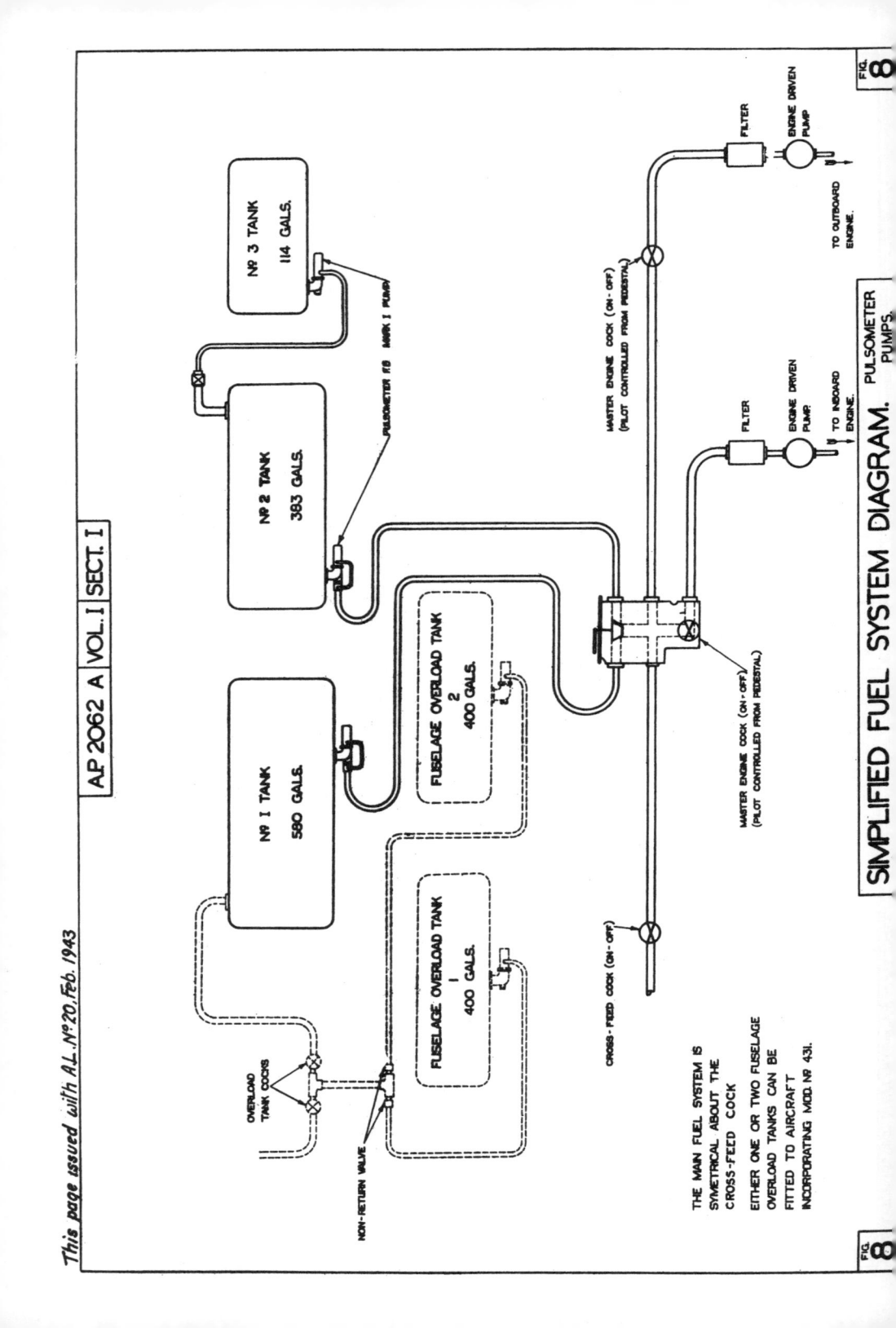

Section 2:
Pilots and flight engineer's notes.

Photo by CHARLES E. BROWN

LANCASTER I, III & X

AIR MINISTRY AIR PUBLICATION 2062A, C, & F—P.N.
May 1944 *Pilot's and Flight Engineer's Notes*

LANCASTER I, III & X
PILOT'S & FLIGHT ENGINEER'S NOTES

LIST OF CONTENTS

PART I—DESCRIPTIVE *Para.*

INTRODUCTION .. 1

FUEL AND OIL SYSTEMS
  Fuel tanks 2
  Fuel cocks 3
  Vapour vent system (Lancaster III and X aircraft only) 4
  Electric fuel booster pumps 5
  Fuel contents gauges 6
  Fuel pressure indicators 7
  Priming pumps 8
  Oil tanks 9
  Oil dilution 10

MAIN SERVICES
  Hydraulic system 11
  Pneumatic system 12
  Electrical system 13

AIRCRAFT CONTROLS
  Trimming tabs 14
  Undercarriage control 15
  Undercarriage indicator 16
  Undercarriage warning horn 17
  Flaps control 18
  Bomb doors 19

ENGINE CONTROLS
  Throttle controls 20
  Mixture control 21
  Propeller controls 22

39

PART I—*continued*　　　　　　　　　　　　　　*Para.*

　　Supercharger controls　　..　　..　　..　　..　　23
　　Radiator shutters　　..　　..　　..　　..　　..　　24
　　Carburettor air-intake heat control　　..　　..　　25

OTHER CONTROLS
　　Intercommunication ..　　..　　..　　..　　..　　26

PART II—HANDLING

Management of fuel system　　..　　..　　..　　..　　27
Preliminaries　　..　　..　　..　　..　　..　　..　　28
Starting engines and warming up　　..　　..　　..　　29
Testing engines and installations..　　..　　..　　..　　30
Check list before taxying ..　　..　　..　　..　　..　　31
Check list before take-off ..　　..　　..　　..　　..　　32
Taking off ..　　..　　..　　..　　..　　..　　..　　33
Climbing　　..　　..　　..　　..　　..　　..　　..　　34
General flying　　..　　..　　..　　..　　..　　..　　35
Stalling　　..　　..　　..　　..　　..　　..　　..　　36
Diving　　..　　..　　..　　..　　..　　..　　..　　37
Check list before landing ..　　..　　..　　..　　..　　38
Approach speeds ..　　..　　..　　..　　..　　..　　39
Mislanding ..　　..　　..　　..　　..　　..　　..　　40
Beam approach　　..　　..　　..　　..　　..　　..　　41
After landing　　..　　..　　..　　..　　..　　..　　42

PART III—OPERATING DATA

Engine data—Merlin XX ..　　..　　..　　..　　..　　43
Engine data—Merlin 22, 28 or 38　　..　　..　　..　　44
Engine data—Merlin 24 ..　　..　　..　　..　　..　　45
Flying limitations ..　　..　　..　　..　　..　　..　　46
Position error corrections　　..　　..　　..　　..　　47
Maximum performance ..　　..　　..　　..　　..　　48
Maximum range ..　　..　　..　　..　　..　　..　　49
Fuel capacity and consumptions ..　　..　　..　　..　　50

PART IV—EMERGENCIES

Engine failure during take-off　　..　　..　　..　　..　　51
Engine failure in flight　　..　　..　　..　　..　　..　　52
Feathering ..　　..　　..　　..　　..　　..　　..　　53
Unfeathering　　..　　..　　..　　..　　..　　..　　54
Damage by enemy action　　..　　..　　..　　..　　55
Undercarriage emergency operation　　..　　..　　..　　56

PART IV—*continued* *Para.*

Flaps emergency operation	57
Bomb doors emergency operation	58
Bomb jettisoning	59
Fuel jettisoning	60
Parachute exits	61
Crash exits	62
Dinghy and ditching	63
Engine fire-extinguishers	64
Hand fire-extinguishers	65
Signal pistol	66
Signal cartridge stowage	67
Parachutes	68
Static line for parachuting wounded men	69
Emergency packs	70
Projectible kite container	71
Crash axes	72
Incendiary bombs	73
First-aid equipment	74

PART V—SUPPLEMENTARY NOTES FOR FLIGHT ENGINEER

Oil system	75
Coolant system	76
Hydraulic system	77
Pneumatic system	78
Electrical system	79
Undercarriage failure	80
Gauges	81

PART VI—ILLUSTRATIONS AND LOCATION OF CONTROLS

Location of controls	Page 46
Instrument panel	*Fig.* 1
Port side of cockpit	,, 2
Flight engineer's panel, Lancasters I & III	,, 3
Flight engineer's panel, Lancaster X	,, 4
Simplified fuel system diagram—Pulsometer pumps	,, 5
Simplified fuel system diagram—Immersed pumps	,, 6

AIR PUBLICATION 2062A, C & F—P.N.
Pilot's and Flight Engineer's Notes

PART I
DESCRIPTIVE

INTRODUCTION

1. The Lancaster I, III and X are heavy bombers, the difference between them lying mainly in the power plants; the Lancaster I is fitted with Merlin XX, 22 or 24 engines which have SU carburettors; the Lancaster III and X are fitted with Merlin 28 or 38 engines which have Bendix Stromberg pressure-injection carburettors; Hydromatic propellers are fitted to all. Lancaster X are Canadian built and differ from British Lancasters in some of the instruments and in the electrical system.

FUEL AND OIL SYSTEMS

2. **Fuel tanks.**—Three self-sealing tanks are fitted in each wing, numbered 1, 2 and 3 outboard of the fuselage between the front and rear spars. On some aircraft the tanks may be marked Inner, Centre and Outer instead of Nos. 1, 2 and 3. The positions are:

No. 1 (Inner): Between the fuselage and the inner engines
No. 2 (Centre): Between the inner and outer engines
No. 3 (Outer): Outboard of the outer engines.
Capacities are:

Port and starboard No. 1:	580 gallons each	
,, ,, ,, No. 2:	383. ,, ,,	
,, ,, ,, No. 3:	114 ,, ,,	
	1,077 ,, ,,	side
	or 2,154 ,,	in all.

Provision is made on some aircraft for carrying one or two 400-gallon tanks fitted in the bomb cells; these tanks are connected so that their contents may be transferred into either or both No. 1 wing tanks and thence to the engines. When the maximum bomb load is carried, the No. 2 tanks should be filled first, and the remainder of the fuel put in No. 1 tanks. This is on account of strength considerations of the aircraft structure.

PART I—DESCRIPTIVE

3. **Fuel cocks.**—The pilot controls four master engine cocks (24, 30). On Lancaster I aircraft, the master engine cocks also control the slow-running cut-outs. The flight engineer controls two tank selector cocks (77) which select No. 1 or No. 2 tank on each side. (No. 3 tank replenishes No. 2, see below). A cross-feed cock (marked BALANCE COCK) connects the port and starboard supply systems, and is on the floor just forward of the front spar, with the handle visible through a hole in the spar cover.

   When the 400-gallon tanks are fitted in the bomb cells they each have an ON-OFF cock situated behind the front spar in the centre of the fuselage.

4. **Vapour vent system** (Lancaster III and X aircraft only).—A vent pipe from each carburettor is connected to the No. 2 tank on the same side of the aircraft, and allows vapour and a small quantity of fuel (approx. ½ gal. per hour, per carburettor, but some later carburettors may have a second vent allowing 10 gallons per hour) to return to the tank. This carburettor is designed to work full of fuel, and it therefore requires the vent to carry away any petrol vapour and dissolved air. It also assists in re-establishing the flow of fuel to the carburettors when the pipe-lines and pump have been run dry due to a tank emptying.

5. **Electric fuel booster pumps**
   (i) Originally, on Lancaster I aircraft, immersed pumps were fitted in all tanks; Mod. 594 (temporary) removed the immersed pumps from No. 1 tanks and fitted stack pipes in their places.

   A later Mod. 512 put back the immersed pumps in No. 1 and No. 2 tanks and incorporated suction by-pass lines to allow fuel to be drawn from the tanks when the pumps are not in use. In aircraft incorporating Mod. 539, including all Lancaster III aircraft, a Pulsometer FB Mk. I pump is fitted in each tank and by-pass lines are incorporated at No. 1 and No. 2 tanks. On Lancaster X aircraft, Thomson pumps, similar to the Pulsometer pumps, and by-pass lines are fitted.

PART I—DESCRIPTIVE

No. 3 tank is used to replenish No. 2 tank (*see* Figs. 5 & 6) by switching on the No. 3 tank pump. When the 400-gallon tanks are fitted in the bomb cells they each have a similar pump fitted to transfer their contents to the No. 1 tanks.

(ii) The main use of the electric fuel pumps in No. 1 and No. 2 tanks is to maintain fuel pressure at altitudes of approximately 17,000 ft. and over in temperate climates, but they are also used for raising the fuel pressure before starting and to assist in re-starting an engine during flight. If one engine fails during take-off and the electric fuel pump is not ON, air may be drawn back into the main fuel system before the master engine cock of the failed engine can be closed, thus causing the failure of the other engine on the same side; therefore at take-off the pumps in Nos. 1 and 2 tanks must be switched on; this is also a precaution against fuel failure during take-off as an immediate supply is available by changing over the tank selector cock. The pump in each tank in use should also be switched on at any time when a drop in fuel pressure is indicated or when it is necessary to run all engines from one tank by opening the cross-feed cock.

6. **Fuel contents gauges.**—On Lancasters I and III, the switch (76) on the flight engineer's panel must be set ON before the fuel contents gauges will indicate. On Lancaster X there is no fuel contents gauge switch; the gauges will indicate whenever electrical power is available.

7. **Fuel pressure indicators**—Fuel pressure warning lights (79) show when the fuel pressure at the carburettor falls below 6 lb./sq.in. on Lancaster I aircraft, and 10 lb./sq.in. on Lancaster III aircraft. They are switched off by the fuel contents gauges switch (76), and this switch must, therefore, always be on in flight. On Lancaster X, fuel pressure gauges (73) are fitted on the flight engineer's panel. They will indicate whenever battery power is available.

8. **Priming pumps.**—There is one cylinder priming pump in each inboard engine nacelle. Each pump serves one inboard and one outboard engine. On Lancasters I and III,

PART I—DESCRIPTIVE

two priming cocks are fitted in each nacelle. On Lancaster X the priming pump handle is turned to the left to prime the left engine, to the right to prime the right engine, and to the mid-position for off.

9. **Oil tanks.**—Each engine has its own tank; capacity 37½ gallons of oil with 4½ gallons air space.

10. **Oil dilution.**—The four push-buttons (81) are on the flight engineer's panel.

MAIN SERVICES

11. **Hydraulic system**

    (i) Each turret is operated by an individual engine-driven pump.

Starboard outer engine:	Mid upper turret
Starboard inner ,,	Front turret
Port inner ,,	Mid under turret, if fitted
Port outer ,,	Tail turret

    (ii) Two pumps (one on each inboard engine), with a hand-pump as an alternative, charge a small accumulator and operate:

    Undercarriage
    Flaps
    Bomb doors
    Carburettor air intake shutters
    Fuel jettisoning

    Owing to the large capacity of the flap and undercarriage jacks, it is not normally possible to operate them by the hand-pump in the time available in an emergency.

12. **Pneumatic system**

    (i) A Heywood compressor on the starboard inboard engine charges an air bottle to 300 lb./sq.in. and operates:

    Wheel brakes
    Radiator shutters
    Supercharger rams (on Lancaster III and X and later Lancaster I aircraft)
    Idle cut-off rams (on Lancaster III and X aircraft only)

PART I—DESCRIPTIVE

A pressure-maintaining valve in the supply line from the air bottle only allows pressure to be supplied to the radiator shutters, superchargers, and idle cut-off rams, if the pressure in the air bottle exceeds 130 lb./sq.in. (This is to ensure sufficient pressure for the brakes, which operate at 80 lb./sq.in.) It is necessary, therefore, to check on the triple pressure gauge that pressure is sufficient before S ratio is engaged or the idle cut-off controls are operated.

(ii) A vacuum pump is fitted on each inboard engine, one for operating the instruments on the instrument flying panel, and the other for operating the gyros of the Mark XIV bombsight; the change-over cock (17) is on the right of the instrument panel beside the suction gauge (23), and in the event of failure of the vacuum pump supplying the flying instruments the changeover cock can be used to connect the serviceable pump with the flying instruments and cut out the bombsight. It is not possible to operate flying instruments and bombsight on one vacuum pump.

(iii) An RAE compressor fitted on the port inboard engine operates the Mark IV automatic controls and the computer unit of the Mark XIV bombsight. For operation of the Mark XIV bombsight, the automatic control cock must be set to OUT.

13. **Electrical system.**—Two 1,500-watt generators (one on each inboard engine), connected in parallel, charge the aircraft batteries (24 volt), and supply the usual lighting and other services, including

    Propeller feathering pumps
    Flap and undercarriage indicators
    Pressure head heating
    Fuel booster pumps
    Radio equipment
    Landing lamps
    Engine starting and booster coils
    Dinghy inflation
    Controls for radiator shutters rams, supercharger gear change rams, and idle cut-off rams (on Lancaster III and X aircraft)

PART I—DESCRIPTIVE

Bomb gear and bombsight
Fire-extinguishers
Fuel contents gauges
Fuel pressure warning lights or gauges
Camera
Heated clothing
DR compass

An alternator may be fitted to each outboard engine, to supply any special radio equipment.

A ground/flight switch on the starboard side of the fuselage, immediately aft of the front spar, isolates the aircraft batteries when the aircraft is parked or when using a ground starter battery.

Two generator switches are provided on the electrical control panel.

AIRCRAFT CONTROLS

14. **Trimming tabs.**—The elevator (62), rudder (63) and aileron (61) tab controls (on the right of the pilot's seat) all operate in the natural sense and each has an indicator.

15. **Undercarriage control.**—The undercarriage lever (64) is locked in the DOWN position by a safety bolt (65) which has to be held aside in order to raise the lever. The bolt engages automatically when the lever is set down. The undercarriage may be lowered in an emergency by compressed air (*see* Part IV, para. 56).

    WARNING.—There is no automatic lock to prevent the undercarriage being raised by mistake when the aircraft is on the ground.

16. **Undercarriage indicator** (39).—On Lancasters I and III the indicators show as follows:

Undercarriage	locked down:	Two green lights
,,	unlocked:	Two red lights
,,	locked up:	No lights

    The indicator switch (4) is interlocked so that it must be on when the port engine ignition switches are on. An auxiliary set of green lights can be brought into operation by pressing the central knob if failure of the main set is suspected. The red lamps are duplicated so that failure of one lamp does not affect the indication of undercarriage

PART I—DESCRIPTIVE

unlocked. The lights can be dimmed by turning the central knob. On Lancaster X a pictorial type of indicator is fitted. When the indicator switch is on and electrical power is available, the pictorial indicator shows the position of the undercarriage wheels and wing flaps at all times. The disappearance of small red flags shows when the wheels are locked up or down.

17. **Undercarriage warning horn.**—The horn sounds if either inboard throttle is closed when the undercarriage is not locked down. The outboard throttles do not operate the horn. A testing pushbutton and lamp are behind the pilot's seat, on the cockpit port rail.

18. **Flaps control.**—The push-pull handle (60) should be moved to the neutral position (located by a spring-loaded catch) after each flap movement. On Lancasters I and III the flap indicator (26) is switched on by a separate switch (27). If the flaps have been selected partly down, and it is desired to lower them fully, it may be found that the flaps will not lower further for some considerable time. This is due to the pressure in the accumulator having fallen below the pressure required to operate the flaps, but not sufficiently to cause the hydraulic pumps to cut in. To overcome this, move the flaps selector to UP, and then immediately put it fully DOWN; this causes the hydraulic pumps to cut in. In an emergency the flaps may be lowered by compressed air after lowering the undercarriage (*see* Part IV, para. 57).

19. **Bomb doors.**—The control (43) has two positions only. The bomb release system is rendered operative soon after the doors begin to open and before they are fully open. The position of the doors must therefore be checked visually before releasing bombs. If the bomb doors open only part way and then stop, it is probably due to icing around the hinges and joints, which raises the hydraulic pressure sufficiently to bring the cut-out into operation, which stops any further movement of the doors. If the bomb doors selector is moved to SHUT and then immediately to OPEN, the doors will usually open further; it may be necessary to repeat this several times to get the doors fully open.

PART I—DESCRIPTIVE

As strenuous pumping for 15 minutes is required to open the doors with engines stopped, they should be opened before stopping engines if the aircraft is to be bombed up before the next flight.

For emergency operation of bomb doors by compressed air, *see* Part IV, para. 58.

ENGINE CONTROLS

20. **Throttle controls**

  (i) *Merlin XX, 22, 28 and 38 engines.*—Climbing boost +9 lb./sq.in. is obtained with the throttle levers (28) at the gate. On Merlin XX installations, and originally on Merlin 22, 28 or 38 installations, going through the gate gives a boost of +12 lb./sq.in. at ground level only. A later modification to Merlin 22, 28 or 38 engines gives +14 lb./sq.in. boost at ground level only with the throttle levers through the gate.

  The boost control cut-out (32) gives +14 lb./sq.in. in M gear and +16 lb./sq.in. in S gear on all the above Merlins.

  (ii) *Merlin 24 engines.*—Originally no boost control cut-out was fitted and no climbing gate. The fully forward position of the throttle lever gave +18 lb./sq.in. boost for take-off and combat. On these installations the automatic boost control does not allow the butterfly to open fully to maintain +9 lb./sq.in. boost up to full throttle height unless the throttle levers are progressively advanced to the fully forward position during the climb. However, a modification is now being introduced which overcomes this, and when this is incorporated a boost control cut-out is fitted which gives +18 lb./sq.in. for take-off and combat; the throttle quadrant is fitted with a gate at +9 lb./sq.in. boost, and the fully forward position gives + 14 lb./sq.in. at ground level only, for take-off at moderate loads.

  (iii) On all Merlins, when climbing with a boost setting less than +9 lb./sq.in. the automatic boost control cannot open the throttle valve fully and the boost will begin to fall off before full throttle height is reached; the throttle lever should then be progressively advanced to maintain boost.

PART I—DESCRIPTIVE

21. **Mixture control**

(i) *Merlin XX, 22 and 24 engines (Lancaster I).*—S.U. carburettors are fitted. The mixture strength is automatically controlled by boost pressure, and the pilot has no separate mixture control. A weak mixture is obtained below +7 lb./sq.in. boost (+4 lb./sq.in on Merlin XX). The carburettor slow-running cut-outs are operated by closing the master engine cocks.

(ii) *Merlin 28 and 38 engines (Lancasters III and X).*—Bendix-Stromberg pressure injection carburettors are fitted. There is no pilot's mixture control, the mixture strength being regulated by the power so that a weak mixture is obtained below +7 lb./sq.in. and 2,650 r.p.m. The carburettor idle cut-outs, which are used in starting, and for stopping the engines, are operated by electro-pneumatic rams controlled by four SLOW-RUNNING CUT-OUT SWITCHES (11) on the pilot's panel just above the engine starter buttons. These switches have each two positions, the top one being the engine RUNNING position and the bottom one the IDLE CUT-OFF position. In the case of electrical or pneumatic failure the rams will return to the RUNNING position.

22. **Propeller controls.**—The speed control levers (29) for the Hydromatic propellers vary the governed r.p.m. from 3,000 down to 1,800. The feathering buttons (19) are on the right of the instrument panel. For feathering and unfeathering procedure *see* Part IV, paras. 53, 54.

23. **Supercharger controls**

(i) On early Lancaster I aircraft the supercharger controls for all four engines are operated mechanically by one lever.

(ii) On later Lancaster I and on all Lancaster III and X aircraft, the superchargers are operated by electro-pneumatic rams of the single-action spring-return type. In the case of electrical or pneumatic failure the rams will return to the M ratio position. A switch, fitted to the pilot's instrument panel immediately below the engine speed indicators, controls all four engines simultaneously, and a red warning light beside it (25) indicates S ratio on the ground only (i.e. when the undercarriage is down).

PART I—DESCRIPTIVE

24. **Radiator shutters.**—The shutters are automatically controlled when the switches forward of the flight engineer's panel are in the up position. When the switches are down, the thermostatic control is over-ridden, and the shutters are opened; this position should be used for all ground running, taxying and marshalling.

25. **Carburettor air-intake heat control.**—A single lever for the hydraulic operation of all four carburettors' hot air intakes is provided beside the pilot's seat. Hot air should not be used unless the air intakes become iced up, and as ice guards are fitted, this should rarely be necessary.

OTHER CONTROLS

26. **Intercommunication.**—On Lancaster X, Bendix interphone station boxes are fitted. For inter-communication the selector switch must be set to INTER and the INCREASE OUTPUT control set full on.

AIR PUBLICATION 2062A, C & F—P.N.
Pilot's and Flight Engineer's Notes

PART II
HANDLING

NOTE.—All speeds quoted are for aircraft with the Pilot's A.S.I. connected to the static vent (*see* para. 47). Speeds given in brackets are for aircraft on which the change to this connection has not been made.

27. **Management of fuel system**

(i) *Testing electric fuel booster pumps.*—Before starting the engines each booster pump should be tested by ammeter (most aircraft have a permanent ammeter fitted on the flight engineer's panel while some early aircraft may have an ammeter test socket into which the ammeter must be plugged); to do this, the switch for each pump should in turn be set to the up (test) position, after ensuring that the idle cut-off switches are in the IDLE CUT-OFF position and air pressure is greater than 130 lb./sq.in. (on Lancaster III and X aircraft); the ammeter reading should be perfectly steady and should be between 4 and 7 amps for a Pulsometer FB Mark I pump, between 3 and 5 amps for a Thomson pump, or between 2 and 4 amps for an immersed pump. Aircraft with Pulsometer pumps may be recognised by the small blisters on the underside of the wings.

(ii) *Use of tanks:*

(*a*) *Starting, warm-up and take-off.*—No. 2 tanks should be used first because the carburettor vents (*see* Part I, para. 4) return to these tanks, also because the contents of No. 1 tanks only can be jettisoned.

The electric fuel booster pumps in Nos. 1 and 2 tanks must be switched on for take-off, so that if for any reason the fuel supply from No. 2 tanks should fail, fuel pressure will be available immediately on turning the tank selectors to No. 1 tanks. *See* also Part I, para. 5.

(*b*) *In flight.*—After climbing to 2,000 feet, switch off booster pumps. Continue running on No. 2 tanks until 200 gallons remains in each, then change over to No. 1

PART II—HANDLING

tanks. Switch on No. 3 booster pumps to transfer their fuel to No. 2 tanks. Switch off the pumps when No. 3 tanks are empty. If overload fuel tanks are carried, continue to fly on No. 1 tanks until enough fuel has been used from them to enable the contents of the fuselage tanks to be transferred to them. Then change over to No. 2 tanks; turn on both long range fuel cocks (behind front spar) and switch on overload tank pump switches and fuel contents gauge. Transfer of fuel from long range tanks takes approximately 1 hour. Watch No. 1 fuel contents gauges and turn off each long range cock as soon as its respective No. 1 tank is filled. Turn off pumps when both No. 1 tanks are filled.

When over enemy territory, keep contents of Nos. 1 and 2 tanks approximately the same by running on each alternately for about half-an-hour.

(iii) *Use of cross-feed cock.*—The cock should be closed at all times, unless it is necessary in an emergency to feed fuel from the tanks in one wing to the engines in the other wing. If the cross-feed cock is open for this purpose, only one tank should be turned on to feed all working engines, and the pump in this tank should be switched on.

(iv) *Changing fuel tanks on Lancaster III and X aircraft.*—If the engine cuts owing to exhaustion of fuel in one tank, back-firing may occur on turning on to another tank. For when the tank empties, the fuel pressure drops, and when the pressure falls to 4 lb./sq.in. fuel injection ceases. When the new tank is turned on, the carburettor restarts and delivers the fuel already in it, but this supply is followed by vapour from the fuel pipelines, causing weak mixture and back-firing until fuel is delivered from the new tank.

When an engine cuts due to exhaustion of one tank:

(*a*) Close the throttle and change over to another tank.

(*b*) Idle the engine till it runs smoothly and open up slowly.

(*c*) The use of the booster pump in the tank turned on will help to restart the engine.

PART II—HANDLING

28. Preliminaries

(i) *Before entering aircraft.*—Check pitot head covers removed.
Check all cowling and inspection panels, and leading edge secured. Check tyres for creep.

(ii) *On entering aircraft.*—Check security of emergency escape hatches
Check emergency air bottle pressure (1,100–1,200 lb./sq.in.)
Check hydraulic accumulator pressure (220 lb./sq.in. minimum, under no hydraulic pressure).
Check fuel cross-feed cock OFF.
Turn ground/flight switch to FLIGHT.
Switch on undercarriage indicator and flaps indicator switches (if fitted) and check indicators.
Switch on fuel contents gauges switch (if fitted) and leave it on, and check fuel contents.
Check master engine cocks OFF.

29. Starting engines and warming up

(i) Test fuel booster pumps by ammeter (*see* para. 27).
On Lancasters III and X aircraft the fuel tank booster pump must *never* be switched on with the master engine cock open and the engine stationary, unless the slow-running cut-out switch is in the IDLE CUT-OFF (down) position and the air supply pressure not less than 130 lb./sq.in.

(ii) Turn ground/flight switch to GROUND and plug in ground starter battery.

(iii) Set engine controls as follows:

Master engine cocks	OFF
Throttles	½ in. open
Propeller controls ..	Fully up
Slow-running cut-out switches	IDLE CUT-OFF
Supercharger control	M ratio (Warning light not showing)
Air intake heat control	COLD
Radiator shutters ..	Over-ride switches at AUTOMATIC

54

PART II—HANDLING

(iv) Have a fire-extinguisher ready in case of emergency.

(v) Turn tank selector cock to No. 2 tank (*see* para. 27 (ii)) and turn on the master engine cock of the engine to be started. On Lancasters III and X aircraft the master engine cocks of all other engines which are not running must be OFF.

(vi) Switch on the booster pump in the No. 2 tank to be used.

(vii) High-volatility fuel (stores ref. 34A/111) should be used, if outside priming connection is fitted, for priming at air temperatures below freezing. The ground crew will work the priming pump until the fuel reaches the priming nozzles; this may be judged by an increase in resistance.

(viii) Switch on the ignition and booster coil, and press the starter button. Turning periods must not exceed 20 seconds with a 30-second wait between each. The ground crew will work the priming pump as firmly as possible while the engine is being turned; it should start after the following number of strokes, if cold:

Air temp., °C.	+30	+20	+10	0	−10	−20
Normal fuel ..	3	4	7	12		
High-volatility fuel ..					4	8	18

It will probably be necessary to continue priming after the engine has fired and until it picks up on the carburettor.

(ix) *On Lancaster III and X aircraft.*—As soon as the engine fires regularly, move the slow-running cut-out control to the ENGINE RUNNING (up) position. If, however, the engine shows signs of being over-rich, return the slow-running cut-out control to the IDLE CUT-OFF (down) position, until it is running smoothly.

(x) When all the engines are running satisfactorily, switch off the booster-coil switch. The ground crew will screw down the priming pumps and turn off the priming cocks (if fitted).

(xi) Have the ground/flight switch turned to FLIGHT and the ground battery removed.

(xii) Open each engine up slowly to 1,200 r.p.m. and warm up at this speed.

(xiii) Switch DR compass ON and SETTING.

PART II—HANDLING

30. **Testing engines and installations**
 While warming up:
 (i) Check temperatures and pressures, and test operation of hydraulic system by lowering and raising flaps and bomb doors—but do not test bomb doors if a bomb load is on board.
 (ii) Switch off electric fuel booster pump so as to test engine-driven pumps.
 After warming up:
 NOTE.—The following comprehensive checks should be carried out after repair, inspection other than daily, or otherwise at the pilot's discretion. Normally they may be reduced in accordance with local instructions.
 (iii) Switch radiator shutters over-ride switches to OPEN.
 (iv) At 1,500 r.p.m. test each magneto in turn to ensure that no magnetos are unserviceable.
 (v) Open up to +4 lb./sq.in. boost and check operation of two-speed supercharger. R.p.m. should fall when S ratio is engaged, and, on aircraft with electro-pneumatically operated supercharger gear change, red warning light should come on. Return to M ratio.
 (vi) At the same boost, check operation of constant-speed propeller. R.p.m. should fall to 1,800 with the control fully down
 (vii) Open throttle to the take-off position and check take-off boost and r.p.m.—*see* Part I, para. 20.
 (viii) Throttle back to +9 lb./sq.in. boost; check that r.p.m. fall below 3,000 and if not throttle back until a drop is shown, to ensure that the propeller is not constant-speeding. Then test each magneto in turn. The drop should not exceed 100 r.p.m.

31. **Check list before taxying**
 Ground/flight switch　FLIGHT
 Navigation lights　..　On if required
 Altimeter　..　..　Set
 Instrument flying panel　Check vacuum on each pump −4½ lb./sq.in.
 Radiator shutter switches　OPEN
 Brakes pressure　..　Supply 250–300 lb./sq.in.

PART II—HANDLING

32. **Check list before take-off**

Auto controls—Clutch		IN
	Cock	OUT
DR compass ..	..	NORMAL
Pitot head heater switch		ON
T —Trimming tabs ..		Elevator slightly forward
		Rudder neutral
		Aileron neutral
P —Propeller controls		Fully up
F —Fuel ..	..	Check contents of tanks
		Master engine cocks ON
		Tank selector cocks to No. 2 tanks
		Crossfeed cock OFF
		Booster pumps in Nos. 1 and 2 tanks ON
Superchargers ..		MOD
Air intake	..	COLD
Radiator shutters switches		AUTOMATIC
F —Flaps ..	..	15°–20° down

33. **Taking off**
 (i) Open the throttles to about zero boost against the brakes to see that engines are responding evenly. Throttle back, release brakes, and open throttles gently checking the tendency to swing to port by advancing port throttles slightly ahead. This will give as good a take off as taking off against the brakes, and renders it easier to correct swing.
 (ii) The tail should be raised as quickly as possible after the throttles are fully open and the aircraft eased off the ground at not less than 95(90) m.p.h. I.A.S. if loaded to 50,000 lb., or 105(100) m.p.h. I.A.S. if loaded to 60,000 lb.
 (iii) Safety speed is 130(125) m.p.h. I.A.S.
 (iv) Raise the flaps at a safe height, not below 500 feet when heavily loaded, and return selector to neutral. Raising flaps causes a nose-down change of trim.
 (v) Switch off electric fuel booster pumps of Nos. 1 and 2 tanks after initial climb, but if a warning light comes on, or fuel pressure drops below 10 lb./sq.in., switch on No. 2 pumps immediately.

PART II—HANDLING

34. Climbing

(i) The recommended speed for a quick climb is 160(155) m.p.h. I.A.S. The most comfortable climbing speed is about 175(170) m.p.h. I.A.S.

(ii) Switch on electric fuel pumps of tanks in use, at any signs of fuel starvation (at approximately 17,000 feet in temperate climates).

35. General flying

(i) *Stability.*—At normal loadings and speeds, stability is satisfactory.

(ii) *Controls.*—The elevators are relatively light and effective, but tend to become heavy in turns. The ailerons are light and effective, but become heavy at speeds over 260 m.p.h. I.A.S.
The rudders also become heavy at high speeds.

(iii) *Change of trim:*

Undercarriage UP..	Slightly nose up
Undercarriage DOWN	Slightly nose down
Flaps up to 25° from fully DOWN	Slightly nose down
Flaps up from 25°	Strongly nose down
Flaps down to 25°	Strongly nose up
Flaps fully DOWN from 25° ..	Slightly nose up
Bomb doors open	Slightly nose up

(iv) *Flying at low airspeeds.*—Flaps may be lowered about 15°–20°, r.p.m. set to 2,650, and the speed reduced to about 130(125) m.p.h. I.A.S.

36. Stalling

(i) Just before the stall, slight tail buffeting occurs.

(ii) There is no tendency for a wing to drop.

(iii) The stalling speeds in m.p.h. I.A.S. at 50,000 lb. are:
   Undercarriage and flaps up   110 (95)
   Undercarriage and flaps down 92 (83)

PART II—HANDLING

37. **Diving**
 (i) The aircraft becomes increasingly nose heavy in a high-speed dive. The elevator tab control should not be used to help the entry into the dive, but it should be used to trim out the pull necessary in the later stages of the dive.
 (ii) The flight engineer should be ready to assist the pilot as required.

38. **Check list before landing**
 Auto-pilot control cock OUT (clutches may be left IN)
 Superchargers .. M (low) ratio
 Air intake .. .. COLD
 Brake pressure .. Supply pressure 250–300 lb./sq.in.
 Reduce speed to below 200 m.p.h. I.A.S. and carry out the following drill:
  Flaps .. .. 20° down on circuit
  U —Undercarriage .. DOWN (check by indicator, visually, and horn)
  P —Propeller .. Controls up to at least 2,850 r.p.m.
  F —Flaps .. .. DOWN on final approach (handle neutral) (*see* para. 18)
  F —Fuel .. .. Booster pumps ON in tanks in use

39. **Approach speeds**
 Recommended speeds for the approach in m.p.h. I.A.S.:

	45,000 lb.	55,000 lb.
Engine-assisted	.. 110(100)	120(110)
Glide	.. 120(110)	130(120)

40. **Mislanding**
 (i) The aircraft will climb satisfactorily with the undercarriage and flaps down.
 (ii) Climb at about 140(130) m.p.h. I.A.S. and, after raising the undercarriage, start raising the flaps a little at a time, retrimming as necessary.

PART II—HANDLING

41. Beam approach

	Indicated height: feet	I.A.S. m.p.h.	R.p.m.	Approx. boost: lb./sq.in.	Actions	Change of trim
Preliminary approach	1,500	135	2,400	−1	Set 25° flap for all manoeuvring	Nose up strongly
On QDR +30°	1,500	135	2,650	+2	Undercarriage down	Nose down slightly
At outer marker	600	130	2,650	−2 to 0 (descent at 400 ft./min.) +2 (level flight)		
At inner marker	150	120	2,850	0 to +2	Flaps fully down	Nose up slightly
Overshoot	up to 300	130–140	2,850	+9	Raise flaps to 25° Raise undercarriage	Nose down slightly Nose up slightly

All four throttles should be used together throughout the approach. An increase in the rate of sink has no effect on the controls.

60

PART II—HANDLING

42. After landing

(i) Before taxying, raise the flaps and open the radiator shutters.

(ii) The outer engines may be stopped and taxying done on the inners. This is preferable to stopping the inner engines, as the brakes compressor is on the starboard inner engine, and the outer engines are more liable to overheat.

(iii) Before stopping the engines, open the bomb doors for bombing up (if required).

(iv) Switch off all booster pumps before stopping engines.

(v) *Stopping engines, Merlin XX,* 22, 24. With the engines running at 800 r.p.m., turn OFF the master engine cocks and switch OFF the ignition after the engines have stopped.

(vi) *Stopping engines, Merlin* 28 *or* 38.—To stop an engine check that the air pressure gauge reads at least 130 lb./sq.in. (*see* para 12 (i)) (if not, open up starboard inner engine which drives the compressor) and move the slow-running cut-out switch to the IDLE CUT-OFF (down) position with the engine running at about 800 r.p.m. Then switch off the ignition and leave the slow-running cut-out switch in the IDLE CUT-OFF (down) position.

NOTE.—Merlin 28 and 38 engines must not be stopped by turning off the master engine cock, as this will empty the carburettor of fuel and fill it with air. This entails much trouble when starting the engine again.

When all engines have been stopped, turn off master engine cocks, check again that all booster pumps are OFF, and then return the slow-running cut-outs to the ENGINE RUNNING position.

NOTE.—If the switches are left in the IDLE CUT-OFF position, the rams will return to the ENGINE RUNNING position as soon as the master switch is turned to GROUND. Then, if any ground maintenance work is carried out which necessitates turning on and off the master switch, the rams are being continually operated.

PART II—HANDLING

(vii) Switch off all electrical switches and turn master electrical switch to GROUND.

(viii) *Oil dilution.—See Pilot's Notes General A.P. 2095.* The correct dilution period for this aircraft is:

    Air temperatures above −10°C. .. One minute
        „   „   below −10°C. .. Two minutes

AIR PUBLICATION 2062A, C & F—P.N.
Pilot's and Flight Engineer's Notes

PART III
OPERATING DATA

43. **Engine data—Merlin XX**
    (i) *Fuel*—100 octane only.
    (ii) *Oil*—See A.P.1464/C.37
    (iii) *Engine limitations* with 100 octane fuel:

		R.p.m.	Boost lb./sq.in.	Temp. °C. Coolant	Oil
MAX. TAKE-OFF TO 1,000 FEET	M	3,000	+12*		
MAX. CLIMBING 1 HOUR LIMIT	M S	2,850	+ 9	125	90
MAX. RICH CONTINUOUS	M S	2,650	+ 7	105	90
MAX. WEAK CONTINUOUS	M S	2,650	+ 4	105	90
COMBAT 5 MINS. LIMIT	M S	3,000 3,000	+14* +16*	135 135	105 105

    *See Part I, para. 20.

    OIL PRESSURE:
      NORMAL .. .. 60/80 lb./sq.in.
      MINIMUM .. .. 45 lb./sq.in.
    MINIMUM TEMPS. FOR TAKE-OFF:
      OIL .. .. 15°C.
      COOLANT .. .. 60°C.

44. **Engine data—Merlin 22, 28 or 38**
    (i) *Fuel*—100 octane only.
    (ii) *Oil*—See A.P.1464/C.37.
    (iii) *Engine limitations* with 100 octane fuel:

		R.p.m.	Boost lb./sq.in.	Temp. °C. Coolant	Oil
MAX. TAKE-OFF TO 1,000 FEET	M	3,000	+14*		
MAX. CLIMBING 1 HOUR LIMIT	M S	2,850	+ 9	125	90
MAX. CONTINUOUS	M S	2,650	+ 7	105	90
COMBAT 5 MINS. LIMIT	M S	3,000 3,000	+14* +16*	135 135	105 105

    *See Part I, para 20.

    OIL PRESSURE:
      NORMAL .. .. 60/80 lb./sq.in.
      MINIMUM .. .. 45 lb./sq.in.
    MINIMUM TEMPS. FOR TAKE-OFF:
      OIL .. .. 15°C.
      COOLANT .. .. 60°C.

PART III—OPERATING DATA

45. Engine data—Merlin 24

(i) *Fuel*—100 octane only.

(ii) *Oil*—See A.P.1464/C.37.

(iii) *Engine limitations* with 100 octane fuel:

		R.p.m.	Boost lb./sq.in.	Temp. °C. Coolant	Oil
MAX. TAKE-OFF TO 1,000 FEET	M	3,000	+18*		
MAX. CLIMBING 1 HOUR LIMIT	M S	2,850	+ 9	125	90
MAX. CONTINUOUS	M S	2,650	+ 7	105	90
COMBAT 5 MINS. LIMIT	M S	3,000	+18*	135	105

* +18 lb./sq.in. boost must not be used below 2,850 r.p.m.

OIL PRESSURE:
   NORMAL .. .. 60/80 lb./sq.in.
   MINIMUM .. .. 45 lb./sq.in.

MINIMUM TEMP. FOR TAKE-OFF:
   OIL .. .. 15°C.
   COOLANT .. .. 60°C.

46. Flying limitations

(i) The aircraft is designed for manœuvres appropriate to a heavy bomber and care must be taken to avoid imposing excessive loads with the elevators in recovery from dives and in turns at high speed. Spinning and aerobatics are not permitted. Violent use of the rudder at high speeds should be avoided.

(ii) *Maximum speeds in m.p.h. I.A.S.:*

Diving	360
Bomb doors open	as for diving
Undercarriage down ..	200
Flaps down	200

PART III—OPERATING DATA

(iii) *Maximum weights:*

Take off and straight flying .. 65,000 lb., provided that the following mods. are incorporated:
Mod. 505 or 518
„ 588 or 598
„ 811 or SI/RDA.660
„ 1004
63,000 lb., if these mods. are not incorporated.

Landing and all forms of flying .. 55,000 lb.

Flying should be restricted to straight and level until weight is reduced to 63,000 lb.

(iv) *Bomb clearance angles:*

Dive .. .. .. 30°
Climb .. .. .. 20°
Bank .. .. .. 10° (with S.B.C. 25°)

47. Position error corrections

All handling speeds are quoted for aircraft with the pilot's A.S.I. connected to the static vent, in the port side of the fuselage. The position error for the static vent connection is −1 m.p.h. at all speeds from 140 m.p.h. I.A.S. upward.

The position error correction for aircraft on which the static vent connection has not been made is as follows:—

From To	120 140	140 160	160 180	180 200	200 250	m.p.h. I.A.S.
Add	12	10	8	6	4	m.p.h.

With bomb doors open, the correction is 2 m.p.h. higher between 160 and 200 m.p.h. I.A.S.

PART III—OPERATING DATA

48. Maximum performance
(i) *Climbing:*
    160 (155) m.p.h. I.A.S. to 12,000 ft.
    155 (150) m.p.h. I.A.S. from 12,000 to 18,000 ft.
    150 (145) m.p.h. I.A.S. from 18,000 to 22,000 ft.
    145 (140) m.p.h. I.A.S. above 22,000 ft.
Change to S ratio when boost has fallen to +6 lb./sq.in.

(ii) *Combat.*—Use S ratio if the boost obtainable in M ratio is more than 3 lb./sq. in. (4 lb./sq.in. with Merlin 24) below maximum combat boost.

49. Maximum range
(i) *Climbing.*—160 (155) m.p.h. I.A.S. at +7 lb./sq.in. boost with Merlin 22, 24, 28 or 38, +4 lb./sq.in. with Merlin XX, and 2,650 r.p.m. Change to S ratio when maximum boost obtainable in M ratio has fallen by 3 lb./sq.in.

(ii) *Cruising* (including descent):

(*a*) Fly in M ratio at maximum obtainable boost not exceeding +4 lb./sq.in. with Merlin XX, +7 lb./sq.in. with Merlin 22, 24, 28 or 38, obtaining the recommended airspeed by reducing r.p.m. which may be as low as 1,800 if this will give the recommended speed. Higher speeds than those recommended may be used if obtainable in M ratio at the lowest possible r.p.m.

(*b*) The recommended speeds are:
Fully loaded (outward journey):
    Up to 15,000 ft.,   170 (165) m.p.h. I.A.S.
    At 20,000 ft. in S ratio, 160 (155) m.p.h. I.A.S.
Lightly loaded (homeward journey):
        160 (155) m.p.h. I.A.S.

(*c*) Engage S ratio when the recommended speed cannot be maintained at 2,500 r.p.m. in M ratio.

(iii) The use of warm intakes will reduce air miles per gallon considerably. On this installation there is no need to use warm air unless intake icing is indicated by a drop of boost. *See* A.P. 2095—Pilot's Notes General.

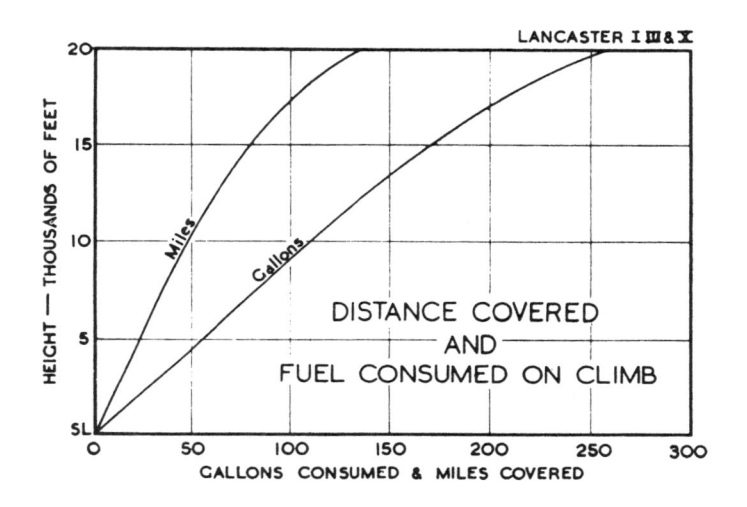

PART III—OPERATING DATA

LANCASTER I, III & X

DISTANCE COVERED AND FUEL CONSUMED ON CLIMB

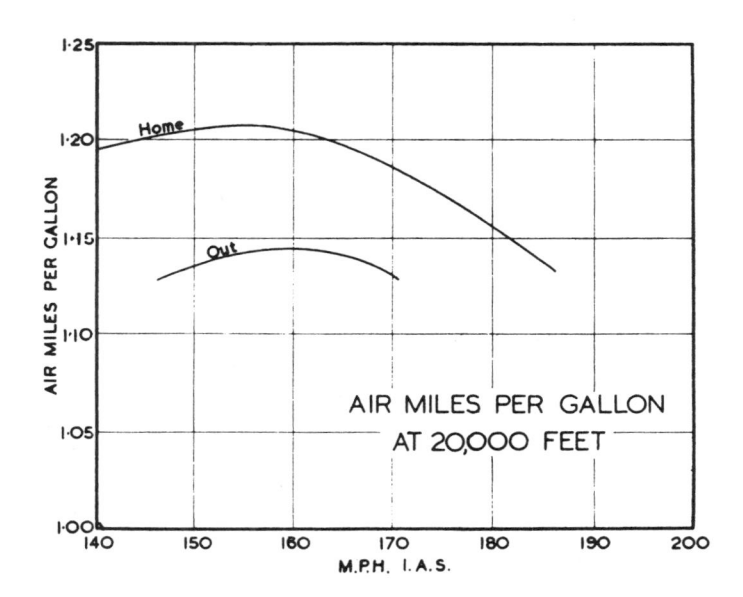

AIR MILES PER GALLON AT 20,000 FEET

PART III—OPERATING DATA

50. Fuel capacity and consumptions

(i) Capacity: Two No. 1 tanks .. 1,160 gallons
Two No. 2 tanks .. 766 gallons
Two No. 3 tanks .. 228 gallons

Total .. 2,154 gallons

(ii) *Weak mixture consumptions, Merlin XX, 22 or 24:*

The following figures are the approximate total gallons per hour and apply in M ratio between 8,000 and 17,000 feet, and in S ratio between 14,000 and 25,000 feet.

Boost lb./sq.in.	R.P.M. 2,650	R.P.M. 2,300	R.P.M. 2,000
+7*	260*	225*	212*
+4	228	204	188
+2	212	188	172
0	192	172	150
−2	172	156	140
−4	152	136	124

* These figures do not apply to Merlin XX.

(iii) *Weak mixture consumptions Merlin 28 and 38 engines:*

The following figures are the approximate total gallons per hour for the aircraft and apply in M ratio at 5,000 ft. and S ratio at 15,000 ft. One gallon per hour should be added for every 1,000 ft. above these heights.

Boost lb./sq.in	R.P.M. 2,650	R.P.M. 2,400	R.P.M. 2,200	R.P.M. 2,000	R.P.M. 1,800
+7	240	235	217	200	—
+4	216	204	196	180	—
+2	196	184	176	164	—
0	172	164	156	144	128
−2	148	140	128	124	112
−4	124	120	108	104	96

PART III—OPERATING DATA

(iv) *Rich mixture consumption, Merlin XX, 22, 24:*

Boost lb./sq.in.	R.p.m.	Total gallons per hour
+14	3,000	500
+12	3,000	460
+ 9	2,850	380
+ 7*	2,650*	320*

* Merlin XX only.

(v) *Rich mixture consumptions, Merlin 28, 38:*

Boost lb./sq.in.	R.p.m.	Total gallons per hour
+9	2,850	420

AIR PUBLICATION 2062A, C & F—P.N.
Pilot's and Flight Engineer's Notes

PART IV

EMERGENCIES

51. Engine failure during take-off

(i) If for any reason the booster pumps in the tanks being used are not ON, the master fuel cock of the failed engine must be turned off before feathering.

(ii) If one outer engine fails, the aircraft can be kept straight provided 130 (125) m.p.h. I.A.S. has been reached.

(iii) Climbing speed on three engines should be 135 (130) m.p.h. I.A.S. at moderate loads, or 140(135) m.p.h. I.A.S. if heavily loaded.

(iv) As soon as the undercarriage is up, raise the flaps a little at a time, retrimming as necessary.

52. Engine failure in flight

(i) If an engine is stopped, air may be drawn into the fuel system through the carburettor of the failed engine. To prevent this, the master fuel cock must be turned off before feathering, unless the booster pump for the tank in use is on. If an engine seizes up, its master fuel cock should be turned off immediately to ensure that the fuel supply to the other engine on the same side is not affected.

(ii) If the failed engine cannot be made to pick up again, feather its propeller and switch off. On Lancaster III and X, set mixture control to IDLE CUT-OFF.

(iii) *Handling on three engines.*—The aircraft will maintain height at full load on any three engines at 10,000 feet, and can be trimmed to fly without foot load. Maintain at least 145 (140) m.p.h. I.A.S. The automatic pilot has sufficient power to maintain a straight course with either outboard engine out of action, but only if assisted by the rudder trimming tab.

PART IV—EMERGENCIES

(iv) *Landing on three engines.*—Lowering of flaps to 20° and of undercarriage may be carried out as normally on the circuit, but further lowering of the flaps should be left until final straight approach. The final approach should be made at 120–125 m.p.h. I.A.S. using as little power as possible, and rudder trim should not be wound off until definitely committed to landing. Use all good engines to regulate approach. (*See* A.P. 2095, Part IV, Note D.)

(v) *Handling on two engines.*—It should be possible to maintain height below 10,000 feet at 140 (135) m.p.h. I.A.S. on any two engines after release of bombs and with half fuel used; but with two engines dead on one side, the foot load will be very heavy. The automatic pilot will not cope with flight with two engines dead on one side.

(vi) *Landing on two engines.*—The circuit should be made with the good engines on the inside of the turn, and undercarriage and flaps left as late as practicable. Keep **extra** height in hand, if possible, and lower the undercarriage later than usual, but have it locked down just before the final approach. The approach should be made at 130–135 m.p.h. I.A.S. in a glide. When certain of getting into the airfield, lower flaps for landing. Do not wind off trim until final approach can be made in a glide, as some power may be necessary in the early stages. (*See* A.P. 2095, Part IV, Notes C and D.)

(vii) Do not attempt to maintain height above 10,000 feet, either on three or two engines.

(viii) *Fuel system.*—The cross-feed cock should only be turned on when it is desired to feed fuel from port (or starboard) tanks to starboard (or port) engines. In this case all live engines should be fed from one tank and the fuel booster pump for this tank should be on. The fuel selector for the tanks on the other side of the aircraft should be off. At all other times, the cross-feed cock should be off.

53. **Feathering**

(i) (*a*) *Practice feathering.*—Check that booster pump in the tank feeding the engine to be stopped is on. *See* para. 52 (i). Set propeller control to low r.p.m. and throttle to give a moderate cruising boost.

PART IV—EMERGENCIES

(b) *Emergency feathering.*—If possible, master fuel cock should be turned off immediately before feathering, but if this is not possible turn fuel cock off immediately after feathering. *See* para. 52 (i).

(ii) Hold the button in only long enough to ensure that it stays in by itself; then release it so that it can spring out when feathering is complete.

(iii) Close the throttle; on Lancaster III and X aircraft move the slow-running cut-out switch to IDLE CUT-OFF position.

(iv) Switch off only when the engine has stopped.

(v) Engine auxiliaries which will be affected by feathering:

Port outer ..	Alternator for special radio, rear turret hydraulic pump.
Port inner ..	Generator, main services hydraulic pump, mid-under turret hydraulic pump, R.A.E. compressor for Automatic Pilot Mark IV and computer unit of Mark XIV bombsight, No. 1 vacuum pump.
Starboard inner	Generator, main services hydraulic pump, front turret hydraulic pump, Heywood compressor for pneumatic system, No. 2 vacuum pump.
Starboard outer	Alternator for special radio, mid-upper turret hydraulic pump.

54. **Unfeathering**

NOTE.—It is preferable not to unfeather at speeds above normal cruising speed to avoid any risk of overspeeding.

(i) Set throttle closed or slightly open, propeller control fully down and ignition on.

(ii) Switch on the fuel booster pump of the tank in use, and turn on master engine cock.

(iii) Hold the button in and, on Lancaster III and X aircraft, as the engine starts turning set the slow-running cut-out switch to RUNNING (up) position. Continue to hold the button in until r.p.m. reach at least 1,500 and not more than 1,800.

(iv) If the propeller does not return to normal constant-speed operation, open throttle slightly.

PART IV—EMERGENCIES

55. Damage by enemy action

(i) *Fires.*—If fire occurs in bomb bay, pilot should open bomb doors, jettison bombs, and dive.

(ii) *Flight engineer's checks:*

Check fuel contents gauges. Should any abnormal consumptions be shown on the tank the aircraft is running on, or should any of the other tanks show a loss of fuel, proceed as follows:

(*a*) Cross-feed cock ON.

(*b*) Run all engines on the damaged tank, and switch on its booster pump. The fuel selector for the tanks on the other side of the aircraft should be off.

(*c*) When contents of damaged tank fall to 20 gallons, turn on fuel selector for the corresponding tank on the other side of the aircraft and turn OFF cross-feed valve.

(*d*) Watch fuel pressure warning lights or fuel pressure gauge and change over to other tank as soon as pressure drops; switch off booster pump in empty tank.

56. Undercarriage emergency operation

If the hydraulic system fails the undercarriage can be lowered by compressed air from a special bottle or bottles, irrespective of the position of the undercarriage lever.

NOTE.—The flap selector should be neutral before using the undercarriage emergency air system.

On early aircraft the control is just aft of the front spar, but on later aircraft the knob (80) for working the air system is just forward of the flight engineer's panel. The undercarriage cannot be raised again by this method. Although the undercarriage will lower by this method, irrespective of the position of the normal undercarriage selector, the latter should be left in the down position for and after landing; otherwise, any leakage of air pressure may cause the undercarriage locks to be released and the undercarriage to collapse.

PART IV—EMERGENCIES

57. **Flaps emergency operation**

   After lowering the undercarriage by turning on the emergency air cock, the flaps may be lowered by operating the flaps control, which admits the air pressure to the flaps system. The flaps can be raised again, but there may not be sufficient air pressure to lower the flaps a second time; furthermore it may cause the header tank to burst. If it is absolutely necessary to raise the flaps by emergency method extreme care must be taken to raise them slowly by stages. If the flaps are lowered by the emergency method before landing, flaps must be left down after landing, owing to the likelihood of bursting the header tank.

58. **Bomb doors emergency operation**

   On aircraft in which Mod. 757 is incorporated, the bomb doors can be operated in an emergency by compressed air from an air bottle (entirely separate from undercarriage and flaps emergency air bottle).

   If, when pilot selects bomb doors open or closed, the doors fail to operate, the air bomber should withdraw the pin on the emergency air control in the nose, and hold the control down against the spring; when the doors have fully opened (or closed), the air bomber should release the control. There is sufficient pressure in the air bottle for three or four operations.

59. **Bomb jettisoning**

   (i) Open bomb doors, and check visually that both are fully open. *See* para. 19.

   (ii) Then jettison containers first by switch (15) on right of dash.

   (iii) Jettison bombs by handle (16) beside container jettison switch.

   (iv) Close bomb doors.

PART IV—EMERGENCIES

60. **Fuel jettisoning**
    NOTE.—Contents of No. 1 tanks only can be jettisoned.
    (i) Reduce speed to 150 (145) m.p.h. I.A.S. and lower flaps 15°.
    (ii) Lift and turn jettison control on left of pilot's seat. Return control after jettisoning.
    (iii) The jettison valve should be closed while there is still about 100 gallons remaining in each tank; if the jettison valve is left open, all the fuel will be jettisoned less approximately 70 gallons, but the last 30 gallons of jettisonable fuel runs out slowly and is inclined to get splashed over the fuselage. The jettison valve may be closed at any time during jettisoning.
    Approximate weight of jettisonable fuel, leaving 100 gallons in each tank, is 6,900 lb.

61. **Parachute exits**
    (i) Hatch in floor of nose should be used by all members of the crew if time is available; it is released by handle in centre, lifted inwards and jettisoned.
    (ii) Main entrance door should be used as a parachute exit only in extreme emergency.

62. **Crash exits**
    Three push-out panels are fitted in the roof, one above the pilot, one just forward of the rear spar, and one forward of the mid-upper turret.

63. **Dinghy and ditching**
    (i) A type J dinghy stowed in the starboard wing may be released and inflated:
    (*a*) from inside by pulling the release cord running along the fuselage roof aft of the rear spar;
    (*b*) from outside by pulling the loop on the starboard side, rear of the tail plane leading edge.
    (*c*) automatically by an immersion switch.
    (ii) The flaps should be lowered 30° for ditching, but if the flaps will not lower by the hydraulic system, do not attempt to lower them by the compressed air system, as this will also cause the undercarriage to lower (*see* paras. 56 and 57).

PART IV—EMERGENCIES

64. **Engine fire-extinguishers**

    Each engine is provided with a fire-extinguisher bottle which can be operated by pushbuttons on the pilot's instrument panel; the fire-extinguishers are also operated automatically by a crash switch (on the starboard side of the nose) and, when the undercarriage is down, by a gravity switch (also on the starboard side of the nose).

    NOTE.—The automatic flame switches have been disnected. Therefore in flight the operation of the engine fire-extinguisher is left entirely to the pilot's discretion.

65. **Hand fire-extinguishers**

    One on port side of air bomber's compartment.
    One on port side of pilot's seat.
    One on starboard side aft of rear spar.
    One on starboard side forward of mid-upper turret.
    One at tail turret.

66. **Signal pistol.**—This is stowed on top of the front spar; the firing position is in the roof forward of the stowed position.

67. **Signal cartridge stowage.**—Starboard side of fuselage just forward of front spar.

68. **Parachutes**

    One in air bomber's compartment, on aft bulkhead.
    One behind pilot's seat.
    One on starboard wall at rest station.
    One on starboard wall forward of mid-upper turret.
    One on port side, opposite entrance door.
    One forward of tail turret.

69. **Static line for parachuting wounded men**

    (i) If possible, fly aircraft at 130 m.p.h. I.A.S. with 15° flap.
    (ii) Assist casualty to air bomber's compartment and place him feet first facing aft.
    (iii) Check casualty's parachute harness, fit parachute, remove helmet.

PART IV—EMERGENCIES

(iv) Remove static line from stowage which is situated on starboard side of front exit. Care should be taken that the threads keeping the static line folded up are not broken. Take snap hook at end of static line and attach to parachute as follows.

(v) Pass the safety becket on the static line through the double 8 cord loop, then pass the small snap hook through the safety becket.

(vi) Snap the hook down on to the rip-cord handle. Insert safety pin to lock the shroud of the snap hook.

(vii) Stow the slack of the static line between the becket and the snap hook under the adjacent pack elastic to prevent this slack length getting caught up on anything and thus pulling the rip-cord too soon.

(viii) Open and jettison front hatch.

(ix) Slide the man through the exit feet first facing aft. Care must be taken to keep his hands to his sides. Do not hold on to the static line by hand.

70. **Emergency packs.**—On starboard side at rest station.

71. **Projectible kite container.**—Along port side at rest station.

72. **Crash axes**

One on port side of fuselage aft of main entrance door. One on starboard wall in front of rear spar.

73. **Incendiary bombs.**—Two are provided on front face of front spar for destruction of aircraft.

74. **First-aid equipment.**—Starboard side of fuselage aft of main entrance door.

PART V

SUPPLEMENTARY NOTES FOR FLIGHT ENGINEER

75. **Oil system.**—A self-sealing oil tank is fitted in each nacelle; the normal capacity is 37½ gallons with 4½ gallons air space. The normal type of oil used is DTD. 472B. A stack pipe in each tank retains 2–3 gallons for feathering the propeller. Normal high-pressure oil feeds the propeller constant speed unit.

   Under cruising conditions, it is recommended that the oil temperature should not exceed 60°C., but up to 90°C. may be used without damage to the engine. The oil consumption should be between 8 and 16 pints per hour.

76. **Coolant system.**—A horseshoe type header tank, filled with 30% Glycol (D.T.D. 344A inhibited) and 70% distilled water, is mounted over the reduction gear of each engine. On the ground with engine running a small coolant discharge is normal, but not in flight.

   From B block on each inboard engine coolant is led to the cabin heating radiator, through which the flow of air is regulated by controls either side of the fuselage at the wireless operator's station.

77. **Hydraulic system**

   The accumulator, supplied by two pumps, has an air charging valve and a pressure gauge which should read 220 lb./sq.in. when there is no pressure in the system. Misleading pressure gauge readings will occur if the accumulator air pressure is incorrect. The gauge should read between 800–900 lb./sq.in. under working pressure, when the cut-out operates isolating the pumps and relieving them of unnecessary strain. The accumulator then provides the initial pressure to operate the various systems. When the pressure falls between 220–300 lb./sq.in. the pumps will automatically be cut in to operate the system and build up accumulator pressure again.

PART V—NOTES FOR FLIGHT ENGINEER

Hydraulic fluids.—The four fluids suitable are mineral oils. They may be mixed if additional supplies of that already in use are not available.

(i) Intava mixture 70% DTD585 + 30% DTD472.

(ii) Intava 695.

(iii) Mixture of two parts DTD44 and one part Intava 694.

(iv) DTD44.

Mixtures containing DTD44 will congeal at a higher temperature than the others. The first-mentioned mixture has the lowest congealing temperature.

Fuel jettison.—When the fuel jettison control is operated an air inlet valve is opened in the top of each No. 1 tank, and at the same time a valve is opened at the bottom of each tank, breaking a small retaining washer and releasing a spring-loaded stocking. Do not jettison below 100 gallons (*see* Part III, para. 60). The valves may be closed at any point but the stocking will not be retracted. When repacking, ensure that the stocking is dry and serviceable. Reseat the inlet and the outlet valves. Before fitting one of the spare shear washers carried in the housing, the spindle must pass centrally through the jettison valve.

78. **Pneumatic system**

The pressure (normally 300-320 lb./sq.in.) is controlled by a pressure regulating valve, which recommences charging when the pressure drops to 270-280 lb./sq.in. If the pressure drops to 130 lb./sq.in. or below, a pressure-maintaining valve closes, rendering the entire pneumatic system, with the exception of the brakes, out of operation. Therefore M supercharger ratio will be engaged, and the idle cut-off and radiator flaps will be inoperative. If pressure cannot be built up, to stop Merlin 28 or 38 engines, throttle down to minimum r.p.m. and close the master fuel cocks. This will drain the carburettor, which should be carefully primed to expel all the air from the fuel chambers before restarting. (*See* Para. 42 (vi).)

PART V—NOTES FOR FLIGHT ENGINEER

79. **Electrical system**

    Four accumulators, connected in series parallel, giving a capacity of 80 ampere hours at 24 volts, are charged by two generators. Two ammeters on the main electrical control panel indicate the total generator output to services and battery charging. On the same panel a voltmeter indicates the state of the accumulators, reading 28–29 volts in flight under normal conditions and over 24 on the ground with engines stopped. On Lancasters I and III, spare fuses and a fuse location table are inside the hinged door. The main generator fuses are at the top inside the main control panel. Spare fuses are carried in the lid of the fuse box.

    The switches below are for ground fault tracing and must be left on and not touched in flight.

    On the front of the panel are two earth warning lights, a resin light switch (locked to prevent its movement) and the air bomber's station light switch of which the push button is for use on the ground in conjunction with the earth warning lights.

    On Lancaster X, overload switches are fitted in the heavier circuits and flick off if the current becomes too great. Allow five or ten minutes for the service to cool down and turn the switch on.

80. **Undercarriage failure**

    Should the red warning lights remain steady or the green lights not appear when the undercarriage is selected down, operate the warning light changeover switch. If this is ineffective select undercarriage up and return the selector down. If this is still ineffective check the accumulator pressure gauge reading. Should it be 300 lb./sq.in. there is probably no pressure in the system. Select the undercarriage up and down again. The pressure may drop between 200 and 300 lb./sq.in. then rise between 850 and 900 lb./sq.in. when the cut-out operates. If about 800 lb./sq.in. is indicated and the undercarriage appears to be down visually the indicator is probably faulty. If there is still some doubt use the emergency air

PART V—NOTES FOR FLIGHT ENGINEER

pressure to make certain the undercarriage is down, turning the cock off when the operation is complete. This conserves the air pressure for further use; if it is necessary to use the flaps emergency system the method of operation is described in para. 57.

81. **Gauges.**—The gauges on the engineer's panel in the Lancaster X are the four point type fitting into sockets and are therefore interchangeable.

AIR PUBLICATION 2062A, C & F—P.N.
Pilot's and Flight Engineer's Notes

PART VI
ILLUSTRATIONS AND LOCATION OF CONTROLS NOT ILLUSTRATED

LOCATION OF CONTROLS

Service	Location
Undercarriage warning horn test pushbutton	Behind pilot's seat.
Cross feed cock	On floor, just forward of the front spar.
Priming pump and cock (if fitted)	In each inboard nacelle.
Air intake heat control	Left of pilot's seat.
Radiator shutter switches	On starboard cockpit wall.
Supercharger gear change lever (on early Lancaster I)	To right of starboard master engine cocks.
Ground/flight switch.	On starboard side aft of front spar.
Cockpit heat controls	One each side of the fuselage just forward of the front spar. Two adjustable louvres in fuselage nose.
Oxygen master valve	At forward end of oxygen crate
Camera pushbutton control	On starboard rail of cockpit.
Reconnaissance flare stowage	On either side of fuselage forward of flare chute.
Flame floats or sea markers stowage	On either side of fuselage adjacent to flare chute.

FUSES

Location	Service
(*a*) Inside junction box at forward end of bomb aimer's compartment	Bomb gear fuses.
(*b*) Pilot's auxiliary fuse panel	Oil and radiator thermometer fuses.
(*c*) Navigation panel	Radio fuses.
(*d*) Mid turret position	Mid-upper and underturret, call lights, and, on early aircraft beam approach fuses.
(*e*) Main electrical control panel	General services.

KEY TO Fig. 1
INSTRUMENT PANEL

1. Instrument flying panel.
2. D.F. Indicator.
3. Landing light switches.
4. Undercarriage indicator switch.
5. D.R. compass repeater.
6. D. R. compass deviation card holder.
7. Ignition switches.
8. Boost gauges.
9. R.p.m. indicators.
10. Booster coil switch.
11. Slow-running cut-out switches.
12. I.F.F. detonator buttons.
13. I.F.F. switch.
14. Engine starter switches.
15. Bomb containers jettison button.
16. Bomb jettison control.
17. Vacuum change-over cock.
18. Oxygen regulator.
19. Feathering buttons.
20. Triple pressure gauge.
21. Signalling switchbox (identification lamps).
22. Fire-extinguisher pushbuttons.
23. Suction gauge.
24. Starboard master engine cocks.
25. Supercharger gear change control panel.
26. Flaps position indicator.
27. Flaps position indicator switch.
28. Throttle levers.
29. Propeller speed control levers.
30. Port master engine cocks.
31. Rudder pedal.
32. Boost control cut-out.
33. Signalling switchbox (recognition lights).
34. Identification lights colour selector switches.
35. D.R. compass switches.
36. Auto controls steering lever.
37. P.4. compass deviation card holder.
38. P.4 compass.
39. Undercarriage position indicator.
40. A.S.I. correction card hold.
41. Beam approach indicator.
42. Watch holder.

KEY TO Fig. 2
PORT SIDE OF COCKPIT

43. Bomb doors control.
44. Navigation lights switch.
45. D switch.
46. Auto controls main switch.
47. Pushbutton unit for T.R. 1196.
48. Seat raising lever.
49. Mixer box.
50. Beam approach control unit.
51. Oxygen connection.
52. Pilot's call light.
53. Auto controls attitude control.
54. Auto controls cock.
55. Auto controls clutch.
56. Brake lever.
57. Auto controls pressure gauge.
58. Pilot's mic/tel socket.
59. Windscreen de-icing pump.
60. Flaps selector.
61. Aileron trimming tab control.
62. Elevator trimming tab control.
63. Rudder trimming tab control.
64. Undercarriage control lever.
65. Undercarriage control safety bolt.
66. Portable oxygen stowage.
67. Harness release lever.

KEY TO *Fig. 3*

FLIGHT ENGINEER'S
PANEL

LANCASTERS I & III

68. Ammeter.
69. Oil pressure gauges.
70. Pressure-head heater switch.
71. Oil temperature gauges.
72. Coolant temperature gauges.
74. Fuel contents gauges.
75. Inspection lamp socket.
76. Fuel contents gauge switch.
77. Fuel tanks selector cocks.
78. Electric fuel booster pump switches.
79. Fuel pressure warning lights.
80. Emergency air control.
81. Oil dilution buttons.

FIG 3

FLIGHT ENGINEER'S PANEL, LANCASTERS I AND III

KEY TO *Fig. 4*

**FLIGHT ENGINEER'S PANEL
LANCASTER X**

68. Ammeter.
69. Oil pressure gauges.
71. Oil temperature gauges.
72. Coolant temperature gauges.
73. Fuel pressure gauges.
74. Fuel contents gauges.
75. Inspection lamp socket.
77. Fuel tanks selector cocks.
78. Electric fuel booster pump switches.
80. Emergency air control.
81. Oil dilution buttons.

FIG 4

FLIGHT ENGINEER'S PANEL, LANCASTER X

FIG 4

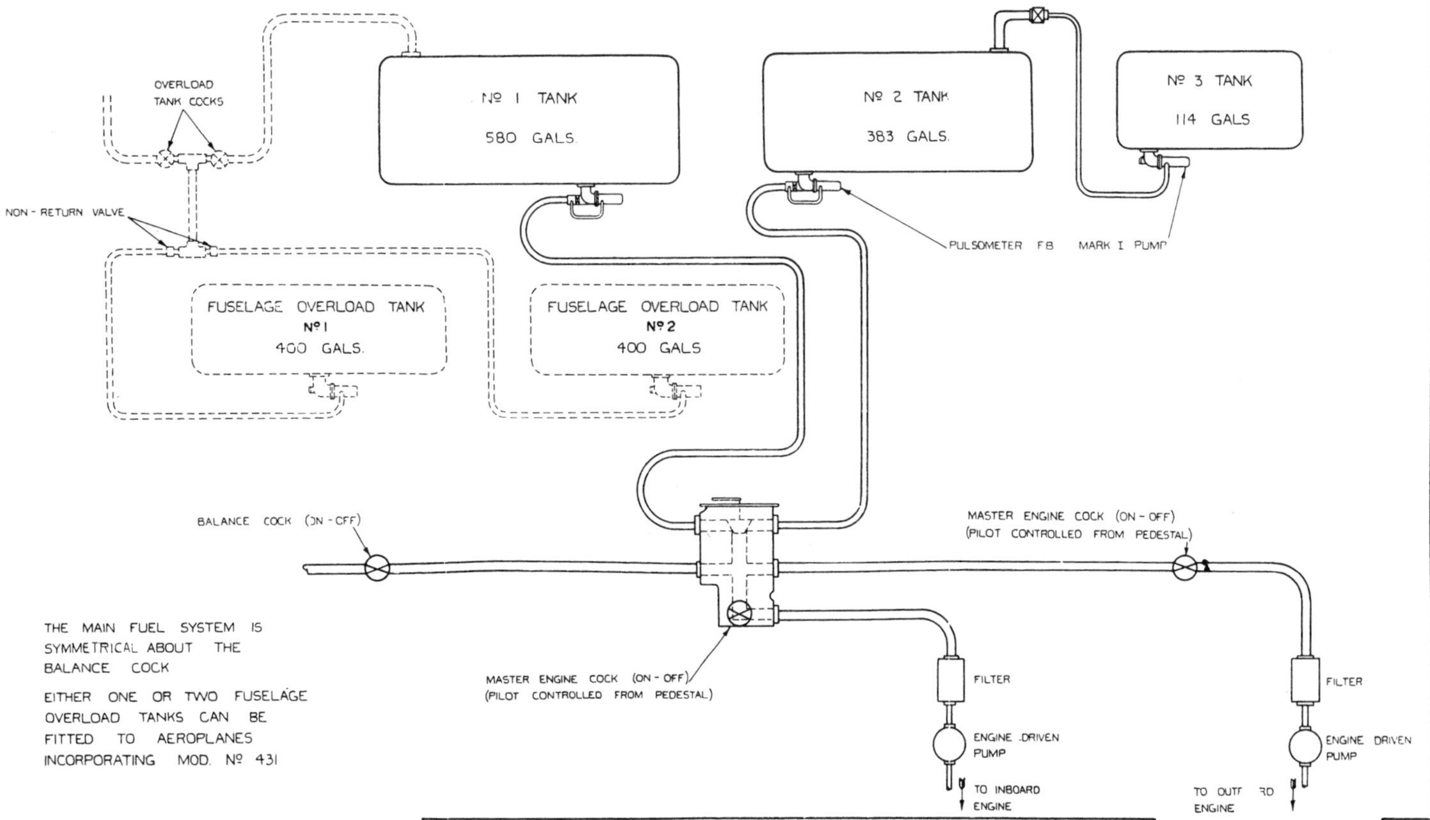

THE MAIN FUEL SYSTEM IS SYMMETRICAL ABOUT THE BALANCE COCK

EITHER ONE OR TWO FUSELAGE OVERLOAD TANKS CAN BE FITTED TO AEROPLANES INCORPORATING MOD. № 431

FIG 5

SIMPLIFIED FUEL SYSTEM DIAGRAM. PULSOMETER PUMPS.

FIG 5

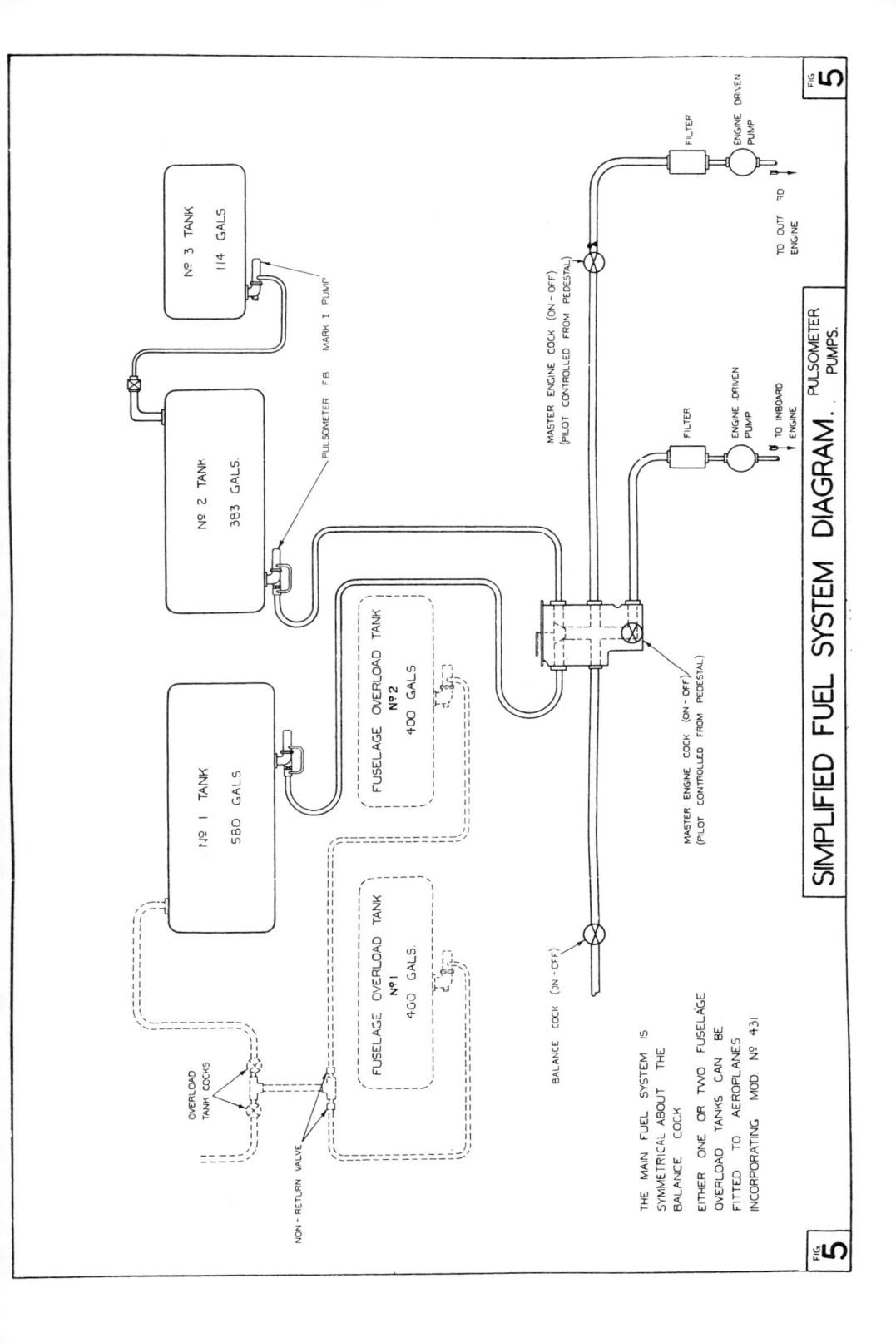

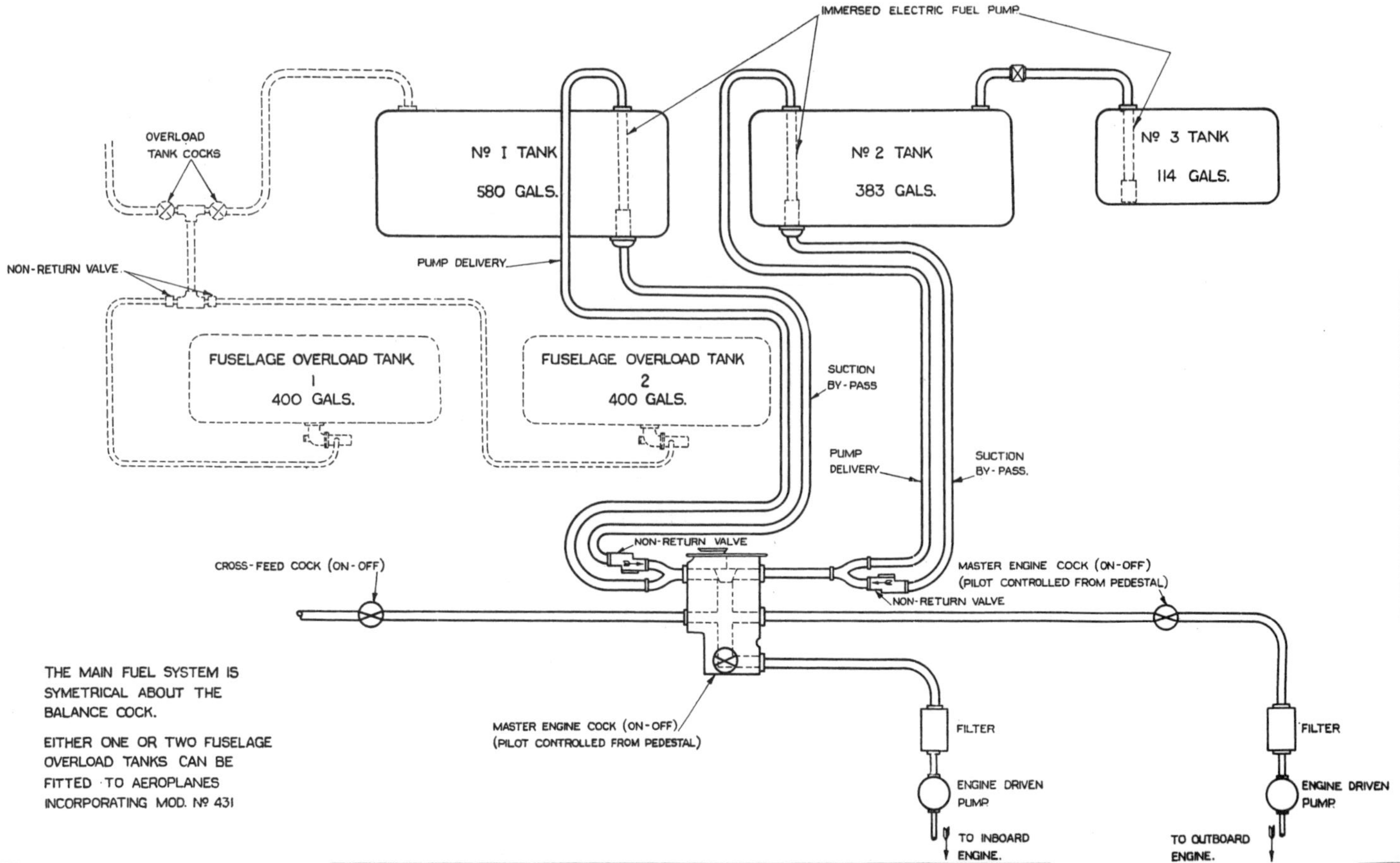

THE MAIN FUEL SYSTEM IS SYMETRICAL ABOUT THE BALANCE COCK.

EITHER ONE OR TWO FUSELAGE OVERLOAD TANKS CAN BE FITTED TO AEROPLANES INCORPORATING MOD. Nº 431

FIG 6

SIMPLIFIED FUEL SYSTEM DIAGRAM. E.P.I. PUMPS

FIG 6

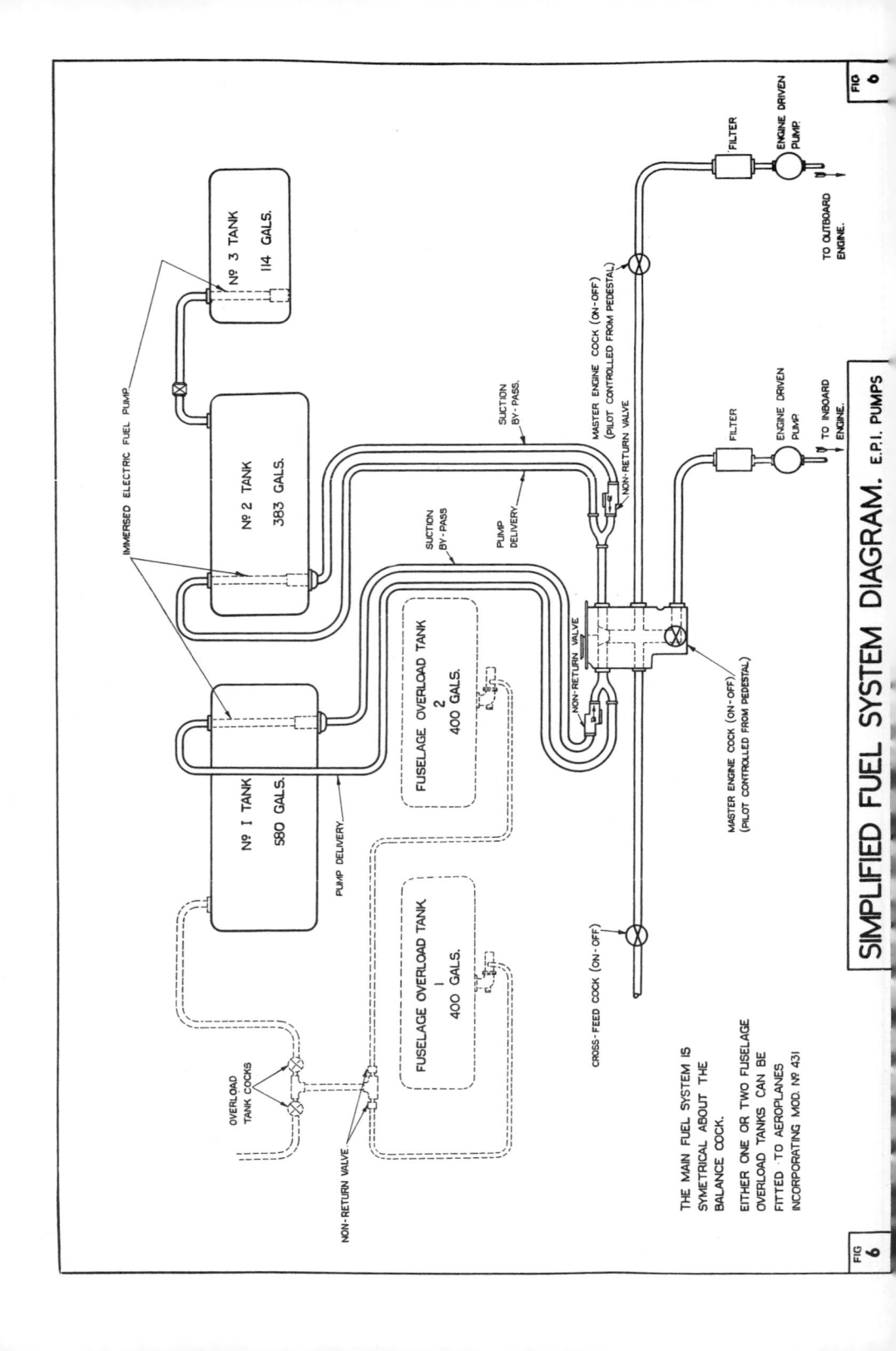

Section 3:
Controls and equipment at crew stations.

This Revised Section issued with A.L. No. 25
(Superseding Sect. 3 issued December, 1941)
April, 1943

A.P.2062A & C, Vol. I

SECTION 3—CONTROLS AND EQUIPMENT AT CREW STATIONS

LIST OF CONTENTS

	Para.
Introductory	1

General equipment

	Para.
Cockpit heating and ventilation	2
Oxygen equipment	3
Intercommunication	4
EMERGENCY exits and equipment	5
Parachutes	6
Parachute and emergency exits	7
Air/sea rescue equipment	9
Fire extinguishers	10
Fireman's axe	11
First-aid outfits	12
Marine distress signals...	13
Hydraulic hand pump	14
Emergency lowering of main wheels and flaps	15
Emergency use of incendiary bombs	15A

Nose

	Para.
General	16
Camera station	17
Air-bomber's station	18
De-icing for air-bomber's window	20

Front centre portion

	Para.
General	21
Air-observer-navigator's station—	
General	22
Instrument panel	23
Fuel contents gauges	24
Fuel cross-feed cock	24A
Navigator's equipment	25
Radio station...	27
Electrical services panel	28

Intermediate centre portion

	Para.
General	29

Rear centre portion

	Para.
General	31
Flares	33
Mid gun stations—	
Upper mid turret	34
Lower mid turret	35

Rear fuselage

	Para.
General	36
Rear turret	37

LIST OF ILLUSTRATIONS

	Fig.
Location of equipment	1

F.S./1

A.P.2062A and C, Vol. I

SECTION 3—CONTROLS AND EQUIPMENT AT CREW STATIONS

Introductory

1. The lay-out of the controls and equipment in the fuselage is illustrated and referenced in fig. 1 at the end of this Section; a key to the items referenced is given facing the illustration. The fuselage is divided, for description, into five portions, viz., nose, front centre portion, intermediate centre portion, rear centre portion and rear fuselage.

GENERAL EQUIPMENT

Cockpit heating and ventilation

2. The cockpit is heated by warm air from two radiators mounted in the main plane leading edge and connected to the inboard engine cooling systems. On each side of the fuselage, just forward of the front spar, is a control knob which operates a shutter in the air duct. When turned counter-clockwise it opens the inlet to the cabin and closes the by-pass to the outer air. To control the escape of the air from the cabin an extractor louvre is provided on each side of the nose of the fuselage.

Oxygen equipment

3. Flexible oxygen connections, with oxygen economisers, flow meters and cut-off valves, are provided at various points throughout the aircraft, and a supply is also taken to the front, upper mid and rear gun turrets. The cut-off valves are opened by the removal of the flexible pipe from the stowage, or in the case of the turret supplies, by the removal of the dummy sockets. The main supply is controlled by the pilot by means of a regulator on his instrument panel. The oxygen bottles are stowed in a crate which forms the frame of the rest couch in the intermediate centre portion of the fuselage, and a main high pressure cut-off valve is provided at the front end of the crate. Portable oxygen bottles are also provided at crew stations.

Intercommunication

4. Microphone-telephone sockets are provided for intercommunication at each of the crew stations. By means of the change-over system in the care of the wireless operator, the microphone-telephone sockets used for intercommunication may also be employed for transmitting and receiving through the general purpose radio installation.

EMERGENCY exits and equipment

5. The location of equipment for use in an emergency is shown in Sect. 1.

6. *Parachutes.*—Stowages for pack-type parachutes are provided at the following points:—
   (i) On the front face of the bulkhead at the rear of the fuselage nose portion.
   (ii) At the forward end of the navigator's table.
   (iii) On the starboard side of the intermediate centre portion, between the rear spar and the armoured bulkhead.

A.P.2062A and C, Vol. I, Sect. 3

(iv) On the starboard side of the rear centre portion above the rear end of the main floor.

(v) On the port side of the rear fuselage aft of the mid gun turrets.

(vi) On the starboard side of the rear fuselage aft of the draughtproof doors.

7. *Parachute and emergency exits.*—If time is available all members of the crew should use the hatch in the floor of the fuselage nose for parachute exits. The main entrance door should be used as a parachute exit only in extreme emergency.

8. Emergency exits of the push-out type (these must not be used as parachute exits) are fitted in the roof, in the following positions:—

(i) In the canopy above the pilot's cockpit.

(ii) In the intermediate centre portion.

(iii) In the rear centre portion above the end of the main floor.

9. *Air/sea rescue equipment.*—A type J dinghy is stowed in the starboard plane and secured by a coiled cord painter. It may be inflated and released by any of the following methods (*see* also A.P.1182, Vol. I):—

(i) By pulling the release cord running inside the fuselage along the roof aft of the rear spar.

(ii) From outside, by means of the loop on the starboard side adjacent to the leading edge of the tail plane.

(iii) Automatically, by an immersion switch.

A special emergency pack is stowed on top of the dinghy, to which it is attached by means of a lanyard. In addition to this pack, standard Type 4 and Type 7 emergency packs are stowed on the starboard side of the fuselage, just aft of the rear spar. No equipment other than that listed in the current Appendix A for the aircraft, may be carried in those emergency packs.

10. *Fire extinguishers.*—Five small hand fire extinguishers are provided inside the fuselage, mounted near the crew stations, and a larger extinguisher is stowed on the starboard side of the fuselage just aft of the front spar.

11. *Fireman's axe.*—A fireman's axe is stowed on the starboard side of the rear fuselage just aft of the entrance door.

12. *First-aid outfits.*—Three first-aid outfits are located just aft of the door on the side of the fuselage. Access to the outfits may be obtained either by a hinged door on the inside or a pull-out panel on the outside.

13. *Marine distress signals.*—Three marine distress signals, together with hand shields, are stowed on the port side of the rear fuselage opposite the door.

14. *Hydraulic hand pump.*—A hydraulic hand pump is mounted on the port side of the intermediate centre portion, between the armoured bulkhead and the front spar. It may be used, in the event of failure of the engine-driven pumps, for the emergency operation of the carburettor air-intake shutters and the fuel jettison system. It is also possible, by fifteen minutes of pumping, to lower the bomb doors.

F.S./2

15. *Emergency lowering of main wheels and flaps.*—If the hydraulic system fails, the main wheels and the flaps can be lowered by compressed air. The control consists either, of a cock just aft of the front spar on the starboard side, or of a knob just forward of the air-observer's instrument panel. When the emergency control is operated, the main wheels are lowered irrespective of the position of the normal control lever and compressed air is admitted to the flaps control valve. After lowering the main wheels the flaps may be lowered by operating the flaps control. The flaps can be raised again, but this should only be done in extreme emergency, as there may not be sufficient air pressure to lower them again. In raising the flaps by this method, *extreme care must be taken to raise them slowly, by stages.*

15A. *Emergency use of incendiary bombs.*—Two 1¼ lb. incendiary bombs, stowed on the forward face of the former above the front spar, are provided for use should the destruction of the aircraft become necessary.

NOSE

General

16. The nose of the fuselage extends forwards from the cockpit instrument panel. The lower part of the nose is dome-shaped and made from transparent material but includes a flat portion of glass in the lower half of the dome for direct vision for the air bomber. A hydraulically-operated gun turret (type F.N.5) is mounted above the air-bomber's station; for further information on the turret, *see* A.P.1659A, Vol. I. The oxygen supply to the turret is controlled by a cut-off valve on the starboard side, immediately behind the turret draughtscreen.

Camera station

17. An F.24 camera is installed on an adjustable framework on the rear port side of the nose above a circular window, and is controlled from a panel on the port side. Two sockets for camera heating connections are mounted below the panel.

Air-bomber's station

18. The air-bomber's station with associated equipment occupies the floor of the nose. The air-bomber is provided with kneeling cushions located on the door in the nose, and an adjustable support. The prone position enables the front gun turret to be used while the air-bomber is at his station. In front of the support provision is made for mounting a Mk. II automatic bomb sight or, in aircraft incorporating Mod. No. 468, a Mk. XIV bomb sight. The computor for the latter is on the port side of the nose, and above the computor is the cock controlling the air supply from the automatic controls system. The bomb sight control panel, the steering control and, when the T.R.1196 installation is fitted, the air-bomber's "Press to Transit" switch, are on the port side at the forward end of the nose. A target map case is provided on the floor below the air-bomber's support. An automatic bomb distributor, a Connell preselector and bomb selector, and fuzing switches, are mounted on a panel on the starboard side. A stowage for the air-bomber's height and speed computor is provided on the starboard panel, and the switch controlling the heating of the 4,000 lb. bomb release gear is mounted above the rear end of the panel.

19. A hinged inspection door for the bomb compartment is formed in the bulkhead at the rear of the nose, and a socket is provided for connecting an inspection lamp. A flexible oxygen connection for the air-bomber is fitted on the port side, and an ivorine writing pad and pencil on the front former.

20. *De-icing for air-bomber's window.*—Glycol de-icing is provided for this window, and is operated by a hand pump on the port side of the fuselage nose (*see* A.P.1464B, Vol. I). If the pump is operated once a minute it delivers fluid at the rate of two pints per hour. The reservoir, which also supplies the pilot's windscreen, is of approximately four gallons capacity, and is fitted below the step at the rear of the nose.

FRONT CENTRE PORTION

General

21. The front centre portion, comprising that part of the aircraft from the front spar to the cockpit instrument panel, houses the following stations: pilot's cockpit (*see* Sect. 1), air-observer-navigator's station, wireless operator's station and fighting control station. The starboard side of the compartment serves as a gangway between the stations, and provides access to the nose of the aircraft. A bullet-proof glass screen is mounted between the top of the fuselage and the canopy on the starboard side, protecting the fighting control station and additional protection is provided by steel plating attached to the top of formers 1, 2, 3 and 4, on the starboard side.

Air-observer-navigator's station

22. *General.*—The air-observer-navigator's station is at the rear of the pilot's seat. The navigator's table and instrument panel are on the port side and the observer's instrument panel is on the starboard side. A swivelling seat at the side of the table is mounted on a vertical strut at former 3.

23. *Instrument panel.*—This panel is hinged at its lower edge and secured at its upper edge to the cockpit rail. On the panel are the following: switches for the electric pumps in the fuel tanks, for the oil dilution system and for the heated pressure head; fuel pressure warning lamps; gauges for fuel contents, oil pressure, oil temperature and coolant temperature. Control handwheels for the fuel tank selector cocks project through holes in the panel. In aircraft L.7527 to L.7532 inclusive and those incorporating Mod. No. 677, a knob for the operation of the emergency air system for main wheel unit and flap lowering (*see* para. 15) is mounted on the face of the former at the front edge of the panel.

24. *Fuel contents gauges.*—Six fuel contents gauges are mounted on the observer's instrument panel (four on aircraft L.7527 to L.7532 inclusive, which are fitted with only four tanks). These show the amount of fuel in each tank when the switch below the gauge is in the ON position. A correction card for the readings when the aircraft is in the tail-down position is fitted on the panel.

  Note.—The fuel pressure warning lamps and the fu1 contents gauges are controlled by the same switch, and this should always be left on in flight.

24A. *Fuel cross-feed cock.*—The cross-feed cock is mounted on the floor just forward of the front spar, with the control handle visible through the front spar cover. Before it is turned ON the tanks that will NOT be in use must be turned OFF at the air-observer's panel. On some aircraft this cock will be labelled "balance cock".

F.S /3

25. *Navigator's equipment.*—The navigator's table is a permanent fixture containing a chart stowage and having an adjustable lamp which may be put in any desired position. In front of the table, on the port wall, are located the navigator's instrument panel and a pencil tray. A T.3135/R.3136 installation in the rear fuselage is supplied from the same control panel and switch as the T.1335, and a T.R.1335 installation is fitted at the forward end of the table. A whip aerial for the latter projects through the canopy aft of the D.F. loop or through the fuselage roof just aft of the front spar, and the control switch, push-buttons and warning lamps are fitted on the instrument panel. Also the on panel is the D.R. compass repeater, and the variation corrector is mounted in the fuselage roof. Above the table is an astrograph.

26. A dome is provided at the aft end of the canopy for taking sextant readings and an anchorage for the air-observer is attached to the floor just forward of the front spar step. The sextant is stowed on a panel at the forward end of the navigator's table. A torch, an Aldis signalling lamp and a hand fire extinguisher are also stowed on this panel. At the base of the main radio panel is a code book stowage box. On the starboard side, opposite the table are the recording drift sight and the navigator's oxygen connection and economiser. The stowage clips for the signal pistol cartridges are just forward of the front spar. A black-out curtain for the navigator's station which can be pulled down within 12 in. of the floor, is fitted at the forward end of the fuselage roof below the canopy and a curtain is also provided in the sextant dome.

Radio station

27. The wireless operator's seat is on the port side integral with the front spar cover and step, and faces forward. A T.1154–R.1155, an amplifier and a crystal monitor are mounted on a transverse table at the rear end of the navigator's panel. A T.R.9F when fitted, is below the table; alternatively a T.R.1196 is mounted on the port side just aft of the rear spar. The wireless operator's oxygen cut-off valve, and the mic-tel distribution panel, are on the port side above the window, and just forward of the window is the R.3003 or R.3090 control unit. At the end of the table is a hinged flap which should be lifted to obtain access to the stowage below. A winch aerial is located on the port side below the table, immediately in front of the wireless operator's seat. This aerial should be reeled in before the bomb doors are opened. Access to the winch is obtained by lowering a sliding door in the cabin heating baffle. A spare reel is stowed under the step at the front spar. In the rear portion of the canopy above the fuselage is mounted a D.F. loop, in conjunction with which two visual indicators are provided, one above the wireless operator's window and the other above the pilot's instrument panel. A spare valve stowage is formed below the step at the front spar.

Electrical services panel

28. The electrical services panel in early aircraft is on the starboard side of the fuselage just forward of the front spar and an auxiliary fuse panel is mounted forward of the adjoining window, near the floor. On the main panel face are the ammeters and voltmeter for both the port and starboard generators, and switches controlling the headlamp and the colour of the wing-tip recognition lamps. Inside the panel are 32 of the fuses. In later aircraft the panel is fitted immediately forward of the window and the auxiliary panel is omitted. The same switches and indicators are provided, with the addition of two earth

A.P.2062A and C, Vol. I, Sect. 3

warning lamps. Inside the panel are the split-negative switches and the majority of the fuses. If a circuit becomes faulty, or an earth is indicated by unequal brightness of the warning lamps, the circuit can be isolated by turning off the relevant split-negative switch.

INTERMEDIATE CENTRE PORTION
General

29. The intermediate centre portion of the fuselage extends between the front and rear spars, and is divided at former 8 by an armour plate bulkhead comprising a frame and two doors. The forward section contains the following equipment. On the top of the front spar is a holster for the signal pistol. On the front spar web are the air cylinder (or in later aircraft two oxygen-type bottles) for the emergency lowering of the main wheels and the main plane flaps, and the distributor block, automatic cut-out and high pressure filter of the hydraulic system. On the port side are the hydraulic reservoir and emergency hand pump. Opposite, on the starboard side, are the battery main switch for the electrical system, a fire extinguisher and a portable oxygen bottle. Prior to the introduction of Mod. No. 677, the control cock for the emergency air system is also on the starboard side at this position (*see* para. 15).

30. A rest couch is provided in the rear compartment, on the port side. The frame forms the stowage for the oxygen bottles, and the main stop cock of the oxygen system is located at the forward end. An emergency exit is formed in the roof. On the port side are the oxygen connection for the rest station and a projectile kite container, and on the starboard side are stowages for the flying control locking gear, a parachute, a portable oxygen bottle, and the pouch for the bomb gear crutch handles.

REAR CENTRE PORTION
General

31. The rear centre portion consists of that part of the fuselage between the rear spar and the transport joint at former 27, and houses the flare station and the upper and lower mid gun turrets. The flap operating jack with its covers is mounted across the main floor. At the end of the main floor on both sides of the fuselage are mounted the ammunition boxes for the rear turret, the ammunition being fed through tracks running along the walls of the compartment. Spare ammunition for the upper-mid and front turrets is stowed in boxes on th port side, just forward of the rear turret ammunition boxes. An emergency exit is formed in the roof above the end of the main floor. The dinghy release cord is led through the conduits on the starboard side of the fuselage, and in case of emergency a pull on the cord releases the dinghy stowed in the trailing edge of the starboard centre section. Handrails, painted yellow, are provided aft of the flare station. Standard emergency packs, one Type 4 and one Type 7, are stowed on the starboard side, just aft of the rear spar.

32. In aircraft incorporating Mod. 612 a T.R.1196 set is mounted just aft of the rear spar, and an R.3003 or R.3090 set at the flare station, both on the port side. On the same side are the oxygen connections for the flare station and lower mid turret, and the oxygen cut-off valve for the upper mid turret. On the starboard side a parachute stowage is provided at the flare station, and stowages for a portable oxygen bottle and hand fire extinguisher at the mid gun station.

F.S./4

Flares

33. Reconnaissance flares are stowed in straps on both sides of the compartment and the flare release chute is provided at the end of the main floor. The following is the procedure to be adopted when releasing a flare:—
  (i) Insert the flare extension tube, stowed on the starboard side of the fuselage, into the flare chute after folding the hinged door on the top of the flare chute forwards.
  (ii) Lower the flare carefully into the tube with the propeller end upwards, and see that it engages the catch on the extension tube.
  (iii) Hook the cord, contained in the reel on the top of the tube, to the pin at the centre of the propeller.
  (iv) Release the flare by means of the catch.
  (v) Rewind the cord on the reel.

Mid gun stations

34. *Upper mid turret.*—A hydraulically-operated rotating gun turret (type F.N.50) is mounted on the top of the fuselage aft of the flare chute. For the operation of this turret, *see* A.P.1659A, Vol. I. A mounting step is provided which swings up against the side of the fuselage when not in use.

35. *Lower mid turret.*—A hydraulically-operated rotating gun turret (type F.N.64) is fitted in the floor of the fuselage at the mid gun station. This turret faces aft and can be turned through an arc of 100 deg. on either side of the centre-line of the aircraft. For the operation of the turret, *see* A.P.1659A, Vol. I. A step on the port side forms the gangway past the turret.

REAR FUSELAGE

General

36. The rear fuselage comprises the tail end of the fuselage, aft of the mid gun station. The main entrance door is located on the starboard side. Forward of the door are stowed the D.R. compass and twelve vacuum flasks; opposite on the port side, are stowages for three marine distress signals and hand shields; aft of these is a fireman's axe, and at the forward end is a parachute stowage. Aft of the door on the starboard side are the fuel and oil tank dipsticks, a crate containing the T.3135/R.3136, the first-aid outfits and the access ladder. In the centre of the floor by the front spar of the tail plane is the Elsan sanitary pan, the lid of which serves as a step to the walkway for access to the rear turret. A flexible oxygen connection is provided on the port side at the lavatory position. Draughtproof doors are fitted above the rear spar of the tail plane. On the starboard side at the rear end are the portable oxygen bottle stowage and parachute stowage for the rear gunner, and on the port side a hand fire extinguisher. The dinghy manual release system is extended through this section to the tail plane, with an external loop fitted on the starboard side adjacent to the leading edge. Handrails are provided on both sides.

Rear turret

37. A rotating gun turret (type F.N.20) is provided at the rear end of the fuselage. For the operation of this turret, *see* A.P.1659A, Vol. I. The spare ammunition for this turret is supplied by means of tracks from boxes on each side of the fuselage at the rear end of the main floor. An external rotating control valve is mounted on the floor on the port side just forward of the tail plane front spar.

P2374   M33453/201   6/43   3950   C & P   **Gp. 1**

Issued with A.L.2

K

1. Headlamp
2. Dimmer switch
3. Cockpit lamp
4. Glycol spray
5. Automatic bomb sight
6. Bomb-aimer's writing pad
7. Front gun turret - F.N.5
8. Inertia switch (R.3003)
9. Gravity switch
10. Extractor louver
11. Stowage for distributor cover
12. Recuperator
13. Oil filter
14. Draught screen
15. Windscreen de-icing sprays
16. Stowage for rudder pedals
17. Handrails
18. 4,000 lb. bomb heating switch
19. Bomb aimer's panel - starboard
20. Stowage for bomb firing switch and bomb sight lead
21. Inertia switch (Fire extinguisher)
22. Empty cartridge chute
23. Bomb-aimer's support and empty case and link container
24. Card holder (Compass deviation)
25. Immersion switch
26. Door and cushions
27. De-icing tank
28. Bomb-aimer's adjustable foot ramp
29. Parachute stowage
30. Portable oxygen stowage
31. Turn regulator (Auto-controls)
32. Control for heated gloves
33. Suppressor
34. Bomb-aimer's panel - port
35. Stowage for gyro azimuth connection
36. Elevator and rudder gyro
37. Cabin lamp
38. Rudder servo motor
39. Brake differential relay valve
40. Elevator servo motor
41. Aileron gyro
42. De-icing pump (Bomb-aimer's window)
43. Fire extinguisher
44. Call light
45. Camera heating panel
46. Tele-mic socket
47. Oxygen economiser
48. Gyro azimuth
49. F.24 camera
50. Camera motor
51. Pressure head
52. T.R.9F radio control
53. Floodlights
54. Pilot's D.R. repeater
55. Bullet-proof glass
56. Loop aerial correction strip
57. D.F. loop aerial
58. Whip aerial, A.I.R.5033

59. Distributor box - D.R. compass
60. Suppressor for D.R. compass
61. Electrical services panel
62. Junction box for D.R. compass
63. General services junction box
64. Oxygen regulator
65. Wedge plate for pilot's camera
66. Second pilot's seat
67. Fuel cock control sprocket box
68. Observer's instrument panel
69. 250 lb. bomb
70. Mounting for drift sight Mk.II
71. Window curtain
72. Oxygen flow indicator
73. General services junction box
74. Auxiliary fuse panel
75. Voltage regulators
76. Spare valve stowage for radio
77. Step at front spar
78. Cabin heating baffle
79. Cover at front spar
80. Visual indicator
81. Pilot's handgrip
82. Pilot's instrument panel
83. Control column
84. Pilot's auxiliary instrument panel
85. Pilot's harness
86. Pilot's armour plate
87. Fire control switch
88. Canopy blinds
89. Black-out curtain
90. Junction box (Intercommunication)
91. Navigator's instrument panel
92. Aldis lamp stowage
93. Astrograph
94. Variation corrector (D.R.compass)
95. Navigator's repeater (Pilot's ty)
96. Angle poise chart lamp
97. Visual indicator
98. Chair support
99. Transmitter
100. Receiver (Navigator)
101. Amplifier
102. Switch type J.
103. Receiver, W/T operator
104. Junction box (Intercommunication)
105. Mounting for signal pistol - upward firing
106.
107. Second pilot's foot rest
108. Computer stowage
109. Map pocket
110. Pilot's de-icing handpump
111. Covers on pilot's floor
112. A.R.I.5033
113. Mk.IX sextant stowage
114. Control panel (A.R.I.5033)
115. A.R.I.5033
116. T.R.9F radio

F.S/6

A.P.2062A, Vol. I, Sect. 3.

Navigator's seat	
H.T. and L.T. power units (W/T)	
Spare reel for trailing aerial	
Stowage for W/T batteries	
Trailing aerial	
Morse key	
Crystal monitor	
Control unit (R.3003)	
W/T operator's harness	
W/T operator's seat and spar cover	
Trough for electrical conduits	
Second pilot's back rest	
Armour plating	
Signal pistol cartridges	
Fuel jettison control valve	
Hot and cold air intake control	
Pilot's seat	
Aerial lead-in	
Navigator's table	
Padding on former 1	
Undercarriage emergency release	
Armour plate bulkhead	
Emergency exit	
Step at front spar	
Ground starting switch	
De-icing rheostats	
Stowage for bomb crutching handles and floor pads for 4,000 lb. bomb	
Stowage for control locking gear	
4,000 lb. bomb	
Junction box	
Automatic cut-out	
H.P. filter	
Signal pistol stowage	
Code book stowage box	
Hydraulic accumulator	
Emergency handpump	
Oxygen bottle crate	
Rest bed	
Back rest	
Hydraulic reservoir	
Emergency air bottle	
Dinghy release cable	
Reconnaissance flares	
Sea markers and flame floats	
Buffer bracket for turret step	
Upper mid gun turret	
Handrails	
Control cover at rear spar	
Flap jack	
Flare chute extension (stowed)	
Ammunition boxes	
Beam approach equipment	
Whip aerial	
Flare chute	
Step	
Mounting step for upper mid turret	
Lower mid turret - F.N.64	

175.	Ammunition ducts
176.	Step at lower mid turret
177.	Junction box
178.	R.3003
179.	
180.	D.R. compass junction box
181.	Card holder
182.	D.R. compass
183.	Door
184.	Ladder
185.	Door switch for cabin lamp
186.	Fireman's axe
187.	Dinghy external release
188.	Draughtproof door
189.	Rear gun turret - F.N.20
190.	Vacuum flasks
191.	Downward identification lights
192.	Step over ammunition ducts at entrance door
193.	Dipsticks stowage
194.	First aid outfit
195.	Sanitary container
196.	Tail wheel unit
197.	Padding over tail plane
198.	Walkway
199.	Tail formation-keeping lamp
200.	Tail navigation lamp
201.	Upward identification lamp
202.	Rear gunner's panel
203.	Dipole aerial
204.	Marine distress signals
205.	Hand shield
206.	External rotation valve for rear turret
207.	Rear turret deflectors
208.	Navigation lamp
209.	Formation-keeping lamps
210.	Cable cutters
211.	Picketing shackles
212.	B.B.P. reinforcing plat
213.	Landing lamps (Port only)
214.	Outer fuel tank
215.	Intermediate fuel tank
216.	Inner fuel tank
217.	Cabin heating duct
218.	Dinghy stowage

100

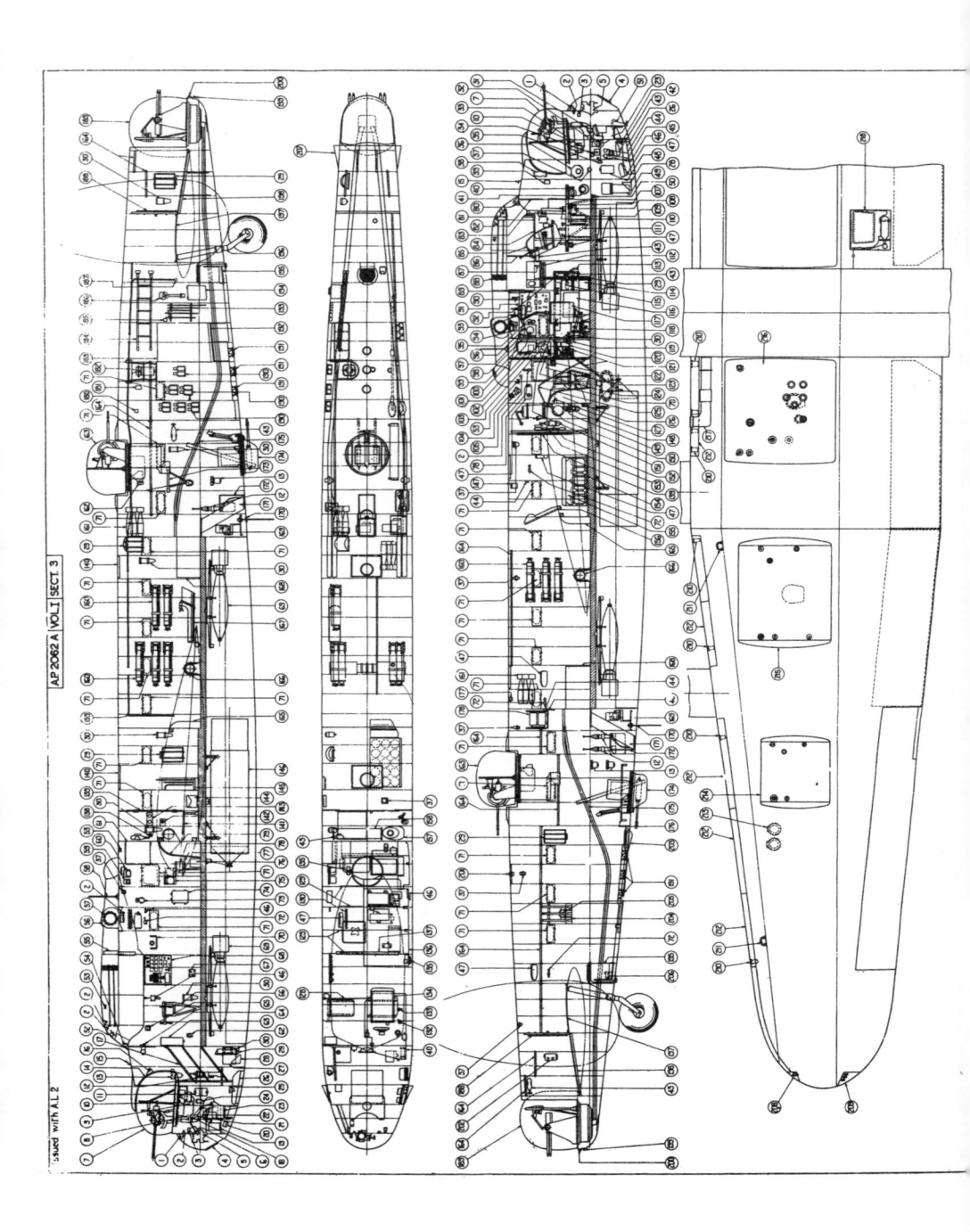

Section 4:
Instructions for ground personnel.

This Revised Chapter issued with A.L.No.24   AIR PUBLICATION 2062A & C
(Superseding Chapter 1 issued with A.L.No.2)   Volume I
April, 1943

SECTION 4 - INSTRUCTIONS FOR GROUND PERSONNEL

CHAPTER 1 - LOADING AND C.G. DATA

LIST OF CONTENTS

	Para.
Introduction	1
Definition of centre-of-gravity position	2
C.G. travel limits	3
Examples on the determination of the C.G. position	4
Effect of modifications	6

LIST OF ILLUSTRATIONS

	Fig.
Loading and C.G. diagram (L.7527 to L.7532)	1
Loading and C.G. charts (L.7527 to L.7532)	2
Loading and C.G. diagram (L.7533 and subsequent)	3
Loading and C.G. charts (L.7533 and subsequent)	4

F.S./1

AIR PUBLICATION 2062A & C
Volume I
SECTION 4

CHAPTER 1 - LOADING AND C.G. DATA

1. <u>Introduction</u>.- The purpose of these data is to enable the aircraft centre-of-gravity position to be determined for any distribution of load, both at the start of flight and at any time during the flight, i.e. after expenditure of fuel, bombs or other consumable loads. For the determination of the C.G. position, the aircraft is considered standing with the thrust line (or rigging datum line) horizontal and the undercarriage down. Since all the data and limits of C.G. travel are quoted with the undercarriage down, no account need be taken of C.G. movement due to undercarriage retraction.

2. <u>Definition of centre-of-gravity position</u>.- The position of the centre of gravity, or C.G. is defined by its distance, in inches, measured parallel to the fuselage datum line, behind a reference point known as the C.G. datum point. The distance is called the moment arm of the C.G., is denoted by the symbol $\bar{x}$, and is given by the expression

$$\bar{x} \text{ (in.)} = \frac{\text{Total moment (Tare and removable items) (lb.ft.)}}{\text{Total weight (Tare and removable items) (lb.)}} \times 12$$

The moment of any item is the product of its weight (lb.) and its moment arm, which is its distance x (ft.) from the datum point, measured parallel to the fuselage datum line. The moment takes the sign of the moment arm x, which is positive when the item concerned is aft of the datum point and negative when it is forward of this point. The weights and moments of the aircraft at tare weight and items of equipment are given in the loading and C.G. diagrams, fig.1 and 3.

3. <u>C.G. travel limits</u>.- The approved limits of C.G. travel are 41.0 to 60.6 in. aft of the C.G. datum point (see fig.2 and 4), measured parallel to the thrust line, and the C.G. position must be kept within these limits, even with the fuel consumed and with bombs and flares expended.

4. <u>Examples on the determination of the C.G. position</u>.- To determine the C.G. position with any particular load, the first step is to ascertain the effect on the basic tare weight and the corresponding moment, of modifications incorporated in the aircraft, but not included in the list in para.6., and the removal of any normally "fixed" items of equipment. The typical service loads are quoted in fig.1 and 3, and these must be adjusted according to the particular loading. In the following examples, the figures are hypothetical; the actual figures must be obtained from the diagrams.

5. Suppose that an aircraft incorporates the following modifications which are not quoted in the diagram, the calculations should proceed as follows (see R.A.F. form 1504), the letters corresponding to those on this form:-

Para. 5 (Contd.)   A.P. 2062A & C. Vol. I, Sect. 4, Chap. 1

	Weight (lb.)		Arm (ft.)	Moment (lb.ft.)	
"Fixed" equipment removed					
Flap jack mounting and cover	19	(B)	12.6	239	(b)
"Fixed" equipment fitted					
New mounting and cover	34	(A)	12.6	429	(a)
Tare condition from diagram, fig. 3	35,354	(C)	3.66	129,445	(c)
Deduct equipment removed	19	(B)		239	(b)
	35,335			129,206	
Add equipment fitted	34	(A)		429	(a)
New tare condition	35,369	(D)		129,635	(d)

The next step is to determine the total weight and moment of the removable items of military load, as follows:-

	Weight (lb.)		Arm (ft.)	Moment (lb.ft.)	
Typical service load less bombs (from diagram, fig. 3)	3,870		10.99	42,565	
Deduct lower mid turret	122		26.5	3,235	
Deduct 2 Browning guns	45		26.5	1,195	
Deduct ammunition 1,500 rds.	99.5		26.5	2,635	
New typical service load less bombs	3,604	(E)		35,500	(e)
3 - 250 lb. bombs	750		- 8.92	- 6,690	
3 - 2,000 lb. bombs	6,000		- 2.54	- 15,240	
3 - 2,000 lb. bombs	6,000		+ 10.21	+ 61,260	
3 - 250 lb. carriers	55		- 8.92	- 490	
3 - 2,000 lb. carriers	165		- 2.54	- 420	
3 - 2,000 lb. carriers	165		+ 10.21	+ 1,685	
Fuel, No. 1 tanks, 1,160 gals. 100 octane at 7.2 lb./gal.	8,352		+ 4.92	+ 41,090	
Fuel, No. 2 tanks, 239 gals. 100 octane at 7.2 lb./gal.	1,720		+ 5.0	+ 8,600	
Oil, inboard, 45 gals. at 9 lb./gal.	405		- 0.5	- 205	
Oil, outboard, 45 gals. at 9 lb./gal.	405		+ 2.34	+ 940	
Total fuel, oil, bombs and carriers	24,017	(F)		+ 90,530	(f)
New tare condition	35,369	(D)		129,635	(d)
New typical service load	3,604	(E)		35,500	(e)
Fuel, oil, bombs and carriers	24,017	(F)		90,530	(f)
Gross take-off weight	62,990	(G)		255,665	(g)

Therefore position of C.G. for take-off = $\frac{255,665}{62,990} \times 12$

= 48.6 in. aft of datum point

F.S./2

A.P.2062A & C, Vol.I, Sect.4, Chap.1

The position of the C.G. when landing after the expenditure of fuel, oil, bombs, ammunition and flares, must then be determined as follows:-

	Weight (lb.)	Moment (lb.ft.)
Fuel - No.1 tanks, 1,056 gals at 7.2 lb./gal.	7,603	+ 37,405
Fuel - No.2 tanks, 239 gals. at 7.2 lb./gal.	1,720	+ 8,600
Oil - inboard, 28 gals. at 9 lb./gal.	252	- 125
Oil - outboard 28 gals. at 9 lb./gal.	252	+ 590
Browning gun ammunition (2,400 rounds from tracks)	159	+ 5,500
Browning gun ammunition (7,600 rounds from boxes)	503.5	+ 10,070
Browning gun ammunition (2,000 rounds from upper mid turret)	132.5	+ 3,445
Reconnaissance flares	200	+ 3,550
Flame floats Mk.II	70.5	+ 1,560
Bombs	12,750	+ 39,330
Total expended load	23,642	109,925

Landing weight 62,990 - 23,642 = 39,348 lb.
Corresponding moment 255,665 - 109,925 = 145,740 lb.ft.

Therefore position of C.G. when landing = $\frac{145,740}{39,348} \times 12$

= **44.4 in.** aft of datum point

This is inside the prescribed limits and therefore no correction is necessary for landing. If, however, one 2,000 lb. bomb was brought back from a flight the C.G. position to cover this must be determined as follows:-

	Weight (lb.)	Moment (lb.ft.)
Expended load (as above)	23,642	109,925
Replace - one 2,000 lb. bomb	2,000	5,080
Corrected expended load	21,642	115,005

Landing weight 62,990 - 21,642 = 41,348 lb.
Corresponding moment 255,665 - 115,005 = 140,660 lb.ft.

Therefore position of C.G. when landing = $\frac{140,660}{41,348} \times 12$

= **40.8 in.** aft of datum point

This is outside the prescribed limits and therefore must be corrected for landing by the movement aft of a member of the crew.

6. **Effect of modification.** - The following is a list of the modifications incorporated in the aircraft as shown in the diagram (see fig.3):-

A.P.2062A & C, Vol.I, Sect.4, Chap.1

397, 399, 410, 415. 424, 432, 436, 447, 455, 459, 461, 466, 467, 470,
471, 473, 483, 484, 485, 489, 490, 493, 494, 500, 503, 504, 507, 510,
511, 519, 521, 532, 536, 538, 540, 541. 553, 555, 557, 559, 565, 574,
585, 589, 594, 598, 609, 610, 675.

Any other modifications which individually or in the aggregate affect the maximum all-up weight for all forms of flying by 1 per cent, or move the C.G. of the tare aircraft by 1 per cent of the mean chord (see fig.2 and 4) whether by incorporation or deletion, must be taken into account when making calculations for any particular aircraft. Under no circumstances must the C.G. be allowed to move beyond the prescribed limits.

7. The following are particulars of modifications approved up to January 31st 1943. They may or may not be included in the diagrams (see para. 6) but are given so that their effect can be taken into account during calculations:-

Mod. No.	Subject	Weight (lb.) Increase or Decrease	Arm (ft.) From C.G. Datum Point	Moment (lb.ft.)
397	Introduction of armour protection for engines (Fixed)	+ 59	+ 1.17	+ 69
399	Adjustable crutches for heavy bombs (Fixed)	+ 5.5	+ 3.83	+ 21
410	Blackout navigator's station and sextant dome (Fixed)	+ 3	- 3.33	- 10
412	Provision for carrying 8,000 lb. bomb (Fixed)	+ 88	+ 11.0	+ 968
413	To modify heavy bomb carrier to provide for 2,000 lb. H.C. bomb (Removable)	+ 1.5	Wt. for 1 carrier only. Arm as shown on loading diagram	
415	Introduction of 1,500 watt generator 24-V, type KX	Negligible		
418	Reposition switch in bomb release circuit	Negligible		

F.S./3

106

Para. 7 (Contd.)   A.P.2002A & C, Vol.I, Sect.4, Chap.1

Mod. No.	Subject	Weight (lb.) Increase or Decrease	Arm (ft.) From C.G. Datum Point	Moment (lb.ft.)
424	Introduction of inspection door for pet cocks in centre plane leading edge	Negligible		
430	Introduction of 6-cell flare launching chute			
	(Fixed)	+ 111	+ 24.67	+ 2,740
	(Removable)	− 50		− 25
431	Introduction of 400 gallon protected tanks in bomb compartment (S.O.O.) One tank installation			
	(Fixed)	+ 30	+ 1.5	+ 45
	(Removable inc. fuel)	+ 3,308	+ 0.91	+ 3,010
	Two tank installation			
	(Fixed)	+ 30	+ 1.5	+ 45
	(Removable inc. fuel)	+ 6,610	+ 4.25	+ 28,090
432	Introduction of T.R.1335			
	(Fixed)	+ 63	− 3.33	− 210
	(Removable)	+ 69	− 6.82	− 472
434	Introduction of arrester gear (Fixed)	+ 94	+ 34.0	+ 3,196
	(Removable)	+ 54	+ 36.25	+ 1,952
436	Introduction of improved type navigator's table (Fixed)	+ 5	− 5.0	− 25
439	Introduction of special armour plate (S.O.O.) (Fixed)	+ 1,710	+ 7.05	+ 12,050
440	To provide 2,000 rounds of reserve ammunition			
	(Fixed)	+ 3	+ 16.67	+ 50
	(Removable)	+ 148	+ 16.67	+ 2,467
446	Mod. to undercarriage retracting strut spring unit	Negligible		

107

Para. 7 (Contd.)   A.P.2062A & C, Vol.I, Sect.4, Chap.1

Mod. No.	Subject	Weight (lb.) Increase or Decrease	Arm (ft.) From C.G. Datum Point	Moment (lb.ft.)
447	To introduce new type emergency air bottle and piping due to revised type winch for 8,000 lb. bomb (Fixed)	− 16	+ 1.67	− 27
455	Introduction of 5-fusing system for 4,000 lb. H.C. bomb Mk.II (Fixed)	+ 1.5	+ 6.33	+ 10
457	To reposition trailing aerial winch (Fixed)	− 3		− 368
459	Introduction of guard on fuel pump switches - outer	Negligible		
461	Heating of automatic bomb distributor Mk.VI	Negligible		
462	Restriction of light on formation lamps	Negligible		
463	Introduction of F.N.64 lower mid turret (Fixed) (Removable)	+ 10 + 266.5	+ 26.5 + 26.5	+ 265 + 7,062
465	Introduction of electro-pneumatic two-speed supercharger control (Fixed)	− 6	+ 1.0	− 6
466	Guard for dipole aerial junction box	Negligible		
467	Introduction of prone bombing support and incorporation of Mk.II bomb sight adaptor plate (Fixed)	− 15	− 15.92	+ 239
468	Introduction of Mk.XIV bomb sight (Fixed) (Removable)	+ 20 + 47	− 15.42 − 13.63	− 310 − 640

F.S./4

Para. 7 (Contd.)   A.P.2062A & C, Vol.I, Sect.4, Chap.1

Mod. No.	Subject	Weight (lb.) Increase or Decrease	Arm (ft.) From C.G. Datum Point	Moment (lb.ft.)
469	Installation of S.A. bomb sight Mk.II (S.O.O.) (Fixed) (Removable)	+ 17 + 31	− 16.42	− 280 − 600
470	Introduction of footrest and back strap for tip-up seat (Fixed)	+ 3	− 10.0	− 30
471	Introduction of new cover at downward identification lamps to improve accessibility	Negligible		
472	Introduction of special self-sealing covered fuel tanks (S.O.O.) (Fixed)	+ 386	+ 5.22	+ 2,015
473	Mod. to undercarriage legs	Negligible		
474	Introduction of desert equipment case and water tank (Fixed) (Removable)	+ 1.5 + 293	+ 14.9 + 14.9	+ 22 + 4,366
476	Introduction of R.3090 to replace R.3003 (Removable)	+ 4	+ 19.58	+ 78
477	Introduction of C.L.E. equipment (S.O.O.) (Fixed) These weights apply only when Mod.463 is fitted (Removable)	− 88 − 742.5	+ 27.5 + 23.6	− 2,422 − 17,527
483	Deletion of sockets on former 41 feeding rear turret	Negligible		
484	Deletion of perspex window in nose for oblique photography (Fixed)	− 1	− 12.5	+ 12

Para. 7 (Contd.) A.P.2062A & C, Vol.I, Sect.4, Chap.1

Mod. No.	Subject	Weight (lb.) Increase or Decrease	Arm (ft.) From C.G. Datum Point	Moment (lb.ft.)
485	Changing the Lord shock-absorber on beam approach units	Negligible		
489	Intercommunication at rest station	Negligible		
490	Improved attachment of hot and cold air-intake lever to operating valve	Negligible		
492	Modification of bomb fusing and release gear	Negligible		
493	Incorporation of automatic valve in fuel transfer pipe from No.3 tank to No.2 tank (Fixed)	+ 0.5	+ 7.0	+ 4
494	Provision of guards for piping in bomb compartment (Fixed)	+ 2	+ 3.92	+ 8
495	To improve weather proofing of pilot's sliding window	Negligible		
497	Replacing upward identification lamp	Negligible		
498	To improve weather proofing of main fuselage entrance door	Negligible		
499	To improve weather proofing of upper exit hatches	Negligible		
500	Introduction of metal couplings in wheel brakes and radiator flap circuits and repositioning of pressure maintaining valve	Negligible		

F.S./5

Para. 7 (Contd.)   A.P.2062A & C, Vol.I, Sect.4, Chap.1

Mod. No.	Subject	Weight (lb.) Increase or Decrease	Arm (ft.) From C.G. Datum Point	Moment (lb.ft.)
501	Stiffening control locking attachment on pilot's seat	Negligible		
502	To replace floating anchor nuts for dinghy covers, by fixed nuts	Negligible		
503	To strengthen stringers in outer plane top surface (Fixed)	+ 87	+ 5.42	+ 472
504	To strengthen mass balance on rudder	Negligible		
505	Introduction of trimmer and controls for port aileron (Fixed)	+ 3	+ 9.0	+ 27
507	Introduction of oxygen cut-off valves for turrets and addition of filter units in change line (Fixed)	+ 2	+ 15.0	+ 30
510	Revision of brake piping to clear undercarriage wheel	Negligible		
511	To improve supercharger control (Fixed)	+ 3	0	0
512	Introduction of by-pass in fuel system (Fixed)	+ 10	+ 3.0	+ 30
516	Tropicalisation - control surface hinge cavity protection (S.O.O.)	Negligible		
517	Sealing and draining of airframe apertures (S.O.O.) (Fixed)	+ 37	+ 5.0	+ 185
518	Strengthening top and bottom stringers on centre portion of outer plane (Fixed)	+ 110	+ 5.42	+ 595

111

Para. 7 (Contd.)   A.P.2062A & C, Vol.I, Sect.4, Chap.1

Mod. No.	Subject	Weight (lb.) Increase or Decrease	Arm (ft.) From C.G. Datum Point	Moment (lb.ft.)
519	Deletion of speed lever and cables (Fixed)	− 1	− 10.0	+ 10
521	Re-arrangement of rear turret piping (Fixed)	+ 4.5	+ 10.0	+ 45
522	Additional temporary taboo cams on F.N.50 upper turret (S.O.O.) (Fixed)	+ 2	+ 24.17	+ 48
523	Introduction of header tanks above each turret recuperator (Fixed)	+ 34	+ 13.33	+ 453
524	New switch and indicator for undercarriage	Negligible		
530	General revision of intercommunication system (Fixed)	− 5	+ 7.0	− 35
531	Introduction of self-sealing flexible fuel pipes (Fixed)	+ 20	+ 2.5	+ 50
532	Introduction of bleed screws in turret pipe-lines (Fixed)	+ 3	+ 1.5	+ 5
536	Rudder trimmer mass balance − rivet attaching steel weight replaced by bolt	Negligible		
537	Introduction of type 117 whip aerial (Fixed)	Negligible		+ 9
538	To invert flame switch	Negligible		
539	Introduction of "Pulsometer F.B. Mk.I" pumps into fuel system (Fixed)	+ 37	+ 5.5	+ 204

F.S./6

Para. 7 (Contd.)   A.P. 2062A & C, Vol. I, Sect. 4, Chap. 1

Mod. No.	Subject	Weight (lb.) Increase or Decrease	Arm (ft.) From C.G. Datum Point	Moment (lb.ft.)
540	Modified general services and intercommunication wiring to under turret	Negligible		
541	Introduction of emergency packs type 4 and 7 (Fixed) (Removable)	+ 1 + 49	+ 11.0 + 10.6	+ 11 + 520
543	Introduction of safety device for 4,000 lb. and 8,000 lb. bomb manual release	Negligible		
544	To introduce new control column head designed to take dual control arm (Fixed)	+ 3.5	− 11.3	− 40
550	To stiffen dinghy sealing	Negligible		
551	Stiffening of attachment to rudder mass balance	Negligible		
553	Deletion of pressure re-fuelling system (Fixed)	− 62	+ 2.0	− 124
554	Guard for glycol pipes in front of pilot's windscreen	Negligible		
555	To prevent instability on R/T	Negligible		
557	To strengthen wing tips (Fixed)	+ 24	+ 6.25	+ 150
559	Stiffening of fin post at top hinge	Negligible		

Para. 7 (Contd.)   A.P.2062A & C, Vol.I, Sect.4, Chap.1

Mod. No.	Subject	Weight (lb.) Increase or Decrease	Arm (ft.) From C.G. Datum Point	Moment (lb.ft.)
562	Introduction of armour protection of outboard engines (rear of oil tanks) (Fixed)	+ 180	+ 3.75	+ 675
565	To improve hook for aileron locking bar	Negligible		
566	Introduction of night photography (Fixed) (Removable)	+ 1 + 1	- 13.0 - 13.0	- 13 - 13
567	Introduction of drip tray between upper and lower turrets (Fixed)	+ 1	+ 26.0	+ 26
570	Red, green and amber downward identification lamps	Negligible		
574	Sealing of emergency boost control in cockpit	Negligible		
575	CO$_2$ gas installation for fire protection of fuel tanks (Fixed)	+ 208	+ 3.75	+ 780
577	Additional static line attachments for containers (C.L.E. requirements) (S.O.O.) (Fixed)	+ 2	+ 9.0	+ 18
579	Provision for carrying heavy armament store (C.S. bomb) (S.O.O.) (Fixed)	- 60	+ 4.67	- 280
584	Introduction of pressure relief valve in undercarriage flap and bomb door hydraulic circuit (Fixed)	+ 2	- 2.08	- 4
585	To stiffen former 35 (Fixed)	+ 8	+ 39.5	+ 315

F.S./7

Para. 7 (Contd.)   A.P.2062A & C, Vol.I, Sect.4, Chap.1

Mod. No.	Subject	Weight (lb.) Increase or Decrease	Arm (ft.) From C.G. Datum Point	Moment (lb.ft.)
586	Introduction of new tanks with protective covering for Pulsometer pumps	Negligible		
588	Introduction of walking tread from ribs 14 to 17 on outer wing (Fixed)	+ 4.5	+ 2.5	+ 12
589	Prevention of incorrect positioning of change-over cock control knobs on spindle	Negligible		
592	Steady supports for D.F. loop corrector strips (Fixed)	+ 1	- 3.83	- 4
594	To replace immersed pumps in inner tanks by suction pipes	Negligible		
598	Increase nose skin on outer wing from 22 s.w.g. to 18 s.w.g. (Fixed)	+ 37	+ 2.5	+ 95
602 and Corrigendum No.1	Introduction of glider towing fixed parts	+ 28.5		+ 1,072
603 and Corrigendum No.1	Introduction of glider towing removable parts (S.O.O.)	+ 46.5		+ 2,150
605	Deletion of azimuth bracket (Fixed) (Removable)	- 1 - 13.5	- 14.25 - 14.25	+ 14 + 193
606	Introduction of low impedance inter-communication (Fixed)	+ 2	- 2.5	- 5
608	Introduction of tug to glider intercommunication system (Fixed)	+ 2	+ 19.18	+ 38

Para. 7 (Contd.)   A.P. 2062A & C, Vol. I, Sect. 4, Chap. 1

Mod. No.	Subject	Weight (lb.) Increase or Decrease	Arm (ft.) From C.G. Datum Point	Moment (lb.ft.)
609	Change of fuse and label on R.3003	Negligible		
610	Increase wire on R.3003 from 5 amp. to 19 amp.	Negligible		
613	Stiffening of rudder post at top hinge	Negligible		
615	Stiffening of rudder at mass balance attachment	Negligible		
616	Stiffening of bomb door jack attachment (Fixed)	+ 3	+ 5	+ 15
617	Introduction of ratchet stop to ammunition tracks	Negligible		
619	Identification of fuel tanks	Negligible		
622	Provision in structure to accomodate 8,000 lb. bomb (Fixed)	+ 52	+ 3.65	+ 189
623	Introduction of 8,000 lb. production bomb doors, and fairings on fuselage (Fixed)	- 5		- 500
624	Provision for 8,000 lb. C.S. bomb (S.O.O.) (Fixed)	+ 50	+ 3.5	+ 175
630	Deletion of mixture control (Fixed)	- 6	+ 1	- 6
635	Deletion of non-essential Avery self-sealing couplings and introduction of substitute adaptors	Negligible		

F.S./8

Para. 7 (Contd.) A.P.206 A & C. Vol.I, Sect. 3, Chap.1

Mod. No.	Subject	Weight (lb.) Increase or Decrease	Arm (ft.) From C.G. Datum Point	Moment (lb.ft.)
637	Introduction of pads and strengthened door stops (S.O.O.)			
	4,000 lb. type (Fixed)	+ 70	+ 4.56	+ 320
	8,000 lb. type (Removable)	+ 50	+ 4.56	+ 230
640	Vent guard for fuel tanks (Fixed)	+ 1	+ 5.25	+ 5
643	Additional adjustment in trimmer controls	Negligible		
644	Engine mountings in material to Spec. D.T.D.563 (Fixed)	+ 81	+ 1.75	+ 142
651	Introduction of static vent to A.S.I. (Fixed)	+ 6	+ 10.8	+ 65
660	Re-introduction of suction gauge Mk.I (Fixed)	+ 1	- 12.25	+ 12
661	Fuel system instruction labels	Negligible		
662	Introduction of high volatility doping in fuel system (Fixed)	+ 1	+ 0.6	+ 1
666	Introduction of stiffeners at push-pull bearings (Fixed)	+ 5.5	+ 14.9	+ 82
668	Installation for Hamilton propellers (Fixed)	- 13	- 1.31	+ 17
	Introduction of Hamilton propellers, type A5/138	Negligible		
	Introduction of Hamilton propellers, type A5/122 (Fixed)	+ 216	- 7.57	- 1,635

Para. 7 (Contd.)   A.P. 2062A & C, Vol. I, Sect. 4, Chap. 1

Mod. No.	Subject	Weight (lb.) Increase or Decrease	Arm (ft.) From C.G. Datum Point	Moment (lb.ft.)
670	Strengthening of fin (Fixed)	+ 3.5	+ 42.5	+ 149
672	Repositioning of engine speed indicator generator	Negligible		
674	Deletion of propeller de-icing (Fixed)	− 148	+ 2.0	− 296
675	Deletion of de-icing for air-bomber's windscreen (Fixed)	− 2	− 16.25	+ 33
676	Deletion of navigator's receiver (Removable)	− 33	− 2.92	+ 96
678	Raising R.3003 aerial up leading edge of fin	Negligible		
681	Introduction of rudder pedal stop bracket with adjustable stops	Negligible		
682	Repositioning Graviner switch	Negligible		
684	Introduction of stronger flap jack mounting (Fixed)	+ 15	+ 12.6	+ 189
685	Strengthening of rudder mass-balance	Negligible		
690	Introduction of navigator's special armour to suit scheme C or E electrics (S.O.O.) (Fixed)	− 14	− 3.75	+ 52
696	Introduction of twin contact tyre on tail wheel (Fixed)	+ 32	+ 41.25	+ 1,320
697	Shortening of finger bars on bullet-proof glass in astro dome	Negligible		

F.S./9

Para.7 (Contd.) A.P.2062A & C, Vol.I, Sect.4, Chap.1

Mod. No.	Subject	Weight (lb.) Increase or Decrease	Arm (ft.) From C.G. Datum Point	Moment (lb.ft.)
705	Detachable covers over ammunition tracks (Fixed)	+ 0.5	+ 34.0	+ 17
707	Introduction of modified beam approach equipment (Fixed) (Removable)	− 6 0		− 248 − 1,070
708	Introduction of modified aileron control rocking lever shaft	Negligible		
709	Modification to Y-piece	Negligible		
710	Provision for Merlin 28 engines (Fixed)	+ 16	+ 1.75	+ 28
	Introduction of Merlin 28 engines (Conversion from Mk.I to Mk.III) (Fixed)	+ 20	− 4.8	− 96
713	To revise clipping of turret delivery pipe for Mk.I	Negligible		
715	Revised piping to suit new position of oil cooler for R.A.E. compressor	Negligible		
717	Strengthening of tail wheel mounting beam (Fixed)	+ 2.5	+ 40.5	+ 102
722	Additional clipping for lower mid turret delivery and return pipes	Negligible		
723	Stiffener for former at push-pull square bearing	Negligible		
724	Modification to F.N.50 turret fairing to clear roller arm and stiffening of rear fairing	Negligible		

Para. 7 (Contd.)   A.P.2062A & C, Vol.I, Sect.4, Chap.1

Mod. No.	Subject	Weight (lb.) Increase or Decrease	Arm (ft.) From C.G. Datum Point	Moment (lb.ft.)
727	Introduction of tug to glider intercommunication system (S.O.O.) (Removable)	+ 2.5	+ 11.33	+ 28
728	To improve ball race housing on elevator cross shaft	Negligible		
729	Modification to navigator's panel (Fixed)	− 2.5	− 4	+ 10
740	Resilient mounting for oil pressure gauges	Negligible		
742	Reinstatement of Lockheed-Avery self-sealing couplings	Negligible		
756	Elevator control bearing at former 34 changed from rear to forward side of former	Negligible		
780	Introduction of deeper perspex nose (Fixed)	+ 6.5	− 18.33	− 119
782	Delete reconnaissance flare stowages in fuselage	Wt. included in Mod.430		
783	Improved version of T.R.1335 (Removable)	+ 23	− 6.9	− 159
805	Introduction of 6-cell launching chute to suit aircraft fitted with 4,000 lb. bomb doors. (This weight applies only when Mod.430 is fitted) (Fixed)	− 4	+ 23.5	− 94

F.S./10

120

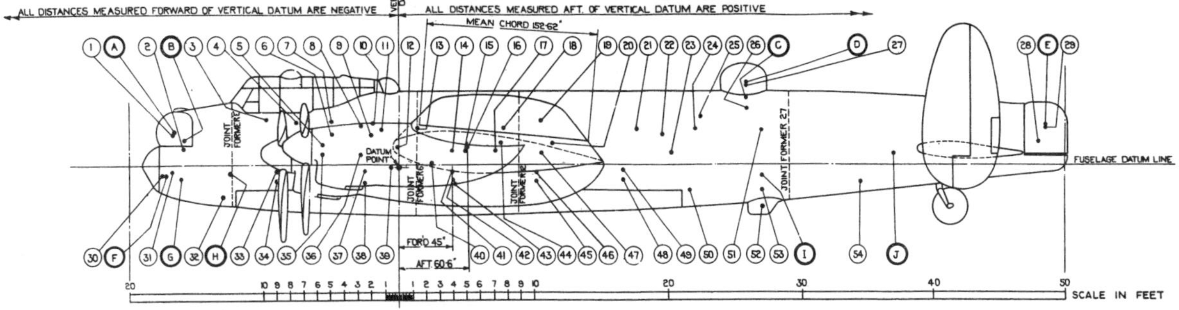

REMOVABLE ITEMS OF MILITARY LOAD

ITEM	No.	WEIGHT (LB)	ARM (FT)	MOMENT (LB. FT.) FORWARD	MOMENT (LB. FT.) AFT
2 BROWNING GUNS (NOSE)	1	46·5	-16·67	775	
AMMUNITION - 2,000 RDS.	2	132·5	-15·83	2,095	
2 BROWNING GUNS (UPPER-MID)	27	46·5	+26·00		1,210
AMMUNITION - 2000 RDS.	26	132·5	+26·00		3,445
2 BROWNING GUNS (LOWER-MID)	52	45	+26·50		1,195
AMMUNITION - 1000 RDS.	53	66·5	+26·50		1,760
4 BROWNING GUNS (REAR)	28	92	+48·33		4,445
AMMUNITION - 2,400 RDS. ON TRACKS	54	159	+34·58		5,500
AMMUNITION - 7,600 RDS. IN BOXES	23	503·5	+20·00		10,070
BOMB SIGHT AUTOMATIC	30	35·5	-17·50	620	
AUTOMATIC BOMB DISTRIBUTOR	31	7	-16·67	115	
MARINE DISTRESS SIGNALS	25	21	+22·33		470
SIGNAL PISTOL & CARTRIDGES	11	6	- 1·25	10	
RECONNAISSANCE FLARES	21	200	+17·75		3,550
ELECTRICAL EQUIPMENT (NOTE 1)	35	12	- 5·83	70	
FLAME FLOATS MK. II (6) (NOTE 2)	24	70	+22·08		1,545
NAVIGATIONAL INSTRUMENTS (NOTE 3)	7	37·5	- 5·00	190	
F.24 CAMERA	32	42	-12·92	540	
OXYGEN CHARGE	17	36	+ 7·08		255
OXYGEN PORTABLE	18	28	+ 7·83		220
DINGHY	47	59	+10·42		615
EMERGENCY RATIONS	19	19	+10·42		200
MISCELLANEOUS	51	33	+27·00		890
RADIO T.1154, R.1155	9	142	- 2·08	295	
R.1155 FOR D.F. LOOP	8	33	- 2·92	95	
INTERCOMMUNICATION	10	5	- 2·08	10	
T.R.9F	5	27	- 5·83	155	
T.R.9F POWER SUPPLY	36	34	- 2·92	100	
BEAM APPROACH EQUIPMENT	50	41	+21·67		890
R.3003	22	31	+19·58		610
CABLE CUTTERS	13	48	+ 1·33		65
CAPTAIN & PARACHUTE	3	200	-10·00	2,000	
2ND PILOT & PARACHUTE	4	200	- 7·50	1,500	
NAVIGATOR & PARACHUTE	6	200	- 5·00	1,000	
RADIO OPERATOR & PARACHUTE	12	200	- 0·33	65	
GUNNER & PARACHUTE (REST SEAT)	44	200	+ 7·08		1,415
REAR GUNNER & PARACHUTE	28	200	+47·92		9,585
				9,635	47,935
TYPICAL SERVICE LOAD (LESS BOMBS)	20	3,391			38,300
POSITION OF C.G.		11·26 FT. OR 135·16 IN. AFT. OF DATUM			

NOTES:-

1:- ITEM 35 ELECTRICAL EQUIPMENT CONSISTS OF ELECTRIC TORCHES SUPPRESSOR & SIGNALLING LAMP.

2:- ITEM 24 STOWAGE PROVIDED FOR 12 FLAME FLOATS OR SEA MARKERS.

3:- ITEM 7 NAVIGATIONAL INSTRUMENTS CONSISTS OF ASTRO. COMPASS MK. II, STANDARDS 05A, RECORDER DRIFT MK. II, ASTROGRAPH MK. I A, NAVIGATIONAL COMPUTER MK. III C, CHART TABLE, PLOTTER MK. I A, SEXTANT MK. IX, MATHEMATICAL DIVIDERS, PRISMATIC BINOCULARS, PILOT'S KNEE TYPE WRITING PAD

4:- ITEM 24 SEA MARKERS MK. III ARE ALTERNATIVE TO FLAME FLOATS MK. II

5:- ITEM 24 SEA MARKERS MK. V ARE ALTERNATIVE TO SEA MARKERS MK. III

6:- C.G. POSITIONS RELATE TO UNDERCARRIAGE DOWN POSITION THE MOMENT DUE TO RETRACTION IS 8,575 LB. FT.

7:- THIS DIAGRAM APPLIES ONLY TO AIRCRAFT NOS L.7527, L.7528, L.7529, L.7530, L.7531, L.7532.

8:- THE WEIGHT OF FUEL IS TAKEN AS 7·2 LB/GAL. AND THE WEIGHT OF OIL IS TAKEN AS 9·0 LB/GAL.

ALTERNATIVE ITEMS OF LOAD NOT INCLUDED IN TYPICAL SERVICE LOAD.

ITEM	No.	WEIGHT (LB)	ARM (FT)	MOMENT (LB. FT.) FORWARD	MOMENT (LB. FT.) AFT
BOMB SIGHT (COURSE SETTING)	F	19	-17·42	330	
BOMB SIGHT (STABILISED AUTOMATIC)	F	60	-17·42	1045	
FLAME FLOATS MK. II (12)	24	140	+22·08		3,090
SEA MARKERS MK. III (6) (NOTE 4)	24	62·5	+22·08		1,380
SEA MARKERS MK. III (12)	24	125	+22·08		2,760
SEA MARKERS MK. V (6) (NOTE 5)	24	47	+22·08		1,040
SEA MARKERS MK. V (12)	24	94	+22·08		2075
CAMERA G.45 (NOSE TURRET)	A	8·5	-16·67	140	
CAMERA G.45 (UPPER-MID)	D	7·5	+26·00		195
CAMERA G.45 (REAR TURRET)	E	7·5	+48·33		360
GUNNER IN (UPPER-MID) TURRET	C	200	+26·00		5,200
GUNNER IN (LOWER-MID) TURRET	I	200	+26·50		5,300
RADIO OPERATOR IN NOSE TURRET	B	200	-15·67	3,135	
NAVIGATOR AS BOMB AIMER	G	200	-15·83	3,160	
RADIO OPERATOR AS FRONT GUNNER	H	200	-12·50	2,500	
CREW MEMBER AT URINAL POSITION	J	200	+37·33		7,465
250 LB. BOMBS / SMALL BOMB CONTAINERS	ARMS ARE AS FOR 500 LB. BOMBS MOMENTS ARE PROPORTIONAL TO WEIGHTS.				
EXPENDABLE PART FRONT AMM.TN	2	59·5	-15·83	940	
EXPENDABLE PART UPPER-MID AMM.TN	26	59·5	+26·00		1,545

14 - 500 LB. BOMBS

ITEM	No.	WEIGHT (LB)	ARM (FT)	MOMENT (LB. FT.) FORWARD	MOMENT (LB. FT.) AFT
AEROPLANE TARE	14	34,835	+ 3·88		134,945
TYPICAL SERVICE LOAD (LESS BOMBS)	20	3,391	+11·26		38,300
3-500 LB. BOMBS	34	1,500	- 8·92	13,380	
3-500 LB. BOMBS	38	1,500	- 2·54	3,810	
2-500 LB. BOMBS	42	1,000	+ 3·83		3,830
3-500 LB. BOMBS	45	1,500	+10·21		15,315
3-500 LB. BOMBS	48	1,500	+16·58		24,870
3-500 LB. CARRIERS	33	55	- 8·92	490	
3-500 LB. CARRIERS	37	55	- 2·54	140	
2-500 LB. CARRIERS	41	37	+ 3·83		140
3-500 LB. CARRIERS	46	55	+10·21		560
3-500 LB. CARRIERS	49	55	+16·58		910
FUEL (1,160 GAL)	15	8,352	+ 4·92		41,090
FUEL (550 GAL)	16	3,960	+ 5·00		19,800
OIL INBOARD (53 GAL)	39	477	- 0·50	240	
OIL OUTBOARD (53 GAL)	40	477	+ 2·34		1,115
				18,060	280,875
ALL UP WEIGHT		58,749			262,815
POSITION OF C.G.		4·47 FT. OR 53·66 IN. AFT. OF DATUM			

1-4,000 LB. & 6-500 LB. BOMBS.

ITEM	No.	WEIGHT (LB)	ARM (FT)	MOMENT (LB. FT.) FORWARD	MOMENT (LB. FT.) AFT
AEROPLANE TARE	14	34,835	+3·88		134,945
TYPICAL SERVICE LOAD (LESS BOMBS)	20	3,391	+11·26		38,300
3-500 LB. BOMBS	34	1,500	-8·92	13,380	
1-4,000 LB. BOMB	43	4,000	+3·96		15,840
3-500 LB. BOMBS	48	1,500	+16·58		24,870
3-500 LB. CARRIERS	33	55	-8·92	490	
3-500 LB. CARRIERS	49	55	+16·58		910
FUEL (1,160 GAL)	15	8,352	+4·92		41,090
FUEL (550 GAL)	16	3,960	+5·00		19,800
OIL INBOARD (53 GAL)	39	477	-0·50	240	
OIL OUTBOARD (53 GAL)	40	477	+2·34		1,115
				14,110	276,870
ALL UP WEIGHT		58,602			262,760
POSITION OF C.G.		4·48 FT. OR 53·78 IN. AFT. OF DATUM			

6 - 1,500 MINES

ITEM	No.	WEIGHT (LB)	ARM (FT)	MOMENT (LB. FT.) FORWARD	MOMENT (LB. FT.) AFT
AEROPLANE TARE	14	34,835	+ 3·88		134,945
TYPICAL SERVICE LOAD (LESS BOMBS)	20	3,391	+11·26		38,300
3-1,500 LB. MINES	38	4,500	- 2·54	11,430	
3-1,500 LB. MINES	45	4,500	+10·21		45,945
3-2,000 LB. CARRIERS	37	165	- 2·54	420	
3-2,000 LB. CARRIERS	46	165	+10·21		1,685
FUEL (1,160 GAL)	15	8,352	+ 4·92		41,090
FUEL (420 GAL)	16	3,024	+ 5·00		15,120
OIL INBOARD (51 GAL)	39	459	- 0·5	230	
OIL OUTBOARD (51 GAL)	40	459	+ 2·34		1,075
				12,080	278,160
ALL UP WEIGHT		59,850			266,080
POSITION OF C.G.		4·45 FT. OR 53·33 IN. AFT. OF DATUM			

6-2,000 LB. & 3-250 LB. BOMBS.

ITEM	No.	WEIGHT (LB)	ARM (FT)	MOMENT (LB. FT.) FORWARD	MOMENT (LB. FT.) AFT
AEROPLANE TARE	14	34,835	+ 3·88		134,945
TYPICAL SERVICE LOAD (LESS BOMBS)	20	3391	+ 11·26		38,300
3-250 LB. BOMBS	34	750	- 8·92	6690	
3-2,000 LB. BOMBS	38	6,000	- 2·54	15,240	
3-2,000 LB. BOMBS	45	6,000	+10·21		61,260
3-250 LB. CARRIERS	33	55	- 8·92	490	
3-2000 LB. CARRIERS	37	165	- 2·54	420	
3-2000 LB. CARRIERS	46	165	+10·21		1685
FUEL (1,100 GAL	15	7,920	+ 4·92		38,965
OIL INBOARD (38 GAL)	39	342	- 0·50	175	
OIL OUTBOARD (38 GAL)	40	342	+ 2·34		800
				23,015	275,955
ALL UP WEIGHT		59,965			252,940
POSITION OF C.G.		4·22 FT. OR 50·60 IN. AFT. OF DATUM			

LOADING & C.G. DIAGRAM.

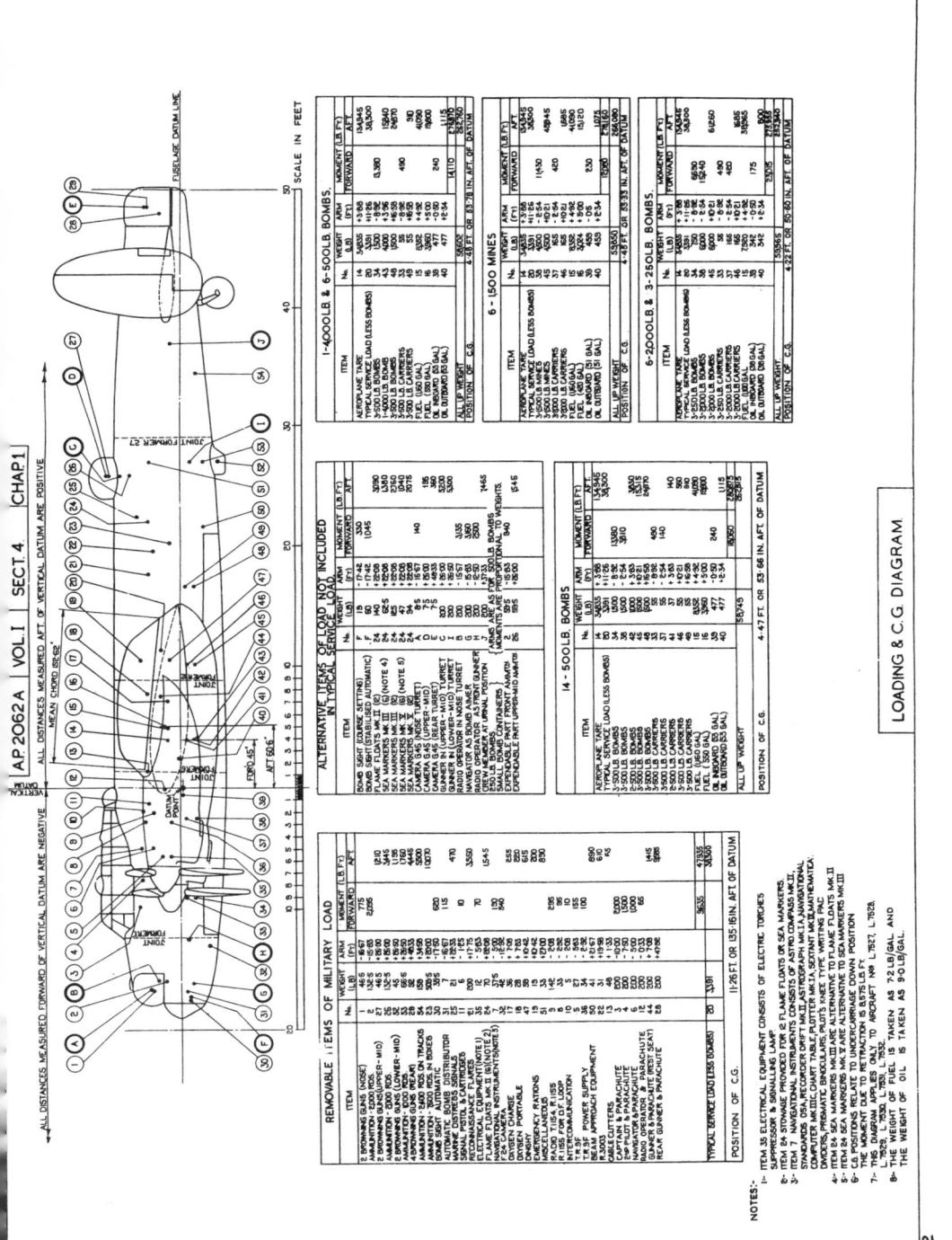

AP. 2062 A | VOL. I | SECT. 4 | CHAP. 1

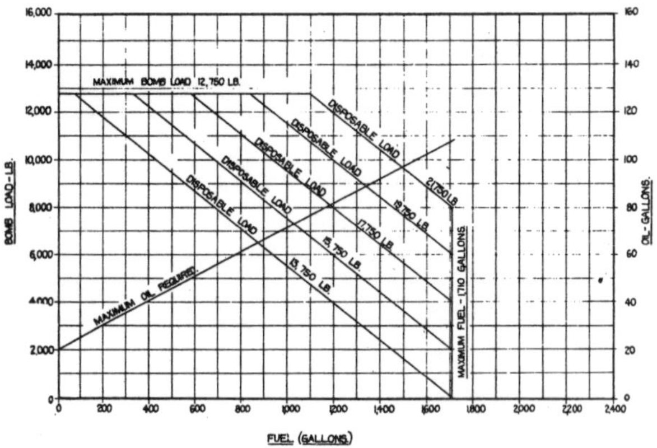

DISPOSABLE LOAD CONSISTS OF BOMBS, CARRIERS, FUEL & OIL. ACCOUNT IS TAKEN IN THE DISPOSABLE LOAD LINES OF THE NECESSARY OIL & CARRIERS TO CORRESPOND WITH THE FUEL & BOMB RESPECTIVELY. THE WEIGHT ASSUMED FOR FUEL IS THAT APPROPRIATE TO 100 OCTANE (7·2 LB. PER GALLON).

TARE WEIGHT 34659 LB

THIS WEIGHT INCLUDES THE FOLLOWING ITEMS:—

FRONT TURRET F.N. 5	261 LB.
UPPER-MID. TURRET F.N. 50	348 LB.
LOWER-MID. TURRET F.N. 64	171 LB.
REAR. TURRET F.N. 20	370 LB.
TURRET HYDRAULICS	320 LB.
AMMUNITION BOXES, TRACKS & MOUNTINGS FOR REAR TURRET	94 LB.
FIXED BOMB & FUSING GEAR	420 LB.
BOMB SIGHT MOUNTINGS	20 LB.
FIXED EQUIPMENT FOR PYROTECHNICS	33·5 LB.
ELECTRICAL EQUIPMENT INCLUDING ACCUMULATORS, LIGHTING, ENGINE DRIVEN GENERATORS, INTERCOMMUNICATION CALL LIGHT SYSTEM, HEATED WINDOW & HEATED GLOVES	770 LB.
FIXED PARTS INSTRUMENT EQUIPMENT FLYING ENGINE & NAVIGATIONAL DR. COMPASS, AUTOMATIC CONTROLS & F.24 CAMERA MOUNTING	314 LB.
FIXED EQUIPMENT FOR OXYGEN INSTALLATION INCLUDING 15 OXYGEN CYLINDERS & CRATE & PORTABLE OXYGEN SYSTEM	310 LB.
FIXED PARTS OF MISCELLANEOUS EQUIPMENT INCLUDING FIRE EXTINGUISHERS, SAFETY BELTS, MOUNTINGS FOR FIRST AID, MOUNTINGS FOR VACUUM FLASKS, ENTRANCE LADDER, PRE-MAN'S AXE, FITTING FOR SUN BLINDS, PARACHUTE STOWAGES, EMERGENCY TOOL KIT & ELSAN	152·5 LB.
FIXED PARTS OF DINGHY INSTALLATION	35 LB.
FIXED PARTS OF RADIO EQUIPMENT INCLUDING D.F. LOOP, INTERCOMMUNICATION, PILOT'S TR.9F STANDARD BEAM APPROACH & R.3003	173 LB.
DE-ICING FOR AIRCREWS, PILOT'S WINDSCREEN & BOMB AIMERS WINDOW	213 LB.
B&F EQUIPMENT	77 LB.
ARMOUR PLATING	300 LB.

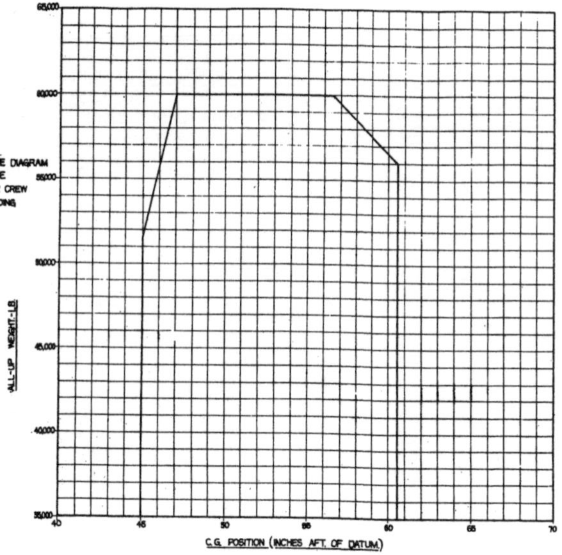

MAXIMUM WEIGHT AT WHICH THIS AEROPLANE HAS BEEN TESTED FOR TAKE-OFF .... 61,500 LB.

MAXIMUM WEIGHT FOR LANDING .... 55,000 LB.

LIMITS OF PERMISSIBLE C.G. TRAVEL
45·0" TO 60·5" AFT OF DATUM ORIGIN MEASURED PARALLEL TO DATUM.

LENGTH OF MEAN CHORD 182·62". (¼ LENGTH OF MEAN CHORD 1·326')

THE C.G. LIMITS GIVEN IN THE DIAGRAM RELATE TO UNDERCARRIAGE DOWN CONDITIONS & ARE FOR CREW IN NORMAL TAKE-OFF & LANDING POSITIONS.

Amended by A.L.2.

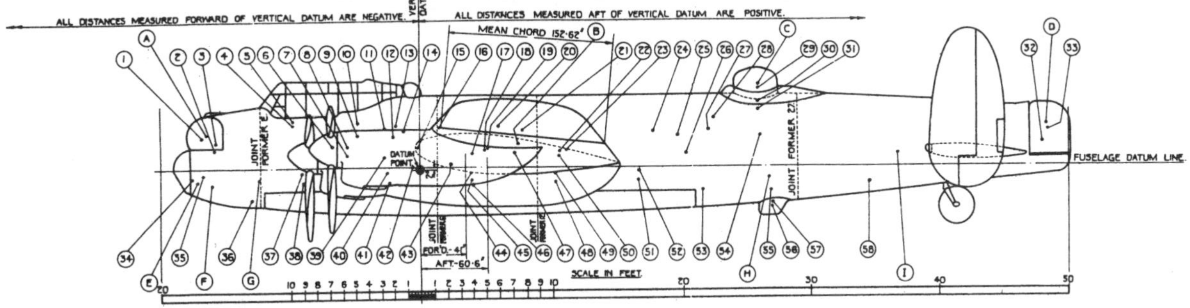

REMOVABLE ITEMS OF MILITARY LOAD					
ITEM	Nº	WEIGHT (LB.)	ARM (FT.)	MOMENT (LB. FT.) FORWARD	MOMENT (LB. FT.) AFT.
2 BROWNING GUNS (NOSE)	1	46·5	-16·67	775	
AMMUNITION - 2,000 RDS.	2	132·5	-15·83	2,095	
2 BROWNING GUNS (UPPER MID.).	29	46·5	+26·00		1,210
AMMUNITION - 2,000 RDS.	31	132·5	+26·00		3,445
UNDER MID TURRET	57	122	+26·50		3,235
2 BROWNING GUNS (LOWER MID.)	56	45	+26·50		1,195
AMMUNITION - 1,500 RDS.	55	99·5	+26·50		2,635
4 BROWNING GUNS (REAR)	33	92	+48·33		4,445
AMMUNITION - 2,400 RDS. ON TRACKS	58	159	+34·58		5,500
AMMUNITION - 7,800 RDS. IN BOXES	26	503·5	+20·00		10,070
BOMB SIGHT (AUTOMATIC)	34	35·5	-17·50	620	
BOMB DISTRIBUTOR	35	6	-16·67	100	
MARINE DISTRESS SIGNALS	28	21	+22·33		470
SIGNAL PISTOL & CARTRIDGES	14	6	- 1·25	10	
RECONNAISSANCE FLARES (8)	24	200	+17·75		3,550
ELECTRICAL EQUIPMENT (NOTE 1)	7	19	- 5·83	110	
FLAME FLOATS MK. II (8)(NOTE 2)	27	70·5	+22·08		1,560
NAVIGATIONAL INSTRUMENTS (NOTE 3)	9	33	- 5·00	165	
F. 24 CAMERA	36	42	-12·92	540	
OXYGEN CHARGE	47	36	+ 7·08		255
OXYGEN PORTABLE	21	28	+ 7·83		220
DINGHY	50	53	+10·42		550
EMERGENCY PACKS	22	49	+10·60		520
MISCELLANEOUS (NOTE 6)	54	42	+24·75		1,040
RADIO T.1154 R.1155	12	142	- 2·08	295	
R.1155 FOR D.F. LOOP	11	33	- 2·92	95	
AMPLIFIER A.1134	13	5	- 2·08	10	
T.R.9.F.	8	28	- 5·83	165	
POWER SUPPLY	39	46	- 2·92	135	
STANDARD BEAM APPROACH	53	45	+21·67		975
R. 3003	25	32	+19·58		625
T. R. 1335	6	69	- 6·83	470	
CABLE CUTTERS	16	50	+1·33		65
CAPTAIN & PARACHUTE	4	200	-10·00	2,000	
PILOT & PARACHUTE	5	200	-10·00	2,000	
NAVIGATOR & PARACHUTE	10	200	- 5·00	1,000	
W/T. OPERATOR & PARACHUTE	15	200	- 0·33	65	
FRONT GUNNER & PARACHUTE	3	200	-15·67	3,135	
MID UPPER GUNNER & PARACHUTE	30	200	+26·00		5,200
REAR GUNNER & PARACHUTE	32	200	+47·92		9,585
				13,785	56,350
TYPICAL SERVICE LOAD (LESS BOMBS)	23	3,870			42,565
POSITION OF C.G.	10·99 FT. OR 131·9 INS. AFT OF DATUM.				

ALTERNATIVE ITEM OF LOAD NOT INCLUDED IN TYPICAL SERVICE LOAD					
ITEM	Nº	WEIGHT (LB.)	ARM (FT.)	MOMENT (LB. FT.) FORWARD	MOMENT (LB. FT.) AFT.
BOMB SIGHT (COURSE SETTING)	E	19	-17·42	330	
BOMB SIGHT (STABILISED AUTOMATIC)	E	60	-17·42	1,045	
FLAME FLOATS MK. II (12)	27	141	+22·08		3,120
SEA MARKERS MK. III (6)(NOTE 4)	27	62·5	+22·08		1,380
SEA MARKERS MK. III (12)	27	125	+22·08		2,760
SEA MARKERS MK. V (6)(NOTE 5)	27	47	+22·08		1,040
SEA MARKERS MK. V (12)	27	94	+22·08		2,075
CAMERA G.45 (NOSE TURRET)	A	8·5	-16·67	140	
CAMERA G.45 (UPPER MID TURRET)	C	7·5	+26·00		195
CAMERA G.45 (REAR TURRET)	D	7·5	+48·33		360
CREW MEMBER ON REST SEAT	B	200	+ 7·08		1,415
GUNNER IN LOWER MID TURRET	H	200	+26·50		5,300
W/T. OP. STANDING BY AS FRONT GUNNER	G	200	-12·50	2500	
NAVIGATOR AS BOMB AIMER	F	200	-15·83	3,160	
CREW MEMBER AT URINAL POSITION	I	200	+37·33		7,465
250 LB. BOMBS SMALL BOMB CONTAINERS	ARMS ARE AS FOR 500 LB. BOMBS MOMENTS ARE PROPORTIONAL TO WEIGHTS.				
EXPENDABLE PART FRONT AMMTN.		59·5	-15·83	940	
EXPENDABLE PART UPPER MID TURRET. AMMUNITION		59·5	+26·00		1,545

FULL FUEL (2,154 GALLS.) & 13-500 LB. BOMBS					
ITEM	Nº	WEIGHT (LB.)	ARM (FT.)	MOMENT (LB. FT.) FORWARD	MOMENT (LB. FT.) AFT.
AIRCRAFT TARE	17	35,354	+ 3·66		129,445
TYPICAL SERVICE LOAD (LESS BOMBS)	23	3,870	+10·99		42,565
3-500 LB. BOMBS	38	1,500	- 8·92	13,380	
3-500 LB. BOMBS	41	1,500	- 2·54	3,810	
1-500 LB. BOMB	45	500	+ 3·83		1,915
3-500 LB. BOMBS	48	1,500	+10·21		15,315
3-500 LB. BOMBS	51	1,500	+16·58		24,870
3-500 LB. CARRIERS	37	55	- 8·92	490	
3-500 LB. CARRIERS	40	55	- 2·54	140	
1-500 LB. CARRIER	44	18	+ 3·83		70
3-500 LB. CARRIERS	49	55	+10·21		560
3-500 LB. CARRIERS	52	55	+16·58		910
FUEL (1160 GALLS.)	18	8,352	+ 4·92		41,090
FUEL (766 GALLS.)	19	5,515	+ 5·00		27,575
FUEL (228 GALLS.	20	1,642	+ 5·92		9,720
OIL INBOARD (65 GALLS.)	42	585	- 0·50	295	
OIL OUTBOARD (65 GALLS.)	43	585	+ 2·34		1,370
				18,115	295,405
ALL UP WEIGHT		62,841			277,290
POSITION OF C.G.	4·42 FT. OR 53·1 INS. AFT. OF DATUM.				

1-4,000 LB. & 6-500 LB. BOMBS					
ITEM	Nº	WEIGHT (LB.)	ARM (FT.)	MOMENT (LB. FT.) FORWARD	MOMENT (LB. FT.) AFT.
AIRCRAFT TARE	17	35,354	+ 3·66		129,445
TYPICAL SERVICE LOAD (LESS BOMBS)	23	3,870	+10·99		42,565
3-500 LB. BOMBS	38	1,500	- 8·92	13,380	
1-4000 LB. BOMB	46	4,000	+ 3·96		15,840
3-500 LB. BOMBS	51	1,500	+16·58		24,870
3-500 LB. CARRIERS	37	55	- 8·92	490	
3-500 LB. CARRIERS	52	55	+16·58		910
FUEL (1160 GALLS.)	18	8,352	+ 4·92		41,090
FUEL (766 GALLS.)	19	5,515	+ 5·00		27,575
FUEL (226 GALLS.)	20	1,628	+ 5·92		9,640
OIL INBOARD (65 GALLS.)	42	585	- 0·50	295	
OIL OUTBOARD (65 GALLS.)	43	585	+ 2·34		1,370
				14,165	293,305
ALL UP WEIGHT		62,999			279,140
POSITION OF C.G.	4·43 FT. OR 53·2 INS. AFT. OF DATUM				

6-1500 LB MINES.					
ITEM	Nº	WEIGHT (LB.)	ARM (FT.)	MOMENT (LB. FT.) FORWARD	MOMENT (LB. FT.) AFT.
AIRCRAFT TARE	17	35,354	+ 3·66		129,445
TYPICAL SERVICE LOAD (LESS BOMBS)	23	3,870	+10·99		42,565
3-1,500 LB. MINES	41	4,500	- 2·54	11,430	
3-1,500 LB. MINES	48	4,500	+10·21		45,945
3-1,500 LB. CARRIERS	40	165	- 2·54	420	
3-1,500 LB. CARRIERS	49	165	+10·21		1,685
FUEL (1160 GALLS.)	18	8,352	+ 4·92		41,090
FUEL (700 GALLS.)	19	5,040	+ 5·00		25,200
OIL INBOARD (58 GALLS.)	42	522	- 0·50	260	
OIL OUTBOARD (58 GALLS.)	43	522	+ 2·34		1,220
				12,110	287,150
ALL UP WEIGHT		62,990			275,040
POSITION OF C.G.	4·37 FT. OR 52·4 INS. AFT. OF DATUM.				

6-2000 LB. & 3-250 LB. BOMBS.					
ITEM	Nº	WEIGHT (LB.)	ARM (FT.)	MOMENT (LB. FT.) FORWARD	MOMENT (LB. FT.) AFT.
AIRCRAFT TARE	17	35,354	+ 3·66		129,445
TYPICAL SERVICE LOAD (LESS BOMBS)	23	3,870	+10·99		42,565
3-250 LB. BOMBS	38	750	- 8·92	6,690	
3-2,000 LB. BOMBS	41	6,000	- 2·54	15,240	
3-2,000 LB. BOMBS	48	6,000	+10·21		61,260
3-250 LB. CARRIERS	37	55	- 8·92	490	
3-2,000 LB. CARRIERS	40	165	- 2·54	420	
3-2,000 LB. CARRIERS	49	165	+10·21		1,685
FUEL (1,160 GALLS.)	18	8,352	+ 4·92		41,090
FUEL (204 GALLS.)	19	1,469	+ 5·00		7,345
OIL INBOARD (45 GALLS.)	42	405	- 0·50	205	
OIL OUTBOARD (45 GALLS.)	43	405	+ 2·34		940
				23,045	284,330
ALL UP WEIGHT		62,990			261,285
POSITION OF C.G.	4·15 FT. OR 49·8 INS. AFT. OF DATUM				

NOTES:-

1. ITEM 7 ELECTRICAL EQUIPMENT CONSISTS OF ELECTRICAL TORCHES SUPPRESSOR & SIGNALLING LAMP.
2. ITEM 27 STOWAGE PROVIDES FOR 12 FLAME FLOATS OR SEA MARKERS.
3. ITEM 9 NAVIGATIONAL INSTRUMENTS CONSISTS OF MK.II ASTRO COMPASS O.S.A. STANDARDS, MK. II RECORDER DRIFT, MK. IA ASTROGRAPH, MK. III C NAVIGATIONAL COMPUTOR, MK. IA CHART TABLE PLOTTER, MK. IX SEXTANT, MATHEMATICAL DIVIDERS, PRISMATIC BINOCULARS, PILOTS KNEE TYPE WRITING PAD.
4. ITEM 27 SEA MARKERS MK. III ARE ALTERNATIVE TO FLAME FLOATS MK. II.
5. ITEM 27 SEA MARKERS MK. V ARE ALTERNATIVE TO SEA MARKER MK. III
6. ITEM 54 MISCELLANEOUS CONSISTS OF FIRST AID PACK, VACUUM FLASKS, SUN BLINDS & FLARE EXTENSION CHUTE.
7. THE WEIGHT OF FUEL IS TAKEN AS 7·2 LB/ GALLON & THE WEIGHT OF OIL IS TAKEN 9/LB. GALLON.

FIG. 3

LOADING & C.G. DIAGRAM (L.7533 AND SUBSEQUENT)

FIG. 3

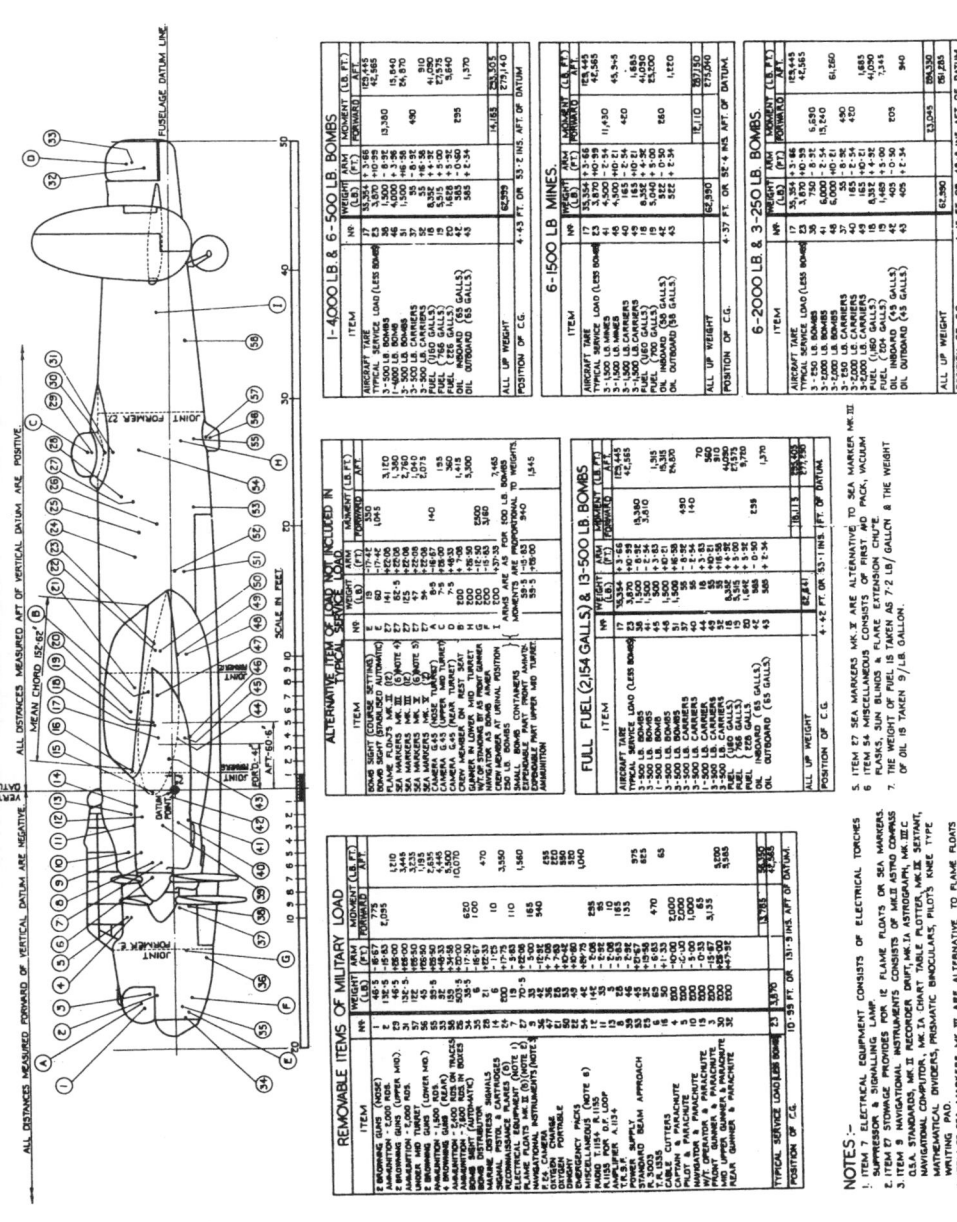

A.P. 2062 A VOL. I SECT. 4 CHAP. I

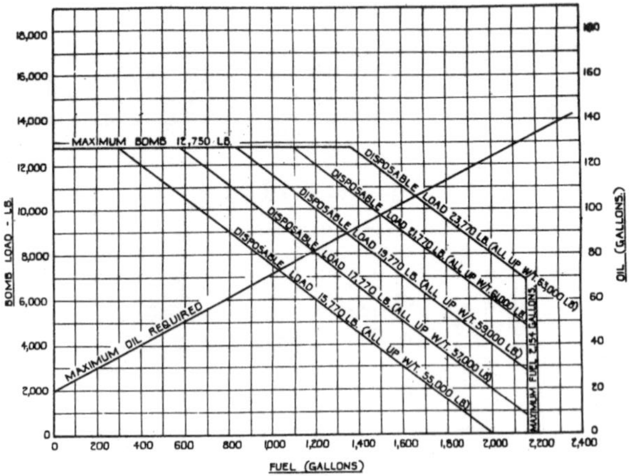

DISPOSABLE LOAD CONSISTS OF BOMBS, CARRIERS, FUEL & OIL. ACCOUNT IS TAKEN IN DISPOSABLE LOAD LINES OF THE NECESSARY OIL & CARRIERS TO CORRESPOND WITH THE FUEL & BOMBS RESPECTIVELY. THE WEIGHT ASSUMED FOR FUEL IS THAT APPROPRIATE TO 100 OCTANE (7·2 LB. PER GALLON)

TARE WEIGHT 35,354 LB.

THIS WEIGHT INCLUDES THE FOLLOWING ITEMS :-

FRONT TURRET F.N.5.	261 LB.
UPPER MID TURRET F.N.50.(M.FAIRINGS)	375 LB.
REAR TURRET F.N.20.	370 LB.
TURRET HYDRAULICS.	320 LB.
AMMUNITION BOXES, TRACKS & MOUNTINGS FOR REAR TURRET.	34 LB.
FIXED BOMB & FUSING GEAR.	425 LB.
BOMB SIGHT MOUNTINGS.	20 LB.
FIXED EQUIPMENT FOR PYROTECHNICS	39 LB.
ELECTRICAL EQUIPMENT INCLUDING ACCUMULATORS, LIGHTING, ENGINE DRIVEN GENERATORS, INTERCOMMUNICATION CALL LIGHT SYSTEM, HEATED WINDOW & HEATED GLOVES.	770 LB.
FIXED PARTS OF INSTRUMENT EQUIPMENT, FLYING, ENGINE & NAVIGATIONAL, D.R. COMPASS, AUTOMATIC CONTROLS & F.24 CAMERA MOUNTING.	339 LB.
FIXED EQUIPMENT FOR OXYGEN INSTALLATION INCLUDING 15 OXYGEN CYLINDERS & CRATE & PORTABLE OXYGEN SYSTEM.	310 LB.
FIXED PARTS OF MISCELLANEOUS EQUIPMENT INCLUDING FIRE EXTINGUISHERS, SAFETY BELTS, MOUNTINGS FOR FIRST AID, MOUNTINGS FOR VACUUM FLASKS, ENTRANCE LADDER, FIREMAN'S AXE, FITTING FOR SUN BLINDS, PARACHUTE STOWAGES, EMERGENCY TOOL KIT & ELSAN.	186 LB.
FIXED PARTS OF DINGHY INSTALLATION & PACKS.	36 LB.
FIXED PARTS OF WIRELESS EQUIPMENT INCLUDING D.F. LOOP, INTERCOMMUNICATION, PILOT'S T.R.9E STANDARD BEAM APPROACH & R.3003 & T.R.1335.	235 LB.
DE-ICING FOR AIRSCREWS, PILOT'S WINDSCREEN & BOMB AIMER'S WINDOW.	213 LB.
CABLE CUTTING EQUIPMENT.	77 LB.
ARMOUR PLATING.	989 LB.

MAXIMUM WEIGHT FOR TAKE-OFF & STRAIGHT FLYING (AT 12 LB./SQ. IN. BOOST PRESSURE) ... 61,500 LB.
MAXIMUM WEIGHT FOR TAKE-OFF & STRAIGHT FLYING (AT 14 LB./SQ. IN. BOOST PRESSURE) ... 63,000 LB.
MAXIMUM WEIGHT FOR LANDING & ALL FORMS OF FLYING ... 55,000 LB.

LIMITS OF PERMISSIBLE C.G. TRAVEL.
FORWARD LIMIT (UP TO 56,000 LB) 41·0 IN. AFT. OF DATUM POINT MEASURED PARALLEL TO DATUM
(ABOVE 56,000 LB) 43·5 IN. AFT. OF DATUM POINT MEASURED PARALLEL TO DATUM
AFT LIMIT (ALL WEIGHTS) 60·6 IN. AFT. OF DATUM POINT MEASURED PARALLEL TO DATUM

NOTE :- MAXIMUM ALL-UP WEIGHTS FOR TAKE-OFF & LANDING IS ONLY PERMISSIBLE FOR AIRCRAFT INCORPORATING MODIFICATIONS 503, 557 & 558. (OR. 558.)

THE C.G. LIMITS GIVEN IN THE DIAGRAM RELATE TO UNDERCARRIAGE DOWN CONDITIONS & ARE FOR CREW IN NORMAL TAKE-OFF & LANDING POSITIONS.

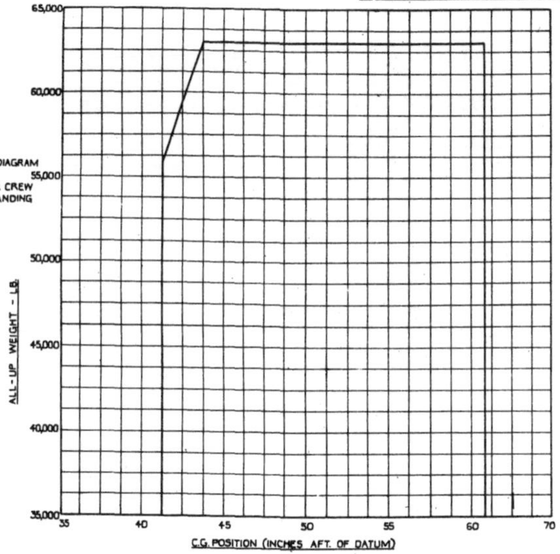

THIS PAGE REVISED BY A.L. 24, APRIL, 1943

This page amended by A.L.No.20
February, 1943
This page amended by A.L.No.26
May, 1943

A.P.2062A and C, Vol.I, Sect.4

CHAPTER 2

GROUND HANDLING AND PREPARATION FOR FLIGHT

LIST OF CONTENTS

	Para.
General	1
Towing	2
Forward towing	3
Backward towing	4
Picketing	5
Jacking	6
Fuel, oil and coolant	7
Pressure refuelling	9
Oil dilution system	10
Ladder for ground starter panel	10A
Bomb loading -	
General	11
Order of loading	13
250 lb. or 500 lb. bombs or containers	14
500 lb. and 600 lb. A.S. bombs	17
1,000 lb. bombs	18
Loading 250 lb., 500 lb. or 1,000 lb. bombs	19
Heavy bombs and mines	21
4,000 lb. bomb	23
8,000 lb. bomb	24B
Flare loading	25
Loading of ammunition -	
Front turret and upper and lower mid-turrets	27
Rear turret	28
Carburettor air intake	29
Method of folding dinghy	30
Salvaging aircraft -	
General	31
First example	32
Second example	33
Third example	34
Fourth example	35

LIST OF ILLUSTRATIONS

	Fig.
Towing diagram	1
Picketing diagram	2
Jacking complete aircraft	3
Outer plane support at rib 7	4
Bomb loadings 1 and 2	5
Bomb loadings 3 and 4	6
Bomb loadings 5 and 6	7
Bomb loadings 7 and 8	8
Bomb loading 9	8A

F.S./1

This page issued with A.L.No.26.　　A.P.2062A and C, Vol.I, Sect.4, Chap.2
May, 1943

	Fig.
Bomb positions and winches required	9
Small-bomb containers	10
Method of fixing 8,000 lb. bomb slip (type G)	10A
Method of fixing 4,000 lb. bomb slip	11
Crutching and fuzing for 4,000 lb. bomb	12
Location of flares and chute	13
Arrangement of covers	14
Method of folding dinghy	15
Lifting crashed aircraft - jacking method 1	16
Lifting crashed aircraft - jacking method 2	17
Lifting crashed aircraft - jacking method 3	18
Lifting crashed aircraft - jacking method 4	19
Method of towing salvaged aircraft	20

June, 1942
Amended (A.L.11)

A.P.2062A, Vol. I, Sect. 4

CHAPTER 2

GROUND HANDLING AND PREPARATION FOR FLIGHT

General

1. This chapter contains information on handling of the aeroplane on the ground and its preparation for flight. Relevant illustrations appear at the end of the chapter. Ancillary equipment for handling and maintenance is listed in the appropriate M leaflet of Vol. II of this publication and special gear and tools are included in the Schedule of Spare Parts of Vol. III, Part 1 of this publication.

Towing

2. The towing arrangements for the aeroplane are shown in fig. 1. Before moving the aeroplane on the ground, care should be taken that the entrance and maintenance ladders are not left against the aeroplane. Before towing the aeroplane, ensure that the undercarriage jury struts, Pt. No. 1.U.631, are in position between the top joint of the shock-absorber strut and the locking joint on the retracting strut.

3. _Forward towing._- The aeroplane is towed forward by a towing bridle, Pt.No.1.U.574, attached to the eyebolt at the bottom of the inner compression leg of each undercarriage unit. The tail wheel steering arm, Pt.No.1.U.572, should be used in conjunction with the towing bridle.

4. _Backward towing._- A towing bar, Pt.No.1.U.573, mounted on two small wheels, is hooked on to the bobbins at the ends of the tail wheel forks, and secured in position by a spring-loaded plunger. The arm is fitted with a spring-loaded mechanism, which releases the aeroplane if the pull applied by the tractor exceeds 3,350 lb. The release is spring operated and is quite simple to re-engage. When using the tail towing bar the elevators must be locked in the neutral position (_see_ Sect. 1).

Picketing

5. A diagram of the picketing of the aeroplane is shown in fig. 2. The main plane is picketed from the shackles on the front spar at rib 6, near the wing tip joint and at rib 21, near the junction of the outer plane and centre section. Doors are provided in the skin on the underside of the plane, for access to these shackles. The fuselage is picketed at the tail end by ropes lashed round the tail wheel axle, and to special eyebolts which are screwed into the sides of the fuselage, just above the rear end of the bomb doors. When the aeroplane is picketed, the main wheels should be chocked and the chocks held in position by stakes. The picketing ropes at the centre fuselage and

F.S./2

Amended (A.L.No.11)
This page amended by A.L.No.26
May, 1943

A.P.2062A and C, Vol.I, Sect.4, Chap.2

wing tip positions should be fitted with one-ton shock-absorbers (see A.P.1464A, Vol.I, Part 8). The picketing points on the aircraft can be used in conjunction with the standard picketing layout. Care should be taken when removing the picketing ropes from the aircraft, to ensure that the special eyebolts in the sides of the fuselage are removed and replaced by standard screwed plugs. The eyebolts are stowed with the bomb gear crutching handles in a pocket in the fuselage intermediate centre portion. Covers are provided for the engines, turrets and canopy (see fig.14).

5A. When an aircraft is picketed out in a wind exceeding 40 m.p.h., the ailerons, elevators and rudders should be secured with external clamps.

Jacking

6. The complete aircraft should be jacked up as shown in fig.3. Bipod jacks are placed under the jacking pads on the front spar of the centre section, and a universal jacking trestle, fitted with a special beam, is placed under the tail end of the fuselage, just forward of the tail wheel at former 35. The jacking pads, Pt.No.2.U.551, must be fitted to the front spar before commencing to jack up and the jacks must be placed with the plane of the jacking legs parallel to the centre-line of the aircraft. It is necessary to lift the hinged nose of the centre section to fit the pads to the stud bolts provided. Steadying trestles and gantries should be placed under the outer planes and fuselage nose, as shown. The jacks have sufficient extension to raise the aircraft from the position of one tyre deflated, to the flying position with the wheels clear of the ground.

Fuel, oil and coolant

7. For the fuel, oil and coolant used with the Merlin XX engines, see Leading Particulars. Diagrams of the systems appear in Chap.3 of this Section.

8. On aircraft not incorporating Mod.553, a pressure refuelling cock is located behind each inboard engine on a bracket below the front spar. From this connection a length of flexible pipe extends downwards, and is secured, when not in use, to a plug mounted on the diagonal strut between the undercarriage support beams. The tanker pipe is connected by means of a 1¼ in. B.S.P. fitting to the lower end of this pipe. The fuel tanks can also be filled through the tank filler caps in the top of the tanks, access being obtained through the appropriate doors in the upper surface of the main plane. Access to the oil tank filler caps is gained through a door in the port fairing panel of each engine nacelle. The coolant tank for each engine is mounted on the front of the engine, just behind the spinner. The filler cap for this tank is located on the top side in such a position as to prevent overfilling. A special spanner is provided to remove this filler cap, Pt.No.1.Z.1377, and is stowed on the inside of the port inboard undercarriage fairing door. To remove the radiator drain plugs spanner, Pt.No.Z.1436 should be used.

Amended (A.L.No.11)   A.P.2062A and C, Vol.I, Sect.4, Chap.2
This page amended by A.L.No.26
May, 1943

9. **Pressure re-fuelling.**- The following is the sequence of operations for each tank :-

   (i)   Fasten the fuel tank bowser to the re-fuelling pipe in the nacelle.

   (ii) Turn the re-fuelling cock, for the tank to be filled, to the ON position. The cock is on the front spar behind the engine.

   (iii) Remove the fuel tank filler cap.

   (iv) Pump in fuel at a pressure not exceeding 30 lb./sq.in., and at a rate not exceeding 60 gals. per minute, at the same time noting the reading of the fuel contents gauge on the observer's panel.

   (v)   After the filling is complete, the re-fuelling cock should be turned to the OFF position, care being taken that the spring-loaded catch has locked.

Oil dilution system

10. The oil dilution valve is mounted on the starboard side of each engine, and the electrical push-button controls are on the observer's instrument panel. A description of the system and the method of its operation is contained in A.P.1464B, Vol.I. The time of operation of the system is :-

    1 minute at air temperatures down to   -10 deg.C.
    2 minutes at air temperatures below   -10 deg.C.

Ladder for ground starter panel

10A. A ladder is provided to give access to the ground starter panels in the inboard nacelles. When in position the top of the ladder rests on the steps on the main wheel retracting struts.

Bomb loading

11. **General.**- Fig.5 to 8 show the layout of the various bomb loads. Before loading bombs, the bomb cell doors should be opened by pushing down the lever on the left-hand side of the pilot's seat. If the inboard engines are running the doors will open automatically, but if not, it will be necessary to operate the emergency hand pump on the port wall of the fuselage just aft of the front spar. The safety brackets, Pt.No.1.U.593, should then be fitted to the four hydraulic jacks to prevent the inadvertent closing of the doors whilst bomb loading operations are in progress.

F.S./3

Amended (A.L.No.15) A.P.2062A and C, Vol.I, Sect.4, Chap.2
This page amended by A.L.No.26
May, 1943

12. Standard bomb loading winches are required, two 2,000 lb. winches being used to hoist the 4,000 lb. bomb. For the location of the two lifting holes for this bomb, forward and aft of the centre bomb gear housing, see Sect.7, Chap.1, fig.7. The adjustable crutches for the 4,000 lb. bomb are removed when other bomb loads are to be carried. For removing bomb carriers and for making final adjustments and checking when the bombs are in position, a step ladder (Stores Ref.4C/86) will be necessary.

13. Order of loading.- The heavy bombs must be loaded in the correct sequence. For this purpose each bomb gear housing is numbered above and below the floor for ease of identification. Fig.9 indicates the housings to be used for the following bombs, and the winches required for lifting them.

(i)   14 - 250 lb., 500 lb. or 1,000 lb. bombs (other than 500 lb. Mk.I, II, III or IV A.S. bombs).

(ii) 6 - mines or heavy bombs.

(iii) 6 - 500 lb. A.S. bombs (Mk.I, II and III only).

(iv) 1 - 4,000 lb. bomb.

Loadings (ii), (iii) and (iv) are location instructions only, and not maximum loads, which are shown in fig.5 to 8.

14. 250 lb. or 500 lb. bombs or containers.- The aircraft can carry 14 - 250 lb. or 500 lb. bombs of the following types :-

(i)   500 lb. G.P. bombs.
(ii)   500 lb. S.A.P. bombs.
(iii) 250 lb. G.P. bombs.
(iv)   250 lb. S.A.P. bombs.
(v)   250 lb. L.C. bombs.
(vi)   250 lb. B. bombs.
(vii) 250 lb. A.S. bombs.
(viii) Small-bomb containers.

15. Although not important, it is more convenient to load the small-bomb containers, the 500 lb. bombs and the 250 lb. bombs in that order.

16. If the number of bombs to be fitted is less than 14, the centre housings should be used.

This page issued with A.L.No.26   A.P.2062A and C, Vol.I, Sect.4, Chap.2
May, 1943

17. **500 lb. and 600 lb. A.S. bombs.**- Fourteen 600 lb. A.S. bombs may be carried but owing to the length of the 500 lb. A.S. bomb it is possible to carry only six Mk.I, II or III or eight Mk.IV bombs of this type. Fig.5 and 6 show the loading of these bombs and the additional bombs which may also be carried. The sequence of loading is in the reverse order to the numbering of the housings.

18. **1,000 lb. bombs.**- Fourteen bombs of the following types can be carried (see fig.5, bomb loading No.1), and should be loaded in the reverse order to the numbering of the housings:-

    (i)   1,000 lb. G.P. (short tail type) bombs.

    (ii) 1,000 lb. U.S.A. bombs.

    (iii) 1,000 lb. M.C. bombs.

Six only of the long type 1,000 lb. bombs can be carried as indicated in fig.6. bomb loading No.4, which also shows the additional bombs which may be carried. The 1,000 lb. bombs should be loaded first at housings 12, 11, 10, 9, 8 and 7, in that order.

19. **Loading 250 lb., 500 lb., or 1,000 lb. bombs.**- The following is the sequence of operations, using the 500 lb. standard winch for 250 lb. or 500 lb. bombs, and the 2,000 lb. standard winch for 1,000 lb. bombs :-

(Continued on next leaf)

.S./3A

Amended (A.L.11)
Para.19 (contd.)

A.P.2062A, Vol.I, Sect.4, Chap.2

(i) Open the bomb doors and fit the safety brackets.

(ii) Remove the cover plates from the bomb gear housings in the floor of the fuselage.

(iii) Using the small crutch handle, Pt.No.2.D.1720 or 1.W.782, wind the front crutch adjustment levers to the maximum up position, i.e., in an anti-clockwise direction. (The crutch handle is stowed in a small pouch on the starboard side of the intermediate centre portion of the fuselage).

(iv) Remove the bomb carriers from inside the bomb cell by releasing the trip levers in the bomb gear housings. This will need one man inside the fuselage to release the lever, and one man in the bomb bay to remove the carrier.

(v) Fit the bomb carrier to the top of the bomb, which should have been wheeled underneath the bomb cell on the ground, and adjust the bomb crutches evenly only sufficient to steady the bomb while it is being raised, otherwise the carrier may distort and prevent its fitting into the housing.

(vi) Adjust the fuze-setting control link from the fuzing box on the carrier to the bomb.

(vii) Set the supporting lever in the bomb gear housing in the cocked position.

(viii) Hold the ratchet on the "quick-wind-in" side of the bomb winch in the FREE position and pull sufficient length of cable off the drum to pass through the housing.

(ix) Lift the winch reaction pad in the housing so that the winch nose can be fitted after the winch cable has been passed through.

(x) Again hold the ratchet in the FREE position, pull the cable to the ground and carefully fit the ball end to the ball socket on the carrier.

(xi) Take up the free length of the cable on the "quick-wind-in".

(xii) After ensuring that the ball end is still engaging the ball socket, proceed to raise the bomb and carrier to the bomb gear housing. The bomb and carrier should be kept in a fore-and-aft position during the lifting operations. (A bomb steadying fork may be used for this purpose).

(xiii) When the carrier is near the bomb housing, ensure that the guide rollers on the carrier engage the guide in the housing, and the supporting pin engages the support hook. This will force the hook upwards and operate the trip lever which will lock the supporting hook round the pin on the carrier.

F.S./4

Amended (A.L.11) A.P.2062A, Vol.I, Sect.4, Chap.2

Para.19 (contd.)

(The completion of this operation will be indicated by a loud click as the trip lever operates). Ensure that the locking pawl is fully engaged.

(xiv) Unwind the cable a few turns to ensure that the carrier is locked in the housing.

(xv) The ball end of the cable should then be disengaged from the socket.

(xvi) Tighten the front carrier crutches by winding the crutch handle in a clockwise direction. Tighten the bomb crutches securely, but take care not to over-crutch or the bomb may be "hung up".

(xvii) The electrical connection between the plug on the carrier and the socket at the rear of the bomb gear housing, should then be made and locked, but first ensure that jettison bars on the selector box are at SAFE.

(xviii) After completion of the bomb loading operations, remove the safety brackets from the bomb door jacks, fit the cover plates to the top of the bomb gear housings, and carry out the usual "light test".

20. The same procedure is used to lift the small-bomb containers as for the 250 lb. or 500 lb. bombs. The electrical connections, however, are slightly different (see fig.10). When the leads between the container and adaptor box have been connected on the ground, the plug on the carrier should be fitted in the socket at the back of the bomb gear housing, as for the ordinary bombs.

21. Heavy bombs and mines.- The aeroplane can carry six heavy bombs or mines of the following types:- 1,900 lb. G.P. bombs, 2,000 lb. A.P. bombs, 2,000 lb. H.C. bombs, or 1,500 lb. mines. These are carried in housings Nos.12, 11, 10, 9, 8 and 7, and must be loaded in that order. When mixed loads are carried the heavy bombs should be loaded first (see figs. 7 and 8). The heavy bomb carrier, Pt.No.1.W.787, is used, and the bomb loading hoist required is the 2,000 lb. standard bomb winch.

22. The loading procedure for heavy bombs and mines is similar to that described in para.19, with the following additions:-

(i) Check the bomb carrier, Pt.No.1.W.787, to ensure that the correct sling is fitted. One of the following slings will be required:-

Amended (A.L.11) A.P.2062A, Vol.I, Sect.4, Chap.2
Para.22 (contd.)

    (a) For 2,000 lb. H.C. bomb   - sling, 54¼ in. long.
         or 1,500 lb. mine   Avro Pt. No. 4.W.787

    (b) For 1,900 lb. G.P. bomb   - sling, 56½ in. long.
                                  Avro Pt. No. 5.W.787

    (c) For 2,000 lb. A.P. bomb   - sling, 40¼ in. long.
                                  Avro Pt. No. 6.W.787

(ii) Slacken the front and rear crutches of the carrier right back.

(iii) Place the carrier on the top of the bomb or mine, with the locating lug in the spring-loaded box on the carrier.

(iv) The tension handle on the strainer should be turned by hand until the sling is slack enough to be passed round the bomb or mine, and for the end to be fastened in the slip release.

(v) The tension handle should now be turned by hand until the sling is tight round the bomb or mine and there is no play on the slip.

(vi) Secure the elastic cord to the sling by passing one side of the loop under the bomb or mine and securing it to the link near the end of the sling.

(vii) The front and rear crutches should be tightened down using finger pressure only. Care must be taken that there is even pressure on the four adjustable pads, otherwise the carrier may be twisted and become difficult to secure. Ensure that the bomb is parallel with the bomb beam, both from the side and from above.

(viii) Adjust the fuze setting control link or links from the fuzing box or boxes on the carrier, taking care that the boxes are set in the correct position on the carrier, and that the fuze setting control links are as near the vertical as possible.

The remainder of the procedure is as described in para.19, except that the crutches used are those forward of the bomb gear housing and not those at the front of the housing, and when mines are carried, the static cord must be attached to the eyebolt in the bomb cell. When lifting heavy bombs or mines, they must be pushed forwards about an inch when a few inches below the carrier housing to ensure engagement of the carrier rollers in the guides and the guide pins in the slots. Care must also be taken to ensure that the ball-end sleeve of the winch cable does not foul the carrier locking lever.

F.S./5

Amended (A.L.11) A.P.2062A, Vol.I, Sect.4,
This page amended by A.L.No.20
February, 1943

23. **4,000 lb. bomb.-** This bomb is carried by an R.A.E. type bomb release in housing No.13 in the floor of the centre portion of the fuselage. The total bomb load is shown in fig.7, the 4,000 lb. bomb being loaded first, followed by the remaining bombs. Two 2,000 lb. standard winches are required to hoist the bomb.

24. The following are the instructions for loading the 4,000 lb. bomb on aircraft not incorporating Mod.412 (bomb release gear for 8,000 lb. bomb):-

(i) Open the bomb doors and fit the safety brackets.

(ii) Remove the cover plates from the bomb gear housing and the two lifting points in the fuselage floor.

(iii) If the front and rear individually adjustable crutches are not in position, fit them by means of the quick-release pins (see fig.12).

(iv) If it is not in position, fit the front fuze bracket (three fuzes), Pt.No.1.W.822, and connect the electric cables of the fuze unit to the terminal block. Ensure that the two fuze units for the bomb side fuzes are in the correct positions (see fig.12).

Note.- Aircraft not incorporating Mod.No.455 are fitted with a single front fuze suitable for the Mk.I bomb only.

(v) Place the bomb under the aircraft and attach the winch connectors to the hoisting lugs.

(vi) Fit a winch reaction socket, Pt.No.1.W.797, at each of the two lifting points in the floor.

(vii) Hold the ratchet on the "quick-wind-in" side in the FREE position and pull sufficient length of cable off the drum to pass through the housing. Thread the cables through the holes in the floor and fit the winches into the reaction sockets.

(viii) Again release the ratchet on the winches, pull down the winch cables, carefully insert the ball-ends into the connectors, and take up the free cables on the "quick-wind-in".

(ix) Ensure that the release jaws are open, if necessary opening them by means of the mechanical release lever. It is essential that the lever be returned to the forward position and LOCKED before the bomb is loaded.

(x) Ensure that the ball-ends are still engaging the sockets and wind the bomb up into position. Take care that the nose of the bomb is lifted first and ensure that the tail of the bomb does not foul the junction box in the floor of the fuselage. The jaws of the slip should close automatically on the bomb supporting lug. If this does not happen, shims should be applied to the top of the bomb lug to ensure this.

Amended (A.L.11)
This page amended by A.L.No.20
February, 1943

A.P.2062A, Vol.I, Sect.4, Chap.2

Para.24 (contd.)

(xi) IMPORTANT. Lock the jaws by means of the small lever on the side of the bomb release, using finger pressure only. DO NOT CONFUSE THIS LEVER WITH THE MECHANICAL RELEASE, OTHERWISE THE BOMB MAY BE DROPPED.

(xii) Check whether the release slip is properly locked by pressing the test button (see fig.11). A sharp point should be felt by the finger if the release is fully locked.

(xiii) Slacken the winch cables, remove the pins securing the winch connectors to the bomb, and remove the two winches, the reaction sockets and the winch connectors.

(xiv) The bomb should then be crutched. The crutches are of the independently adjustable type and should be operated until the four points are finger-tight on the bomb. After this a final tightening should be made and the crutches finally locked by means of the locknuts provided. The tail of the bomb should be crutched lower than the nose to avoid fouling the junction box.

(xv) Make the fuzing connections by fitting three cables to the front fuzes and one on each side of the bomb (see fig.12).

Note.- In aircraft not incorporating Mod.No.455 and suitable therefore for the Mk.I bomb, make only the single fuzing connection to the bomb nose fuze.

(xvi) Fit the covers to the release slips and the lifting holes, taking care that the emergency hand release is fitted into the spring clip on the housing.

24A. In aircraft incorporating Mod.No.412 (introducing bomb release gear for an 8,000 lb. bomb), the following is the loading procedure for the 4,000 lb. bomb:-

(i) Open the bomb doors and fit the safety brackets.

(ii) Remove the cover plates from the bomb gear housing and the two lifting points in the fuselage floor.

(iii) If the combined slip and release type G (for an 8,000 lb. bomb) is in position, it must be adapted as follows:-

 (a) Remove the combined slip and release by withdrawing the two bolts (A) (see fig.13) from the housing and disconnecting the electrical wiring from the five-way terminal block.

 (b) Fit the adaptors, Pt.No.7.D.3128 and replace the 4,000 lb. bomb release type F (see fig.12).

(iv) If the front and rear individually adjustable crutches are not in position fit them by means of the quick-release pins (see fig.14).

F.S./6

This page amended by A.L. No. 18
September, 1942
This page amended by A.L. No. 20
February, 1943

A.P.2062A, Vol. I, Sect. 4, Chap. 2

Para. 24A (contd.)

(v) If it is not in position, fit the front fuze bracket (three fuzes), Pt. No. 1.W.822, and connect the electrical cables of the fuze unit to the terminal block. Ensure that the two fuze units for the bomb side fuzes are in the correct position (see fig. 14).

(vi) Place the bomb under the aircraft and attach the winch connectors to the hoisting lugs.

(vii) Fit a winch reaction socket, Pt. No. 1.W.817, at the front lifting point and 1.W.823 at the rear lifting point. Fit an adaptor, Pt. No. 1.W.819, in each socket.

(viii) Hold the ratchet on the "quick-wind-in" side in the FREE position and pull about 3 ft. of cable from each winch. Thread the cables through the holes in the floor and fit the winches into the reaction sockets.

(ix) Again release the ratchet on the winches, pull down the winch cables, carefully insert the ball-ends into the connectors, and take up the free cable on the "quick-wind-in".

(x) See that the release jaws are open, if necessary opening the jaws by means of the mechanical release lever. It is essential that the lever be returned to the rear position and LOCKED before the bomb is loaded.

(xi) Ensure that the ball-ends are still engaging the sockets and wind the bomb up into position. The jaws should automatically close on the bomb supporting lug. If this does not happen, shims should be applied to the top of the bomb lug to ensure that it does.

(xii) IMPORTANT. Lock the jaws by means of the small lever on the side of the bomb release, using finger pressure only. DO NOT CONFUSE THIS LEVER WITH THE MECHANICAL RELEASE, OTHERWISE THE BOMB MAY BE DROPPED.

(xiii) Check whether the release slip is properly locked by pressing the test button (see fig. 13). A sharp point should be felt by the finger if the release is fully locked.

(xiv) Slacken the winch cables, remove the pins securing the winch connectors to the bomb, and remove the two winches, the reaction sockets and the winch connectors.

(xv) The bomb should then be crutched. The crutches are of the independently adjustable type and should be operated until the four points are finger-tight on the bomb. After this, a final tightening should be made and the crutches then locked by means of the locknut.

(xvi) Make the fuzing connections by fitting three cables to the front fuzes and one on each side of the bomb (see fig. 14).

(xvii) Fit the covers to the release slips and lifting holes, taking care that the emergency hand release is fitted into the spring clip on the housing.

This page issued with A.L. No. 20
February, 1943

A.P. 2062A, Vol. I, Sect. 4, Chap. 2

24B. **8,000 lb. bomb.** - This bomb also is carried by housing No. 13 in the centre portion of the fuselage floor (see fig. 9). Two heavy bomb winches are required to hoist the bomb and the loading procedure is as follows:-

(i) Place the bomb on trolley type E.

(ii) Open the bomb doors and fit the safety brackets.

(iii) Remove the cover plates from the bomb gear housing and the two lifting points in the fuselage floor.

(iv) If the combined slip and release type G (8,000 lb. bomb) is not in place, due to the release being adapted for carrying a 4,000 lb. bomb, the adaptors (Pt. No. 7.D.3128) and the bomb release must be removed, and the combined slip and release type G fitted, (see fig. 13).

(v) If the front and rear individually adjustable crutches are not in position fit them by means of the quick-release pins (see fig. 15).

(vi) If it is not in position, fit the front fuze bracket (three fuze) Pt. No. 1.W. 822, and connect the electric cables to the terminal blocks. See that the two fuze units for the bomb side fuzes are in the correct positions (see fig. 15).

(vii) Fit a winch reaction socket, Pt. No. 1.W. 817, at the front lifting point, and Pt. No. 1.W. 823 at the rear lifting point.

(viii) Take the two winches and, using the ratchet lever on the "quick-wind-in" side, pull about 3 ft. of cable from each winch.

(ix) Thread the cables through the holes in the floor, and fit the winches into the reaction sockets.

(x) The bomb trolley with the bomb should then be pushed into position below the bomb gear housing, from the front of the aircraft only.

(xi) Attach the winch connectors to the hoisting lugs on the bomb by means of the quick-release pins.

(xii) Again releasing the ratchets on the winches, pull down the winch cables, carefully insert the ball-ends into the connectors, and take up the free cable on the "quick-wind-in".

(xiii) See that the slip is in the OPEN position, if necessary opening the jaws by means of the mechanical release lever. It is essential that the lever be returned to the rear position and LOCKED before the bomb is loaded.

(xiv) Ensure that the ball-ends are still engaging the sockets, and wind the bomb up into position. The lug on the bomb will engage the hook in the slip, causing the jaws of the release to close automatically on the pin at the end of the supporting hook.

(xv) IMPORTANT. Lock the jaws on the release by means of the

F.S./7

This page issued with A.L. No. 20 A.P.2062A, Vol.I, Sect.4, Chap.2
February, 1943

Para. 24B (contd.)

small lever on the side of the bomb release slip, using finger pressure only. DO NOT CONFUSE THIS LEVER WITH THE MECHANICAL RELEASE OTHERWISE THE BOMB MAY BE DROPPED.

(xvi) Check whether the release slip jaws are properly locked by pressing the test button (see fig. 10A). A sharp point should be felt by the finger.

(xvii) Slacken the winch cables, remove the pins securing the winch connectors to the bomb and remove the two winches, the reaction sockets and the winch connectors.

(xviii) The bomb should then be crutched. The crutches, which are of the independently adjustable type, should be operated until the four points are finger tight on the bomb. A final tightening should be made, and the crutches locked by means of the locknuts.

(xix) Make the fuzing connections by fitting three cables to the front fuzes and two on the starboard side of the bomb.

(xx) Fit the covers to the release slip and the lifting holes, taking care that the emergency hand release is fitted into the spring clip on the housing.

Flare loading

25. The arrangement of the reconnaissance flares in the fuselage is shown in fig. 13, which also shows the flare chute fitted with the extension tube ready for dropping the flares and the stowage position for the extension tube.

26. The procedure for loading the reconnaissance flares is as follows:-

(i) Open the lid of the flare tube.

(ii) Remove the flare tube extension from the stowed position in the fuselage side and insert it in position in the top of the flare tube (see fig. 13).

(iii) Remove a flare from the stowed position on the side of fuselage and insert into the tube with the propeller end uppermost. Ensure that the release mechanism on the flare tube extension engages the stop on the flare.

(iv) Connect the cable from the pulley on the top of the extension tube to the pin at the centre of the flare propeller.

Loading of ammunition

27. <u>Front turret and upper and lower mid turrets.</u>- The ammunition for these turrets is carried inside the turrets, in boxes which are easily handled for loading purposes. The ammunition boxes for the front turret should be lifted into the aircraft through the access door in the floor of the nose, and for the upper and lower mid turrets through

This page issued with A.L.No.20 February, 1943
This page amended by A.L.No.26 May, 1943

A.P.2062A and C, Vol.I, Sect.4, Chap.2

the main door of the fuselage. Spare ammunition for the front and upper mid turrets is carried in boxes stowed on the port side near the end of the main floor, just forward of the boxes for the rear turret.

28. *Rear turret.-* The ammunition for the rear turret is stowed in boxes on each side of the fuselage floor at the rear end of the bomb compartment, and is led by tracks along each side of the fuselage to the rear turret. To load these boxes it is necessary to remove the access door underneath the rear turret, when the ammunition can be fed through the opening on to the ammunition track and then be drawn along the fuselage and fed into the boxes.

Carburettor air intake

29. On aircraft not incorporating Mod.No.432, this control is underneath the navigator's seat, but on subsequent aircraft, it is on the port side of the cockpit floor. After the air-intake scoops are attached, and before take-off, the operation of this control should be checked for freeness of the butterflies. If their movement is too stiff, the jubilee clips should be slackened slightly.

Method of folding dinghy

30. When folding the type J, Mk.III dinghy care must be taken to make it as compact as possible (see fig.15), otherwise difficulty will be encountered when fixing the lid of the stowage compartment. Before folding, the dinghy must be thoroughly deflated by means of a pump. Deflation is complete only when all creases appear as knife edges. When stowing the dinghy it is essential to keep it clear of the short portion of manual release between the operating head and the fairlead on the stowage wall.

Salvaging aircraft

31. *General.-* Four methods for the quick removal of a crashed aircraft are described in para.32 to 35 and fig.20. These instructions assume that the aircraft can be moved intact and that no dismantling is necessary. The trolley arms should be to the rear so that a man on each handle can assist in manoeuvring the trolley on turns. In each example, as soon as convenient, open the bomb doors, remove the bombs and close the doors.

32. *First example.-* An aircraft lands with one main wheel unit retracted but undamaged. It is required to lift the aircraft in order to lower the wheel. The procedure is as follows (see fig.16):-

   (i) Obtain the following equipment :-

      (a) One 15-ton hydraulic bipod single extension jack - 4 ft. 0 in. closed height, 6 ft. 0 in. extended.

F.S./8

This page issued with A.L.No.26 A.P.2062A and C, Vol.I, Sect.4, Chap.2
May, 1943

Para.32 (contd.)

    (b) Two 15-ton hydraulic bipod double extension jacks - 5 ft. 6 in. closed height, 11 ft. 6 in. extended.

(ii) Place the 15-ton single extension jack below the outboard jacking pad on the lower side of the aircraft.

(iii) Place a 15-ton double extension jack below the outboard pad on the high side of the aircraft.

(iv) Take the initial load on both jacks. Raise the jack on the lower side to its fullest extent, keeping the other jack adjusted so that the extended wheel clears the ground.

(v) Place the second 15-ton double extension jack below the inboard jacking pad on the lower side and raise to its full extent together with the jack on the higher side. Remove the single extension jack and lower the main wheel unit.

(vi) The aircraft may then be towed away by attaching cables to the inboard propeller hubs after the removal of the spinners.

33. **Second example.**- An aircraft lands with one main wheel unit retracted. It is required to lift the aircraft on to salvage trolleys (see fig.17):-

(i) Obtain the following equipment :-

    (a) Two 10-ton salvage trolleys.

    (b) One 15-ton hydraulic bipod single extension jack - 4 ft. 0 in. closed height, 6 ft. 0 in. extended.

    (c) One 15-ton hydraulic bipod double extension jack - 5 ft. 6 in. closed height, 11 ft. 6 in. extended.

    (d) Chocks for tail wheel.

(ii) Place the 15-ton single extension jack below the inboard jacking pad on the lower side of the aircraft, and take the initial load by raising the jack to approximately 6 ft. 0 in.

(iii) Place the 15-ton double extension jack under the inboard jacking pad on the higher side of the aircraft, and chock the tail wheel. Raise this jack sufficiently to allow the main wheel unit to be retracted, and then lower the jack to approximately 6 ft. 0 in.

(iv) Remove both inboard engine cowlings and radiators and all other equipment below the undercarriage support beams (see Sect.5).

This page issued with A.L.No.26   A.P.2062A and C, Vol.I, Sect.4, Chap.2
May, 1943

Para.33 (contd.)

- (v) Place the salvage trolleys centrally below the undercarriage support beams.

- (vi) Lower the jacks until the beams rest on the trolleys and secure the beams to the trolleys.

- (vii) Remove the tail wheel chocks. The aircraft may then be towed away by attaching cables to the inboard propeller hubs after the removal of the spinners.

34. **Third example.-** An aircraft lands with both main wheel units retracted but undamaged. It is required to lift the aircraft in order to lower both wheels (see fig.18).

- (i) Obtain the following equipment :-

  - (a) Two 25-ton hydraulic bipod double extension jacks - 2 ft. 0 in. closed height, 4 ft. 0 in. extended.

  - (b) Two 15-ton hydraulic bipod single extension jacks - 4 ft. 0 in. closed height, 6 ft. 0 in. extended.

  - (c) Two 15-ton hydraulic bipod double extension jacks - 5 ft. 6 in. closed height, 11 ft. 6 in. extended.

  - (d) Chocks for the tail wheel.

- (ii) Place the 25-ton jacks below the outboard jacking pads and raise to the fully extended position. Chock the tail wheel.

- (iii) Place the 15-ton single extension jacks below the inboard jacking pads and raise to the fully extended position. Remove the 25-ton jacks.

- (iv) Place the 15-ton double extension jacks below the outboard jacking pads and raise to allow the main wheel units to be lowered.

- (v) Remove the jacks.

- (vi) Remove the tail wheel chocks. The aircraft may then be towed away by attaching cables to the inboard propeller hubs after removing the spinners.

35. **Fourth example.-** An aircraft lands with both main wheel units retracted. It is required to lift the aircraft on to salvage trolleys (see fig.19).

F.S./9

This page issued with A.L.No.26   A.P.2062A and C, Vol.I, Sect.4, Chap.2
May, 1943

Para.35 (contd.)

- (i) Obtain the following equipment :-
    - (a) Two 25-ton hydraulic bipod double extension jacks - 2 ft. 0 in. closed height, 4 ft. 0 in. extended.
    - (b) Two 15-ton hydraulic bipod single extension jacks - 4 ft. 0 in. closed height, 6 ft. 0 in. extended.
    - (c) Two 10-ton salvage trolleys.
- (ii) Place the 25-ton jacks under the outer jacking pads, and raise to the full extension of 4 ft. 0 in.
- (iii) Place the 15-ton jacks under the inner jacking pads, and raise to the full extension of 6 ft. 0 in.
- (iv) Remove both inboard engine cowlings and radiators and all other equipment below the undercarriage support beams (see Sect.5).
- (v) Place the salvage trolleys centrally below the undercarriage support beams.
- (vi) Lower the jacks until the beams rest on the trolleys and secure the beams to the trolleys.
- (vii) The aircraft can then be towed by cables attached to the inboard propeller hubs, after removing the spinners.

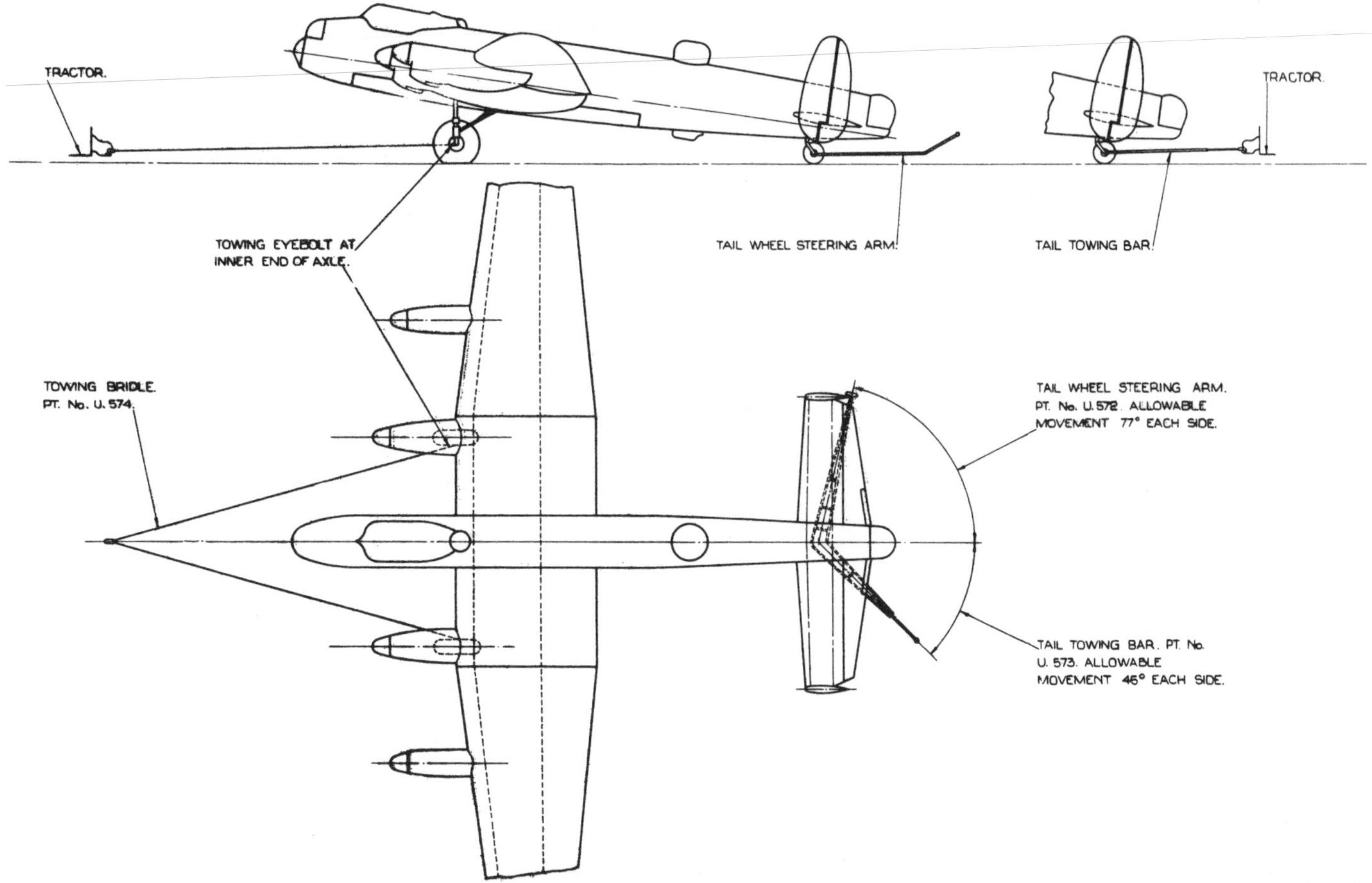

TOWING DIAGRAM

A.P. 2062 A | VOL. 1 | SECT. 4 | CHAP. 2

FIG. 1

PICKETING DIAGRAM

A.P. 2062 A | VOL. I | SECT. 4 | CHAP. 2

JACKING COMPLETE AEROPLANE

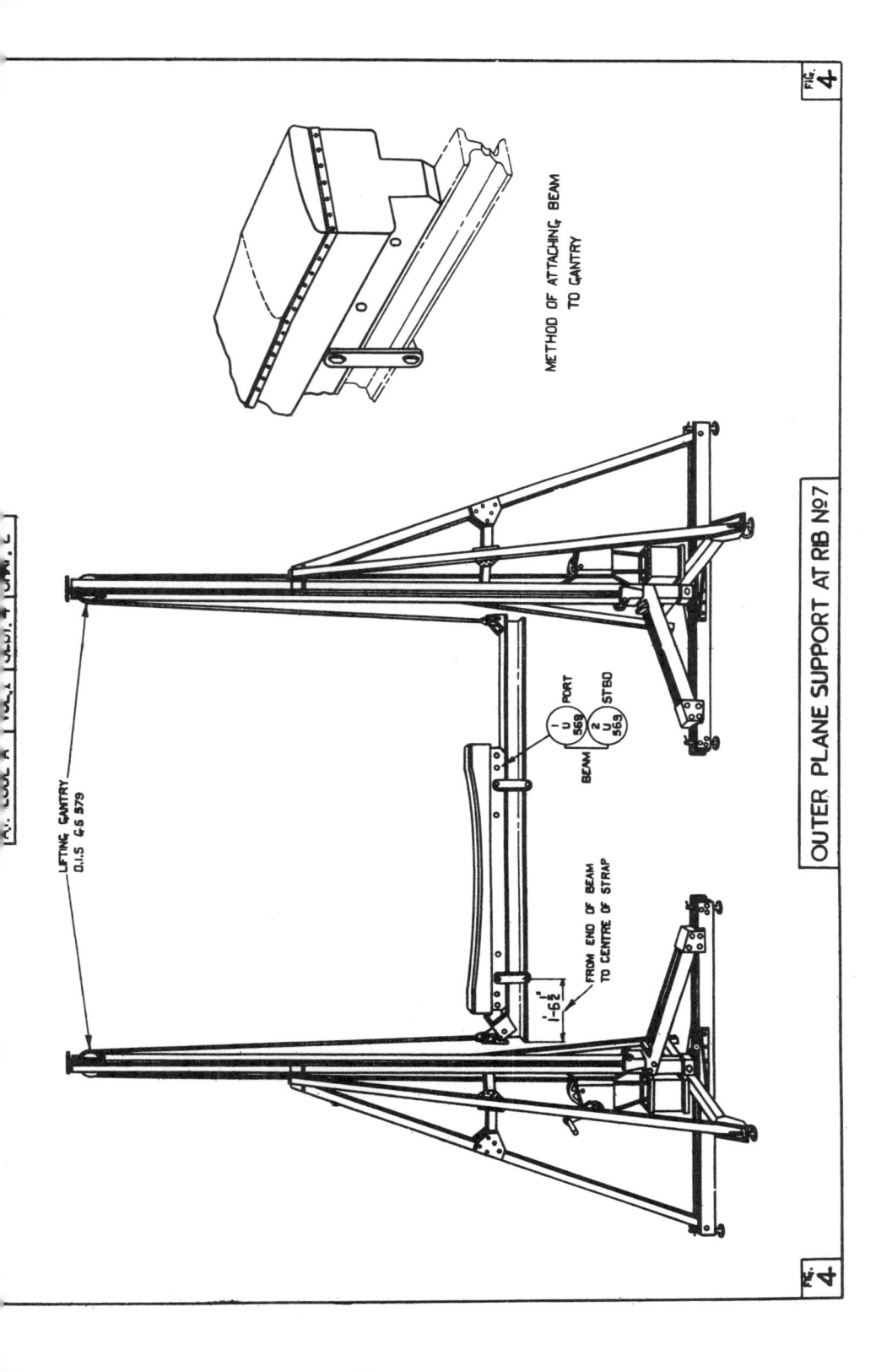

METHOD OF ATTACHING BEAM TO GANTRY

LIFTING GANTRY
D.I.S G S 579

1 U 569 PORT
2 U 569 STBD
BEAM

FROM END OF BEAM TO CENTRE OF STRAP
1-6½"

OUTER PLANE SUPPORT AT RIB Nº7

FIG. 4

THIS PAGE AMENDED BY A.L. 26, MAY, 1943

A.P. 2062A | VOL. I | SECT. 4 | CHAP. 2

1.

500 LB. G.P. | 500 LB. G.P. | 500 LB. G.P. | 500 LB. G.P. | 500 LB. G.P.

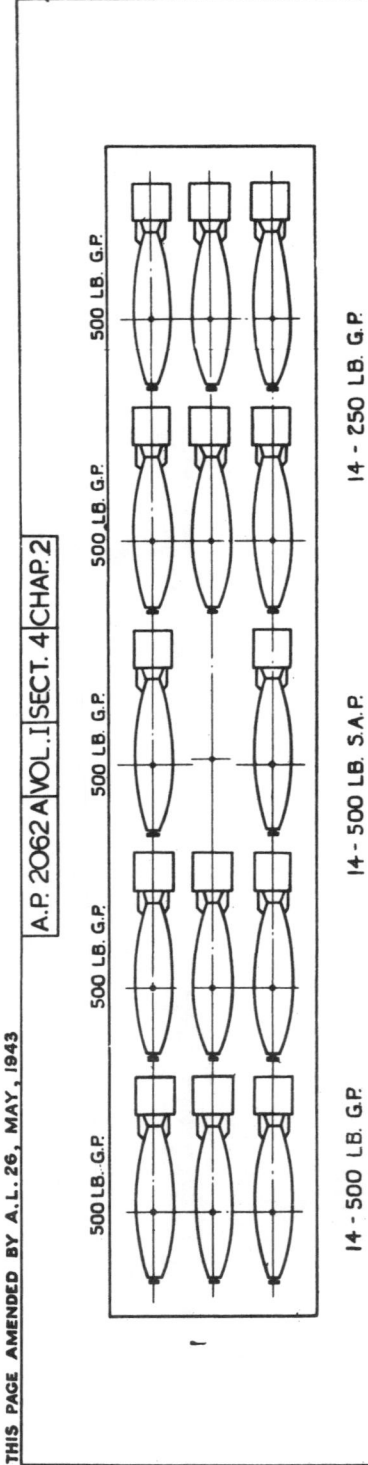

14 - 500 LB. G.P.
14 - 250 LB. S.A.P.
14 - 250 LB. B. MK. III
14 - 1,000 LB. U.S.A. TYPE

14 - 500 LB. S.A.P.
14 - 250 LB. A.S
14 - 600 LB. A.S.
14 - 1,000 LB. M.C.

14 - 250 LB. G.P.
14 - 250 LB. L.C.
14 - 250 LB. SMALL - BOMB CONTAINERS
14 - 1,000 LB. G.P SHORT TAIL TYPE

ANY ONE OF THE ABOVE LOADINGS MAY BE USED.

2.

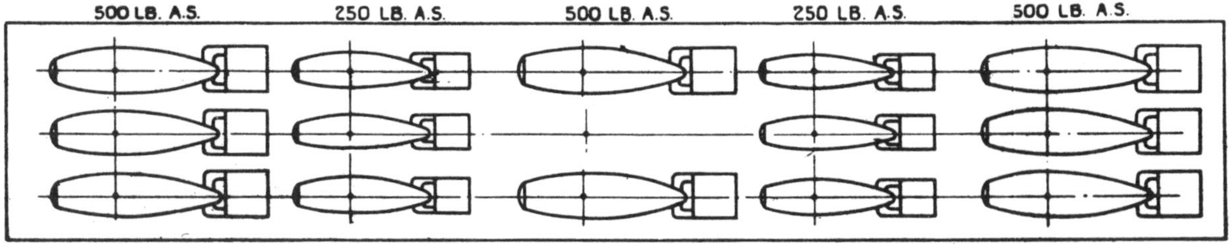

500 LB. A.S. | 250 LB. A.S. | 500 LB. A.S. | 250 LB. A.S. | 500 LB. A.S.

8 - 500 LB. & 6 - 250 LB. A.S. (MK. IV ONLY)

BOMB LOADINGS 1 & 2

A.P. 2062A | VOL. I | SECT. 4 | CHAP. 2

FIG. 6

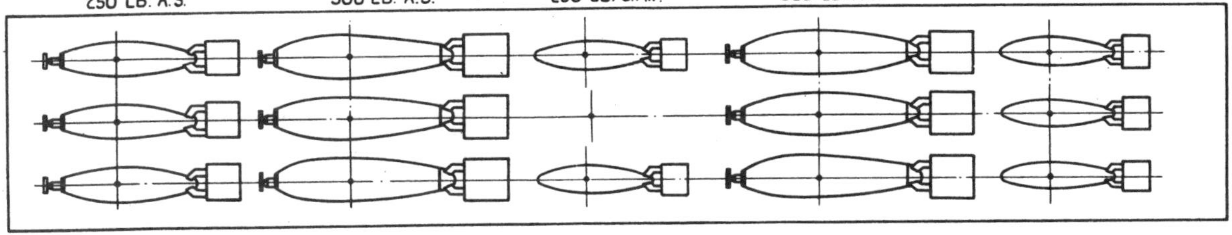

6 - 500 LB. & 3 - 250 LB. A.S. (MK. I, II & III) AND 5 - 250 LB. S.A.P.

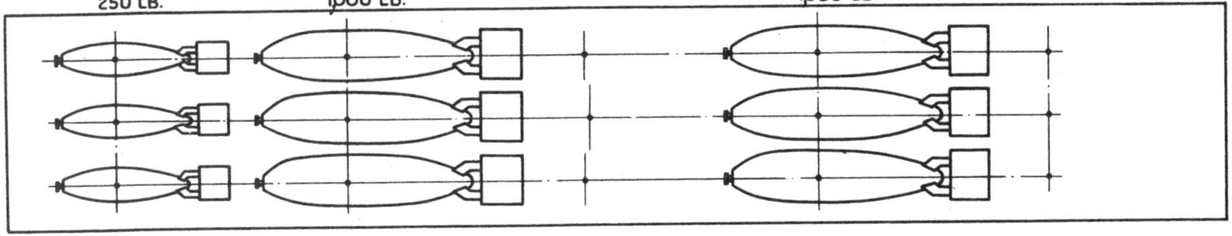

6 - 1,000 LB. & 3 - 250 LB. G.P.

BOMB LOADINGS 3 & 4.

FIG. 6

THIS PAGE AMENDED BY A.L.26, MAY, 1943

A.P. 2062A | VOL. I | SECT. 4 | CHAP. 2

1,000 LB. G.P. 4,000 LB. H.C. 1,000 LB. G.P.

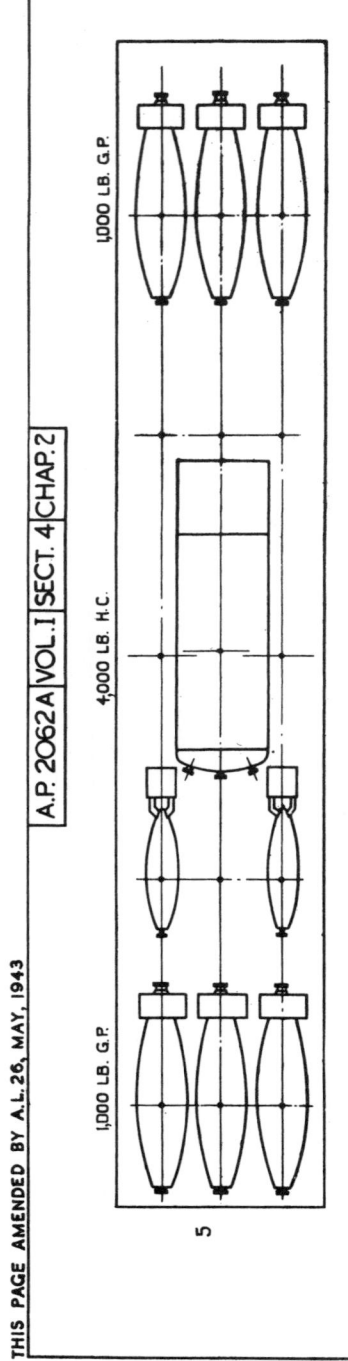

1-4,000 LB. H.C. & 6-1,000 LB. G.P. (SHORT TAIL TYPE)* & 2-250 LB. G.P. BOMBS.

*OR 6-1,000 LB. U.S.A. BOMBS OR 1,000 LB. M.C. BOMBS.

5

1,500 LB. A. MINES.

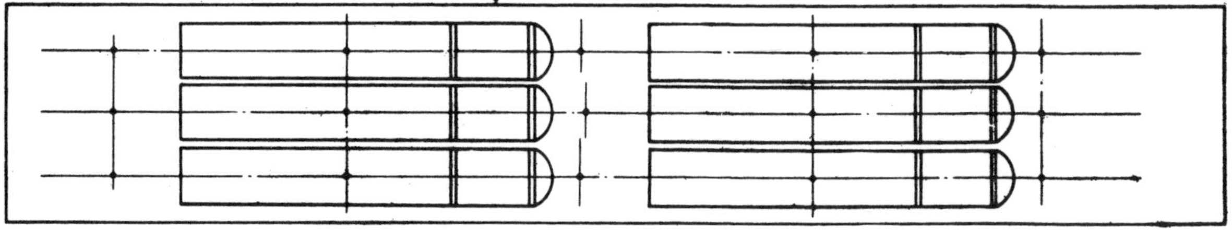

6-1,500 LB. A MINES OR 6-2,000 LB. H.C. BOMBS.

6

BOMB LOADINGS 5 & 6

A.P. 2062A|VOL.1|SECT. 4|CHAP.2

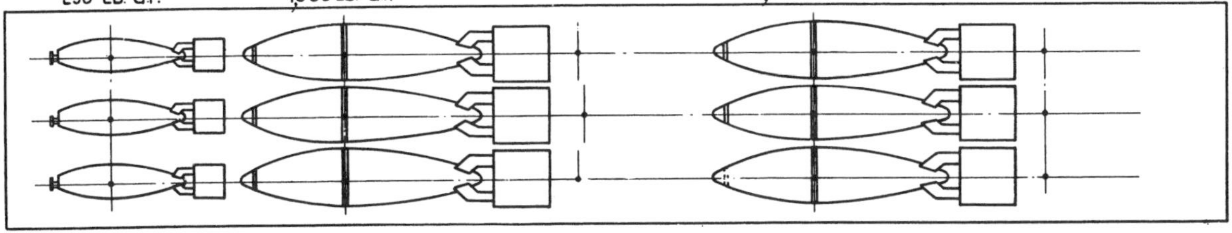

250 LB. G.P.   1900 LB. G.P.   1900 LB. G.P.

6 - 1,900 LB. & 3 - 250 LB. G.P.

7

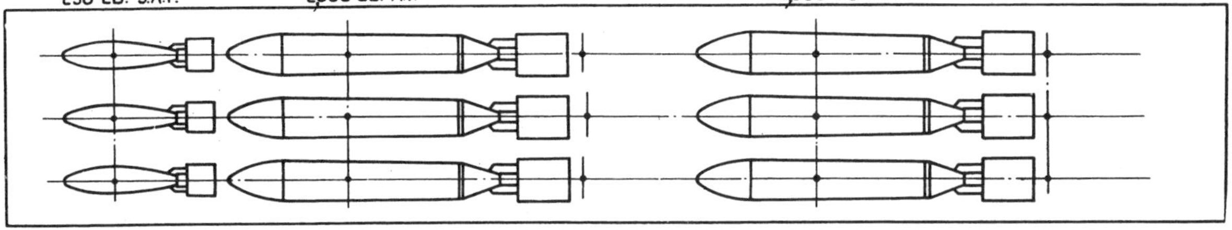

250 LB. S.A.P.   2,000 LB. A.P.   2,000 LB. A.P.

6 - 2,000 LB. A.P. & 3 - 250 LB. S.A.P.

8

BOMB LOADINGS 7 & 8.

FIG. 8

THIS PAGE ISSUED WITH A.L. 20, FEB. 1943

A.P. 2062A | VOL. I | SECT. 4 | CHAP. 2

500 L.B. G.P. BOMB

1-8,000 L.B. BOMB AND
6-500 L.B. G.P. BOMBS

8,000 L.B. BOMB

500 L.B. G.P. BOMB

FIG. 8A — BOMB LOADING 9 — FIG. 8A

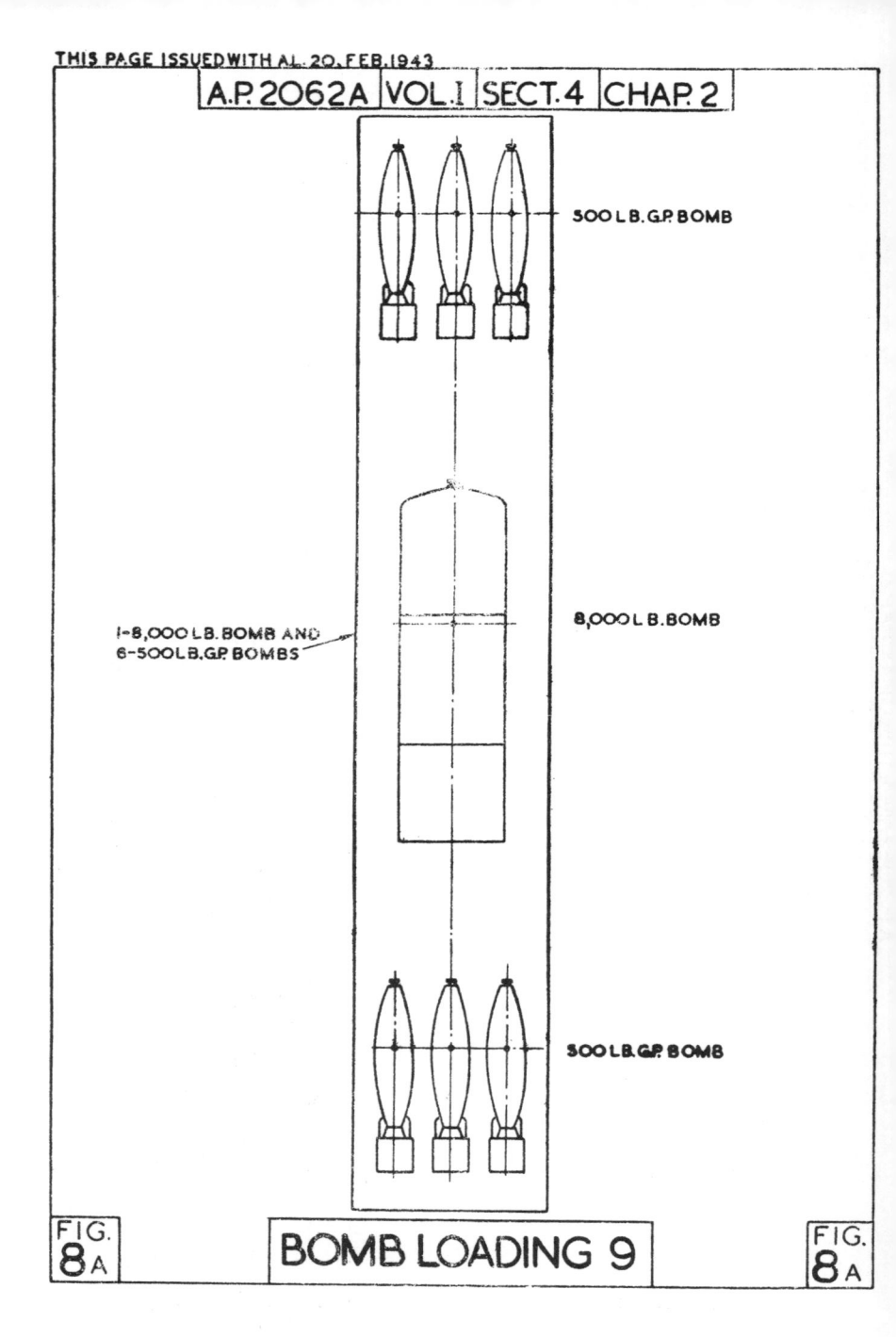

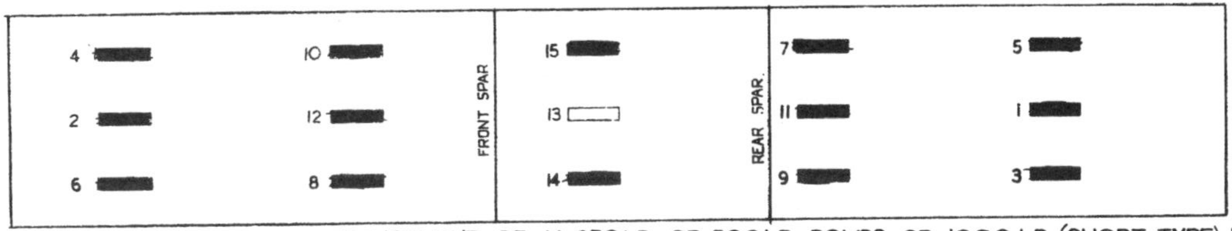

FIG. 9 — BOMB POSITIONS & WINCHES REQUIRED

A.P.2062A VOL.1 SECT.4 CHAP.2

ARRANGEMENT OF 14-250LB. OR 500LB. BOMBS, OR 1,000 LB. (SHORT TYPE) BOMBS.
USE 500LB 'GYRAL' WINCH, FOR 250 LB. OR 500 LB. BOMBS.
USE 2,000LB 'GYRAL' WINCH FOR 1,000 LB. BOMBS.

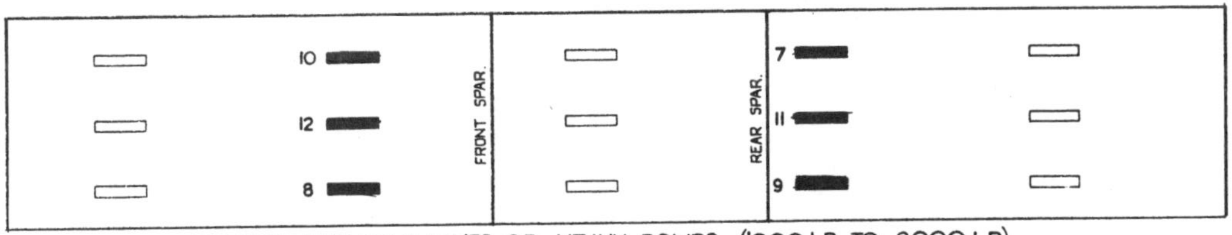

ARRANGEMENT OF 6 MINES OR HEAVY BOMBS (1000 LB. TO 2000 LB)
USE 2000 LB. 'GYRAL' WINCH.

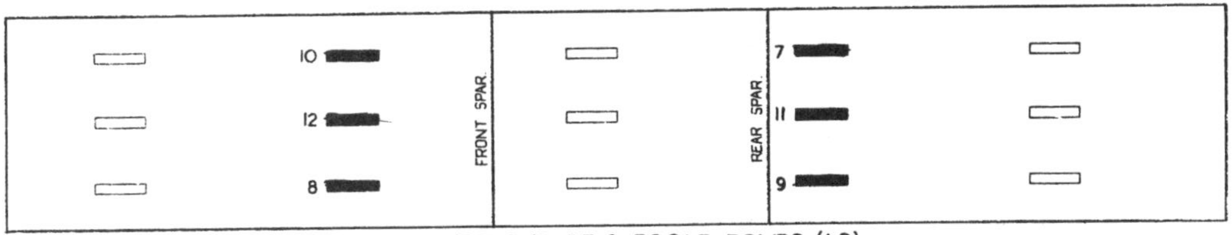

ARRANGEMENT OF 6-500LB. BOMBS. (A.S)
USE 500LB 'GYRAL' WINCH.

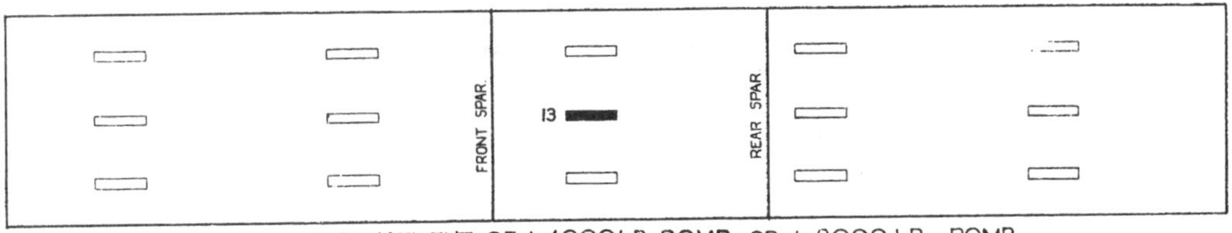

ARRANGEMENT OF 1-4000LB. BOMB, OR 1-8,000 LB. BOMB.
FOR 4000LB BOMB USE 2-2000LB 'GYRAL' WINCHES
FOR 8,000 LB. BOMB USE 2 SPECIAL 'GYRAL' WINCHES

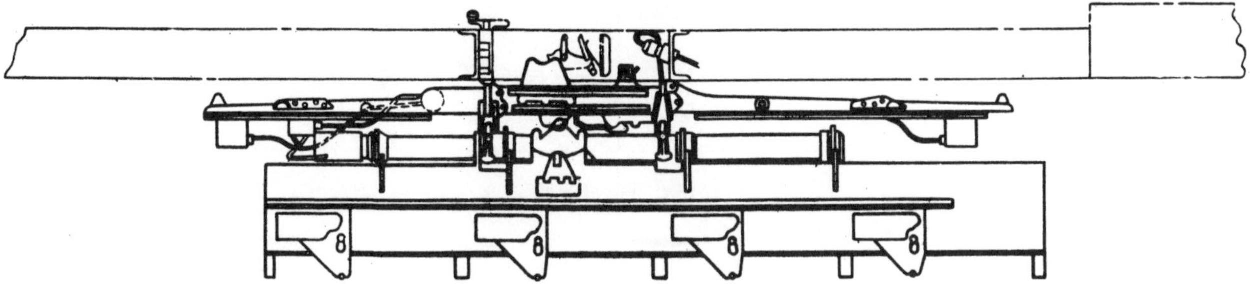

A.P. 2062 A | VOL. I | SECT. 4 | CHAP. 2

ARRGt. OF CONTAINER ON CARRIER

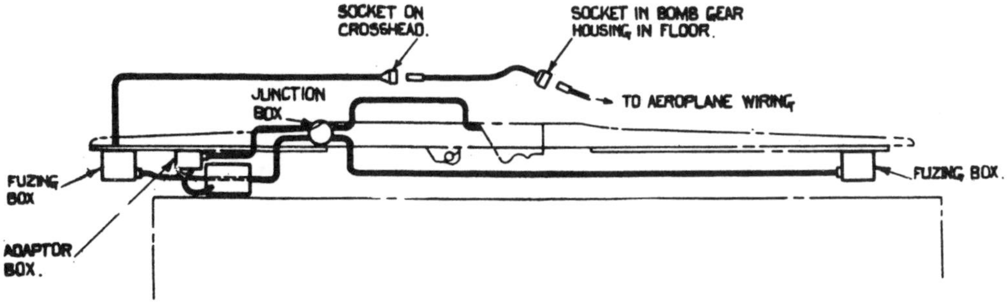

WIRING DIAGRAM FOR EACH CARRIER

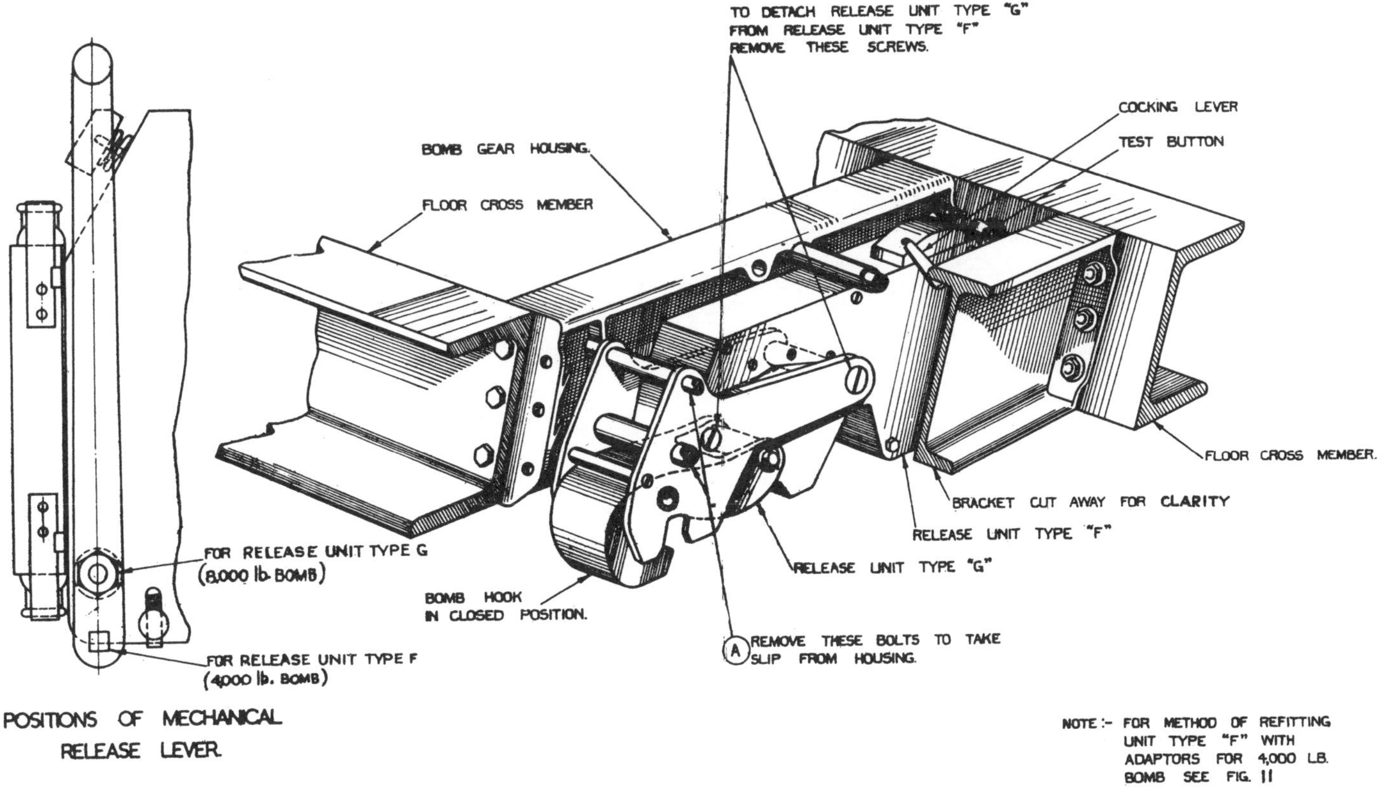

METHOD OF FIXING 8,000 LB. BOMB SLIP (TYPE G)

FIG. 10A — A.P. 2062 A, VOL. I, SECT. 4, CHAP. 2

A.P. 2062A VOL.I SECT. 4 CHAP. 2

1. VIEW SHOWING BOMB GEAR HOUSING WITH BOMB SLIP REMOVED.

ADAPTORS

BOLTS PICK UP THESE HOLES TO SECURE BOMB SLIP.

2. VIEW SHOWING ADAPTORS BOLTED IN POSITION

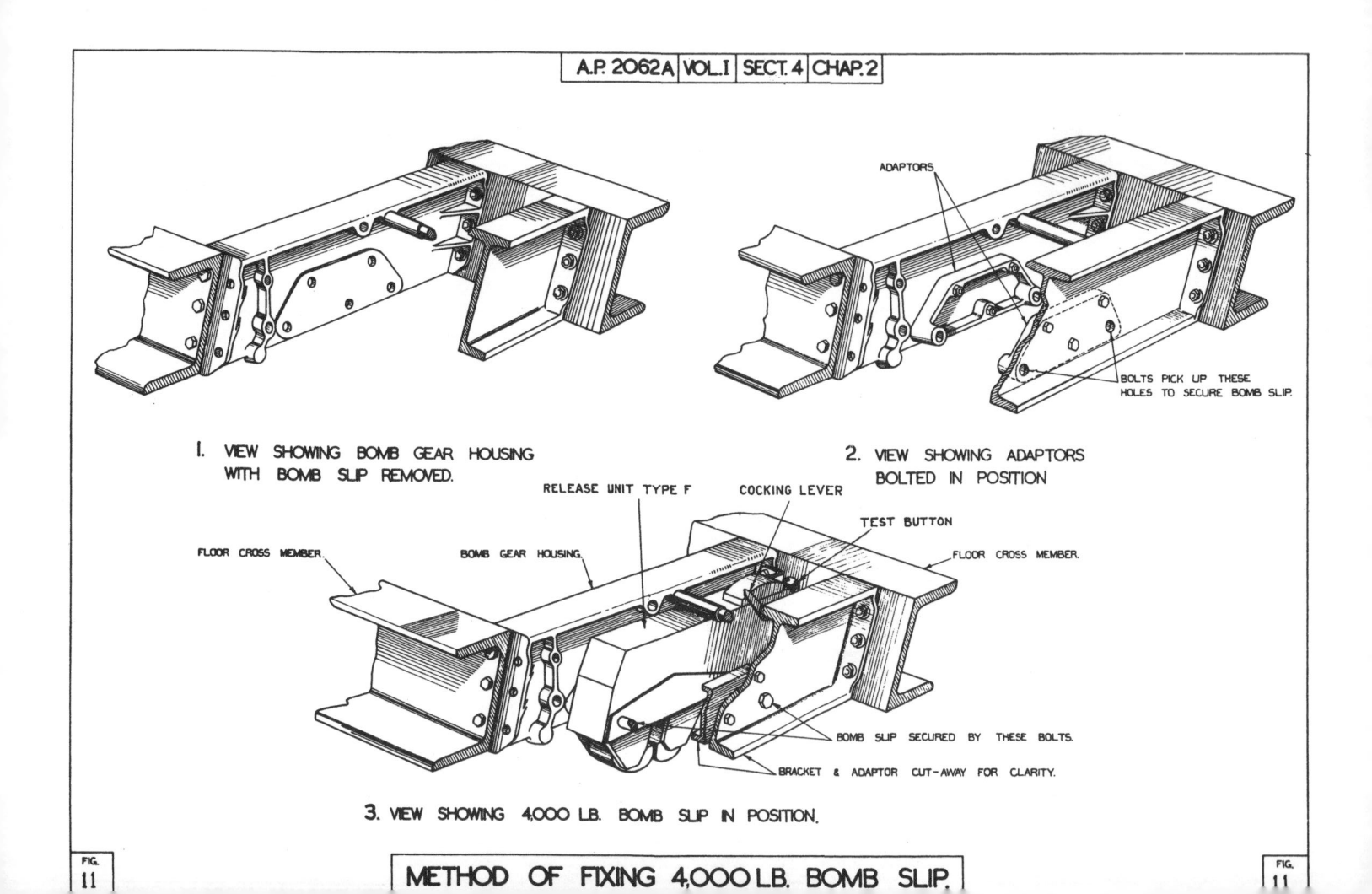

RELEASE UNIT TYPE F

COCKING LEVER

TEST BUTTON

FLOOR CROSS MEMBER.

BOMB SLIP SECURED BY THESE BOLTS.

BRACKET & ADAPTOR CUT-AWAY FOR CLARITY.

BOMB GEAR HOUSING

FLOOR CROSS MEMBER.

3. VIEW SHOWING 4,000 LB. BOMB SLIP IN POSITION.

METHOD OF FIXING 4,000 LB. BOMB SLIP.

FIG. 11

CRUTCHING AND FUZING FOR 4,000 LB. BOMB

A.P. 2062 A | VOL I | SECT. 4 | CHAP. 2

FORMER 27

FORMER 12

RELEASE MECHANISM

ENLARGED VIEW OF
FLARE EXTENSION TUBE

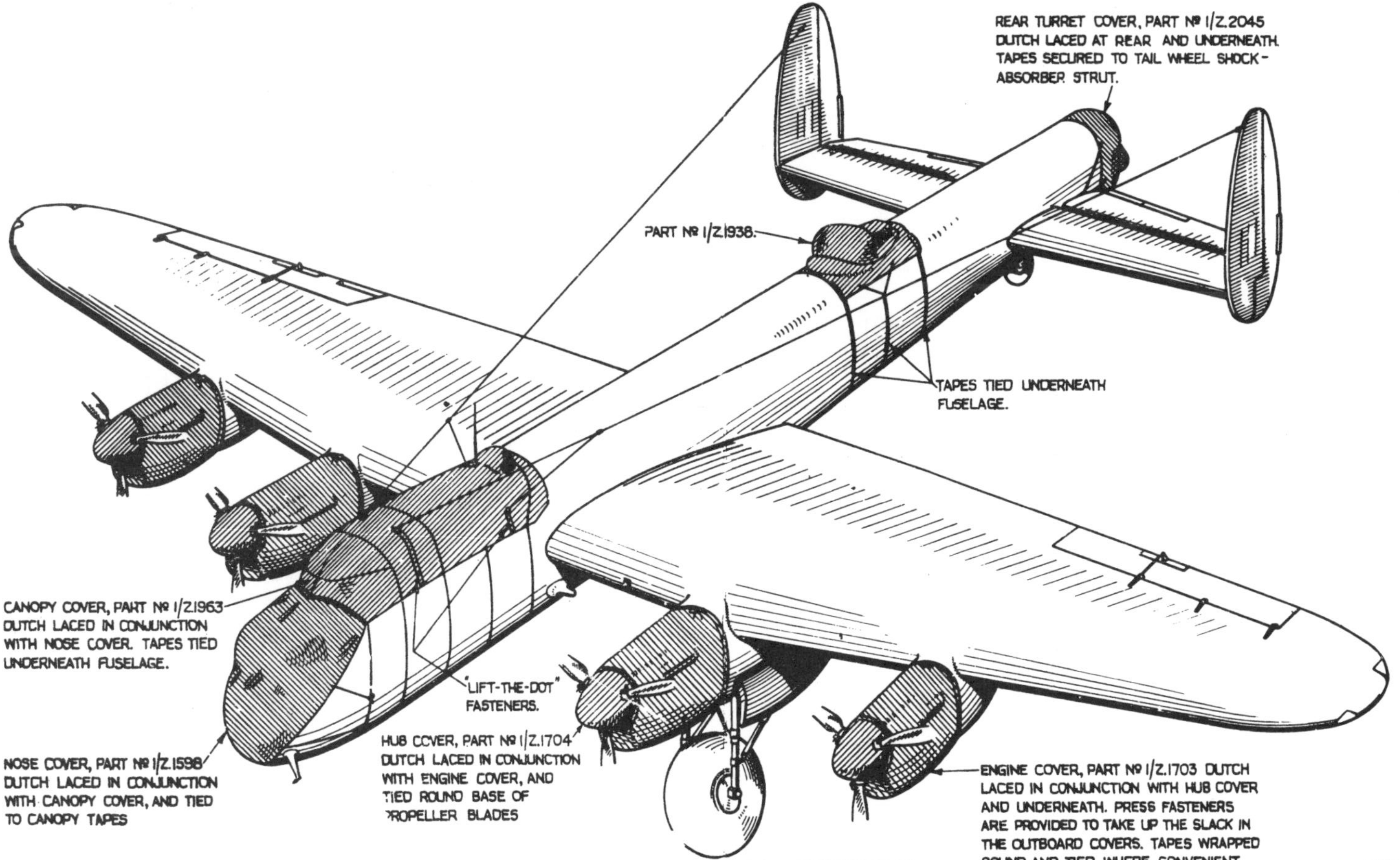

ARRANGEMENT OF COVERS

FIG 15 — METHOD OF FOLDING DINGHY

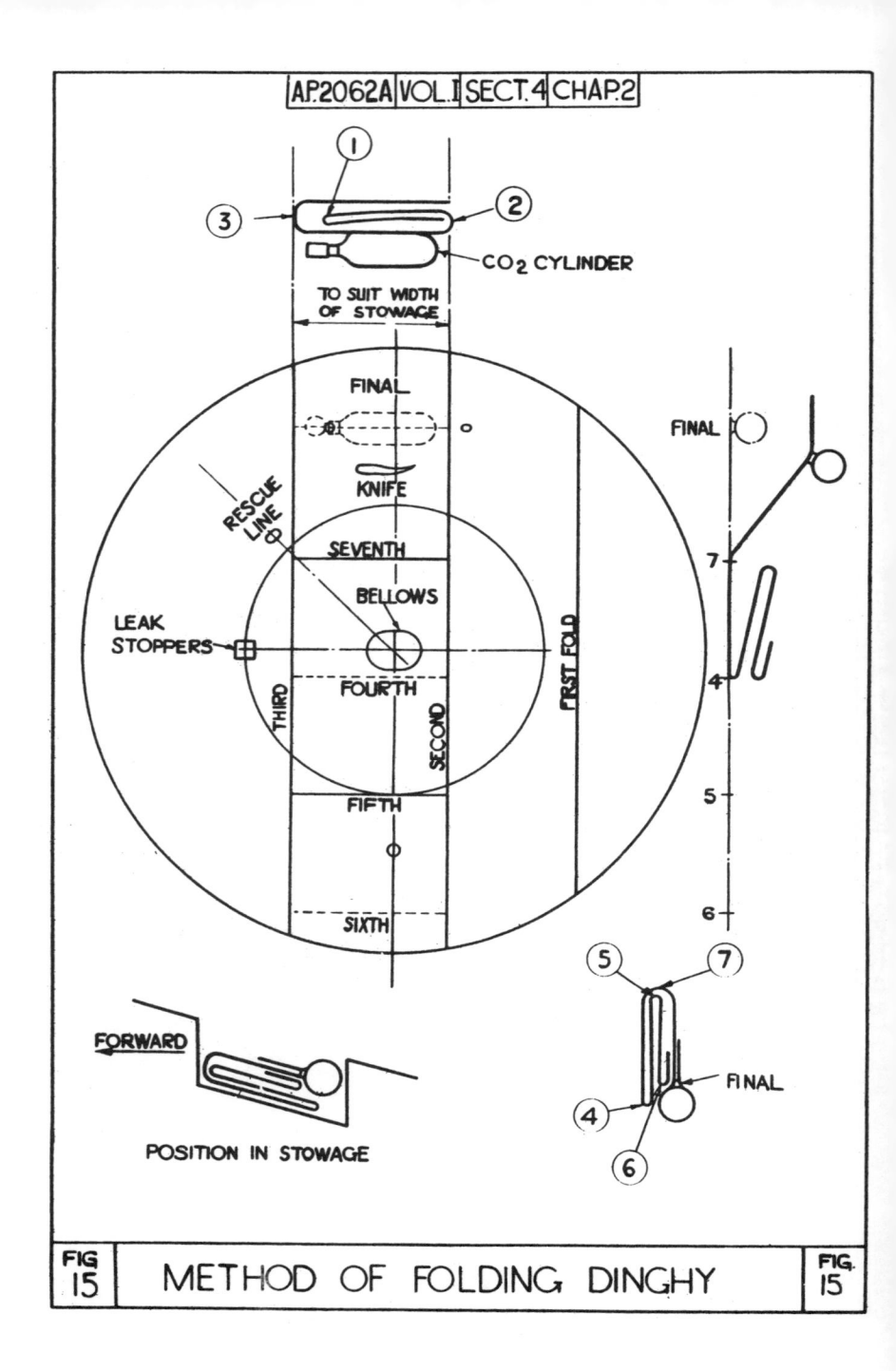

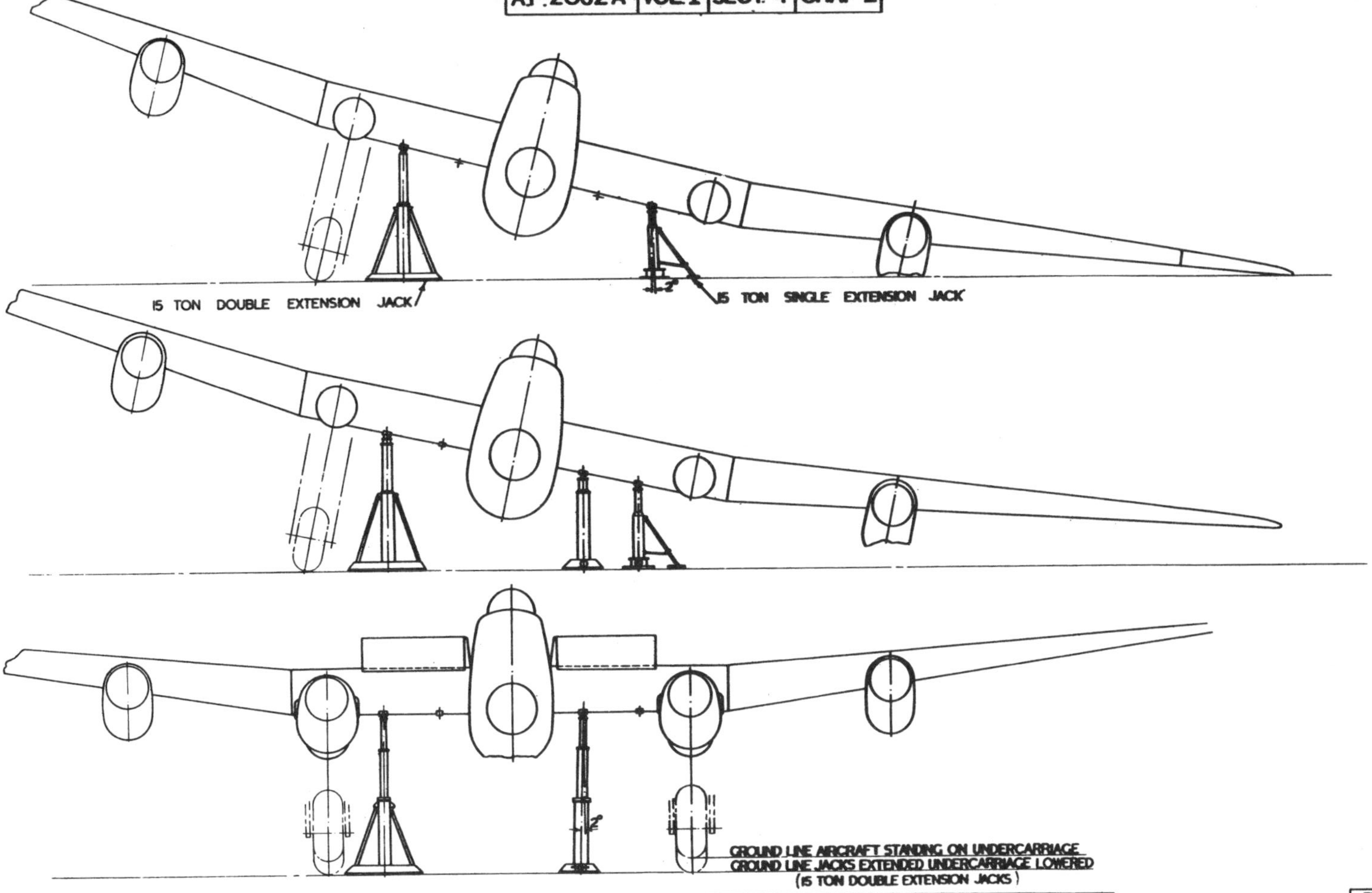

LIFTING CRASHED AIRCRAFT — JACKING METHOD 1

FIG. 16

THIS PAGE ISSUED WITH A.L. 20, MAY, 1943

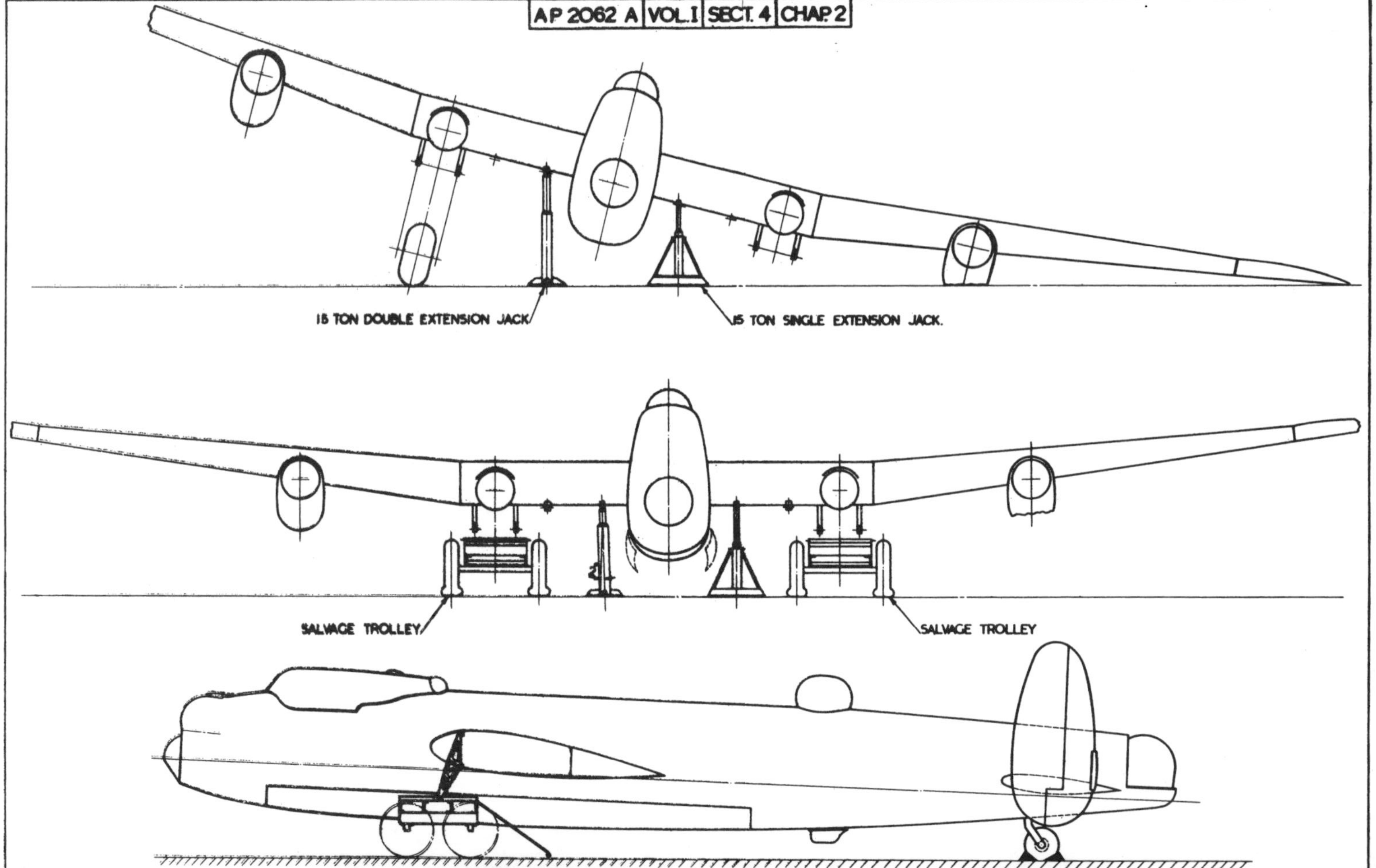

FIG.

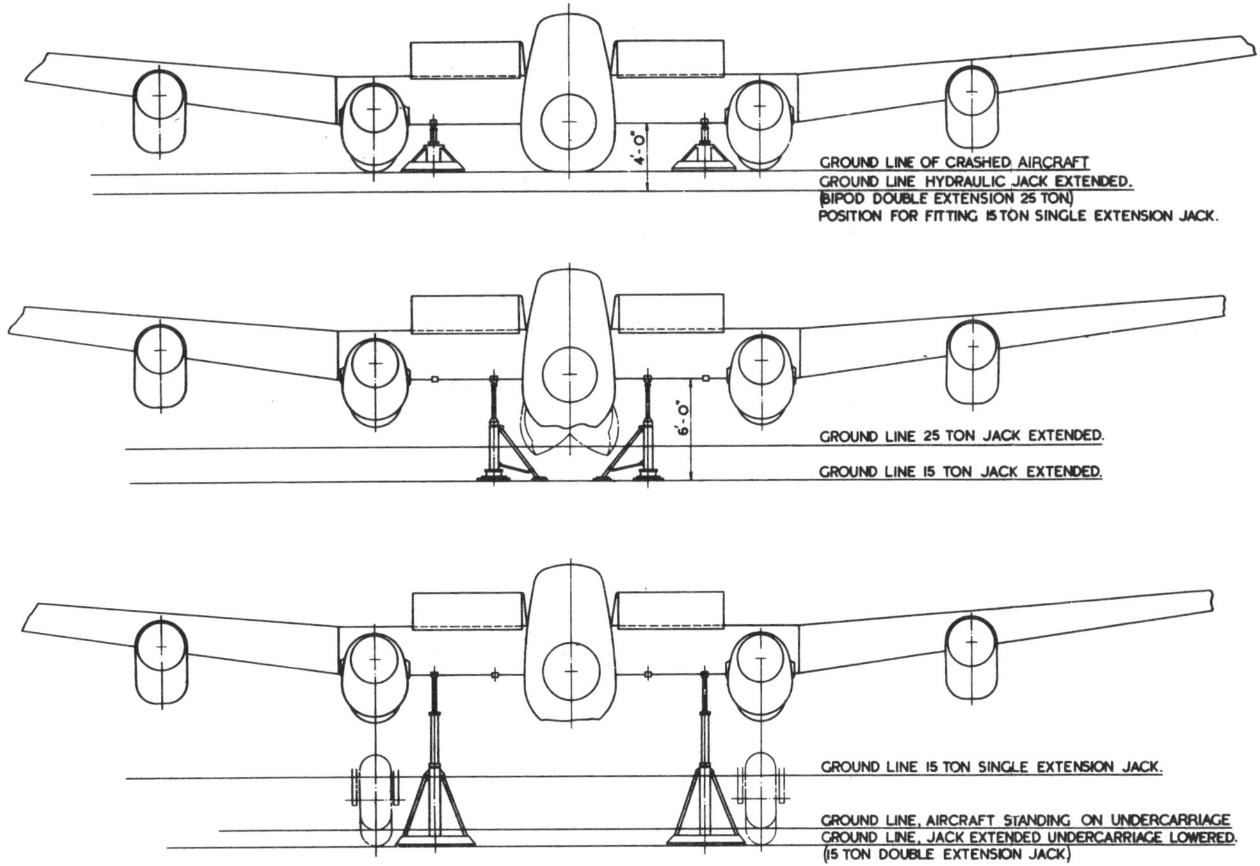

LIFTING CRASHED AIRCRAFT – JACKING METHOD 3.

FIG. 18

AP. 2062 A | VOL. I | SECT. 4 | CHAP. 2

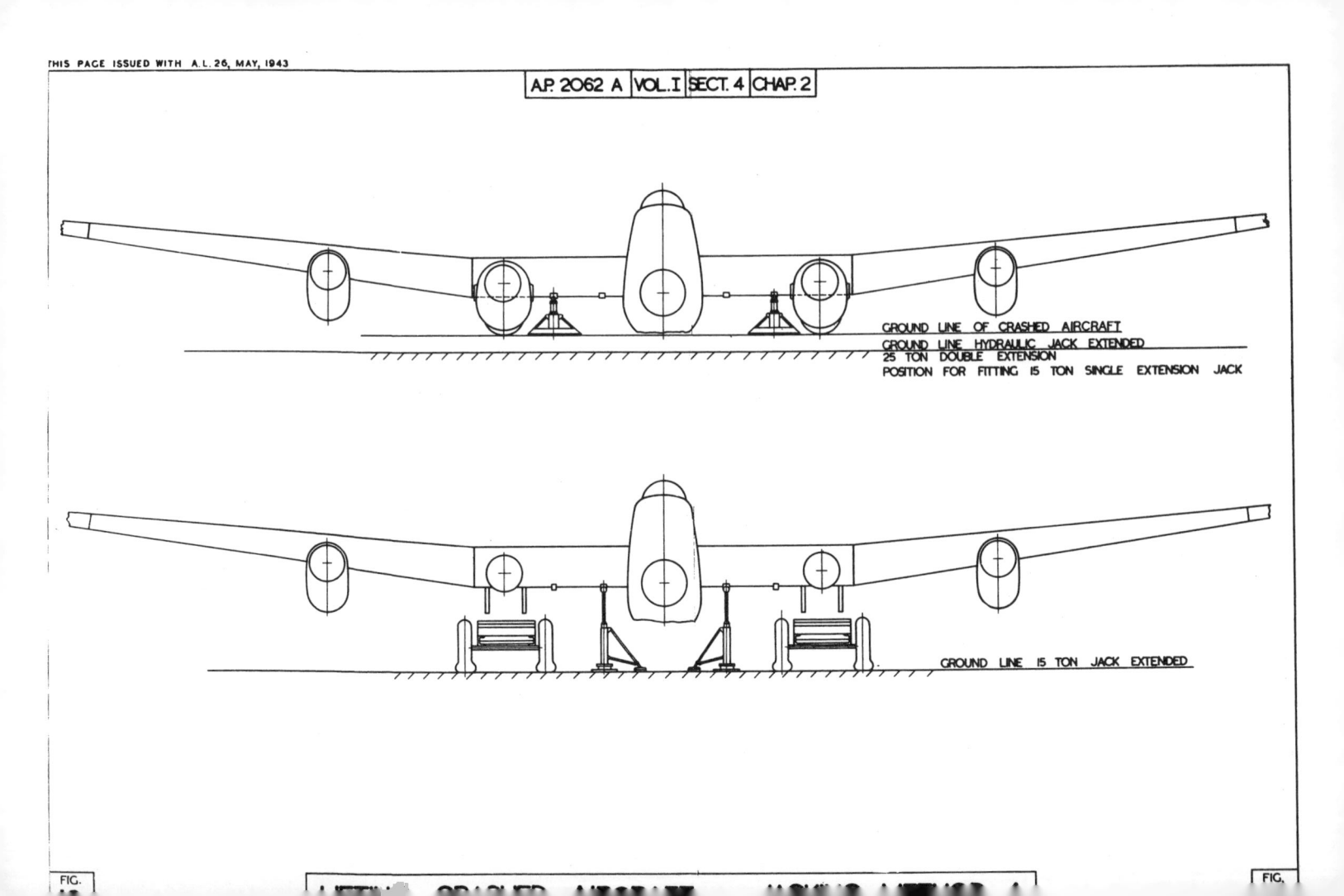

GROUND LINE OF CRASHED AIRCRAFT
GROUND LINE HYDRAULIC JACK EXTENDED
25 TON DOUBLE EXTENSION
POSITION FOR FITTING 15 TON SINGLE EXTENSION JACK

GROUND LINE 15 TON JACK EXTENDED

THIS PAGE ISSUED WITH A.L. 26, MAY, 1943

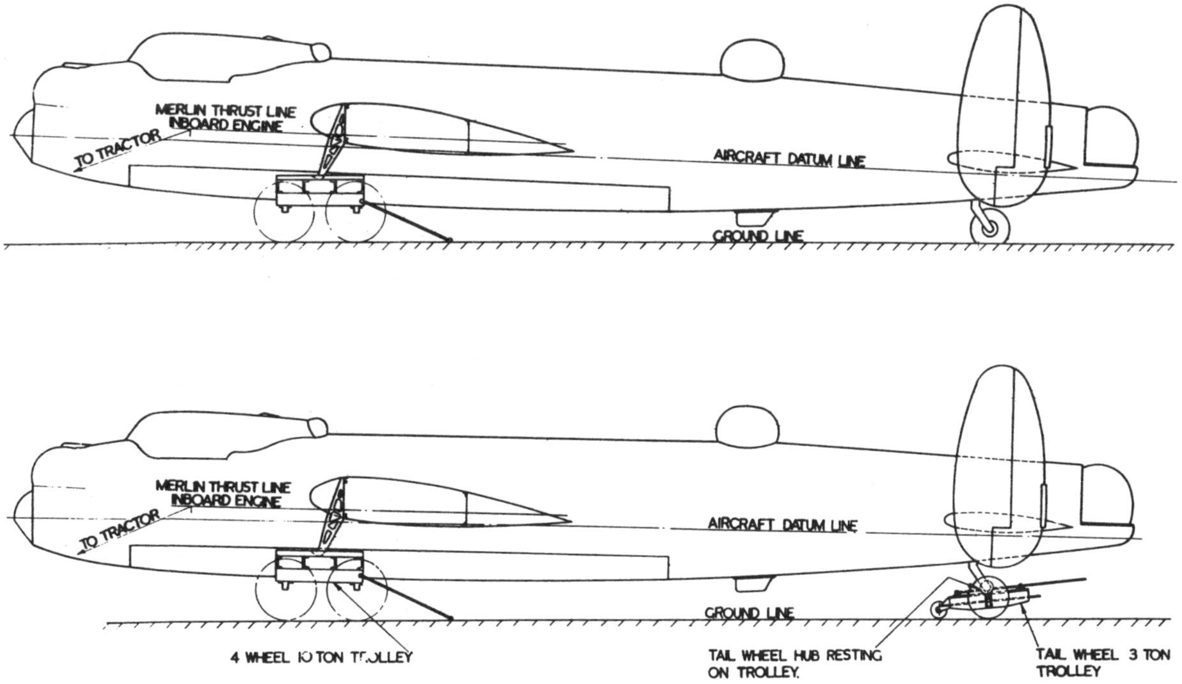

METHOD OF TOWING SALVAGED AIRCRAFT

March, 1942

Issued with A.L.No.4

A.P.2062A, Vol.I, Sect.4.

CHAPTER 3 – MAINTENANCE

LIST OF CONTENTS

	Para.
General	1
List of references	2
Lubrication	3
Jacking	4
Maintenance ladder	7
Former positions and inspection panels	8

Rigging

General	9
Rigging position	10
Main plane	11
Tail plane	12
Fins	13
Setting of flying controls	14
Ailerons	15
Rudders	16
Elevators	17
Push-pull controls (rudder and elevator)	18
Aileron trimming tab	19
Rudder and elevator trimming tabs	20
Elevator balance tabs	21
Setting of automatic controls	22
Ailerons	23
Rudders	24
Elevators	25

Undercarriage

General	26
Main wheel units –	
General	27
Removal of wheel	28
Removing tyre from wheel	29
Refitting tyre on wheel	30
Main wheel shock-absorber strut –	
General	31
Oil level check	32
Air charging	33
Deflation	34
Warning	35
Dismantling shock-absorber strut	36
Topping up with oil	37
Oil filling	38

F.S./1

Issued with A.L. No. 4
This page amended by A.L. No. 20
February, 1943

A.P. 2062A, Vol. I, Sect. 4, Chap. 3

	Para.
Testing shock-absorber struts	39
Leakage of oil or loss of pressure	40
Adjustment of main wheel units -	
UP and DOWN latches	41
Hydraulic jacks	42
Tail wheel unit -	
General	43
Removing tail wheel	44
Tail wheel shock-absorber strut -	
Oil level check	45
Inflation pressure check	46
Deflation	47
Warning	48
Dismantling tail wheel strut	49
Re-assembly of tail wheel strut	50
Topping up with oil	51
Oil filling	52
Testing tail wheel strut	53
Leakage of oil or loss of pressure	54
Adjustment of friction clip	56

Engine installation

Fuel, oil and coolant systems -	
Cleaning the fuel tanks	57
Cleaning the oil tanks	58
Cleaning the oil filters	59
Draining the coolant header tank and radiators	60
Engine controls -	
General	61
Throttle, mixture, supercharger and propeller controls	62
Boost cut-out control	63
Slow running cut-out controls	64
Hand turning gear	65

Hydraulic system

General	66
Filling	68
Bleeding	69
To bleed the main wheel and bomb door circuits	70
To bleed the flap circuit	71
To bleed the air-intake circuit	72
Operational tests -	
General	73
Main wheel units	74
Flaps	75
Bomb doors	76
Air-intake shutters	77
Fuel jettison system	78
Pressure tests	80

Issued with A.L.No.4 A.P.2062A and C, Vol.I, Sect.4, Chap.3
This page amended by A.L.No.26
May, 1943

	Para.
Faults and their remedies	81
Maintenance of components	83
Re-setting the fuel jettison valve	84
Cleaning hydraulic fluid filter	85

Miscellaneous

	Para.
Propeller feathering tests	86
Landing lamp adjustment	87
"Fixed olive" pipe couplings	88
Method of adjusting the bomb door jacks	89
Method of setting main wheel unit doors	90
De-icing hand pumps	91
Propeller de-icing fluid tank dipstick	92
Packing the dinghy	93
Bonding	94
Fixed aerial	95
Swinging D.R. compass	96
Sanitary closet	97

LIST OF ILLUSTRATIONS

	Fig.
Rigging diagrams -	
Rigging instructions	1
Main plane - incidence check	2
Tail plane - incidence check	3
Method of setting elevator and trimming and balance tabs	4
Method of setting fin and rudder	5
Movement of flying controls	6
Setting of rudder and elevator controls	7
Method of removing tail wheel	8
Diagram of pneumatic system	9
Diagram of fuel system	10
Diagram of fuel system (Pulsometer F.B.Mk.I pumps)	10A
Diagram of oil system - inboard engine	11
Diagram of oil system - outboard engine	12
Cooling system	13
Hydraulic feed system	14
Former and rib positions	15
Lubrication diagram	16
Hydraulic system - bomb doors	17
Hydraulic system - undercarriage	18
Hydraulic system - flaps	19
Hydraulic system - air intakes	20
Fuel jettison system	21
Emergency air system	22
Engine auxiliaries - port	23
Engine auxiliaries - starboard	24
Main wheels shock-absorber strut inflation	25

F.S./2

Issued with A.L.No.4　　　　　A.P.2062A, Vol.I, Sect.4, Chap.3

	Fig.
Tail wheel shock-absorber strut inflation	26
Diagram of automatic controls	27
Diagram of pipes for automatic controls	28
Vacuum system	29
Access and inspection panels	30
Locking catch undercarriage retracted	31
Hydraulic system ground test rig	32
Hydraulic system component test rig	33
Main wheels strut inflation check	34
Tail wheel strut inflation check	35
Hydraulic system - front gun turret	36
Hydraulic system - upper mid gun turret	37
Hydraulic system - lower mid gun turret	38
Hydraulic system - rear gun turret	39
Differential control for brakes	40
Main wheel shock-absorber struts	41
Tail wheel shock-absorber unit	42

March, 1942   A.P.2062A, Vol.I, Sect.4
Issued with A.L.4
This page amended by A.L.No.20
February, 1943

CHAPTER 3 - MAINTENANCE

General

1. This Chapter describes the maintenance operations for certain components, and is intended to implement the Maintenance Schedule, Vol.II, Part 2, of this Publication; some maintenance notes on the electrical equipment are, however, given in Section 6. The ancillary ground equipment required for the maintenance of the aircraft is listed in the appropriate M leaflet of Vol.II, Part 1, of this Publication. Tools, rigging boards and other special items of equipment are included in the Schedule of Spare Parts, Vol.III, Part 1, of this Publication. Relevant illustrations appear at the end of this Chapter.

List of references

2. The following handbooks describe the maintenance operations involved on certain units fitted to the aircraft:-

Propeller (D.H. hydromatic)	A.P.1538D,	Vol.I
Power plants (Merlin XX, Mk.I)	A.P.2140A,	Vol.I
Air compressor (Heywood S.H.6/2)	A.P.1519,	Vol.I
Gun turrets	A.P.1659A,	Vol.I
Guns	A.P.1641C,	Vol.II
Gun firing controls	A.P.1641E,	Vol.II
Bomb carriers	A.P.1664,	Vol.II
Automatic controls Mk.IV	A.P.1469A,	Vol.I
Pneumatic brakes (Dunlop)		
Dinghy (type J)		
Fire extinguisher system	A.P.1464B,	Vol.I
De-icing equipment		
Oil dilution system		
Instruments	A.P.1275,	Vol.I
Hydraulic components	A.P.1803,	Vol.I
Cable cutters (balloon barrage protection)	A.P.2051A,	Vol.I

Lubrication

3. The lubrication diagram is given in fig.16. All points are lubricated with anti-freezing oil, type 417A (Stores Ref.34A/86 and 87) except shielded ball and roller bearings which are packed on assembly with anti-freezing grease (Stores Ref.34A/49 and 103) and need no further maintenance.

Jacking

4. The jacking pads should be mounted on the front spar, two on

F.S./3

A.P.2062A, Vol.I, Sect.4, Chap.3

each side of the fuselage (see Chap.2, fig.3). They are secured by special stud bolts which pass through the spar boom.

5. For jacking up the tail of the aeroplane to remove the tail wheel or inflate the strut, a special jacking trestle (Pt. No.1.U.591) is used (see fig.8).

6. Further details of jacking, trestling and slinging are given in Sect.4, Chap.2, and in Sect.5.

Maintenance ladder

7. A maintenance ladder, Pt. No.1.U.575, which can be used as a single ladder or as a step ladder, is provided for maintenance operations. When used as a single ladder the two portions are held together by two quick-release pins, and two bolts and wing nuts. When used as s step ladder the bolts and wing nuts are removed and the top portion is swung down and a tie-cable fitted between the two legs.

Former positions and inspection panels

8. The positions of the fuselage formers and main plane ribs are shown in fig.15, and the inspection doors and access panels are shown in fig.30. The layout of the assembly panels and the types of rivets used to secure them are shown in Sect.5, fig.7.

RIGGING

General

9. The main plane and tail plane are fixed cantilever structures and cannot be adjusted. Shims, however, may be fitted in either the top or the bottom of the centre joint of the tail plane, to correct any slight error in the verticality of the fin and rudder. Apart from this, the only rigging operations are those of checking the diagonal measurements and the incidence and dihedral of the main plane and tail plane and checking the movements of the control surfaces. The methods of making these checks are shown in figs.1 - 5.

Rigging position

10. Datum points for longitudinal levelling are the two rear jacking points in the fuselage. Pegs, Pt. No.1.Z.1353, are provided to screw into these holes, so that a straightedge, Pt. No.1.Z.1427, can be placed across them. For transverse checking, blocks are provided on formers 12 and 35 inside the fuselage. Straightedges, Pt. Nos.1.Z.1422 and 1.Z.1421, are provided for use on these points (see fig.1). The rear jacking point in the front centre portion is the C.G. datum point.

This page amended by A.L.No.18   A.P.2062A, Vol.I, Sect.4, Chap.3
September, 1942

Main plane

11. This should be checked to conform to the diagonal measurements shown in fig.1. In addition the incidence of the main plane should be checked as shown in fig.2. The dihedral of the outer plane should be checked with the special board provided, Pt.No.1.Z.1778. This should be held in position under the rear spar and checked with a level (see fig.1).

Tail plane

12. To check the incidence, two rigging boards, Pt.Nos.1.Z.1286 and 1.Z.1287, should be placed on the upper surface of the tail plane at the front and rear spars (see fig.3) and a level placed along the tops of the boards. The horizontal level may be checked by placing a straightedge and level across the tops of the two boards.

Fins

13. To check the verticality of the fin, remove the rudder, and fit checking board, Pt.No.1.Z.1895, to the top and bottom rudder hinges. Check longitudinally (see fig.5) using an inclinometer. Turn the board through 90° and check laterally.

Setting of flying controls

14. The ranges of movement of the control surfaces and their limits are shown in fig.6. The diagrams of the flying and trimming tabs controls are shown on the relevant illustrations in Sect.7, Chap.4.

15. <u>Ailerons.</u>- Turnbuckles for adjusting the cables are provided on the port side of the fuselage, just forward of the front spar. The push-pull connections in the main planes should normally require no further adjustment after the outer plane transport joints have been correctly made. With the handwheel central, the ailerons should be set with 5/8 in. droop, measured at the inboard end of the aileron trailing edge. This setting should be tested on flight trials, when it may be found that one of the following conditions exists, owing to slight variations in the manufacture of the main planes and ailerons:-

(i) The aileron control may be heavy.

(ii) A slight snatch may occur on the ailerons at about two-thirds of their travel when manoeuvring at fairly high speeds.

The aileron control becomes lighter as the droop is reduced, and condition (i) may therefore be corrected by reducing the droop to a minimum of

F.S./4

This page amended by A.L.No.20
February, 1943
This page amended by A.L.No.26
May, 1943

A.P.2062A and C, Vol.I, Sect.4, Chap.3

3/8 in., provided that condition (ii) is not induced. If, however, snatch is present as described in (ii) the droop may be increased to a maximum of $\frac{3}{4}$ in.

15A. **Flaps.-** The flaps should be adjusted as follows in order to minimise drooping of the port flaps when the aircraft is airborne :-

(i) Allow the flaps, port and starboard, to droop to the extent of one inch; assuming that all the flaps have previously been set to close completely (see Sect.5, para.15).

(ii) Adjust the interconnection link at the port end of the jack piston rod so that the port flaps just touch the trailing edge while the starboard flaps are maintained at one inch droop.

(iii) Select FLAPS UP on the flap control, pump with the hand pump, and check that the starboard flaps close. A maximum droop of 3/16 in. to $\frac{1}{4}$ in. is permissible.

16. **Rudders.-** To set the rudders in the neutral position, fit setting board, Pt. No.1.Z.1924, (see fig.5). For adjustment of the push-pull connections, see para.18.

17. **Elevators.-** To set the elevators in the neutral position, fit setting board, Pt.No.1.Z.1988, at tail plane rib 6, (see fig.4). For adjustment of the push-pull controls, see para.18.

18. **Push-pull controls (rudder and elevator).-** Normally no adjustment should be required after the initial setting (see fig.7). When adjustment is necessary, it can be made at the following points :-

(i) Forward of the front spar in the fuselage front centre portion.

(ii) Aft of the rear spar, in the fuselage rear centre portion.

(iii) At the outboard ends of the push-pull connections in the tail plane.

To adjust, the joint should be disconnected, the locknut slackened off, and the eyebolt screwed in or out as necessary.

18A. The controls should be checked for full left rudder and elevator in full nose down position. In this position the free end of the guide at formers 33 and 34 should protrude at least 1.0 in. to avoid the risk of the controls jamming.

19. **Aileron trimming tabs.-** Turnbuckles for the adjustment of the aileron trimming tabs are provided in the trailing edge of the main plane

This page amended by A.L.No.20 February, 1943
This page amended by A.L.No.26 May, 1943

A.P.2062A and C, Vol.I, Sect.4, Chap.3

centre section, or, in aircraft not incorporating Mod.No.505, in the starboard trailing edge only. Access to the cables is gained by lowering the flaps. When the tab is in the mid position, the turnbuckle on the starboard forward cable should be equi-distant between the fairlead on the bridge bracket and rib 32 and the turnbuckle on the aft cable equi-distant between the fairlead and rib 25. On the port side the positions are reversed. In aircraft not incorporating Mods.No.505 or 643 the turnbuckle on the forward cable should be equi-distant between ribs 29 and 32, and that on the aft cable equi-distant between ribs 26 and 29.

20. <u>Rudder and elevator trimming tabs</u>.- Before these tabs can be set, the rudders and elevators must be locked in the neutral position (<u>see</u> Sect.1). Turnbuckles for both rudder and elevator tabs are provided on the port side of the rear fuselage between formers 30 and 31. Turnbuckles for the rudder trimming tab are also provided between the spars of the tail plane, one on the upper cable at the centre of the fuselage and one on the lower cable between tail plane ribs 12 and 13; access to the turnbuckle in the fuselage is gained through an inspection door in the upper surface of the tail plane. The elevator trimming tabs are adjusted by means of a turnbuckle at the centre of the fuselage, just aft of the tail plane rear spar. The settings are correct when the indicator in the cockpit reads 0 deg. and the tabs are in line with the trailing edges of the rudders and elevators. To set the elevator tabs, the setting board, Pt.No.1.Z.1831, should be fitted above and below the elevator (<u>see</u> fig.4) and the tab adjusted equally between the boards. A system of colour identification is used to ensure that the elevator trimming tab cables are correctly fitted. The ends of the cables are marked at the intermediate joints and at the joints with the chains; the elevator spar and the edge of the pilot's floor are also marked adjacent to the latter joints.

21. <u>Elevator balance tabs</u>.- If it is found during flight trials that to trim the aircraft in level flight at cruising speed the trimming tabs must be adjusted by more than 1 to $1\frac{1}{2}$ graduations on the indicator, the balance tabs should be set, on the ground, to provide the necessary correction. The adjustment required will be approximately 5/8 of the linear displacement of the trimming tab trailing edge from neutral, and in the same direction. Before setting the trimming tabs, the rudders and elevators must be locked in the neutral position (<u>see</u> Sect.1).

Setting of automatic controls

22. Instructions for the setting of Mk.IV automatic controls in

(Continued on next leaf)

F.S./4A

This page amended by A.L.No.18 A.P.2062A, Vol. I, Sect.4, Chap.3
September, 1942

conjunction with the main controls are given in paras.23 to 25, and the positions of the units are shown in fig.27. Care must be taken in all cases that the stops in the automatic controls servo motors come into operation before those on the main control. For all other particulars of automatic controls Mk.IV, see A.P.1469A, Vol.I.

23. **Ailerons.-**

 (i) Lock the control column handhweel in the mid-travel position (see Sect.1).

 (ii) Set the aileron servo motor at the mid-stroke.

 (iii) Slacken the nuts on the bolts securing the servo motor to the base plate, and unscrew the adjusting screws.

 (iv) Place the chain round the aileron torque shaft and servo motor sprockets and connect the ends. Use the vernier adjustment provided by the sprocket attachment holes to position the sprocket correctly relative to both chain and motor.

 (v) Tighten the adjusting screw on the servo motor base plate and take up any slack in the chain.

 (vi) Tighten the nuts on the bolts securing the servo motor to the base plate.

24. **Rudders.-**

 (i) Lock the rudder pedals in the mid-travel position (see Sect.1).

 (ii) Set the rudder servo motor at the mid-stroke position by adjusting the two turnbuckles in the chain between the sprocket on the servo motor and the quadrant on the end of the rudder pedal torque shaft. Check that there is no slack in the chain.

 (iii) Tighten the locknuts on the turnbuckles and lock with wire.

25. **Elevators.-**

 (i) Lock the control column in the mid-travel position, i.e. $\frac{1}{2}^o$ aft of the vertical (see Sect.1).

 (ii) Set the elevator servo motor at mid-stroke.

 (iii) Adjust the turnbuckles on the chains running from the sprocket on the servo motor to the quadrant on the end of the control column shaft. Check that no slack occurs in the chain.

 (iv) Tighten the locknuts on the turnbuckles and lock with wire.

 (v) Move the control column to the neutral position, i.e. $3\frac{3}{4}^o$ forward of the vertical and lock (see Sect.1).

 (vi) Connect up the follow-up cables.

F.S./5

This page amended by A.L.No.18　　　A.P.2062A, Vol.I, Sect.4, Chap.3
September, 1942

UNDERCARRIAGE

General

26. The main wheels and tail wheel should be kept clean and free from mud, particularly at the knee joints on the retracting struts. In wet weather this joint should be cleared of mud and dirt and lubricated after each flight. When the main wheel units are down and the aeroplane is resting on the wheels, the jury struts, Pt.No.1.U.631, must be fitted between the top joint of the shock-absorber strut and the joint at the centre of the retracting strut. These will enable the aeroplane to be towed, or other maintenance work to be done, without any danger of the main wheel units being retracted inadvertently.

Main wheel units

27. _General._- The main wheel unit is illustrated in Sect.7, Chap.5, the hydraulic and emergency lowering systems are shown in figs.18 and 22, and the method of setting the undercarriage doors is described in para.90.

27A. The alignment of the retracting struts in the DOWN position is designed so that the hinge pin of the knuckle joint is not more than 0.05 in. below a line joining the hinge pins at either end of the strut. In practice the offset may be up to a maximum of 0.2 in., the amount being checked by means of a thread stretched between the hinge pins.

28. _Removal of wheel._- If a tyre is burst or is deflated, the aeroplane should be jacked up (see Chap.2, fig.3) using the A.M.gantries to support the outer planes. The tail wheel should be chocked instead of being supported with the universal jacking trestle. When the aeroplane is in this position the following operations are necessary:-

(i) Disconnect the pneumatic brake pipe at the bottom of the flexible tubing.

(ii) Remove the bolts securing the brake drum to the shackles on each side of the wheel.

(iii) Support the wheel with blocks of wood.

(iv) Remove the eyebolt securing the axle to the lower end of the shock-absorber strut, and lower the wheel.

29. _Removing tyre from wheel._- This procedure is fully described in A.P.2337, Vol.I.

30. _Refitting tyre on wheel._- This procedure is fully described in A.P.2337, Vol.I.

Main wheel shock-absorber strut

31. _General._- The main wheel shock-absorber struts are illustrated

This page amended by A.L.No.18
September, 1942   A.P.2062A, Vol.I, Sect.4, Chap.3

in fig.41. For the method of filling the struts with oil, see paras.37 and 38, and for inflating the struts, see para.33. The oil to be used is D.T.D.44D (Stores Ref.34A/43 and 141).

32. <u>Oil level check.</u>- The oil level should not be checked immediately after use as a froth will have collected on top of the oil. To check the level, proceed as follows:-

        Allow the unit to support the aeroplane. Remove the dust cap from the inflation valve, fit adaptor, Pt.No.C.7704, (see fig.25) and permit air to escape gradually until the struts are fully compressed. If, just prior to the struts becoming compressed, a spray of oil and air is blown off, the oil level is correct. The strut can then be re-inflated (see para.33). If only air is blown off, the strut requires topping up (see para.37).

33. <u>Air charging.</u>- When testing the pressure, and charging if necessary, proceed as follows, with the aeroplane standing on the ground:-

(i) Remove the dust cap from the inflation valve.

(ii) Connect the adaptor, Pt.No.C.7704, to the inflation valve (see fig.25).

(iii) Test the air pressure in the struts by turning the knob (A) on the adaptor in a clockwise direction.

(iv) Measure the extension of the strut (see fig.34) and compare it with the dimension given in the table.

(v) If the pressure is below the minimum given for the dimension concerned, unscrew the knob (A) (see fig.25) to close the inflation valve, remove the dust cap from the end of the adaptor and attach an air pump. Re-open the inflation valve by means of knob (A) and inflate the strut, checking the dimension at intervals, until the pressure and extension are within the limits given in the table.

(vi) Disconnect the adaptor and replace the dust cap on the inflation valve.

34. <u>Deflation.</u>- To deflate the strut, remove the dust cap and fit the adaptor, Pt.No.C.7704. Release the pressure by screwing up knob (A) and unscrewing knob (B) on the adaptor (see fig.25).

35. <u>WARNING.</u>- On no account should any bolts or connections etc. be removed before the strut is deflated. Failure to do this may result in a serious accident.

36. <u>Dismantling shock-absorber strut.</u>- This should only be necessary after a long period of service or after accidental damage. The following is the sequence of operations involved in dismantling a strut (see fig.41) which has been removed from the aeroplane:-

F.S./6

Para. 36 (Contd.) A.P.2062A, Vol.I, Sect.4, Chap.3

(i) Deflate both struts in the unit (see para.34).

(ii) Disconnect the balance pipe connections and the bracing, and separate the struts.

(iii) Remove the two bolts (U1). Withdraw the fork (N1) and brake torque link (N) from the lower sliding member (M).

(iv) Unlock and remove the inflation valve (O) and the balance pipe connection (G1).

(v) Unscrew the ferrules from the two screwed rods (S1) and remove the two setscrews to free the end fitting (G) and inner tube assembly from the main outer tube.

(vi) Withdraw the shock-absorber assembly together with the lower sliding member (M) from the top of the main outer tube. Slide down the distance piece (K) until the locking screw (R1) is accessible through the clearance hole. Remove the locking screw.

(vii) Unscrew the lower sliding member (M) and then remove the locking pin and unscrew the stop nut (Z1) to free the fitting (V1).

(viii) Remove the locking screw and then unscrew the oil cylinder from the piston rod (Y1) and remove the cylinder. Unscrew the damping valve assembly (H1) from the end of the air chamber (H) using spanner, S.T.205.

(ix) Slide the damping valve assembly (H1) off the piston rod (Y1) and unscrew the cover plate of the valve assembly to free the valve. Examine the sealing washer for wear or damage, and if necessary renew it. Clean out the oil holes in the damping valve and cover and also in the piston.

(x) Unlock and unscrew the gland nut (Q1) using spanner, S.T.699, and examine the inside surface for wear.

(xi) Remove the spacer rings and gland ring (J). Examine the gland ring for wear or damage, and if necessary renew it.

(xii) Remove the circlip locking end cap (W1), and unscrew the end cap, using spanner, S.T.164.

(xiii) Unlock and remove the grease nipples and studs from the attachment sleeves (A1) and (B1), and unscrew sleeve (B1) toward the bottom of the main outer tube. Withdraw the sleeves (A1) and (B1) and unscrew them from each other.

(xiv) The bronze liner (L1) should be examined for wear without removing it from the tube (A). If necessary a new tube (A) complete with liner (L1) must be fitted.

A.P.2062A, Vol.I, Sect.4, Chap.3

37. **Topping up with oil.-** If after checking the oil level (see para.32), the strut requires topping up, the aeroplane should be jacked up and the following procedure adopted:-

(i) With the unit in a vertical position and the strut fully compressed, and using the adaptor, Pt. No.C.7704, connect the inflation valve to the component test rig (see fig.33).

(ii) Pump oil into the strut until the pressure begins to rise rapidly. The pressure must not exceed 2,325 lb./sq.in.

(iii) Release the pressure slowly by means of the adaptor (see para.34), and then fully compress the strut.

(iv) Disconnect the test rig and connect the adaptor to an air pump.

(v) Inflate with air to 995 lb./sq.in. allowing the strut to extend fully.

(vi) Remove the air pump and inflation adaptor and replace the inflation valve dust cap.

38. **Oil filling.-** When, after complete dismantling, the strut requires filling with oil, the following instructions must be carefully carried out (see fig.41):-

(i) With the oil cylinder and air chamber completely assembled and in an upright position, but before assembling the end fitting (G), remove the stack pipe (L) and fully compress the strut.

(ii) Fill the strut with oil and, gradually extend the oil cylinder, pouring in additional oil until the strut is fully extended.

(iii) Replace the stack pipe and the end fitting (G)

(iv) Complete the filling (see para.37).

39. **Testing shock-absorber struts.-** With the strut deflated, connect the component test rig (see fig.33) through the inflation adaptor, Pt. No.C.7704, and pump in oil to a pressure of 2,325 lb./sq.in. This pressure should be maintained. Any fall in pressure unaccompanied by visible leakage at the sealing washer under the inflation valve, will be due to leakage at the following points:-

(i) At the fitting (L). Leakage will be visible on removal of the end cap (G).

(ii) At the gland ring (J). Oil may eventually appear at the bottom of the main outer tube (A).

F.S./7

This page amended by A.L. No. 20 A.P.2062A, Vol.I, Sect.4, Chap.3
February, 1943

40. **Leakage of oil or loss of pressure.-**

(i) If leakage occurs round the sealing washer under the inflation valve, first tighten the valve body. If this is ineffective, deflate the strut. remove the valve and renew the washer.

(ii) If leakage occurs from the inflation valve itself, deflate the strut and renew the complete inflation valve unit.

(iii) Should leakage occur from the sealing washer under the stack pipe (L), deflate the unit, remove the stack pipe and renew the washer.

(iv) If leakage of oil or loss of pressure occurs and cannot be traced to the inflation valve or sealing washer, deflate the strut and then dismantle (see para.36, (i) to (iii)). If, after removal of the fork (N), oil is to be found in the lower sliding member, leakage from the sealing washer (X1) is indicated. To remedy this, it will probably be necessary to renew the sealing washer, since further tightening is not likely to be effective. Proceed as in para.36, (iv) to (vii).

(v) If no leakage is apparent from the sealing washer (X1) continue dismantling as in para.36 (iv) to (viii) and (x). Then tighten the gland nut (Q1), using spanner S.T.699, and if this is ineffective renew the gland.

Adjustment of main wheel units

41. **UP and DOWN latches.-** The arrangement of these latches is shown in fig.31 and in Sect.7, Chap.5, fig.3. They are set correctly before leaving the manufacturers and should need no adjustment. If, however, the undercarriage is damaged or new retracting struts are fitted, the latches may be re-set by means of the adjustable side stays (C). These should be adjusted so that the lever (K) will contact the stop (M) when the upper and lower retracting struts (D1) and (C1) are truly in line. It is important that when the unit is locked in the UP position, the UP latch (J) is forced back 1/32 in. to ensure a positive bearing on the UP catch tube (see fig.31). This condition can be obtained by means of the two turnbuckles at each end of the catch. It is also important that a clearance of $\frac{1}{8}$ in. be maintained between the top of the catch tube and the latch (J).

42. **Hydraulic jacks.-** If adjustment is required proceed as follows:-

(i) Remove the bolt passing through the lower end of the jack piston rod and see that the rod is at the bottom of its stroke.

(ii) Adjust the length of the piston rod, by screwing the fork-end into or out of the rod, so that the lever (K) is against the stop (M) and the bolt (H), when replaced, will bear against the lower end of the slotted hole in lugs (G), i.e. the end nearest the knuckle joint of the retracting struts.

This page amended by A.L. No.20   A.P.2062A, Vol.I, Sect.4, Chap.3
February, 1943

(iii) Unscrew the fork-end an additional half turn and replace and lock the bolt (H). This ensures that the jack piston will not bottom before the struts (D1) and (C1) are truly in line.

Tail wheel unit

43. **General.-** The tail wheel unit is illustrated in fig.42. For the method of filling the strut with oil and inflating with air, see para. 51 and 46 respectively.

44. **Removing tail wheel.-** To remove the tail wheel proceed as follows:-

(i) Jack up the aircraft (see fig.8).

(ii) Remove the setscrews locking the axle plugs.

(iii) Unscrew the axle plugs, using spanner, S.T.659.

(iv) Remove the two bolts on the underside of the axle, at each end.

(v) The wheel and axle will now drop away. (For the method of removing the shock-absorber strut from the aircraft, see Sect.5).

(vi) Screw plug, Pt.No.S.T.530, into the axle. Fit tube, Pt.No.S.T.531, over the plug, and drive the axle from the wheel.

Tail wheel shock-absorber strut

45. **Oil level check.-** The oil level should not be checked immediately after use as a froth will have collected on the top of the oil. Allowing the unit to support the aircraft, proceed as follows:-

(i) Remove the dust cap from the inflation valve and fit the adaptor, Pt.No.C.7704 (see fig.25).

(ii) Screw in the knob (A) to open the inflation valve and by unscrewing the knob (B) allow the air to escape gradually until the unit is fully compressed. If at the final stage of compression a spray of oil and air is blown off, the oil level is correct and the strut can be re-inflated (see para.46).

(iii) If only air is blown off, the oil level requires topping up (see para.51).

46. **Inflation pressure check.-** The strut inflation pressure should be checked with the aircraft standing on the ground:-

(i) Remove the dust cap from the inflation valve. Connect the adaptor, Pt.No.C.7704 (see fig.26).

(ii) Test the pressure by turning the knob (A) on the adaptor (see fig.25).

(iii) Measure the extension of the strut (see fig.35) and compare it with the dimension given in the table. If the pressure is within the limits given, the strut is serviceable.

(iv) If the pressure is below the minimum given for the dimension concerned, unscrew the knob (A) (see fig.25) to close the

F.S./8

This page amended by A.I. No. 20 A.P.2062A, Vol.I, Sect.4, Chap.3
February, 1943

inflation valve, remove the dust cap from the end of the adaptor, and connect an air pump. Re-open the inflation valve and inflate the strut, checking the dimension at intervals, until the pressure and extension are within the limits given in the table.

(v) Jack up the aircraft until the strut is fully extended. The pressure in the strut in this condition must be that given in the Leading Particulars. If it is not, the unit must be partly dismantled and then re-filled with oil (see para.52).

47. **Deflation.** - Should it be necessary to deflate the strut, the adaptor, Pt.No.C.7704, should be fitted to the inflation valve. The pressure should then be released by screwing up knob (A) and unscrewing knob (B) on the adaptor.

48. **WARNING.** - On no account should any bolts, connections, etc. be removed before the strut is deflated. Failure to do this may result in a serious accident.

49. **Dismantling tail wheel strut.** - To dismantle the tail wheel strut proceed as follows:-

(i) Remove the complete unit (see Sect.5).

(ii) Deflate the strut (see para.47).

(iii) Remove the wheel and axle (see para.44).

(iv) Slacken the friction clip bolt (O) (see fig.42) and remove the setscrews (B) and the inflation valve (E1). This will release the main outer tube (B1) which must then be drawn down from the top of the strut to expose the plugs (C).

(v) Extract the plugs (C) and remove the top end cap (D). The main outer tube including the attachment bracket (N) can then be drawn over the top of the strut and removed.

(vi) Using spanner, Pt.No.S.T.658, unscrew the gland nut (F) and remove the distance piece (G), gland ring (H), and spacer.

(vii) Using spanner, Pt.No.S.T.719, unscrew the self-centring cam retaining nut (J). The air cylinder assembly, together with both self-centring cams (Z) and (M), can then be withdrawn from the lower sliding member (U). When withdrawing the upper cam, retrieve the cam locking key which will be released.

(viii) Remove the four setscrews to free the cam (M) and damping valve assembly (X) from the inner cylinder (K).

(ix) Examine the edge of the inner cylinder (K) between the diaphragm (X) and the lower cam (M) for signs of distortion due to elongation of the cam securing bolt holes in the cylinder. Distortion exceeding 1/32 in. renders the assembly unacceptable for re-assembly and it must be renewed.

This page amended by A.L.No.20   A.P.2062A, Vol.I, Sect.4, Chap.3
February, 1943

- (x) Remove the setscrews to free the filter (A1).
- (xi) Remove the nut from the bolt (L) to free the cover plate, sealing washer and damping valve from the diaphragm (X).
- (xii) Using special tool, Pt.No.S.T.721, unscrew the ferrules from the screwed rods securing the fork (T) to the lower sliding member (U) and extract the rods to free the fork.
- (xiii) With spanner, Pt.No.S.T.252, unscrew the gland nut and free the gland ring (W) from the fork (T).
- (xiv) To remove the friction clip (O) from the main outer tube, unscrew the ten setscrews to release the lower end of the main outer tube (B1) which will allow the friction clip assembly (O) to be slid from its housing.

50. **Re-assembly of tail wheel strut.-** In general, re-assembly is a reversal of the dismantling procedure, but the following points should also receive attention:-

- (i) When inserting the wheel fork assembly (T) into the end of the lower sliding tube (U), care should be taken to ensure that the gland ring (W) is not damaged when passing the holes drilled in the tube.
- (ii) Assembly sleeves, Pt.Nos.S.T.528 and S.T.720. should be used when assembling the gland ring (H).
- (iii) The nuts retaining gland rings (W) and (H) must not be overtightened or the efficiency of the gland will be impaired.
- (iv) When assembling the top cam (Z), the nut (J) and the gland assembly (H), the inner cylinder assembly should be held by means of the expanding collet, Pt.No.S.T.526, which fits into the recess in the top end of the cylinder (K).
- (v) The clamp, Pt.No.S.T.722, should be used to prevent the inner cylinder assembly from falling into the lower sliding tube during assembly.

51. **Topping up with oil.-**

- (i) With the unit in an upright position, remove the dust cap from the inflation valve.
- (ii) Connect the inflation valve, through the adaptor, Pt.No.C.7704, to the component test rig (see fig.33).
- (iii) Pump in oil until the pressure begins to rise rapidly. It must not exceed 1,200 lb./sq.in.
- (iv) Release the pressure gradually, and fully compress the strut.
- (v) Remove the test rig and connect an air supply to the inflation adaptor.
- (vi) Inflate with air to the normal pressure at full extension (see Leading Particulars).
- (vii) Remove the air pump and inflation adaptor and replace the inflation valve dust cap.

F.S./9

This page amended by A.L. No. 18
September, 1942
This page amended by A.L. No. 20
February, 1943

A.P. 2062A, Vol. I, Sect. 4, Chap. 3

52. **Oil filling and inflation.** - New or replacement struts to issue 18 or subsequent will be delivered fully extended and filled with oil only (indicated by red stencilled note on strut). These struts are to be inflated with air after installation in the aircraft, as instructed in sub-para. (ii). Struts which are dismantled and refilled by Service personnel are to be filled as instructed in sub-para. (i) and a note that the strut is filled only with oil is to be painted in red on the outer tube.

(i) When the tail wheel strut requires refilling proceed as follows:-

 (a) With the inner cylinder assembly, top cam (Z) and nut (K) reassembled in the lower sliding member (U), i.e. with the strut in the condition as at the end of para. 49 (vi), and the unit upright and fully extended, pump in oil through the inflation valve (E1) until it completely fills member (U) and overflows from the top edge. The adaptor, Pt. No. C. 7704, will facilitate connection of the oil pump to the valve.

 (b) With the gland housing filled with oil and the unit fully extended re-insert the spacer and gland ring (H), using sleeves Pt. Nos. S.T. 720 and S.T. 528. A smooth metal "spoon" may be used to release oil from beneath the gland ring as the ring is slid down into position, but great care must be taken not to damage the gland while doing this. Refit the distance ring (G) and the gland nut (F), using spanner Pt. No. S.T. 781, and lock with the grubscrew. Then complete the assembly of the strut, temporarily fitting plug, Pt. No. S.T. 784 in place of valve (E1), and not forgetting to tighten friction clip bolt (O). Also ensure that the cam locking key is correctly replaced between the upper cam and the lower sliding tube, before fitting nut (J).

 (c) Pump in oil to extend the strut fully, then compress the strut, allowing oil to escape. Repeat this until no air bubbles are ejected with the oil and then finally pump in oil to extend the strut fully, disconnect the oil pump and fit the inflation valve dust cap.

(ii) To fit and inflate the strut:-

 (a) With the strut adjacent to but not installed in the aircraft, open the inflation valve and fully compress the strut, keeping it in a vertical position. Oil will be ejected from the valve.

 (b) Keeping the unit as nearly vertical as possible, install the strut in the aircraft

 (c) Using the adaptor, Pt. No. C. 7704, connect an air supply line to the valve (E1) and inflate the strut to the correct pressure at full extension (see Leading Particulars).

 (d) Remove the jacks and allow the strut to support the aircraft, then carry out the check described in para. 46.

53. **Testing tail wheel strut.** - With the unit deflated, connect the component test rig (see fig. 33) through the inflation adaptor, Pt. No. C. 7704, and pump in oil to a pressure of 1,200 lb./sq. in. This

A.P.2062A, Vol.I, Sect.4, Chap.3

pressure should be maintained. Fall in pressure not due to leakage from the inflation valve or its sealing washer may be caused by leakage at the following points:-

(i) At the gland ring (W). Leakage at this point will eventually cause oil to appear at the junction of the wheel fork and lower sliding member (U).

(ii) At the gland ring (H). Oil will eventually appear at either the top or bottom ends of the main outer tube (B1).

(iii) At the end plug (A). Oil will be visible when the end cap (D) is removed.

54. **Leakage of oil or loss of pressure.-** If leakage occurs from the sealing washer under the inflation valve, first tighten the inflation valve. If leakage persists, deflate the strut and fit a new washer. If leakage occurs from the inflation valve itself, deflate the strut and fit a complete new valve assembly.

55. If loss of oil or pressure occurs which cannot be traced to a faulty inflation valve or washer, deflate and dismantle the strut (see para.49). Inspect, and if necessary renew the gland rings (W) and (H) and the damping valve assembly (X).

56. **Adjustment of friction clip.-** Excessive shimmying of the tail wheel should be corrected by tightening the friction clip screw (O). Care should be taken that the friction clip is not tightened to such an extent that it prevents proper castoring and self-centring of the wheel.

ENGINE INSTALLATION

Fuel, oil and coolant systems

57. **Cleaning the fuel tanks.-**

(i) Remove the fuel tank (see Sect.5).

(ii) Remove all access doors, sumps and pipe connections.

(iii) Support the tank on its rear end, and flush out the inside with filtered petrol by spraying the petrol on the sides of the tank.

(iv) Drain off the flushing petrol.

(v) Clean the sumps and other fittings removed, and refit them to the tank.

(vi) Refit the tank in the main plane (see Sect.5).

F.S./10

A.P.2052A, Vol.I, Sect.4, Chap.3

58. **Cleaning the oil tanks.-**

   (i) Drain and remove the tank (see Sect.5).

   (ii) Plug up all holes.

   (iii) Remove the access door in the tank.

   (iv) Wash out the tank by spraying with flushing oil (Stores Ref. 34A/68) and finally spray the sides with petrol.

   (v) Drain off the flushing oil and the petrol. Make sure that the petrol is all cleared away before filling the tank with new oil.

   (vi) Refit the access door in the tank and refit the tank (see Sect.5).

59. **Cleaning the oil filters.-** When cleaning the oil filter the following procedure should be adopted:-

   (i) Remove the locking wire and unscrew the handscrew.

   (ii) Turn the special nut through 90° until the arms coincide with the slots in the casing, and remove the handle and nut.

   (iii) The filter element will now slide out under the pressure of the spring-loaded plunger which descends and seals the oil inlet. Should the element stick, it may be released by grasping the projection at the bottom.

   (iv) Clean the inside of the filter and the element with flushing oil (Stores Ref.34A/68) and finally flush with filtered petrol.

60. **Draining the coolant header tank and radiators.-** Should it be necessary to drain the header tank and radiators, proceed as follows:-

   (i) Open the inspection door in the underside of the cowling.

   (ii) Open the drain tap at the base of the circulating pump. This tap should remain open until the system is refilled.

   (iii) Remove the drain plug at the base of the radiator. The cabin heating radiator connected to each inboard system is separately drained from the drain plug in its base.

   Note.- Pet cocks are fitted in the tops of the cabin heating radiators and at the highest points in the return pipes. Access to the pet cocks is obtained through doors in the leading-edge skin.

Engine controls

61. **General.-** The engine control levers, chains and tie-rods will

This page amended by A.L.No.26   A.P.2062A and C, Vol.I, Sect.4, Chap.3
May, 1943

normally only need adjustment after the dismantling of components (see para. 62 - 65). Instructions are given for setting manually operated supercharger and mixture controls, but in aircraft incorporating Mod. No. 465, electro-pneumatic supercharger controls are fitted, and Mod.No.630 deletes the mixture control. In Mk.III aircraft the slow-running cut-out controls are also electro-pneumatically operated by the pilot. For details of the controls in the power plant see A.P.2140A and B, Vol.I.

62. **Throttle, mixture, supercharger and propeller controls.-**

   (i) Set the levers on the pilot's control quadrant to the mid-travel position. The mixture lever should be tied in this position.

   (ii) Disconnect the spring from the mixture lever on the engine control box on the front spar behind the fireproof bulkhead.

   (iii) On the inboard engine control boxes set the levers at 6¾ deg. forward of the vertical to obtain the mid-travel position. (The spar web is vertical when the aircraft is in the rigging position).

   (iv) On the outboard engine control boxes, set the levers at 31 deg. forward of the vertical to obtain the mid-travel position.

   (v) Connect up all chains on the sprockets so that the chain ends are approximately equi-distant from the sprockets. Attach the tie-rods and adjusters and take up all slack.

   (vi) See that the differential links at the divisions of the supercharger and mixture controls are vertical. The links are fitted at the division of the inboard and outboard controls between the fuselage and the inboard nacelles.

   (vii) To obtain the mid-travel position on the inboard engine fireproof bulkheads, set the levers for the rods passing through the bulkhead as follows, (the bulkheads are vertical when the aircraft is in rigging position):-

      Throttle and mixture levers   9 deg. forward of vertical
      Propeller and supercharger levers 6¾ deg. forward of vertical

      These levers should be set to their maximum radius of 4 in. at the centre-line of the joints with the rods, and may be adjusted to a reduced radius if required when the controls are finally tested.

   (viii) On the outboard engine fireproof bulkheads set the levers as follows :-

F.S./11

This page amended by A.L.No.26 A.P.2062A and C, Vol.I, Sect.4, Chap.3
May, 1943.

Para.62 (contd.)

        Throttle lever   35 deg. forward of vertical
        Mixture lever $35\frac{1}{2}$ deg. forward of vertical
        Propeller and supercharger levers 31 deg. forward of vertical

        The mixture lever should be set to a radius of 3 25/32 in. but may be further adjusted as necessary. The throttle, propeller and supercharger levers should be set as described for the inboard engine.

(ix) Fit the connecting rods between the levers at the front spar and the fireproof bulkhead, adjusting the lengths of the rods to suit the positions of the levers as previously set.

(x) Replace the spring on the mixture lever on the engine control box. It is important that it should be done at this stage before the controls are connected to the engines.

(xi) Pull the control levers in the cockpit to the fully back position and set the control levers on the engine against the rear stops.

(xii) Connect the control rods between the engine controls and the levers on the countershaft on the fireproof bulkhead, adjusting the length of the rods as required.

(xiii) Move the levers in the cockpit to the fully forward position and check that the levers on the engine are against the forward stop. The levers may be checked at the forward and rear stops by ascertaining that a piece of thin paper placed on the stop is trapped by the lever when the control lever in the cockpit is pushed fully forward or pulled fully backwards.

(xiv) Make any adjustment required on the control connections on the engine (see A.P.2140A and B, Vol.I).

(xv) If required, the adjustments referred to in sub-paras.(vii) and (viii) may be made in the lengths of the levers.

63. **Boost cut-out control.**- When setting the boost cut-out control, the control lever in the cockpit and the quadrant on the countershaft at the front spar should be set at mid-travel position, and the chains fitted with the ends approximately equi-distant from the sprockets. The quadrant is at mid-position when the centre-line of the bolt at its outer edge is 3.96 in. below the lower surface of the skin of the main floor. To adjust the cables the lever in the cockpit must be pulled back to the stop, and the cables tensioned by means of the turnbuckles. When the cockpit lever is released the engine lever must return to its stop, and the cables must be slack.

64. **Slow-running cut-out controls (Mk.I aircraft).**- These controls are inter-connected with the engine fuel cock controls by means of lost-

This page issued with A.L.No.26   A.P.2062A and C, Vol.I, Sect.4, Chap.3
May, 1943

motion links between the fuselage and the inboard nacelles. Teleflex controls connect the lost-motion links with the engines. For information regarding Teleflex controls, see A.P.1464B, Vol.I. The lost-motion link should be adjusted to suit the difference in movement between the fuel cock control and the lever of the slow-running cut-out control on the engine, and to take up any backlash.

Hand turning gear

65. A hand turning handle is stowed on the bulkhead at the rear of the port main wheel compartment. It is intended for maintenance purposes only and should not be used for starting the engine.

HYDRAULIC SYSTEM

General

66. Installation diagrams of the hydraulic system circuits are given in figs.14 and 17 to 22, and of the turret systems in figs. 37 to 40. These diagrams show also the identification markings and pipe

(Continued on next leaf)

F.S./11A

A.P.2062A, Vol.I, Sect.4, Chap.3

numbers. In all maintenance operations on the hydraulic system absolute cleanliness is essential. Clean fluid only should be used when filling or topping up, and the containers, funnels, etc., used for holding the fluid and for the reception of drained fluid must be scrupulously clean. It is preferable that after the container has been carefully cleaned it should be swilled out with a small quantity of clean fluid, which should then be discarded.

67. Whenever pipe-lines are disconnected the unions and pipe ends should be blanked off against entry of dirt. Whenever drain plugs or other components are removed they must be carefully examined to see that they are free from dirt before they are reassembled. Any new length of pipe or new coupling should be thoroughly flushed out to ensure freedom from dirt before being fitted.

Filling

68. The following procedure should be adopted when it is necessary to fill the complete circuit:-

(i) Jack up the aeroplane by means of hydraulic jacks under the pads on the front spar (see Sect.4, Chap.2).

(ii) Fill the hydraulic reservoir with fluid, D.T.D.44D (Stores Ref.34A/43 and 46).

(iii) See that the inboard fuel tanks have been drained.

(iv) Detach the sealing washers and allow the jettison pipes to extend.

(v) Connect the ground test rig (see fig.32) to the external supply and return valves in each inboard nacelle. These valves are mounted on the panels between the undercarriage support beams.

(vi) Fill the system by running the motor in low gear, at the same time maintaining the fluid level in the reservoir. When filling it is important that all jacks should be in the extended position.

(vii) Operate each circuit several times each way in order to fill all the jacks and the jettison circuit.

Important.- Screw down the reservoir cap while operating any circuit, and fill when necessary with the test rig stopped.

(viii) Reinstate the jettison pipes as described in para.84, except that the original sealing washers should be used.

Bleeding

69. The system should be bled after any component has been removed or a new length of pipe inserted, and during the bleeding operation, the aeroplane should be jacked up. Connect the ground test rig (see fig.32) to the external supply and return valves.

70. To bleed the main wheel and bomb door circuits.-

(i) Set the main wheel and bomb door control valves in the UP position.

F.S./12

Para.70 (Contd.)　　　　　　A.P.2062A, Vol.I, Sect.4, Chap.3

- (ii) Disconnect the jack piston rods from the bomb doors, and disconnect the operating links from the undercarriage doors.
- (iii) Pump with the ground test rig until the jacks are fully compressed and then switch off the test rig.
- (iv) Slacken off the bleeder plugs on the rod side of the piston.
- (v) Pump with the hand pump in the fuselage until air bubbles cease to appear and fluid is ejected.
- (vi) Tighten and lock the bleeder plugs.
- (vii) Top up the reservoir.
- (viii) Move the undercarriage and bomb door control valves to the DOWN position.
- (ix) Pump with ground test rig until the jacks are fully extended and switch off test rig.
- (x) Slacken off the bleeder plugs on the piston head side of the jack.
- (xi) Pump with hand pump until air bubbles cease to appear and fluid is ejected.
- (xii) Tighten and lock the bleeder plugs.
- (xiii) Reconnect the jack piston rods to the bomb doors and the operating links to the undercarriage doors.

71. To bleed the flap circuit.-

- (i) Move the operating lever on the control valve to the flaps DOWN position.
- (ii) Pump with ground test rig until the stroke is completed and switch off the test rig.
- (iii) Slacken off the bleeder plugs at the end of the jack into which fluid is being fed.
- (iv) Pump with hand pump until air bubbles cease to appear and fluid is ejected.
- (v) Tighten and lock the bleeder plugs.
- (vi) Move the operating lever on the control valve to the flaps UP position.
- (vii) Repeat the procedure, this time slackening off the bleeder plugs at the opposite end of the jack when the stroke is completed.

72. To bleed the air-intake circuit.-

- (i) Move the control handle in the pilot's cockpit to the HOT AIR position.
- (ii) Pump fluid through by means of the hand pump until the jacks are fully compressed.

A.P.2062A, Vol.I, Sect.4, Chap.

- (iii) Slacken the connection on the rod side of the piston, sufficiently to allow air to escape.
- (iv) Operate the hand pump until air bubbles cease to appear and fluid is ejected.
- (v) Tighten the connection.
- (vi) Repeat the procedure with the control in the COLD AIR position, this time bleeding the circuit through the connection on the piston head side of the jack.

Operational tests

73. *General*.- When the system has been filled and bled it is necessary to test each circuit. Before any operational tests are carried out it is necessary to jack up the aeroplane (*see* Sect.4, Chap.2) and connect the test rig to the external supply and return valves. The operation of the main wheels, bomb doors, flaps, air intake and the fuel jettison should also be tested by the hand pump in conjunction with their respective control valves.

74. *Main wheel units*.-
- (i) To retract the main wheels, release the spring catch and move the control valve lever to the UP position.
- (ii) To lower the main wheels move the control valve lever to the DOWN position. When the jacks are fully extended the retracting strut joint should lock in the DOWN position.

75. *Flaps*.-
- (i) To lower the main plane flaps, move the operating handle to the DOWN position; when the desired angle is reached the handle should be returned to the neutral position and the movement of the flaps should stop immediately.
- (ii) To raise the flaps, move the operating handle on the control valve from the neutral position to the UP position. When the desired angle is reached or the flaps are in the fully UP position the handle should be returned to the neutral position.

76. *Bomb doors*.-
- (i) To lower the bomb doors move the control valve lever to the DOWN position.
- (ii) To raise the bomb doors move the control lever to the UP position. For the method of adjusting the bomb door jacks, *see* para.89.

P.S./13

This page amended by A.L.No.20 A.P.2062A, Vol.I, Sect.4, Chap.3
February, 1943

77. **Air-intake shutters.**- To operate the air-intake shutters move the control handle to the HOT AIR and COLD AIR positions successively, checking that the correct movement of the shutters is obtained.

78. **Fuel jettison system.**- To operate the fuel jettison system move the lever on the pilot's floor from the NORMAL to the JETTISON position. See that the jettison valve and the air valve open. Now return the lever to the NORMAL position and check that the jettison valve and the air valve are closed.

> Note.- The above operations should be carried out with the inboard fuel tanks empty. After this test has been carried out the jettison pipe should be replaced (see para.84).

79. When it is required to operate the jettison system to prevent the sticking of the synthetic rubber rings to the valve piston barrels and spindles, the following procedure may be used if the tanks are not drained :-

(i) Detach the sealing washers and allow the jettison pipes to extend.

(ii) Place a 50-gallon container beneath each pipe.

(iii) If necessary pump up the hydraulic system until the accumulator gauge shows 700 lb./sq.in.

(iv) Operating the control quickly, so as to jettison the minimum amount of fuel, move the lever to JETTISON, then return it to NORMAL. The operation of the air inlet valves should be carefully checked at the same time.

(v) Allow the jettison pipes to dry, (see para.84).

(vi) Replace the jettison pipes, using the original sealing washers and re-set the valves.

79A. If the air inlet valve has stuck in the open position after the jettison system has been tested proceed as follows :-

(i) Ensure that the jettison control handle on the pilot's floor has been returned to NORMAL.

(ii) Open the inspection door in the top skin of the main plane, above the hydraulic pipe connection in the top of the fuel tank, and remove the drilled plug from the jettison system air vent adjacent. Connect an air pump or other source of compressed air supply to the ¼ in. B.S.P. female connection exposed by the removal of the plug.

(iii) Apply increasing air pressure until the valve closes. The pressure must not exceed 850 lb./sq.in.

(iv) Disconnect the air line and replace the drilled plug in the vent.

Note.- This operation does not ensure that the valve will not stick again when next the jettison system is tested, and it may be necessary to close the valve by this method on each occasion.

This page amended by A.L.No.20   A.P.2062A, Vol.I, Sect.4, Chap.3
February, 1943

Pressure tests

80. After filling and bleeding, the system should be pressure tested as follows :-

(i) Disconnect the coupling on the suction side of the hand pump. An Avery self-sealing coupling is fitted at this point.

(ii) Connect the external hand pump (reservoir type) to the open end of the pipe.

(iii) Blank off the main reservoir by means of the sliding blanking plate at the top of the junction block. In order to move the plate the bolts at the joint must be slackened, and then tightened again evenly with the plate in the new position.

(iv) If the jettison system is to be tested, see that the inboard fuel tanks are empty, remove the sealing washers, and allow the jettison pipes to extend.

(v) Place the flap control valve in the UP or DOWN position, the carburettor air-intake valve in the HOT AIR or COLD AIR position, and the undercarriage and bomb door control valves in the mid positions. If the jettison system also is to be tested move the control handle to the JETTISON position.

(vi) Operate the hand pump until a pressure of 850 lb./sq.in. is shown by the pressure gauge on the hydraulic accumulator. This pressure should be maintained for five minutes.

(vii) Release the pressure by means of the valve on the test pump.

Faults and their remedies

81. Faulty operation of the hydraulic system may be caused through defect either in the system or in the mechanical layout. The faults can usually be traced by noting the behaviour of each hydraulic circuit, and this must be done before removing the component from the aircraft. If any circuit responds correctly to both the engine-driven pumps and the hand pump, then it follows that the pumps are satisfactory. Investigation of faults may be considered under the headings :- loss of pressure, air in system, increase in load.

82. A study of the diagram of the system (see Sect.9) together with evidence obtained from the working of the system, will usually suffice to locate the fault. In all cases, the removal of a component should be at the end and not at the beginning of an investigation. A list of likely faults, their causes and the remedial action are given in Table I.

Maintenance of components

83. For the maintenance, and testing of the hydraulic components, see A.P.1803, Vol.I.

F.S./14

A.P.2062A, Vol.I, Sect.4, Chap.3

TABLE I

HYDRAULIC SYSTEM FAULT LOCATION AND RECTIFICATION

Fault	Indication	Probable cause	Remedy
All services inoperative.	Loss of pressure.	Failure of pump(s).	Fit new unit(s).
All services operative but no pressure shown on gauge.	Loss of pressure.	Faulty gauge.	Fit new unit.
External leakage.	Loss of pressure.	Faulty connections.	Tighten connections and if necessary fit new sealing washers or couplings.
Sluggish movements of all services.	Internal leakage.	Excessive clearance in engine-driven pump(s), allowing fluid to escape from the pressure side to the suction side of the pump(s).	Fit new unit.
Sluggish movement of a particular service.	Internal leakage.	Fluid leakage past glands in control valve.	Fit new gland.
Sagging of flaps or lifting when lowered in flight.	Internal leakage.	Fluid leakage past valve in cut-out.	Dismantle valve and inspect for wear. If necessary fit new unit.

A.P.2062A, Vol.I, Sect.4, Chap.3

TABLE I (Contd.)

HYDRAULIC SYSTEM FAULT LOCATION AND RECTIFICATION

Fault	Indication	Probable cause	Remedy
Circuit operating times excessive after bleeding.	Internal leakage.	Fluid leakage past glands in jacks.	Fit new glands.
Operating times slow. ⎫ Backlash at flaps. ⎬ Load on hand pump very light and spongy. ⎭	Air in the system.		Bleed the circuit (see paras.69-72).
Increase of load.		Mal-alignment of jacks. (i) Causing side load on extended ram-rod (ii) Mechanical interference between moving parts. (iii) Presence of foreign matter between moving parts. (iv) Increase of friction due to excessive tightening of glands etc.	

F.S./15

A.P.2062A, Vol.I, Sect.4, Chap.3

Resetting the fuel jettison valve

84. When the fuel jettison system has been operated, it is necessary to reset the valve as follows:-

(i) Ensure that the jettison pipe is dry between the double walls, in order to avoid deterioration due to prolonged contact with fuel. To dry the pipe after it has drained, close and re-open it several times, repeat the process five minutes later and allow the pipe to dry in the extended position for a further 30 minutes.

(ii) Ensure that the air vent valve is correctly closed.

(iii) See that the jettison valve lever in the cockpit is in the NORMAL position.

(iv) Detach a spare sealing washer from inside the hinged cover.

(v) Push the jettison pipe up into the pipe casing and swing the cover plate back into place.

(vi) Remove the nut at the end of the spindle, allowing the inner and outer housings and enclosed spring to slide off the spindle.

(vii) Place the new sealing washer over the outer housing, and replace the outer housing, the spring, the inner housing and the nut on the spindle. The nut should be tightened until it is hard against the seat on the spindle.

Note.- This valve is described and illustrated in A.P.1803, Vol.I.

Cleaning hydraulic fluid filter

85. A high pressure filter is fitted just behind the rear spar on the port side of the fuselage. When it is necessary to clean this filter, proceed as follows:-

(i) Relieve all pressure in the system.

(ii) Drain the fluid from the filter by removing the plug at the bottom.

(iii) Unscrew the bottom half of the filter.

(iv) Withdraw the filter element and the by-pass spring.

(v) Unscrew the wing-nut at the bottom of the filter element, remove the end cages and take the filter element out of the perforated cylinder.

A.P.2062A, Vol.I, Sect.4, Chap.3

(vi) Remove the spring clip from the filter element and unroll.

(vii) Wash the element thoroughly in filtered petrol, also the filter casing and the spring.

(viii) Re-roll the element and assemble the filter.

MISCELLANEOUS

Airscrew feathering tests

86. When airscrew feathering tests are to be made on the ground, an external battery must be used. It is essential that this should be fully charged, in order to avoid damage to the switch solenoids.

Landing lamp adjustment

87. Two landing lamps, type J, are mounted in the lower surface of the port main plane. For instructions on making adjustments, and for other maintenance notes, see A.P.1095, Vol.I.

"Fixed olive" pipe couplings

88. The "fixed olive" couplings used in the pipe systems on the aeroplane differ from standard couplings in that the nipples, or "fixed olives" are integral with the fittings. The instructions for making joints are given in A.P.1464A, Vol.I.

Method of adjusting the bomb door jacks

89. (i) Drain the bomb door circuit.

(ii) Open the emergency release valve.

(iii) Disconnect the four main door jacks at their lower pins.

(iv) Fully close each jack by hand.

(v) Close each door in turn and hold it flush with the fuselage to ascertain the adjustment required for each jack.

(vi) Lower the doors, then extend the jacks and connect to the doors.

(vii) To check the adjustment close each door in turn, then close both together. They should meet evenly along the whole

F.S./16

A.P.2062A, Vol.I, Sect.4, Chap.3

length of the joint. Any sag should not exceed 3/8 in.

(viii) Sagging above 3/8 in. may be remedied by closing the door which sags slightly inside the skin line and closing the other door slightly outside the skin line.

Method of setting main wheel unit doors

90. (i) Jack up the aeroplane by means of the hydraulic jacks under the pads on the front spar. The tail wheel should be chocked.

(ii) Remove both the pins securing the adjustable ends of the arms to the rotating pins on the doors.

(iii) Retract the main wheels.

(iv) Push one of the doors into the closed position and adjust the adjustable end of the arm until the door is held in the closed position by the arm when the pin is fitted.

(v) Repeat this procedure with the other door.

(vi) The wheels should now be lowered and the pins fitted to the rotating pins on both doors.

(vii) Raise the wheels to ensure that the doors both close correctly.

De-icing hand pumps

91. The hand pumps for the windscreen and bomb-aimer's window de-icing, require to be primed if they have been drained in the course of maintenance or from any other cause.

Airscrew de-icing fluid tank dipstick

92. The calibrations on the dipstick attached to the airscrew de-icing fluid tank filler cap, are made with the cap just resting on the top of the seating and not screwed down.

Packing the dinghy

93. When packing the dinghy it is essential to keep it clear of the short portion of manual release between the operating head and the fairlead on the stowage wall.

A.P.2062A. Vol.I. Sect.4. Chap.3

Bonding

94. The bonding of the aeroplane structure to fittings and pipes etc. is given in Sect.6. When fitting new parts to the aeroplane care should be taken to ensure that all contacting faces are metal to metal, and that all bonding clips are correctly replaced.

Fixed aerial

95. It is important that when replacing or repairing the main fixed aerial, the insulator immediately forward of the fin should be fitted with a 3/32 in. dia. aluminium rivet instead of the standard split-pin. This is to provide a weak link in the aerial and so prevent damage by over-tensioning.

Swinging D.R. compass

96. When swinging the D.R. compass the entrance door must be closed.

Sanitary closet

97. It is important that the sewage should always be covered with liquid; if necessary, add water occasionally. When cleaning the closet, the sewage container can be removed by means of a wire handle attached to it. It should then be emptied and swilled out. Before recharging the closet, the "Elsanol" chemical should be well stirred. One pint of the chemical should be then added to $\frac{1}{2} - \frac{3}{4}$ gals. of water and well mixed. Care should be taken to see that the chemical is not exposed to naked light.

F.S./17

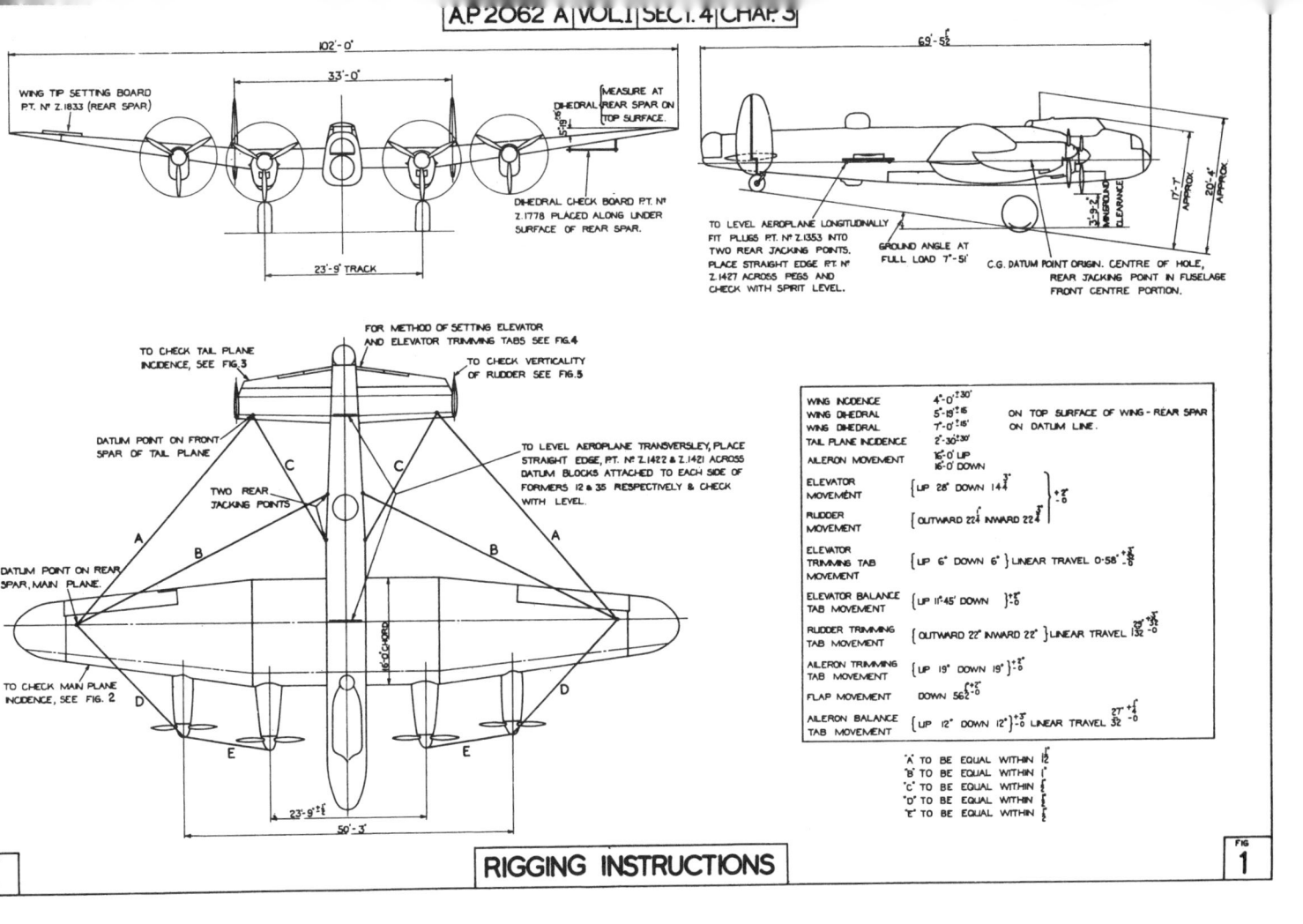

RIGGING INSTRUCTIONS

AP 2062 A | VOL I | SEC.1.4 | CHAP. 3

WING INCIDENCE	4°-0' $^{+30'}_{-0}$
WING DIHEDRAL	5°-15' ± 15'
TAIL PLANE INCIDENCE	7°-0' ± 15'
AILERON MOVEMENT	2°-30'/20'
ELEVATOR MOVEMENT	$\begin{cases} \text{UP } 16°\text{-0'} \\ \text{DOWN } 16°\text{-0'} \end{cases}$
RUDDER MOVEMENT	$\begin{cases} \text{UP } 28° \text{ DOWN } 14\frac{3}{4}° {}^{+2°}_{-0} \end{cases}$
ELEVATOR TRIMMING TAB MOVEMENT	$\begin{cases} \text{OUTWARD } 22\frac{1}{4}° \text{ INWARD } 22\frac{1}{4}° \end{cases}$
ELEVATOR BALANCE TAB MOVEMENT	$\begin{cases} \text{UP } 6° \text{ DOWN } 6° \end{cases}$ LINEAR TRAVEL 0·58" $^{+\frac{1}{32}}_{-0}$
RUDDER TRIMMING TAB MOVEMENT	$\begin{cases} \text{UP } 1°45' \text{ DOWN } \end{cases}$ $1°45'_{-0}$
AILERON TRIMMING TAB MOVEMENT	$\begin{cases} \text{OUTWARD } 22° \text{ INWARD } 22° \end{cases}$ LINEAR TRAVEL $\frac{13}{32}$"$^{+\frac{1}{32}}_{-0}$
FLAP MOVEMENT	$\begin{cases} \text{UP } 15° \text{ DOWN } 15° \end{cases}^{+2°}_{-0}$
AILERON BALANCE TAB MOVEMENT	DOWN $56\frac{1}{2}°{}^{+2°}_{-0}$
	$\begin{cases} \text{UP } 12° \text{ DOWN } 12° \end{cases}^{+3°}_{-0}$ LINEAR TRAVEL $\frac{27}{32}$"$^{+\frac{1}{16}}_{-0}$

'A' TO BE EQUAL WITHIN $\frac{1}{2}$"
'B' TO BE EQUAL WITHIN $\frac{1}{4}$"
'C' TO BE EQUAL WITHIN $\frac{1}{4}$"
'D' TO BE EQUAL WITHIN $\frac{1}{4}$"
'E' TO BE EQUAL WITHIN $\frac{1}{4}$"

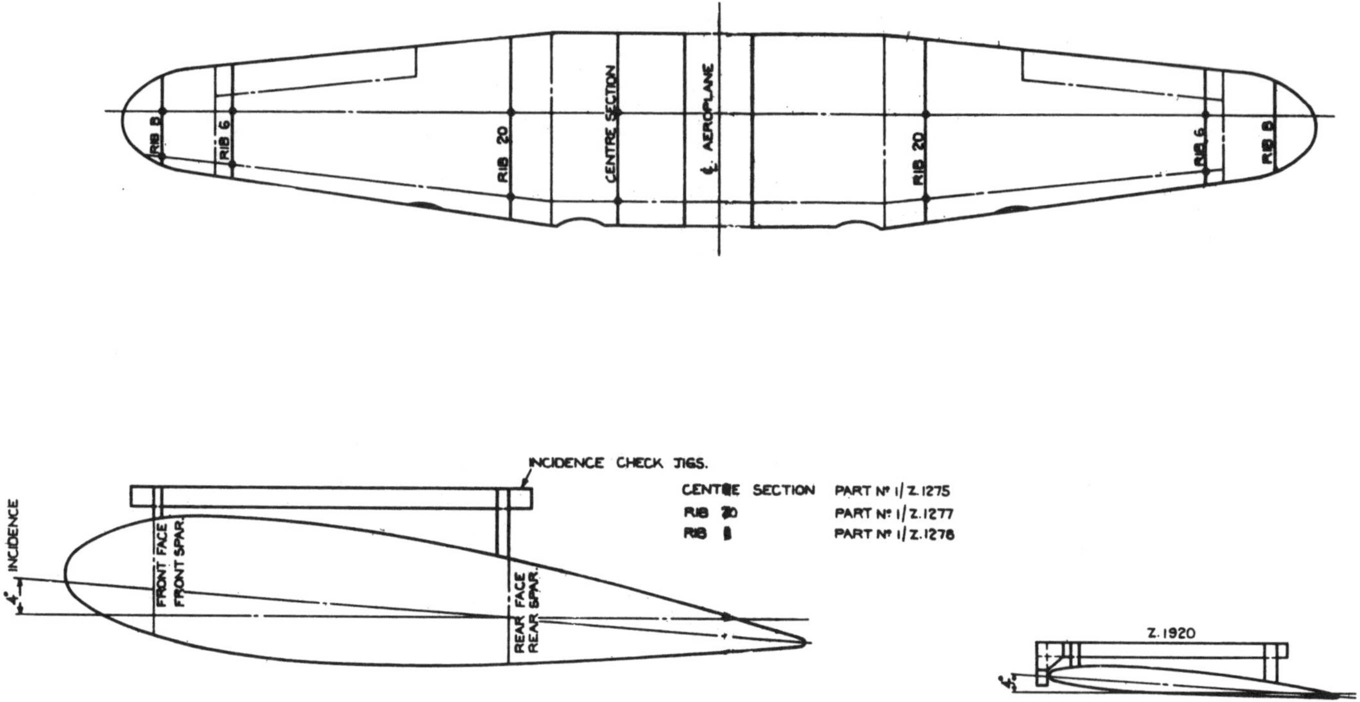

AP 2062 A VOL. I SECT. 4 CHAP. 3

SECTION AT RIB 'B' SHOWING
INCIDENCE CHECK JIG IN POSITION

CENTRE SECTION   PART N° 1/Z.1275
RIB 20   PART N° 1/Z.1277
RIB B   PART N° 1/Z.1276

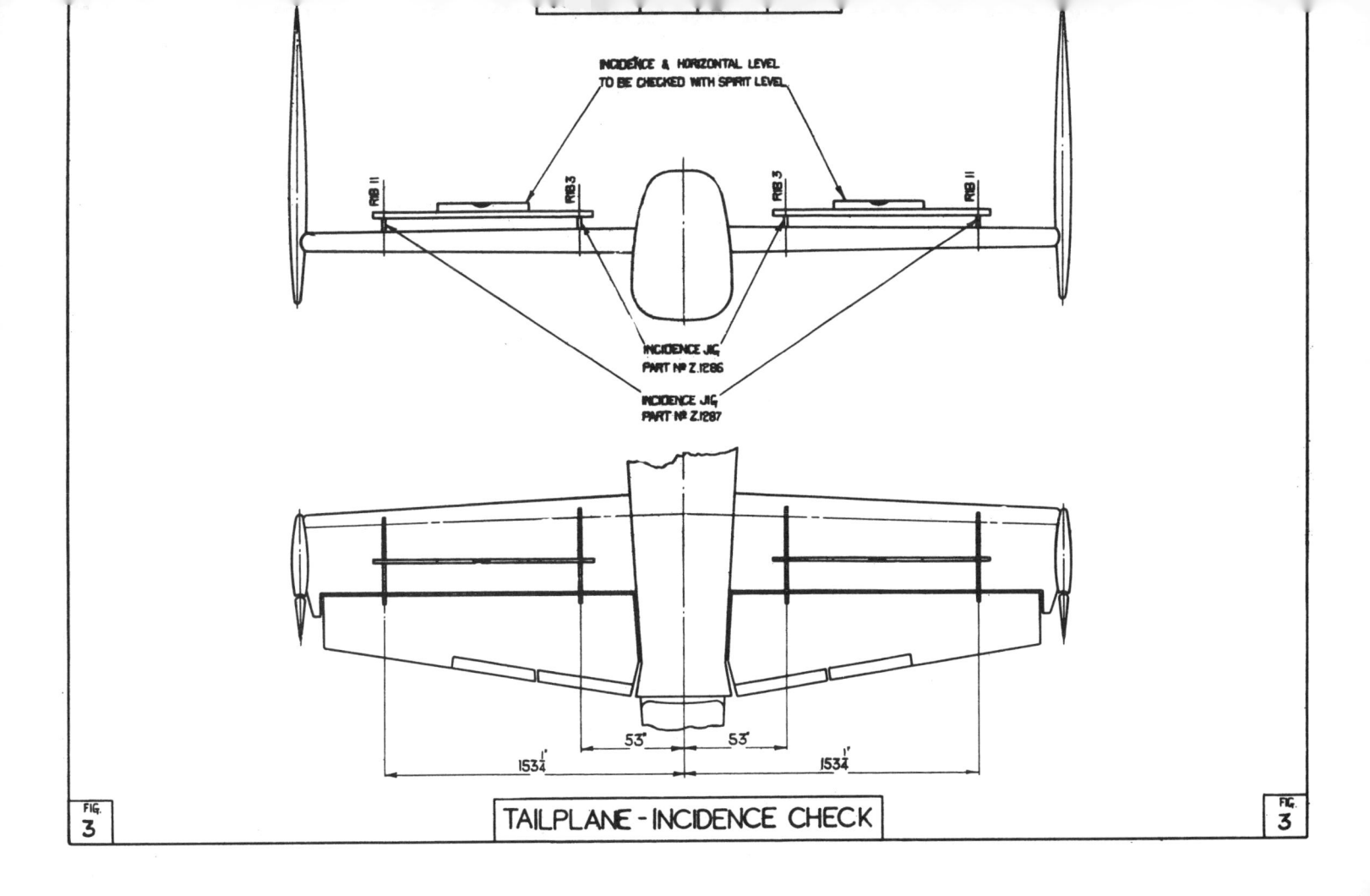

TAILPLANE - INCIDENCE CHECK

FIG. 3

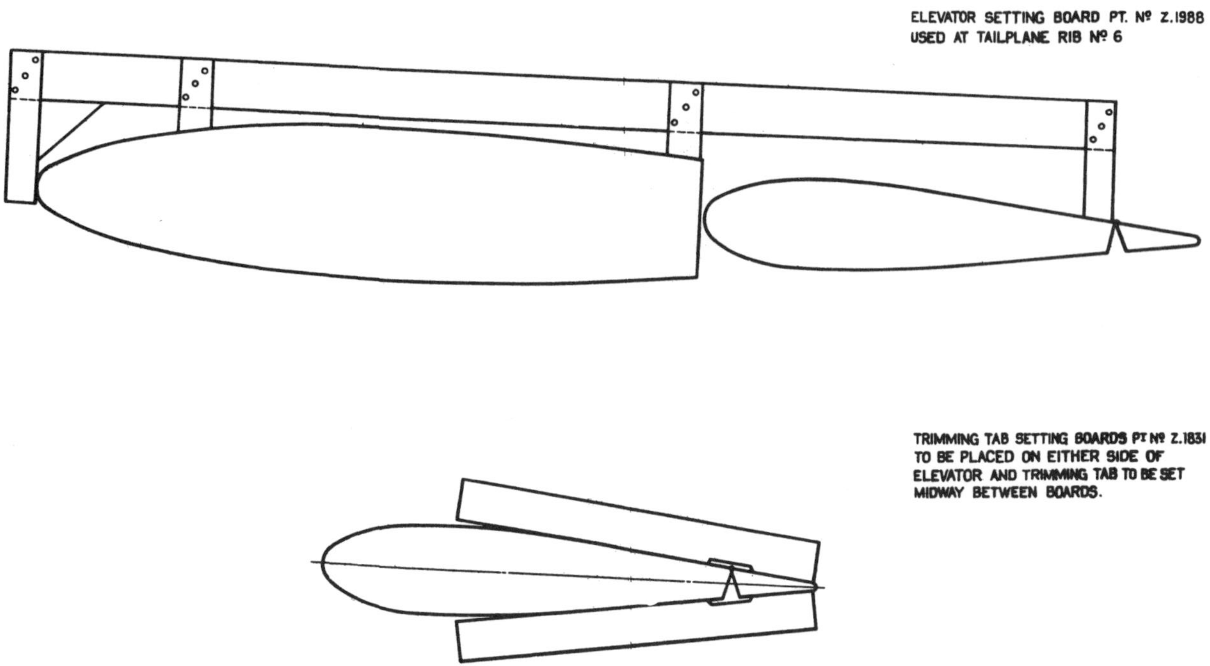

A.P.2062 A | VOL.I | SECT. 4 | CHAP. 3

ELEVATOR SETTING BOARD PT. N° Z.1988
USED AT TAILPLANE RIB N° 6

TRIMMING TAB SETTING BOARDS PT N° Z.1831
TO BE PLACED ON EITHER SIDE OF
ELEVATOR AND TRIMMING TAB TO BE SET
MIDWAY BETWEEN BOARDS.

FIG. 4. METHOD OF SETTING ELEVATOR AND TRIMMING AND BALANCE TABS

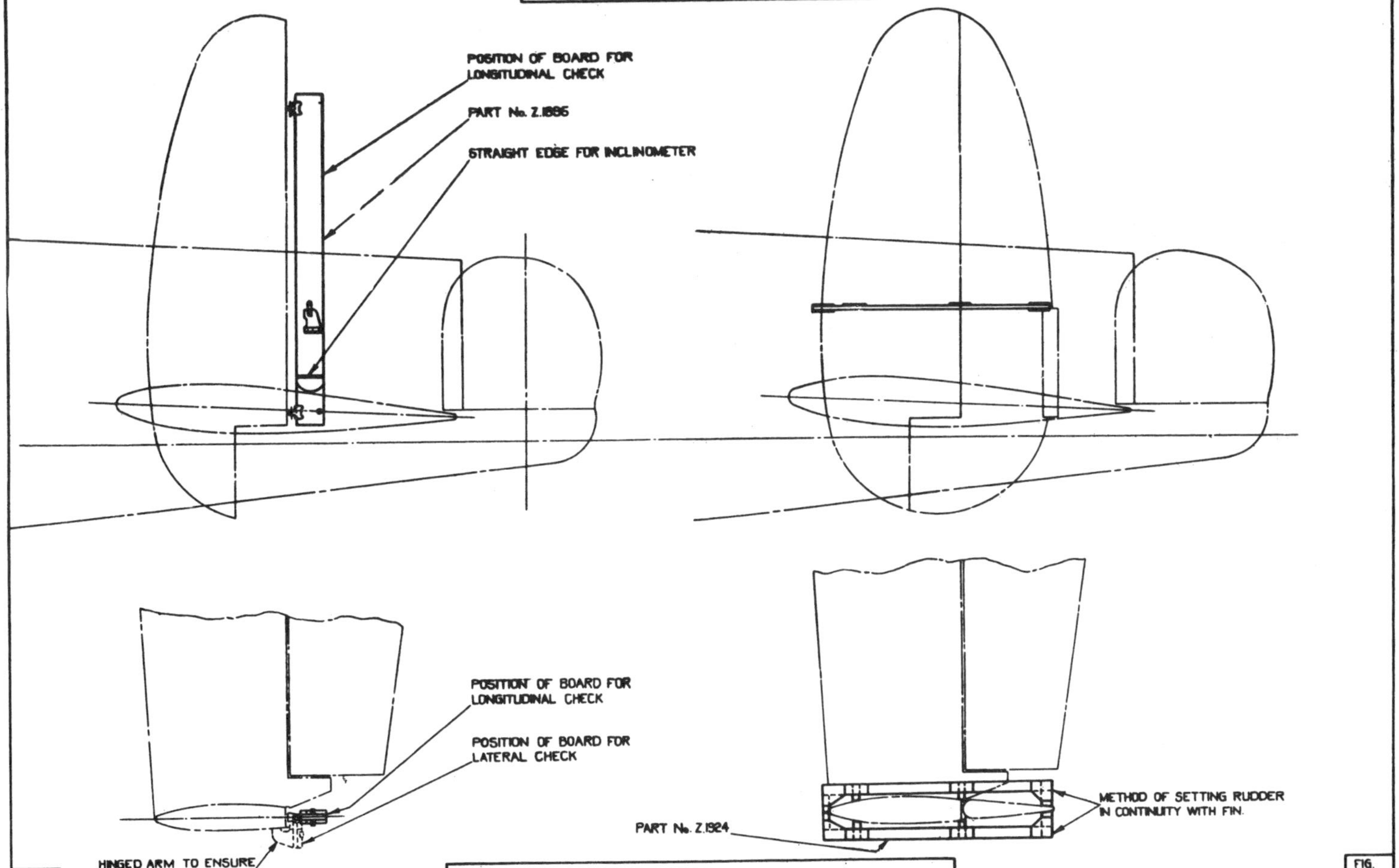

AP.2062 A. VOL.I SECT.4 CHAP.3

METHOD OF SETTING FIN & RUDDER.

FIG. 5

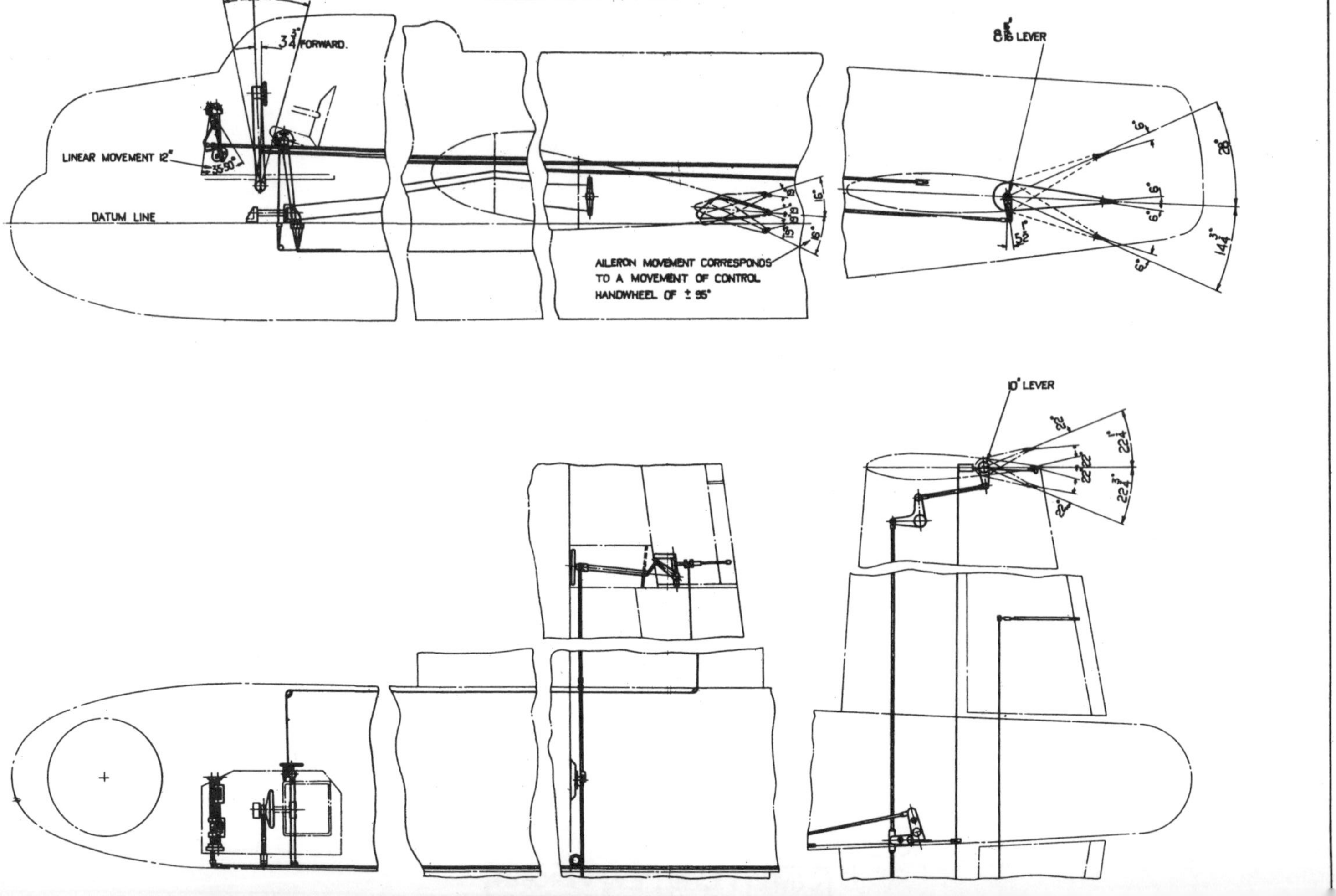
LINEAR MOVEMENT 5·27"
LINEAR MOVEMENT 10·17"
SEAT DOWN.
3¾° FORWARD.
LINEAR MOVEMENT 12"
DATUM LINE
AILERON MOVEMENT CORRESPONDS
TO A MOVEMENT OF CONTROL
HANDWHEEL OF ± 95°
8 5/16" LEVER
28°
14¼°
6°
16°
10" LEVER
22½°
22°

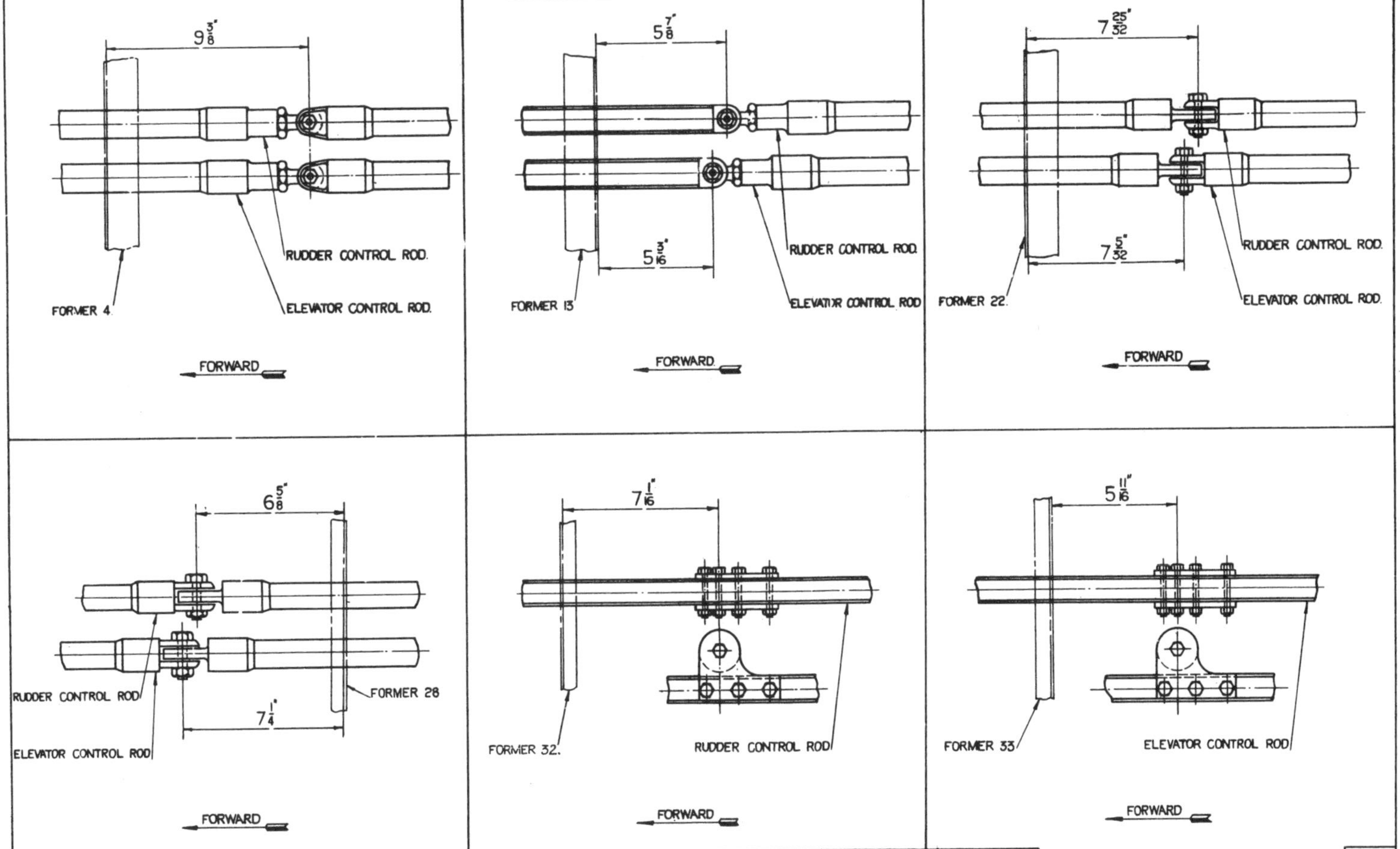

AP 2062A, VOL.I, SECT.4, CHAP.3

FIG. 7

SETTING OF ELEVATOR & RUDDER CONTROLS

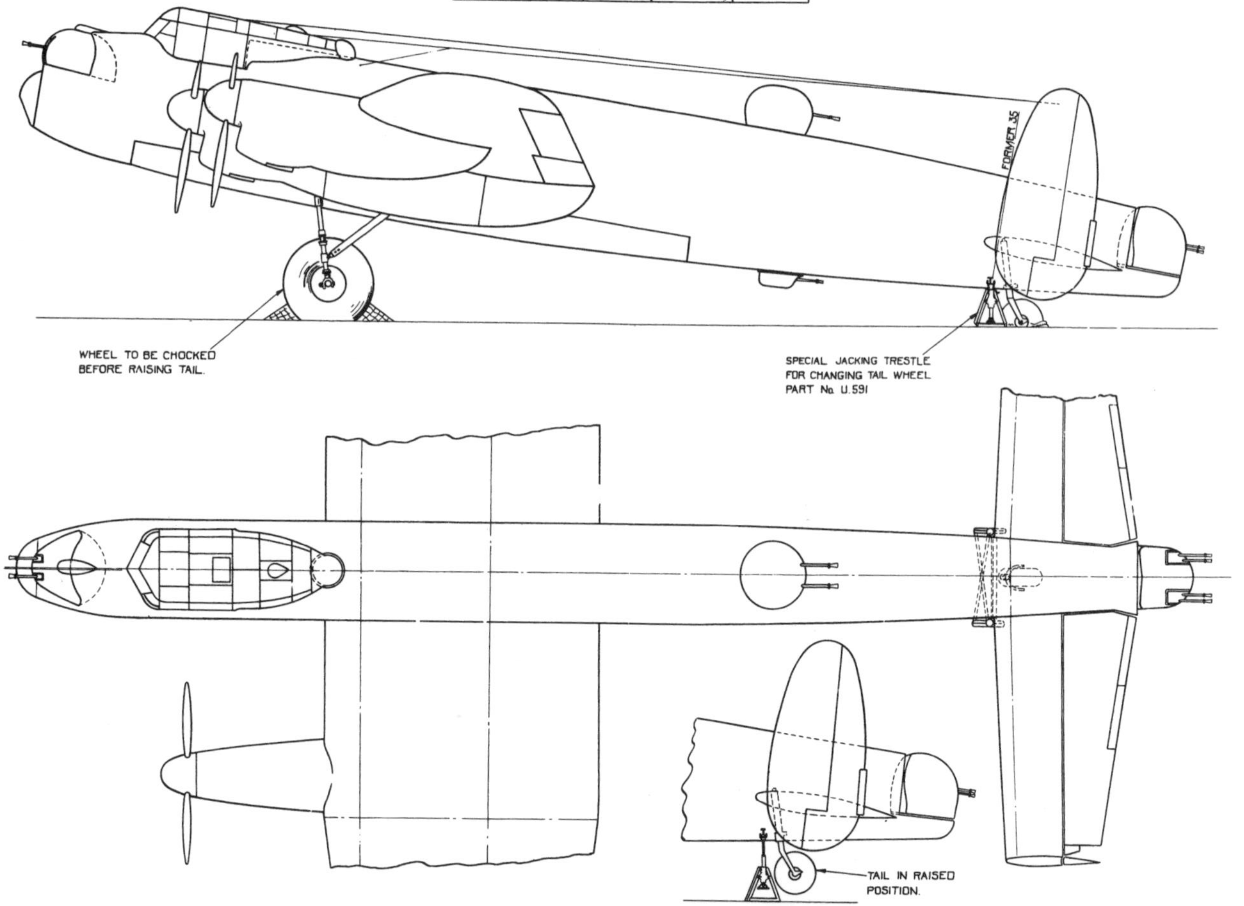

FIG. 8

METHOD OF REMOVING TAIL WHEEL

FIG. 8

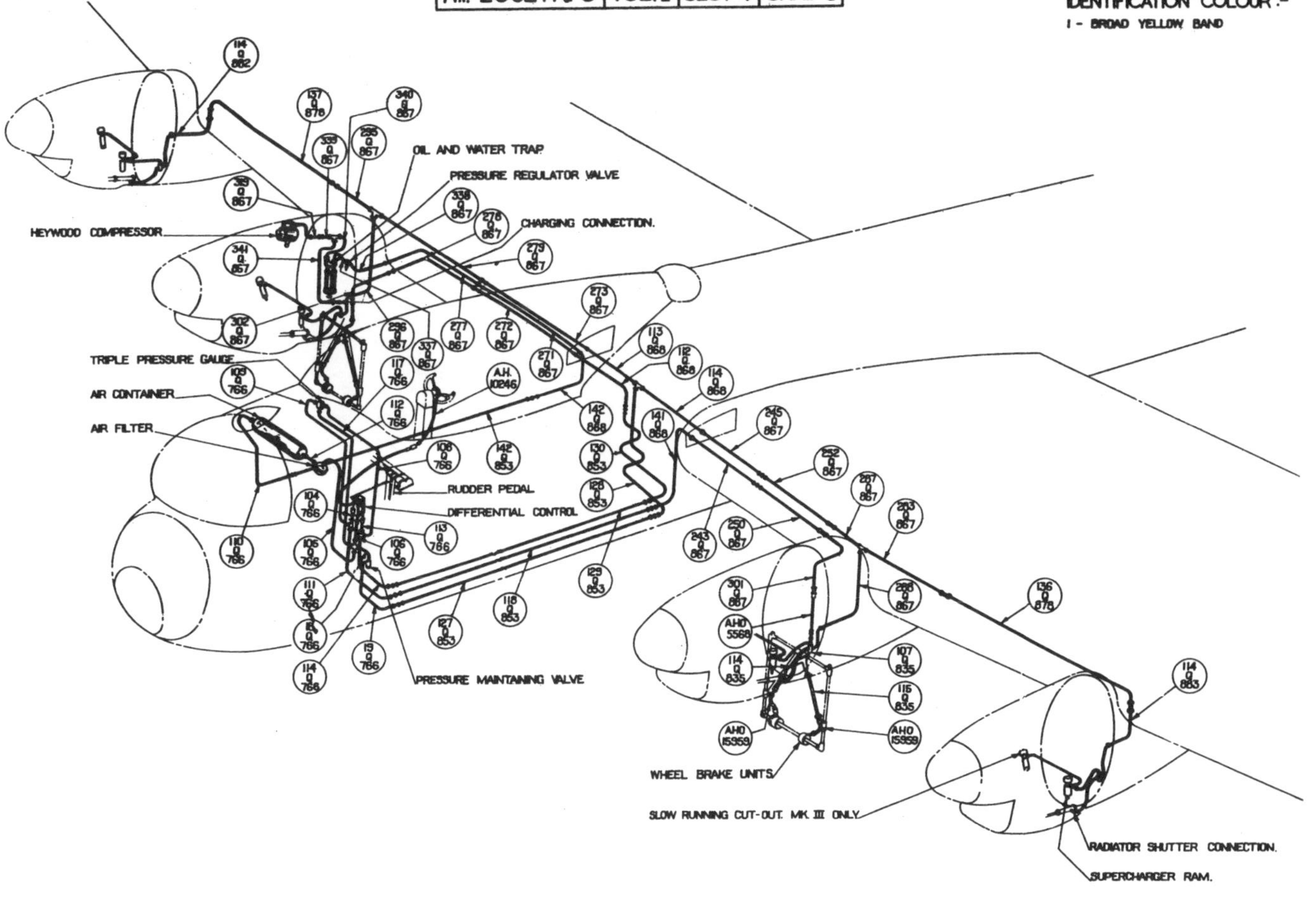

DIAGRAM OF PNEUMATIC SYSTEM

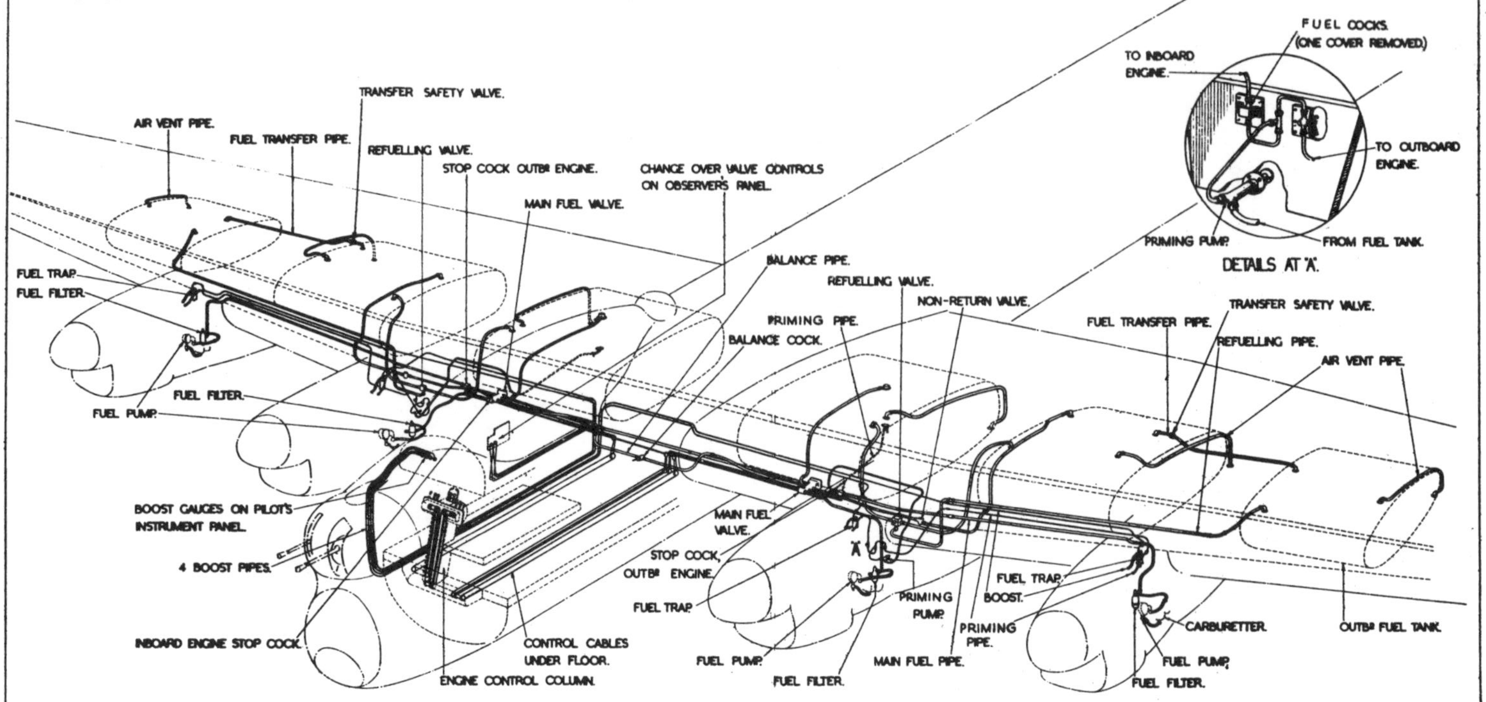

DIAGRAM OF FUEL SYSTEM

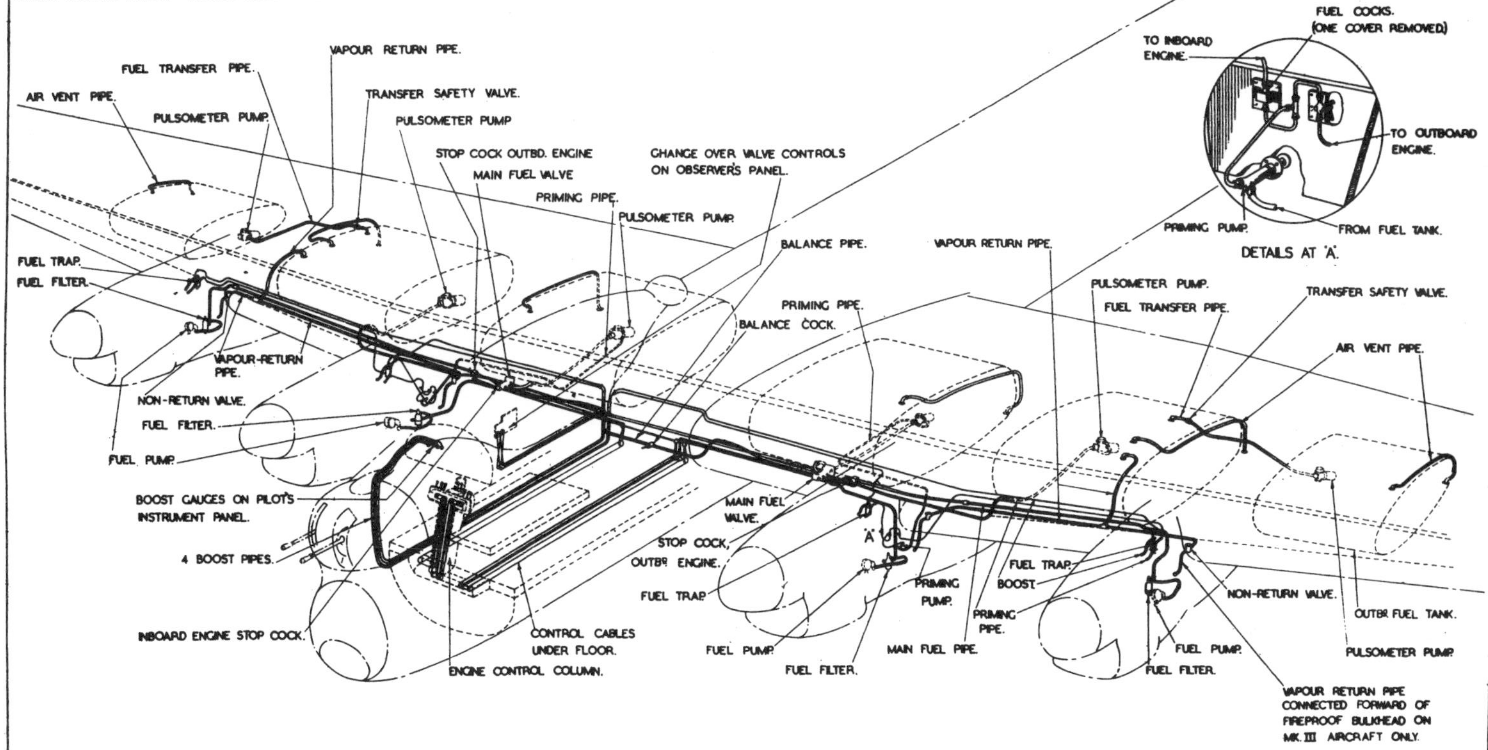

FIG. 10A

DIAGRAM OF FUEL SYSTEM
PULSOMETER F.B. MK. I PUMPS

FIG. 10A

DIAGRAM OF OIL SYSTEM - INBOARD ENGINE

A.P.2062A | VOL.I | SECT.4 | CHAP.3

IDENTIFICATION MARKING
1 BROAD BLACK BAND.

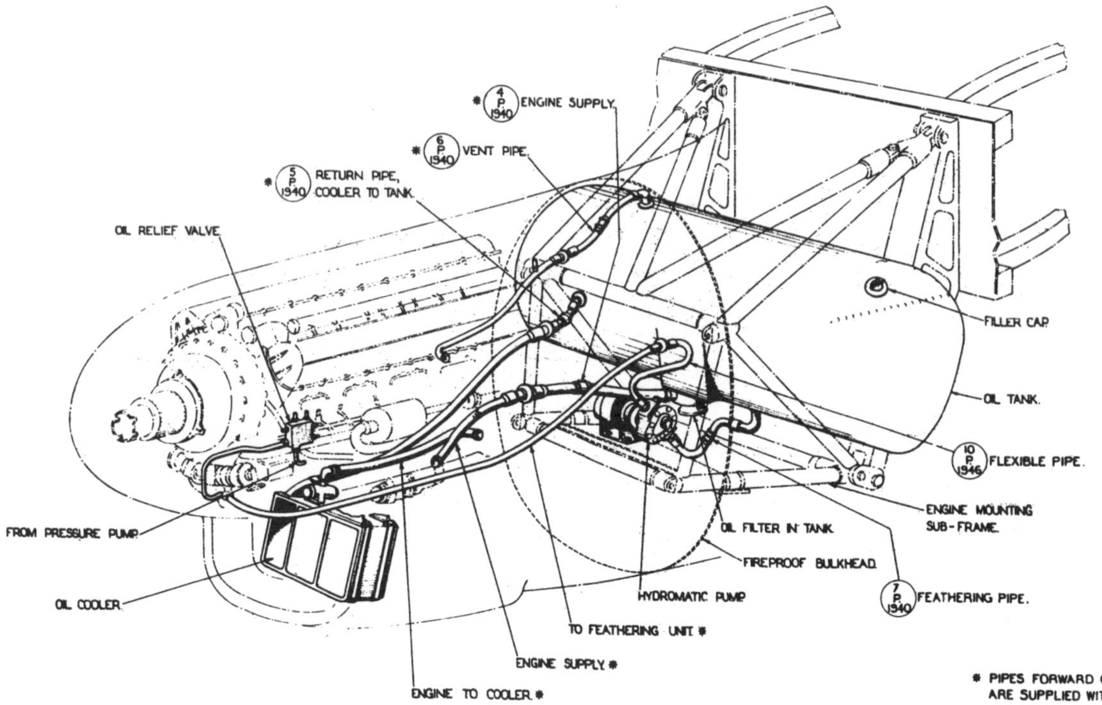

* PIPES FORWARD OF BULKHEAD ARE SUPPLIED WITH THE POWER UNIT

FILLER CAP
OIL TANK.
FLEXIBLE PIPE.
(10) P (546) ENGINE MOUNTING SUB-FRAME.
(7) P (540) FEATHERING PIPE.
FIREPROOF BULKHEAD
OIL FILTER IN TANK
HYDROMATIC PUMP
TO FEATHERING UNIT *
ENGINE SUPPLY *
ENGINE TO COOLER *
(4) P (540) ENGINE SUPPLY.
(6) P (540) VENT PIPE.
(5) P (540) RETURN PIPE, COOLER TO TANK.
OIL RELIEF VALVE
FROM PRESSURE PUMP
OIL COOLER

FIG. 11

IDENTIFICATION MARKING
I BROAD BLACK BAND.

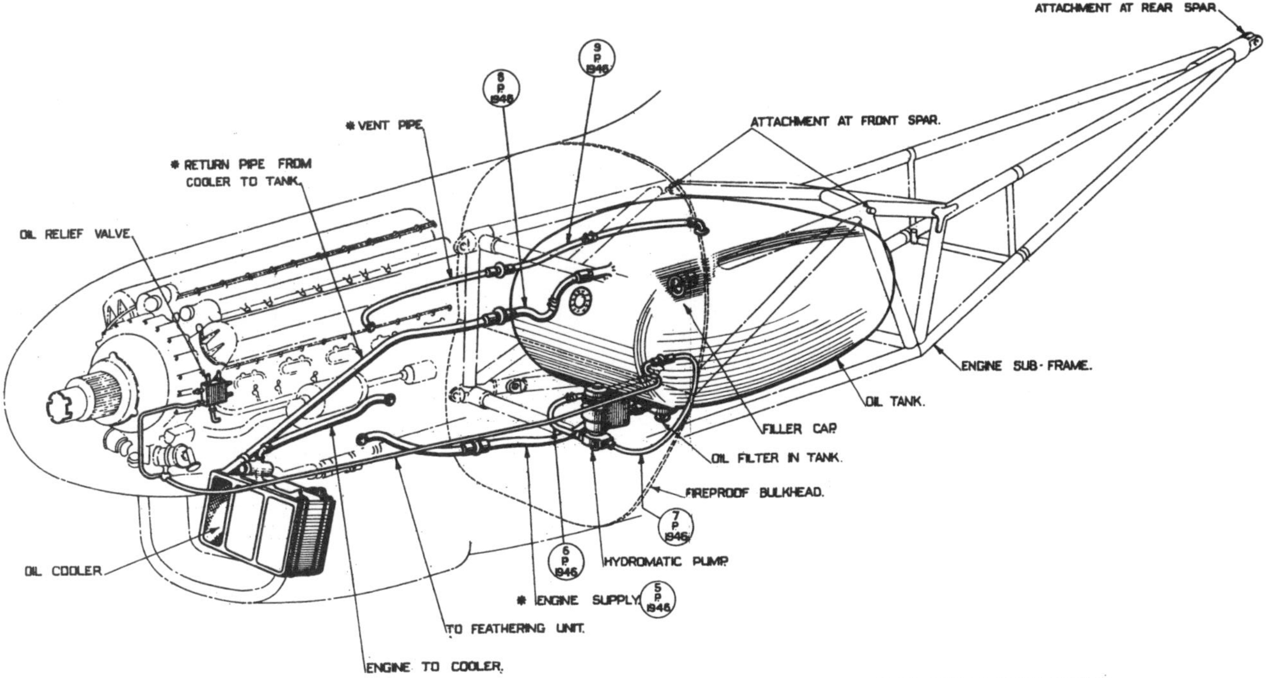

* ALL PIPES FORWARD OF BULKHEAD ARE SUPPLIED WITH THE POWER UNIT

FIG. 12

DIAGRAM OF OIL SYSTEM – OUTBOARD ENGINE.

FIG. 12

COOLING SYSTEM

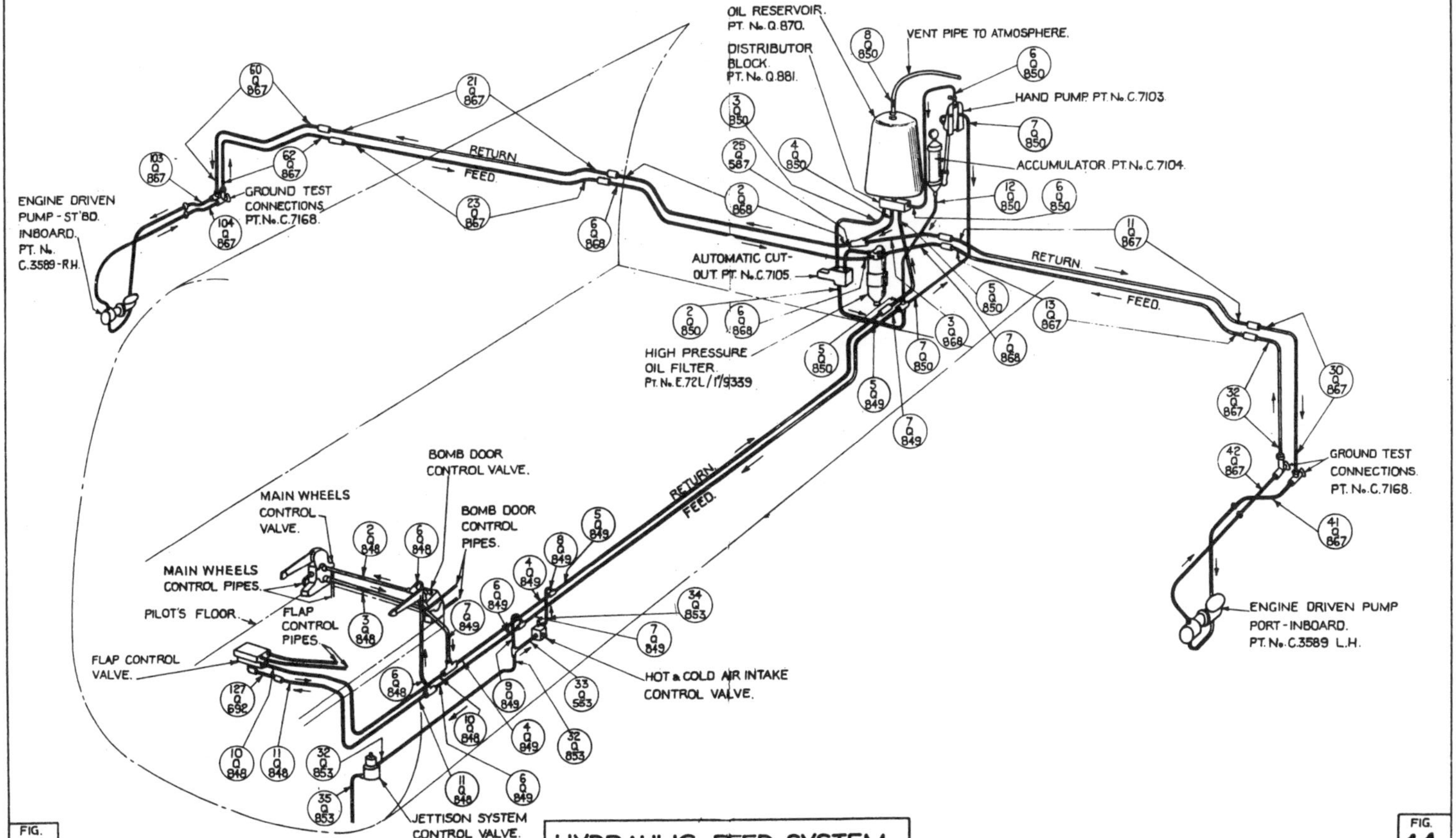

FIG. 14 HYDRAULIC FEED SYSTEM

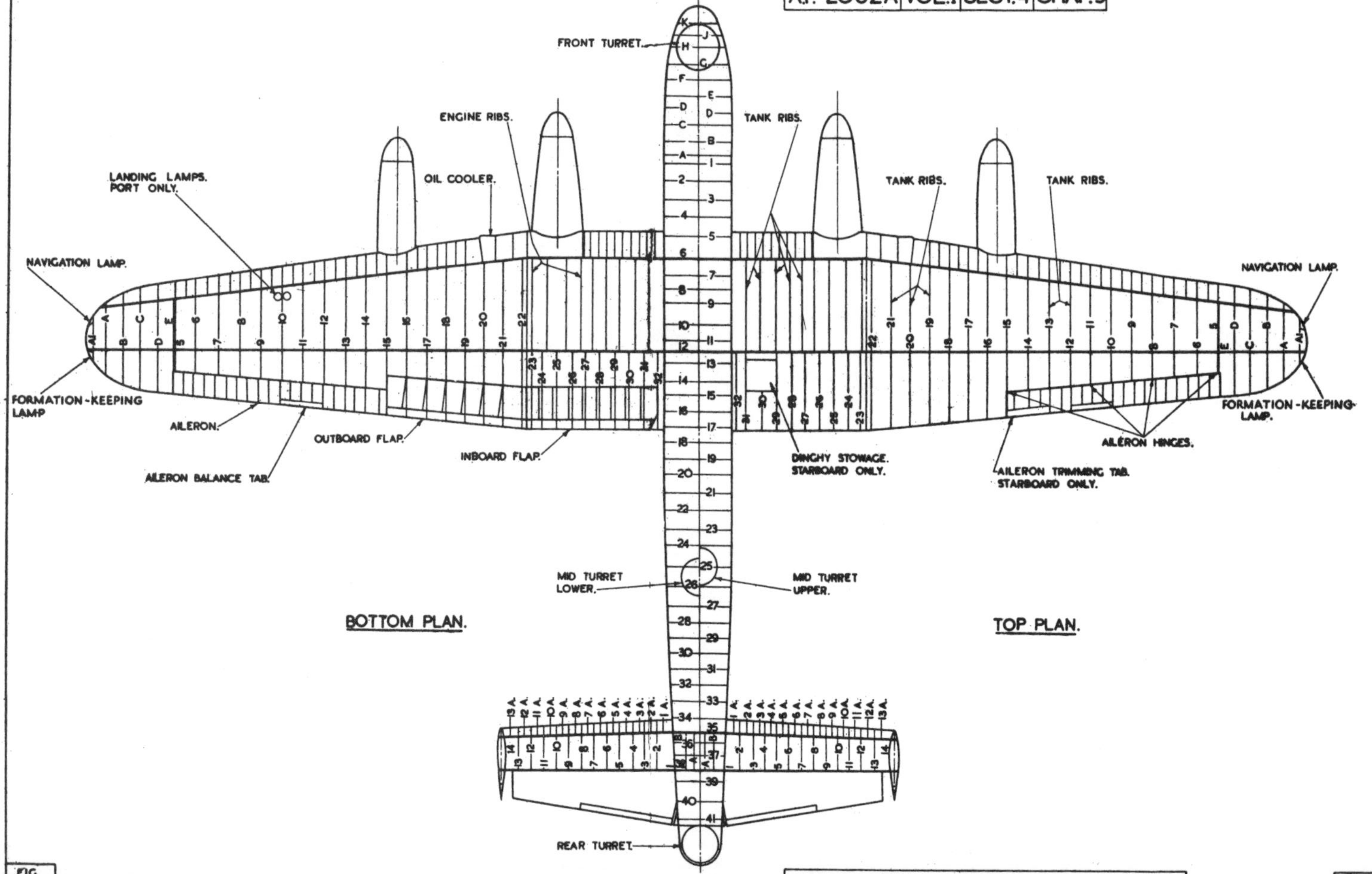

FIG. 15

FORMER & RIB POSITIONS

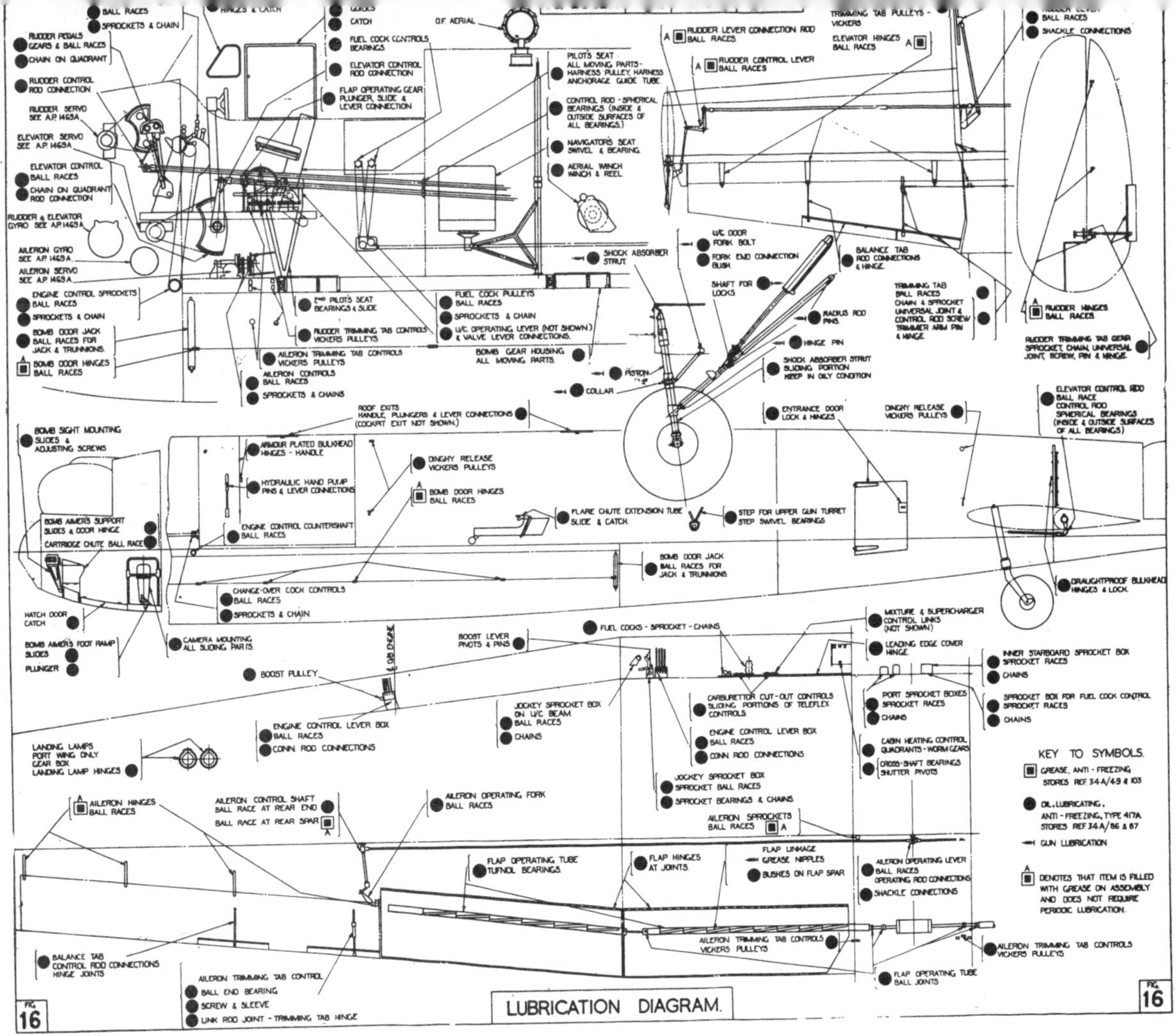

LUBRICATION DIAGRAM.

IDENTIFICATION MARKING.

1 - NARROW WHITE BAND
1 - BROAD YELLOW BAND
1 - NARROW WHITE BAND

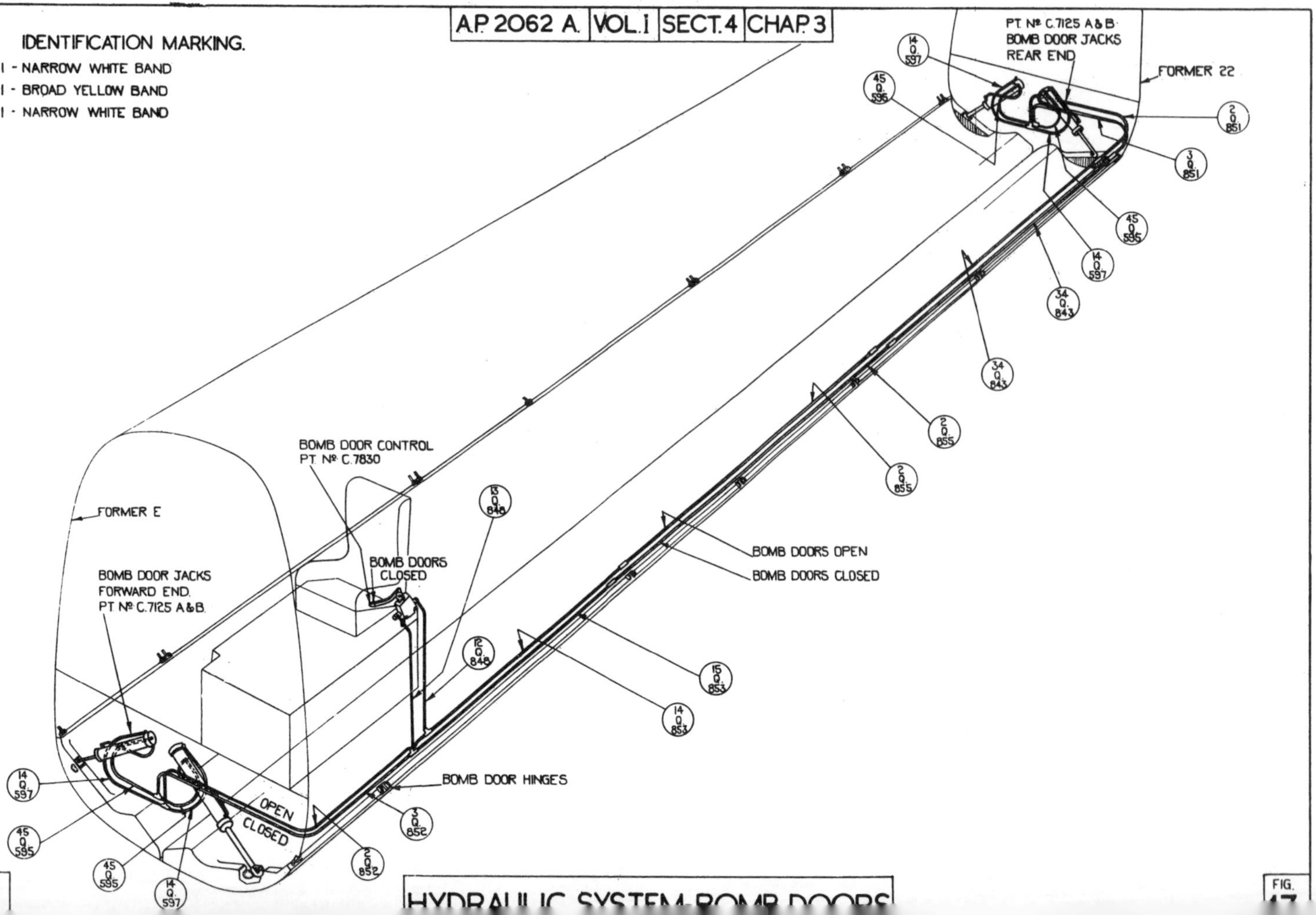

FIG. 17

HYDRAULIC SYSTEM-BOMB DOORS

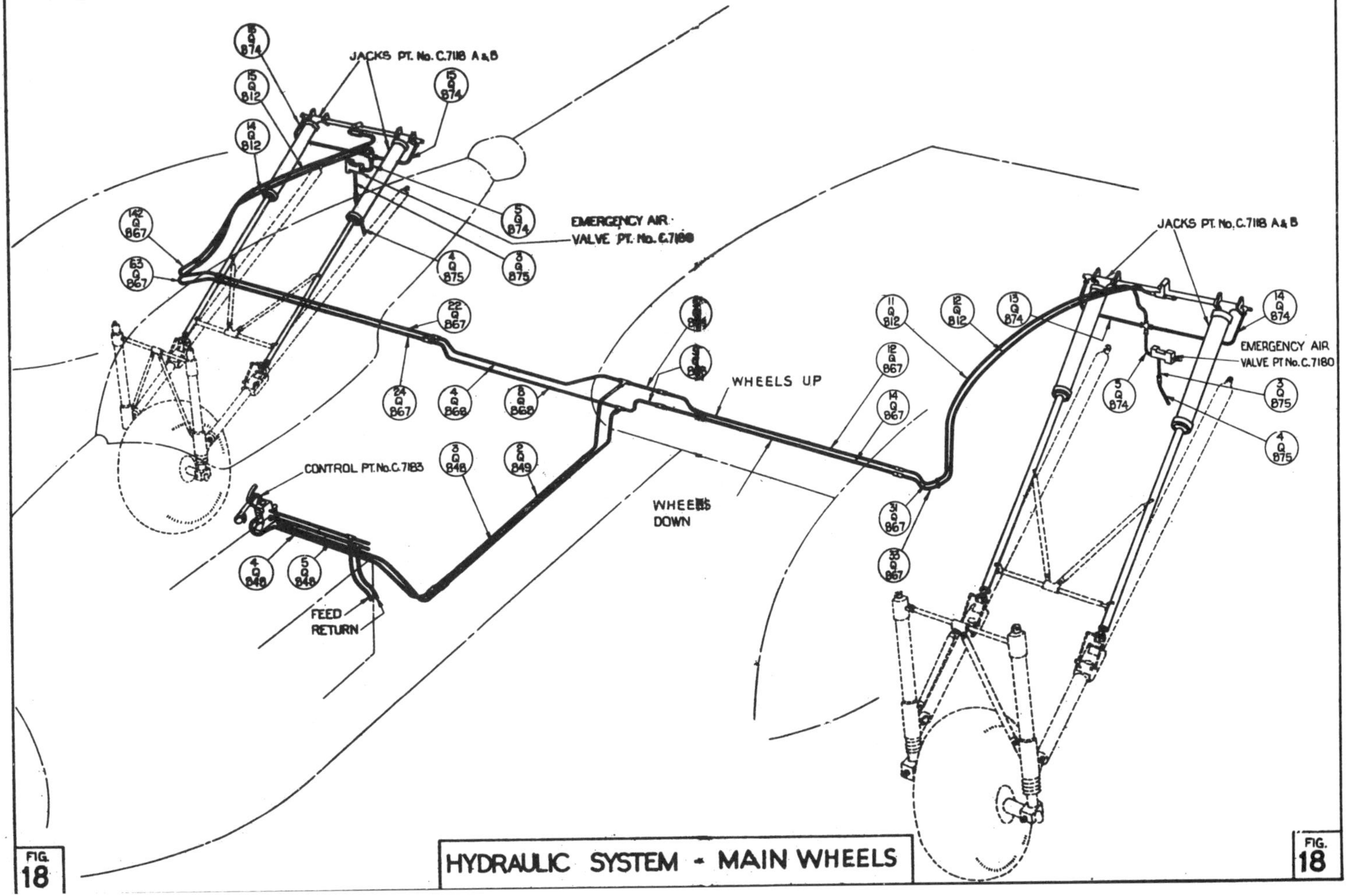

HYDRAULIC SYSTEM - MAIN WHEELS

1 - NARROW WHITE BAND
1 - BROAD RED BAND
1 - NARROW WHITE BAND

FIG. 18

IDENTIFICATION MARKING.

1 - NARROW WHITE BAND.
1 - BROAD GREEN BAND.
1 - NARROW WHITE BAND.

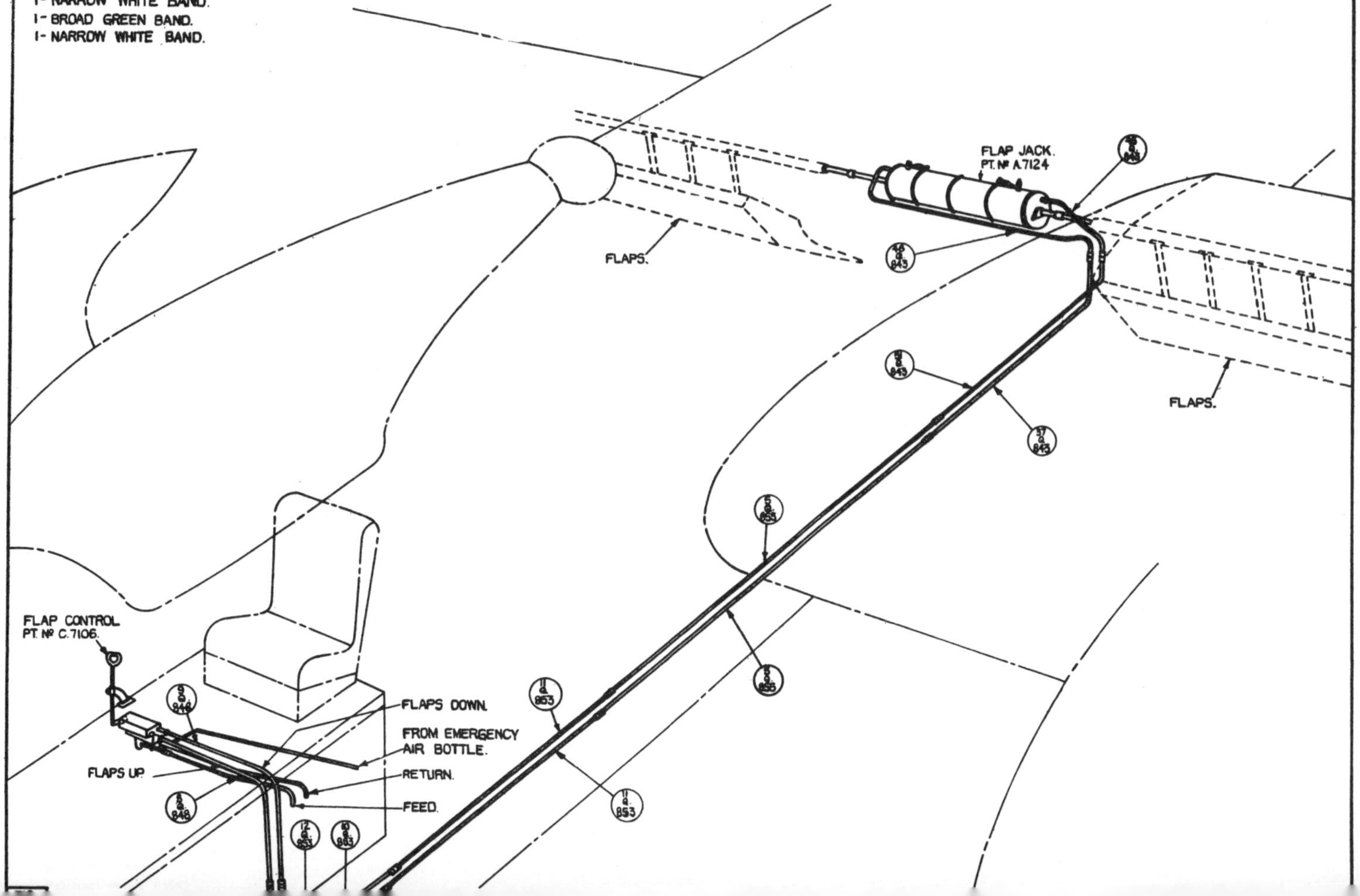

IDENTIFICATION MARKING.
1 - NARROW WHITE BAND.
1 - BROAD BROWN BAND.
1 - NARROW WHITE BAND.

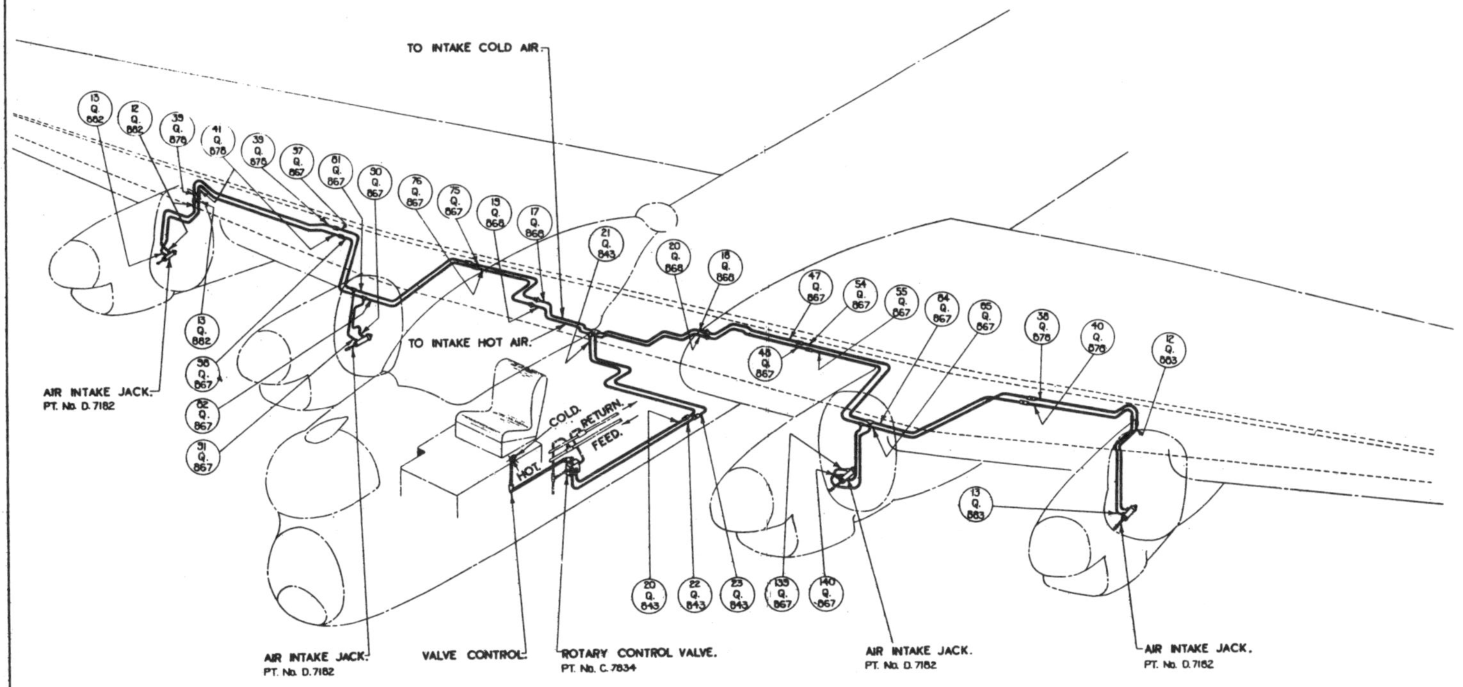

FIG. 20

HYDRAULIC SYSTEM - AIR INTAKES.

FIG. 20

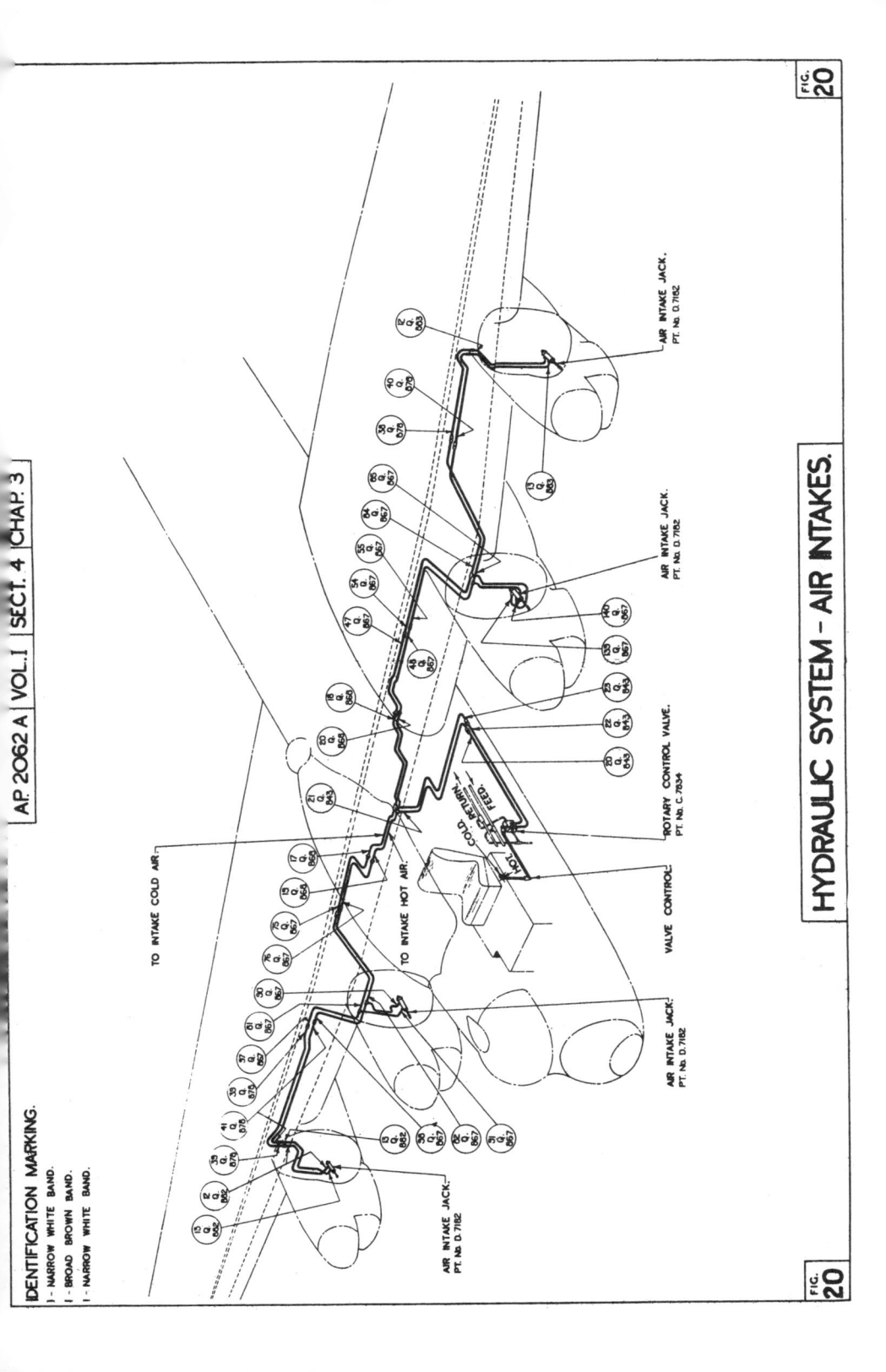

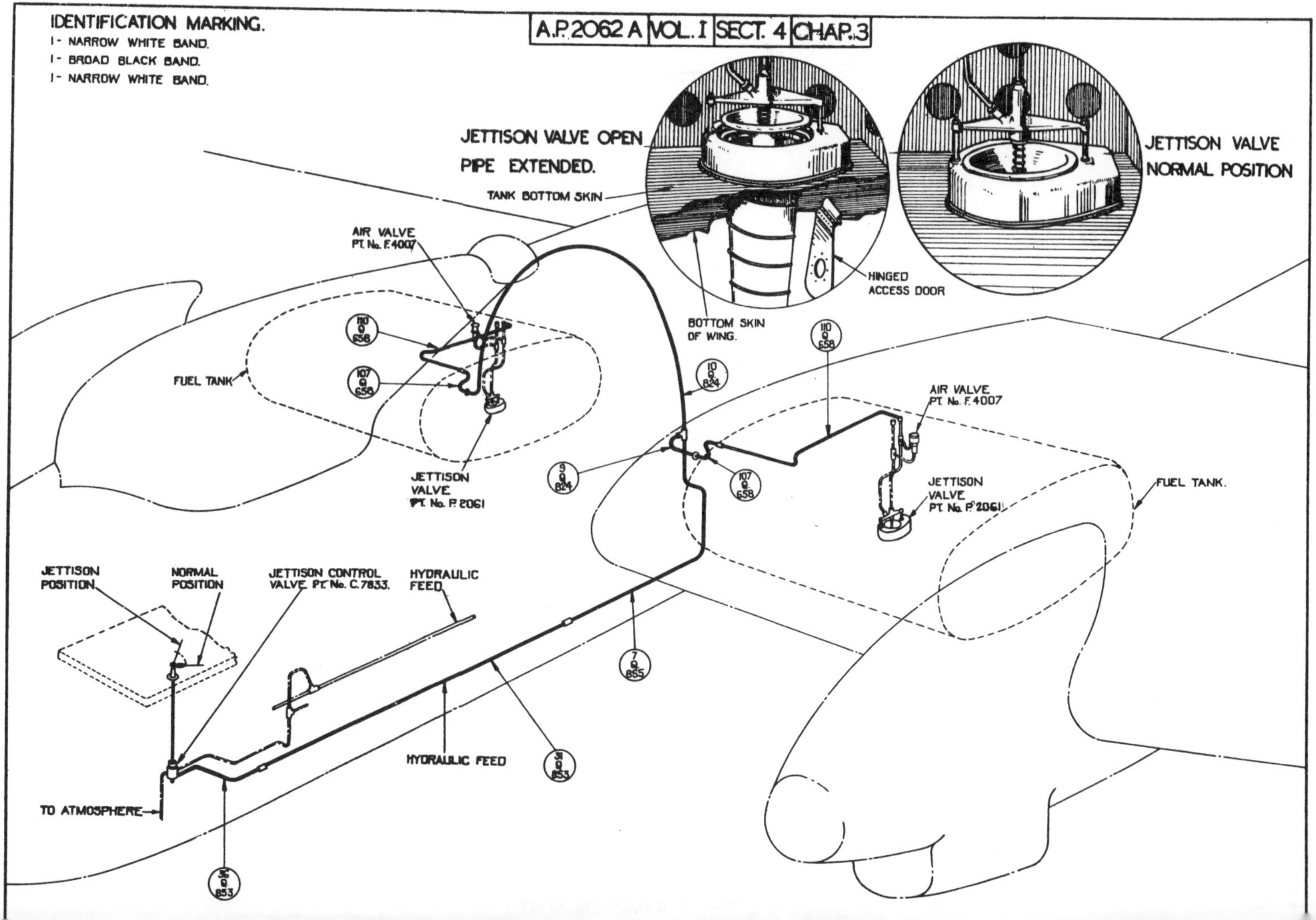
IDENTIFICATION MARKING.
1- NARROW WHITE BAND.
1- BROAD BLACK BAND.
1- NARROW WHITE BAND.
JETTISON VALVE OPEN
PIPE EXTENDED.
TANK BOTTOM SKIN
JETTISON VALVE
NORMAL POSITION
HINGED
ACCESS DOOR
BOTTOM SKIN
OF WING.
AIR VALVE
PT. No. F.4007
FUEL TANK
110 Q 658
107 Q 658
JETTISON
VALVE
PT. No. P. 2061
10 Q 824
9 Q 824
AIR VALVE
PT. No. F.4007
JETTISON
VALVE
PT. No. P. 2061
FUEL TANK.
JETTISON
POSITION
NORMAL
POSITION
JETTISON CONTROL
VALVE PT. No. C.7833.
HYDRAULIC
FEED
7 Q 855
HYDRAULIC FEED
31 Q 853
TO ATMOSPHERE
36 Q 853

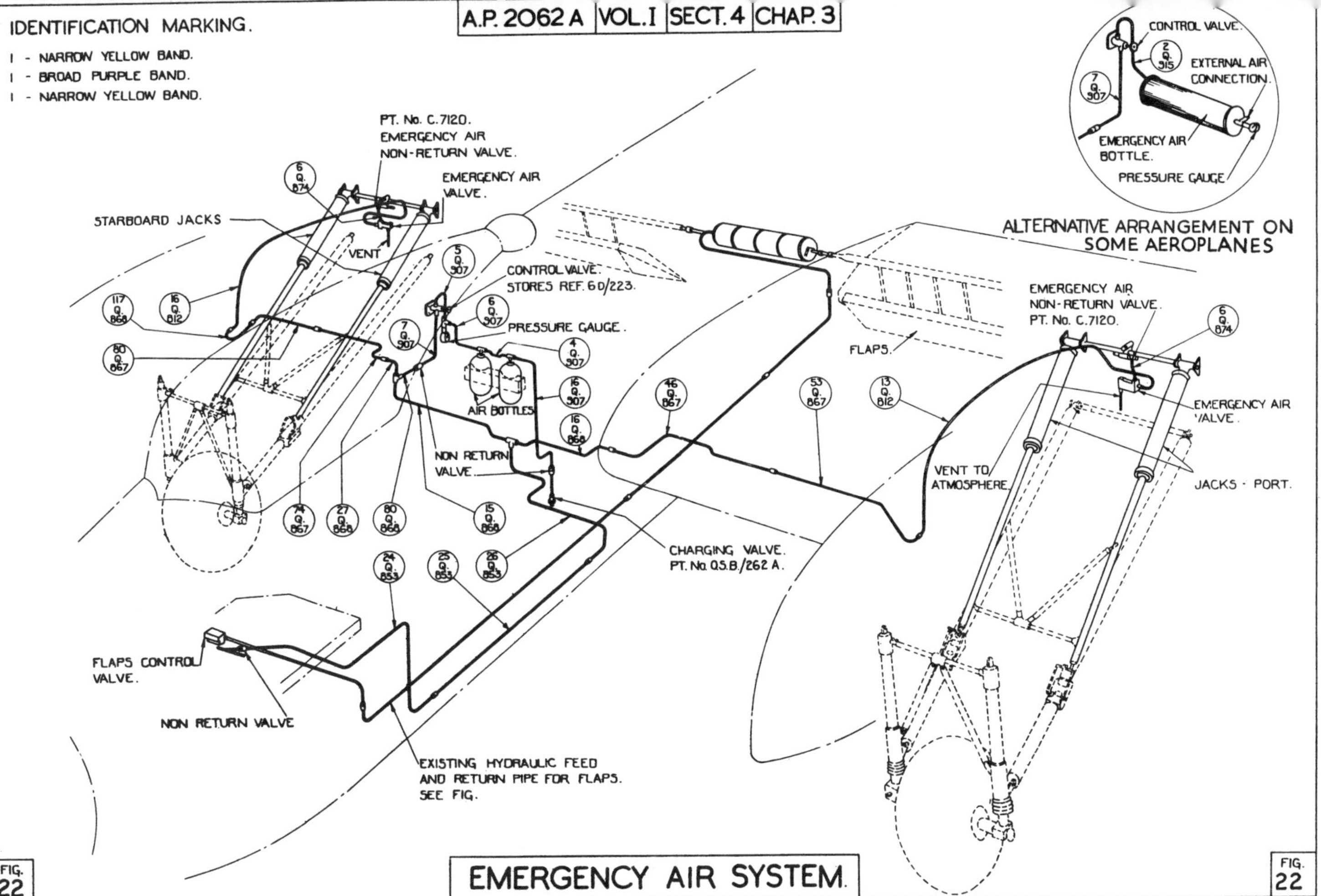

EMERGENCY AIR SYSTEM.

FIG. 22

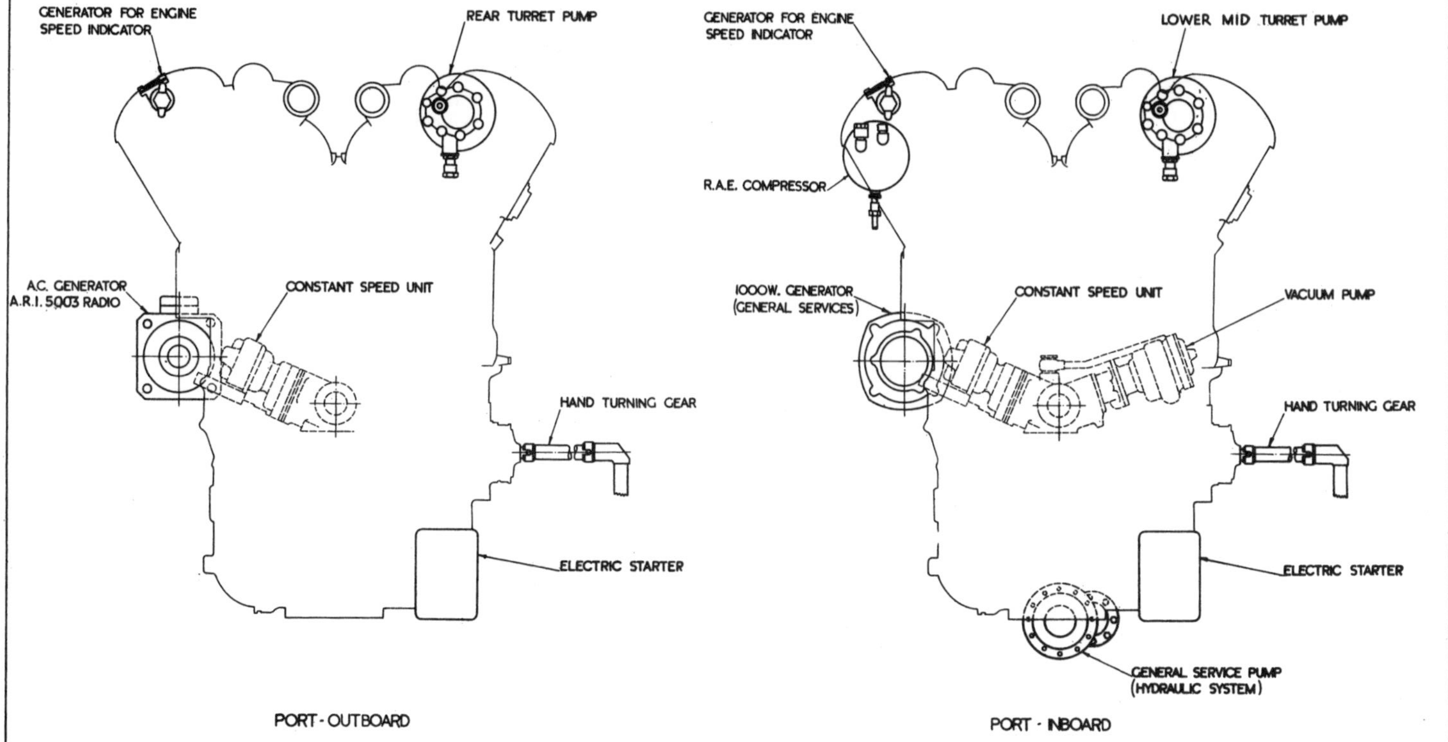

VIEW ON BACK OF ENGINE
LOOKING FORWARD

FIG 23

ENGINE AUXILIARIES - PORT

FIG 23

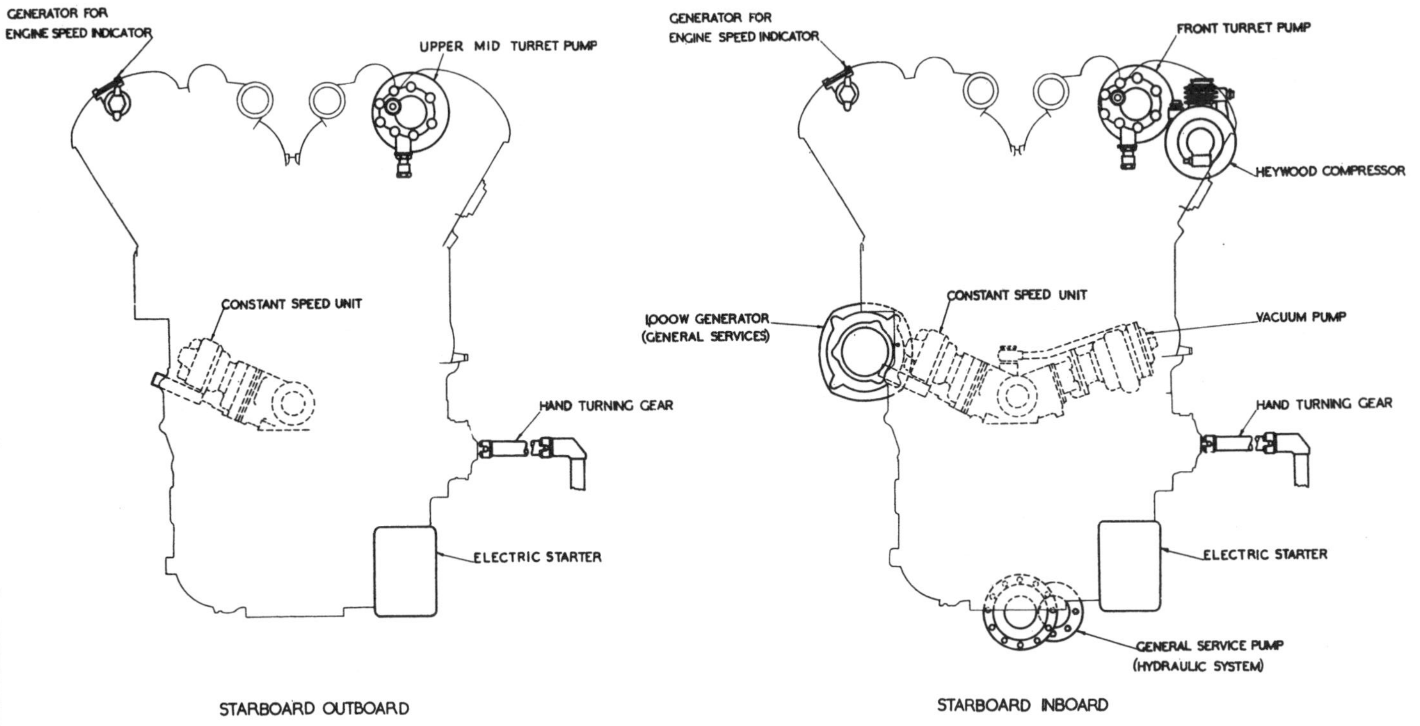

ENGINE AUXILIARIES - STARBOARD

FIG. 24

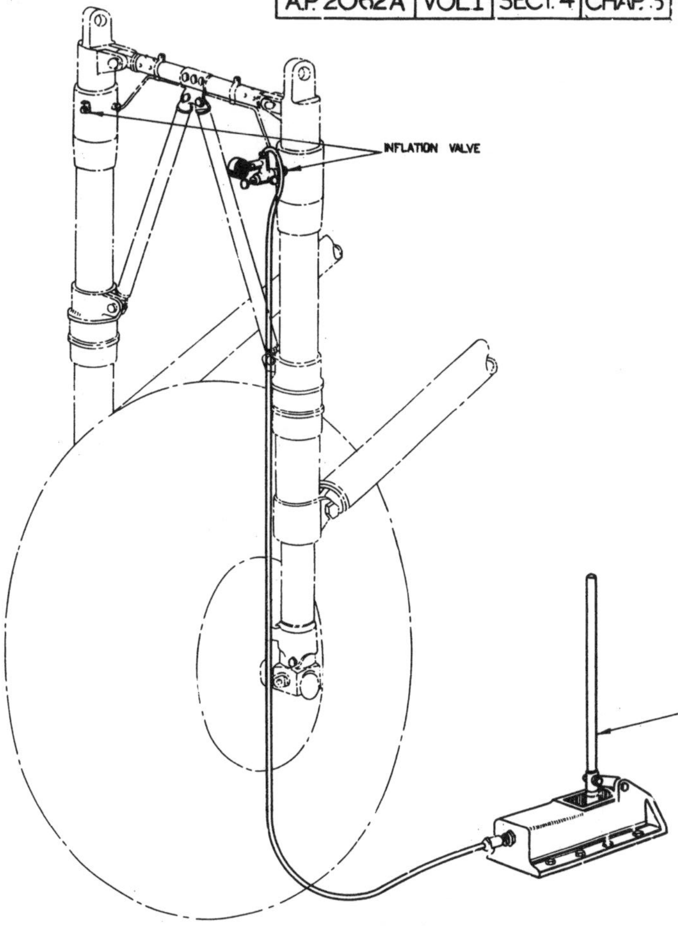

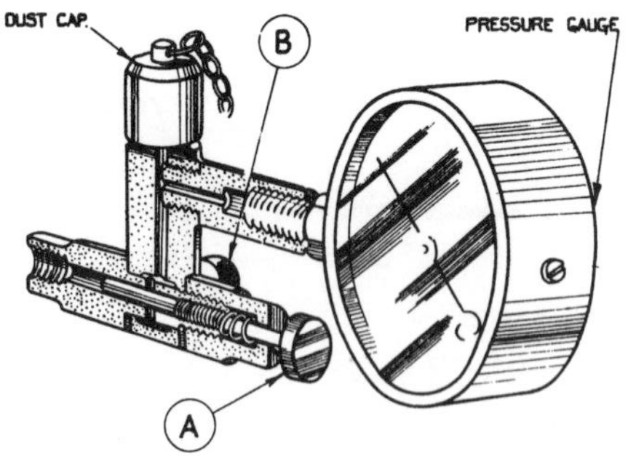

DETAIL OF INFLATION ADAPTOR PART Nº C.7704

FIG. 25

MAIN WHEELS SHOCK-ABSORBER STRUT INFL[illegible]ION

FIG.

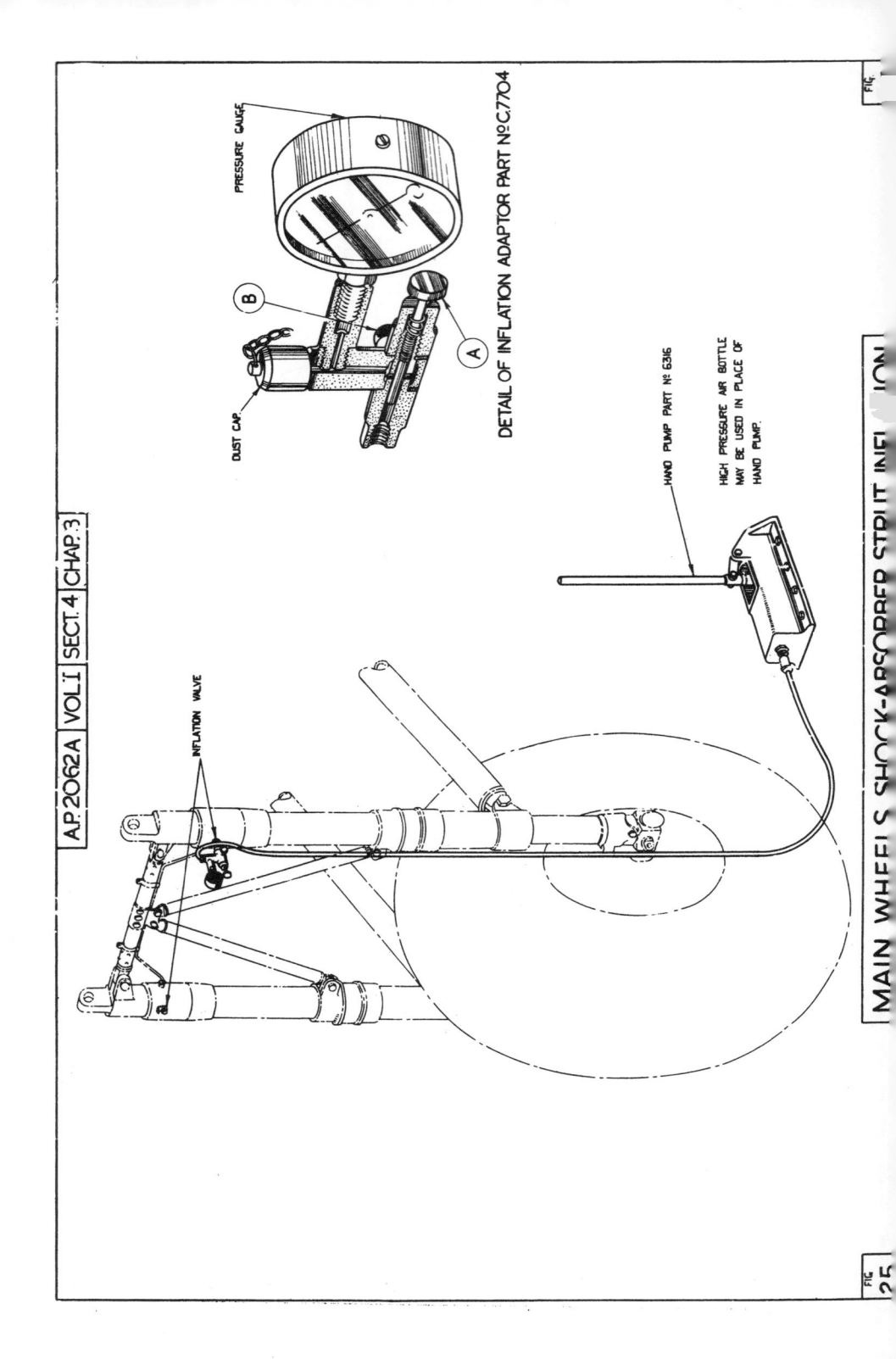

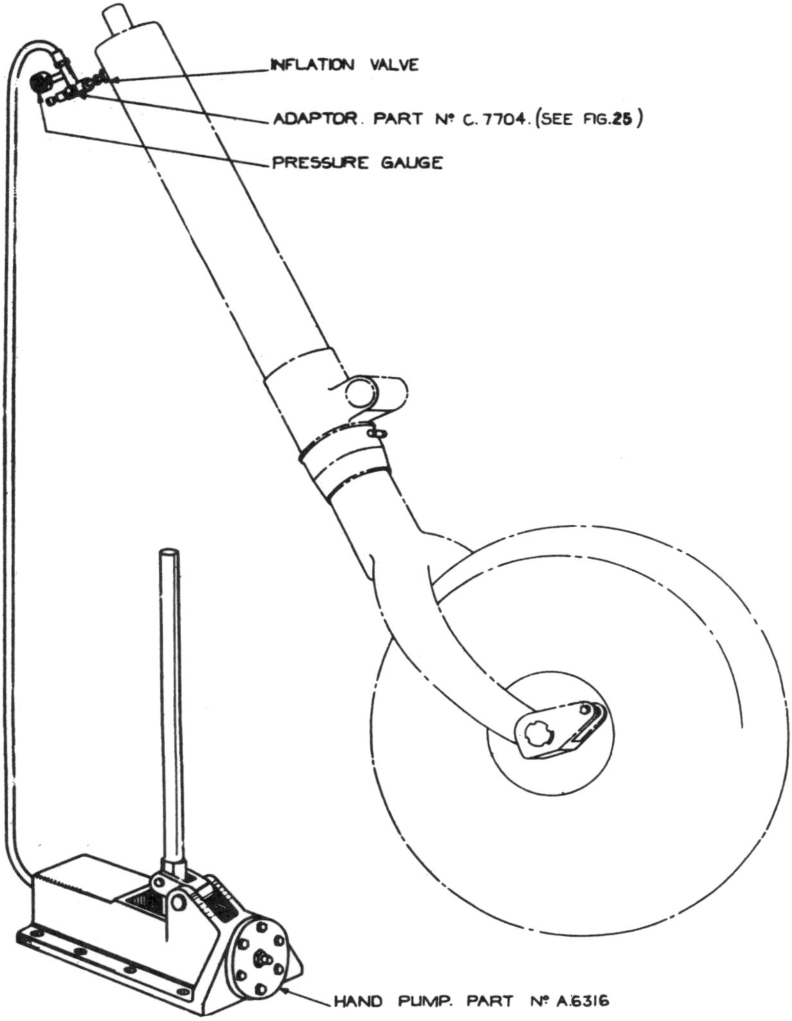

FIG. 26 — TAIL WHEEL SHOCK-ABSORBER STRUT INFLATION

A.P. 2062 A | VOL. I | SECT. 4 | CHAP. 3

- INFLATION VALVE
- ADAPTOR. PART Nº C.7704. (SEE FIG. 25)
- PRESSURE GAUGE
- HAND PUMP. PART Nº A.6316

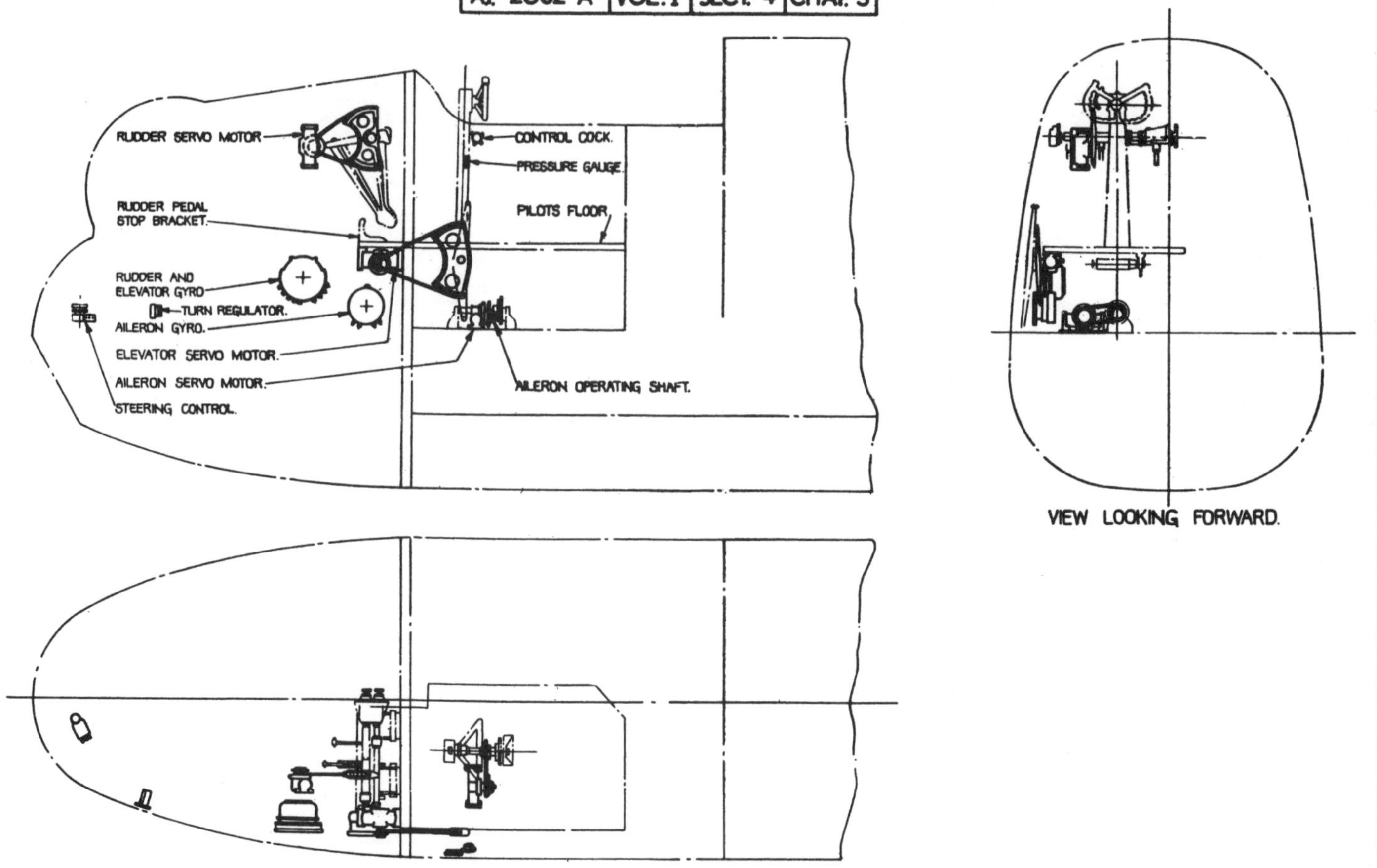

AP 2062 A | VOL. I | SECT. 4 | CHAP. 3

VIEW LOOKING FORWARD.

- CONTROL COCK
- PRESSURE GAUGE
- PILOTS FLOOR.
- AILERON OPERATING SHAFT.
- RUDDER SERVO MOTOR.
- RUDDER PEDAL STOP BRACKET.
- RUDDER AND ELEVATOR GYRO.
- AILERON GYRO.
- TURN REGULATOR.
- ELEVATOR SERVO MOTOR.
- AILERON SERVO MOTOR.
- STEERING CONTROL.

DIAGRAM OF AUTOMATIC CONTROL S

FIG. 27

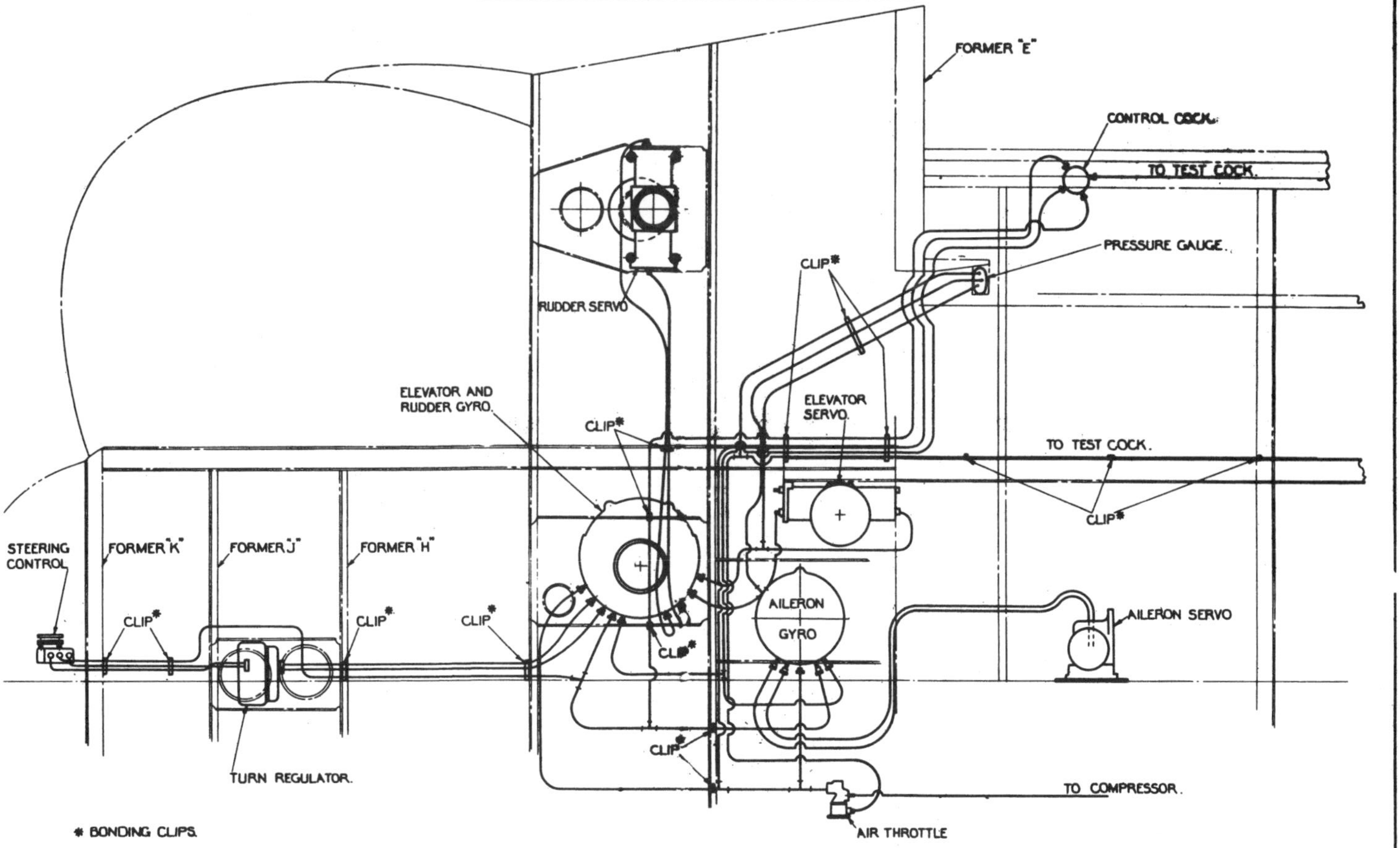

A.P. 2062A | VOL.I | SECT.4 | CHAP. 3.

FIG. 28

DIAGRAM OF PIPES FOR AUTOMATIC CONTROLS.

VACUUM SYSTEM

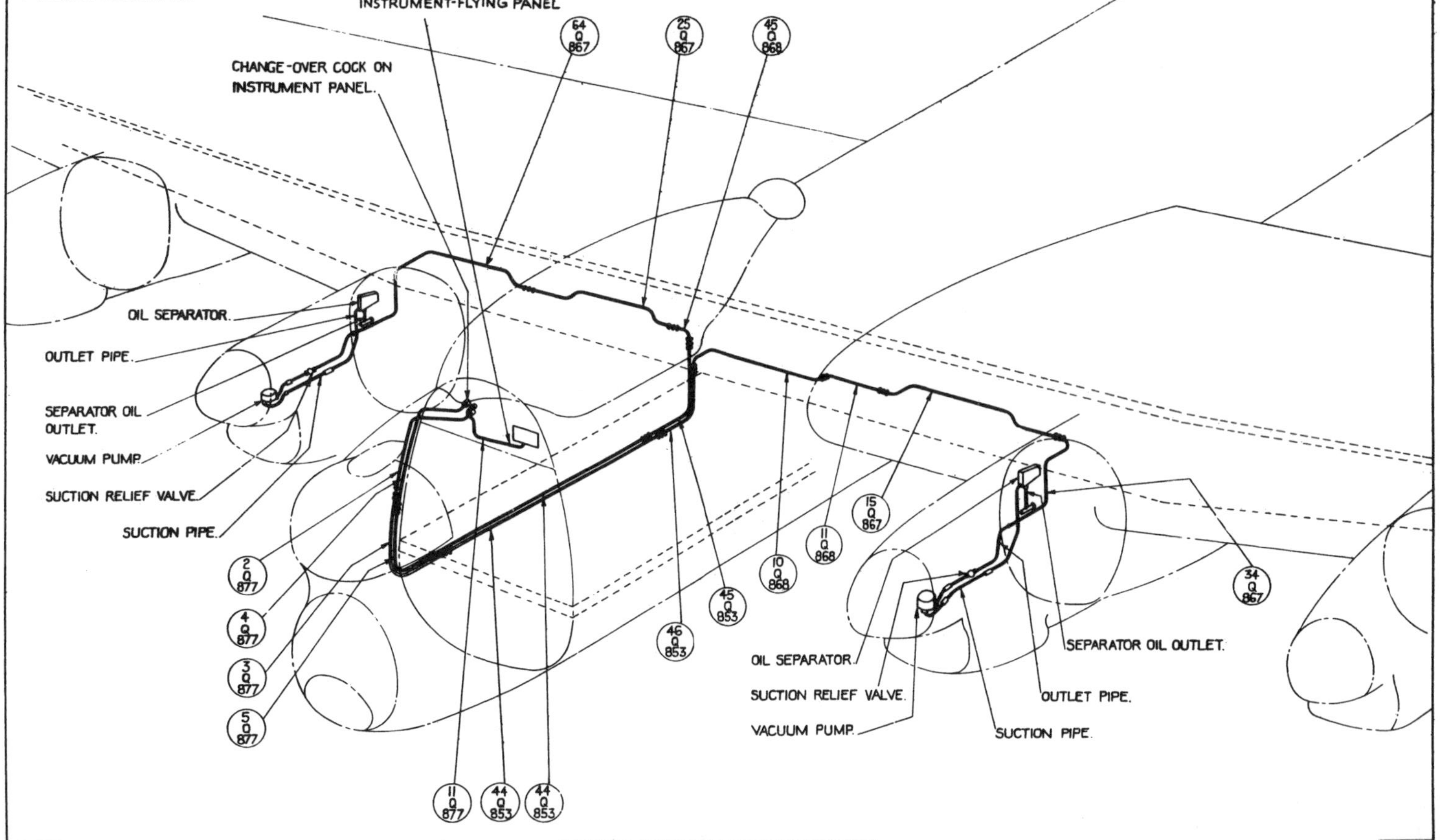

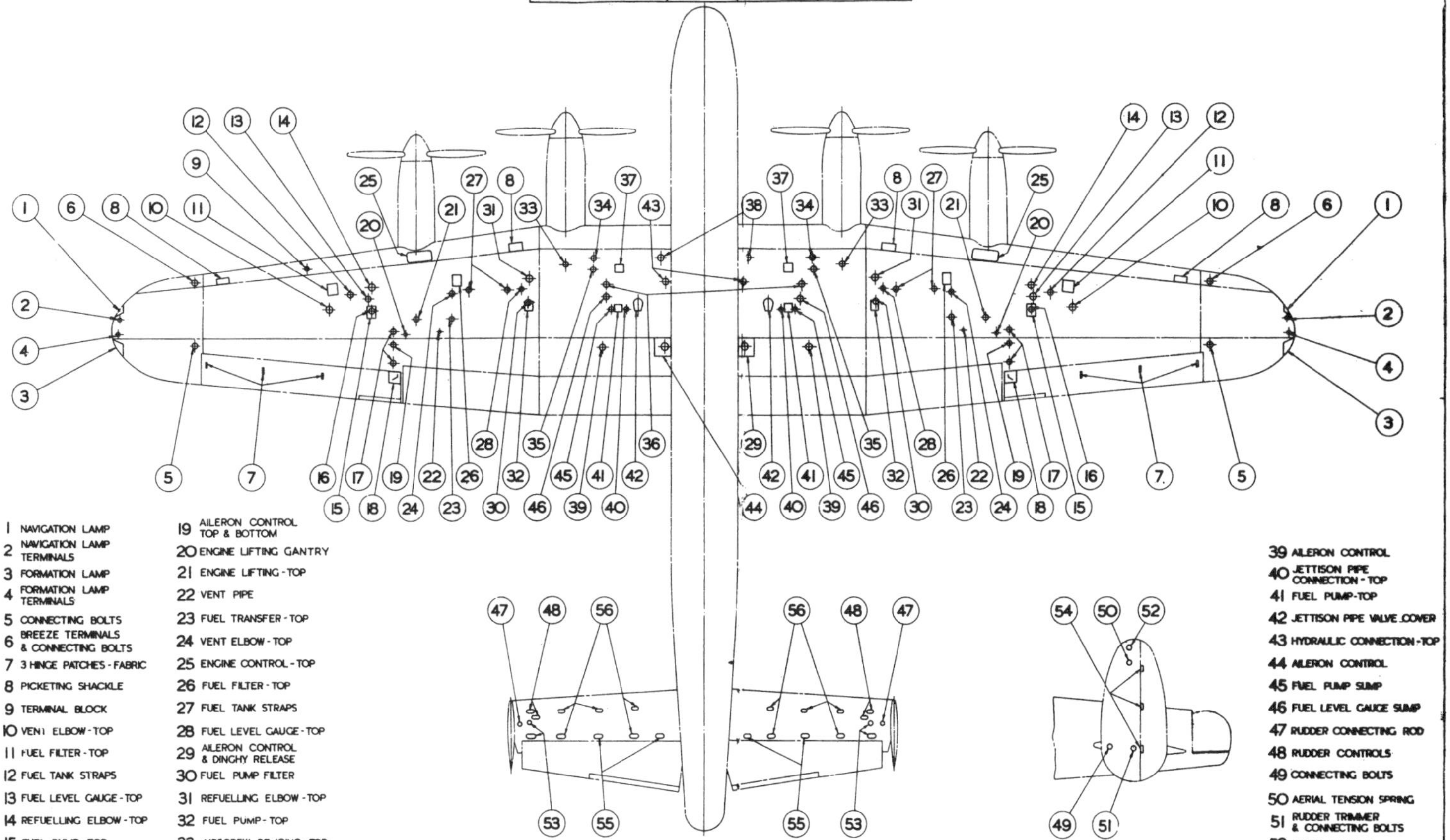

ACCESS & INSPECTION PANELS

1. NAVIGATION LAMP
2. NAVIGATION LAMP TERMINALS
3. FORMATION LAMP
4. FORMATION LAMP TERMINALS
5. CONNECTING BOLTS
6. BREEZE TERMINALS
7. 3 HINGE PATCHES - FABRIC & CONNECTING BOLTS
8. PICKETING SHACKLE
9. TERMINAL BLOCK
10. VENT ELBOW - TOP
11. FUEL FILTER - TOP
12. FUEL TANK STRAPS
13. FUEL LEVEL GAUGE - TOP
14. REFUELLING ELBOW - TOP
15. FUEL PUMP - TOP
16. FUEL PUMP FILTER
17. AILERON CONTROL
18. AILERON CONTROL ARM
19. AILERON CONTROL TOP & BOTTOM
20. ENGINE LIFTING GANTRY
21. ENGINE LIFTING - TOP
22. VENT PIPE
23. FUEL TRANSFER - TOP
24. VENT ELBOW - TOP
25. ENGINE CONTROL - TOP
26. FUEL FILTER - TOP
27. FUEL TANK STRAPS
28. FUEL LEVEL GAUGE - TOP
29. AILERON CONTROL & DINGHY RELEASE
30. FUEL PUMP FILTER
31. REFUELLING ELBOW - TOP
32. FUEL PUMP - TOP
33. AIRSCREW DE-ICING - TOP
34. REFUELLING CONNECTION - TOP
35. AIR VENT - TOP
36. FUEL LEVEL GAUGE - TOP
37. FUEL FILLER - TOP
38. EXTRA REFUELLING ELBOW - TOP (WHEN REQUIRED)
39. AILERON CONTROL
40. JETTISON PIPE CONNECTION - TOP
41. FUEL PUMP - TOP
42. JETTISON PIPE VALVE COVER
43. HYDRAULIC CONNECTION - TOP
44. AILERON CONTROL
45. FUEL PUMP SUMP
46. FUEL LEVEL GAUGE SUMP
47. RUDDER CONNECTING ROD
48. RUDDER CONTROLS
49. CONNECTING BOLTS
50. AERIAL TENSION SPRING
51. RUDDER TRIMMER & CONNECTING BOLTS
52. AERIAL PULLEY
53. RUDDER CONTROLS TOP & BOTTOM
54. RUDDER HINGE CUFFS
55. HINGE BOLTS
56. FAIRLEAD

ALL PANELS ARE IN THE BOTTOM SKIN EXCEPT WHERE STATED OTHERWISE

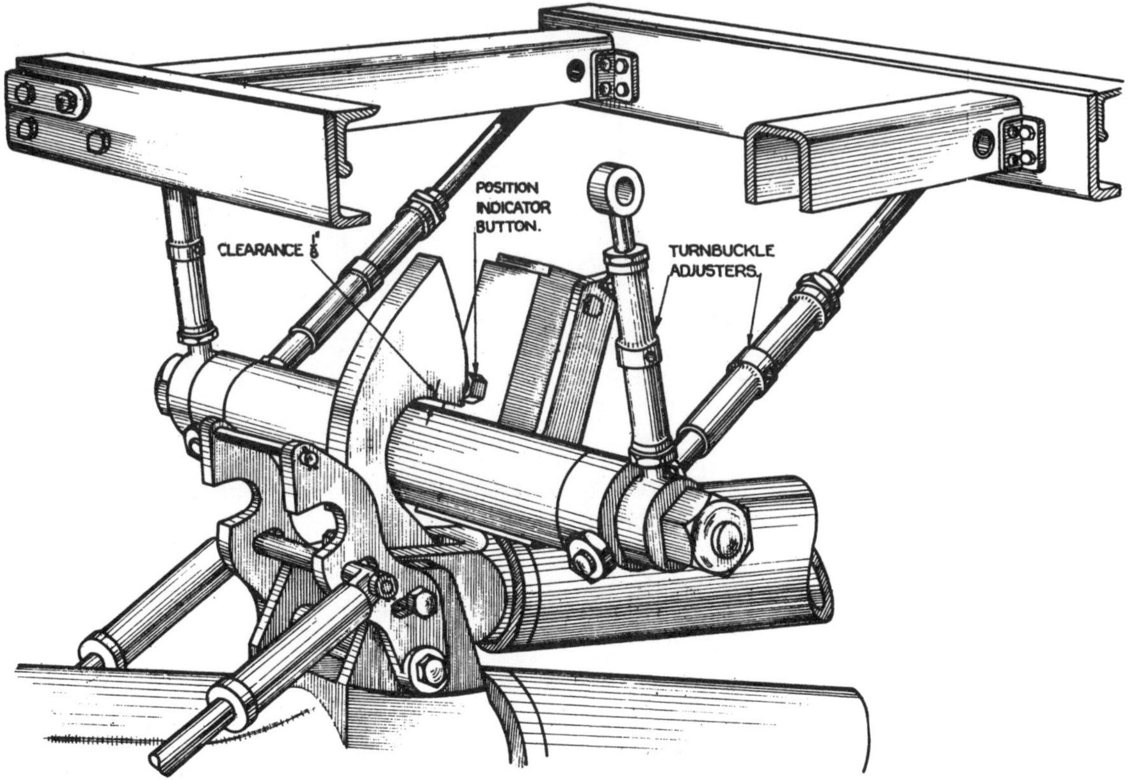
POSITION
INDICATOR
BUTTON.
CLEARANCE $\frac{1}{8}''$
TURNBUCKLE
ADJUSTERS.

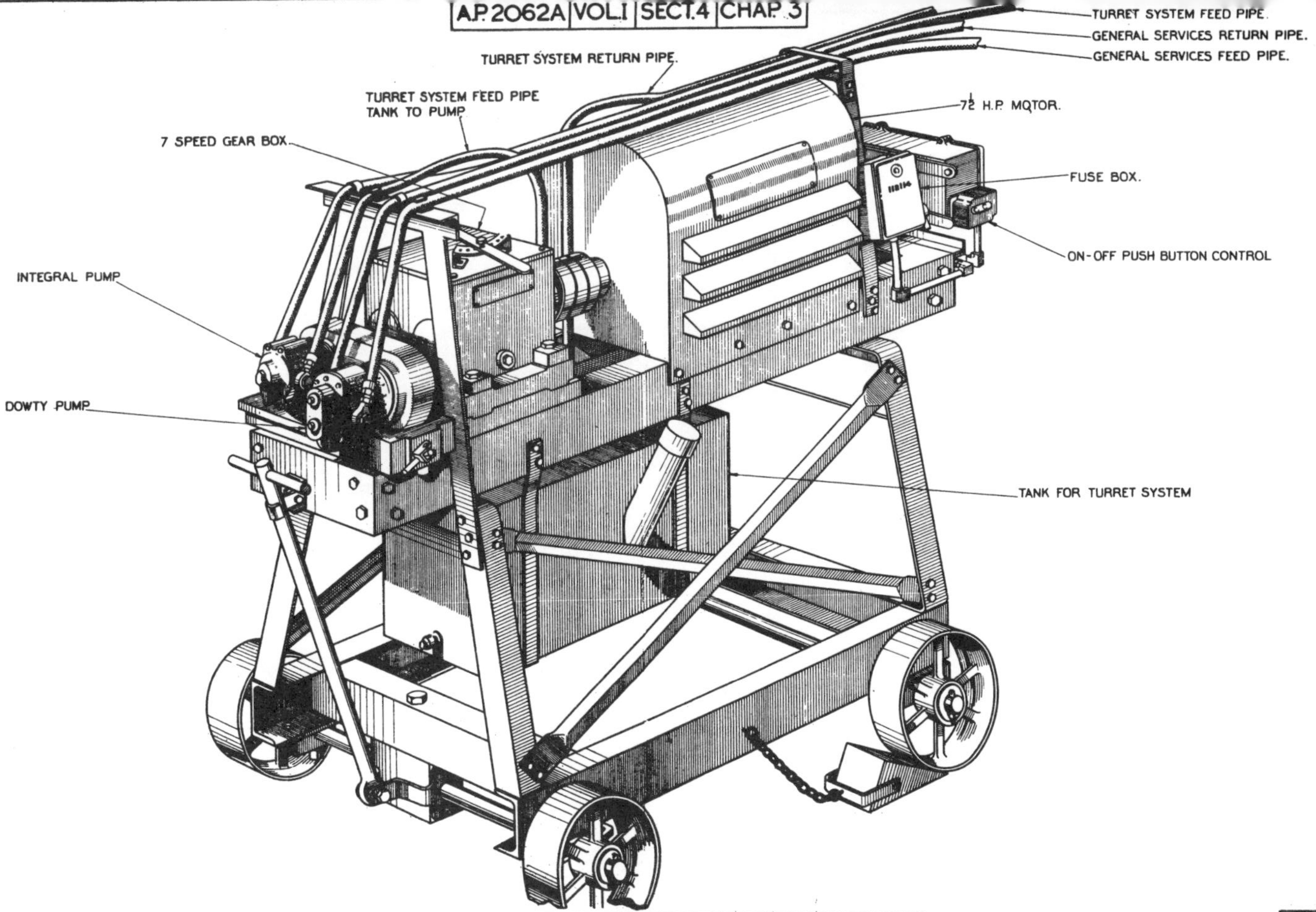

FIG. 32

HYDRAULIC SYSTEM GROUND TEST RIG

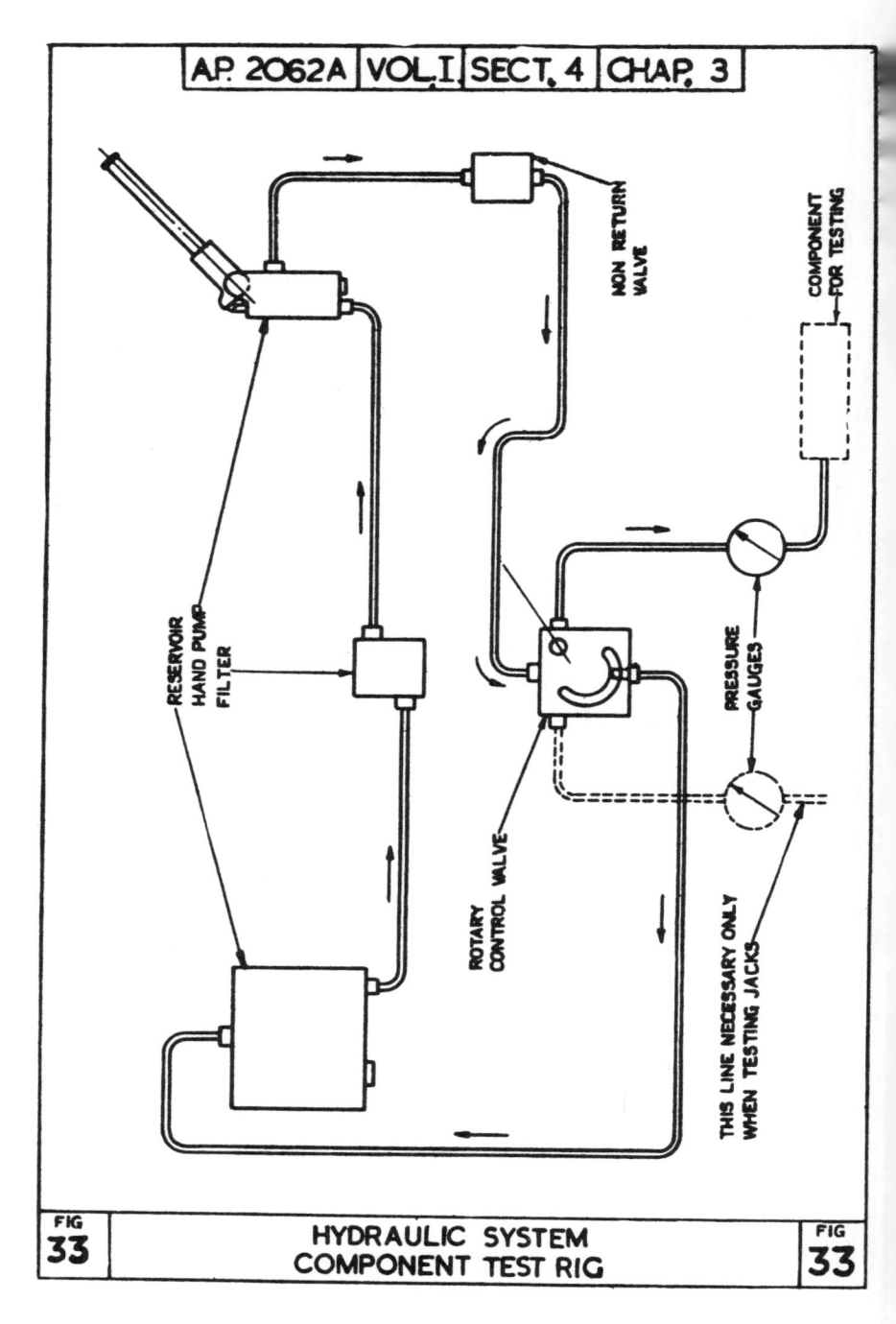

A.P. 2062A | VOL.I | SECT. 4 | CHAP. 3

HYDRAULIC SYSTEM COMPONENT TEST RIG

FIG 33

THIS PAGE AMENDED BY A.L. Nº 20

A.P. 2062 A | VOL. I | SECT. 4 | CHAP. 3

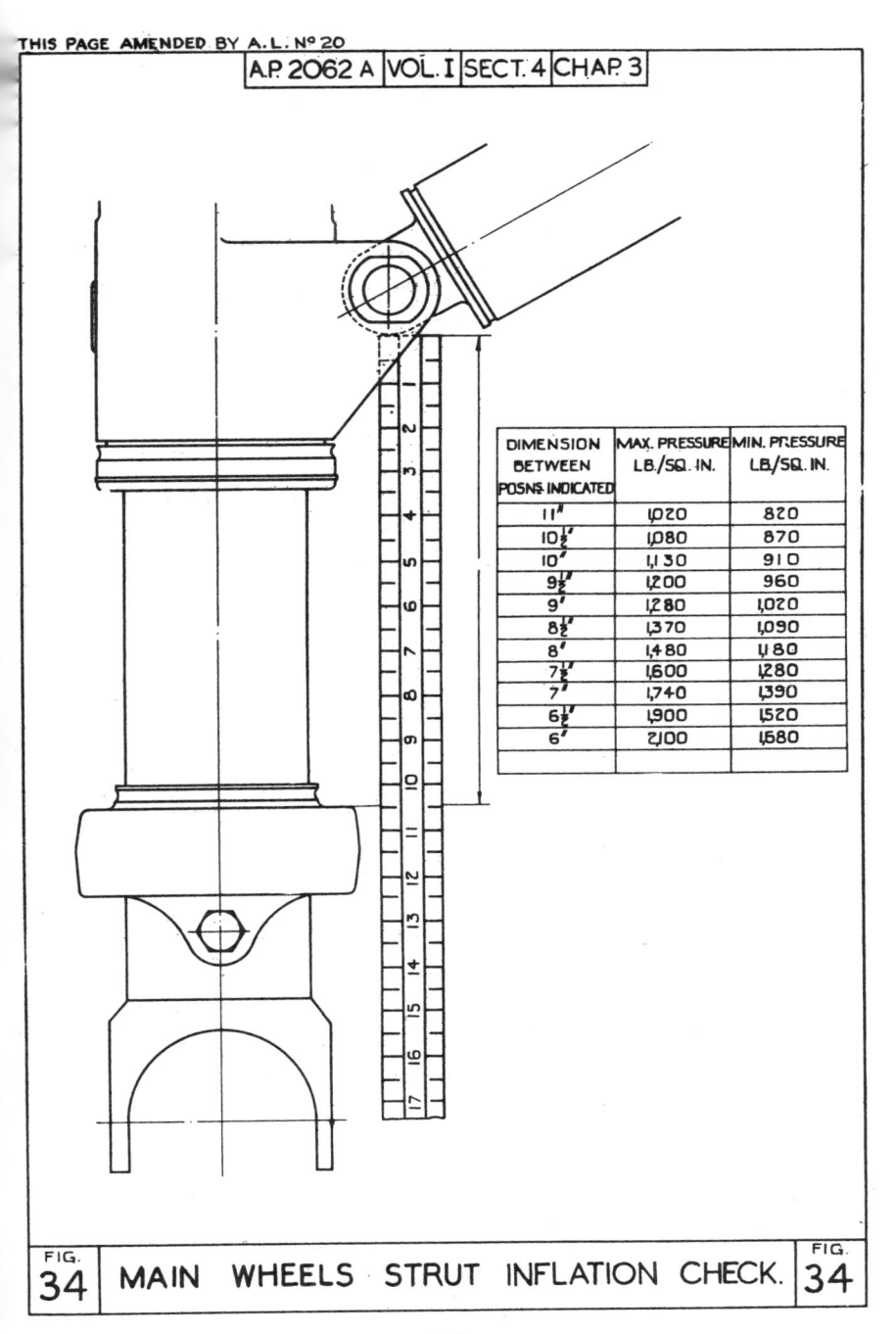

DIMENSION BETWEEN POSNS INDICATED	MAX. PRESSURE LB./SQ. IN.	MIN. PRESSURE LB./SQ. IN.
11"	1,020	820
10½"	1,080	870
10"	1,130	910
9½"	1,200	960
9"	1,280	1,020
8½"	1,370	1,090
8"	1,480	1,180
7½"	1,600	1,280
7"	1,740	1,390
6½"	1,900	1,520
6"	2,100	1,680

FIG. 34 — MAIN WHEELS STRUT INFLATION CHECK.

A.P. 2062 A | VOL. I | SECT. 4 | CHAP. 3

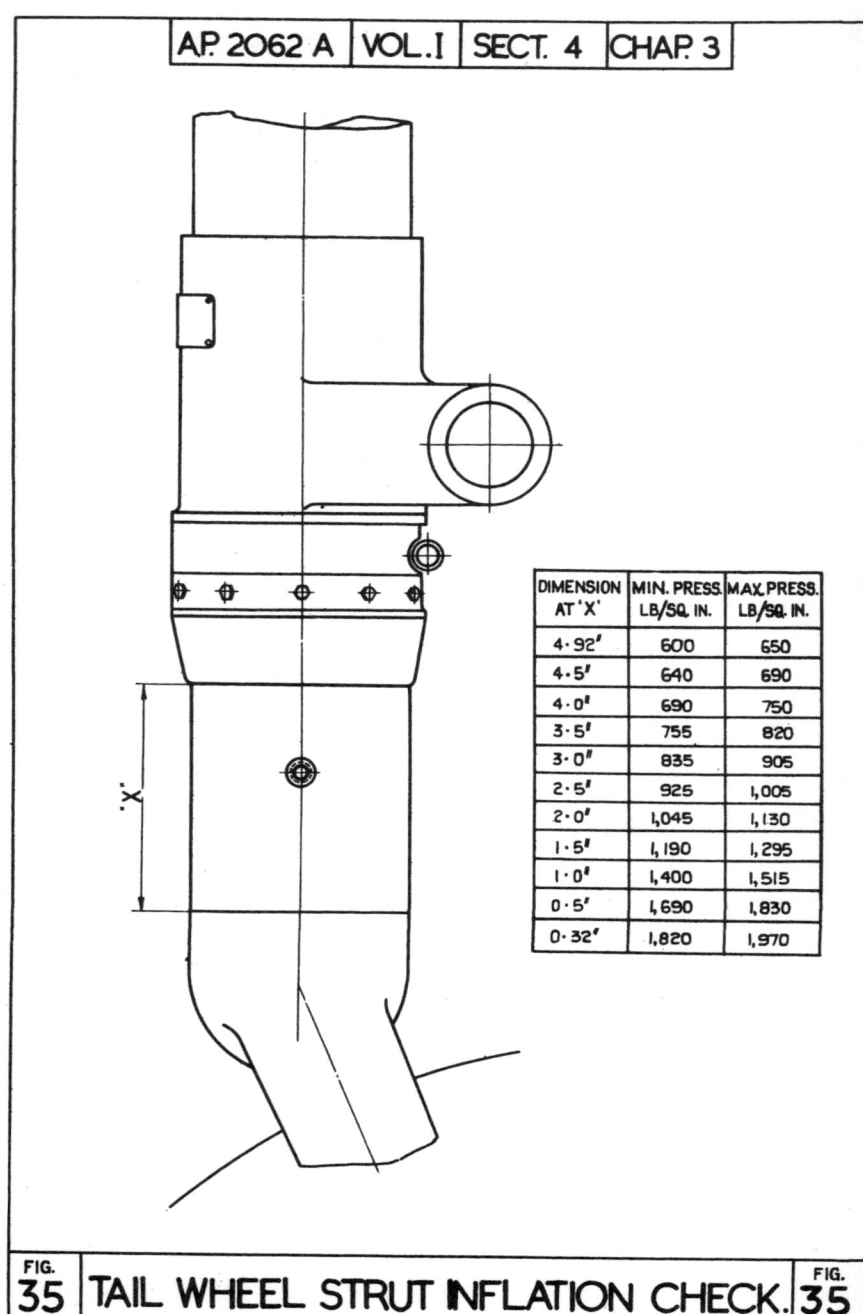

DIMENSION AT 'X'	MIN. PRESS. LB/SQ. IN.	MAX. PRESS. LB/SQ. IN.
4·92"	600	650
4·5"	640	690
4·0"	690	750
3·5"	755	820
3·0"	835	905
2·5"	925	1,005
2·0"	1,045	1,130
1·5"	1,190	1,295
1·0"	1,400	1,515
0·5"	1,690	1,830
0·32"	1,820	1,970

FIG. 35 TAIL WHEEL STRUT INFLATION CHECK.

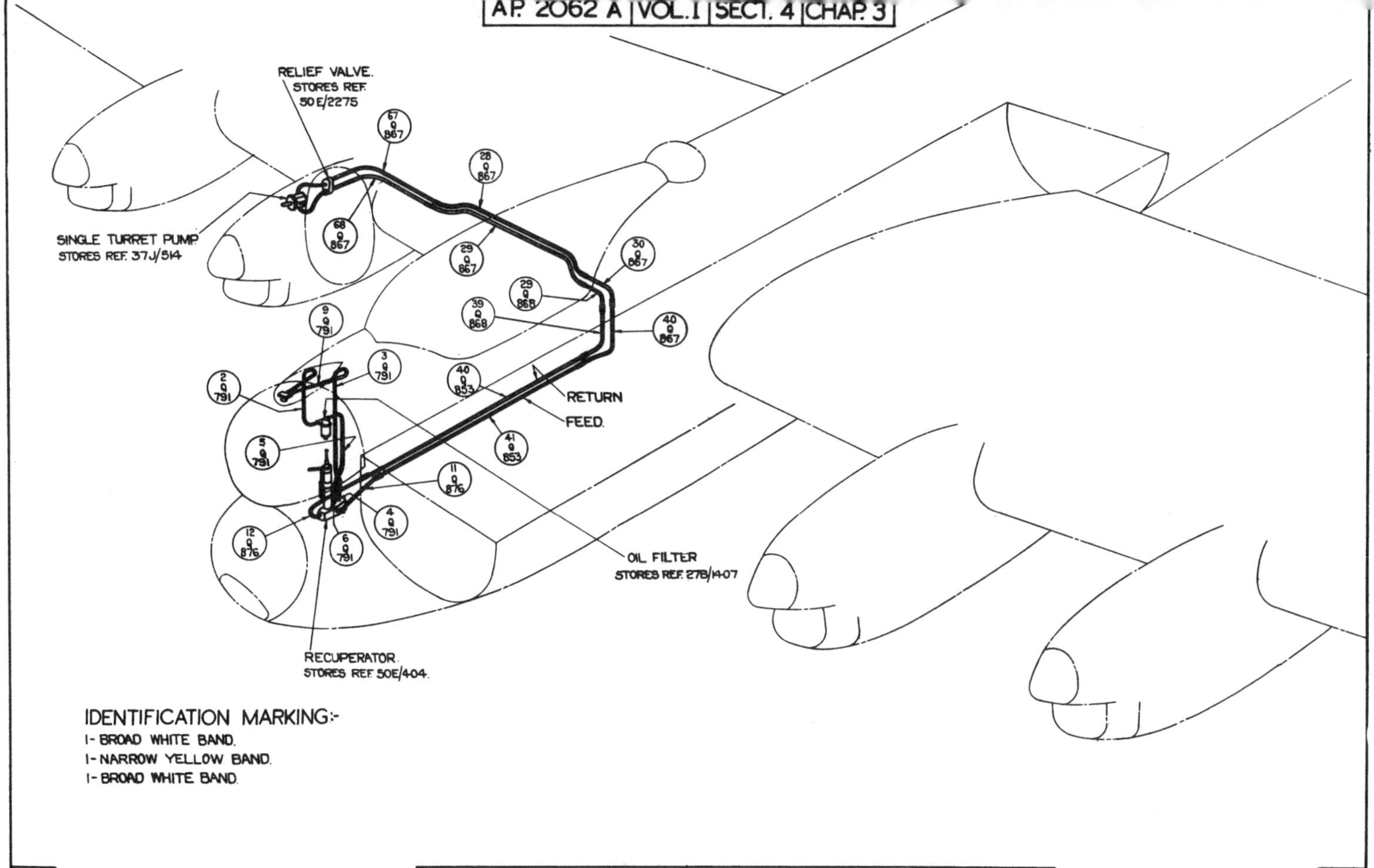

A.P. 2062 A | VOL. I | SECT. 4 | CHAP. 3

HYDRAULIC SYSTEM - FRONT GUN TURRET

IDENTIFICATION MARKING:-
1 - BROAD WHITE BAND.
1 - NARROW YELLOW BAND.
1 - BROAD WHITE BAND.

RELIEF VALVE.
STORES REF. 50E/2275

SINGLE TURRET PUMP
STORES REF. 37J/514

OIL FILTER
STORES REF. 27B/4-07

RECUPERATOR.
STORES REF. 50E/4-04.

RETURN
FEED.

FIG. 36

IDENTIFICATION MARKINGS:-

1 – BROAD WHITE BAND
1 – NARROW BLUE BAND
1 – BROAD WHITE BAND

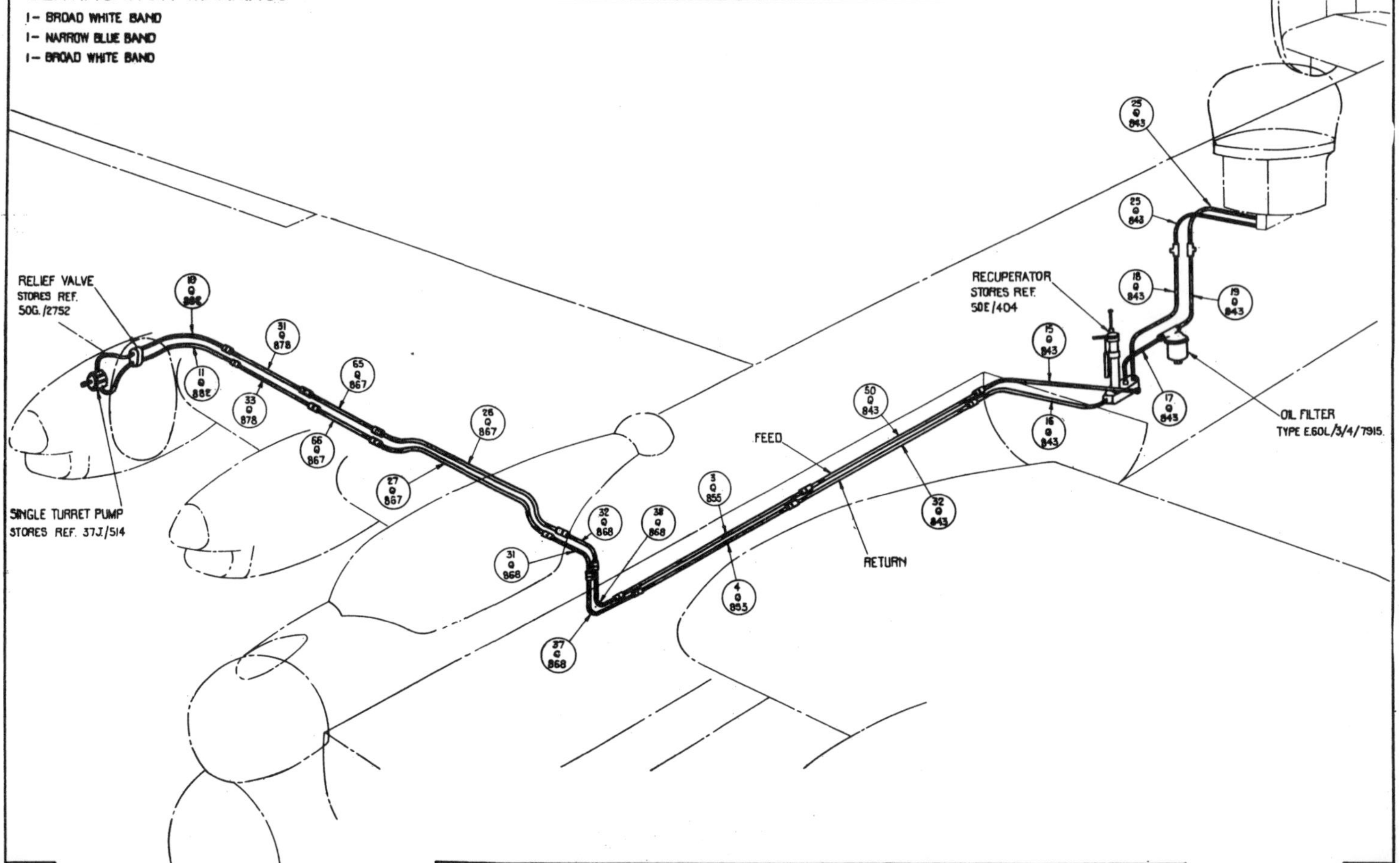

FIG. 37

HYDRAULIC SYSTEM

FIG.

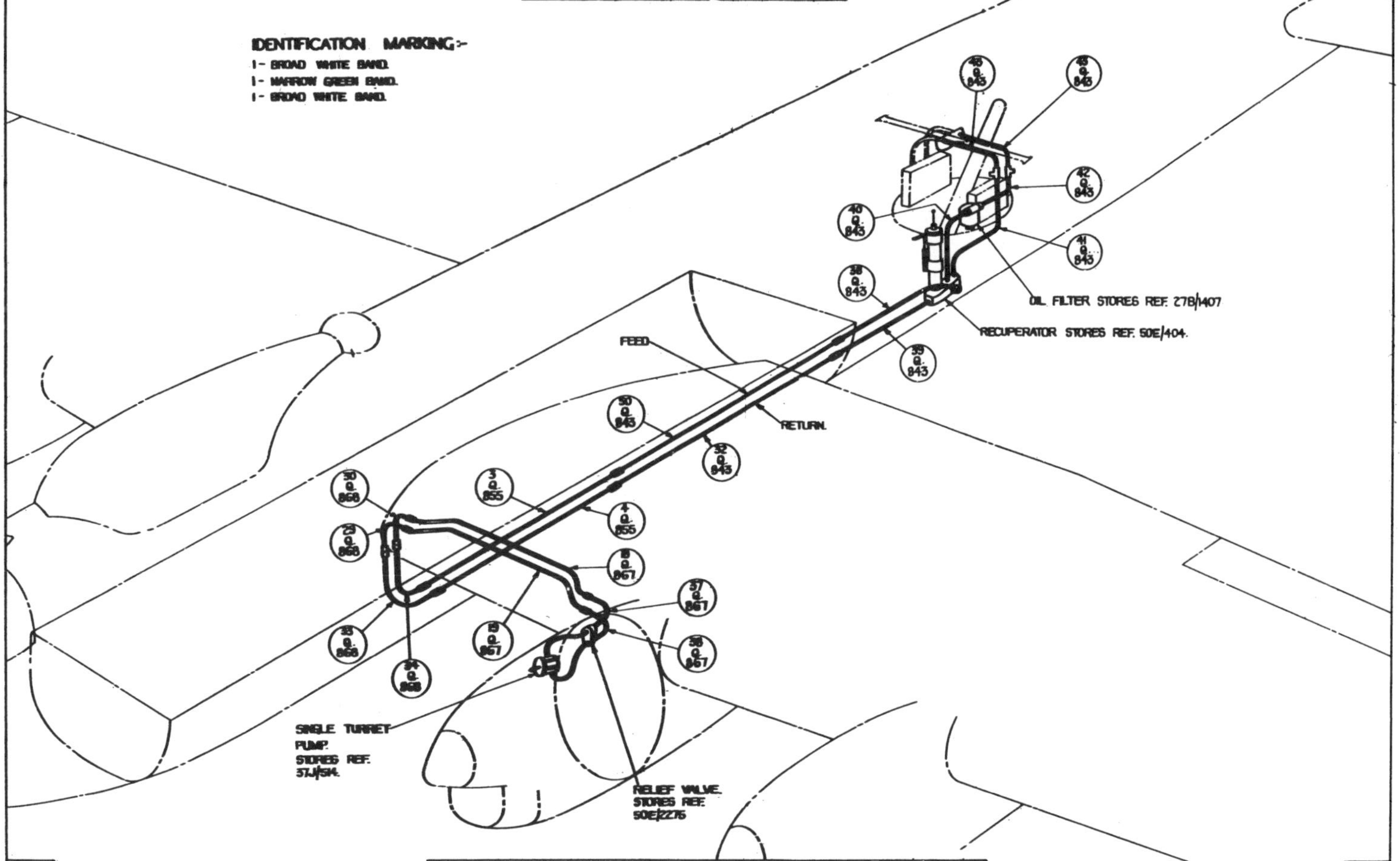

FIG. 38

HYDRAULIC SYSTEM-LOWER MID GUN TURRET

FIG. 38

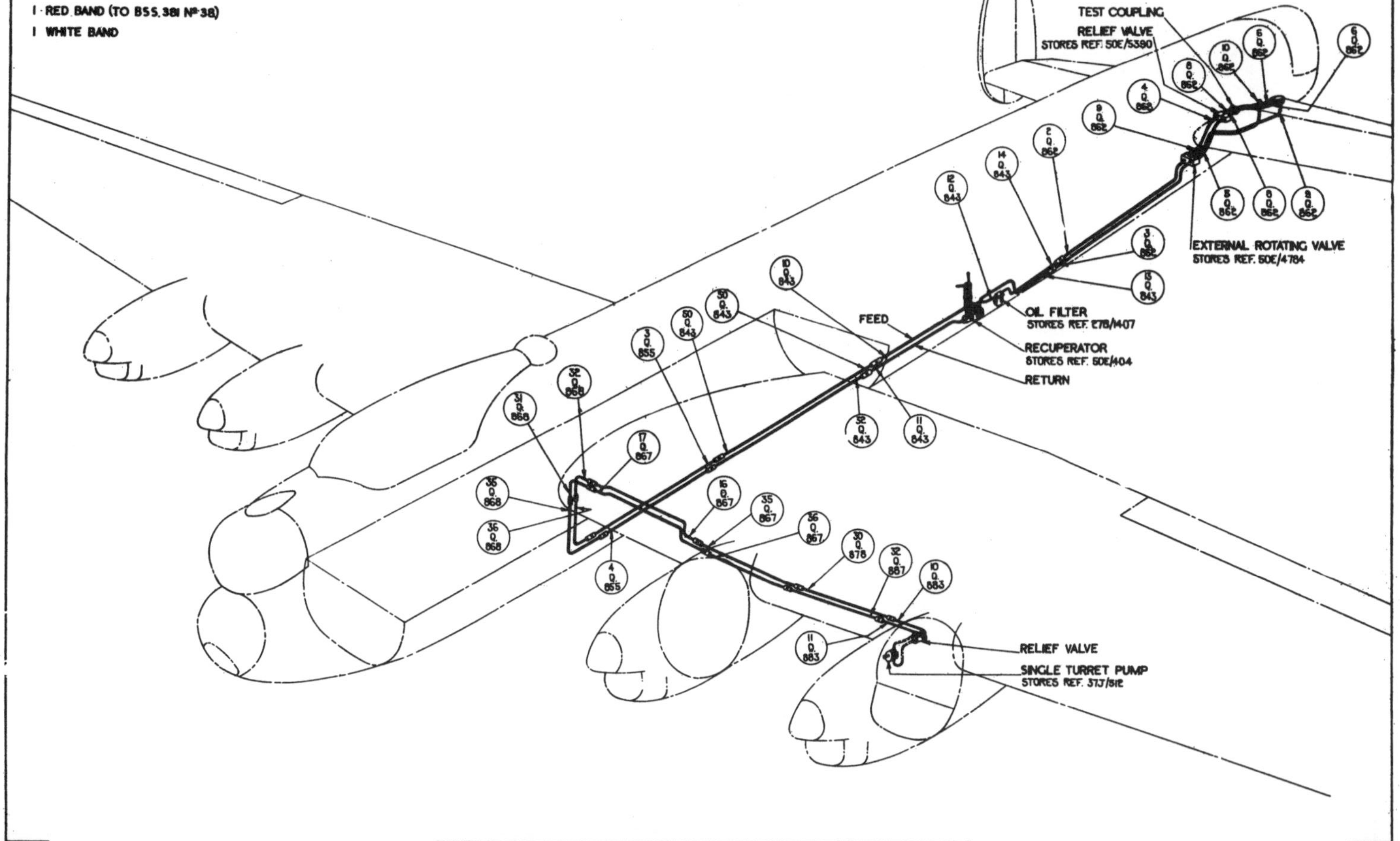

HYDRAULIC SYSTEM—REAR GUN TURRET

FIG. 39

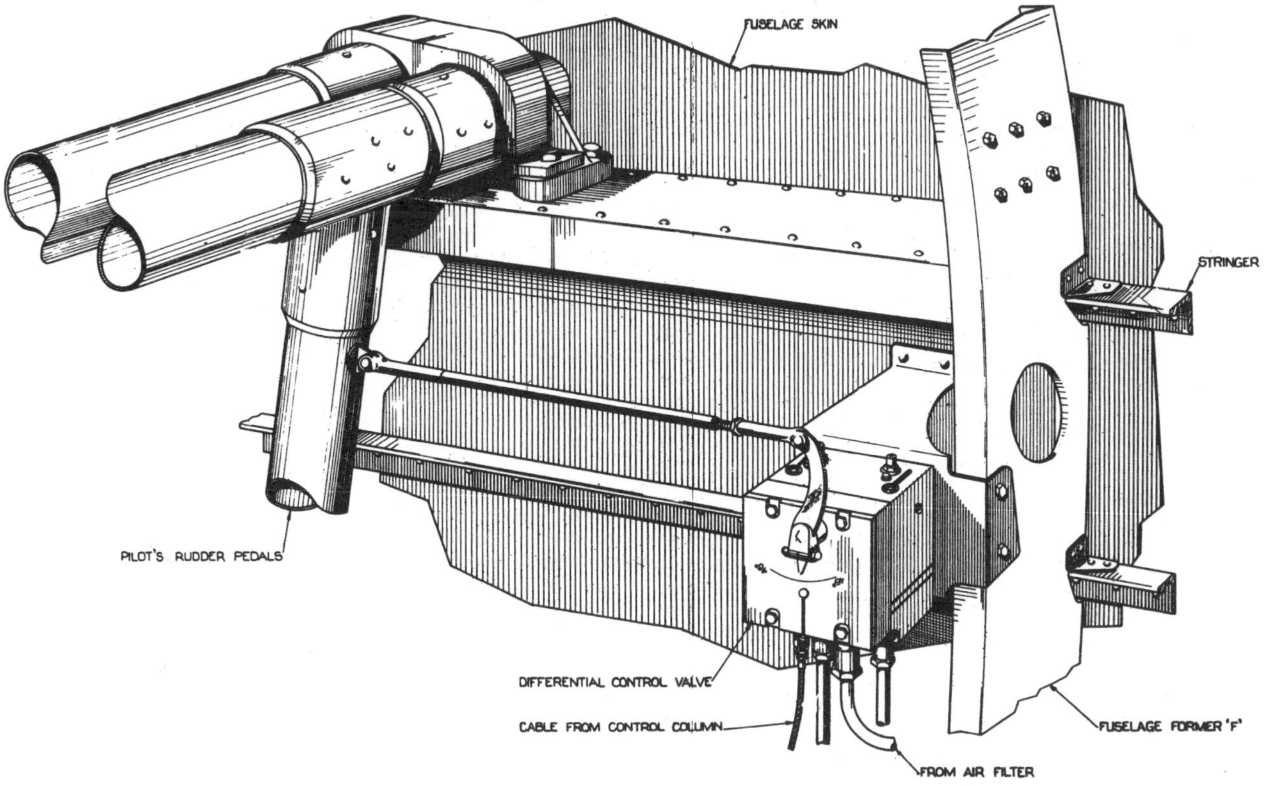

FIG. 40: DIFFERENTIAL CONTROL FOR BRAKES

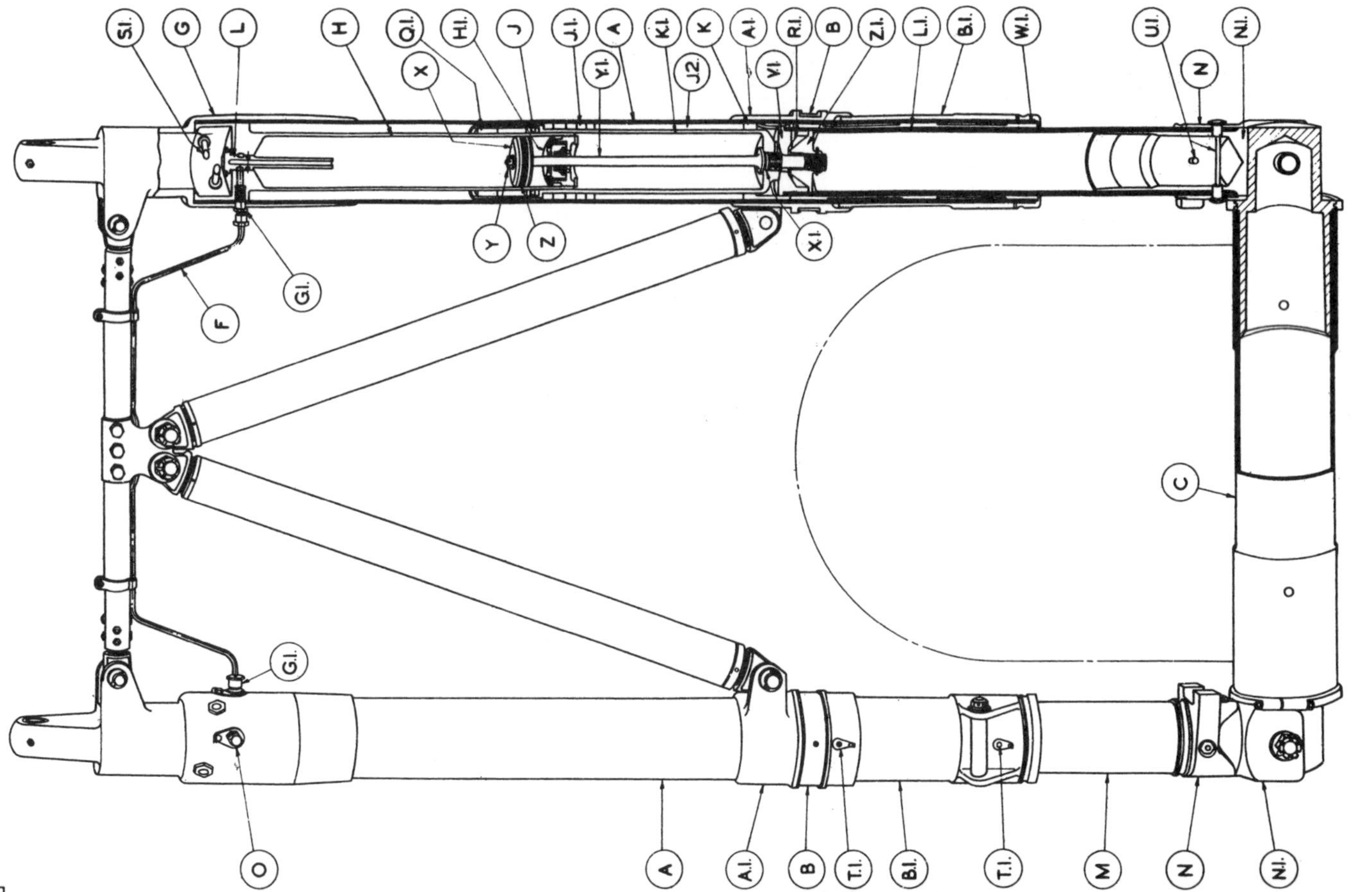

MAIN WHEEL SHOCK-ABSORBER STRUTS

FIG. 41

A.P. 2062 A | VOL. I | SECT. 4 | CHAP. 3

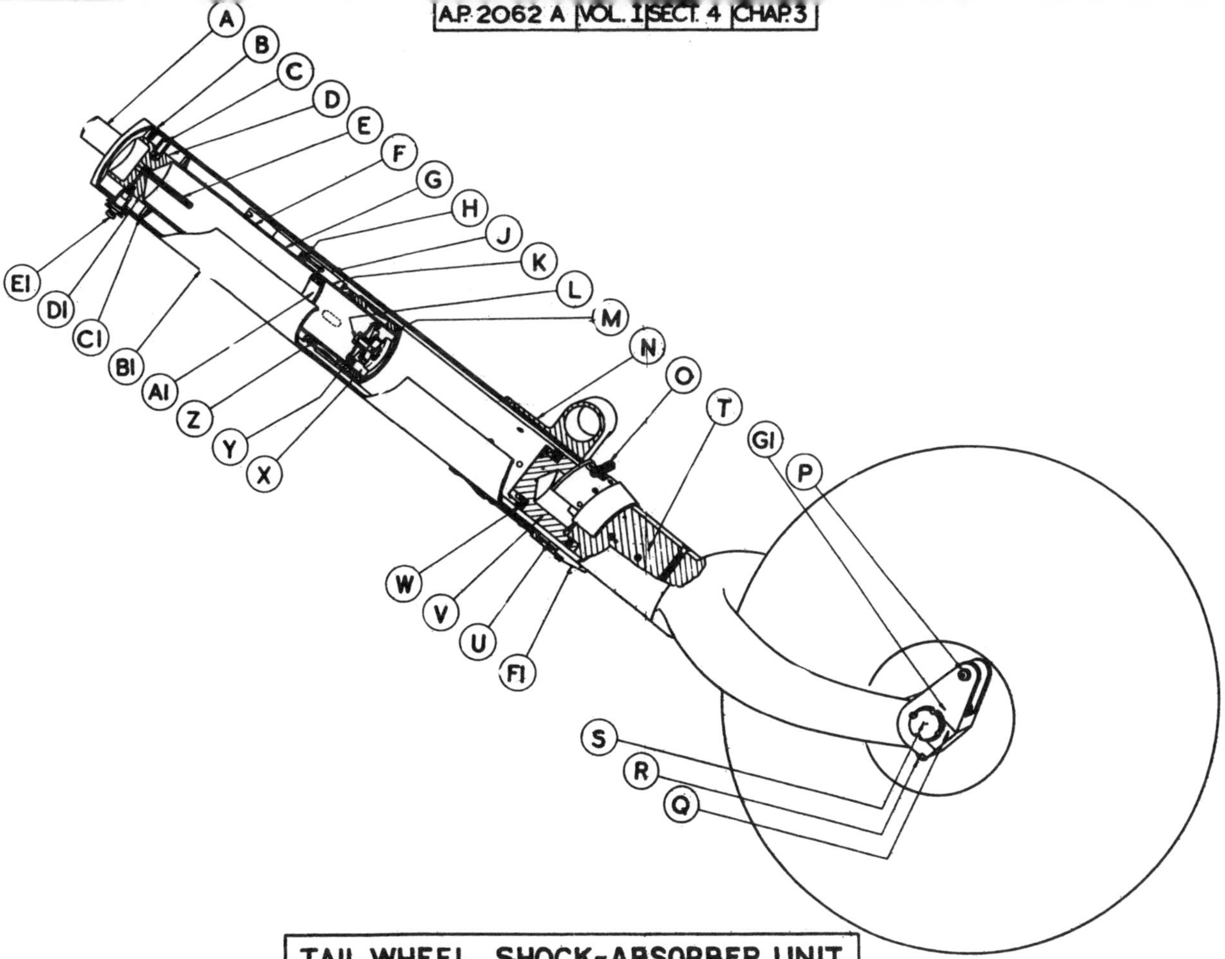

TAIL WHEEL SHOCK-ABSORBER UNIT

FIG. 42

Section 5:
Removal and assembly operations.

March, 1942
Issued with A.L.4

A.P. 2062A, Vol. I

SECTION 5 – REMOVAL AND ASSEMBLY OPERATIONS

LIST OF CONTENTS

	Para.
Introductory	1
Pop-riveted panels	2
Engine cowling	3
Nacelle fairings aft of fireproof bulkhead	4
Rear fairing of outboard nacelle	5
Power plant changing gantry	6
Airscrew	7
Power plants –	
Removal	8
Installation	9
Engine sub-frame	10
Main wheel unit beams	11
Main plane –	
Aileron	12
Main plane flaps, centre portion	13
Main plane flaps, outer portion	14
Assembly of flap operating tubes to jack	15
Trailing edge, centre portion	16
Trailing edge, outer plane	17
Outer plane	18
Fuel tanks	19
Oil tanks	20
Main wheel door and valance fairing	21
Main wheel units	22
Wing tip	23
Tail unit –	
Elevator	24
Rudder	25
Fin	26
Tail plane and elevator	27
Tail wheel strut	28
Fuselage –	
Rear portion	29
Rear centre portion	30
Bomb doors	31
Front spar cover and cabin heating baffles	32
Front centre portion	33
Centre portion of main plane and fuselage	34
Miscellaneous –	
Removal of Mk.IV automatic control units	35
Aileron gyro unit	36
Aileron servo motor	37

F.S./1

A.P.2062A, Vol. I, Sect. 5

	Para.
Rudder servo motor	38
Rudder and elevator gyro unit	39
Elevator servo motor	40
Front turret	41
Upper mid turret	42
Lower mid turret	43
Rear turret	44
Flap hydraulic jack	45
Cabin heating ducts and radiators	46

LIST OF ILLUSTRATIONS

	Fig.
Slinging and jacking sections of aeroplane	1
Slinging outer plane	2
Engine and radiator cowling	3
Method of erecting engine changing gantry	4
Removal of inboard power plant	5
Removal of outboard power plant	6
Diagram of transport sections	7
Assembly panels	8
Pop riveter and drill	9

March, 1942
Issued with A.L.4

A.P.2062A, Vol. I

SECTION 5 - REMOVAL AND ASSEMBLY OPERATIONS

Introductory

1. In most of the following cases only the removal operation is described and where no additional notes are given the assembly operation is in the reverse order. Slinging and jacking equipment is listed in the appropriate M leaflet of Vol. II, and tools and other special items of equipment are included in the Schedule of Spare Parts, Vol. III, Part 1 of this publication. The trestling of the various parts of the aeroplane is illustrated in fig.1.

Pop-riveted panels

2. Most of the assembly panels shown in fig.8 are secured by pop rivets which must be drilled out before the panels can be removed. Drill, Pt.No. 1.Z.1473, should be used for this purpose; it is fitted with a screwdriver end which prevents the special pop rivet from revolving with the drill. The mandrel heads should be punched out of the rivets before the latter are drilled. When replacing these assembly panels they should be riveted with the same type of rivets that were removed. Fig.8 shows the layout of the assembly panels and the types of rivets used in each case, and fig.9 illustrates the tools required.

Engine cowling

3. The engine cowling panels should be removed in the following order, by releasing the Dzus fasteners (see fig.3):-

- (i) Port and starboard side panels (1) and (2).
- (ii) Top panel (3).
- (iii) Door in radiator duct roof and air-intake fairings (4) and (5), after slackening the clips securing the cold air intake ducts.
- (iv) Main bottom panel (6) after detaching the radiator flap rods.
- (v) Front bottom scoop (7); on the port inboard engine, two pipes must first be disconnected at the oil cooler on the inboard side for the R.A.E. compressor.
- (vi) Front diaphragm (if required).
- (vii) Cowling rails (if required).

F.S./2

A.P.2062A, Vol. I, Sect.5

In order to avoid unnecessary removal of the cowling for minor inspection, full use should be made of the detachable air intakes and inspection doors. Further details on the removal of the cowling panels are contained in A.P.2140A, Vol. I.

Nacelle fairings aft of fireproof bulkhead

4. To remove the four detachable panels aft of the fireproof bulkheads of the inboard and outboard nacelles, release the Dzus fasteners and remove the panels in order of the numbers (see fig.3).

5. *Rear fairing of outboard nacelle.-* To remove this fairing, which is detachable as a unit, proceed as follows:-

(i) Remove the side, top and main bottom cowling panels (see para. 3).

(ii) Remove the screws securing the fairing rails to the brackets on the fireproof bulkhead.

(iii) Release the clips securing the front former of the fairing to the engine sub-frame.

(iv) Support the fairing and release the Dzus fasteners securing it to the undersurface of the main plane, after removing the doped-on fabric strips.

(v) Lower the fairing from the plane.

Power plant changing gantry

6. A special gantry, Pt.No. 1.U.634, which can be erected on the main plane, is provided for use when a normal hangar roof crane is not available. The aeroplane must be in the tail down position in order to use the gantry, (see figs. 5 and 6). The gantry should be erected as follows:-

(i) Remove the cowling and fairing panels (see paras. 3 and 4). For power plant removal purposes it is not necessary to detach the front bottom scoop, the front cowling diaphragm or the cowling rails.

(ii) Place the wooden platform in position above the power plant and erect the gantry in accordance with the operations numbered 1 to 10 (see fig.4). This procedure, and the instructions on the labels on the parts of the gantry, should be followed carefully. The differences in the erection of the gantry for inboard and outboard power plants are:-

A.P. 2062A, Vol. I, Sect. 5

(a) For outboard power plants a single rear bracing unit is fitted in place of the two struts required for the inboard power plant.

(b) The front fixing points inboard consist of ball-and-socket brackets which should be bolted to the tops of the main wheel unit mounting beams, while the sockets on the main outer plane are screwed into the top of the front spar boom.

(c) The lengths of the front and rear side struts must be adjusted as required by the instructions on the label.

Airscrew

7. The general handling of the airscrew is dealt with in A.P.1538, Vol. I. The airscrew can be removed from the engine by means of an overhead crane, if available, or by using the gantry fitted with the extension struts, Pt.Nos. 1.U.647 and 1.U.653, (see fig.4). The outer extension strut should be adjusted to the correct length as indicated by the label on the strut. The airscrew can be attached to the crane or gantry hook by means of the standard airscrew lifting sling, Ref. No.4L/1347.

Power plants

8. Removal.- Each power plant can be removed from the aeroplane by disconnecting the joints of the pipes, cables and controls at the fireproof bulkhead (with certain exceptions mentioned below) and detaching the mounting from the sub-frame. The following is a list of operations necessary:-

(i) Remove the cowling and fairing panels (see para. 6).

(ii) Erect the gantry if required (see para.6).

(iii) Remove the airscrew (see para. 7).

(iv) Turn off the fuel supply by turning the knob on the observer's panel and the lever on the pilot's control quadrant to OFF, and see that the balance cock just forward of the front spar in the fuselage is turned to OFF.

(v) Drain the oil tank by opening the filler cap and removing the drain plug

(vi) Drain the coolant system (see Sect. 4, Chap.3).

Amended (A.L.No.11)　　　A.P.2062A and C, Vol.I, Sect.5
This page amended by A.L.No.26
May, 1943

Para. 8 (contd.)

- (vii) Disconnect all pipes provided with joints at the bulkhead.
- (viii) Disconnect the oil feed pipe joint forward of the bulkhead.
- (ix) Disconnect the capillaries at the engine.
- (x) Disconnect the pipes at the oil separator (inboard only).
- (xi) Disconnect the engine drain pipe at the oil tank drain (inboard only).
- (xii) Disconnect the boost gauge connection at the fuel trap.
- (xiii) Disconnect all electrical cables at the sockets at the bulkhead.
- (xiv) Disconnect the magneto lead at the booster coil.
- (xv) Disconnect the flexible drive at the engine-speed indicator.
- (xvi) Disconnect the four engine control rods at the countershaft.
- (xvii) Disconnect the boost cut-out control cables on the engine.
- (xviii) **Mk.I aircraft.-** Disconnect the slow-running cut-out Teleflex control at the connector just aft of the bulkhead, and at the securing clip at the front face of the bulkhead.
  Mk.III aircraft.- In this case it is only necessary to release the clip at the bulkhead and withdraw the Teleflex control, which is sealed at this point and has no engine connection.
- (xix) Disconnect the connecting rod of the hot and cold air intake jack at the joint with the jack-piston rod.
- (xx) Remove the exhaust stub second from the rear of the engine, on each side.
- (xxi) Attach the sling, Pt.No.1.U.629, to the slinging points on the engine and to the crane or gantry hook. The front leg of the sling can be shortened for use when the aircraft is in the tail down position, or lengthened for use with a crane when the aircraft is in flying position. Before lifting, the stirrup on each side of the sling must be secured to the lug on the engine mounting by the pin provided (see A.P.2140A, Vol.I).
- (xxii) Take the load by means of the crane or gantry lifting gear, and remove the four bolts securing the engine mounting to the sub-frame, using extractors, Pt.No.1.Z.1715 and 1.Z.1716.
- (xxiii) If the gantry is employed the power plant should first be lifted away from the sub-frame, then moved forward by means of the screw luffing mechanism, turned through 90 deg., and lowered on to the special stand.

This page amended by A.L.No.26   A.P.2062A and C, Vol.I, Sect.5
May, 1943

(xxiv) Other details on the removal of a power plant are included in A.P.2140A, Vol.I.

9. **Installation**.- The installation of the engine is described in A.P.2140A. Vol.I.

Engine sub-frame

10. To remove the engine sub-frame (inboard or outboard) proceed as follows :-

(i) Remove the power plant (see para.6 to 8).

(ii) Remove the oil tank (see para.20).

(iii) Remove the rear nacelle fairing (outboard nacelle only, see para.5).

(iv) Disconnect all pipes and electrical cables at the bulkhead.

(v) Disconnect the hydraulic pipes to the hot and cold air intake jack.

(vi) Release all clips supporting pipes, stays and cables on the sub-frame struts, and release electrical cables where attached to the struts.

(vii) Remove all pipes now loose in the sub-frame by disconnecting at the nearest joint.

(viii) Disconnect the engine control rods and withdraw the slow-running cut-out and boost cut-out controls. On Mk.III the slow-running cut-out is installed but not connected.

(ix) Remove the fuel filter. Withdraw the fuel supply pipe.

(x) Remove the hot and cold air intake jack.

(xi) Remove the propeller feathering pump.

(xii) Remove the fire extinguisher (outboard nacelles only).

(xiii) Release the bulkhead stabilising struts, clips and fastening plates and remove the bulkhead.

(xiv) Support the sub-frame, remove the attachment bolts (three for the outboard and four for the inboard sub-frames) and lower the sub-frame from the aircraft.

Main wheel unit beams

11. To remove the main wheel unit support beams proceed as follows :-

F.S./4

Para.11 (contd.)   A.P.2062A, Vol.I, Sect. 5

- (i) Remove the engine sub-frame (see para.10).
- (ii) Remove the main wheel units or disconnect the bolts at the top of the shock-absorber struts (see para.22).
- (iii) Disconnect the pipes and electrical cables at the accessories panel between the beams.
- (iv) Remove the accessories panel.
- (v) Remove the diagonal strut between the beams.
- (vi) Remove the bolts securing the main wheel door hinge beams to the brackets on the support beams.
- (vii) Remove the nuts and bolts securing the beams to the front spar. To remove the bolts in the upper spar booms use special spanner, Pt.No. 1.Z.1267.

Main plane

12. **Aileron.-** To remove an aileron, proceed as follows:-

- (i) Cut out the fabric patch doors below each hinge bracket.
- (ii) Lower the trailing edge flaps.
- (iii) Remove the detachable nose cover at the inboard end.
- (iv) Remove the vertical bolt securing the aileron actuating fork to the bracket on the end of the aileron spar.
- (v) Disconnect the aileron trimming tab operating cables (starboard aileron only) at the turnbuckles, release the fairleads and withdraw the cables from the inner and outer trailing edges.
- (vi) Disconnect the balance tab operating rod at the aileron hinge bracket.
- (vii) Support the aileron, remove the securing bolts from the hinge brackets mounted on the top of the plane, and release the bonding connection at the centre hinge bracket.
- (viii) Remove the aileron by lowering it at the outer end and withdrawing it outwards from the self-centring ball race at the inner end.

A.P.2062A, Vol. I, Sect. 5

13. **Main plane flaps, centre portion.**- To remove the main plane flaps from the centre portion trailing edge, proceed as follows:-

   (i) Remove the detachable covers from the flap jack in the centre of the fuselage just aft of the rear spar.

   (ii) Disconnect the operating rod between the transmitter and the flap (port side only).

   (iii) Support the flap and disconnect the flap operating tube connecting link from the hydraulic flap jack, using C-spanners Pt.No. 1.Z.1268, and lower the flaps.

   (iv) Remove the screws securing the rear of the nacelle to the flap and remove the section of the nacelle.

   (v) Disconnect the flap operating tube at the universal joints at the junction of the centre and outer main plane.

   (vi) Remove the circlips from the flap link pins in the operating tube, and withdraw the pins. (Use special circlip pliers, screw a $\frac{1}{4}$ in. B.S.F. bolt into the end of the pin and withdraw the pin).

   (vii) Remove the bolts securing the flap hinge to the main plane dummy spar.

   (viii) Lower the flap from the main plane.

14. **Main plane flaps, outer portion.**- To remove the flaps from the outer main plane proceed as follows:-

   (i) Fully lower the flaps.

   (ii) Disconnect the flap operating tube at the universal joints at the junction of the centre and outer main plane.

   (iii) Remove the circlips from the flap link pins in the operating tube and withdraw the pins. (Use special circlip pliers, screw a $\frac{1}{4}$ in. B.S.F. bolt into the end of the pin, and withdraw the pin).

   (iv) Remove the bolts securing the flap hinge to the main plane dummy spar.

   (v) Carefully lower the flap from the plane.

15. **Assembly of flap operating tubes to jack.**- To assemble he flap operating tubes to the jack, proceed as follows:-

   (i) Lower all the flaps and fit the links. Individual links may have the length slightly adjusted to ensure alignment of the flap trailing edge.

F.S./6

The bomb aimer's compartment, with the bombsight computer on the left, sighting head in front of the cushion, and the bomb selector and fuzing switches on the right.

The flight engineer's seat has been lowered – it has to be raised to give access to the nose. Note the open sliding window.

The engineer was responsible for managing the engines and fuel. His main panel includes temperature and pressure gauges, as well as the fuel tank selectors and contents gauges.

The rear turret is a Frazer-Nash FN 20: note the two control handles in the centre, and the gunsight mounted on a bracket above. The fourth Browning gun is just out of shot on the left.

The Wireless Operator sits on the port side just aft of the navigator's position, facing forward. The T1154 and R1155 radio sets are mounted on the right, and the circular display on the left is for the *Fishpond* warning device.

Para.15 (contd.) A.P. 2062A, Vol. I, Sect. 5

- (ii) Ensure that the jack is at the end of the stroke. This is indicated by the red line on the port side being opposite to the pointer.

- (iii) Adjust the ball-end connection until the inner flaps just close. Check that the jack shaft has not moved during this adjustment.

- (iv) Lower the inboard flaps. Raise the starboard outer flap and clamp it in position. Raise the inner flaps till the trunnion can be connected, then shorten the connection to raise the inner flaps.

- (v) Clamp the inner flaps raised. Partly raise the port outer flap, screw on the connecting trunnion, and shorten the connection until the port outer flap is completely raised.

16. **Trailing edge, centre portion.**- To remove the trailing edge from the main plane proceed as follows:-

- (i) Remove the screws securing the top and bottom trailing edge fairing strips along the side of the fuselage and trailing edge. Remove the panels.

- (ii) Remove the flap jack covers in the fuselage, just aft of the rear spar.

- (iii) Support the flaps and disconnect the flap operating tube connecting link from the hydraulic flap jack. Use C-spanners, Pt.No. 1.Z.1268.

- (iv) Lower the flaps fully.

- (v) Disconnect the flap operating tube at the universal joints at the junction of the centre section and the outer main plane.

- (vi) Remove the screws securing the top fairing strip between the centre and outer main plane trailing edges.

- (vii) Open the access doors in the bulkhead at the rear end of the main wheel compartment and remove the bolts securing the rear ends of the main wheel door hinge beams.

- (viii) Support the rear fixed section of the inboard nacelle and remove the screws securing it to the underside of the main plane trailing edge.

- (ix) Remove inspection and assembly panels secured to the underside trailing edge, just aft of the rear spar, by screws and pop rivets (see para.2).

- (x) Disconnect the flap indicator electric cable (port side only).

Para.16 (contd.)

(xi) Disconnect the dinghy manual release cable and electrical release cable (starboard side only).

(xii) Disconnect the aileron operating push-pull rod between the inboard and outboard trailing edges, by unscrewing the turnbuckle after removing the two locking bolts, and at the joint inside the inboard end of the trailing edge.

(xiii) Disconnect the aileron trimming tab operating cables at the turnbuckles, release the fairleads, and withdraw the cables from the inboard trailing edge (starboard aileron only).

(xiv) Support the trailing edge and remove the nuts securing the top and bottom of the trailing edge spar to the rear spar of the centre section.

(xv) Carefully draw the trailing edge aft from the centre section and then lower the outer end so that the trailing edge can be drawn outward to clear the projection of the aileron push-pull control rod.

17. **Trailing edge, outer plane.-** To remove the trailing edge from the outer plane proceed as follows:-

(i) Remove the inspection and assembly panels secured to the underside trailing edge, just aft of the rear spar, by screws and rivets (see para.2).

(ii) Remove the detachable fairing strip between the centre section and the outer main plane trailing edge.

(iii) Fully lower the flaps.

(iv) Disconnect the trailing edge flap operating tube at the universal joint.

(v) Disconnect the aileron operating push-pull rod between the inboard and outboard trailing edges, by removing the two locking bolts and unscrewing the turnbuckle at the inboard end and removing the bolt at the outboard end joint with the aileron lever.

(vi) Disconnect the aileron trimming tab operating cables (starboard only) at the turnbuckles, release the fairleads and withdraw the cables from the inner and outer trailing edges.

(vii) Support the trailing edge and remove the nuts securing the top and bottom of the trailing edge rear spar to the rear spar of the centre portion.

(viii) Carefully draw the trailing edge aft and then lower it.

F.S./6

This page amended by A.L.No.26   A.P.2062A and C, Vol.I, Sect.5
May, 1943

18. **Outer plane.**- To remove the outer plane proceed as follows :-

(i) Remove the outboard power plant (see para.6 to 8).

(ii) Remove the outboard engine sub-frame (see para.10).

(iii) Remove the inboard engine fairing panels between the fireproof bulkhead and the front spar (see para.4).

(iv) Remove the outboard undercarriage door and valance (see para.21).

(v) Remove the transport joint cover panels at the junction of the centre portion and outer main plane by removing the screws securing them.

(vi) Remove the access panel below the leading edge of the outer plane.

(vii) Ensure that the fuel tank selector cock control at the observer's panel and the outboard engine master cock control on the pilot's quadrant are turned to the OFF position.

(viii) Drain the No.2 and No.3 fuel tanks (see Sect.4, Chap.3).

(ix) In aircraft retaining the pressure re-fuelling system, remove the appropriate access door and disconnect the No.2 tank re-fuelling pipe at the tank. Release the pipe clips, withdraw the pipe from the outer main plane and tie the loose end in the main plane centre portion.

(x) Disconnect the outboard engine fuel supply pipe, priming pipe and boost pipe at the transport joints. Disconnect the vapour vent pipe (when fitted) at the non-return valve on the inboard engine sub-frame.

(xi) Disconnect the No.2 tank delivery pipe at the tank selector cock in aircraft fitted with Pulsometer pumps (Mod.No.539). Disconnect the delivery pipe at the joint just aft of the front spar in aircraft fitted with immersed pumps and suction by-pass (Mod.No.512), release the pipe clips and withdraw the pipe from the outer plane.

(xii) Disconnect the slow-running cut-out control at the connector and the remainder of the outboard engine controls at the turnbuckles.

(xiii) Disconnect all pipes and electrical wiring carried on the front face of the front spar.

(xiv) Open the fairleads securing the capillaries in the leading edge of the outer plane. Coil the capillaries, remove them from the outer plane, and tie up the coils in the main plane centre portion.

(xv) Remove the two locking bolts and disconnect the aileron push-pull control rod at the turnbuckle.

This page amended by A.L.No.26   A.P.2062A and C, Vol.I, Sect.5
May, 1943

Para.18 (contd.)

(xvi) Disconnect the trailing edge flap operating tube at the universal joint.

(xvii) Lower the flaps and disconnect the aileron trimming tab operating cables (starboard only in aircraft not incorporating Mod.505) at the turnbuckles, release the fairleads and withdraw the cables from the inboard trailing edge.

(xviii) Support the outer plane on bearers, or sling from a crane (see fig.1 and 2) using slings Pt.No.1 and 2.U.571 and 1.U.627.

(xix) Remove the web plates at the front and rear spar webs.

(xx) Remove the nuts and drive out the main bolts securing the link plates to the spar booms.

(xxi) Lower the outer plane from the aircraft.

Fuel tanks

19. To remove the fuel tanks from the aircraft proceed as follows :-

(i) Place a suitable platform beneath the tank assembly panel in the main plane.

(ii) Remove the nut from the end of the spindle securing the jettison pipe door to the underside of the main plane (No.1 tank only).

(iii) Remove the tank assembly panel from the underside of the main plane (see fig.8). To remove the No.1 tank panel, first remove the inboard undercarriage door and valance (see para.21). When removing or replacing the No.2 and No.3 tank panels it is necessary to take the weight of the outboard engine by means of an external crane which is not mounted on the main plane (i.e. the engine gantry should not be used). When refitting a panel it should first be attached by at least two screws at diagonally opposite corners, and the rivet holes examined to see that they line up with those in the main plane. If they do not the engine should be raised or lowered until they do. The remaining attachment screws, followed by the pop rivets, should then be fitted.

(iv) Remove the access doors in the upper surface of the plane.

(v) Ensure that the tank selector cock is turned off and drain the tank, using a Bowser to pump the fuel out through the filler neck. Complete the draining by removing the plug in the sump.

F.S./ 7

This page amended by A.L.No.26 A.P.2062A and C, Vol.I, Sect.5
May, 1943

Para.19 (contd.)

(vi) Disconnect all pipes and electrical leads at the top of the tank. On No.2 tank, if an immersed pump or a pressure re-fuelling connection are fitted, use spanners Pt.Nos.1.Z.1998 and 1.Z.1999 respectively.

(vii) Disconnect the main delivery pipe on aircraft fitted with Pulsometer pumps or the suction by-pass pipe on aircraft with immersed pumps. On No.1 tank disconnect the doper pump supply pipe also.

(viii) Remove the Pulsometer pump as follows :-

    (a) Disconnect the pump delivery pipe at the pump.

    (b) Disconnect the electrical supply at the socket on the pump.

    (c) Remove the securing bolts and detach the pump.

    (d) Remove the non-return valve from the sump by unscrewing the securing bolts.

    (e) Remove the nuts from the studs securing the sump to the tank, and remove the clamping plate.

    (f) Remove the sump by unscrewing the studs.

Note.- After re-assembly to the tank, the following pressure test should be made :-

    Fit a pressure gauge at the main delivery pipe joint, run a small quantity of fuel into the tank and switch on the pump. A pressure of approximately 12 - 13 lb./sq.in. should be registered. Any loss of pressure or leaks should be investigated. Drain the fuel from the tank and remove the pressure gauge.

(ix) Support the tank and unscrew the turnbuckle in each strap.

(x) Lower the rear end of the tank and withdraw it from the main plane.

Oil tanks

20. To remove the inboard or outboard oil tank proceed as follows :-

(i) Remove the nacelle fairings aft of the fireproof bulkhead.

(ii) Drain the tank by removing the plug from the bottom and opening the filler cap.

This page issued with A.L.No.26   A.P.2062A and C, Vol.I, Sect.5
May, 1943

Para.20 (contd.)

- (iii) Disconnect and remove the oil pipes.
- (iv) To remove the inboard tank, unscrew the turnbuckle in each strap and withdraw it through side of sub-frame.
- (v) In the outboard nacelle, disconnect the electrical lead from the hydromatic pump, and the pipes from the fuel filter.

F.S./7A

A.P.2062A, Vol. I, Sect. 5

  (vi) To remove the outboard tank (with bearers) remove the bottom diagonal sub-frame struts, remove the bolts securing the bearers and lower the tank from the sub-frame.

Main wheel door and valance fairing

21. To remove the door and valance fairing proceed as follows:-

  (i) Remove the bolt securing the door operating link to the rotating pin in the lower edge of the door.

  (ii) Support the door and remove the screws securing the top of the valance to the underside of the main plane. These screws are on each side of the top edge of the valance.

  (iii) Remove the inspection door in the face of the rear fairing bulkhead, and remove the bolts securing the door rail to the rear fairing.

  (iv) Remove the two bolts securing the front end of the door rail to the main wheel support beam bracket.

  (v) Lower the door and valance from the aeroplane.

Main wheel units

22. To remove the unit from the aeroplane proceed as follows:-

  (i) With the unit fully lowered jack the complete aeroplane as illustrated in Sect.4, Chap.2, with the wheel about 2 in. off the ground.

  (ii) Release the air pressure in the shock-absorber struts (see Sect. 4, Chap.3).

  (iii) Remove the wheel (see Sect.4, Chap.3).

  (iv) Disconnect the hydraulic pipe connections at the jack fulcrum at the top rear spar flange.

  (v) Disconnect the position indicator cables at the terminal box positioned above the bottom rear spar flange.

  (vi) Remove the bolts securing the caps to the jack fulcrum bracket on the top rear spar flange and remove the caps.

  (vii) Remove the pins connecting the jack piston rods to the lower ends of the upper radius rods and remove the jack.

  (viii) Remove the pins connecting the lower radius rods to the shock-absorbers.

F.S./8

A.P.2062A, Vol.I, Sect. 5

(ix) Remove the fulcrum pins at the top of the shock-absorbers and remove the shock-absorbers.

(x) Remove the pins from the upper radius rods at the brackets on the bottom rear spar flange, and remove the upper and lower radius rods complete.

Wing tip

23. To remove the wing tip from the outer plane proceed as follows:-

(i) Remove the screws securing the joint plates to the main plane spar.

(ii) Tear off the fabric strip at the joint of the wing tip to the outer plane.

(iii) Remove the underside assembly panel at the joint of the wing tip and outer plane by removing the rivets (see fig.8); the joint occurs at ribs 4 and 5.

(iv) Unscrew and disconnect the Breeze plug for air-to-air recognition and navigation lamps, at the junction box inside the wing tip.

(v) Support the outer end of the wing tip, remove the nuts securing rib 4 to the studs on rib 5 between the spars, and the nuts and bolts aft of the rear spar, and draw the wing tip outwards from the outer plane and aileron.

Tail unit

24. Elevator.- To remove the elevator proceed as follows:-

(i) Disconnect the elevator connecting rod at the torque shaft at the rear of the fuselage.

(ii) Remove the bonding lead at the inboard end of the torque shaft.

(iii) Disconnect the coupling at each side of the elevator torque shaft and remove the centre portion of the shaft.

(iv) Disconnect the elevator trimming tab cable turnbuckle at the centre of the fuselage behind the rear spar.

(v) Disconnect the elevator trimming tab cables at the turnbuckles forward of the tail plane front spar.

(vi) Remove the four Vickers pulleys mounted at former 39,

Para. 24 (contd.)   A.P.2062A, Vol.I, Sect. 5

       remove the fairleads and draw the cables through the tail plane.

(vii)   Remove the fairlead in the fuselage side and pass the cables through the opening.

(viii)   Remove the three taper pins securing the outer ends of the elevator torque shaft to the inner ends of the elevator spars and draw the ends of the torque shaft inside the fuselage.

(ix)   Remove the fabric patch access doors in the undersurface of the elevator just aft of the hinges.

(x)   Support the elevator, remove the split-pins from the hinge bolts and draw the elevator from the tail plane.

25. **Rudder.-** To remove the rudder proceed as follows:-

(i)   Remove the three hinge inspection covers at the nose of the rudder.

(ii)   Remove the access panel on the outer face of the fin by removing the rivets (see fig.8).

(iii)   Remove the access door in the upper surface of the tail plane outer end.

(iv)   Disconnect the rudder trimming tab operating cable, detach the guard and remove the chain from the sprocket in the fin.

(v)   Disconnect the trimming tab operating rod at the tab, unscrew and remove (The sprocket must be prevented from turning while the rod is unscrewed).

(vi)   Remove the nuts securing the sprocket bearing housing to the outer end of the tail plane rear spar, and withdraw the housing complete with the universal joint and the screwed fork-end.

(vii)   Remove the bolt securing the rudder actuating lever to the connecting rod in the tail plane.

(viii)   Support the rudder, remove the three hinge bolts and lower the rudder from the fin.

26. **Fin.-** To remove the fin proceed as follows:-

(i)   Remove the rudder (see para.25).

(ii)   Remove the fairings at tail plane tip and fin junction.

F.S./9

A.P. 2062A, Vol. I, Sect. 5

(iii) Disconnect the aerial by removing the aluminium "weak link" rivet at the rear insulator.

(iv) Remove the bolts securing the front and rear fin posts to the front and rear tail plane spars. Lower the fin from the tail plane.

27. **Tail plane and elevator.-** To remove the tail plane from the aeroplane proceed as follows:-

(i) Remove all the tail plane root fairings.

(ii) Disconnect the aerial attached to the top of each fin by removing the aluminium "weak link" rivet at the rear insulator.

(iii) Disconnect the aerial at the end of the tail plane. Care must be taken on reassembly to ensure sound electrical contact at this point.

(iv) Disconnect the elevator connecting rod at the torque shaft in the rear end of the fuselage.

(v) Disconnect the couplings at each end of the elevator torque shaft.

(vi) Remove the three taper pins securing the outer ends of the elevator shaft to the inner ends of the elevator spars on each side of the fuselage, and draw the ends of the torque shaft inside the fuselage.

(vii) Remove the bolts securing the walkway across the top of the tail plane in the centre of the fuselage and securing the walkway in the rear end of the fuselage to the angle brackets located on the tail plane rear spar.

(viii) Remove the four inspection panels on the top surface of the tail plane inside the fuselage.

(ix) Disconnect and remove the rod connecting the rudder push-pull controls in the rear fuselage to the lever between the tail plane spars in the fuselage.

(x) Disconnect the starboard rudder push-pull control at the lever between the tail plane spars in the fuselage.

(xi) Tie the rudder trimming tab control cables with string at the control box in the pilot's cockpit to prevent the cables unwrapping over the sides of the drum.

(xii) Disconnect the elevator and rudder trimming tab control cables at the turnbuckles on the port side of the fuselage

Para. 27 (contd.)   A.P.2062A, Vol.I, Sect. 5

       forward of the tail plane front spar.

(xiii) Remove the fairleads on the fuselage formers between the turnbuckles and the tail plane rear spar.

(xiv) Remove the four Vickers pulleys between the tail plane spars and draw the rudder trimming tab cables into the tail plane.

(xv) Disconnect the rudder trimming tab cable turnbuckle at the centre of the fuselage between the tail plane spars.

(xvi) Disconnect the elevator trimming tab cable turnbuckle at the centre of the fuselage aft of the tail plane rear spar.

(xvii) Remove the four Vickers pulleys at the first former aft of the tail plane rear spar, and remove the fairlead on each side of the fuselage.

(xviii) Withdraw the cables leading forward and pass them through the sides of the fuselage.

(xix) Remove the four bolts securing the draught-proof plate to the rear spar of the tail plane.

(xx) Detach the canvas bulkhead below the front spar of the tail plane and remove the fastener studs from the spar.

(xxi) Remove the eight bolts securing the tail wheel strut anchorage plate on the top of the tail plane.

(xxii) Remove the fibre packing blocks positioned between the ends of the fuselage formers, and at the top and bottom skin of the tail plane.

(xxiii) Support the tail plane at each side of the fuselage on the special tail plane supporting trolley.

(xxiv) Remove the attachment bolts at the top and bottom joints at the centre of the tail plane.

(xxv) Remove the main attachment bolts securing the tail plane front and rear spars to fuselage formers 35 and 38. Unscrew the rear spar bolt bushes until flush with the former. Withdraw the tail plane horizontally from each side of the fuselage. Care should be taken not to damage the fuselage formers, or the trimming tab cables.

Tail wheel strut

28. To remove the tail wheel strut from the rear end of the fuselage proceed as follows:-

F.S./10

A.P.2062A, Vol. I, Sect. 5

(i) Trestle the aeroplane as shown in Sect.4, Chap.3.

(ii) Remove the tail wheel (see Sect.4, Chap.3).

(iii) Remove the inspection panels from the underside of the fuselage round the tail wheel strut.

(iv) Remove the bolts securing the tail wheel strut spindle at each side of the fuselage beam (access is obtained under tail plane inside the fuselage).

(v) Withdraw the tubular spindle from the side of the fuselage beam, inside the fuselage, and slide the strut down through the bearing from the fuselage.

Fuselage

29. Rear portion.- To remove the rear portion of the fuselage from the aeroplane proceed as follows:-

(i) Chock the main wheels.

(ii) Remove the di-pole aerial. Disconnect the main aerials by removing the aluminium rivet at the rear insulator. Disconnect the aerials of the A.R.I. 5000.

(iii) Trestle the rear end at former 30 and former 41 (see fig.1).

(iv) Trestle the rear centre portion (see fig.1).

(v) Disconnect the electric wiring, the control rods and cables and the hydraulic pipe lines at former 27. (The ends of the pipes must afterwards be plugged to prevent dust entering the system).

(vi) Disconnect the ammunition tracks.

(vii) Remove the bolts at the flanged joint at former 27 and draw the rear portion of the fuselage aft.

30. Rear centre portion.- To remove the rear centre portion of the fuselage from the aeroplane proceed as follows:-

(i) Chock the undercarriage wheels.

(ii) Remove the di-pole aerial, and disconnect the main aerials by removing the aluminium rivet at the rear insulator.

(iii) Remove the bomb doors (see para.31).

Para. 30 (contd.)   A.P.2062A, Vol.I, Sect. 5

(iv) Trestle the rear end, the rear centre portion, intermediate centre portion and front centre portion (see fig.1).

(v) Remove the screws which secure the top and bottom trailing edge panels along the side of the fuselage and the trailing edge. Remove the panels.

(vi) Remove the flap jack cover in the centre of the fuselage, just aft of the rear spar.

(vii) Disconnect the flap operating tube connecting link from the hydraulic flap jack using C-spanners, Pt.No.1.Z.1268.

(viii) Pull the port side flap to the fully down position, leaving the starboard side flap in the closed position.

(ix) Disconnect all flying controls.

(x) Disconnect all pipes and elecfric cables at former.12.

(xi) Disconnect the dinghy manual release.

(xii) Disconnect the flap indicator electrical lead at the socket on the port side of the fuselage.

(xiii) Remove the transport joint bolts at former 12, and remove the rear centre portion of the fuselage.

31. **Bomb doors.-** To remove the bomb doors proceed as follows:-

(i) Open the bomb doors by setting the lever on the control pedestal in the cockpit to OPEN. (see Sect.4, Chap.2).

(ii) Withdraw the solid pins at the lower end of the hydraulic jacks at each end of the doors.

(iii) Support the bomb door and remove the Simmonds nuts from the top hinge eyebolts securing the bomb door to the fuselage rail.

Note:- Do not try to remove the hinge pins, as the hinges are made as complete units and damage will be caused by removing the pins with the door in position.

32. **Front spar cover and cabin heating baffles.-** To remove the front spar cover in the fuselage proceed as follows:-

(i) Release the two fasteners at the front edge of the side panel of the radio operator's seat, fold up the step and fold the side panel back.

F.S./11

Para.32 (contd.)   A.P.2062A, Vol.I, Sect. 5

(ii) Release the two fasteners at the bottom of the seat front panel, fold up the seat and the front panel down.

(iii) Pull the projecting handle of the securing bolt at the top of the cover towards the port side. This bolt is spring-loaded and must be held back.

(iv) Raise the cover to release the floor pegs, supporting it carefully, and draw it forward from the spar.

(v) Fold the upper portion of the cover backward and down to the floor.

(vi) Secure the portions in the folded position by means of a strap on each side.

(vii) To remove the port or starboard baffles, raise the flap of the radio operator's table (port baffle only) release the fasteners at the top of the baffle, and raise the baffle to disengage the floor pins.

    Note:- On reassembly, the baffles must be replaced first. It is important when replacing the radio operator's seat to ensure that the pins in the fixed tubular supports engage the holes in the seat.

33. **Front centre portion.**- To remove the front centre portion of the fuselage from the aeroplane proceed as follows:-

(i) Chock the main wheels.

(ii) Disconnect the main aerials by removing the aluminium rivet at the rear insulators.

(iii) Remove the bomb doors (see para.31).

(iv) Trestle the intermediate centre portion and the rear portion of the fuselage (see fig.1).

(v) Remove the front spar cover and cabin heating baffles (see para.32).

(vi) Disconnect all flying controls.

(vii) Disconnect all pipes and electrical cables at former 6. The ends of the pipes should be plugged and covered to prevent dust from entering the system.

(viii) Disconnect all pipes and electrical cables leading from the sides of the fuselage to the leading edge of the main plane. The ends of the pipes should be plugged and

A.P.2062A, Vol. I, Sect. 5

        covered to prevent dust from entering the system.

(ix) Disconnect all engine and fuel cock control tie-rods at the first turnbuckles outboard of the fuselage.

(x) Disconnect the control tie-rods and the boost cut-out control cable at the turnbuckles or connectors just inside the fuselage (the cable should be removed from the thimble at the end of the turnbuckle).

(xi) Remove the locknuts, withdraw the tie-rods and cable from the fuselage, and replace the locknuts.

(xii) Raise the hinge leading edge and disconnect the hot air inlet valve and operating rod on each side of the fuselage.

(xiii) Remove the transport joint bolts at former 6 and remove the fuselage front centre portion.

34. **Centre portion of main plane and fuselage.-** To remove the intermediate centre portion from the aeroplane proceed as follows:-

(i) Remove the power plant (see paras. 6 to 8).

(ii) Remove the outer main plane (see para.18).

(iii) Remove the centre section trailing edge (see para.16).

(iv) Remove the bomb doors (see para. 31).

(v) Trestle the intermediate centre portion (see fig.1).

(vi) Disconnect the fuselage rear centre portion. (see para.30).

(vii) Disconnect the fuselage front centre portion. (see para.33).

Miscellaneous

35. **Removal of Mk.IV automatic control units.-** Before removing any of the units open the test cock to allow the air to escape from the system.

36. **Aileron gyro unit.-** To remove the aileron gyro unit proceed as follows:-

(i) Disconnect the pipes from the underside of the aileron gyro unit.

(ii) Remove the bowden cables leading to the aileron servo, and the cables for the speed lever and attitude control.

(iii) Remove the nut and washer from the top fixing bolt,

F.S./12

Para. 36 (contd.)   A.P. 2062A, Vol. I, Sect. 5

    loosen the locknuts and remove the setscrews from the
    two lower angle brackets attached to the mounting
    between formers E and F.

  (iv) Remove the gyro unit.

  37. **Aileron servo motor.-** To remove the aileron servo motor
proceed as follows:-

  (i) Slacken off the chain by slackening the four fixing
    bolts securing the aileron servo motor to the base
    plate on the main floor. Unscrew the two adjusting
    screws on the base plate just sufficiently to disconnect
    the removable link of the chain.

  (ii) Disconnect the chain at the servo motor.

  (iii) Disconnect the pipes at the banjo fittings on the aileron
    servo motor.

  (iv) Disconnect the bowden cables at the servo motor.

  (v) Remove the four bolts securing the servo motor to the rails
    on the main floor.

  (vi) Remove the aileron servo motor.

  38. **Rudder servo motor.-** To remove the rudder servo motor
proceed as follows:-

  (i) Remove the chain from the sprocket to the quadrant at the
    turnbuckles.

  (ii) Disconnect the pipes at the banjo fittings on the rudder
    servo motor.

  (iii) Disconnect the bowden cables at the rudder servo motor.

  (iv) Remove the four fixing bolts securing the rudder servo
    motor to the bracket on formers (F) and (G), and remove the
    rudder servo motor.

  39. **Rudder and elevator gyro unit.-** To remove the rudder and
elevator gyro unit proceed as follows:-

  (i) Disconnect the pipes on the underside of the rudder and
    elevator gyro unit.

  (ii) Disconnect the bowden cables at the gyro unit.

  (iii) Remove the electric plug from the socket.

  (iv) Remove the five fixing bolts securing the gyro unit to
    the bracket on the port side between formers (F) and (G),

Para.39 (contd.)   A.P.2062A, Vol. I, Sect. 5

and remove the gyro unit.

40. **Elevator servo motor.-** To remove the elevator servo motor proceed as follows:-

(i) Remove the chain from the elevator servo motor sprocket to the quadrant at the turnbuckles provided.

(ii) Disconnect the pipes at the banjo fittings on the servo motor.

(iii) Disconnect the bowden cables at the servo motor.

(iv) Remove the four fixing bolts securing the servo motor to the underside of the pilot's floor at the forward end.

(v) Remove the elevator servo motor.

Front turret

41. To remove the front turret proceed as follows:-

(i) Remove the guns and ammunition boxes.

(ii) Remove the turret hood by removing the 10 screws securing it to the top skin and fairing.

(iii) Remove the two bolts securing the pipe clip to the top cross tube of the fairing.

(iv) Remove the fairing by removing the screws round former (G) and the nuts under the side of the turret frame.

(v) Disconnect the two hydraulic connections at the top of former (G).

(vi) Disconnect the two electrical plugs for the general services and intercommunication from the top of former (G).

(vii) Remove the 16 holding-down bolts securing the turret base ring to the fuselage.

Note:- Access to these bolts is obtained through two small handholes in the cupola base ring. This means that the turret is to be rotated to bring a hole over each bolt in turn.

(viii) After removing these bolts rotate the turret in either direction until it comes up against a stop. Then force the turret round a further $22\frac{1}{2}°$.

F.S./13

Para.41 (contd.)   A.P.2062A, Vol. I, Sect. 5

  (ix) With the turret in this position, raise the back so that the turret pivots on the centre line of the aeroplane at the front of the nose. Use sling, Pt.No. 1.U.655, to remove the turret.

Upper mid turret

42. To remove the upper mid turret proceed as follows:-

  (i) Support the tail of the aeroplane in approximately rigging position.

  (ii) Disconnect the intercommunication and general service cables at the base of the turret.

  (iii) Disconnect the oxygen supply pipe at the base of the turret.

  (iv) Disconnect the hydraulic pipes at the base of the turret.

  (v) Remove the holding-down bolts securing the turret base ring to the support ring.

  (vi) Fit four sling attachment bolts in the holes in the sides of the turret above the fuselage.

  (vii) Attach the sling, Pt.No. 1.U.656, to the bolts and lift the complete turret from the aeroplane.

Lower mid turret

43. To remove the lower mid turret proceed as follows:-

  (i) Turn the turret to face aft.

  (ii) Disconnect the flexible hydraulic pipes at the self-sealing couplings and the electrical leads, at the bracket on the transverse stay above the turret.

  (iii) Withdraw the four quick-release pins securing the fixed ring of the turret in the mounting.

  (iv) Supporting the turret, turn the fixed ring through 15° in either direction. The supporting lugs will then be clear of the brackets on the mounting ring, and the turret may be lowered from the aeroplane.

Rear turret

44. To remove the rear turret proceed as follows:-

  (i) Remove the access door in the end fairing below the turret.

Para.44 (contd.) A.P.2062A, Vol. I, Sect. 5

- (ii) Disconnect the two hydraulic pipes at the bottom of the turret.
- (iii) Disconnect the oxygen pipe at the bottom of the turret.
- (iv) Disconnect the intercommunication and general services electrical cables.
- (v) Remove the sixteen holding-down bolts securing the turret base ring to the fuselage.
- (vi) Attach a cable sling, Pt.No. 1.U.657, to the four lugs provided on the top and sides of the turret and lift the complete turret from the aeroplane.

Flap hydraulic jack

45. To remove the flap jack from the rear centre portion of the fuselage proceed as follows:-

- (i) Remove the bolts securing the two covers to the jack mounting and lift off the covers.
- (ii) Disconnect the flap operating tube connecting link from the hydraulic flap jack. Use C-spanners, Pt.No. 1.Z.1268.
- (iii) Disconnect the pipe connection at each end of the hydraulic jack.
- (iv) Remove the four nuts securing the ends of the jack to the mounting.
- (v) Raise the jack and remove it from the mounting.

Cabin heating ducts and radiators

46. To remove the cabin heating air ducts and radiators proceed as follows:-

- (i) Drain the radiator by removing the drain plug and opening the pet cocks.
- (ii) Disconnect the water pipes at the radiator.
- (iii) Detach the outboard duct at the outer end.
- (iv) Remove the bolts securing the inlet valve box to the fuselage, and disconnect the operating rod of the valve.
- (v) Disconnect the clips securing the radiator and withdraw the ducts and radiator as a unit. The radiator and ducts can then be separated if required.

F.S./14

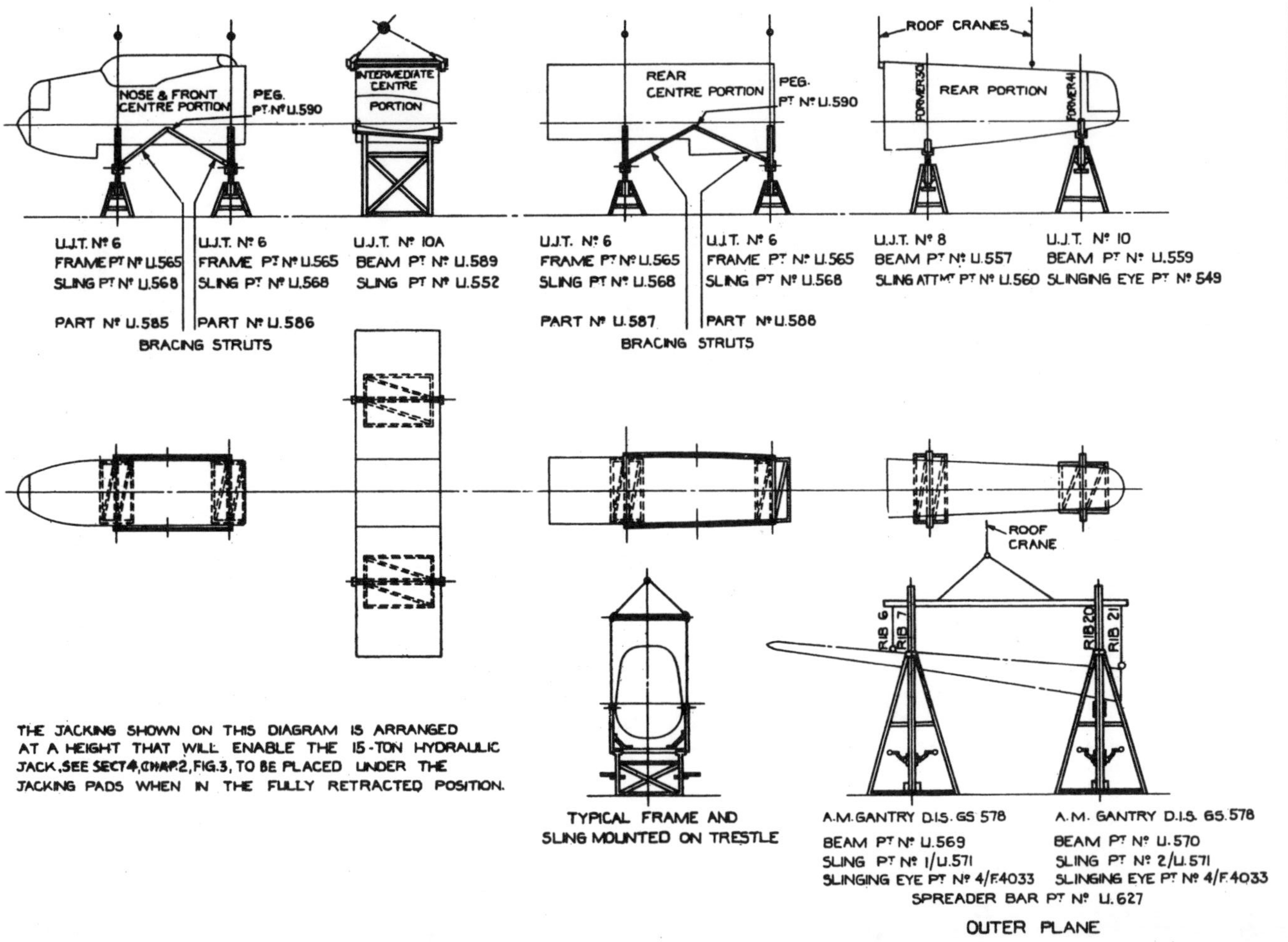

THE JACKING SHOWN ON THIS DIAGRAM IS ARRANGED AT A HEIGHT THAT WILL ENABLE THE 15-TON HYDRAULIC JACK, SEE SECT. 4, CHAP. 2, FIG. 3, TO BE PLACED UNDER THE JACKING PADS WHEN IN THE FULLY RETRACTED POSITION.

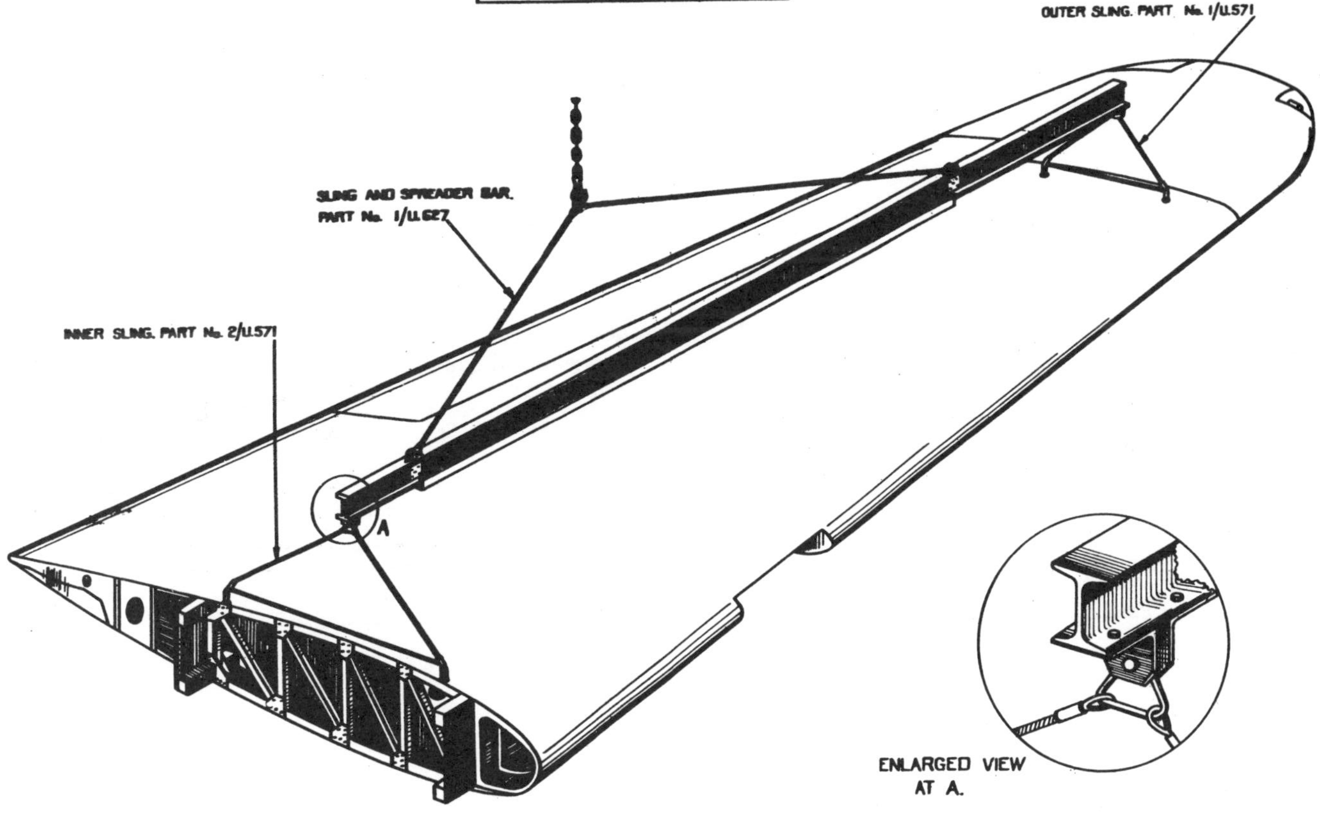

FIG. 2

SLINGING OUTER PLANE

FIG. 2

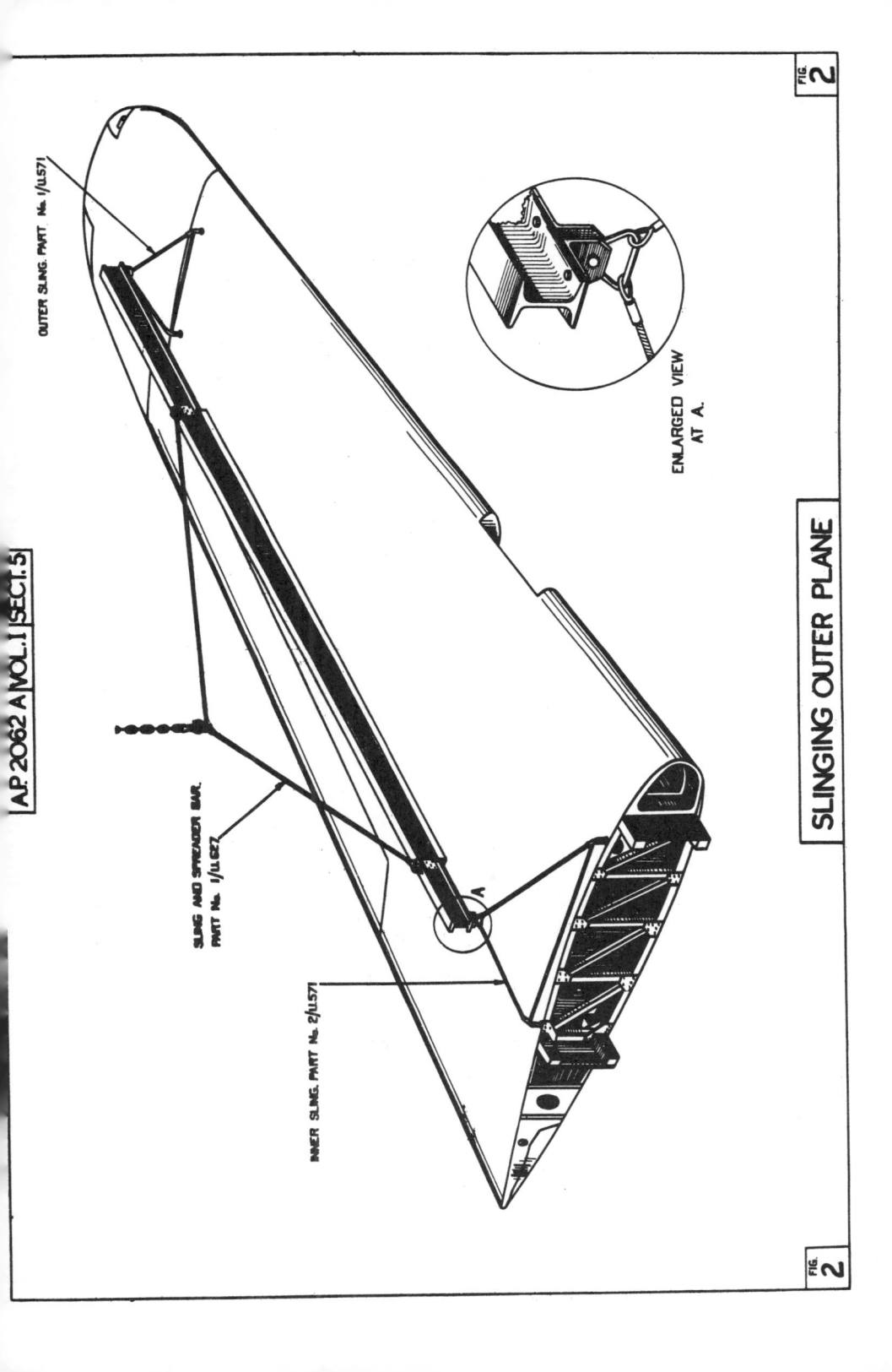

A.P. 2062A VOL.I SECT.5

OUTBOARD ENGINE

INBOARD ENGINE.

ENGINE & RADIATOR COWLING

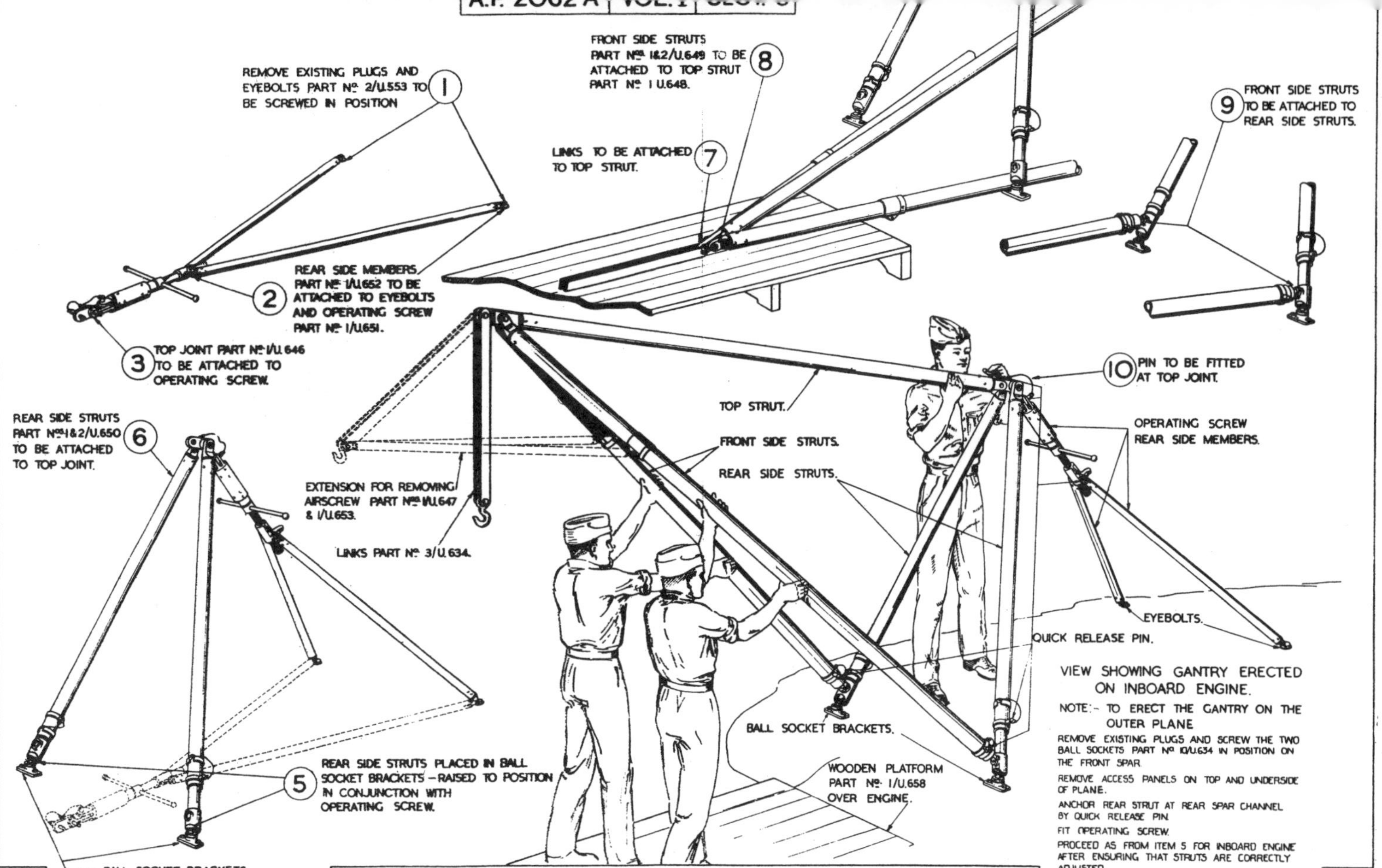

FIG. 4

METHOD OF ERECTING ENGINE CHANGING GANTRY

AMENDED (A.L.14)

A.P. 2062A | VOL. I | SECT. 5

BLOCK & TACKLE OMITTED IN THIS VIEW FOR CLARITY

SAFETY PIN AND LUG

MAINTENANCE LADDER
PART No. I/U.575

LUFFING HANDLE

EXTENSION STRUTS FOR USE WHEN REMOVING PROPELLER

1½-TON PULLEY BLOCK & TACKLE

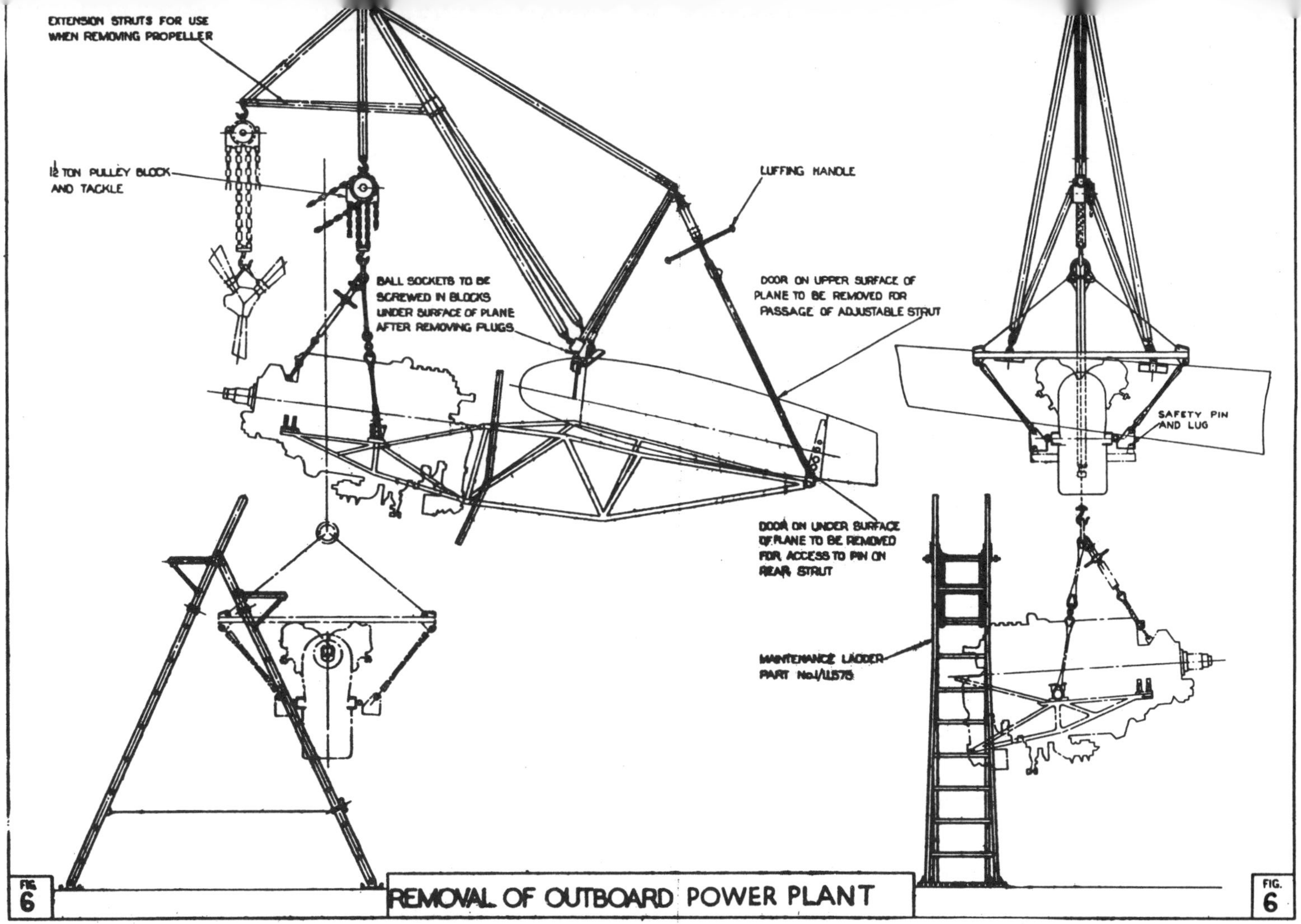

REMOVAL OF OUTBOARD POWER PLANT

FIG. 6

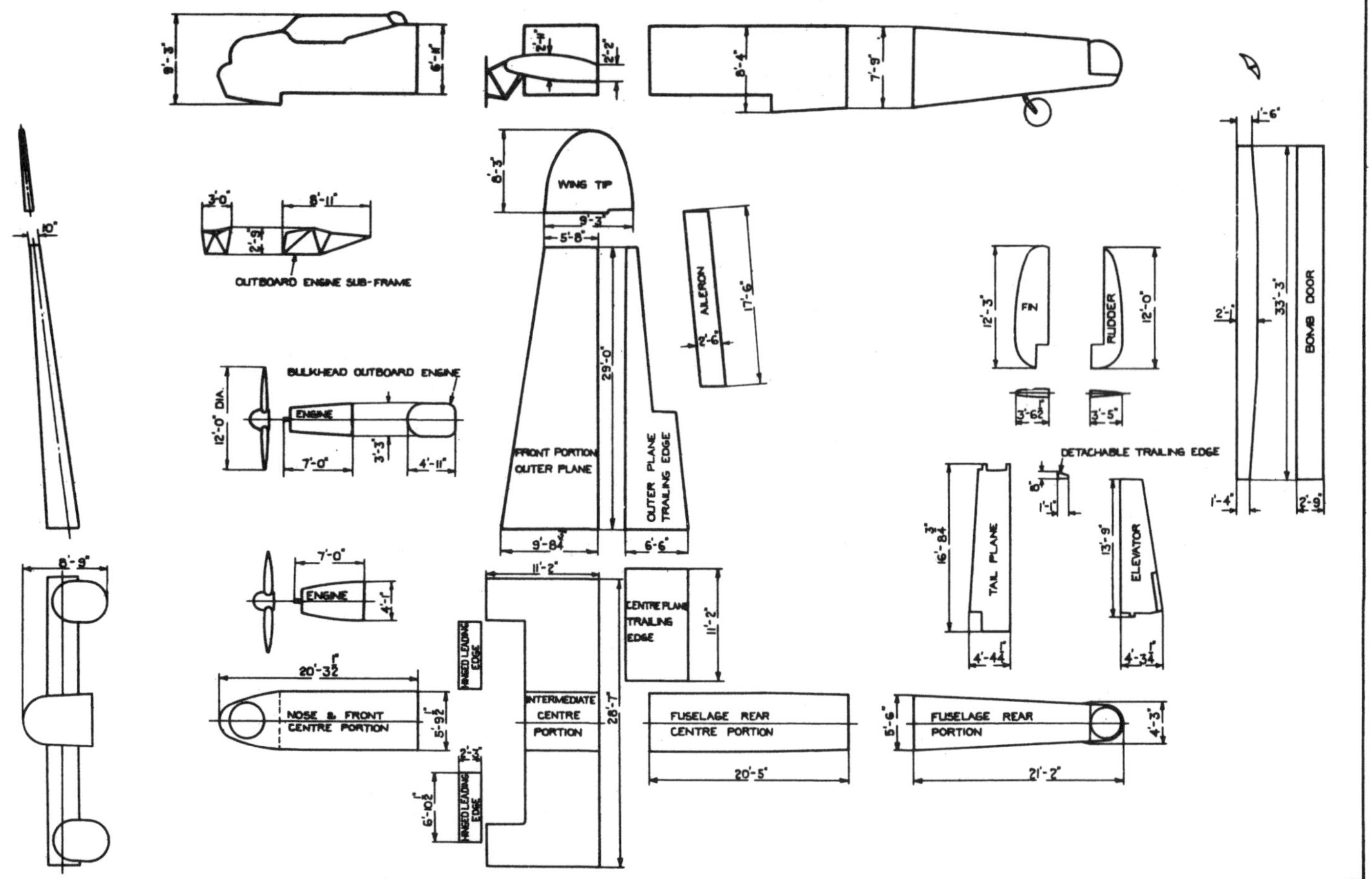

DIAGRAM OF TRANSPORT SECTIONS

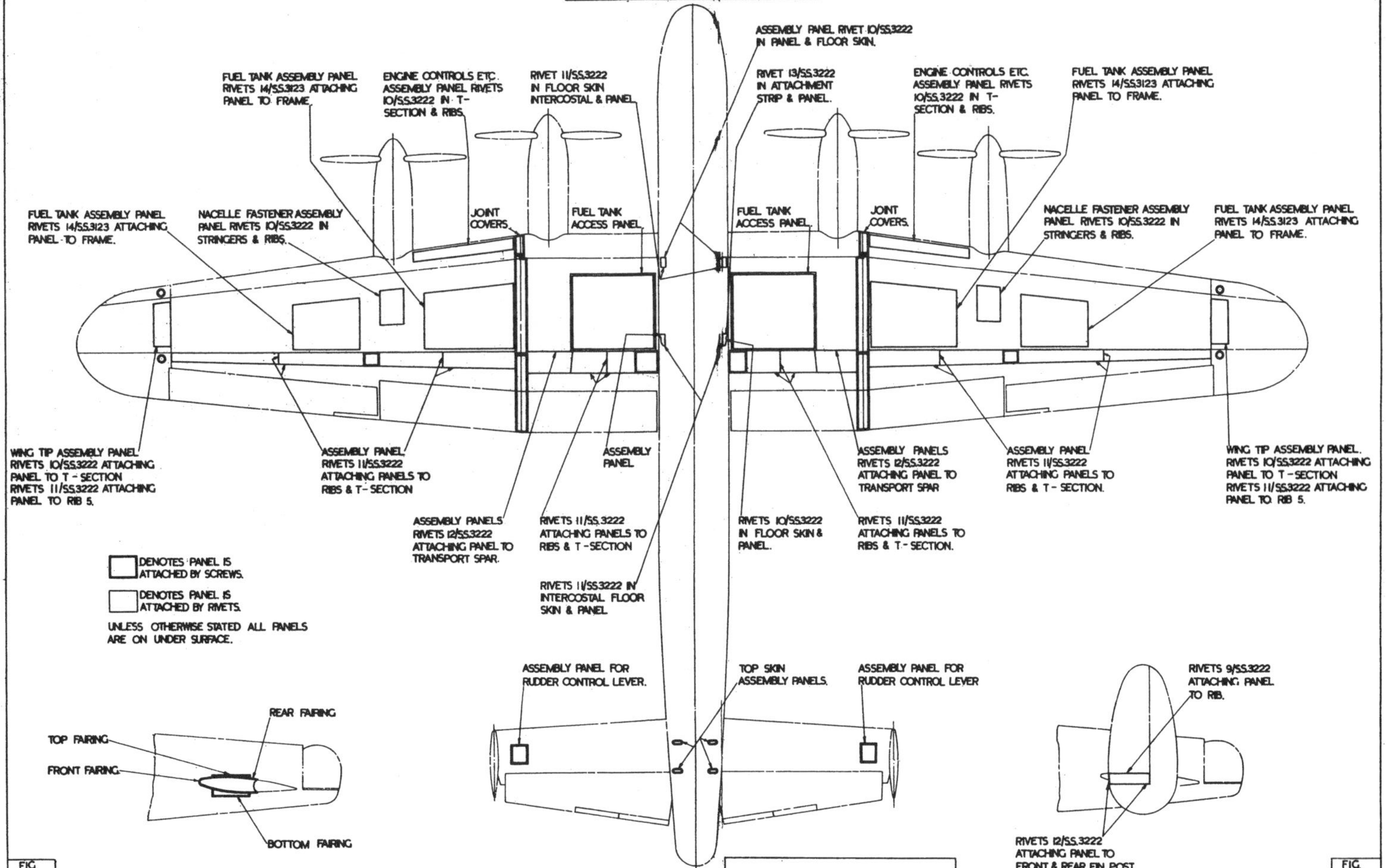

FIG. 8

ASSEMBLY PANELS.

FIG. 8

A.P. 2062A Vol. I Sect. 5

POP RIVETING DRILL
PART No. I/Z.1473

GRIP FOR RIVET EXTRACTOR.

POP RIVETING EQUIPMENT
PART No. I/Z.1474

POP RIVETER.

FLEXIBLE PIPE.

FOOT PUMP.

Section 6:
Electrical and radio installation-Maintenance.

This Section revised by A.L.No.21
February, 1943

AIR PUBLICATION 2062A
Volume I

SECTION 6

ELECTRICAL AND RADIO INSTALLATION MAINTENANCE

LIST OF CONTENTS

	Para.
Introduction	1
Schematic diagrams	3
Interpretation of routing charts	4
Referencing of fuses (scheme B)	6
Referencing of fuses (scheme C and E)	7
Referencing of conduits	8
Referencing of junction boxes	9
Referencing of plugs and sockets	10
Referencing of terminals blocks in junction boxes	11
Method of reading routing charts	12
General	13
Access to components	19
Maintenance notes	20
Undercarriage position indicator	21
Warning horn	22
Control switch	23
Oil dilution system	24
Bonding	25

LIST OF ILLUSTRATIONS

	B	Schemes C	E
		Fig. Nos.	
Location diagrams -			
General services	1	35	35
Bomb fuzing and release	2	36	36
R/T intercommunication	3	3	3
D.R. compass, etc.	4	4	4
Schematic diagrams -			
Electrical services	5	37	37
Electrical services (continued)	5A	37A	37A
Bomb fuzing and release	5B	37B	37B
Routing charts -			
Generator controls	6	38	38
General lighting, compass, turrets, beam approach and call light supply	7	39	39
Navigation recognition and identification lamps	8	40	55
Oil dilution system	} 9	41	56
Dinghy release			
Engine speed indicators	} 10	42	57
Auto controls			
Flap indicators			
Fire extinguishers	} 11	43	58
Radiator flaps			
Fuel pressure warning lamps	} 12	44	59
L.T. and H.T. supply			

F.S./1

This page amended by A.L.27
June, 1943

	Schemes		
	B	C	E
		Fig. Nos.	
Hydromatic propeller	13	45	60
Engine starting and ignition	14	46	61
Immersed fuel pumps	15	47	47
Undercarriage indicators	16	48	48
Fuel contents gauges	17	49	49
Landing lamps }	18	50	50
Heated pressure head }			
Camera supply }			
Bomb fuzing and release supply }			
Negative distribution }	19	–	–
De-icing }			
Bomb fuzing and release	20	51	51
A.R.I. 5000 and A.R.I. 5033 }	21	52	52
Auto bomb sight }			
Engine supercharger controls }	–	53	53
De-icing }			
Slow-running cut-off controls	–	–	62
Installation diagrams –			
Intercommunication call lights }	22	22	22
Heated gloves, camera and bombs }			
Camera circuit }			
D.R. compass installation	23	23	23
Beam approach	24	24	24
A.R.I. 5000	25	25	25
Intercommunication installation, T.1154, R.1155, T.R.9F and amplifier type A.1134	26	26	26
T.1154, R.1155 and radio wiring	27	27	27
A.R.I.5033 installation }	28	28	28
A.R.I.5000 detonator circuit }			
Bonding diagrams –			
General services	29	29	29
Hydraulic system	30	30	30
Pneumatic system	31	31	31
Undercarriage position indicator	32	32	32
Control switch	33	33	33
Warning horn	34	34	34

A.P.2062A, Vol. I

SECTION 6

ELECTRICAL AND RADIO INSTALLATION—MAINTENANCE

Introduction

1. This section contains the wiring diagrams of the various circuits presented in the form of routing charts, notes on the interpretation of the charts, access to electrical components and the maintenance of equipment peculiar to these aircraft.

2. The wiring of the first 250 aircraft (i.e. scheme B) is contained mainly in protected and screened flexible conduits. The wiring of the 251st onwards (i.e. scheme C and E) is contained in flexible insulated polivyŋal tubing except for circuits comprising ignition, intercommunication, beam approach, and D.R. compass and on the screened portion of the W/T installation, when bonded braided cable or screened flexible metal conduits are employed; where it is necessary to break down conduits and cables, either plugs and sockets, junction boxes, or terminal blocks are provided. The wiring for the outer plane services is contained in open ended tubular conduits.

Schematic diagrams

3. The schematic diagrams give a theoretical representation of the whole electrical system and show the two parallel engine-driven generators, and the loads carried by them. The various lines are indicated as follows:—

The main supply lines are identified on the schematic diagram as A+ for generator and accumulator positive and A− for common negative. Where the symbol R+ and R− are used on the scheme B theoretical diagram they should be read as A+ and A−

Interpretation of routine charts

4. The routing charts are laid out in tabular form, the first column on the left-hand side gives the title of each circuit, and further columns denote the junction box, panel or item of equipment where breaks in the circuit occur. While all the possible points for circuit breaks are given at the head of each column, only those appropriate to the individual circuit are used. Interposed at convenient positions are columns headed "Equipment", in which are items of equipment peculiar to each circuit. Further columns headed "Con.Ref./Pin" are placed beside the junctions box columns to indicate conduit references and pin designations.

5. Identification reference letters and numbers are marked on the fuses, conduits, junction boxes and plugs and sockets; these references being indicated on the routing charts and marked on the components as described in the following paragraphs.

6. *Referencing of fuses (scheme B).*—Fuses are mounted in the control panel, the auxiliary control panel adjacent to the control panel, the navigator's panel and at the mid-turret position. The fuses for the bomb gear are mounted

F.S./2

inside junction box A at the forward end of the bomb compartment and a fuse for the auto-bomb sight is mounted in the port bomb sight panel. Labels mounted on each fuse box give the number of each fuse, whilst a chart engraved on the inside of the panel access door gives the current rating and services. The fuses in the control panel are numbered 1 to 32, fuses 18, 20, 21, 26, 29 and 32 being spare. Fuses 33 to 48 are positioned in the auxiliary control panel, fuse 48 being spare. The fuses at the navigator's panel are numbered 1 to 4.

        No. 1.   Detonator
        No. 2.   R.3003
        No. 3.   T.R.1335
        No. 4.   T.R.9F Vibro pack

The fuses at the mid turret position are numbered No. 1 (beam approach), No. 2 (upper mid turret), No. 3 (lower mid turret) No. 4 (call lights).

7. *Referencing of fuses (scheme C and E).*—Fuses are mounted in the control panel, the navigator's panel, the mid turret position and on the starboard bomb aimer's panel. Labels mounted near each fuse box give the number of each fuse, a list of the fuses giving rating and service being mounted inside the door of the control panel. The fuses in the control panel are numbered 1 to 56; where no service is shown on the list of fuses, these are spare. The fuses at the navigator's panel are numbered 1 to 4.

        No. 1   Detonator
        No. 2   R.3003
        No. 3   T.R.1335
        No. 4   T.R.9F

The fuses at the mid turret are numbered No. 1 (beam approach), No. 2 (upper mid turret), No. 3 (lower mid turret), No. 4 (call lights). On the starboard bomb aimer's panel is a fuse box with fuses numbered No. 1 (nose fuzing), No. 2 (tail fuzing), No. 3 (spare), No. 4 (distributor heating).

8. *Referencing of conduits.*—All conduits are marked with the Air Ministry reference number, the conduit reference and the Plessey drawing number. Conduits for general service wiring are prefixed with the letter F, P or S for the fuselage, port and starboard planes respectively (e.g. F.13—fuselage, P.20—port plane, and S.6—starboard plane). Conduits for the radio and intercommunication, bomb fusing and release are referenced as follows:—

(i) Wireless and intercommunication—series of numbers with the prefix W.T. (e.g. W.T.3).

(ii) Bomb fuzing and release (scheme B). Conduit references consist of the combined letters of the junction boxes they connect (e.g. conduit A.C. connects junction boxes J.B.A. and J.B.C.).

(iii) Bomb fusing and release (scheme C and E). In addition to the Air Ministry reference number the conduit references are numbered or lettered.

9. *Referencing of junction boxes.*—The general service junction boxes are referenced numerically with the prefix J.B. (e.g. J.B.13). The junction boxes for the radio and intercommunication are referenced alphabetically with the prefix W (e.g. W.D. W.E., etc). For the bomb fuzing and release the junction boxes are also referenced alphabetically but with the prefix J.B. (e.g. J.B.C). For schemes C and E, only one junction box is fitted in this circuit.

10. *Referencing of plugs and sockets.*—The plugs and sockets are numbered with either a series of numbers or a series of letters, the number or letter being repeated in the appropriate pin or hole at the other end of the conduit. The markings will be found on the mouldings adjacent to the appropriate plug and socket.

11. *Referencing of terminals in junction boxes.*—The terminals inside the junction boxes have a prefix which is the circuit reference letter and a suffix which is one of a series of numbers for that particular circuit (e.g. circuit reference Z, terminal reference Z4). The circuit letters are given on the routing charts.

12. *Method of reading routing chart.*—To follow any particular circuit, commence at the fuse, generally shown in the column marked "Control Panel". Where a dot is shown on a vertical line this indicates a "break" at the plug or terminal at the position shown at the top of that particular column, e.g. Circuit P camera supply (*see* fig. 18). Commencing at A+ in control panel, thence to fuse No. 9, the first "break" occurs at the vertical line representing the plug and socket at the outer casing of the tontrol panel to which is connected the lead in conduit F.35 pin "A". This continues without further breaks until it connects to the plug and socket on the outer casing of junction box J.B.13, then to terminal P1 inside this junction box and on to the plug and socket emerging from the same junction box at pin B to conduit F.47. This wire continues to the plug and socket on the air bomber's panel, port. An internal connection is made on this panel to the common negative A−, and thence via junction box 13 to common negative A− in the control panel.

13. *General.*—The conduit wiring system is bench assembled in units and is fitted in the aircraft by means of multiple plugs and sockets.

14. Conduit assemblies consist of V.I.R. or "cel" wiring enclosed in flexible conduits terminating at either or both ends in multiple sockets. Cable assemblies are composed of metal braided cables, terminating in either sockets or cable ends for connection to terminal blocks, lamps, switches, etc.

15. The junction boxes and panels contain terminals or terminal blocks for services using them. Multiple plugs to take the appropriate sockets are fitted to junction boxes and most panels.

16. Multi-pin bulkhead plugs which act as disconnecting points are used to take the wiring through the fireproof bulkheads. On scheme B this method is also employed at the wing root.

17. Fault location is facilitated by the fact that each wire is designated at both ends. Fault rectification is simplified in that the entire conduit assembly or component can be removed and either bench repaired or replaced from stock.

18. The services to the outboard engines and outer planes pass through the main junction boxes (J.B.1 and J.B.2). These boxes are situated on the front spar at the centre of the inboard nacelles. The cables for these services pass through solid conduit tubes mounted in the nose of the wing between the

F.S./3

inboard and outboard engines. These cables are pushed through from the inboard side and are identified to correspond with the labelled terminals mounted on the panels attached to the bearers on the outboard engine frame. Cables from the outboard engine services and from the outer wings connect to these panels also and are identified to connect to the labelled terminals in a similar manner.

Access to components

19. Where required, provision has been made to give access to items of electrical equipment. In the wing the leading edge between fuselage and inboard engine is hinged to give access to the equipment forward of the front spar. The overhanging portion of the wing forward of the front spar at the inboard engine is also hinged. Equipment forward and aft of the engine bulkheads can be reached by removal of the engine cowling panel. Access to the following components is provided as follows:—

Component.	Means of access.
Navigation recognition lamps ...	Remove transparent moulding from wing tip
T.B.7, 8, 9, 10, 11, 12, 21, 22 and 23	Access doors in underside of main plane skin
J.B.4 and J.B.5	Access door in underside of main plane skin
Fuel contents gauge tank units and immersed fuel pumps	Access door in upper surface of main plane skin

Maintenance notes

20. Information regarding the maintenance of electrical equipment not covered in A.P.1095 is given in the following paragraphs.

21. *Undercarriage position indicator.*—The indicator is illustrated in fig. 32, and the unit is described in Sect. 10. The following notes give the maintenance dismantling and re-assembly for the undercarriage position indicator:—

(i) *Maintenance.*—The plunger contacts (12) are lubricated before delivery and because the assembly is effected by a spinning operation it is not practicable to make any repair. The only trouble likely to be experienced with the plunger itself is sticking which may be remedied by additional lubrication. If, however, this treatment is not effective the complete plunger assembly should be replaced. It is important that the tops of the plungers, which make contact with the lamp contacts, should be clean and free from grease or other substances which increase electrical resistance. The connecting wires from the terminal block to the contact plungers are looped at the terminal block end, the loops being passed over the terminal screws and clamped in position by means of locknuts. To free this end it is, therefore, only necessary to remove the locknut. The other ends of the wire are attached to soldered tags which in turn are soldered to the contact plunger (12). Should a tag become detached from its contact plunger the tag must be re-positioned and soldered in the usual way, care being taken to avoid a dry joint. To replace a defective lamp it will only be necessary to withdraw the lamp mounting (5) by unscrewing the bezel, etc., and it may be found in some cases that this lamp mounting will be withdrawn simultaneously with the dial and spider assembly from which the lamp mounting may be separated by a gentle pull. When a new lamp is fitted care should be taken to see that it is screwed firmly home in its socket to prevent its working loose due to vibration. The terminal cover should always be firmly in position as it not only affords protection to the terminals but also clamps the cables in position. To ensure that the lamp mounting (5) is always correctly positioned in the case, a groove is provided in the top and should clear the two fillets moulded integrally with the case. Also when the dial and spider assemblies (2) and (3) are returned to the case the vertical spider web must be offered so as to pass along the groove formed by the two fillets previously referred to, thereby ensuring correct alignment. Finally the bezel ring must be screwed reasonably tight. The action of screwing home the bezel ring forces the lamp mounting (5) rearward and establishes electrical contact between the lamps, contact stud and the spring loaded plungers.

(ii) *Dismantling.*—Removal of the bezel ring (1) by unscrewing (right-hand thread) permits the withdrawal of the dial and spider assemblies (2) and (3) and the lamp mounting assembly (5). These two assemblies are withdrawn through the front of the case. The spring plunger contact plate terminal block assembly (9) may be dismantled from the case by unscrewing the two 6 B.A. screws (7). The terminal block (9) and contact plunger assembly (8) are withdrawn rearwards. Slackening of the four fixing screws (11) permits the cover plate (10) to be removed, exposing the terminals and cable leads thereto.

(iii) *Re-assembly.*—If it has been necessary to remove the contact plunger assembly plate (8) and the terminal block (9) from the instrument these two assemblies must be returned to the case simultaneously; all connections between the terminal block and the contact plungers having been made before attempting to return these two assemblies to the case. It will be discovered that the contact plunger plate (8) can only be returned to the case in one way, that is when the two semi-circular gaps diametrically opposite to each other are passed over the two semi-circular lugs moulded integrally with the case, which carry the retaining screws (7). The contact plunger plate (8) must then be partially rotated so as to bring the two 6 B.A. clearance holes in line with the previously mentioned lugs and the two retaining screws (7) be passed through the plate and the lugs and allowed to project to the rear, on this instrument. The screws may now be offered to the inserts in the terminal block (9) and tightened down, thus clamping the terminal block firmly to the back of the instrument. It is important in doing this to make sure that any of the connecting wires do not touch the screws as should they do so the insulation may be chaffed due to vibration.

22. *Warning horn.*—The warning horn is illustrated in fig. 34 and the unit is described in Sect. 10. The following sub-paragraphs give instructions for maintenance, dismantling, reassembly and testing:—

(i) *Maintenance.*—The tungsten contacts of the "make" and "break" device may require cleaning after a period of service. This should be done by light rubbing with fine emery cloth or a smooth file and only

F.S./4

the minimum amount of cleaning should be attempted. It is also important to avoid any rounding of contacting surfaces. Overheating of the magnet winding due to the application of an excessive voltage or to sticking of the "make" and "break" contacts may result in permanent damage through breakdown of insulation and the only remedy is to rewind the bobbin. The shunting resistance is wound with nickel chrome wire and is very robust. Should the wire break, the resistance must be completely rewound.

(ii) *Dismantling.*—To remove the unit from its case, first remove the locknuts (7) and withdraw the unit. It may not normally be necessary to remove the connecting wires from the terminals to effect any slight repair or to clean the contacts and the leads should be left in position if possible. It is not necessary to dismantle the "make" and "break" device to clean the contacts but it may be necessary to slacken the adjusting screw (8) to allow sufficient clearance between the contacts for the application of the abrasive or file. The "make" and "break" mechanism may, however, be completely removed by unscrewing the studs (10). To remove the resistance winding, the locknuts on the studs (9) must be removed and the resistance may then be lifted off its supports. It is also necessary to remove these nuts and the resistance in order to detach the armature plunger and flat spring assembly. The magnet winding is wound on a metal former with insulated cheeks, the metal former being riveted permanently to the main assembly plate (1). Dismantling of this bobbin is necessary in order to rewind and this process should only be attempted at a maintenace depot. To remove the cover plate (5) the three captive screws (6) must be first slackened.

(iii) *Re-assembly.*—The re-assembly of this unit is merely the reverse of the dismantling. Care, however, should be taken when re-assembling to observe the following points:—

(a) If the "make" and "break" device has been dismantled care must be exercised to see that the live metal parts are properly isolated and that the insulating sleeving which covers the shanks of the two studs (10) is correctly positioned, otherwise short circuiting and therefore failure to function may result.

(b) If the resistance winding, the armature, or flat spring assembly have been removed the locknuts must be very firmly tightened in position when these parts are reassembled.

(c) If dismantling to this extent has taken place readjustment for optimum sound output will be essential. This is essentially a trial and error process and the optimum is achieved by adjusting in combination the striking plunger (11) and the "make" and "break" adjusting screw (8). It is very important that when the correct settings have been found these two screws be very firmly locked in position.

(d) On returning the unit to its case it is necessary to avoid the fouling of any parts by the two leads, particular attention being given to those parts that vibrate. Furthermore the distance washers (13) must be in position on the two studs (12) before the ends of these studs are passed through the holes in the moulded case.

(iv) *Testing.*—This should be done with a D.C. supply of 24 volts.

23. *Control switch.*—The unit is illustrated on fig. 33 and described in Sect. 10, the following notes describe the maintenance, dismantling and re-assembly of the central switch:—

(i) *Maintenance.*—The contacting surfaces are silver plated and may be cleaned with a jeweller's cloth. During any cleaning process the phosphor-bronze contact springs must not be bent out of shape. The extending springs must be replaced should they break or become unduly fatigued causing loss of snap in the switch action.

(ii) *Dismantling.*—If it is necessary at any time to gain access to the switch mechanism it is preferable to remove the switch completely from the instrument panel. To do this the cables should be first disconnected. Removal of the two screws (17) retaining the moulded terminal cover in position allows this part to be slipped along the cables that pass through the centre hole of the cover. The terminals are now exposed and the cables can be disconnected. To remove the switch from the instrument panel the four retaining screws, one at each corner of the top mounting plate (14), should be withdrawn. Removal of the two round-head screws (12) which retain the top mounting plate (14) in position will free this part and also the sliding bar (13), the rectangular aperture of which is passed over the ON-OFF section lever (8) and also the die-cast distance piece (15). The metal case may now be withdrawn and the switch mechansim exposed. The two sections of the switch are held together by four long transverse screws (5) the ends of which are riveted over on the locknuts. The spade-ended terminals (4) are riveted to their respective phosphor-bronze contacting springs but the end terminal plate (3) is retained by nine round-headed slotted screws. The various other sub-assemblies of the switch are also riveted together. The transverse tension spring pivots (10) are held in position by circlips, and the looped ends of the tension springs rest in grooves in these pivots and are readily removable.

(iii) *Re-assembly.*—If new tension springs have been fitted it is important to place a small quantity of lubricant on the looped ends to minimize wear, and a small quantity of lubricant should also be placed on the lever bearings. The small dumb-bell-shaped roller is carried loose in a slot at the end of the insulated lever arm and must not be lubricated, neither should the lubricant be placed on any of the silvered surfaces. To replace the metal case, the two levers should be set in the dead centre position and carefully held thus (avoiding distortion of the contacting springs) to allow the levers to pass readily through the arc-shaped slots in the end of the case. The terminal shroud should next be fitted and it is correctly positioned when the figures 3, 6 and 9 read vertically downwards co-incide with the three terminals associated with the ON-OFF section, i.e. the section of the switch which is actuated by the fork lever (8). The shroud is retained in position by friction only. Having replaced the case (7) in position, the die-cast distance piece (15) should now be positioned and the sliding bar (13) placed in position by passing the ON-OFF section lever (8) through the rectangular aperture in same. The chamfered edges of the sliding bar should be outward. The mounting plate (14) may now be replaced and held in position by the two round headed retaining screws (12)

F.S./5

fitted with spring washers. The mounting plate is correctly in position relative to the terminal shrouds when the wording INDICATOR LAMPS on the mounting plate is on the same side as the figures 3, 6, and 9 on the shroud.

Oil dilution system

24. The solenoid on each electro-magnet valve should be checked for continuity. The action of the valve plunger may be checked by disconnecting the petrol feed pipe from the valve unit and operating the push switch. If the plunger is found to be sticking, the unit should be replaced.

Bonding

25. Bonding diagrams for the general services, the hydraulic and pneumatic systems are shown in figs. 29 to 31.

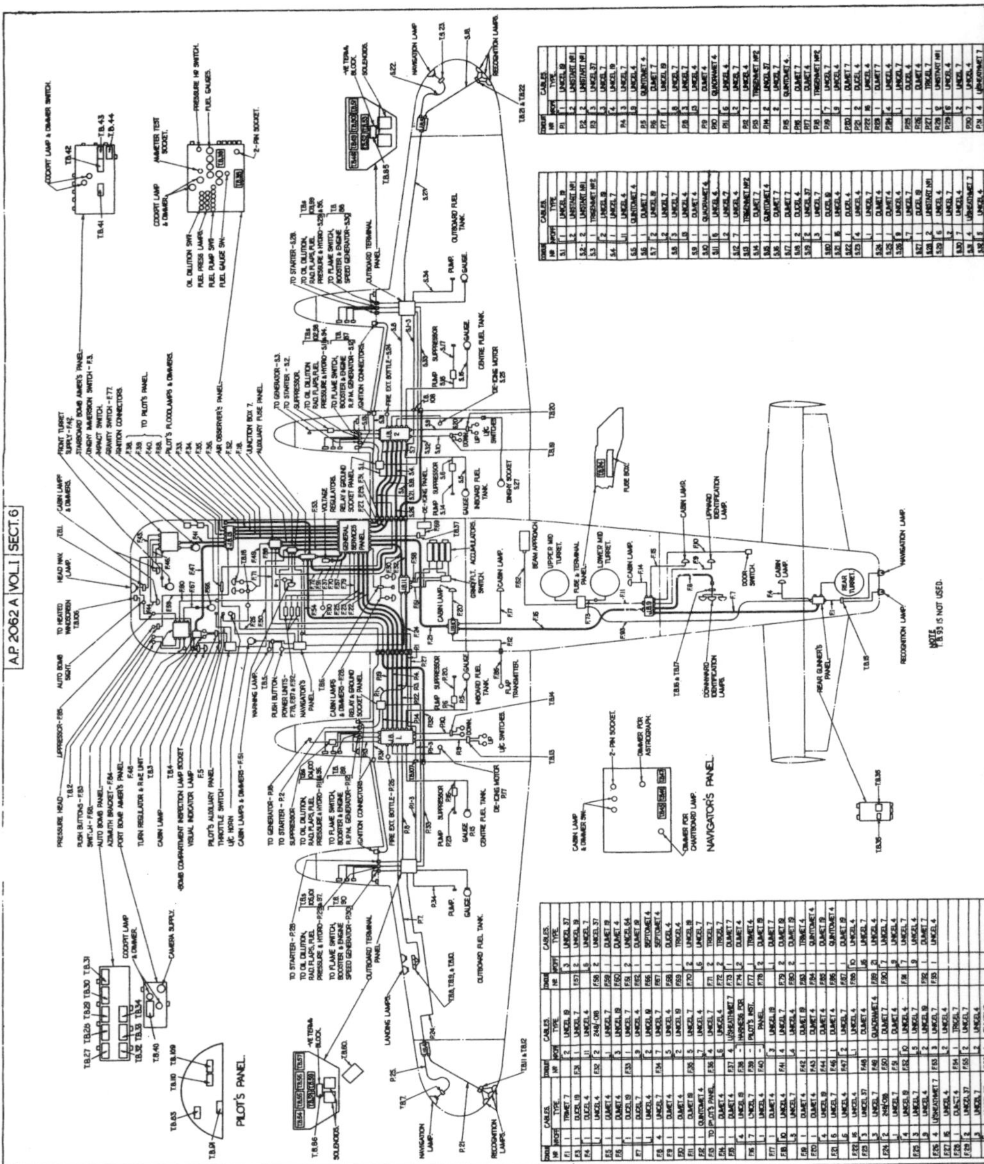
A.P. 2062 A VOL.I SECT.6
PILOT'S PANEL.
NAVIGATOR'S PANEL.
NOTE T.B.93 IS NOT USED.

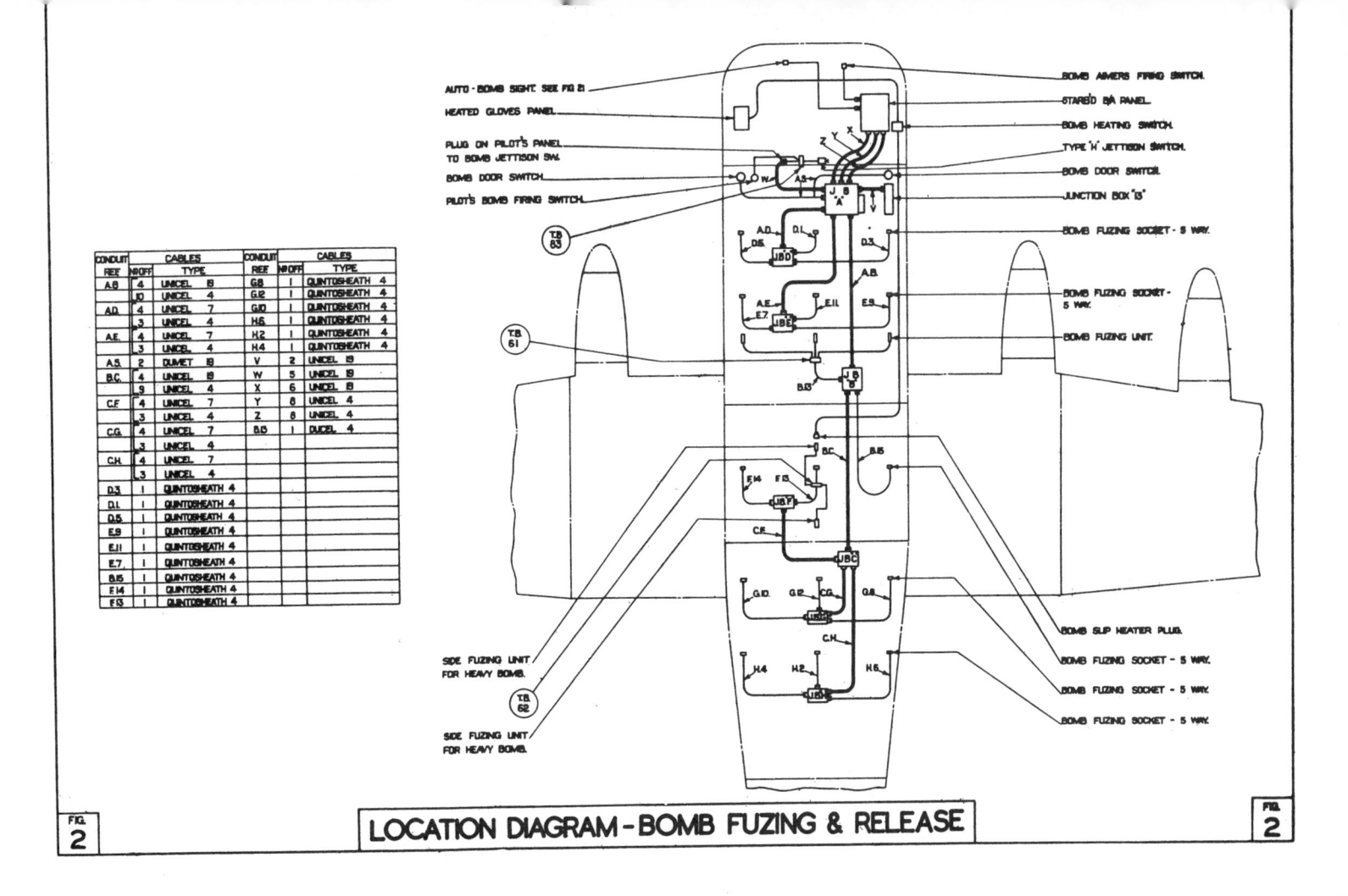

LOCATION DIAGRAM - BOMB FUZING & RELEASE

FIG. 2

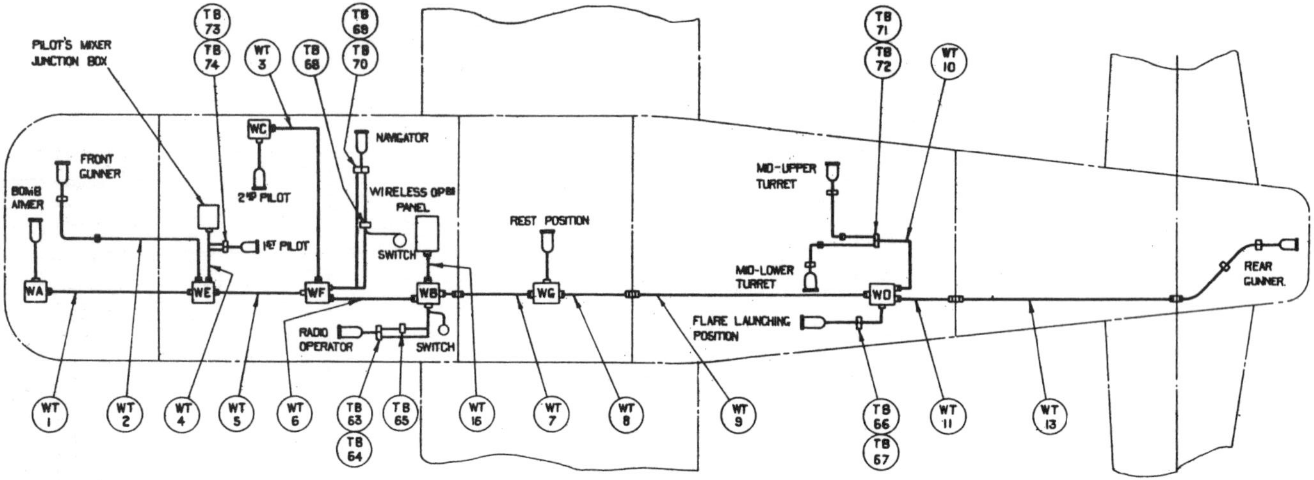

CONDUIT REF.	CABLES	
	Nº OFF	TYPE
WT 1	2	DUMET 4
WT 2	2	DUMET 4
WT 3	2	DUMET 4
WT 4	2	DUMET 4
WT 5	2	DUMET 4
WT 6	2	DUMET 4
WT 7	2	DUMET 4
WT 8	2	DUMET 4
WT 9	2	DUMET 4
WT 10	2	DUMET 4
WT 11	2	DUMET 4
WT 13	2	DUMET 4
WT 16	3	DUMET 4

FIG 3

LOCATION DIAGRAM — INTERCOMMUNICATION

FIG 3

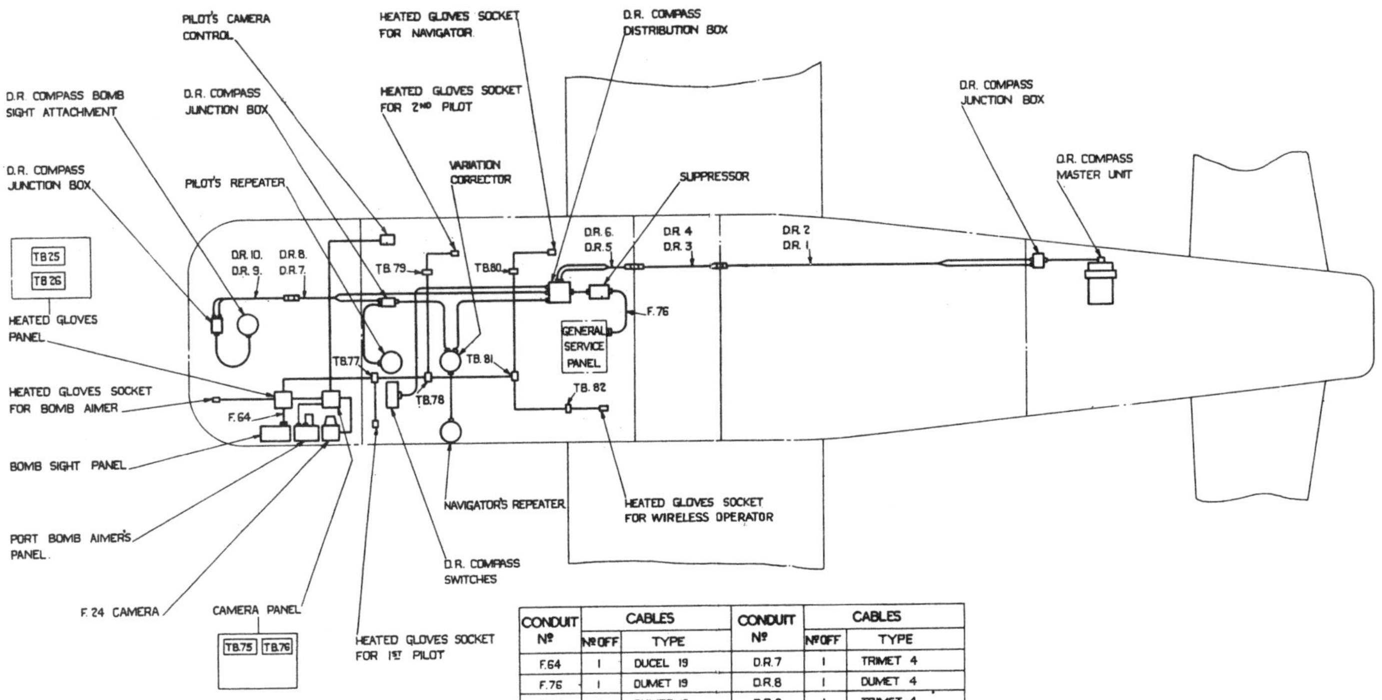

AP.2062A, VOL.I, SEC.I.6

CONDUIT	CABLES		CONDUIT	CABLES	
Nº	Nº OFF	TYPE	Nº	Nº OFF	TYPE
F.64	1	DUCEL 19	D.R.7	1	TRIMET 4
F.76	1	DUMET 19	D.R.8	1	DUMET 4
D.R.1	1	DUMET 19	D.R.9	1	TRIMET 4
D.R.2	1	SEXTOMET 4	D.R.10	1	DUMET 4
D.R.3	1	DUMET 19			
D.R.4	1	SEXTOMET 4			
D.R.5	1	DUMET 19			
D.R.6	1	SEXTOMET 4			

FIG. 4

LOCATION DIAGRAM
D.R. COMPASS, HEATED GLOVES CAMERA & CAMERA SUPPLY.

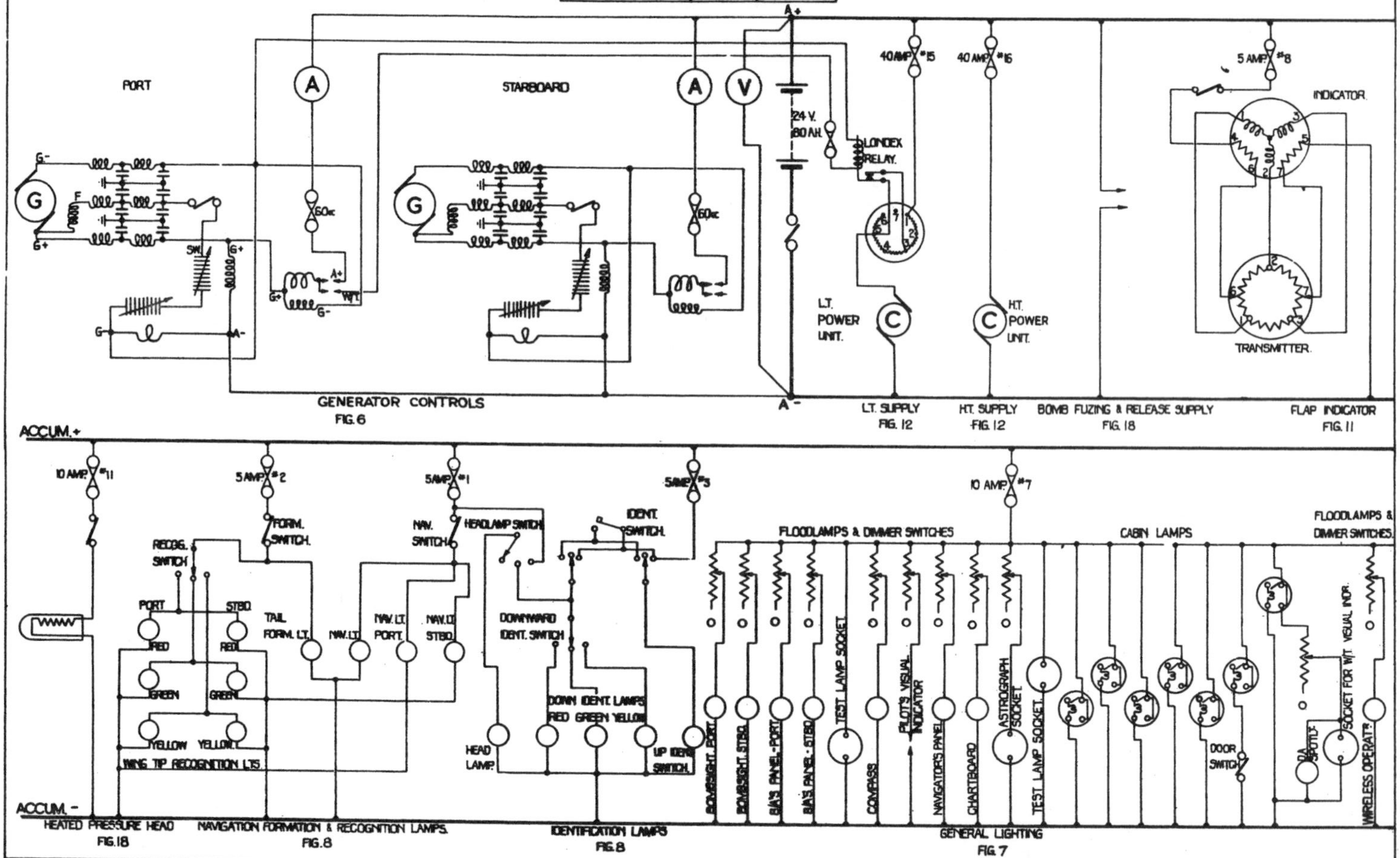

FIG 5 SCHEMATIC DIAGRAM

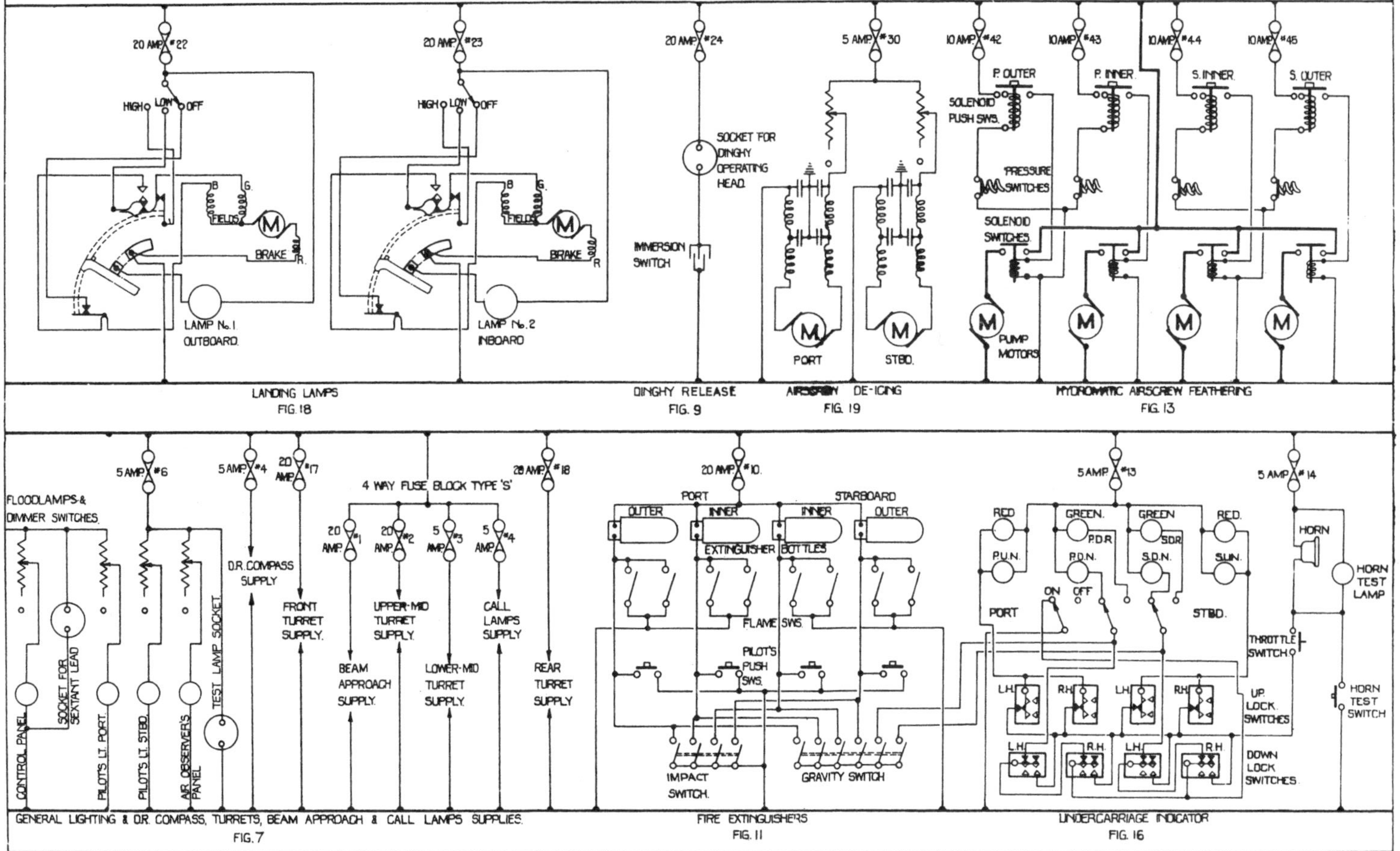

ELECTRICAL SERVICES

FIG. 5

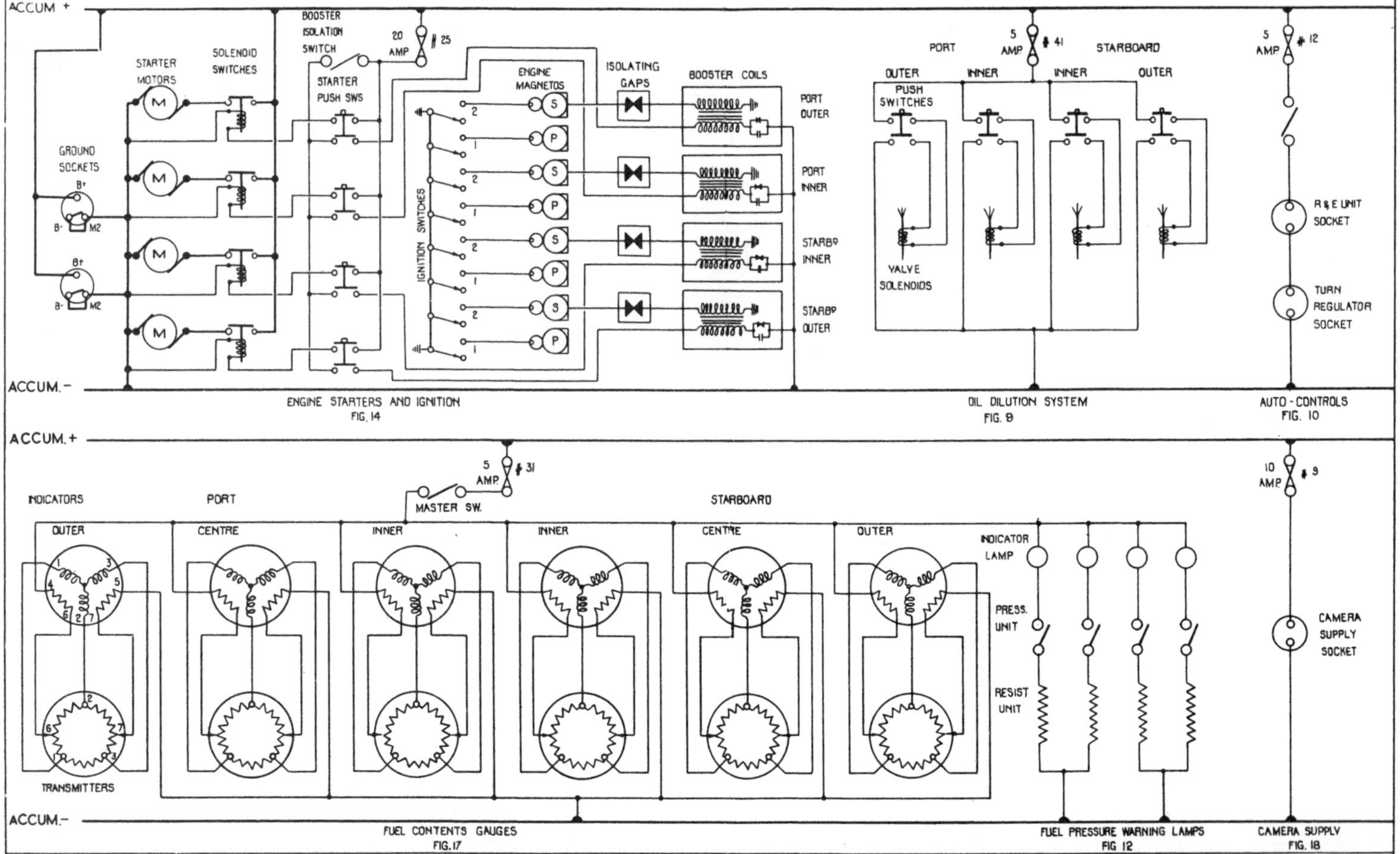

ACCUM +
ACCUM. −
ACCUM. +
ACCUM. −
STARTER MOTORS
SOLENOID SWITCHES
GROUND SOCKETS
B+
B-
M2
BOOSTER ISOLATION SWITCH
STARTER PUSH SWS
20 AMP
25
ENGINE MAGNETOS
IGNITION SWITCHES
ISOLATING GAPS
BOOSTER COILS
PORT OUTER
PORT INNER
STARBD INNER
STARBD OUTER
ENGINE STARTERS AND IGNITION
FIG. 14
PORT
STARBOARD
OUTER
INNER
5 AMP
41
PUSH SWITCHES
VALVE SOLENOIDS
OIL DILUTION SYSTEM
FIG. 9
12
R & E UNIT SOCKET
TURN REGULATOR SOCKET
AUTO-CONTROLS
FIG. 10
INDICATORS
CENTRE
31
MASTER SW.
TRANSMITTERS
FUEL CONTENTS GAUGES
FIG. 17
INDICATOR LAMP
PRESS. UNIT
RESIST UNIT
FUEL PRESSURE WARNING LAMPS
FIG 12
10 AMP
9
CAMERA SUPPLY SOCKET
CAMERA SUPPLY
FIG. 18

FIG. 5A

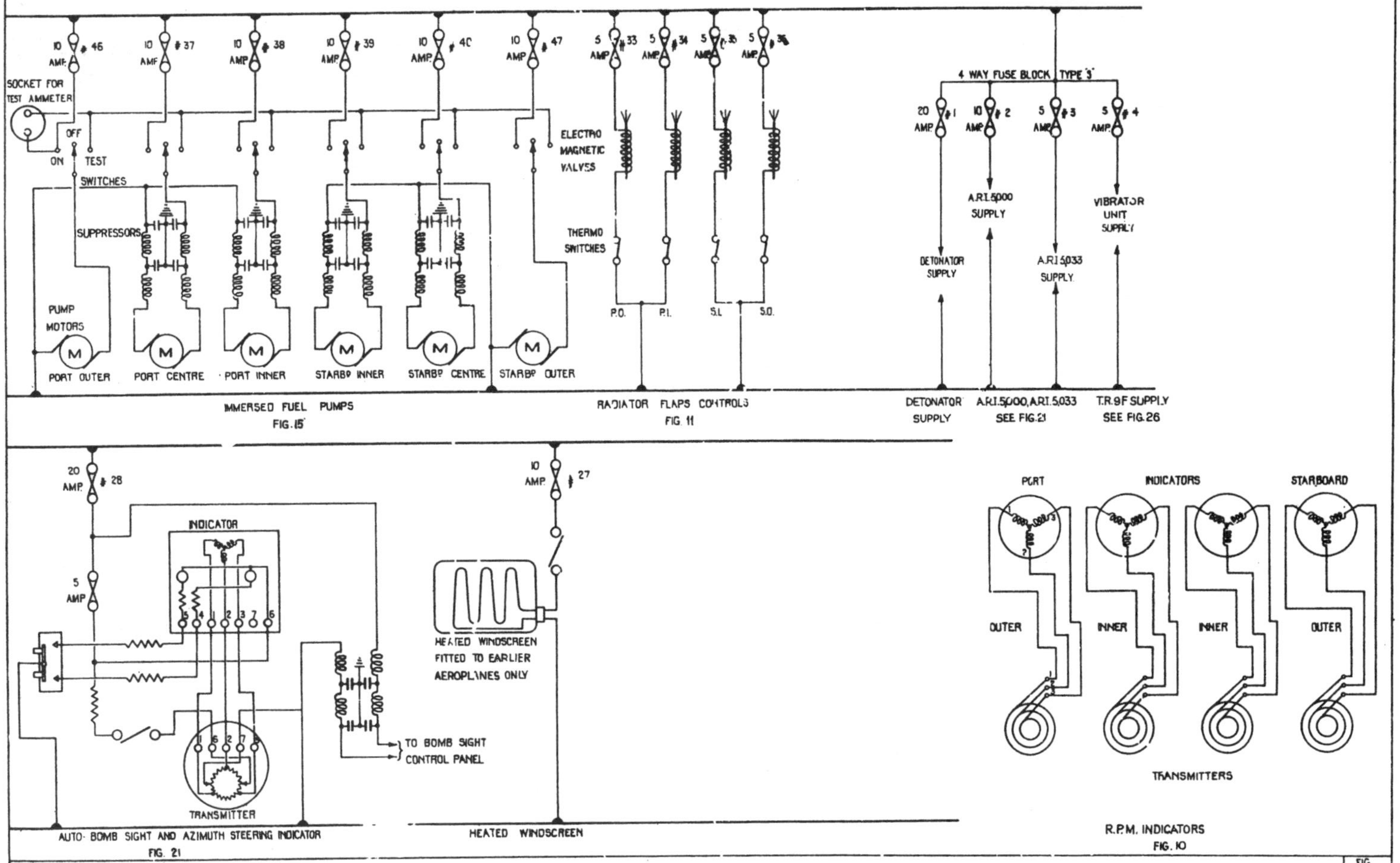

ELECTRICAL SERVICES (CONTINUED) FIG. 5A

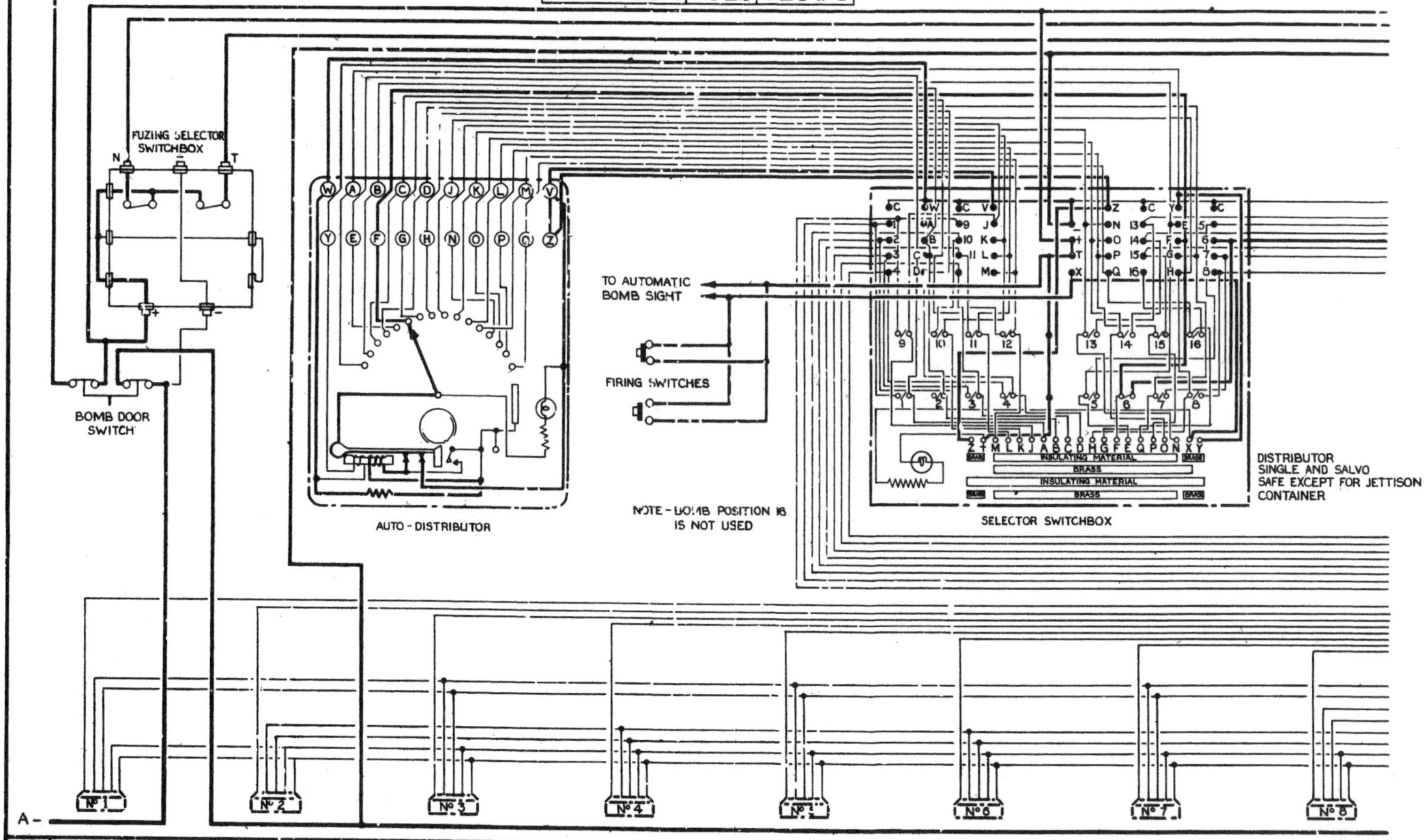

FIG. 5B SCHEMATIC DIAGRAM OF

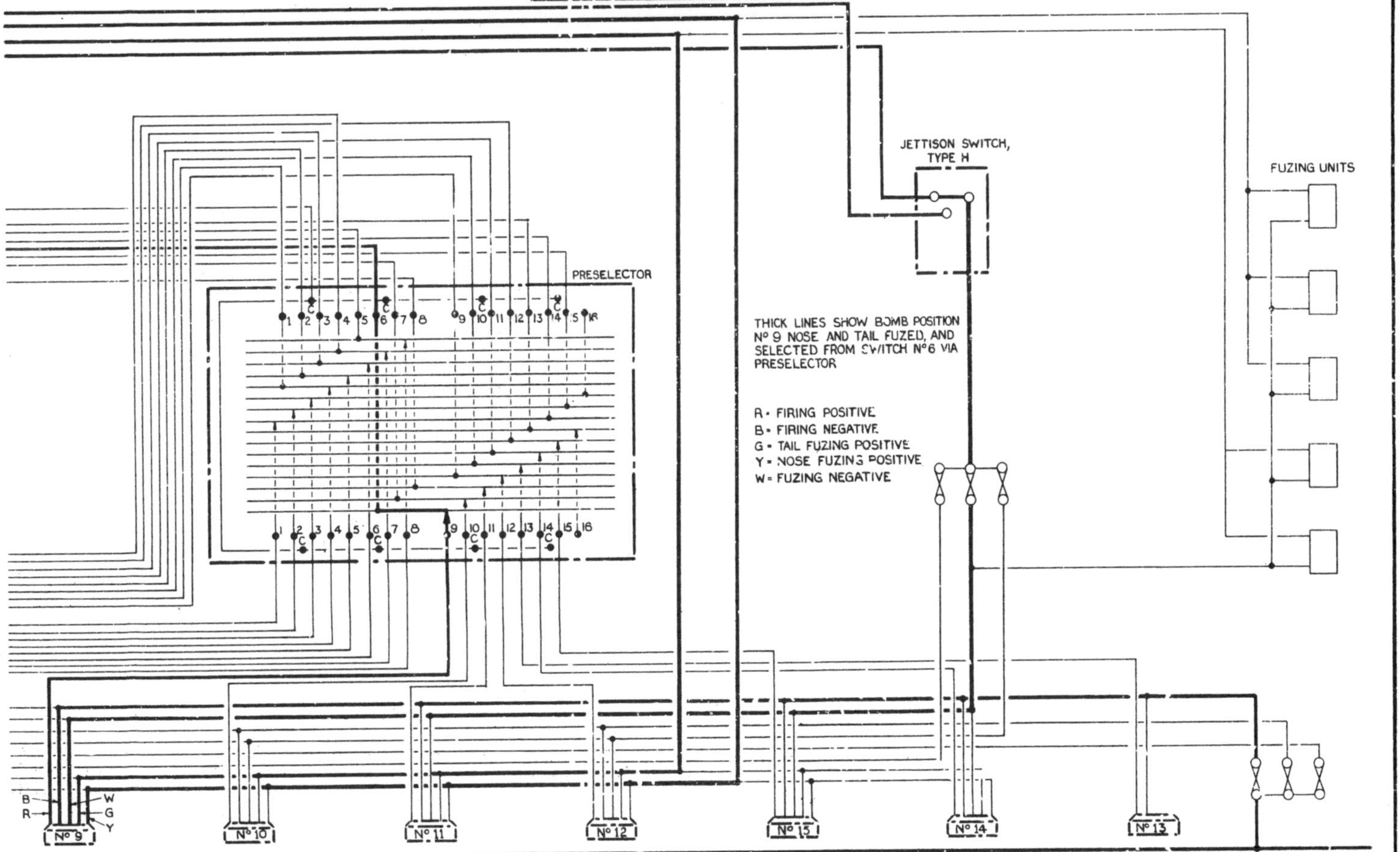

BOMB FUZING AND RELEASE

FIG. 5B

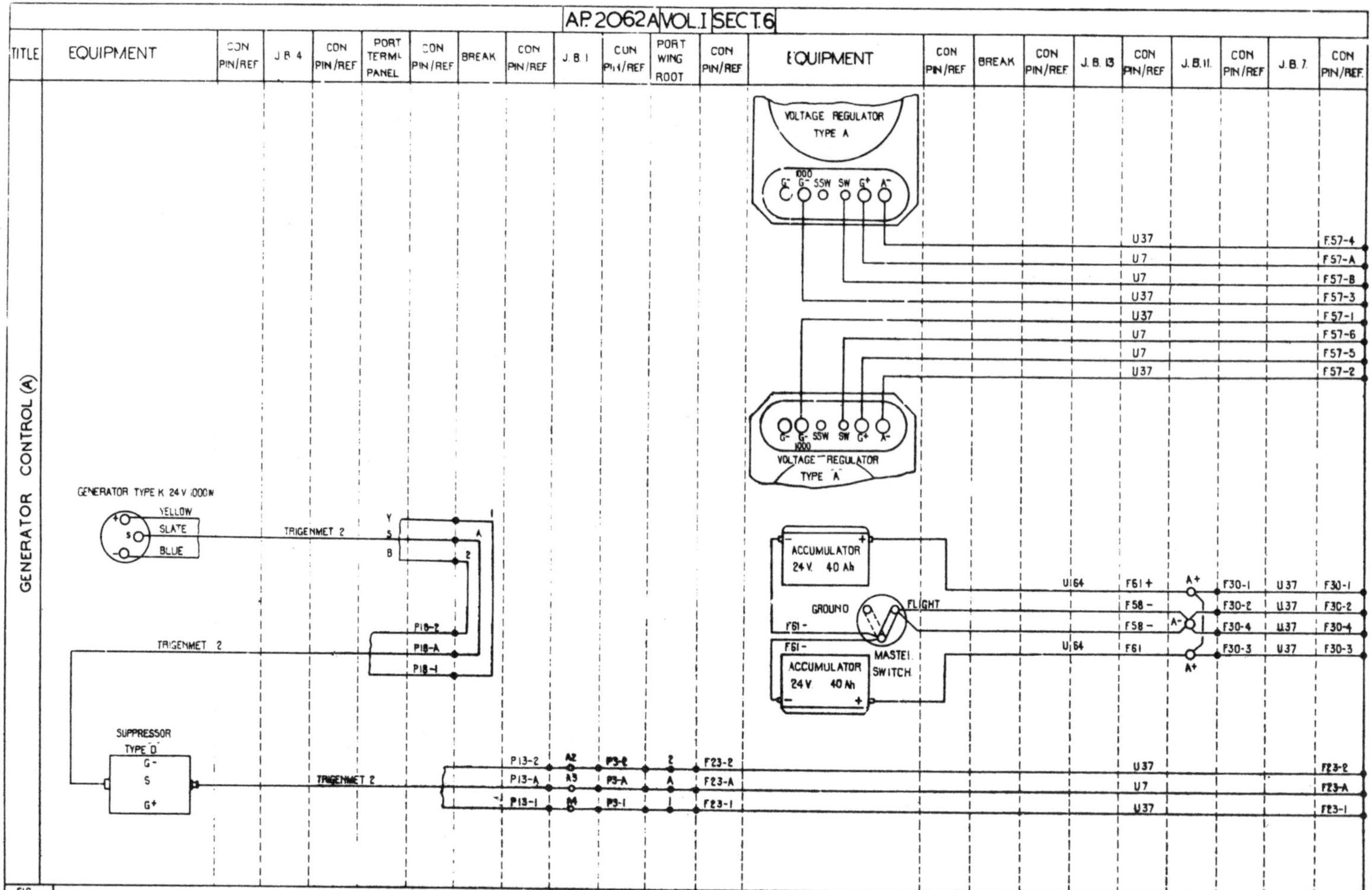

FIG 6

ROUTING CHART

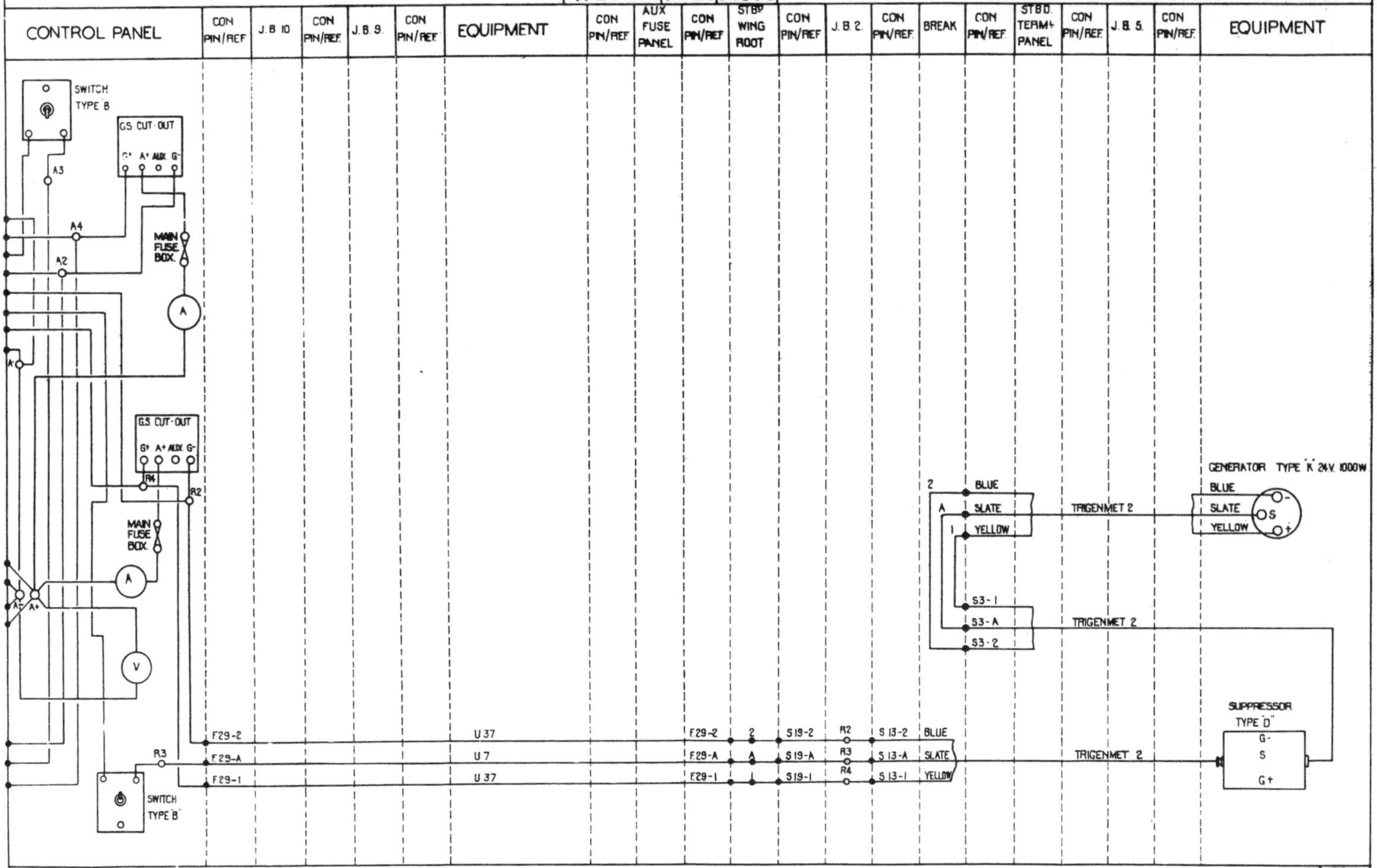

GENERAL SERVICES

FIG 6

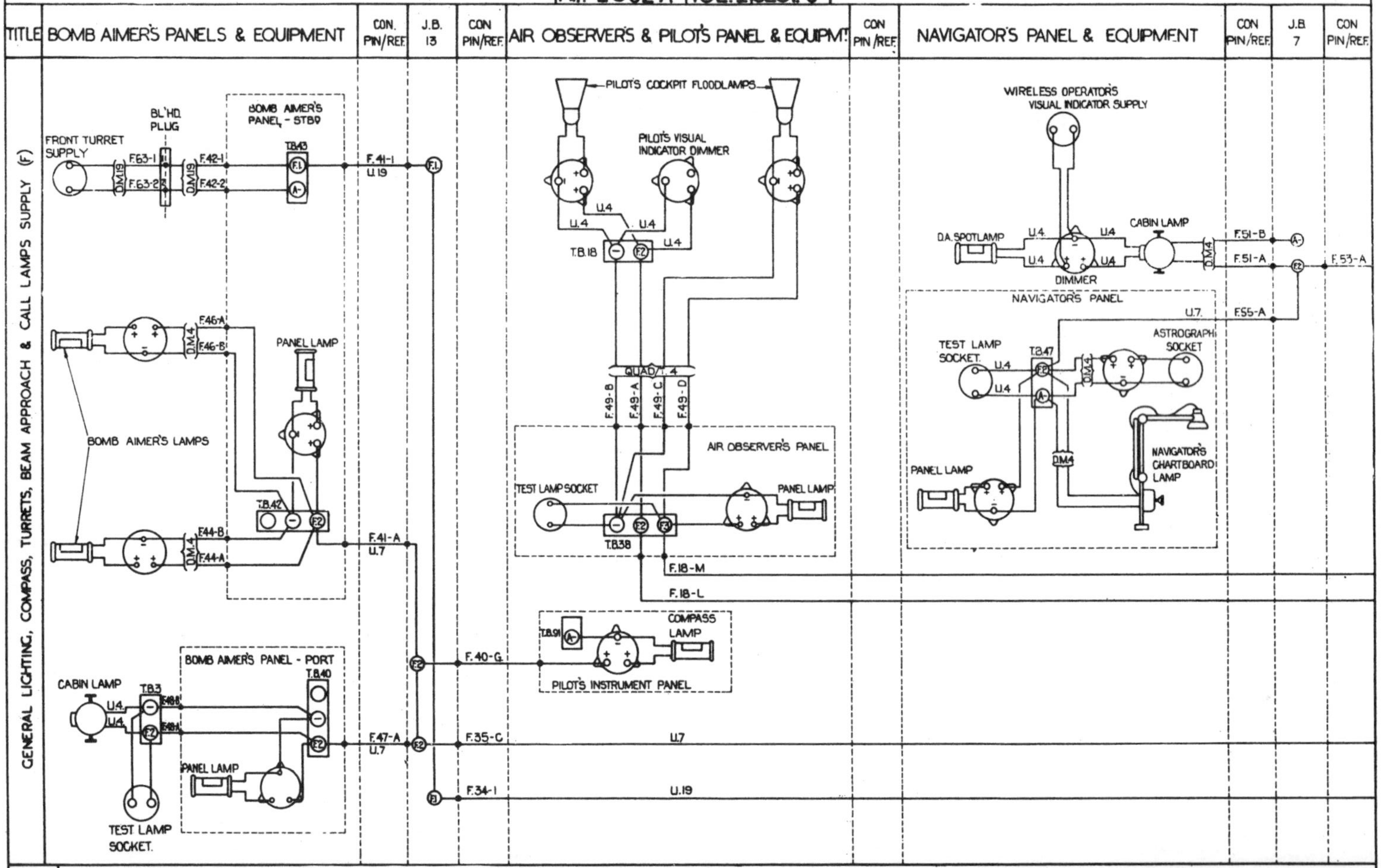

FIG. 7

ROUTING CHART

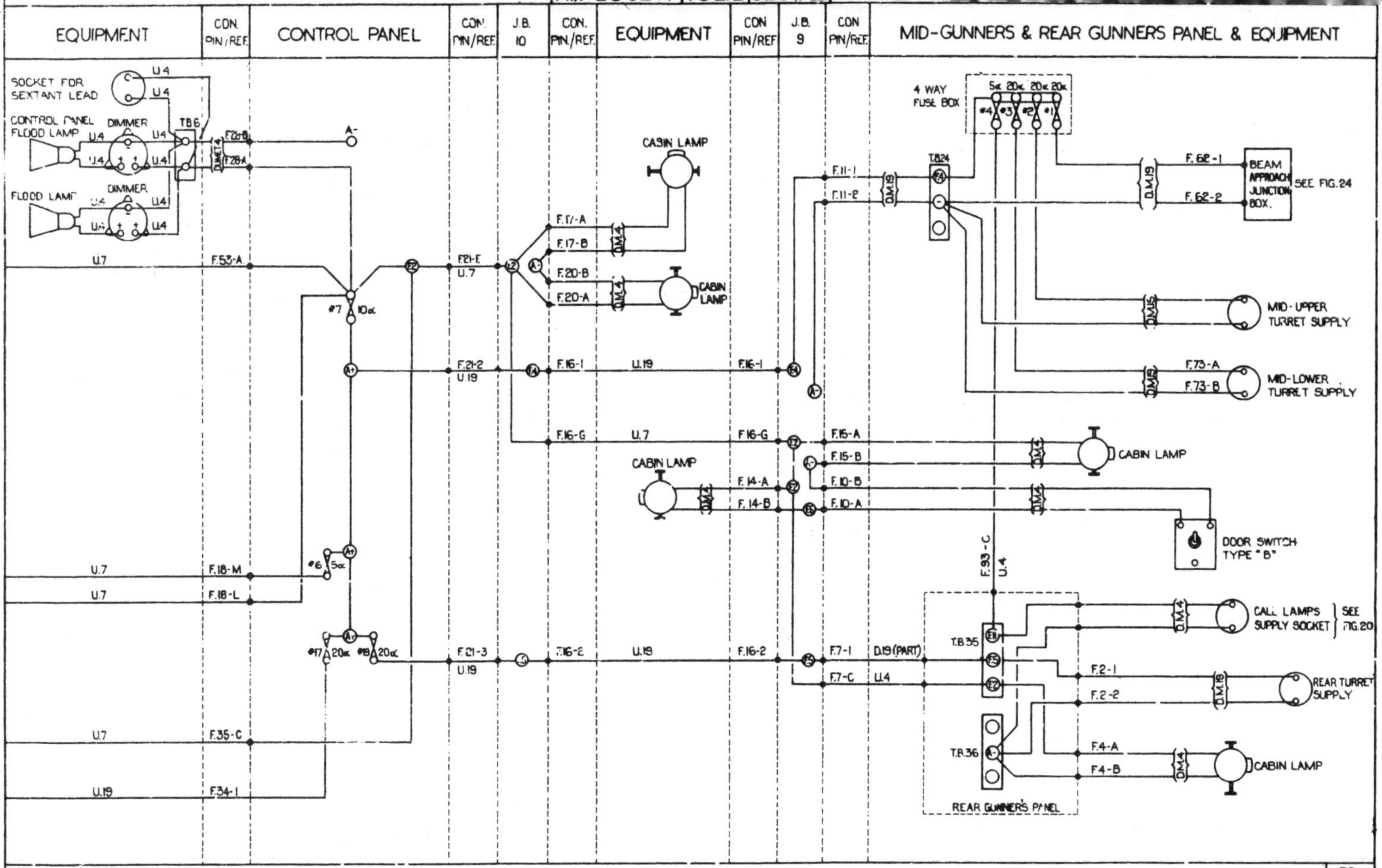

GENERAL SERVICES

FIG 7

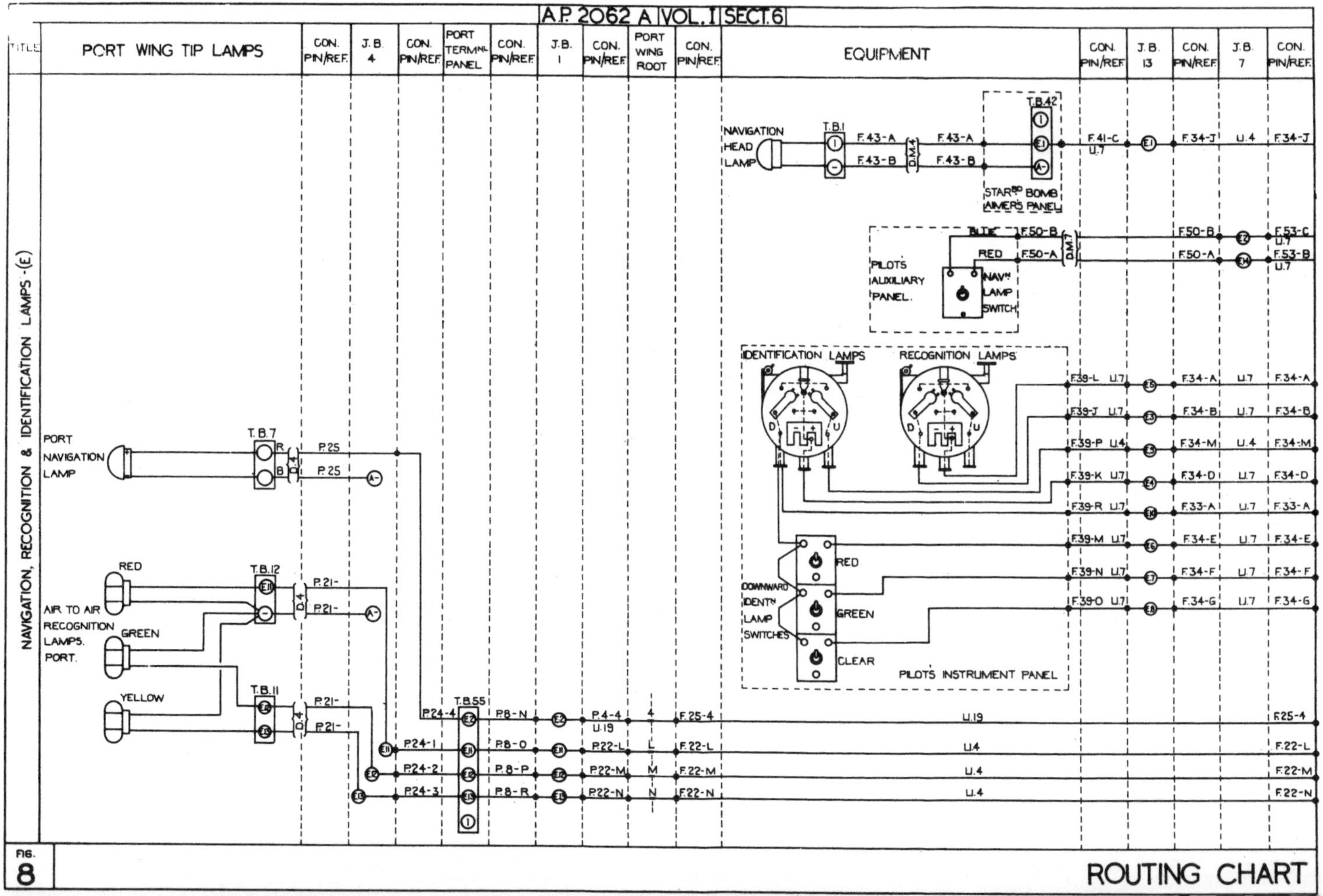

FIG. 8

ROUTING CHART

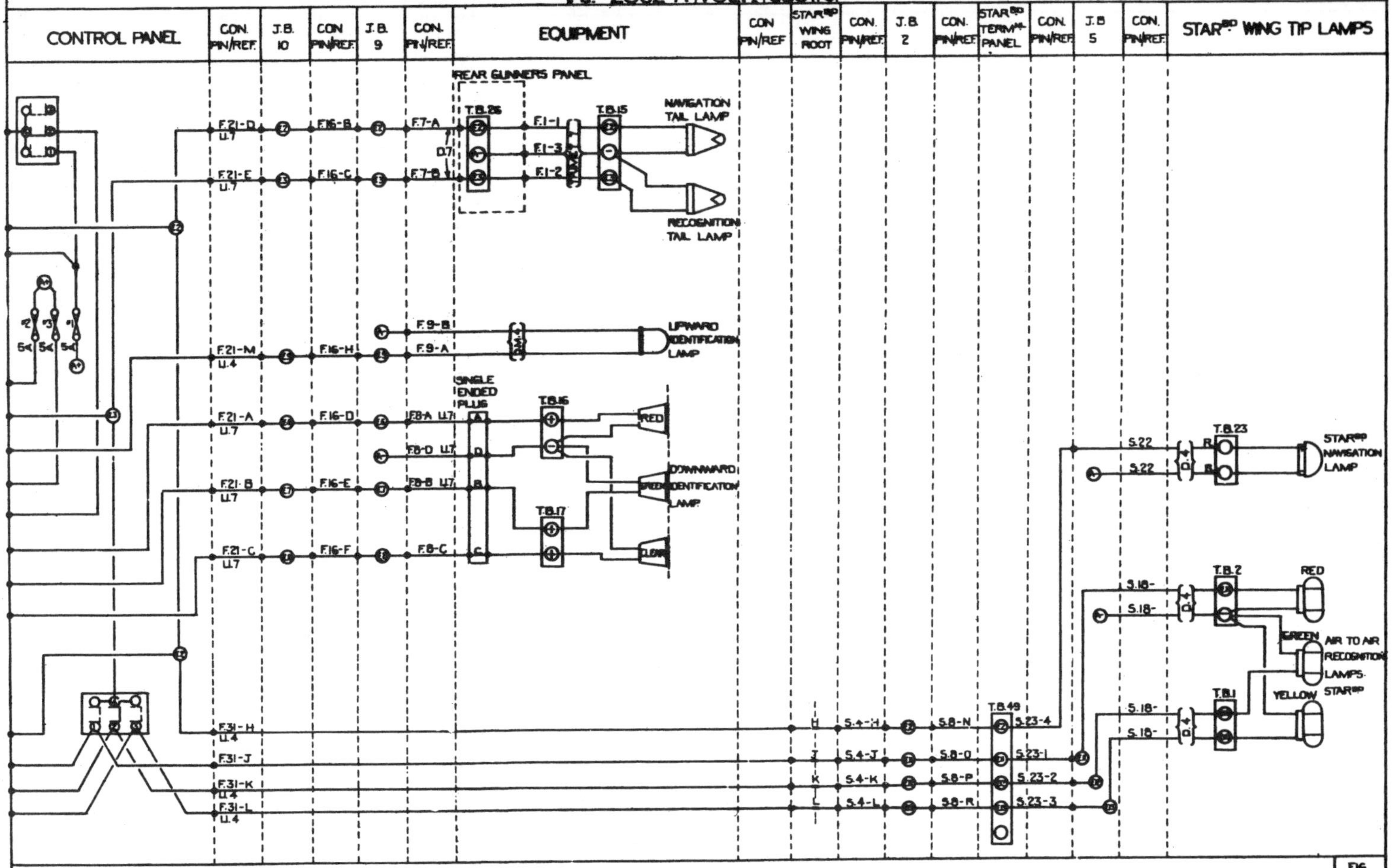

GENERAL SERVICES

FIG. 8

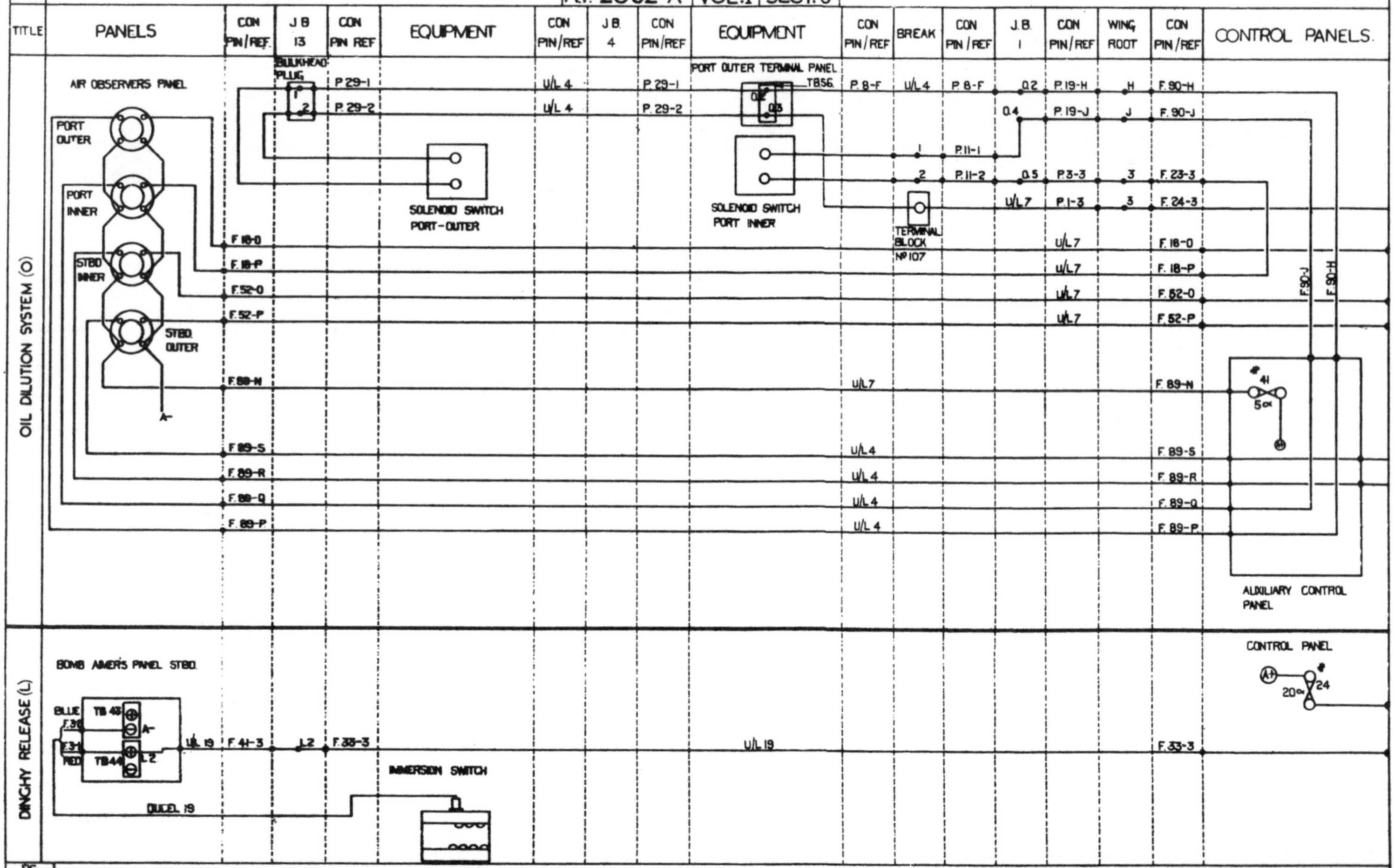

FIG 9

ROUTING CHART

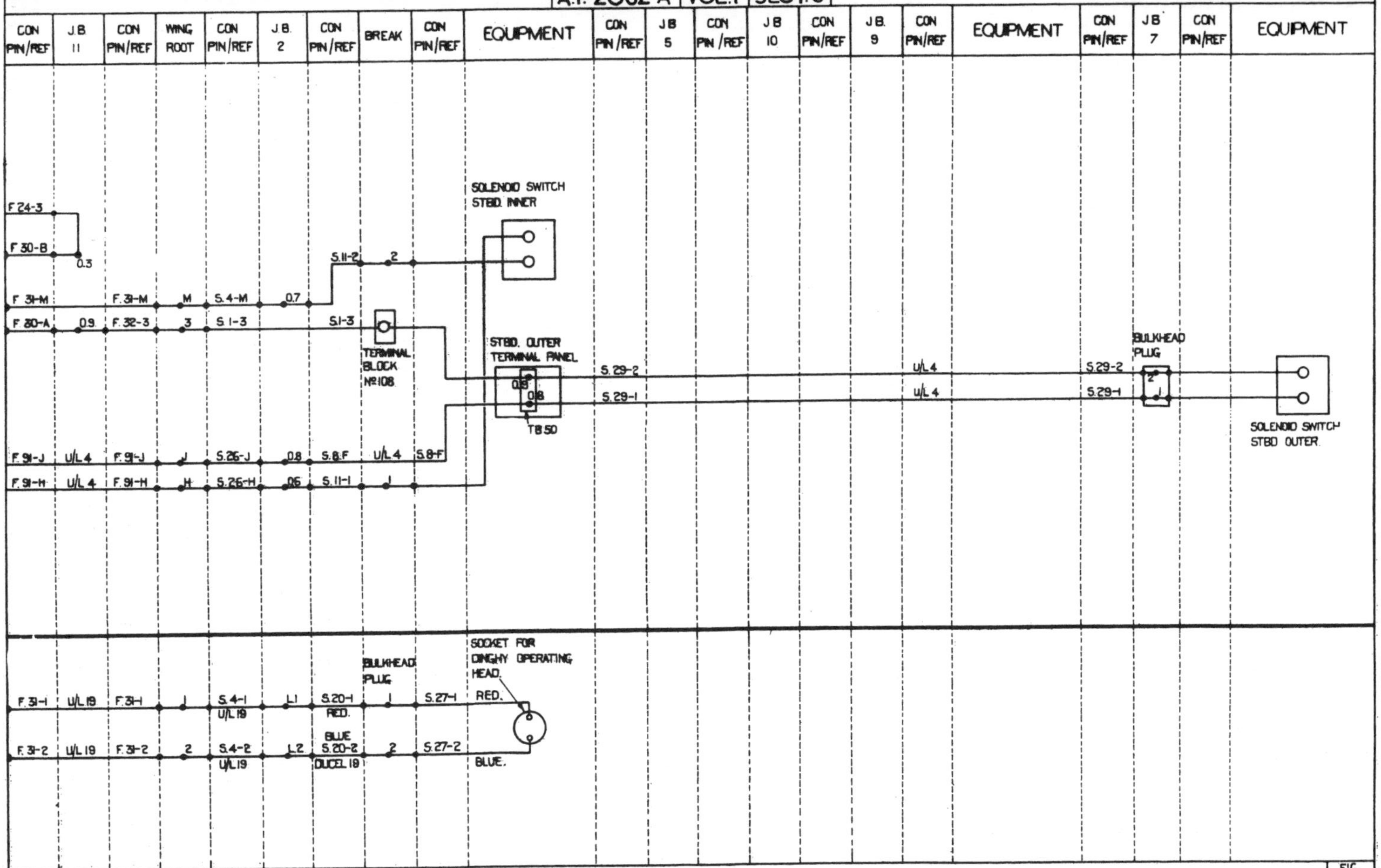

GENERAL SERVICES

FIG. 9

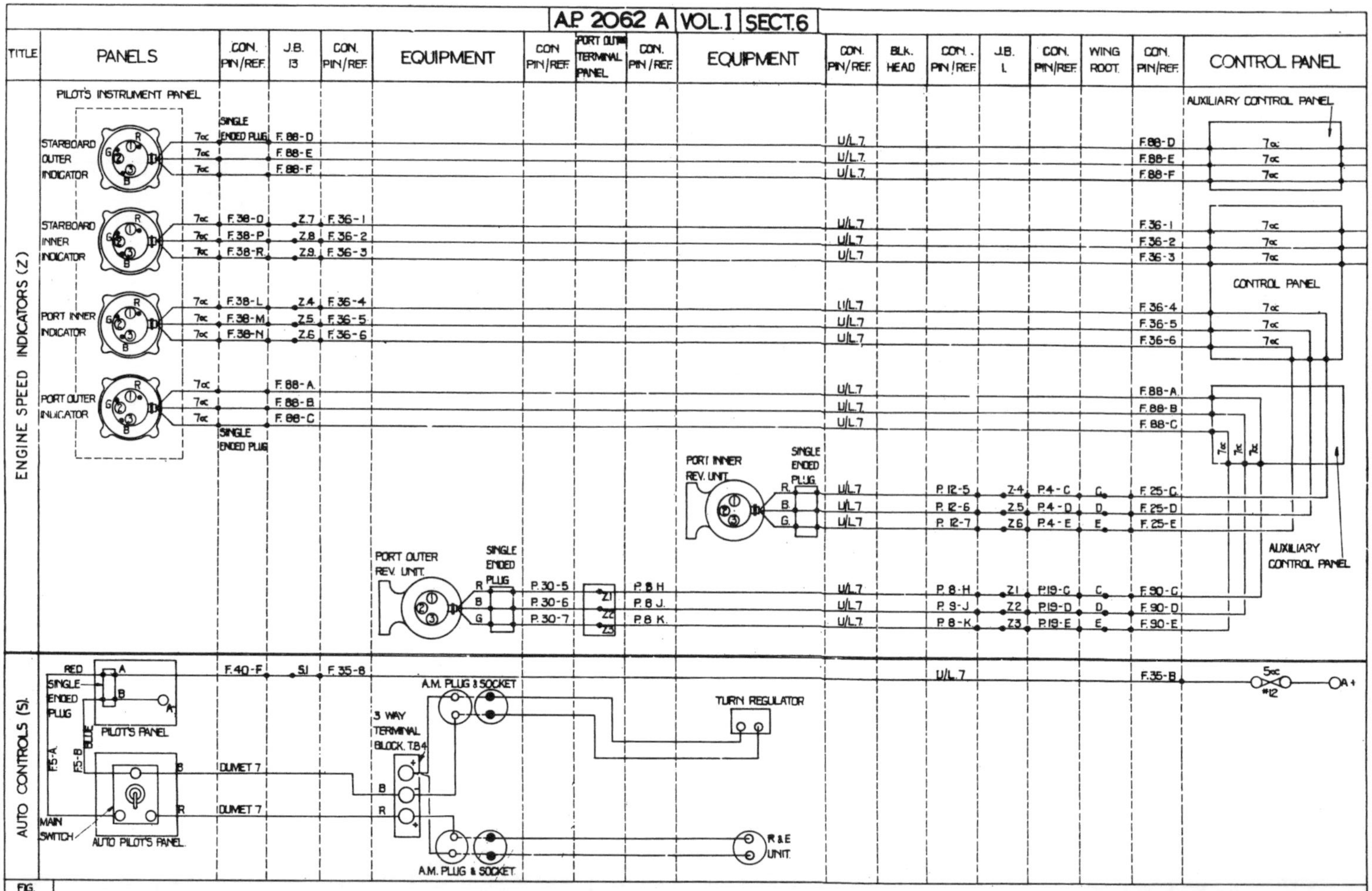

FIG. 10 ROUTING CHART

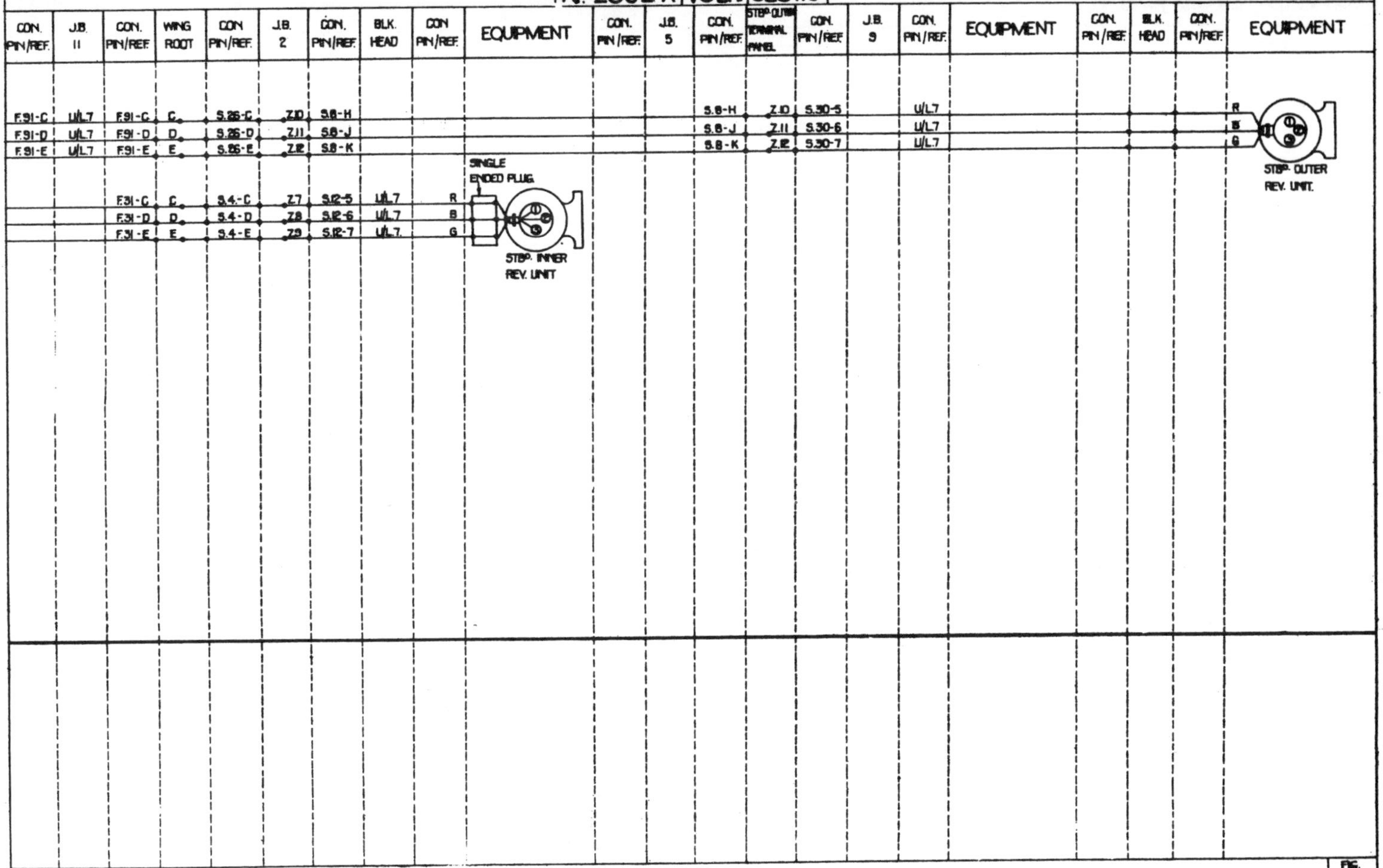

CON. PIN/REF	J.B. 11	CON. PIN/REF	WING ROOT	CON. PIN/REF	J.B. 2	CON. PIN/REF	BLK. HEAD	CON. PIN/REF	EQUIPMENT	CON. PIN/REF	J.B. 5	CON. PIN/REF	STBD OUTER TERMINAL PANEL	CON. PIN/REF	J.B. 9	CON. PIN/REF	EQUIPMENT	CON. PIN/REF	BLK. HEAD	CON. PIN/REF	EQUIPMENT
F.91-C	U/L7	F.91-C	C	5.26-C	Z10	5.8-H						5.8-H	Z10	5.30-5		U/L7					STBD OUTER REV. UNIT R B G
F.91-D	U/L7	F.91-D	D	5.26-D	Z11	5.8-J						5.8-J	Z11	5.30-6		U/L7					
F.91-E	U/L7	F.91-E	E	5.26-E	Z12	5.8-K						5.8-K	Z12	5.30-7		U/L7					
								SINGLE ENDED PLUG	STBD INNER REV. UNIT R B G												
F.91-C		F.91-C	C	5.4-C	Z7	5.12-5	U/L7														
F.91-D		F.91-D	D	5.4-D	Z8	5.12-6	U/L7														
F.91-E		F.91-E	E	5.4-E	Z9	5.12-7	U/L7														

AP.2062 A, VOL.1, SECT.6

GENERAL SERVICES

FIG. 10

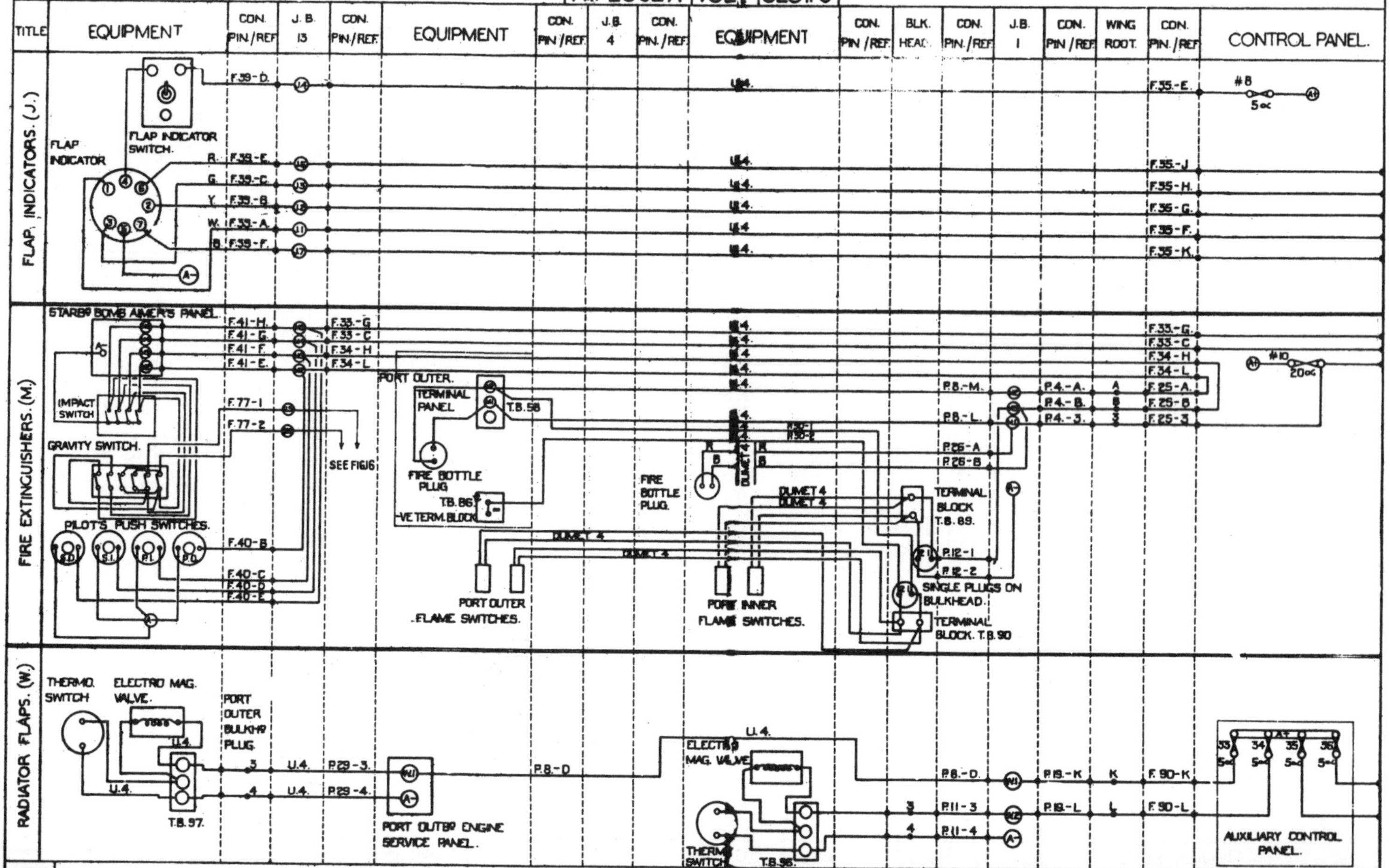

FIG. 11

ROUTING CHART

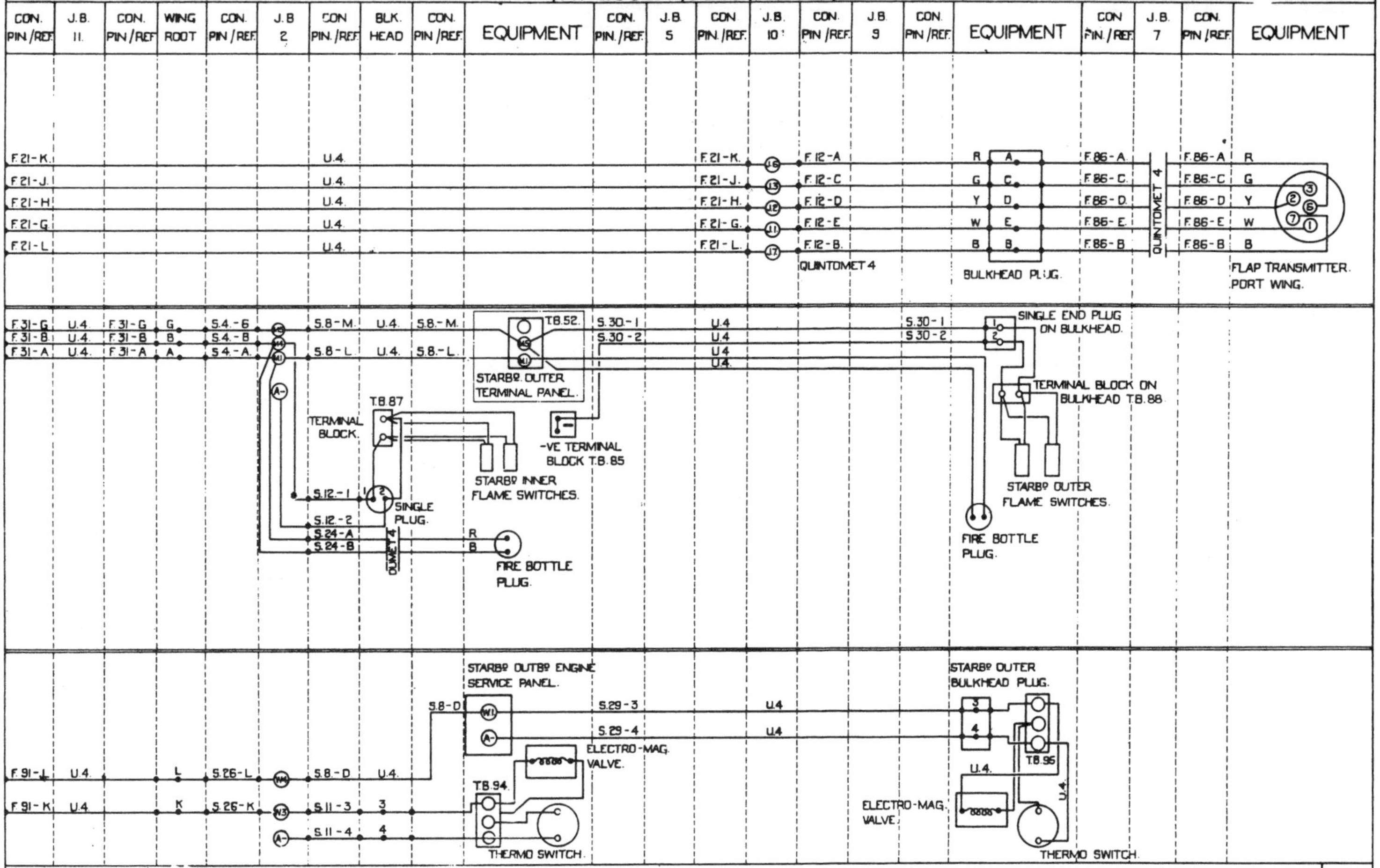

GENERAL SERVICES

FIG. 11

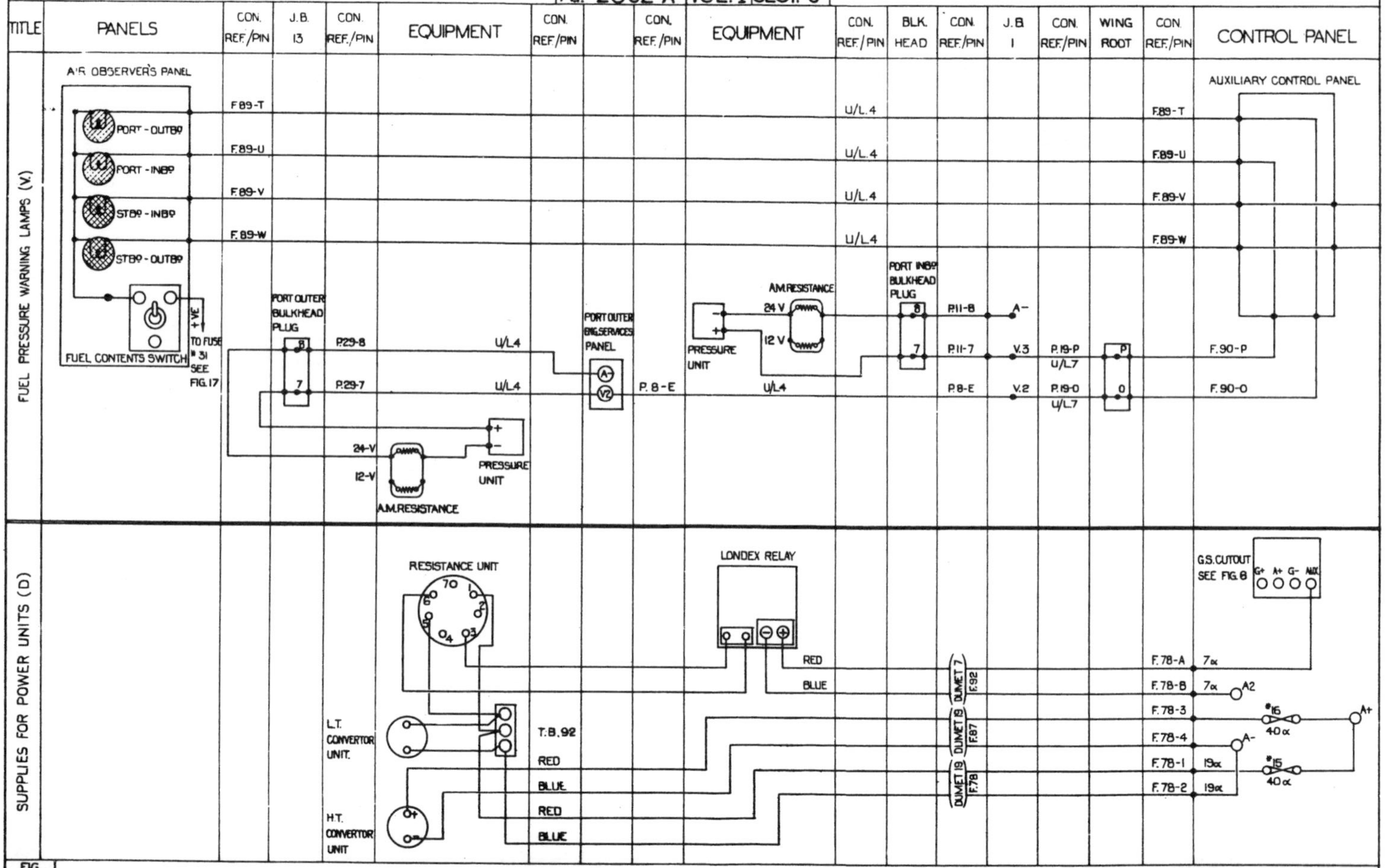

FIG. 12 ROUTING CHART

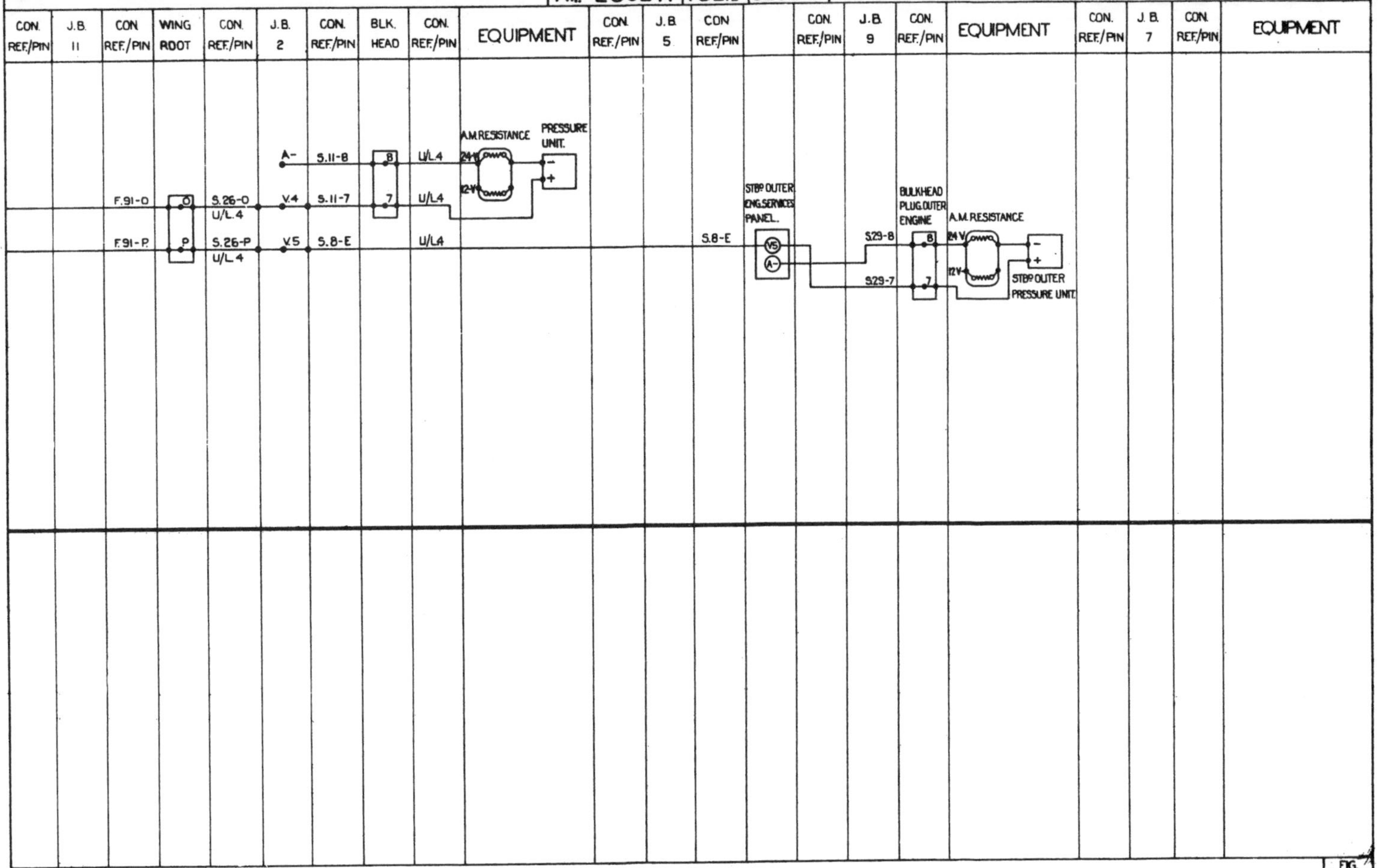

CON REF/PIN	J.B 11	CON REF/PIN	WING ROOT	CON REF/PIN	J.B 2	CON REF/PIN	BLK. HEAD	CON REF/PIN	EQUIPMENT	CON REF/PIN	J.B 5	CON REF/PIN	EQUIPMENT	CON REF/PIN	J.B 9	CON REF/PIN	EQUIPMENT	CON REF/PIN	J.B 7	CON REF/PIN	EQUIPMENT
F.91-O		S.26-O U/L 4	O	S.11-8	A-	S.11-8	B U/L4		A.M RESISTANCE PRESSURE UNIT												
F.91-P		S.26-P U/L 4	P	S.11-7	V4	S.11-7	7 U/L4														
				S.8-E	V5	S.8-E	U/L4			S.8-E			STBD OUTER WING SERVICES PANEL	S29-8			BULKHEAD PLUG OUTER ENGINE				A.M RESISTANCE STBD OUTER PRESSURE UNIT
														S29-7							

GENERAL SERVICES

FIG. 12

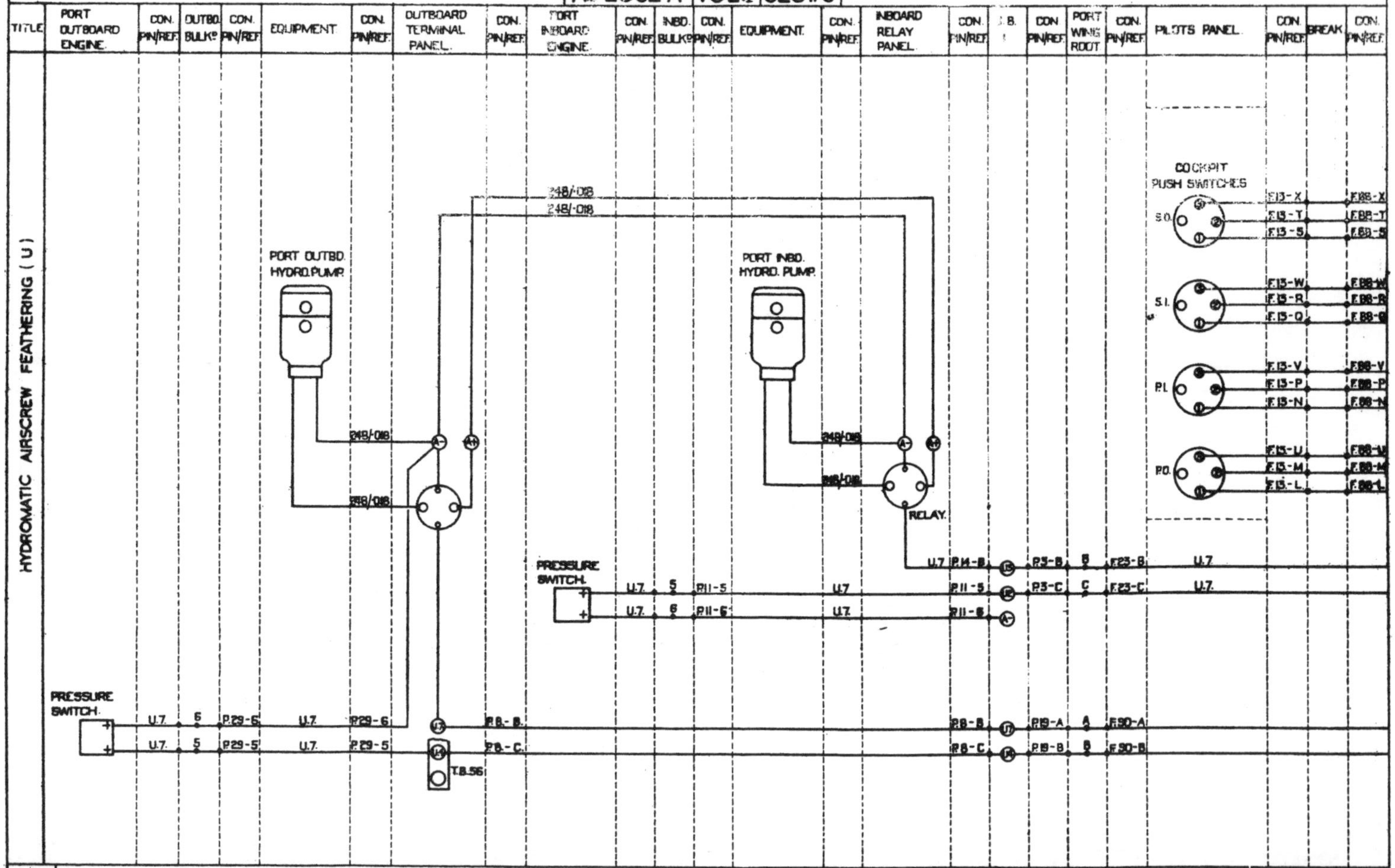

FIG. 13 ROUTING CHART

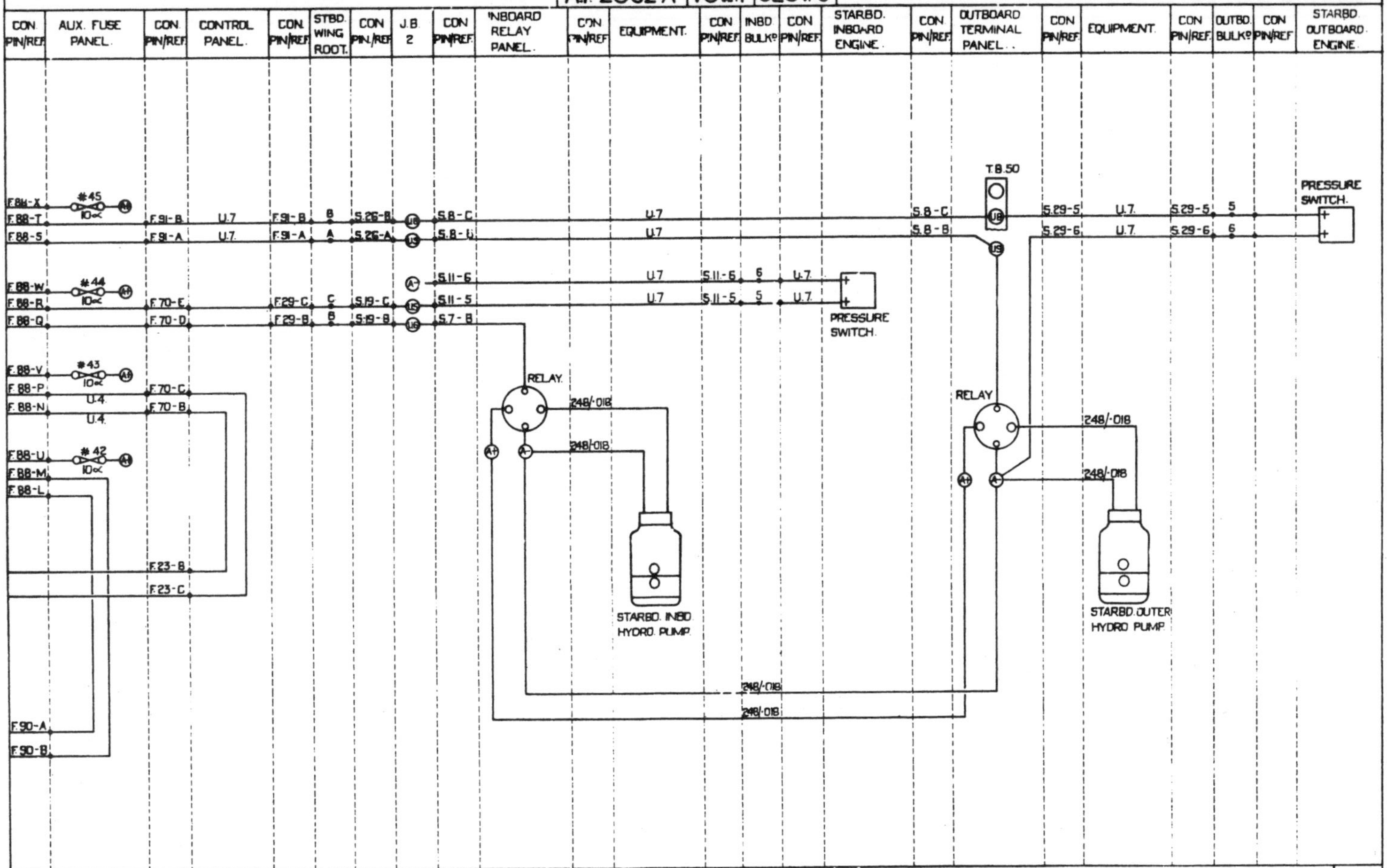

FIG. 13 — GENERAL SERVICES (AP2062A VOL.1 SEC.1.6)

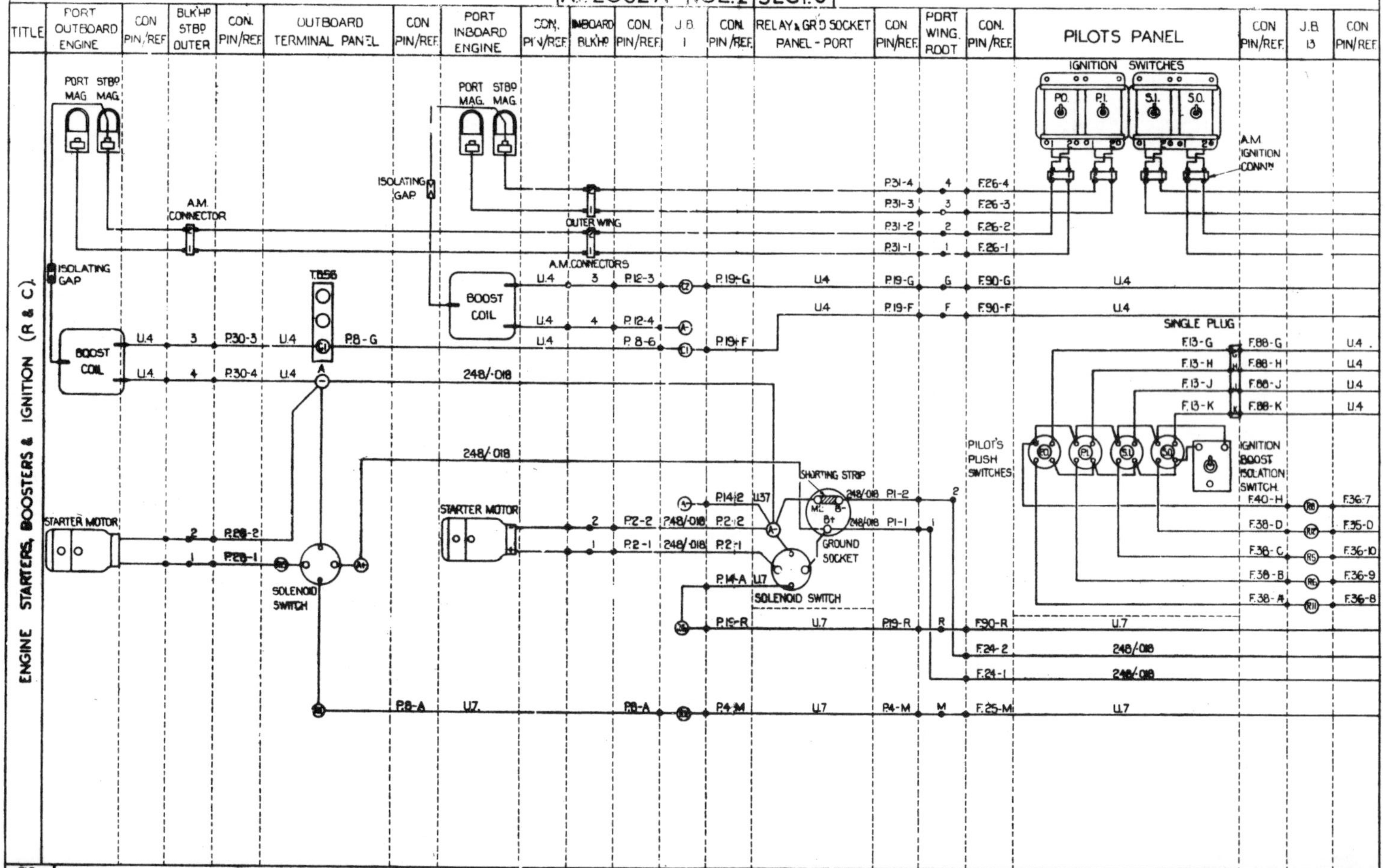

FIG. 14

ROUTING CHART

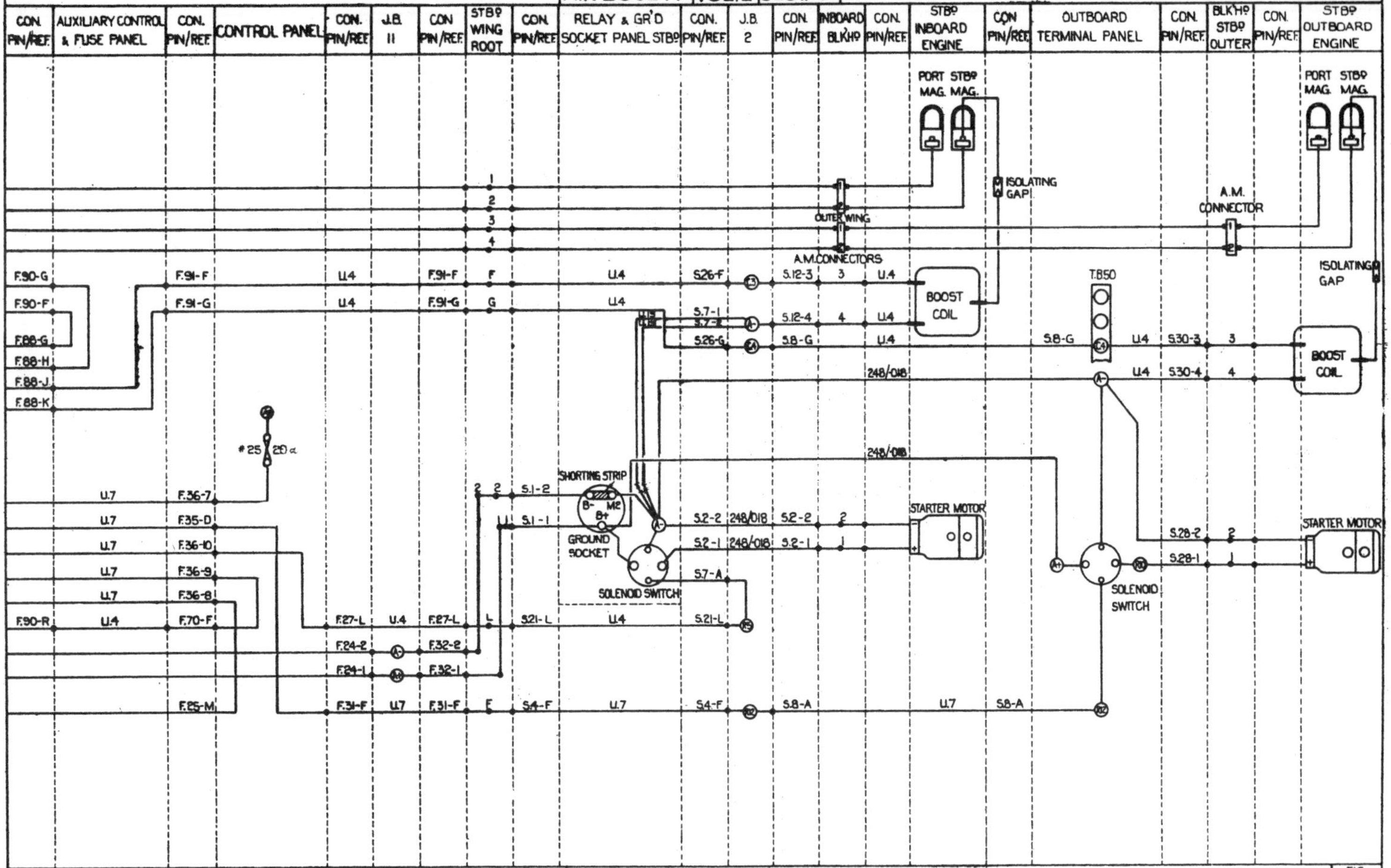

GENERAL SERVICES

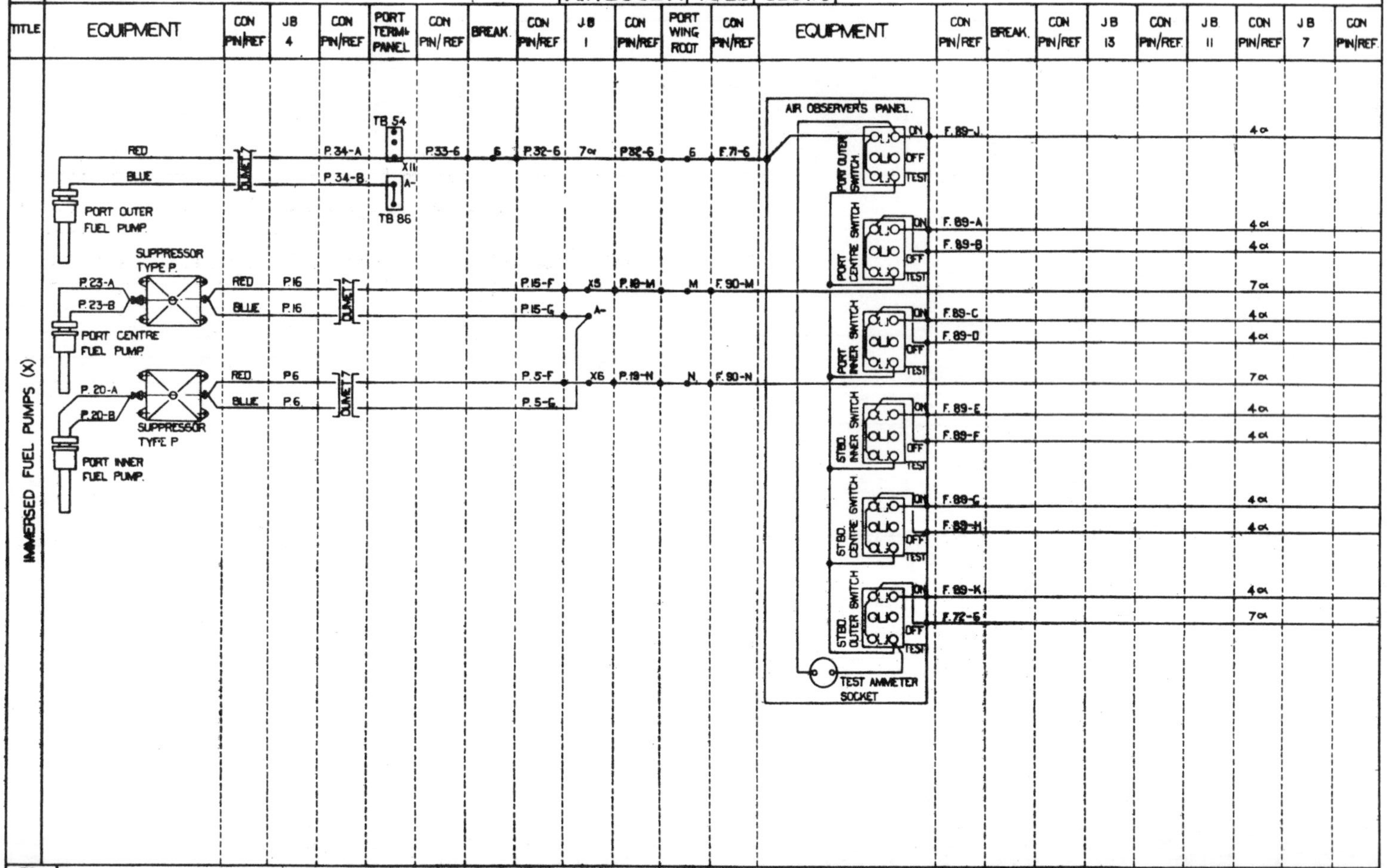

ROUTING CHART

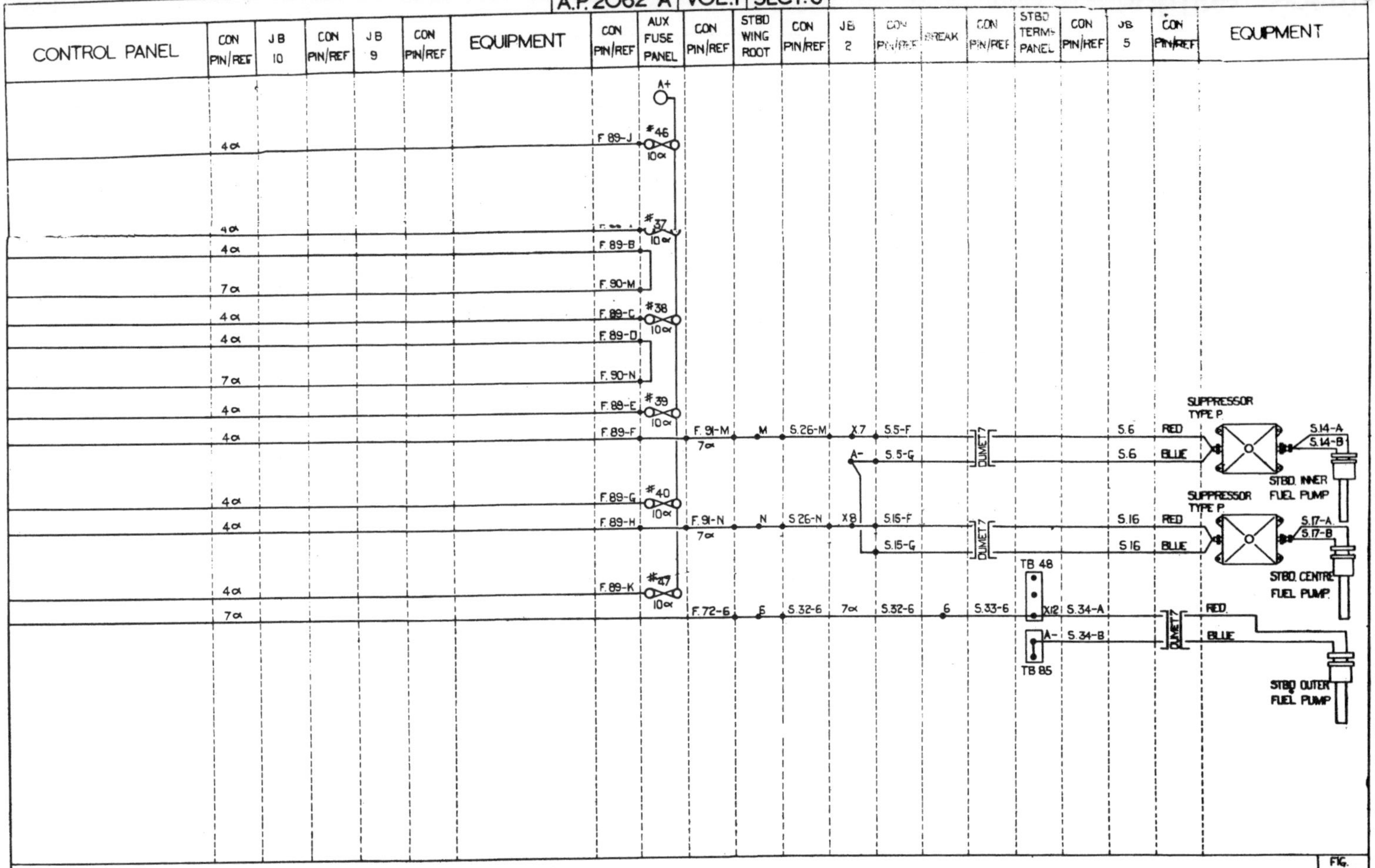

GENERAL SERVICES

FIG. 15

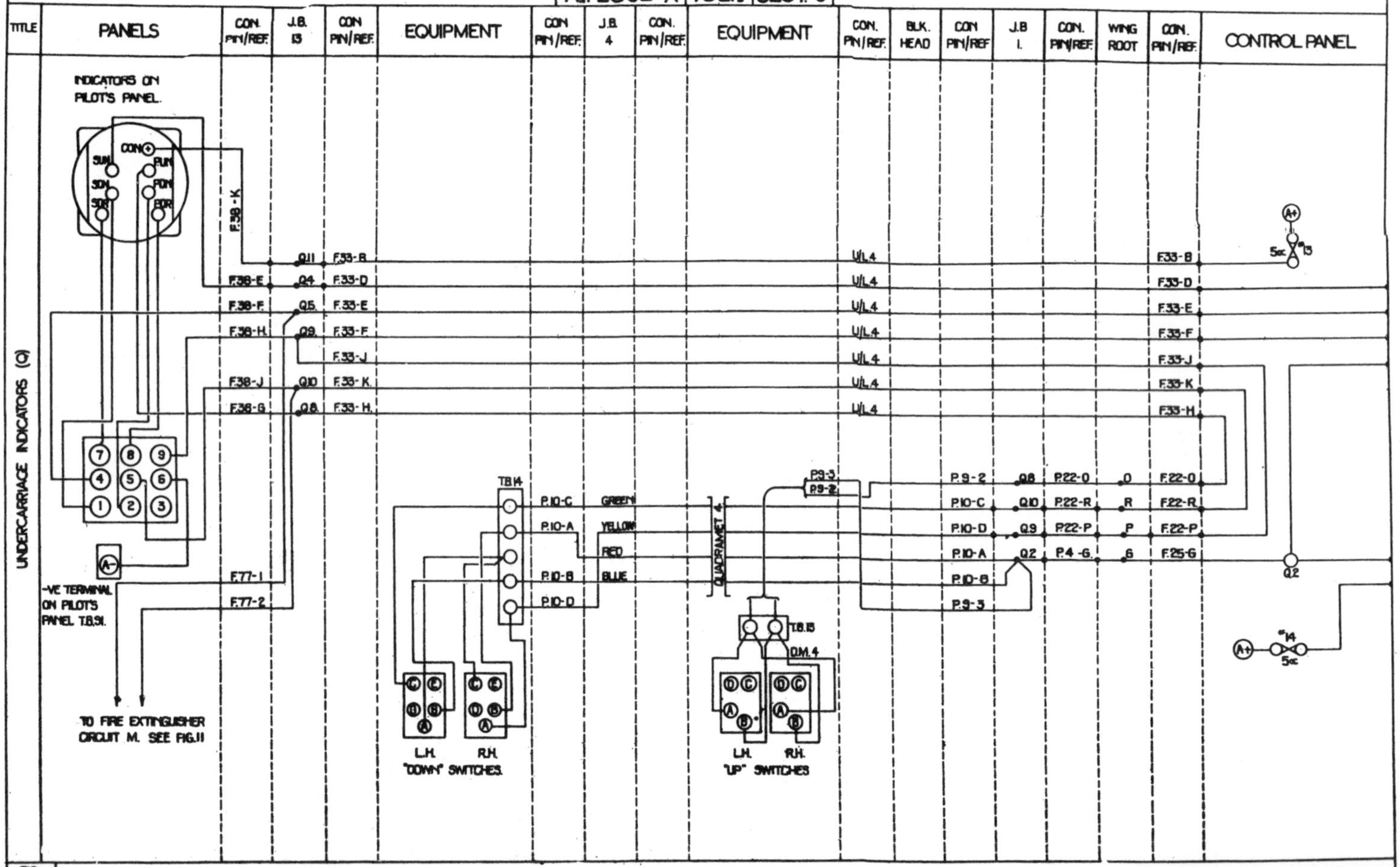

FIG. 16

ROUTING CHART

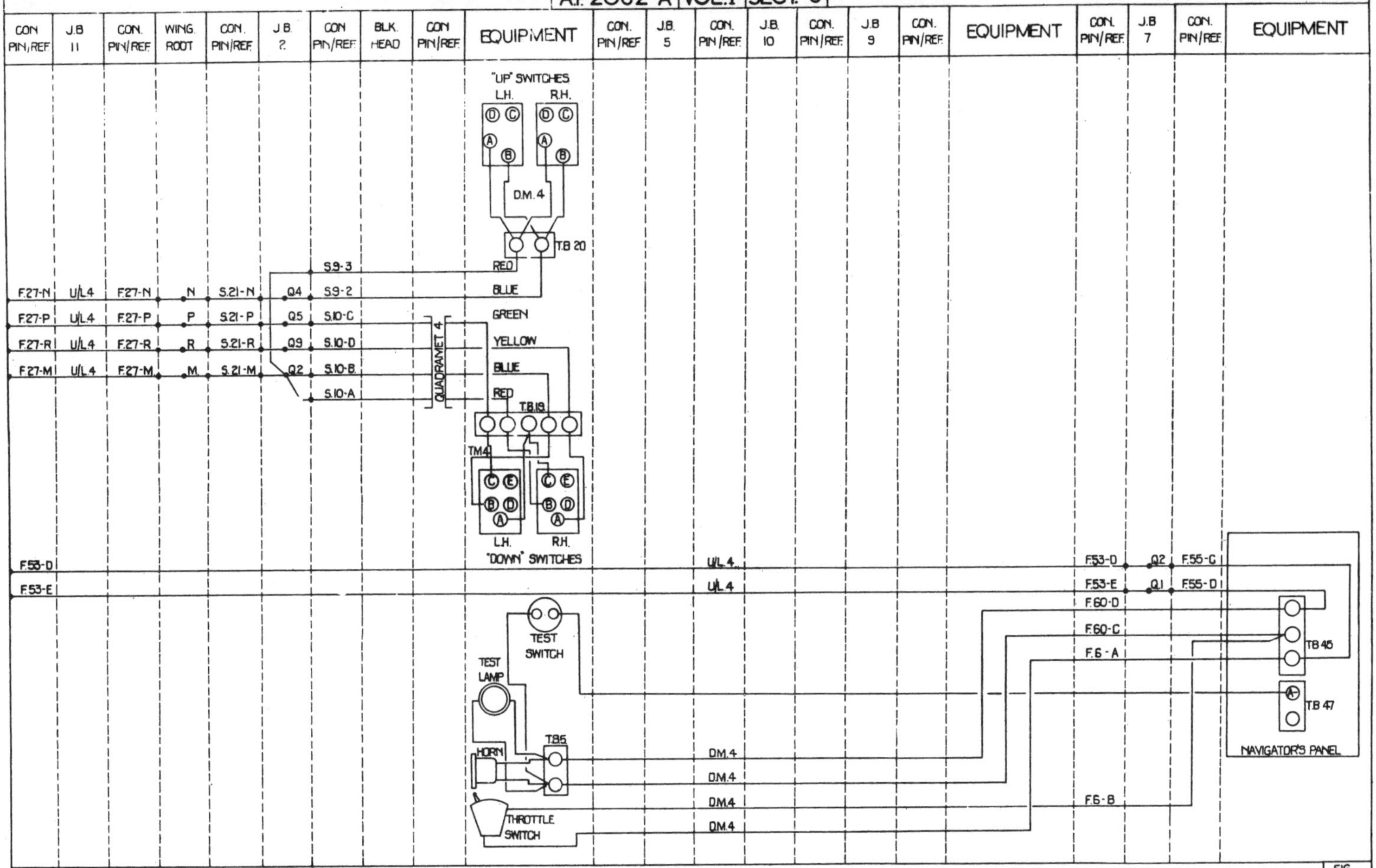

FIG. 16

GENERAL SERVICES

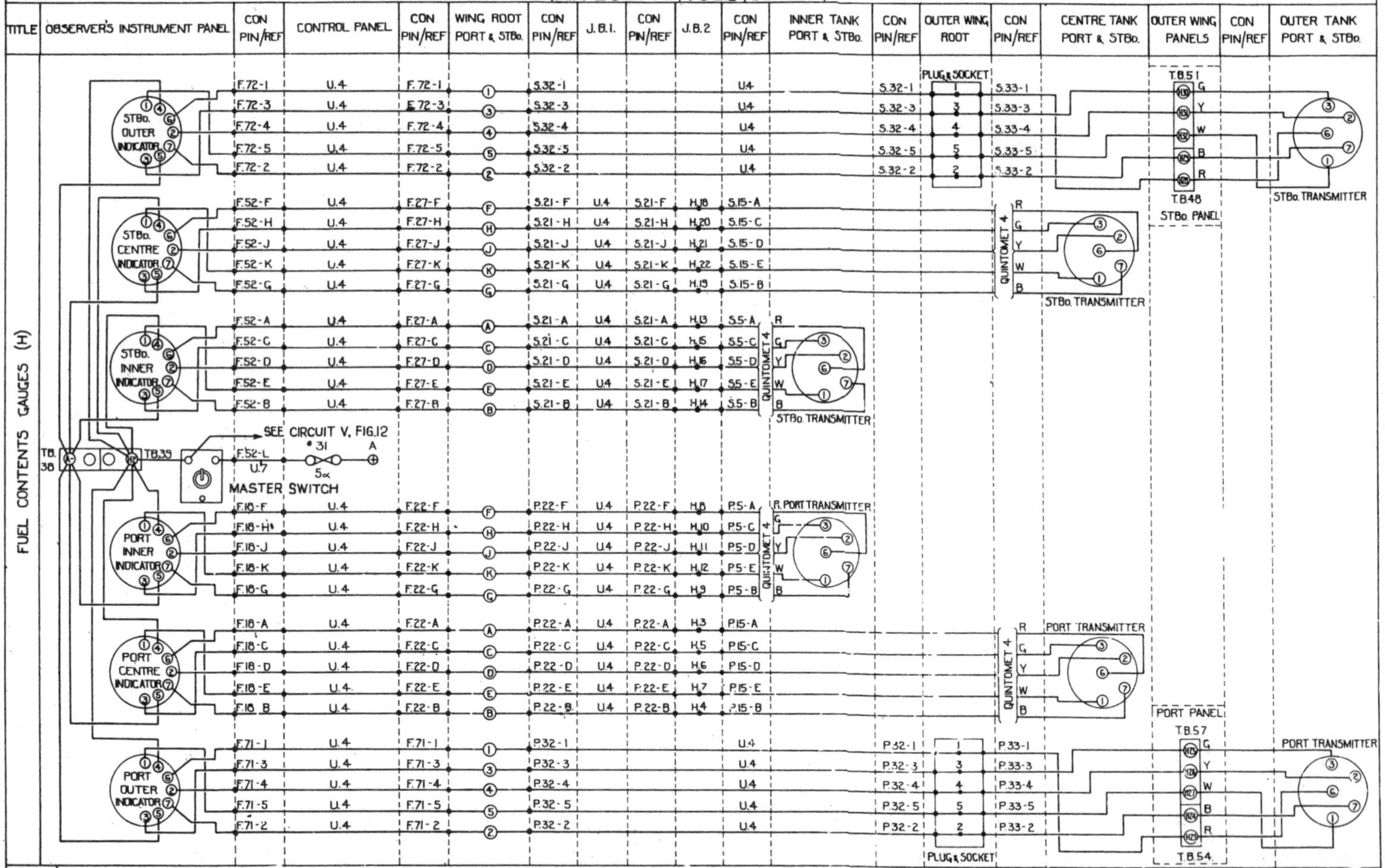

FIG. 17 ROUTING CHART - GENER[AL] SERVICES

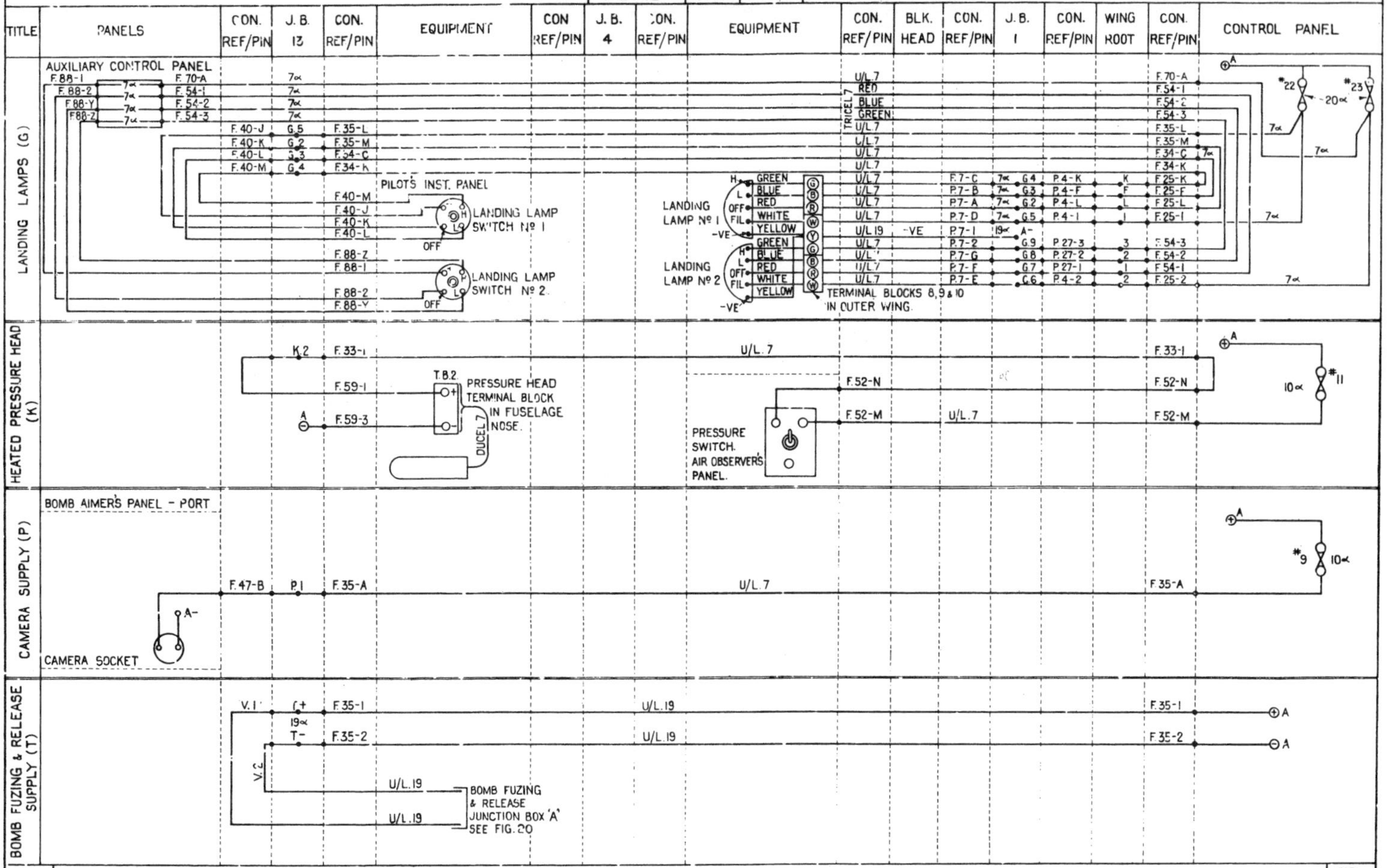

FIG. 18 ROUTING CHART - GENERAL SERVICES FIG. 18

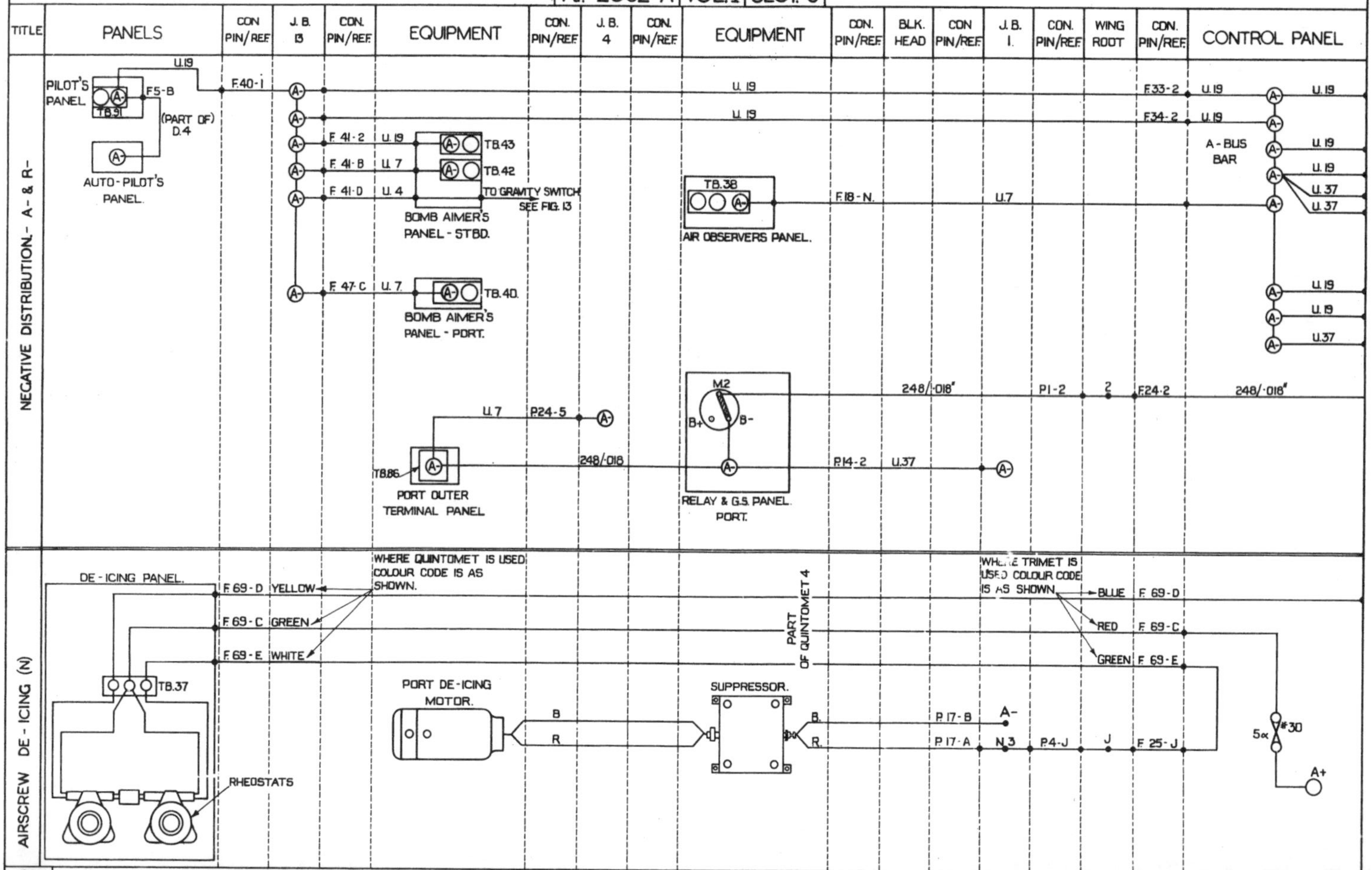

FIG. 19 ROUTING CHART

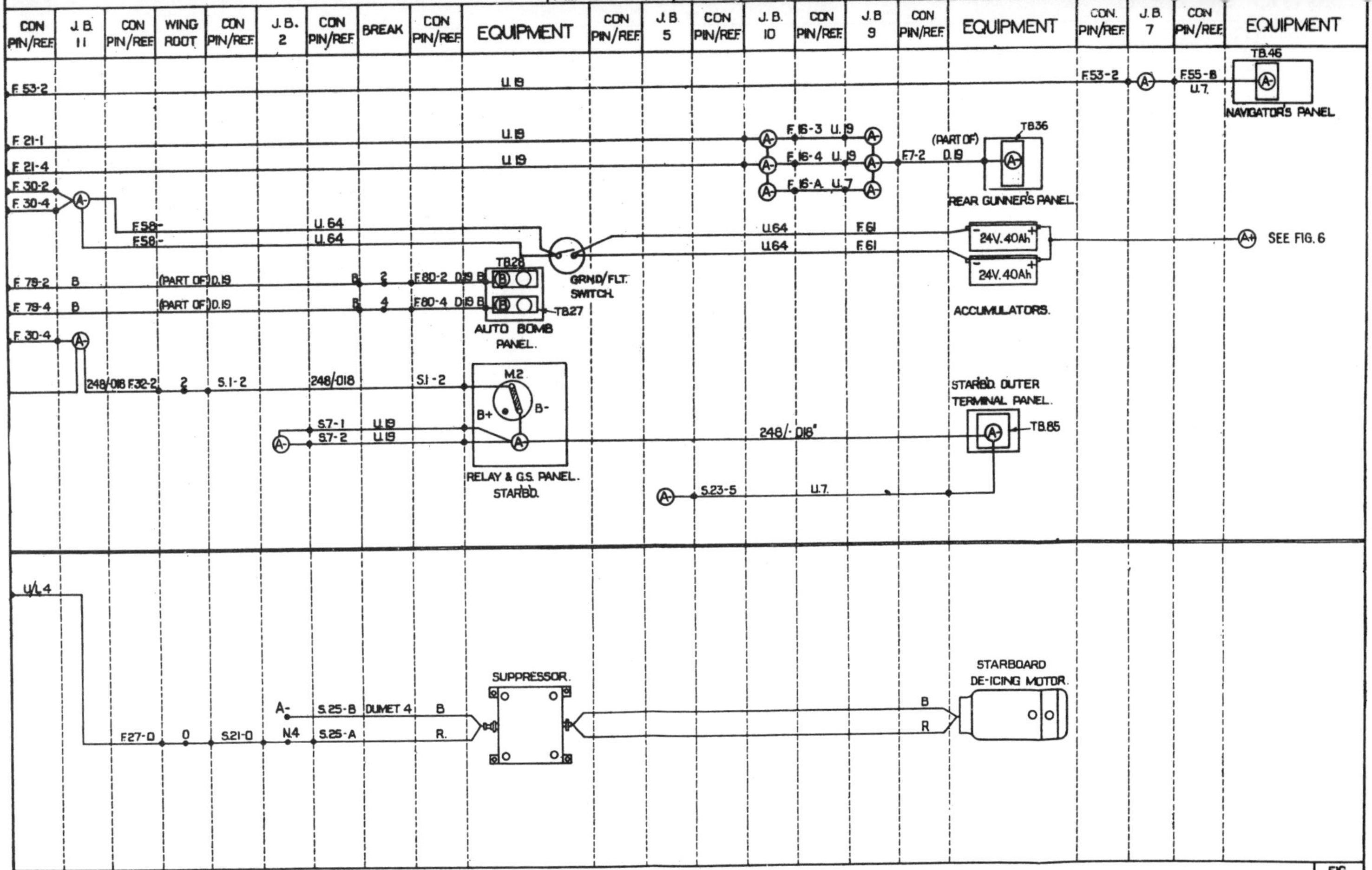

GENERAL SERVICES

FIG. 19

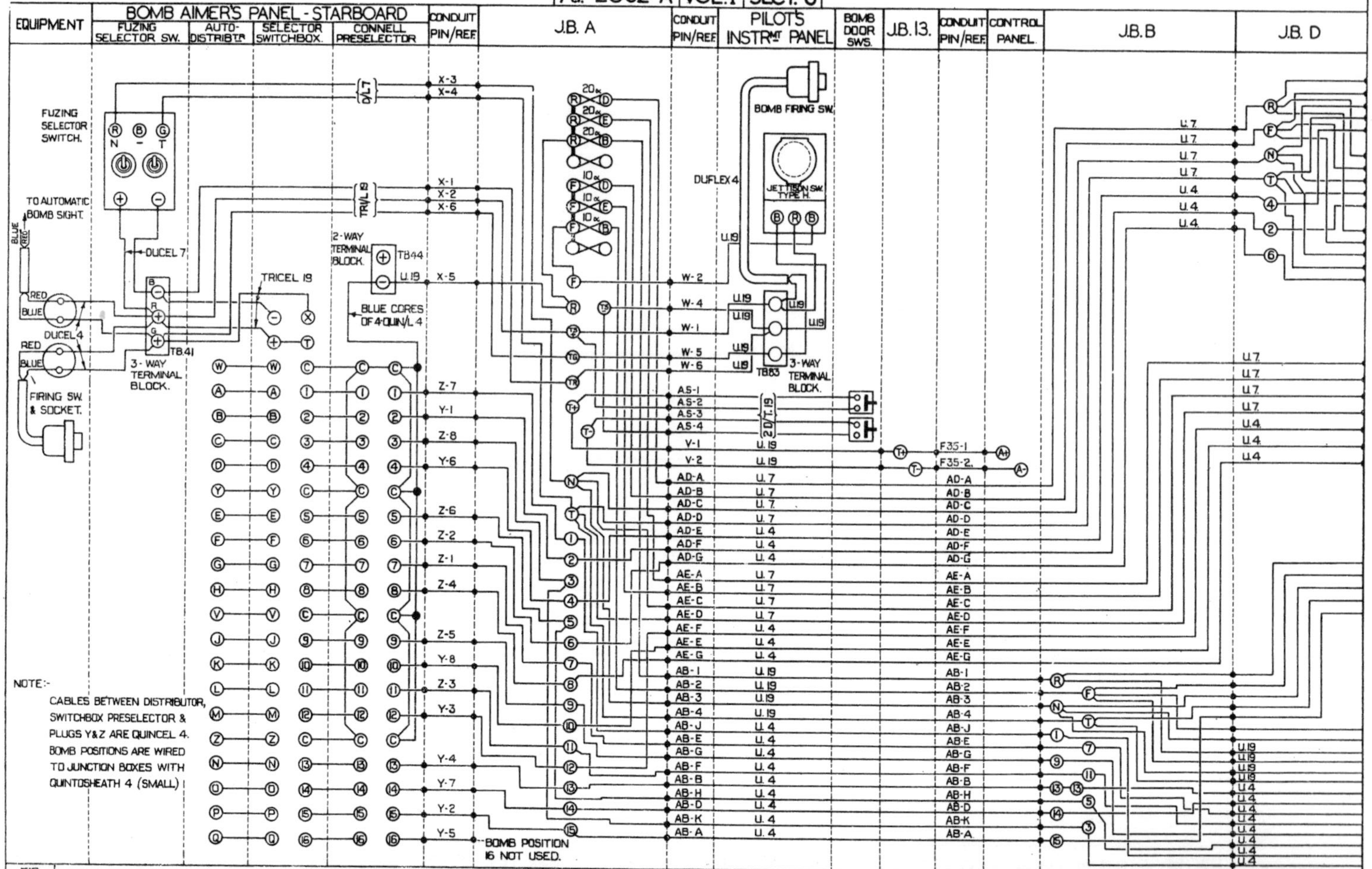

FIG. 20

ROUTING CHART

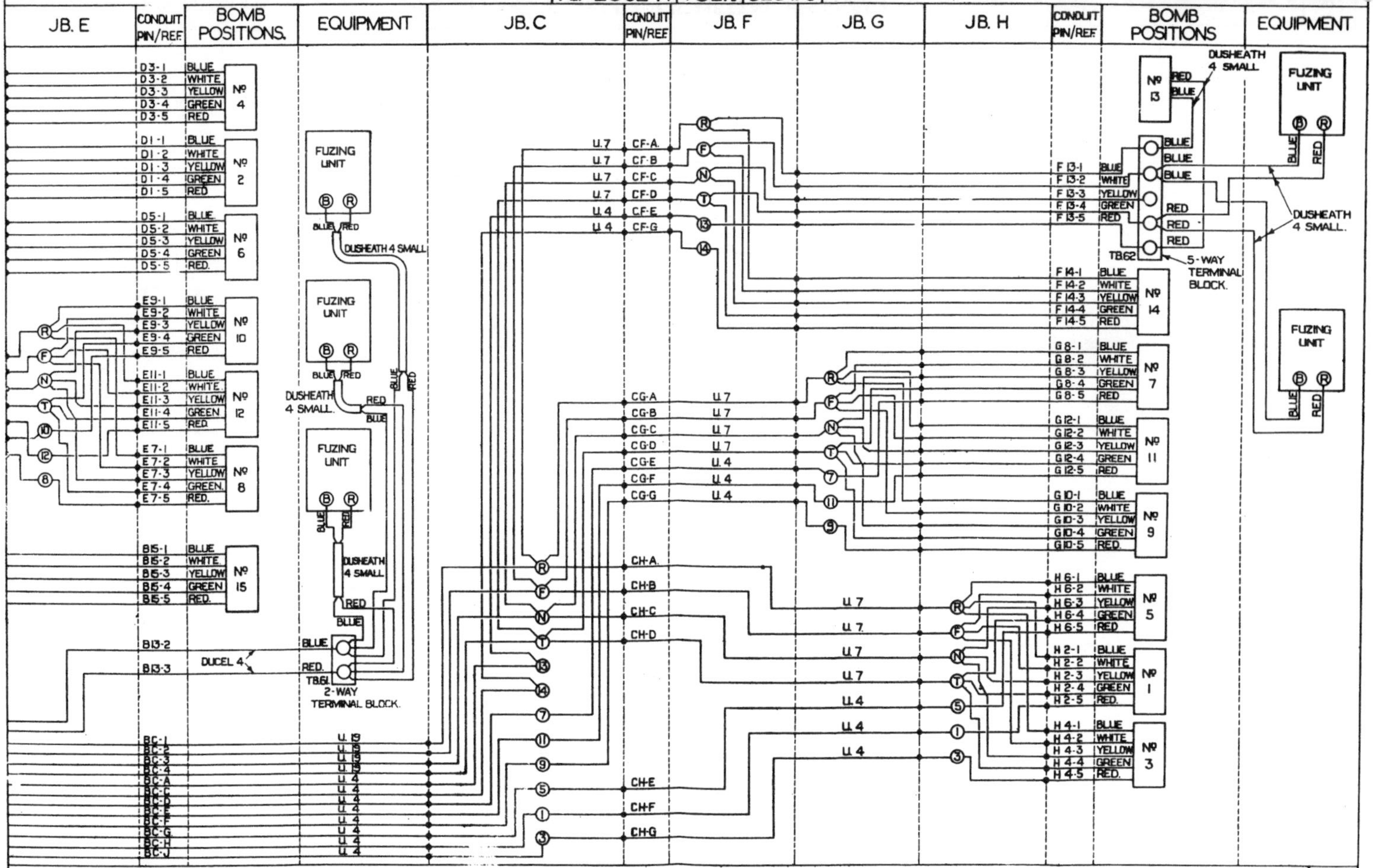

BOMB FUZING & RELEASE.

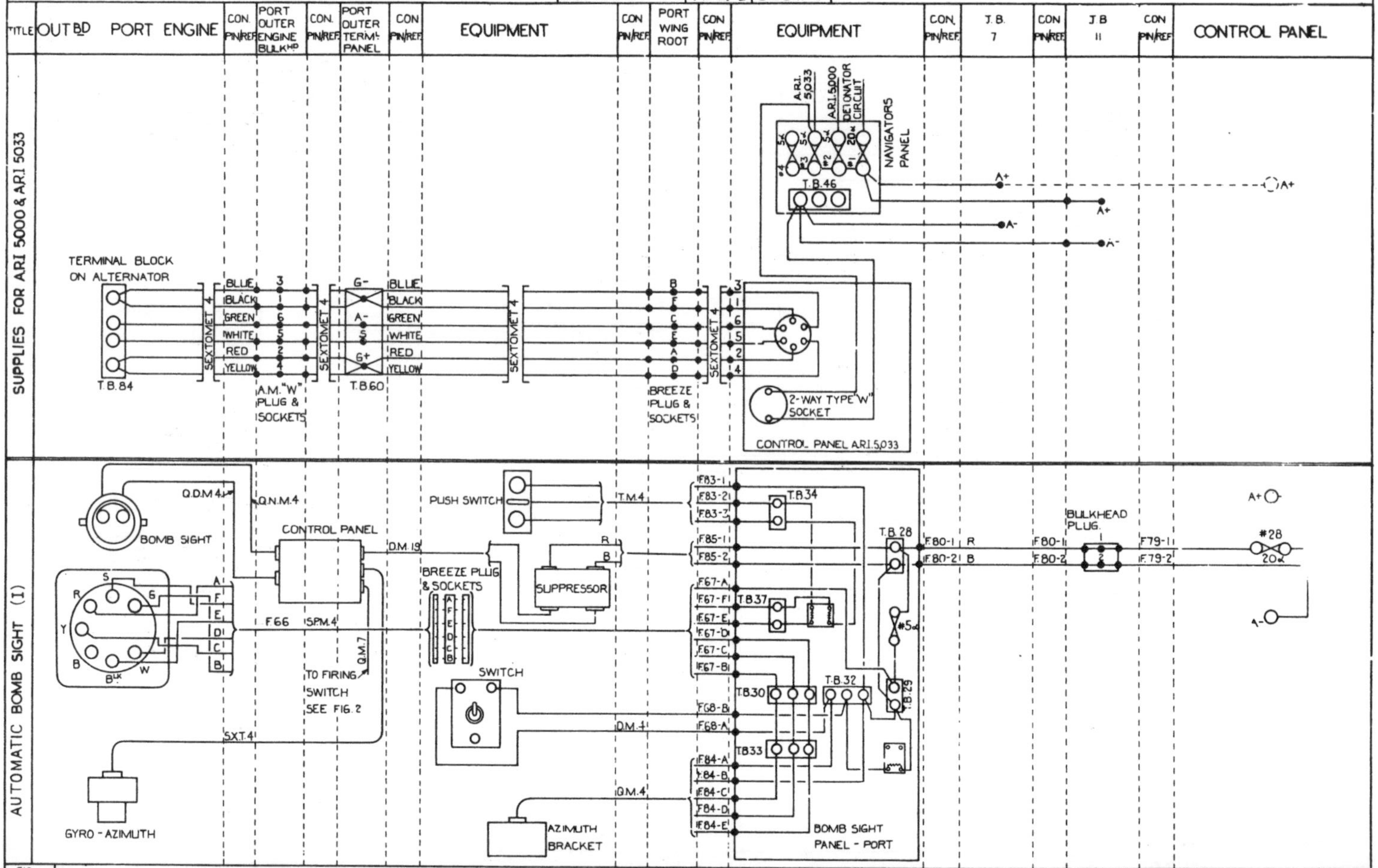

FIG. 21

ROUTING CHART - GENERAL SERVICES

FIG 21

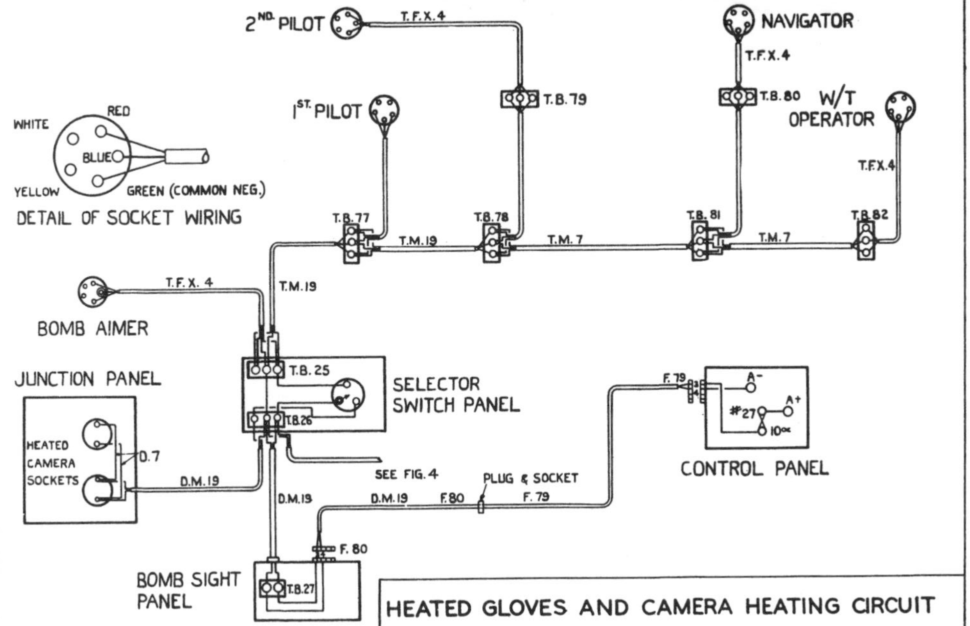

FIG. 22 — INTERCOMMUNICATION CALL LAMPS

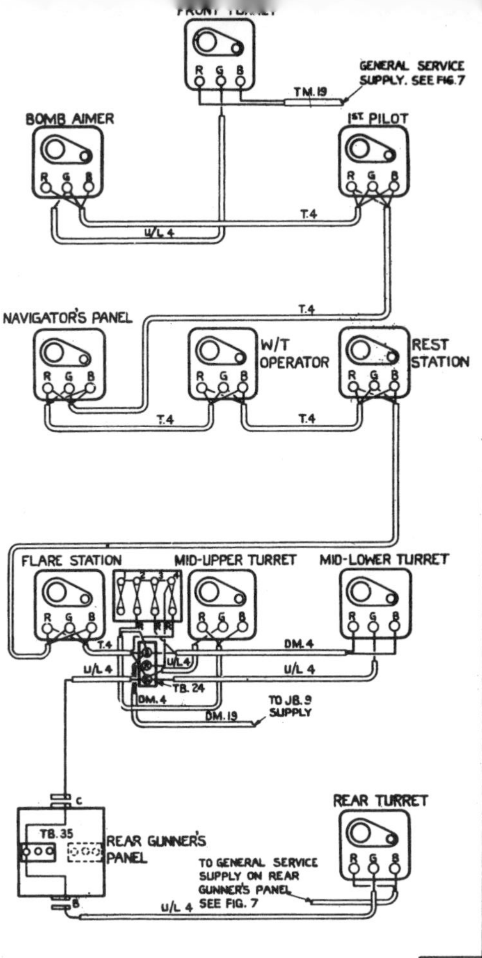

FIG. 22 — CAMERA CIRCUIT / HEATED GLOVES AND CAMERA HEATING CIRCUIT

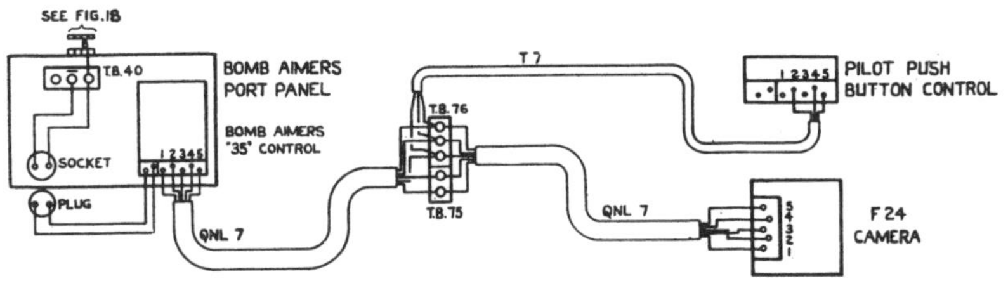

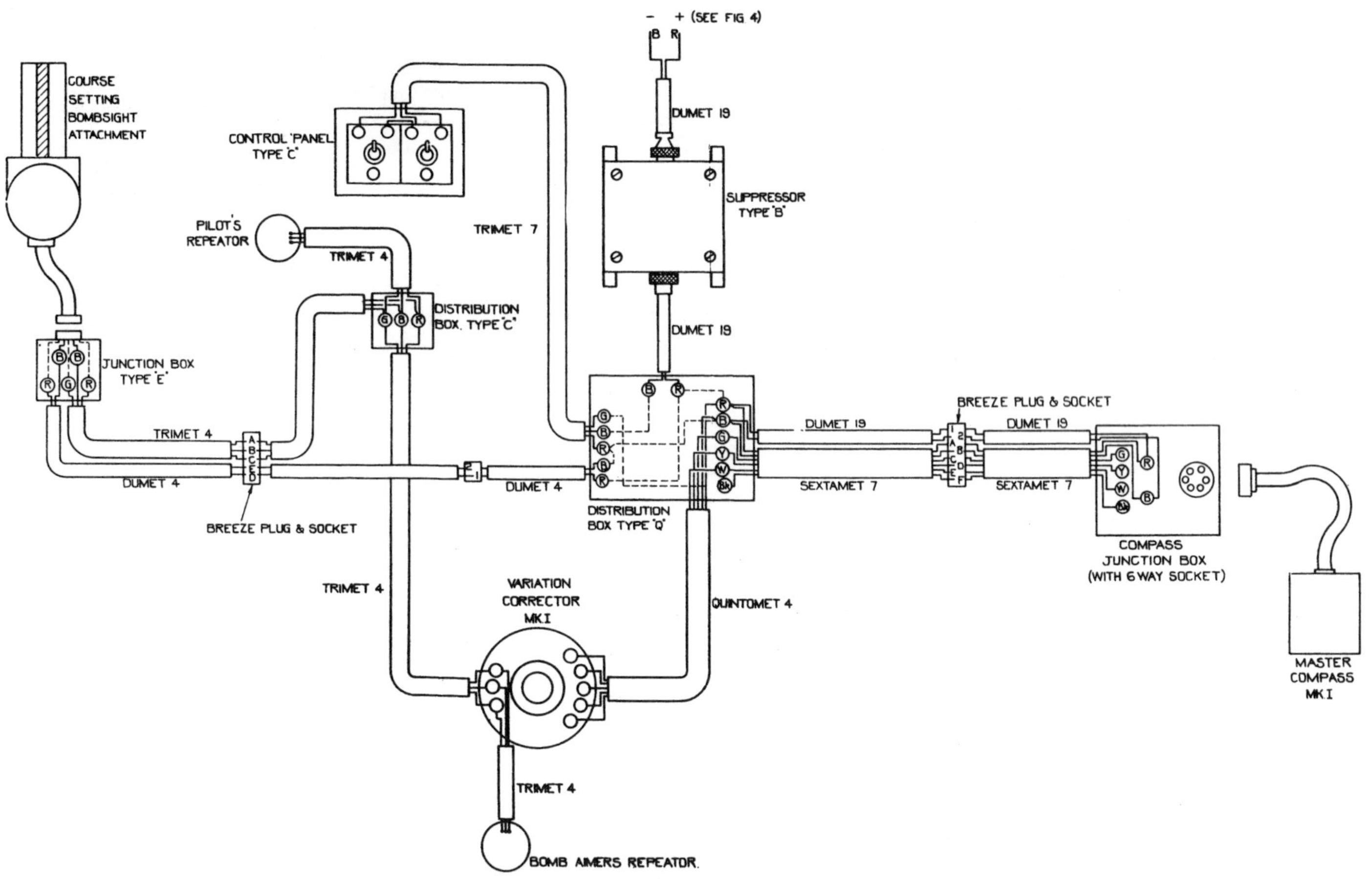

FIG. 33

D.R. COMPASS INSTALLATION

FIG.

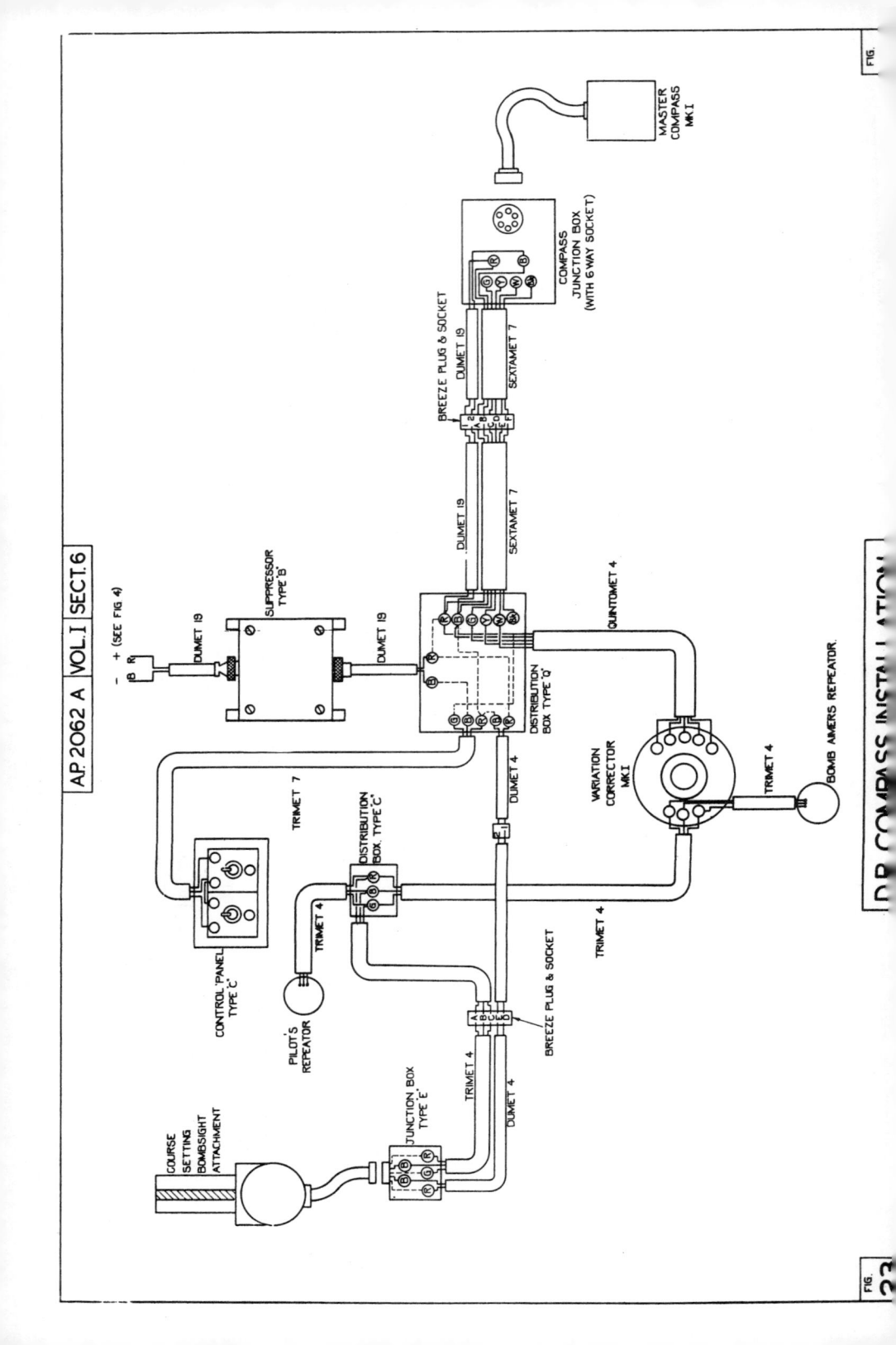

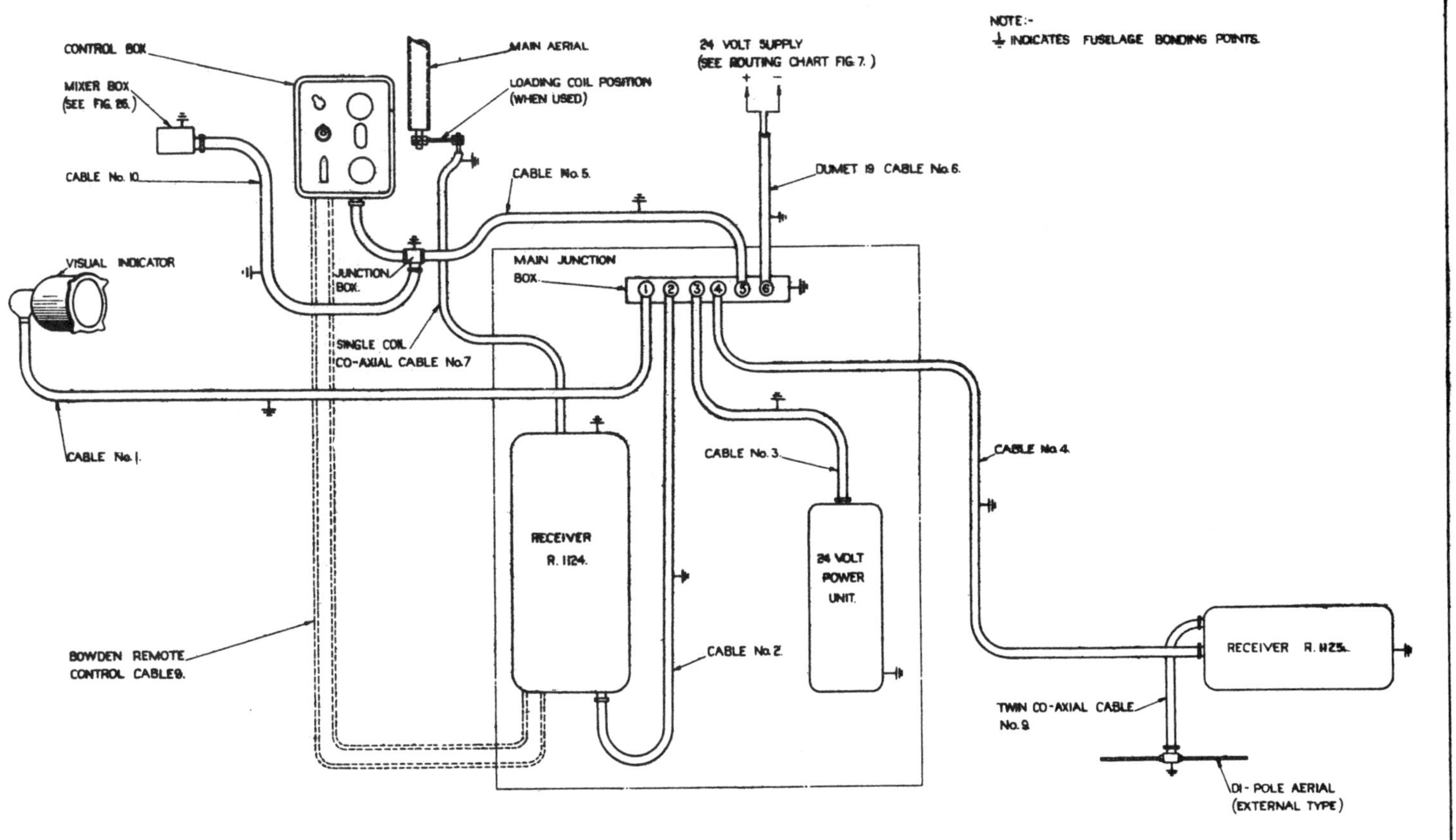

FIG. 24

BEAM APPROACH INSTALLATION

FIG. 24

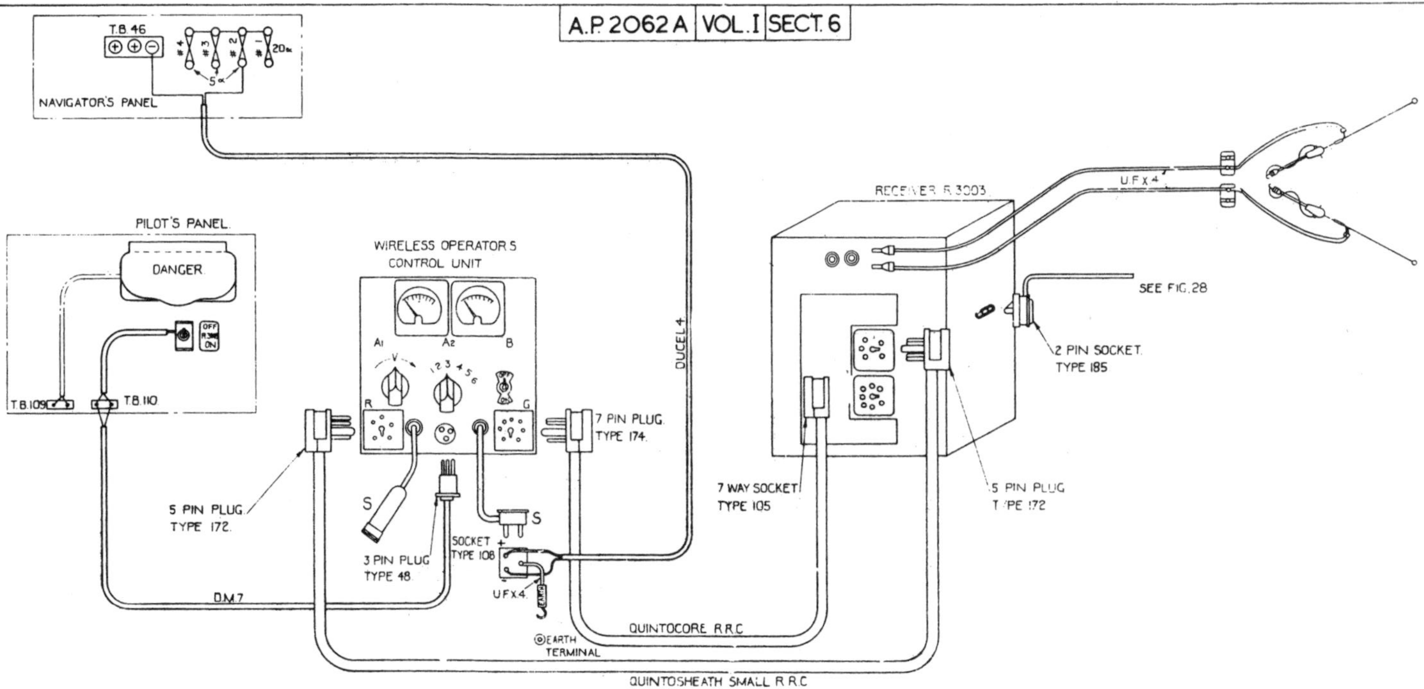

NOTE:-LEADS TO BE AT LEAST 4 FEET LONG & HELD WITH ONE TURN OF FINE COTTON THREAD
ITEMS MARKED S ARE SUPPLIED WITH THE INSTRUMENTS

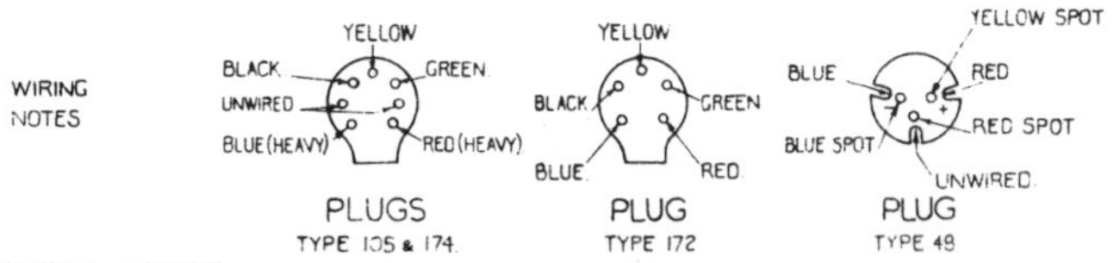

FIG. 25

A.R.I. 5,000

FIG. 25

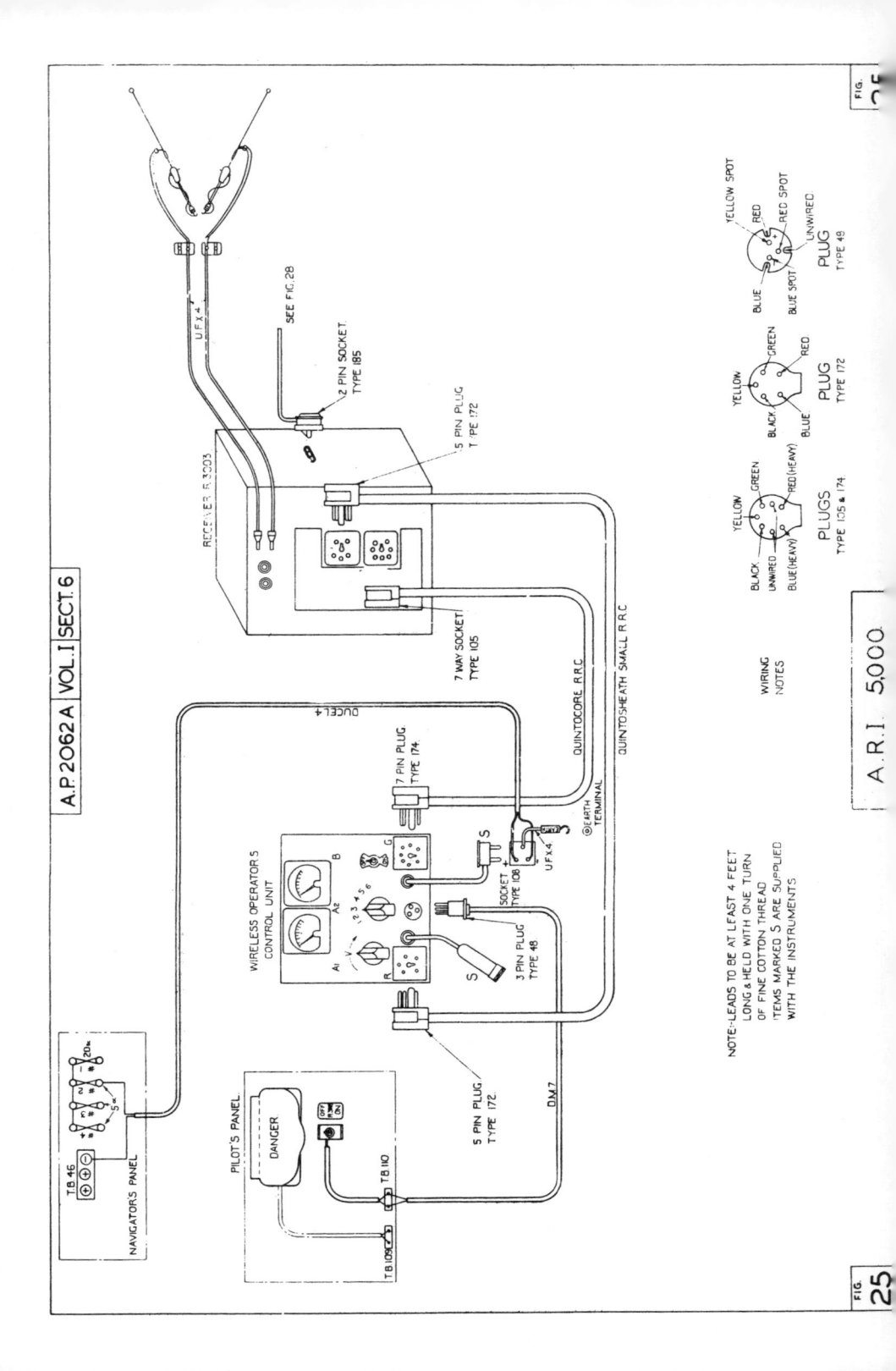

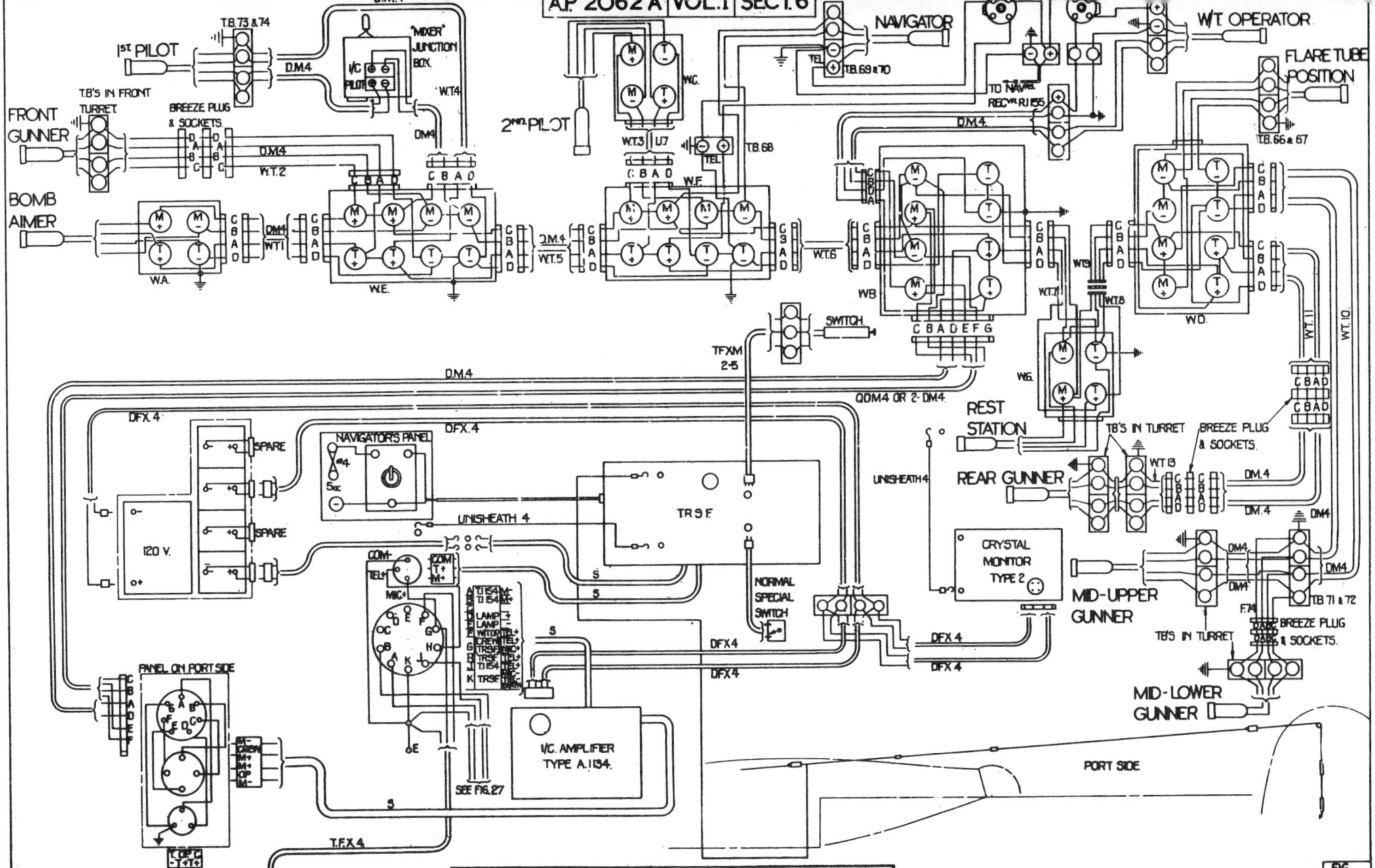

T.R.9F & A.1134 INSTALLATION

FIG. 26

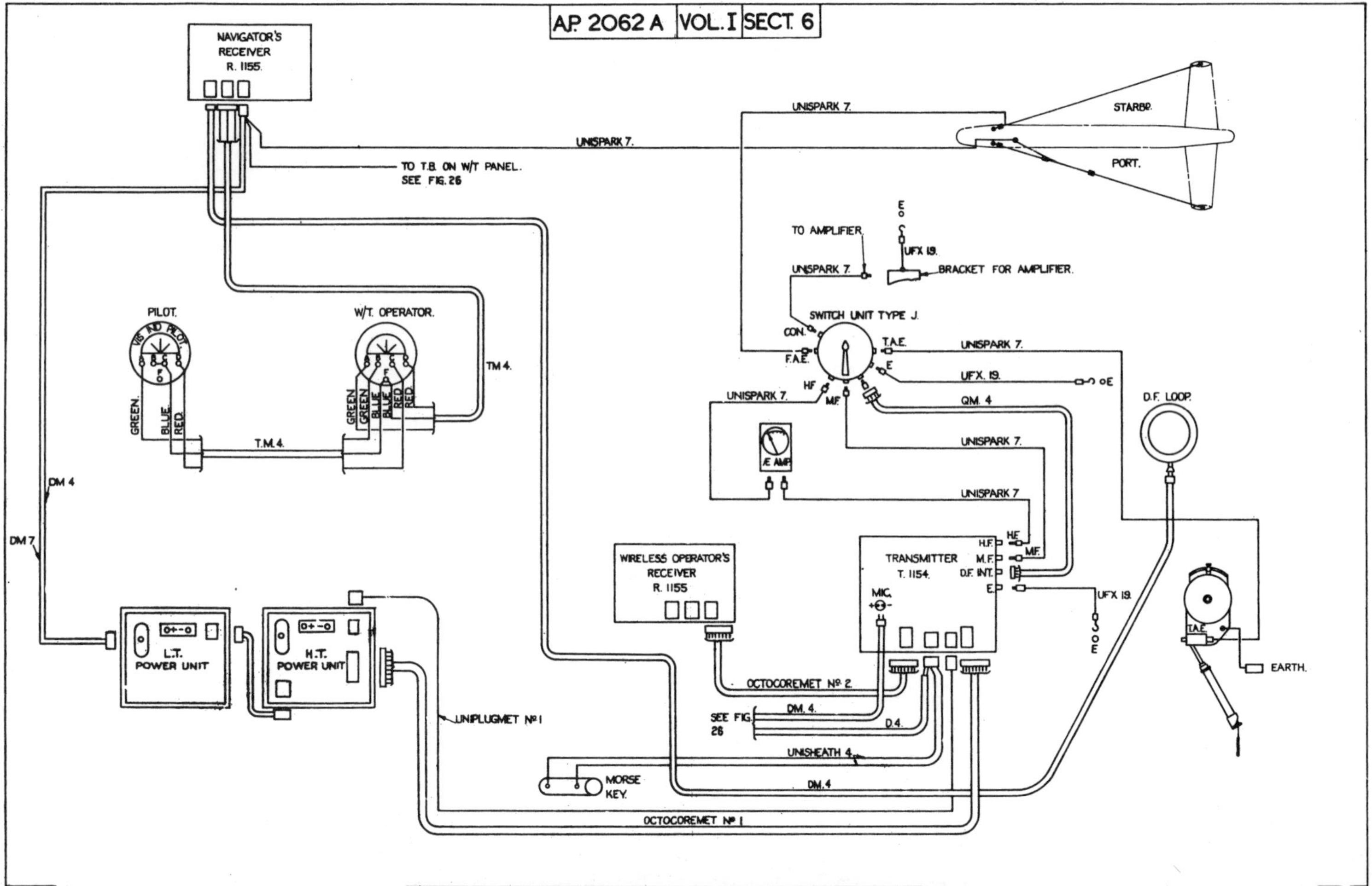

FIG. 27

T 1154 AND R 1155 INSTALLATION

FIG.

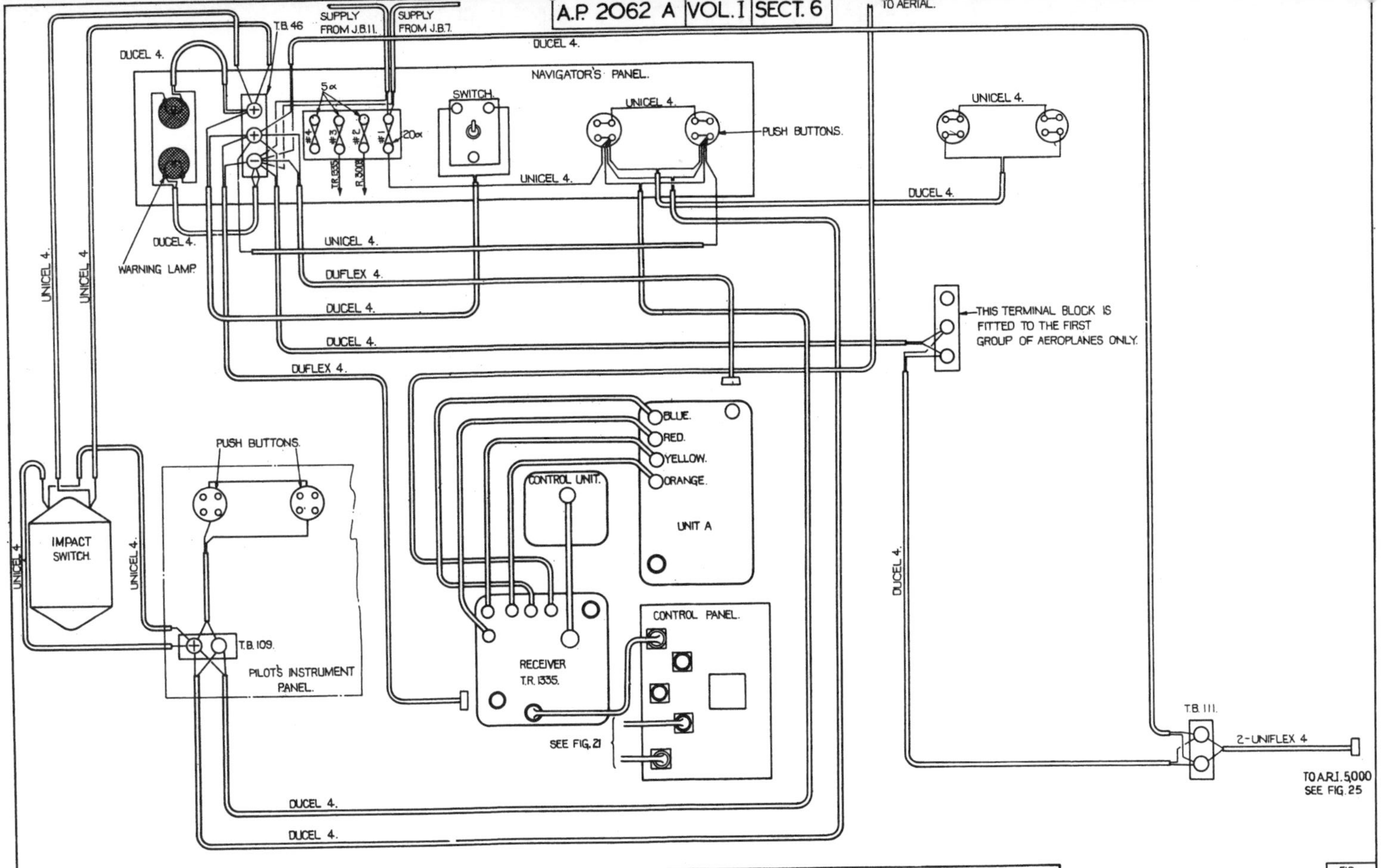

A.R.I. 5033 CIRCUIT, AND A.R.I. 5000 DETONATOR CIRCUIT

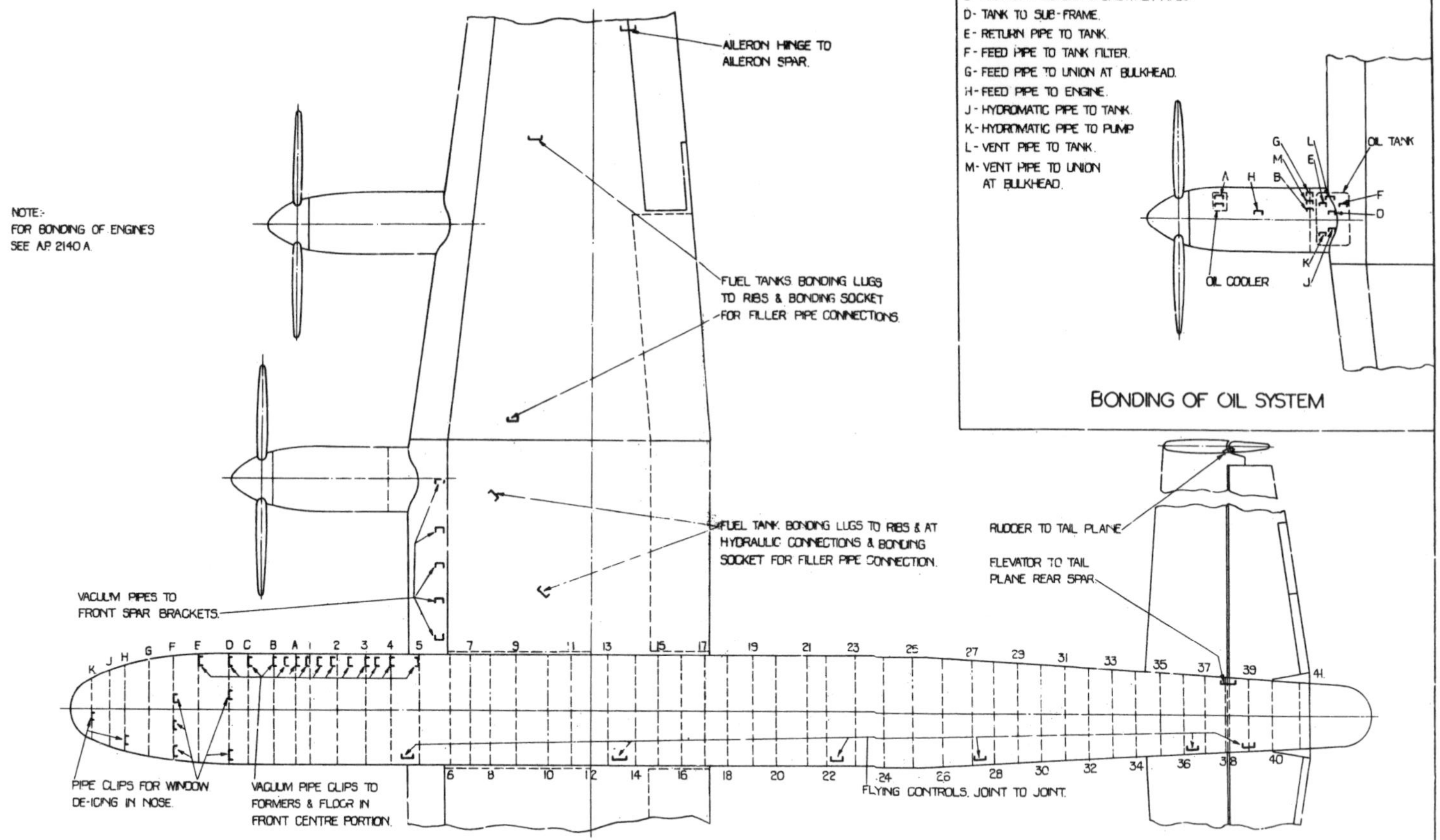

NOTE:-
FOR BONDING OF ENGINES SEE A.P. 2140 A.

NOTE:-
FOR BONDING OF HYDRAULIC SYSTEM SEE FIG. 31
FOR BONDING OF AUTOMATIC CONTROLS SEE SECT. 4. CHAP. 3 FIG. 28

FIG. 29

BONDING OF GENERAL SERVICES

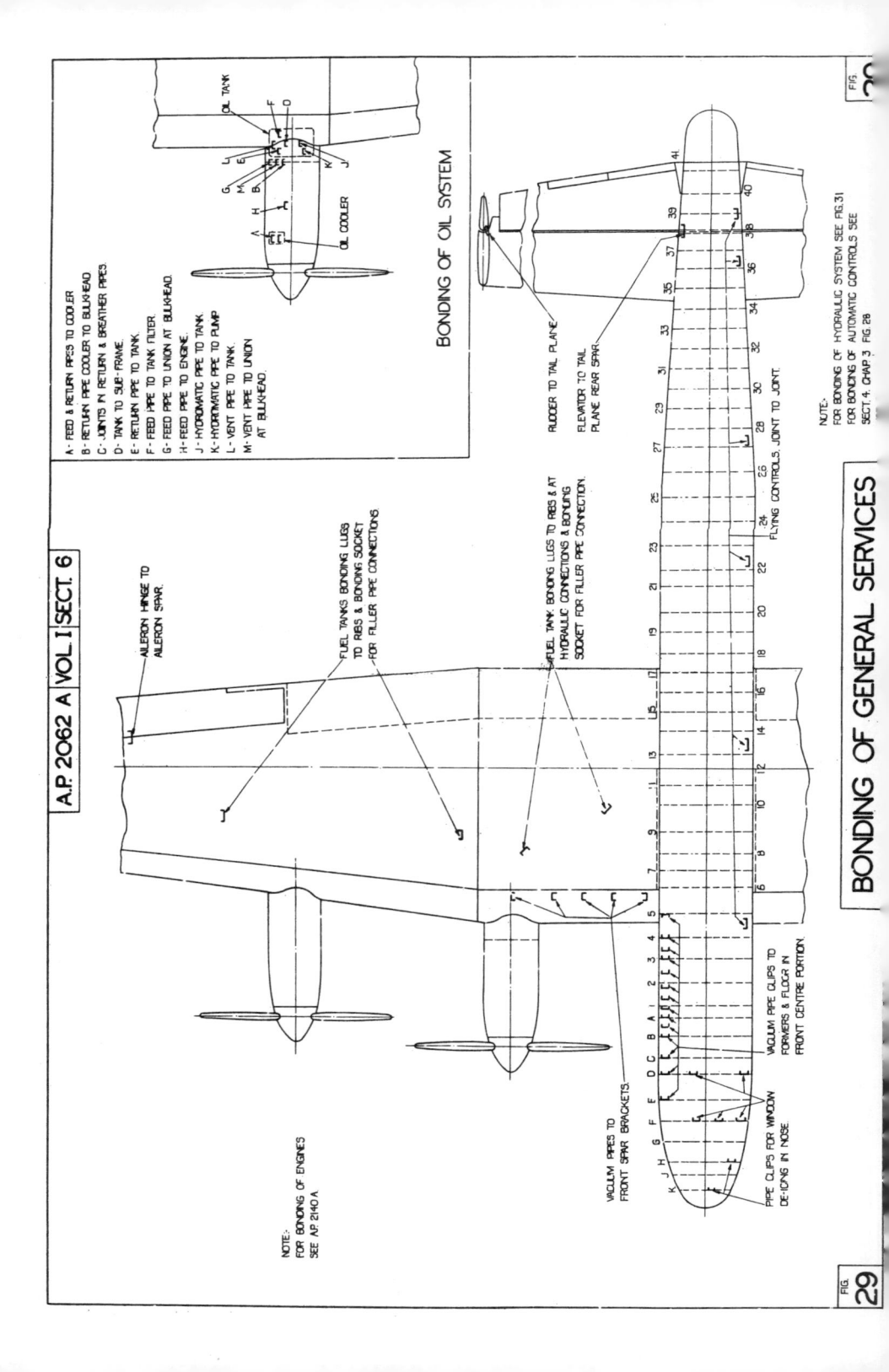

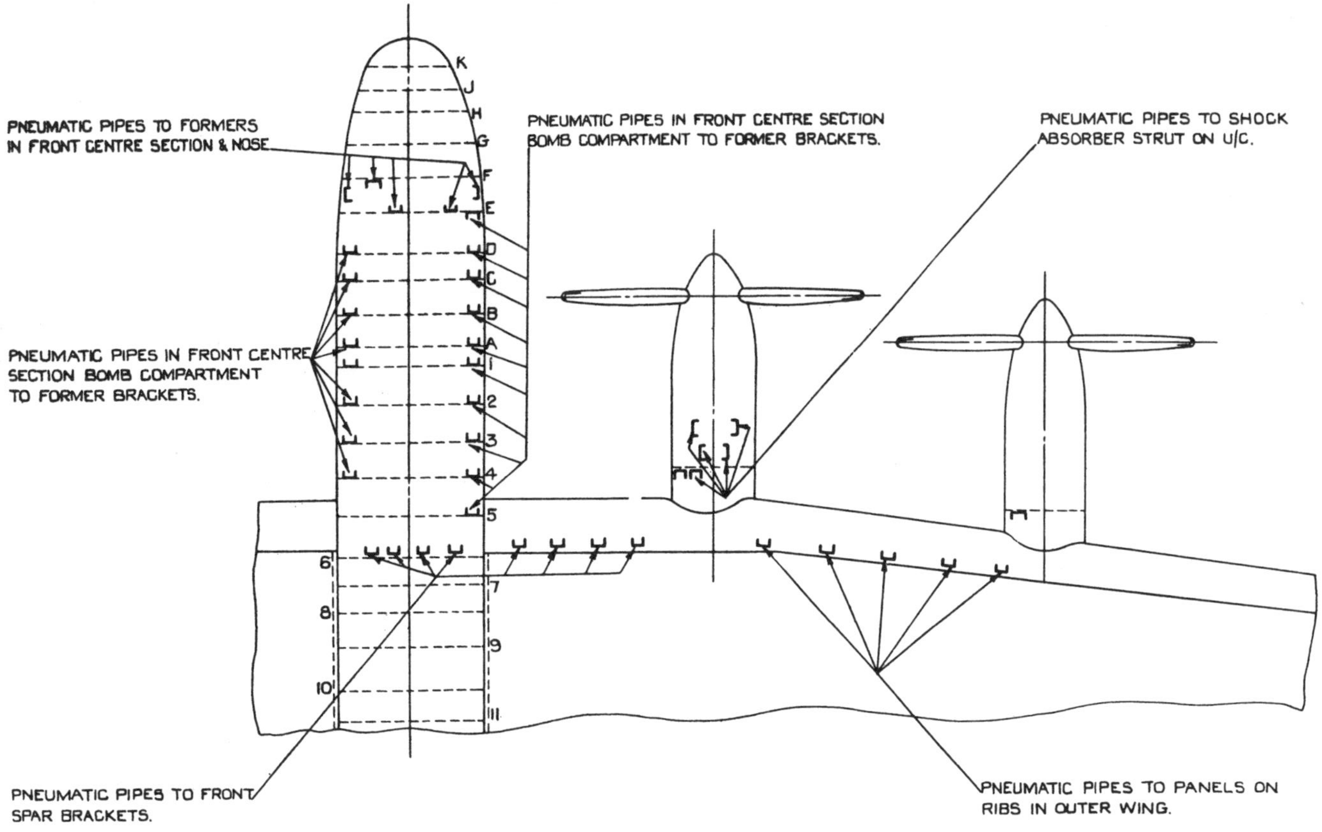

FIG. 30

BONDING OF PNEUMATIC SYSTEM

FIG. 30

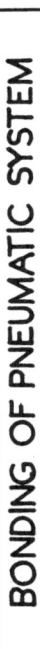

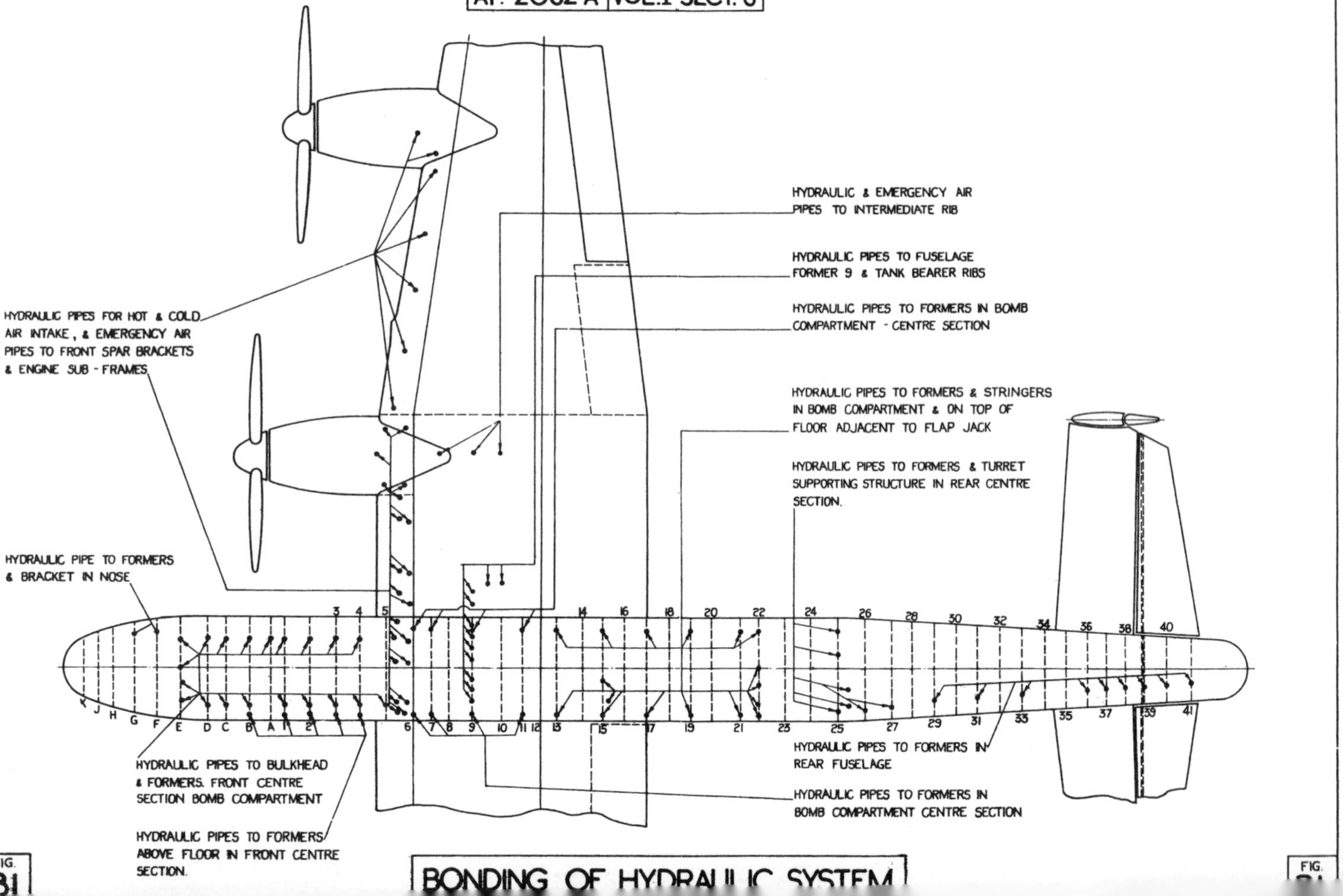

BONDING OF HYDRAULIC SYSTEM

AP 2062 A | VOL.I SECT.6

FIG. 31

- HYDRAULIC PIPES FOR HOT & COLD AIR INTAKE, & EMERGENCY AIR PIPES TO FRONT SPAR BRACKETS & ENGINE SUB-FRAMES
- HYDRAULIC PIPE TO FORMERS & BRACKET IN NOSE
- HYDRAULIC PIPES TO BULKHEAD & FORMERS, FRONT CENTRE SECTION BOMB COMPARTMENT
- HYDRAULIC PIPES TO FORMERS ABOVE FLOOR IN FRONT CENTRE SECTION.
- HYDRAULIC & EMERGENCY AIR PIPES TO INTERMEDIATE RIB
- HYDRAULIC PIPES TO FUSELAGE FORMER 9 & TANK BEARER RIBS
- HYDRAULIC PIPES TO FORMERS IN BOMB COMPARTMENT - CENTRE SECTION
- HYDRAULIC PIPES TO FORMERS & STRINGERS IN BOMB COMPARTMENT & ON TOP OF FLOOR ADJACENT TO FLAP JACK
- HYDRAULIC PIPES TO FORMERS & TURRET SUPPORTING STRUCTURE IN REAR CENTRE SECTION.
- HYDRAULIC PIPES TO FORMERS IN REAR FUSELAGE
- HYDRAULIC PIPES TO FORMERS IN BOMB COMPARTMENT CENTRE SECTION

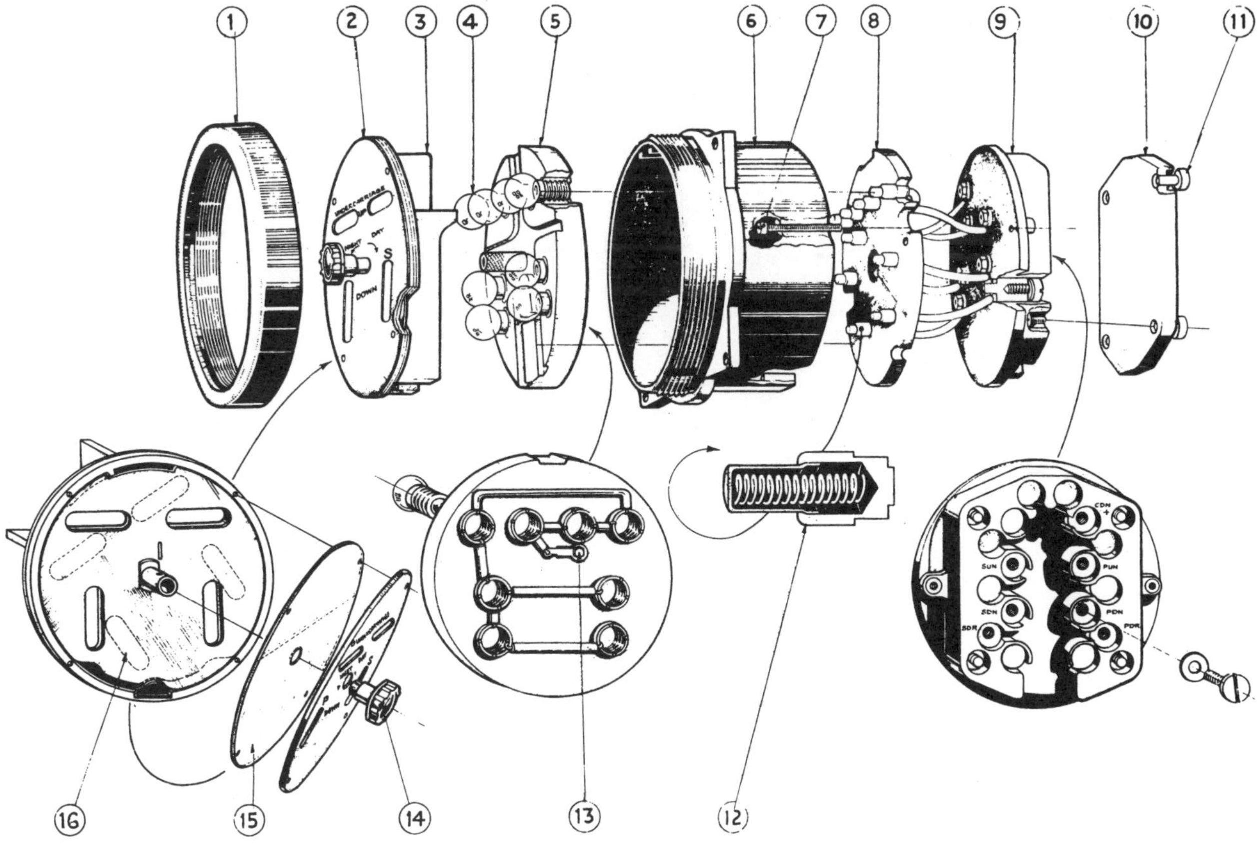

A.P. 2062 A | VOL.1 | SECT. 6

FIG. 32

UNDERCARRIAGE POSITION INDICATOR

FIG. 32

A.P.2062A | VOL.I | SECT.6

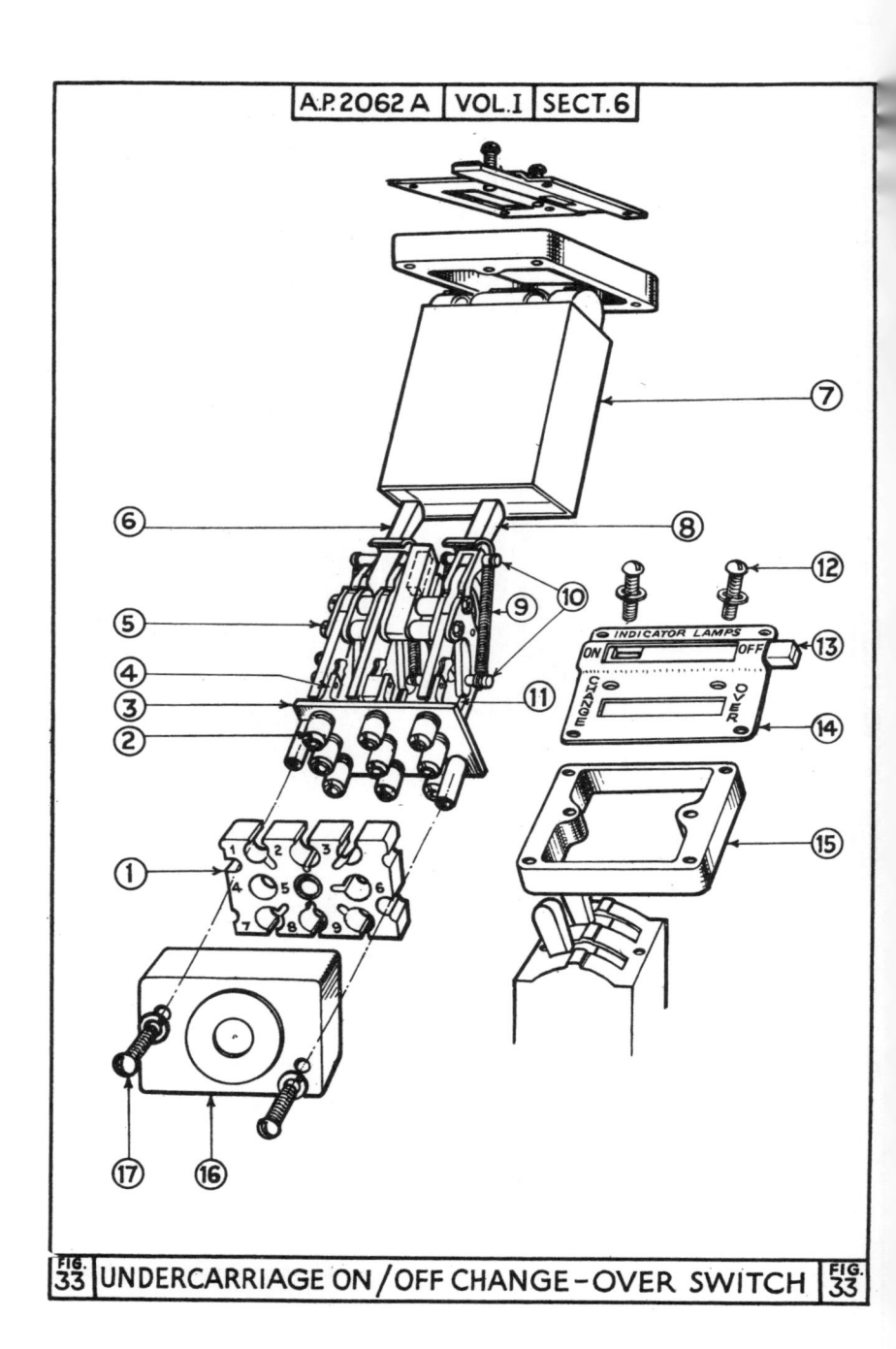

FIG. 33 UNDERCARRIAGE ON/OFF CHANGE-OVER SWITCH FIG. 33

344

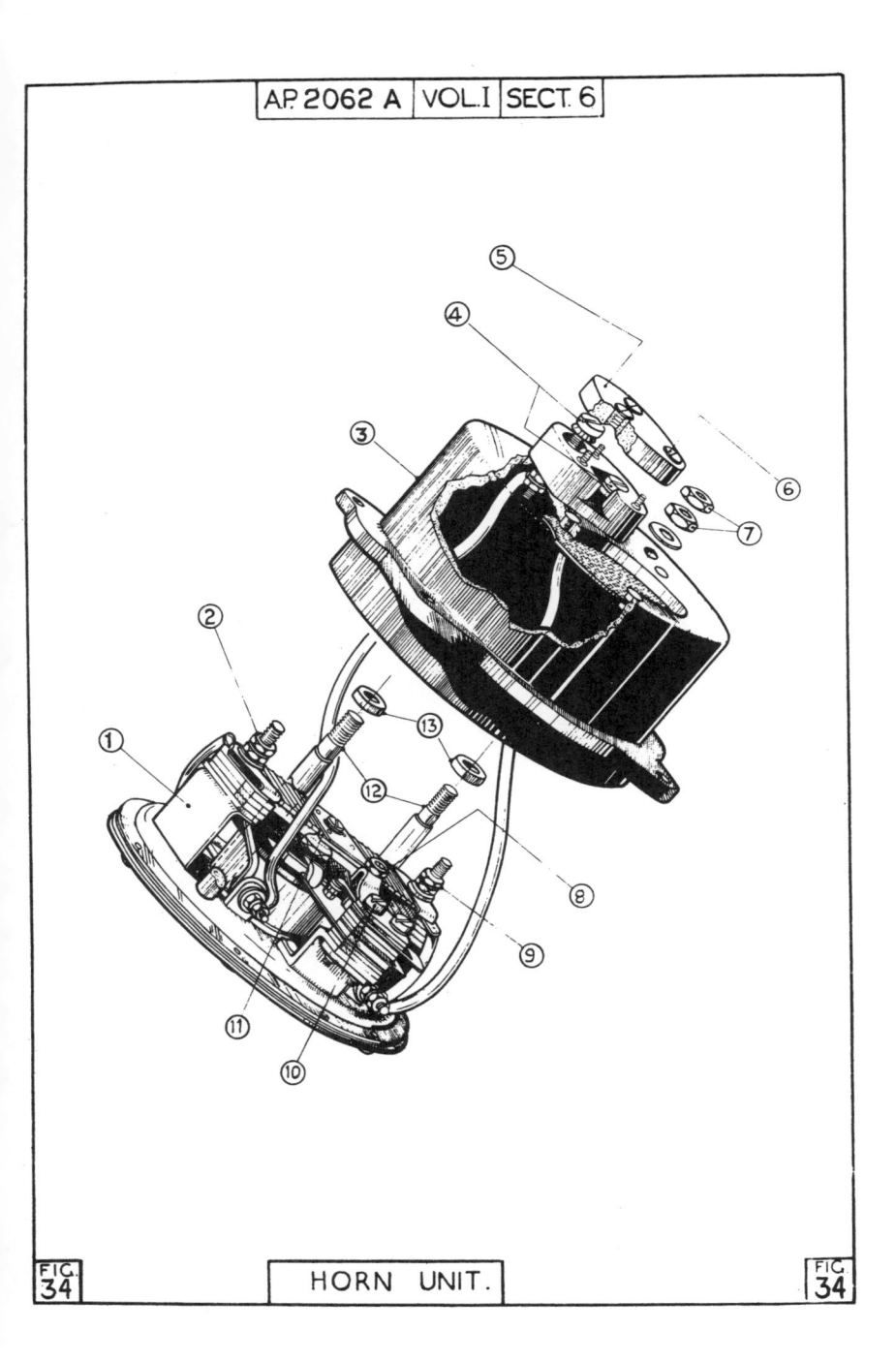

A.P. 2062 A | VOL. I | SECT. 6

FIG. 34

HORN UNIT.

345

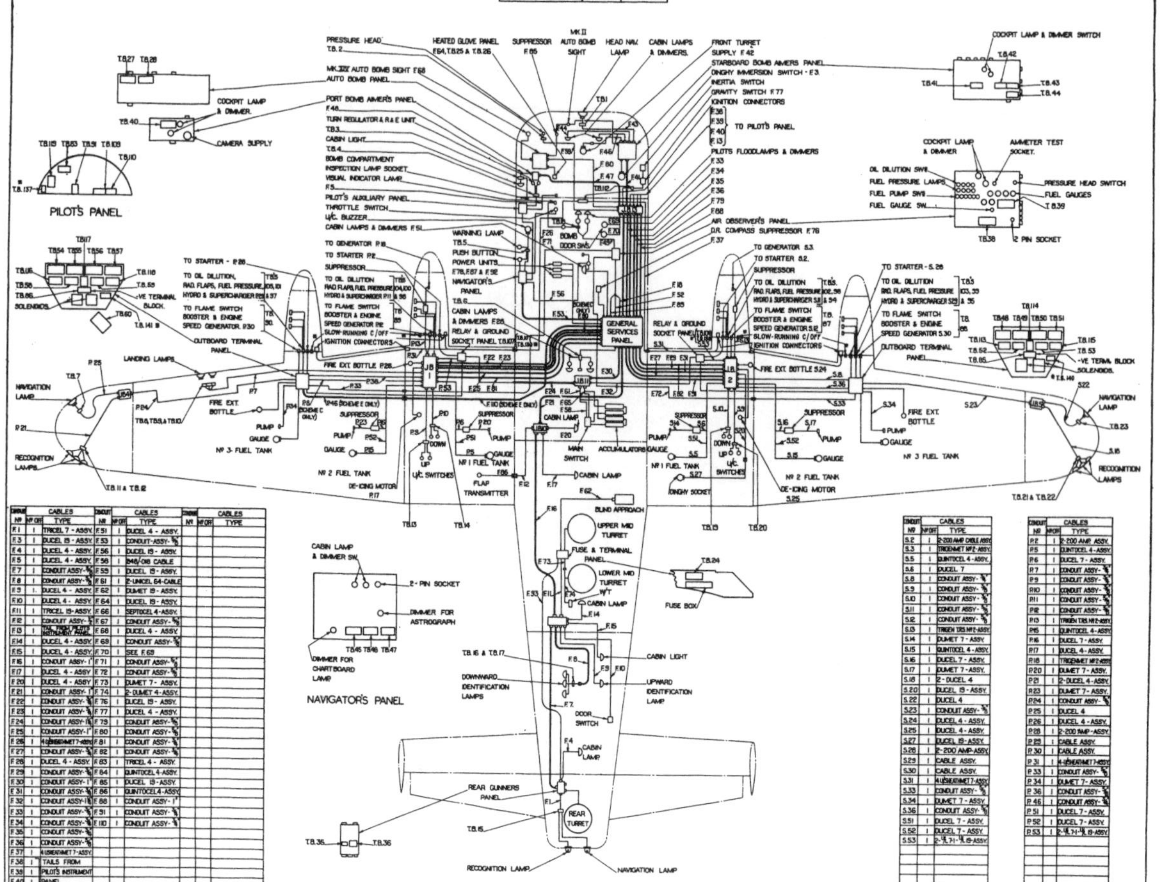

CONDUIT	CABLES		CONDUIT	CABLES	
REF.	Nº OFF	TYPE	REF.	Nº OFF	TYPE
A.S.	2	UNICEL 19			
			12A	1	QUINCEL 4
W	6	UNICEL 19	13A	1	DUCEL 4
X	6	UNICEL 19			
Y	9	UNICEL 4			
Z	9	UNICEL 4			
1	1	QUINCEL 4			
2	1	QUINCEL 4			
3	1	QUINCEL 4			
4	1	QUINCEL 4			
5	1	QUINCEL 4			
6	1	QUINCEL 4			
7	1	QUINCEL 4			
8	1	QUINCEL 4			
9	1	QUINCEL 4			
10	1	QUINCEL 4			
11	1	QUINCEL 4			
12	1	QUINCEL 4			
13	1	QUINCEL 4			
14	1	QUINCEL 4			
15	1	QUINCEL 4			

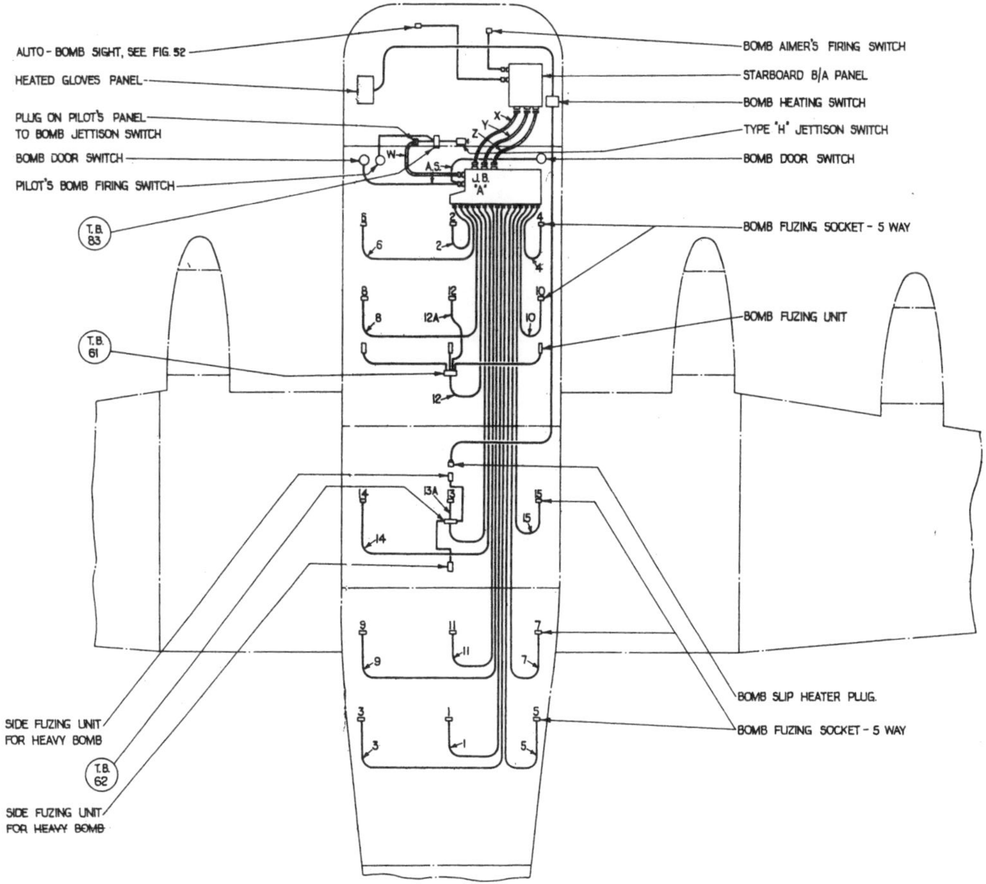

FIG. 36

LOCATION DIAGRAM - BOMB FUZING & RELEASE - SCHEMES 'C' & 'E'

FIG. 36

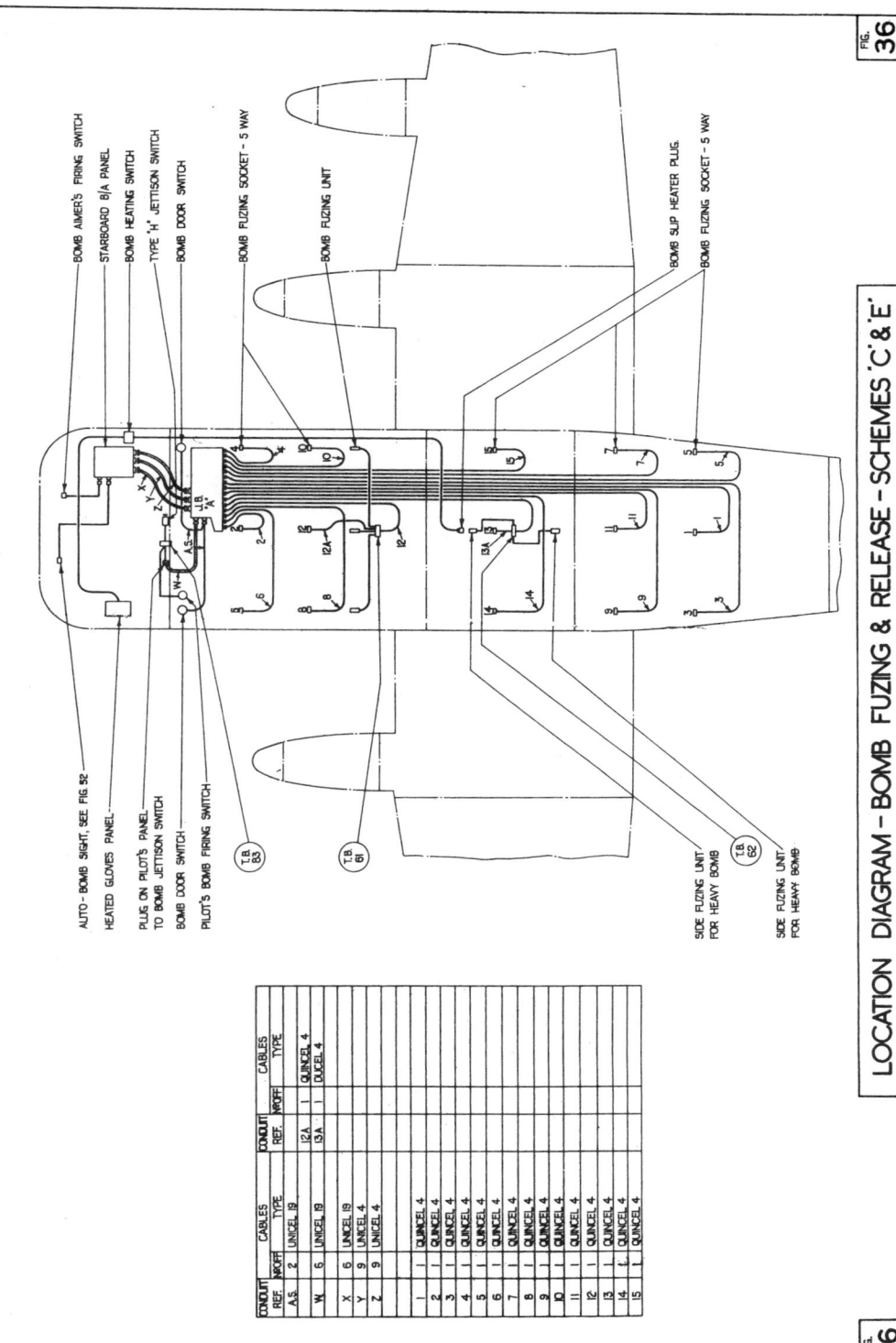

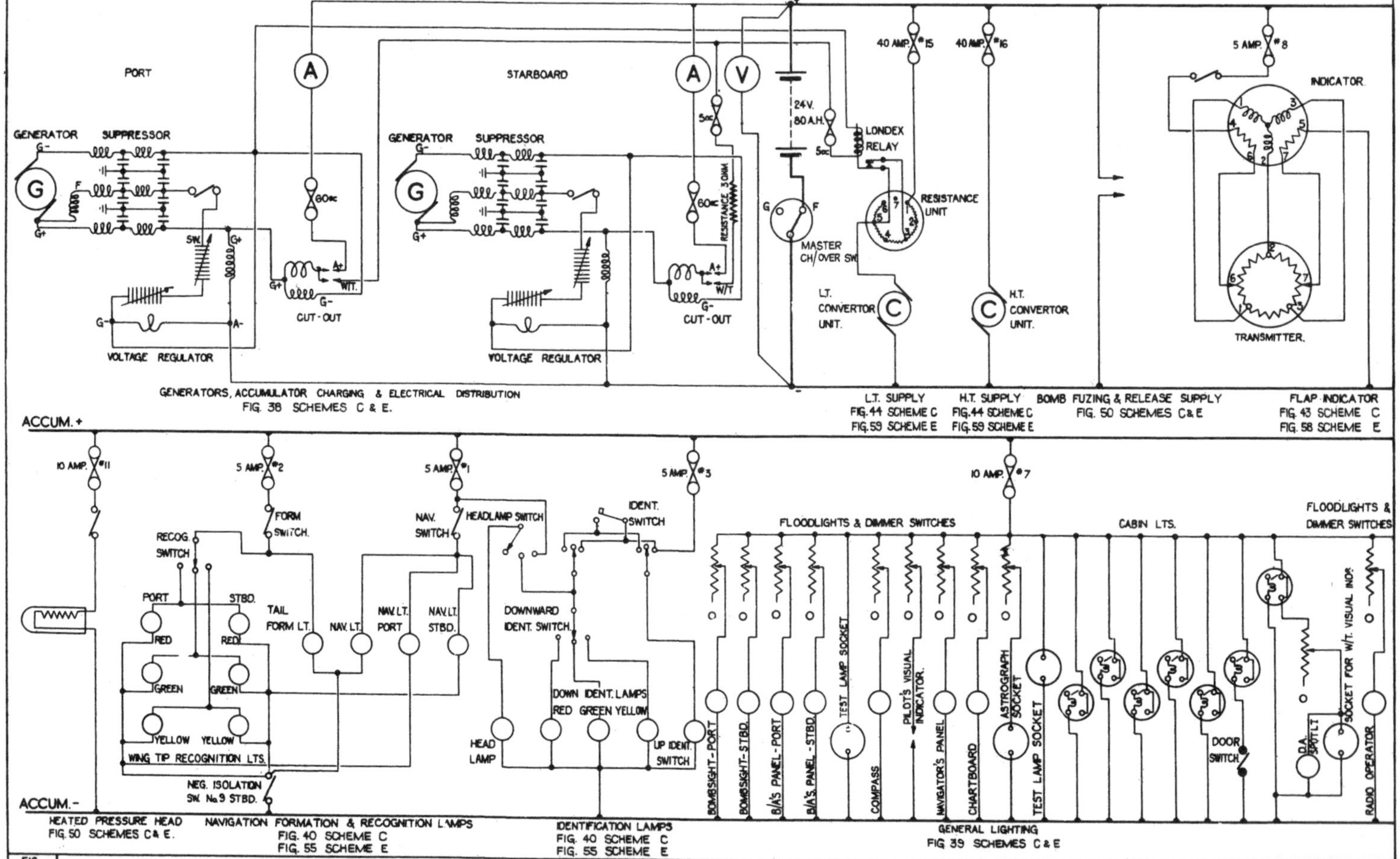

FIG. 37 SCHEMATIC DIAGRAM

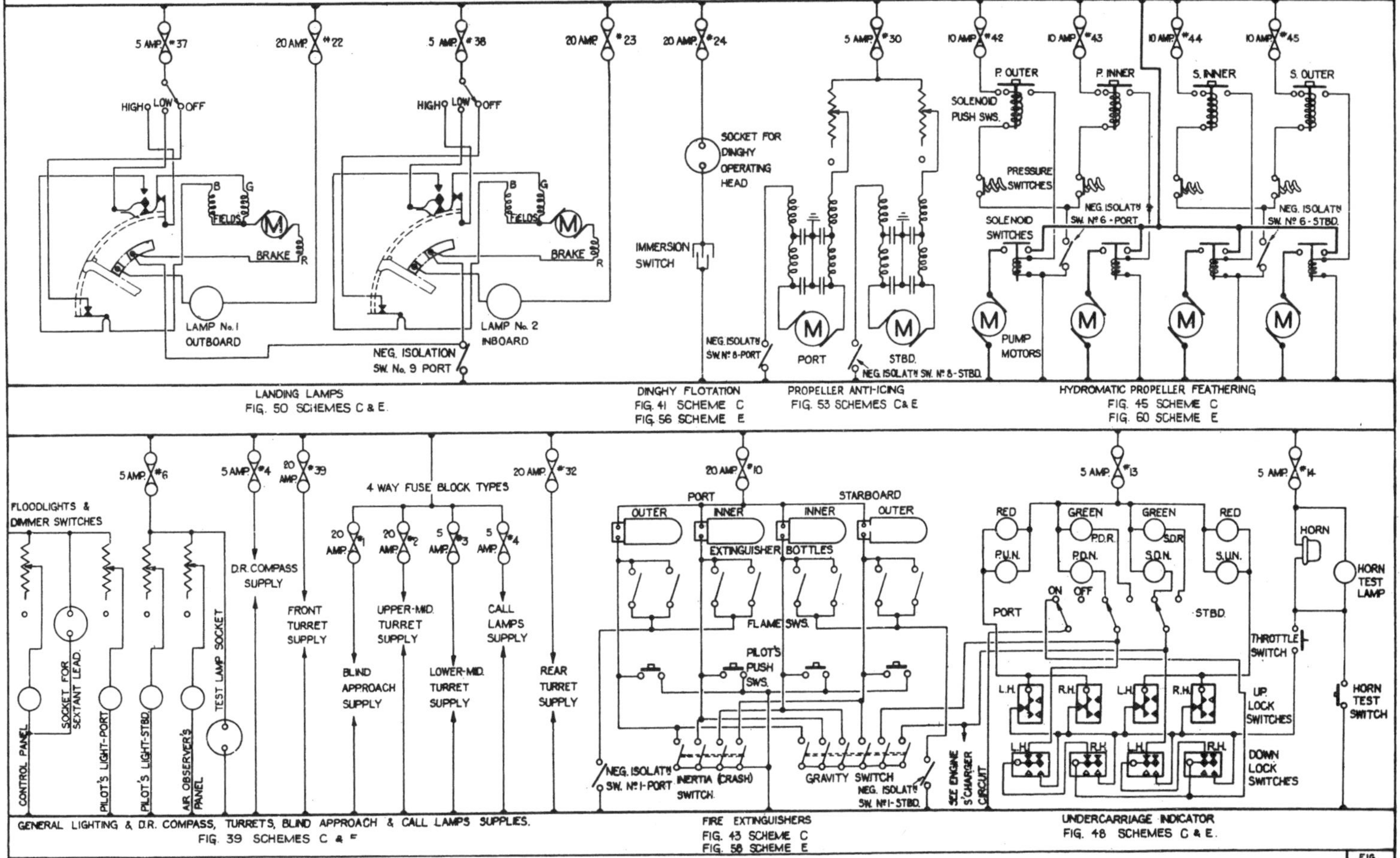

ELECTRICAL SERVICES SCHEMES C & E

FIG. 37

PP2080 M /1095 3/43 3950 C & P Gp. 959 (4)

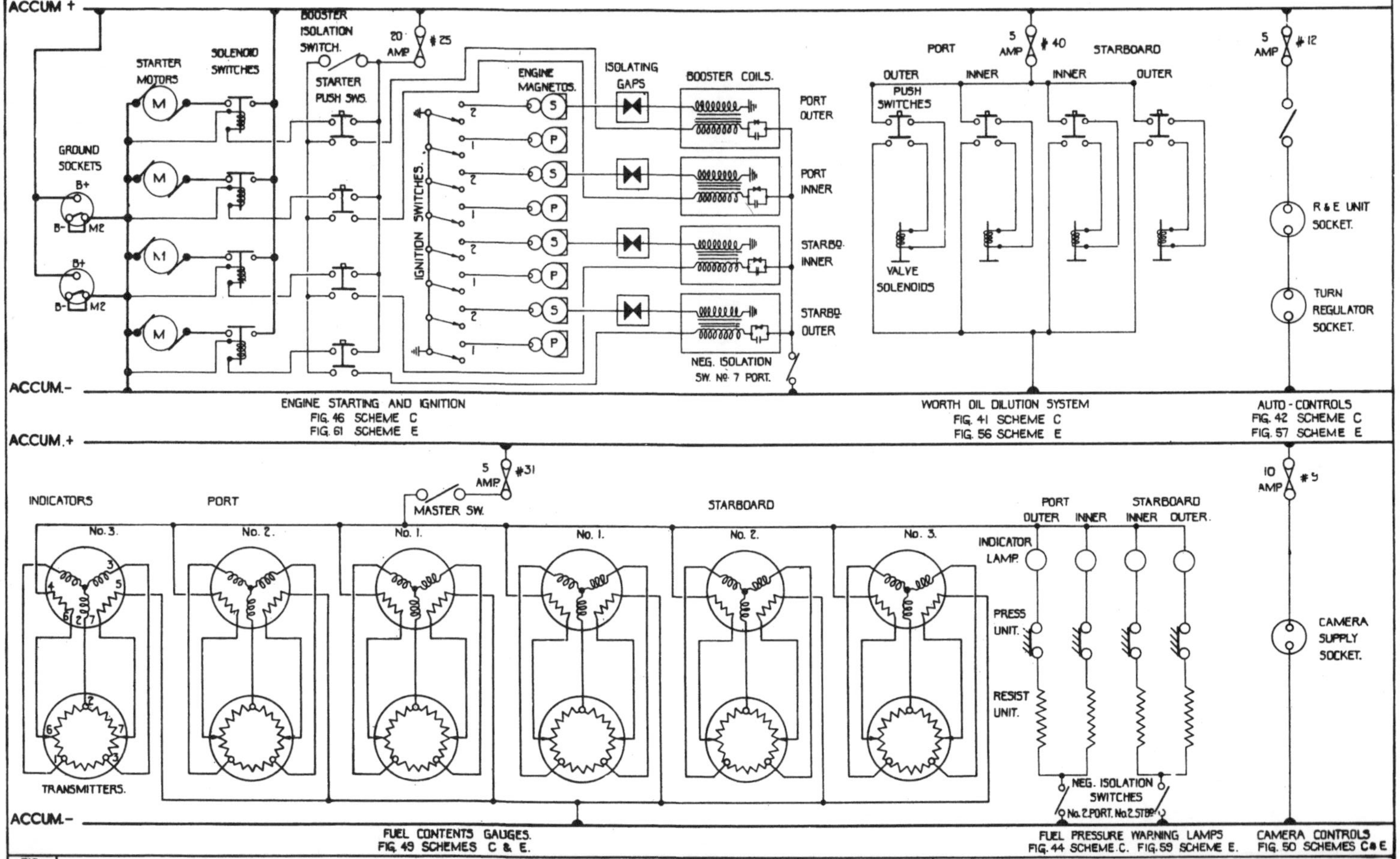

FIG. 37A

SCHEMATIC DIAGRAM

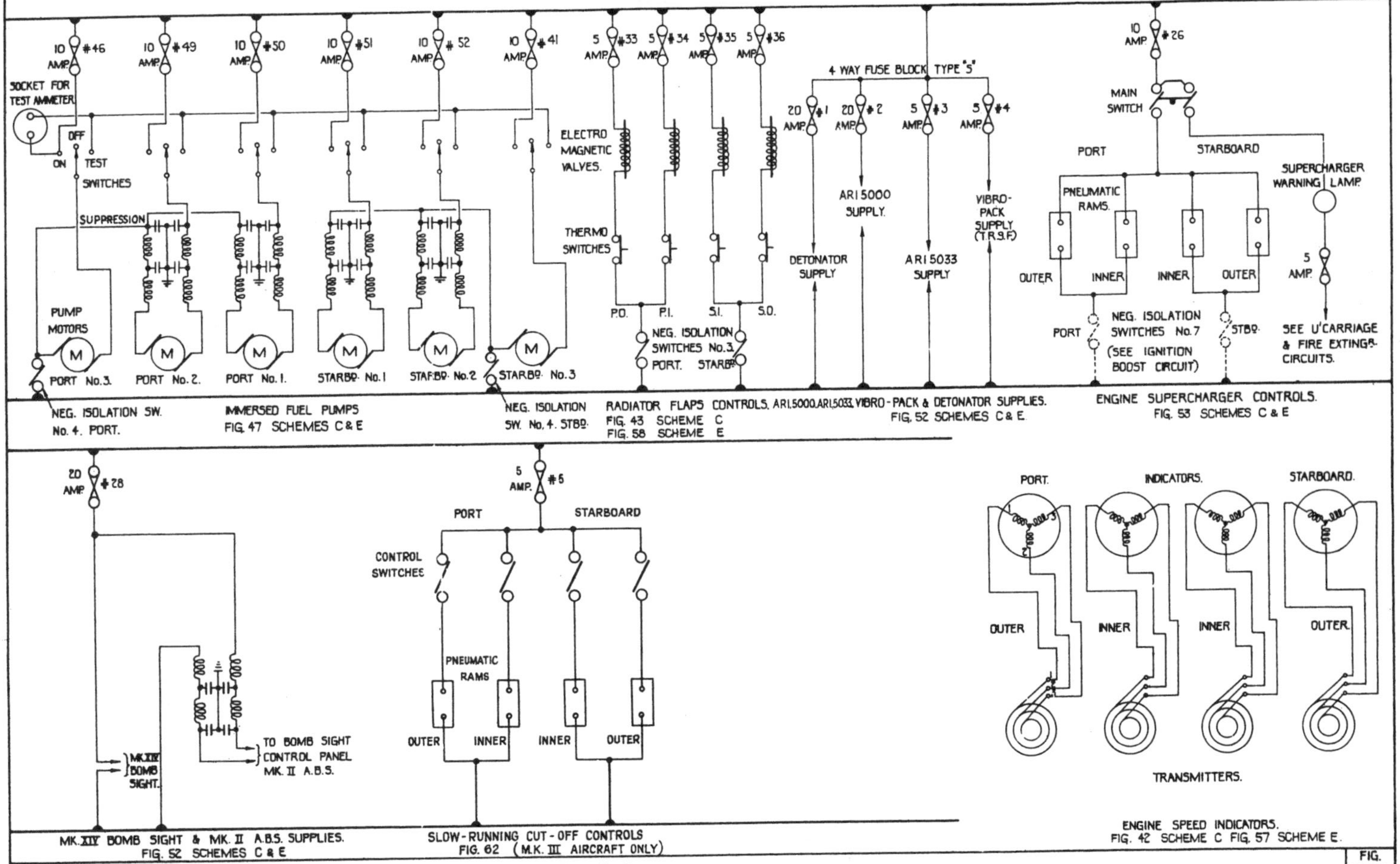

FIG. 37A

ELECTRICAL SERVICES – SCHEMES 'C' & 'E'.

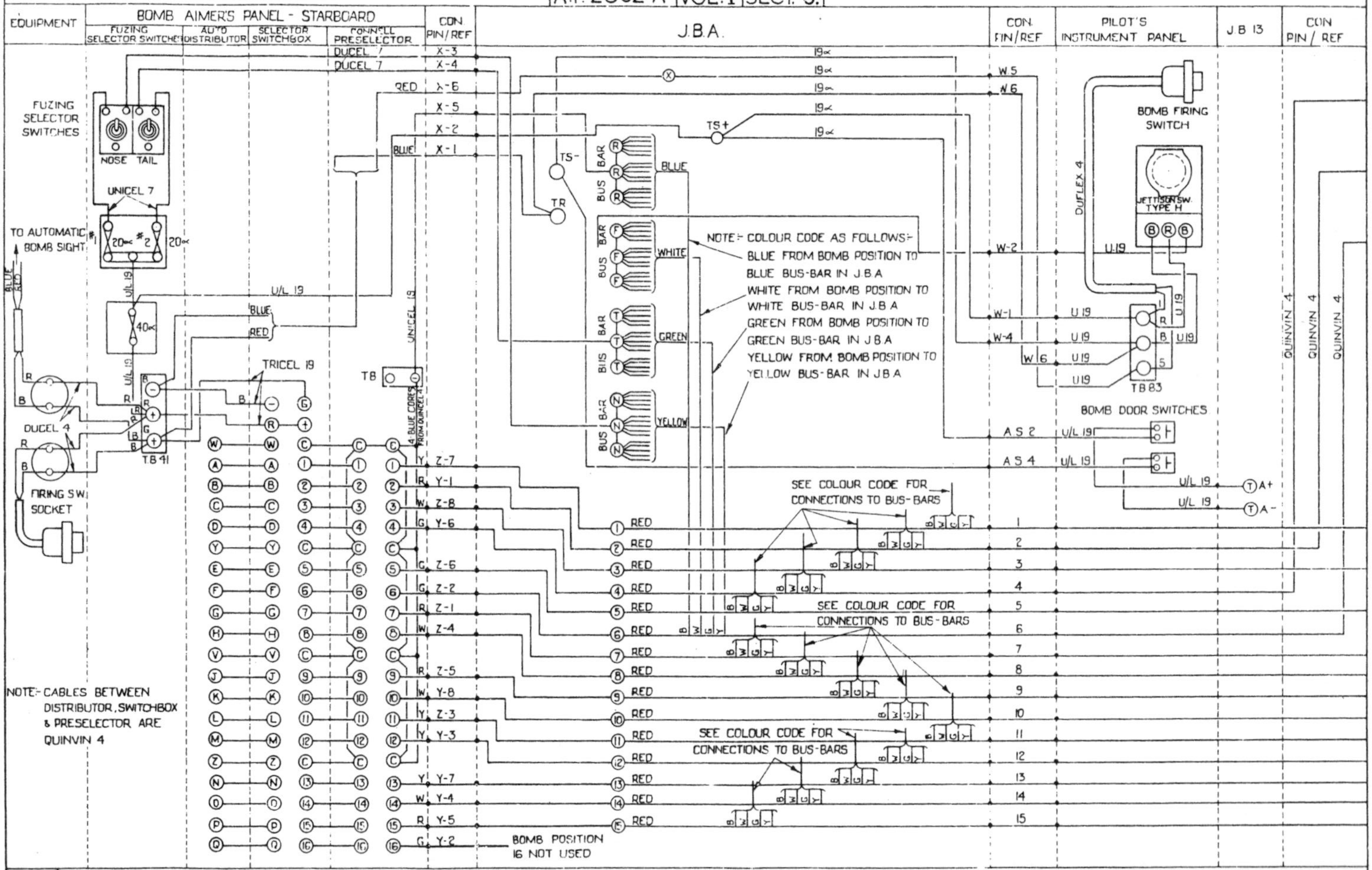

FIG 37B

ROUTING CHART

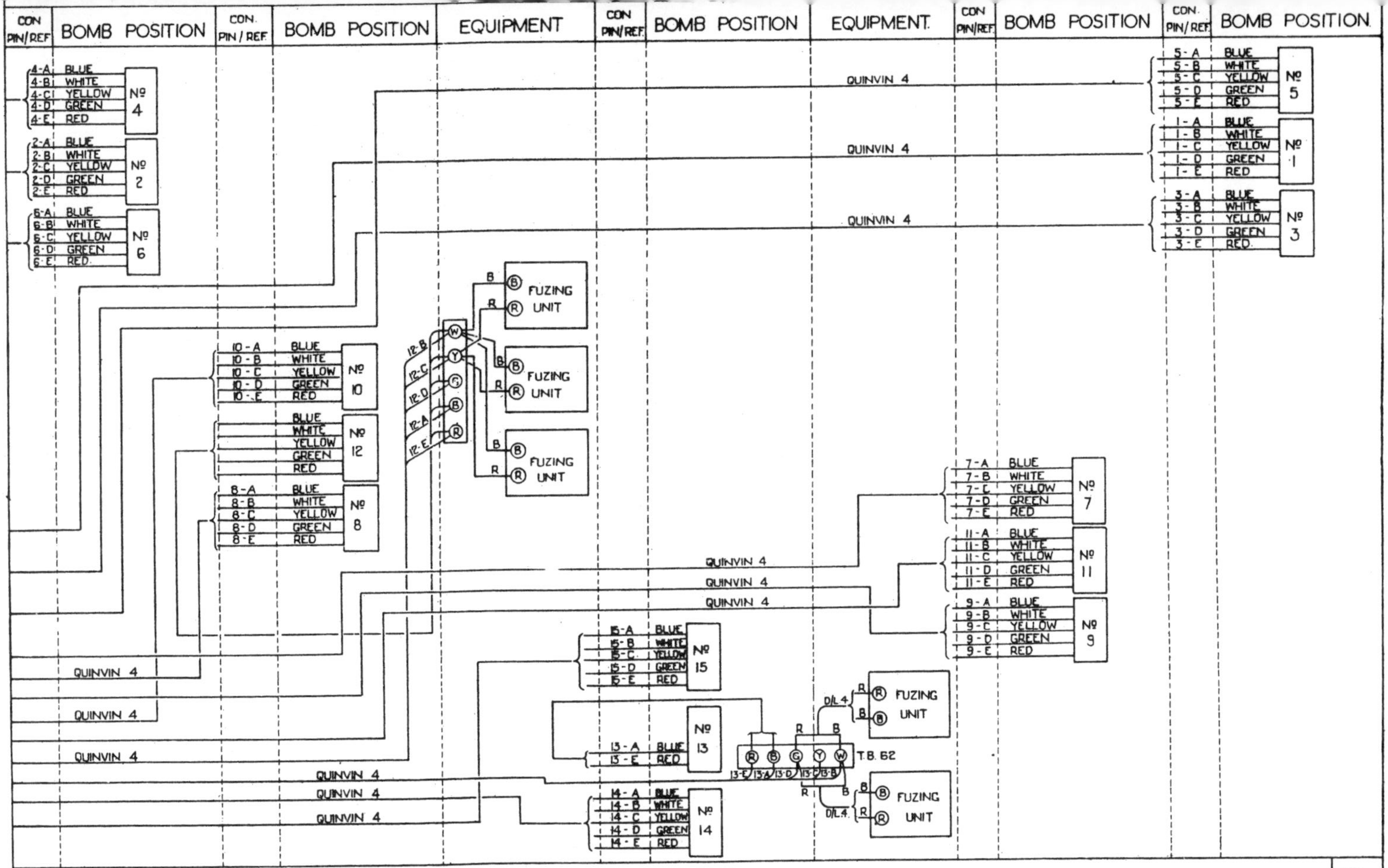

BOMB FUZING & RELEASE - SCHEMES C & E.

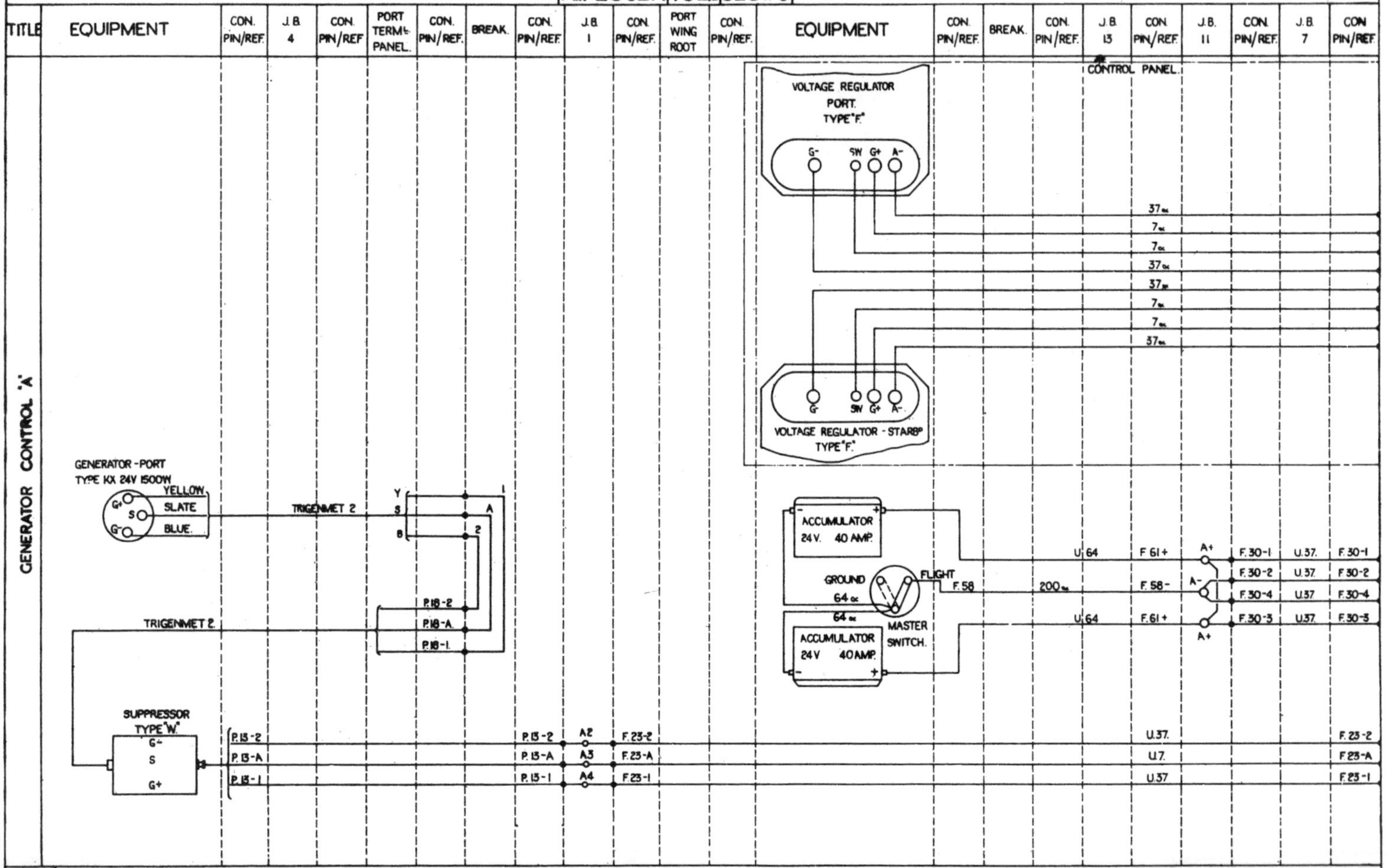

TITLE
EQUIPMENT
CON. PIN/REF.
J.B. 4
CON. PIN/REF
PORT TERM'L PANEL.
CON. PIN/REF.
BREAK.
CON. PIN/REF
J.B. 1
CON. PIN/REF.
PORT WING ROOT
CON. PIN/REF.
EQUIPMENT
CON. PIN/REF.
BREAK.
CON. PIN/REF.
J.B. 13
CON. PIN/REF.
J.B. 11
CON. PIN/REF.
J.B. 7
CON. PIN/REF.
GENERATOR CONTROL 'A'
CONTROL PANEL.
VOLTAGE REGULATOR PORT. TYPE "F."
G- SW G+ A-
37 7 7 37 37 7 7 37
VOLTAGE REGULATOR - STARB'D TYPE "F."
GENERATOR - PORT TYPE KX 24V 1500W
G+ S G-
YELLOW SLATE BLUE.
TRIGENMET 2
Y S B
1 A 2
P.18-2 P.18-A P.18-1
TRIGENMET 2.
SUPPRESSOR TYPE "W."
G- S G+
P.13-2 P.13-A P.13-1
A2 A3 A4
F.23-2 F.23-A F.23-1
U.37. U.7. U.37
ACCUMULATOR 24V. 40 AMP.
GROUND 64
64
FLIGHT F.58
MASTER SWITCH.
200
U.64 F.61+ F.58- U.64 F.61+
A+ A- A+
F.30-1 F.30-2 F.30-4 F.30-3
U.37.

FIG. 38

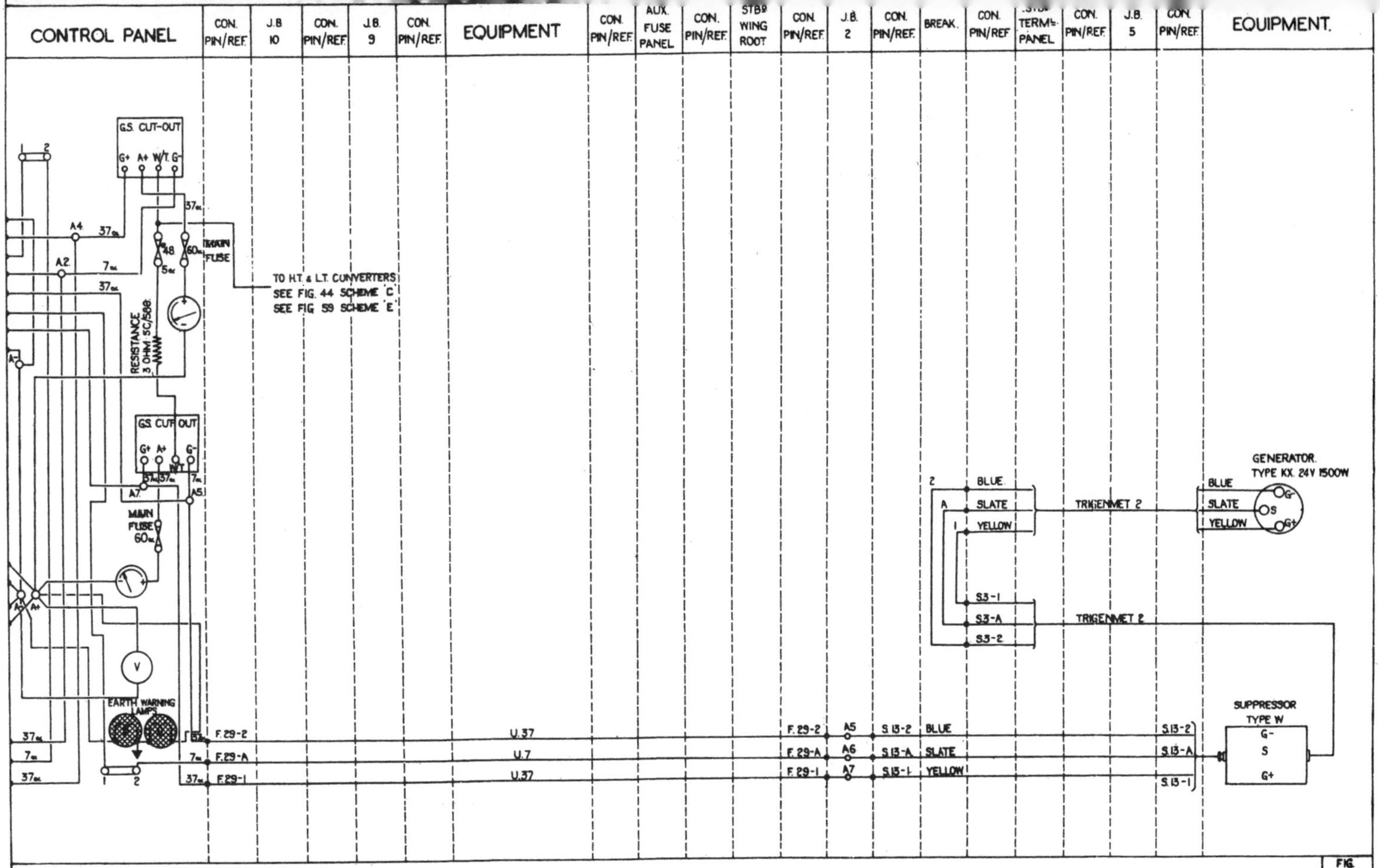

GENERAL SERVICES. SCHEME C & E.

FIG. 38

PP2080 M /1095 3/43 3950 C & P Gp. 959 (4)

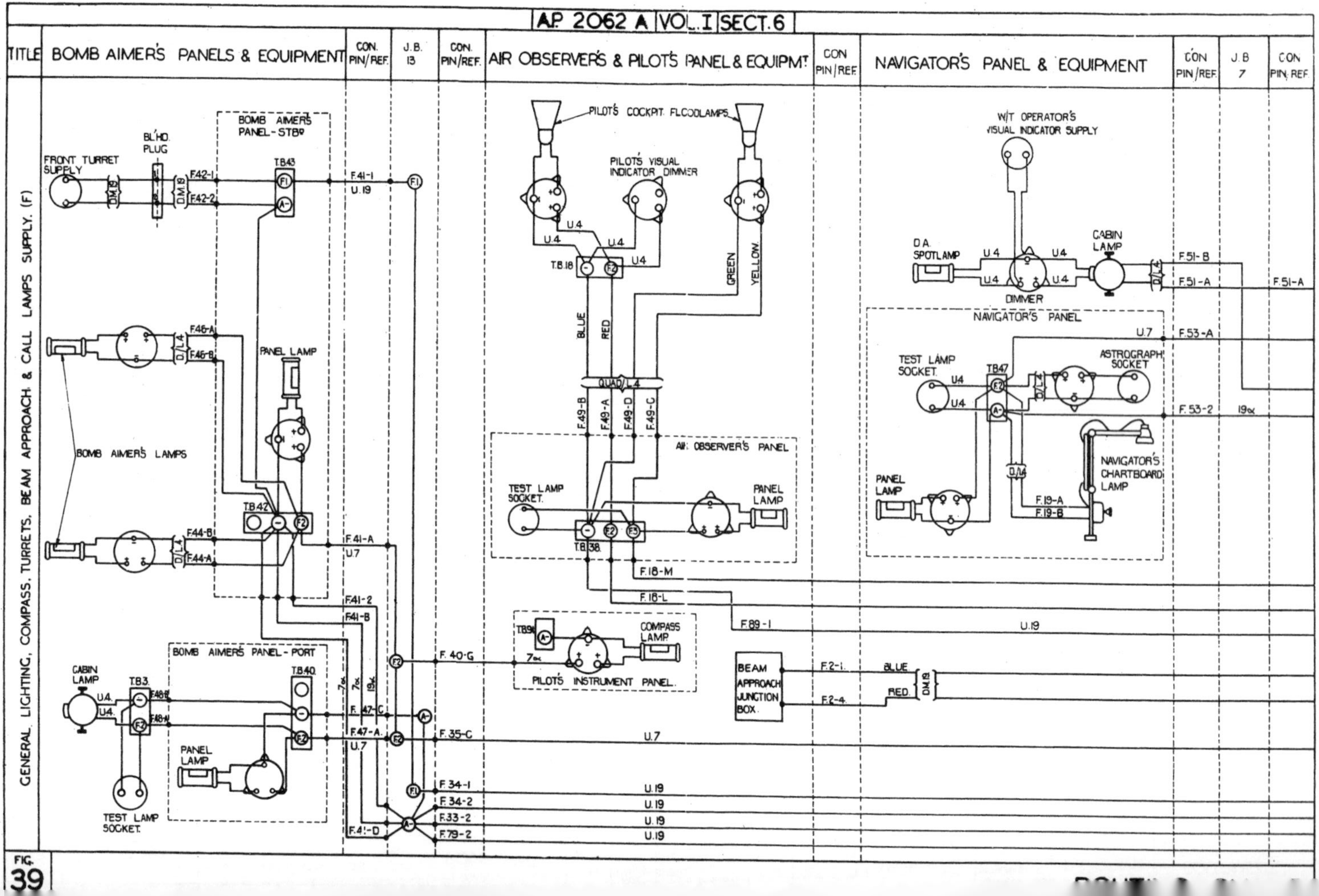
TITLE
GENERAL LIGHTING, COMPASS, TURRETS, BEAM APPROACH & CALL LAMPS SUPPLY. (F)
BOMB AIMER'S PANELS & EQUIPMENT
CON. PIN/REF.
J.B. 13
CON. PIN/REF.
AIR OBSERVER'S & PILOT'S PANEL & EQUIPMT
CON PIN/REF
NAVIGATOR'S PANEL & EQUIPMENT
CON PIN/REF
J.B 7
CON PIN REF
FRONT TURRET SUPPLY
BL'HD. PLUG
D.M.19
F.42-1
F.42-2
BOMB AIMER'S PANEL-STBD
T.B.43
F.41-1
U.19
F.46-A
F.46-B
D/L4
PANEL LAMP
BOMB AIMER'S LAMPS
T.B.42
F.44-B
F.44-A
F.41-A
U.7
F.41-2
F.41-B
CABIN LAMP
U.4
T.B.3
F.48-B
F.48-A
BOMB AIMER'S PANEL - PORT
T.B.40
PANEL LAMP
TEST LAMP SOCKET
7α
19α
F. 47-C
F.47-A
F.41-D
F. 40-G
F. 35-C
F. 34-1
F. 34-2
F. 33-2
F. 79-2
PILOT'S COCKPIT FLOODLAMPS
PILOT'S VISUAL INDICATOR DIMMER
T.B.18
GREEN
YELLOW
BLUE
RED
QUAD/L4
F.49-B
F.49-A
F.49-D
F.49-C
AIR OBSERVER'S PANEL
TEST LAMP SOCKET
PANEL LAMP
T.B.38
F.18-M
F.18-L
F.89-1
TB.94
COMPASS LAMP
PILOT'S INSTRUMENT PANEL
BEAM APPROACH JUNCTION BOX
F.2-1
F.2-4
BLUE
RED
W/T OPERATOR'S VISUAL INDICATOR SUPPLY
D.A. SPOTLAMP
CABIN LAMP
DIMMER
F.51-B
F.51-A
NAVIGATOR'S PANEL
U.7
F.53-A
TEST LAMP SOCKET
TB47
ASTROGRAPH SOCKET
F. 53-2
19α
D/L4
PANEL LAMP
NAVIGATOR'S CHARTBOARD LAMP
F.19-A
F.19-B
FIG. 39

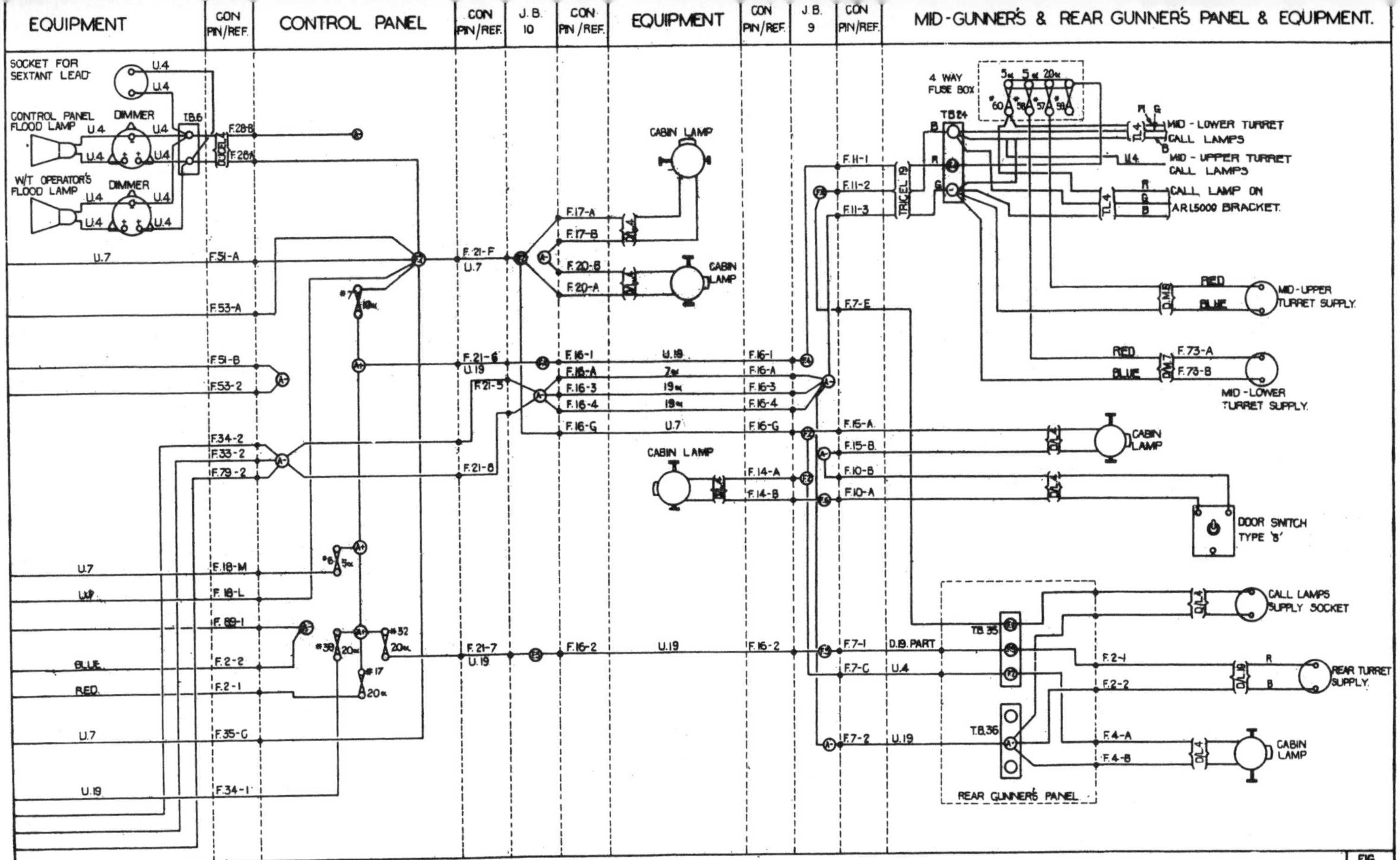

GENERAL SERVICES - SCHEME 'C & E'

FIG 39

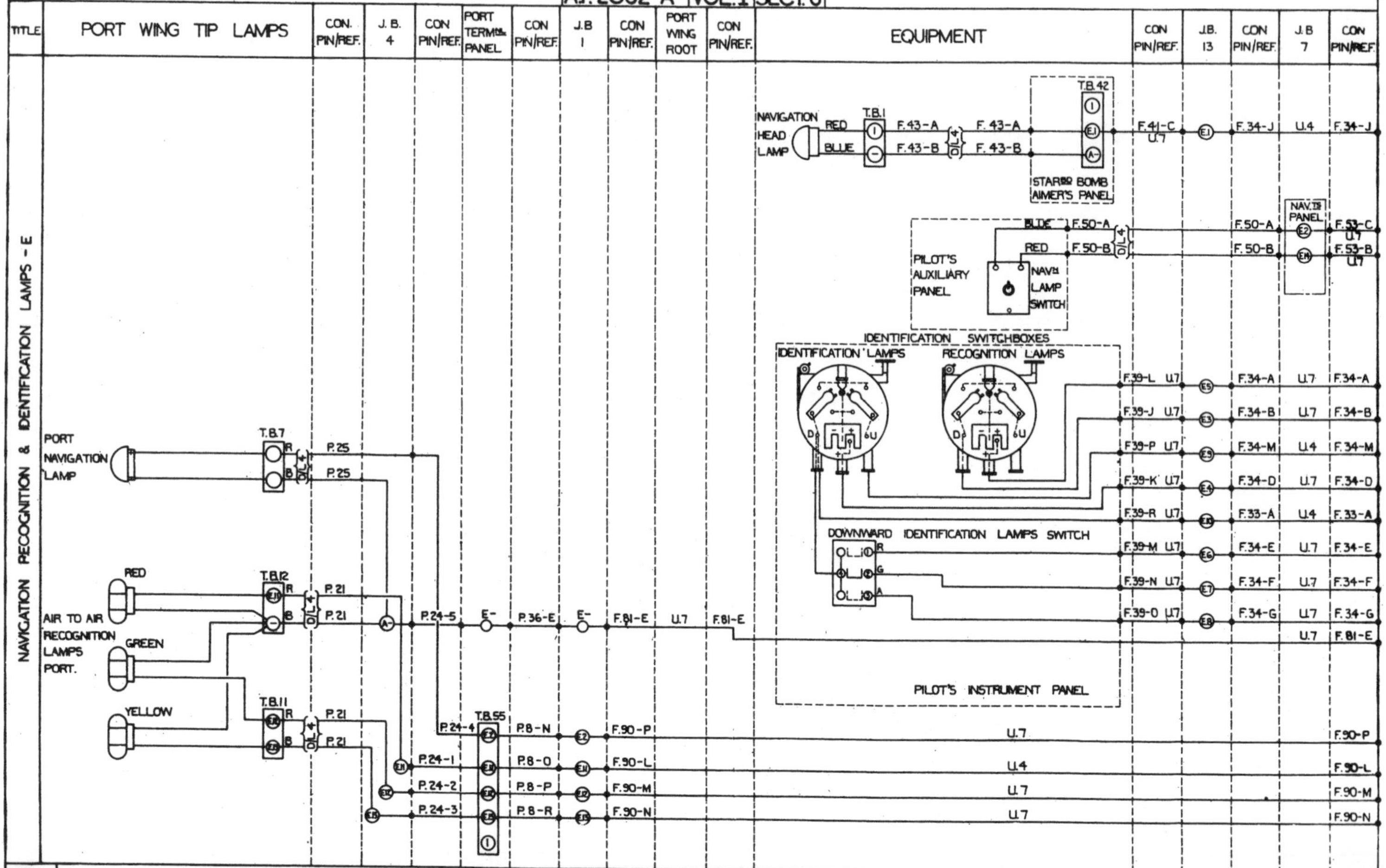
TITLE
NAVIGATION RECOGNITION & IDENTIFICATION LAMPS - E
PORT WING TIP LAMPS
CON. PIN/REF.
J.B. 4
CON PIN/REF.
PORT TERML. PANEL
CON PIN/REF.
J.B 1
CON PIN/REF.
PORT WING ROOT
CON PIN/REF.
EQUIPMENT
CON PIN/REF.
J.B. 13
CON PIN/REF.
J.B 7
CON PIN/REF.
PORT NAVIGATION LAMP
T.B.7
P.25
P.25
RED
AIR TO AIR RECOGNITION LAMPS PORT.
GREEN
YELLOW
T.B.12
T.B.11
P.21
P.21
P.21
P.21
P.24-5
E-
P.36-E
E-
F.81-E
U.7
F.81-E
T.B.55
P.24-4
P.24-1
P.24-2
P.24-3
P.8-N
P.8-O
P.8-P
P.8-R
F.90-P
F.90-L
F.90-M
F.90-N
U.7
U.4
U.7
U.7
NAVIGATION HEAD LAMP
RED
BLUE
T.B.1
F.43-A
F.43-B
F.43-A
F.43-B
T.B.42
STARBD BOMB AIMER'S PANEL
F.41-C U.7
F.34-J
U.4
F.34-J
PILOT'S AUXILIARY PANEL
BLUE
RED
NAVN LAMP SWITCH
F.50-A
F.50-B
F.50-A
F.50-B
NAV.N PANEL
F.53-C U.7
F.53-B U.7
IDENTIFICATION SWITCHBOXES
IDENTIFICATION LAMPS
RECOGNITION LAMPS
DOWNWARD IDENTIFICATION LAMPS SWITCH
PILOT'S INSTRUMENT PANEL
F.39-L U.7
F.39-J U.7
F.39-P U.7
F.39-K U.7
F.39-R U.7
F.39-M U.7
F.39-N U.7
F.39-O U.7
F.34-A U.7 F.34-A
F.34-B U.7 F.34-B
F.34-M U.4 F.34-M
F.34-D U.7 F.34-D
F.33-A U.4 F.33-A
F.34-E U.7 F.34-E
F.34-F U.7 F.34-F
F.34-G U.7 F.34-G
U.7 F.81-E

FIG. 40

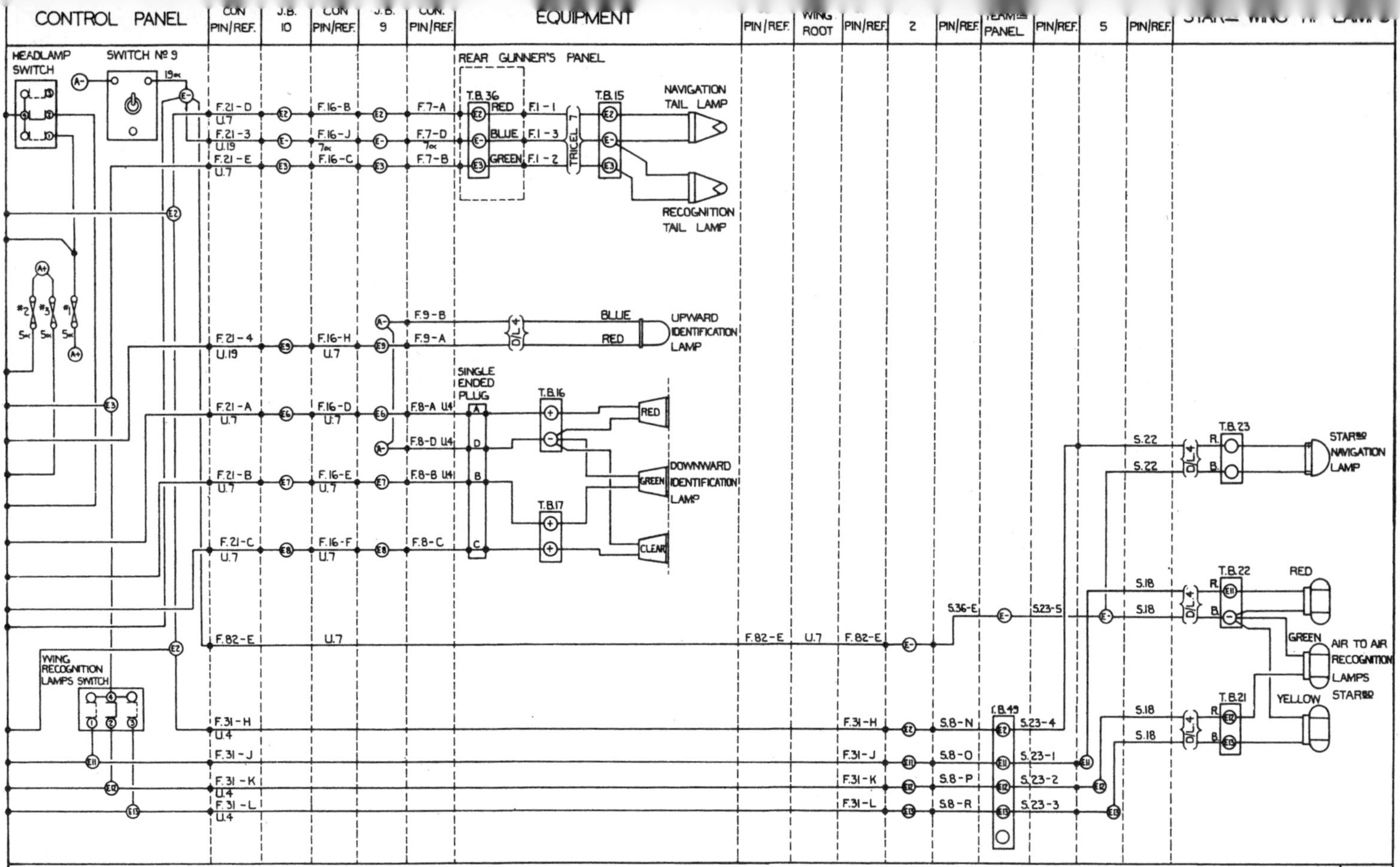

GENERAL SERVICES - SCHEME "C"

FIG. 40

PP2080 M /1095 3/43 3950 C & P Gp. 959 (4)

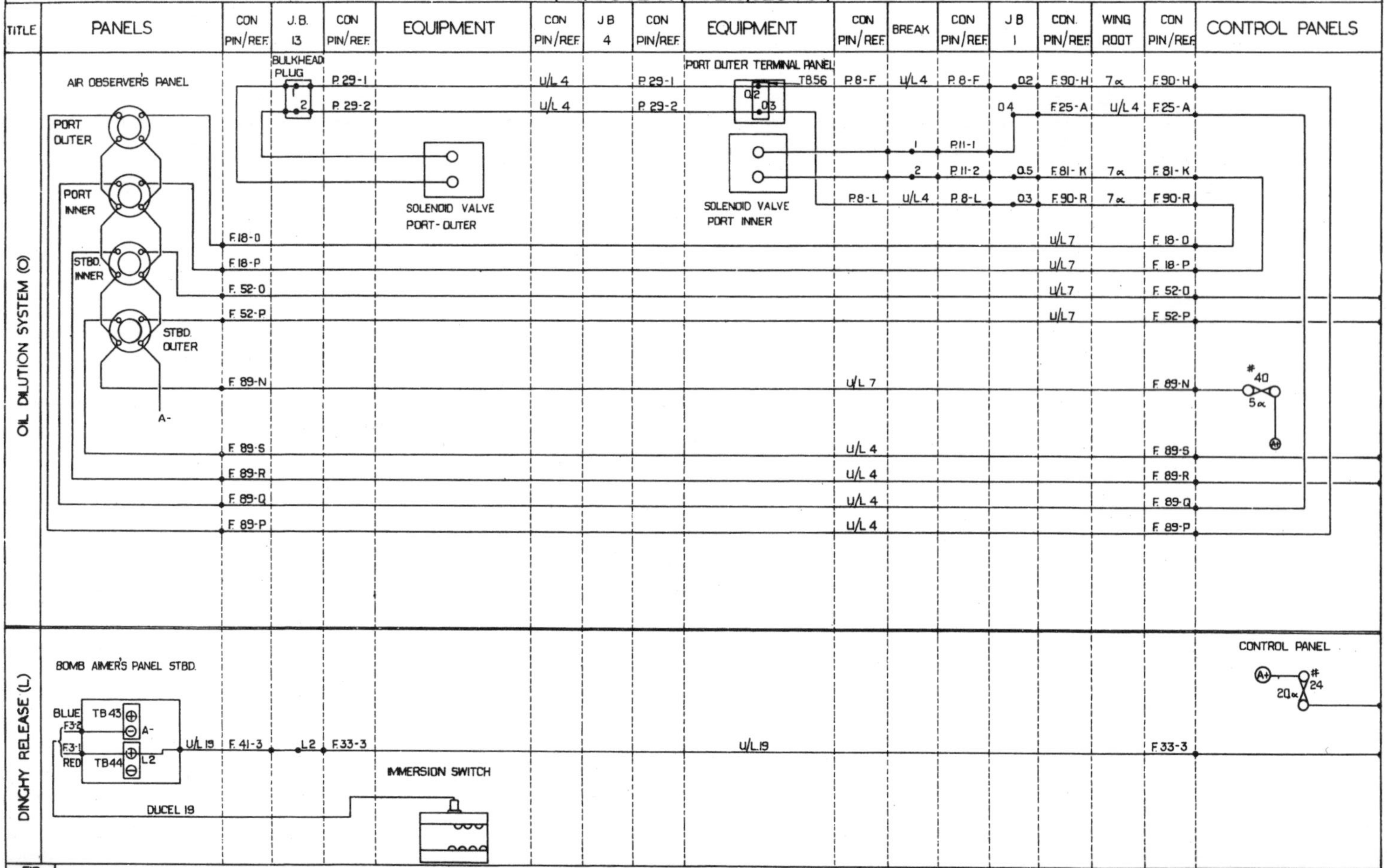
TITLE
PANELS
CON PIN/REF.
J.B. 13
CON PIN/REF.
EQUIPMENT
CON PIN/REF.
J B 4
CON PIN/REF.
EQUIPMENT
CON PIN/REF.
BREAK
CON PIN/REF.
J B 1
CON. PIN/REF.
WING ROOT
CON PIN/REF.
CONTROL PANELS
OIL DILUTION SYSTEM (O)
AIR OBSERVER'S PANEL
PORT OUTER
PORT INNER
STBD. INNER
STBD. OUTER
A-
BULKHEAD PLUG
P. 29-1
P. 29-2
SOLENOID VALVE PORT-OUTER
U/L 4
PORT OUTER TERMINAL PANEL
TB56
SOLENOID VALVE PORT INNER
P. 8-F
P. 8-L
P. 11-1
P. 11-2
F. 90-H
F. 25-A
F. 81-K
F. 90-R
7∝
U/L 7
F. 18-O
F. 18-P
F. 52-O
F. 52-P
F. 89-N
F. 89-S
F. 89-R
F. 89-Q
F. 89-P
#40
5∝
DINGHY RELEASE (L)
BOMB AIMER'S PANEL STBD.
BLUE
RED
TB43
TB44
F3-2
F3-1
A-
L2
U/L 19
F. 41-3
F. 33-3
DUCEL 19
IMMERSION SWITCH
CONTROL PANEL
#24
20∝

FIG. 41

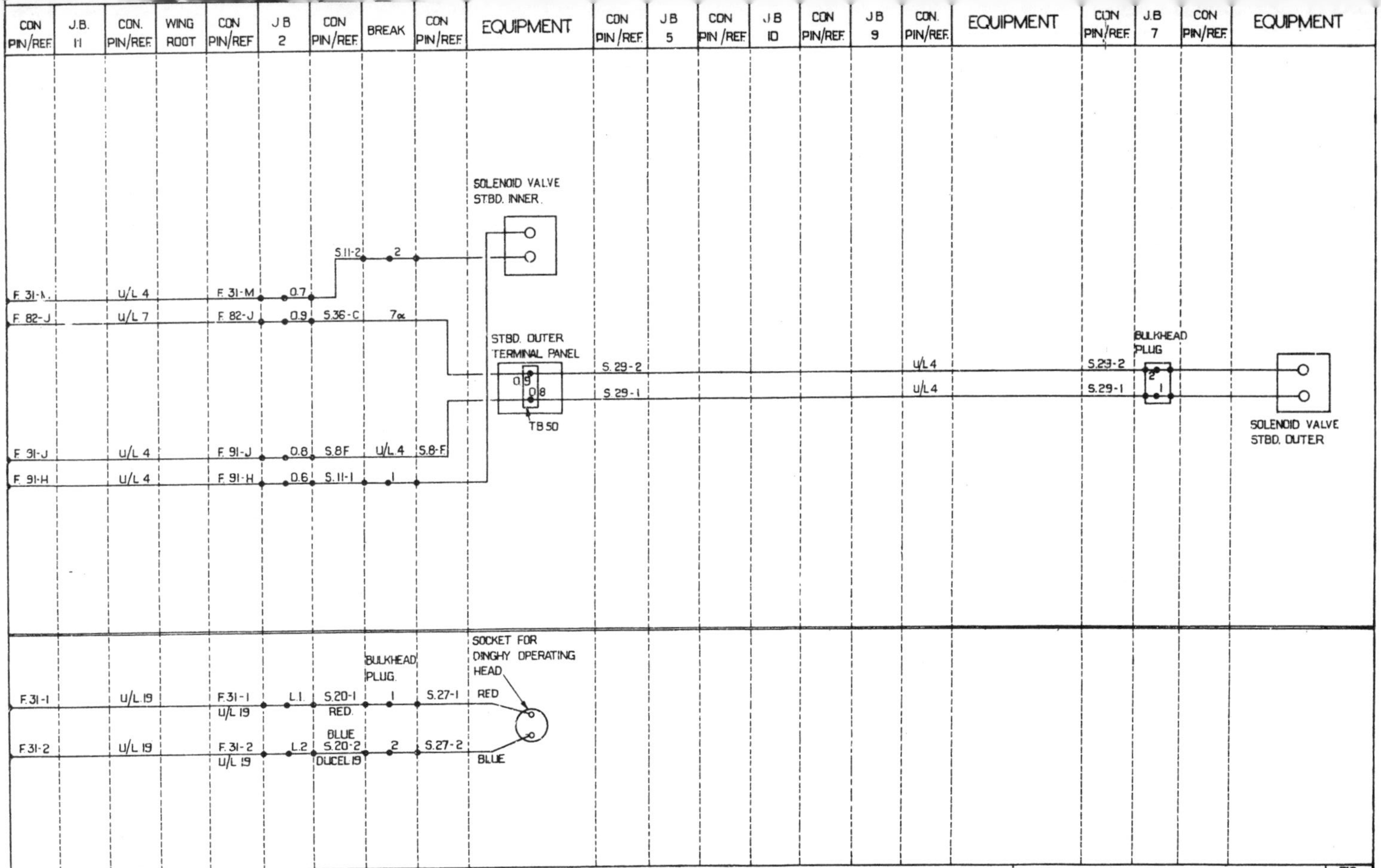

GENERAL SERVICES SCHEME C

FIG. 41

PP2080 M /1095 3/43 3950 C & P Gp. 959 (4)

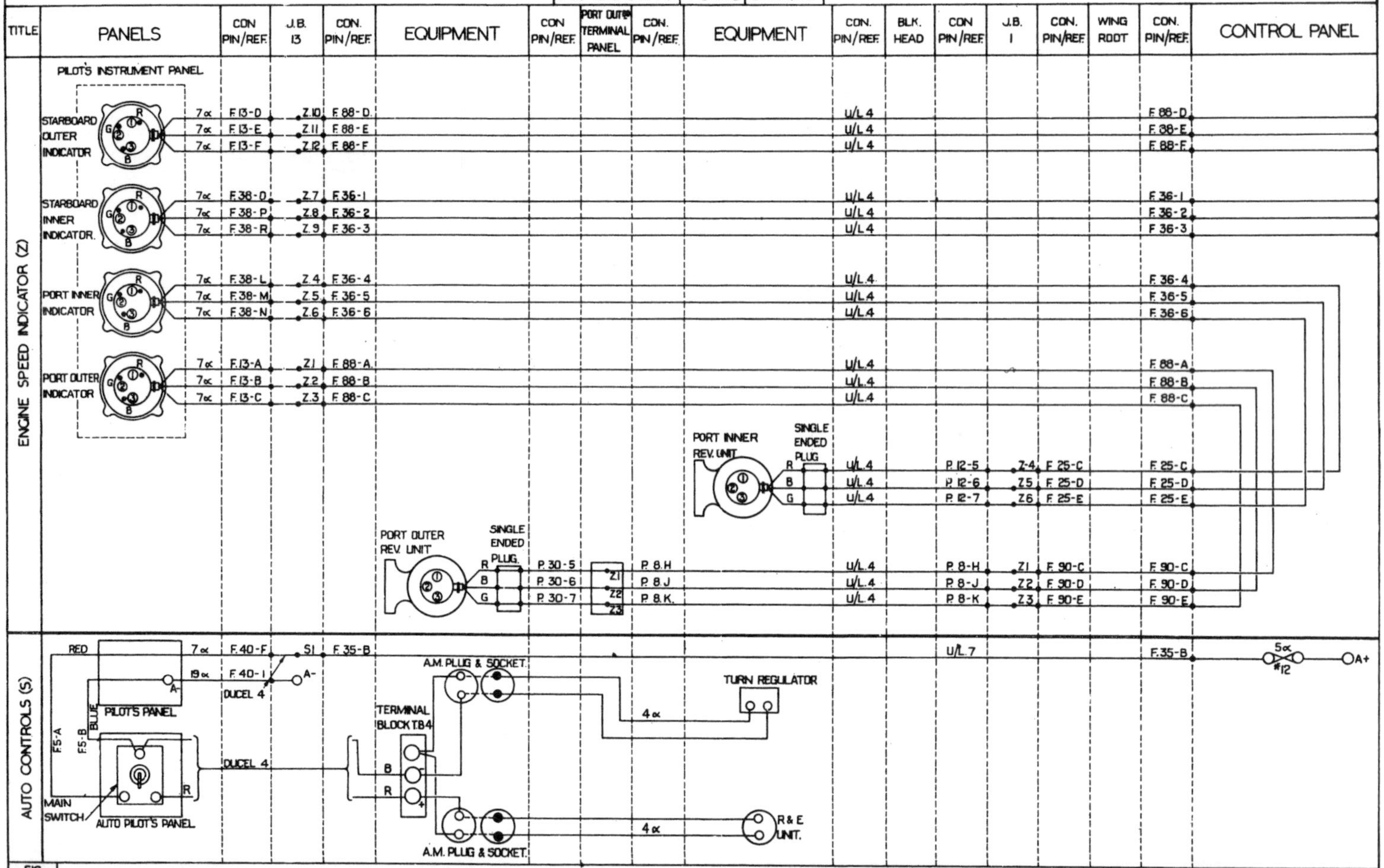

FIG. 42

ROUTING CHART

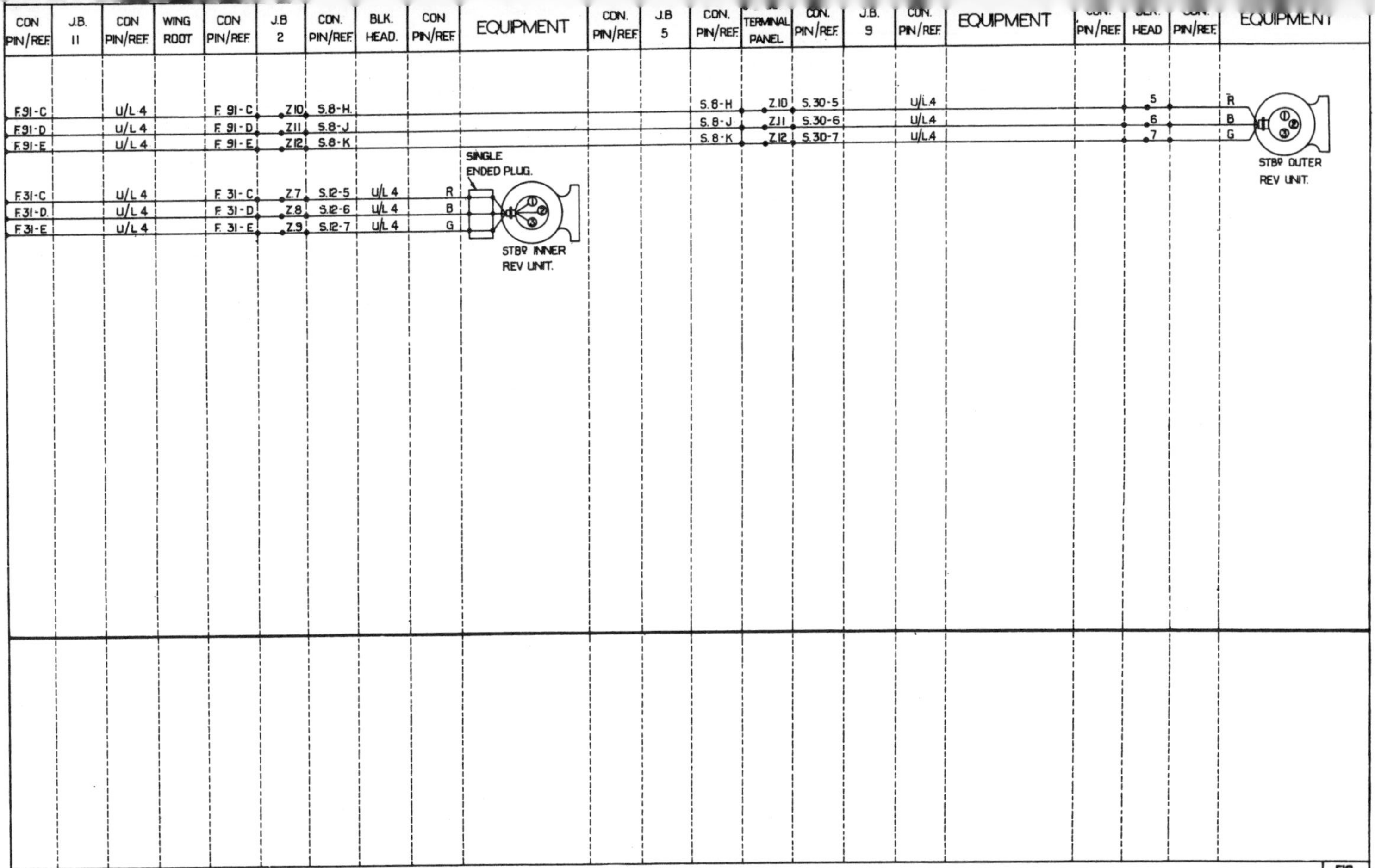

GENERAL SERVICES SCHEME C

FIG. 42

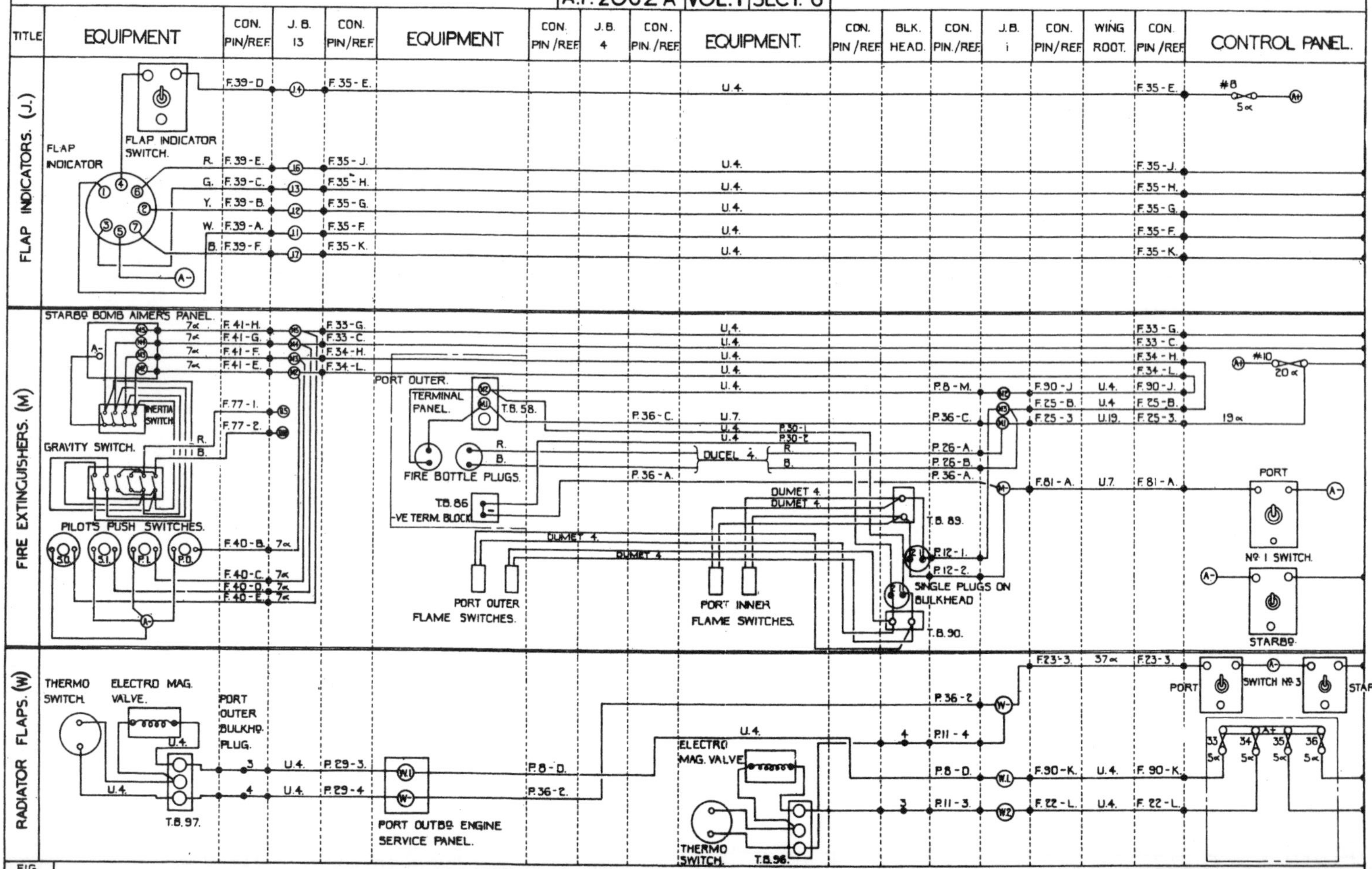

FIG. 43

ROUTING CHART

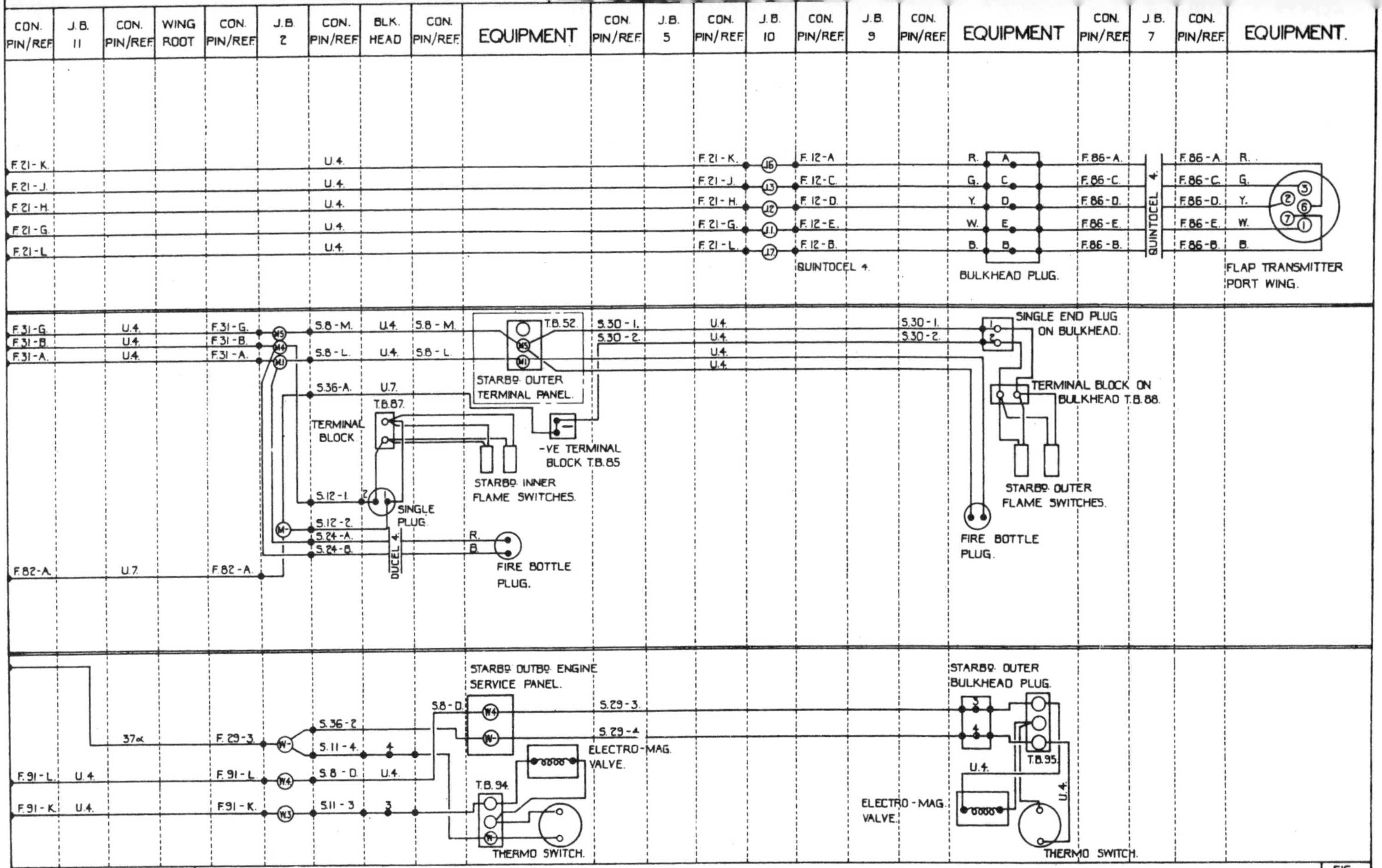

GENERAL SERVICES. SCHEME C.

FIG. 43

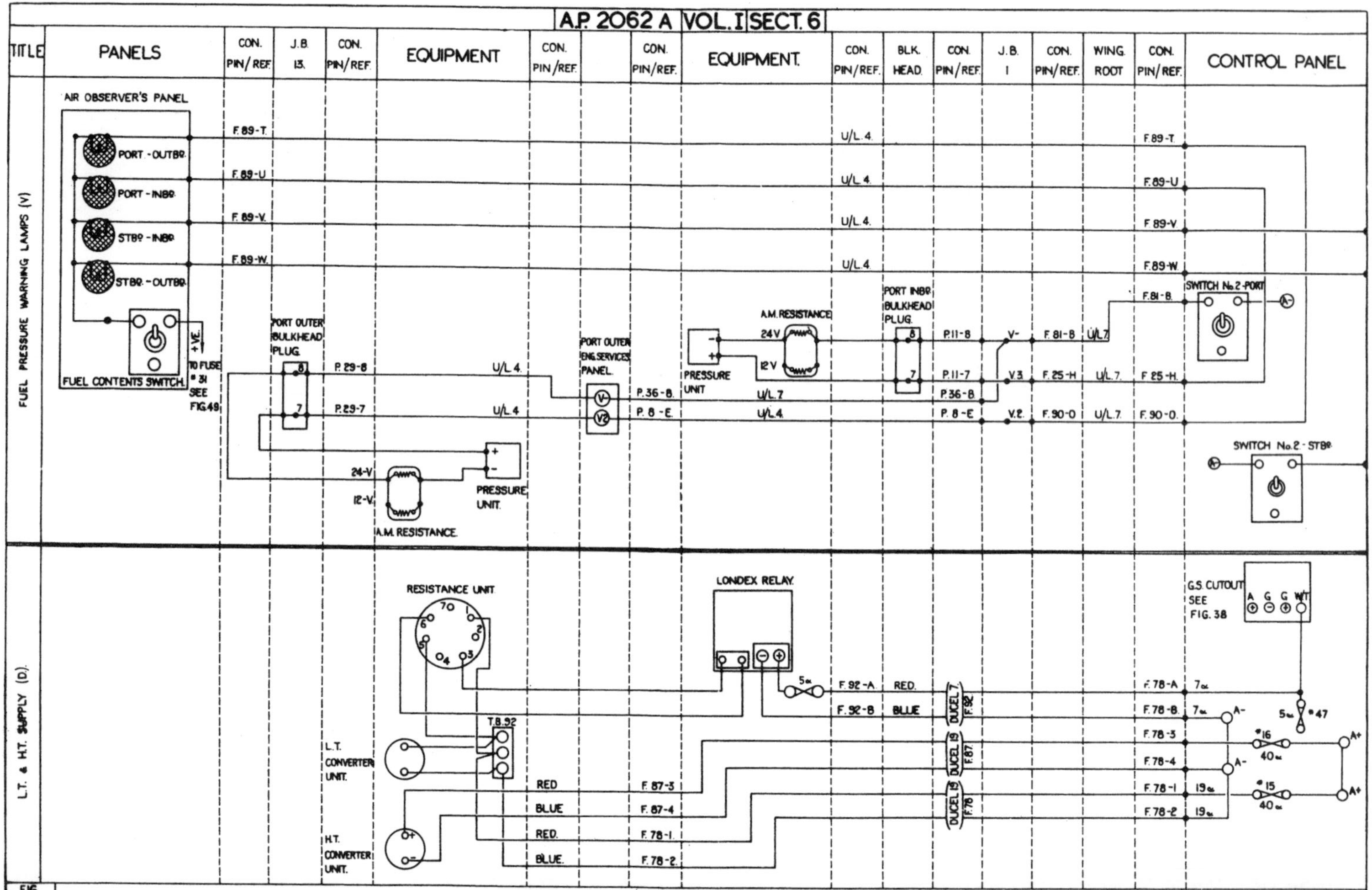

FIG. 44

ROUTING CHART

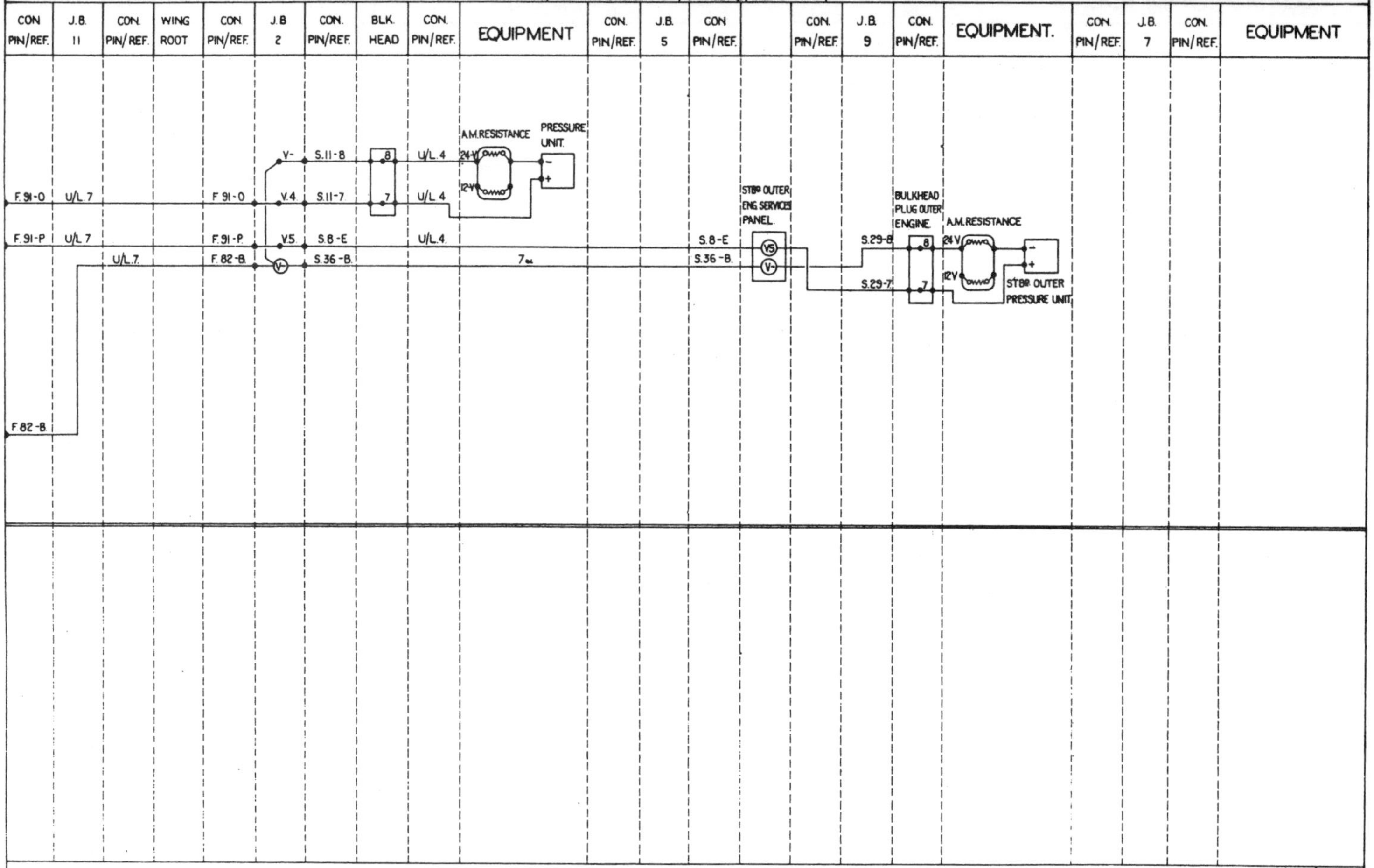

GENERAL SERVICES. SCHEME C.

FIG. 44

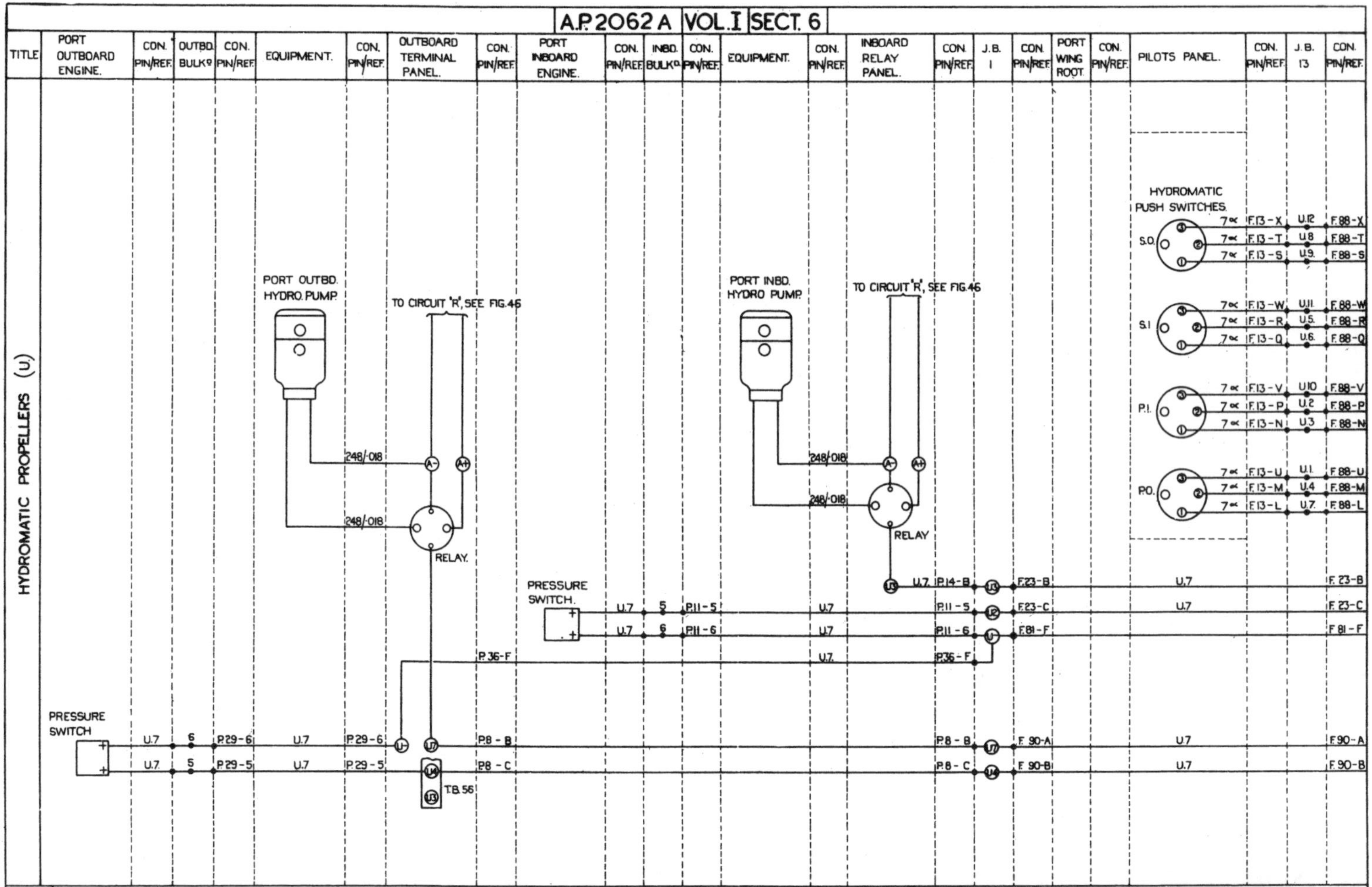

FIG. 45 ROUTING CHART

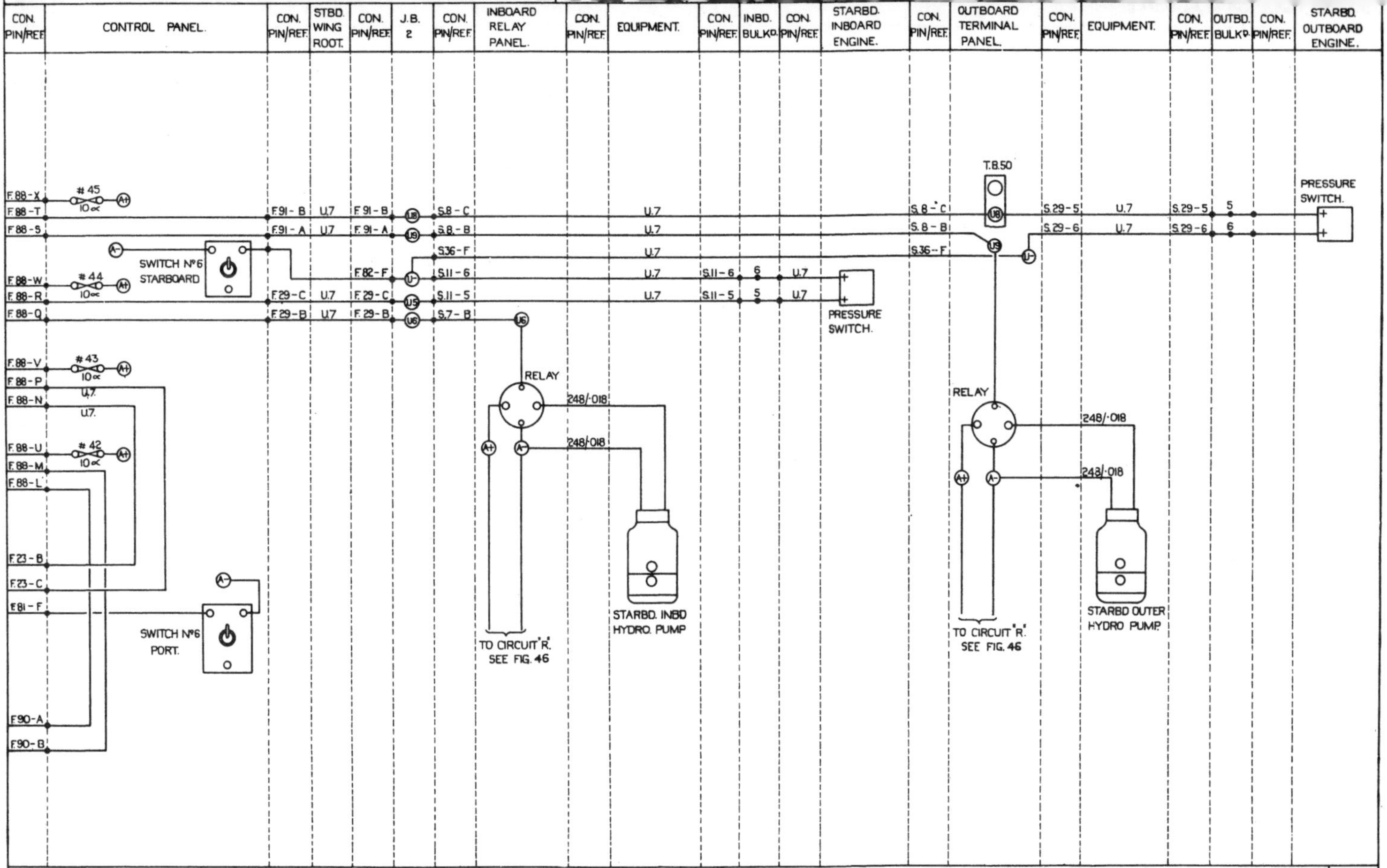

GENERAL SERVICES. SCHEME C.

FIG. 45

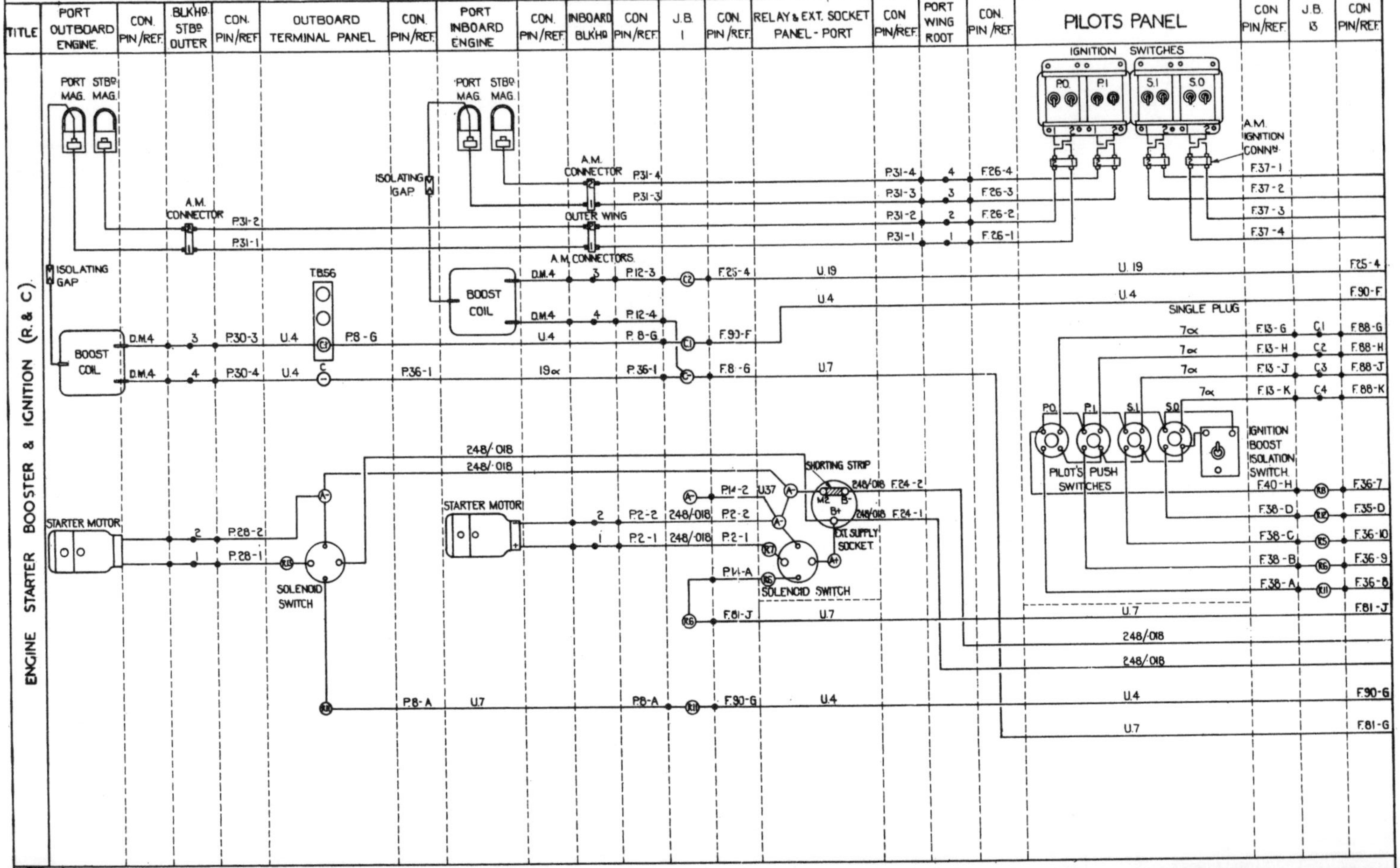

ROUTING CHART

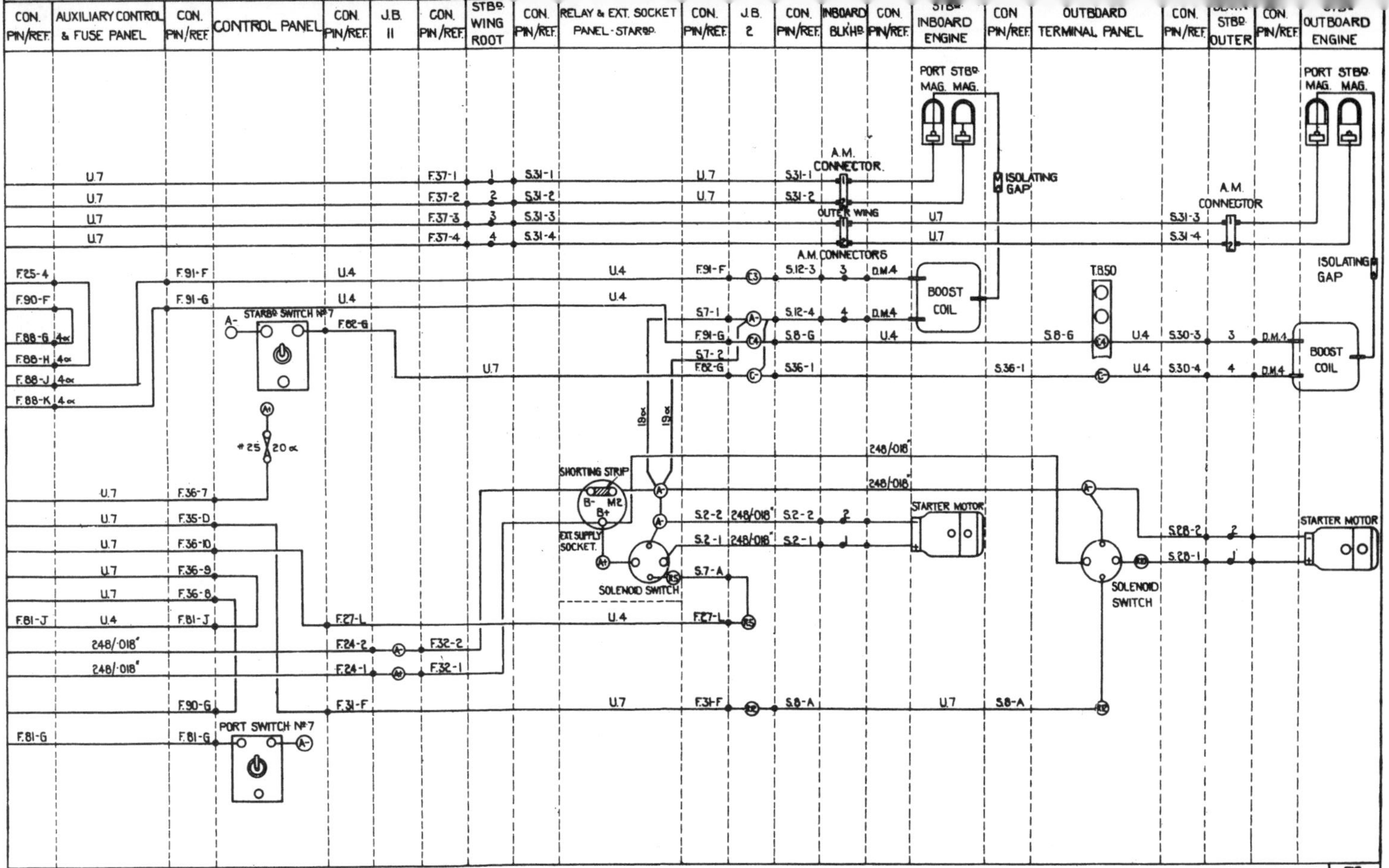

GENERAL SERVICES. SCHEME C.

FIG. 46

PP2080 M /1095 3/43 3950 C & P Gp. 959 (4)

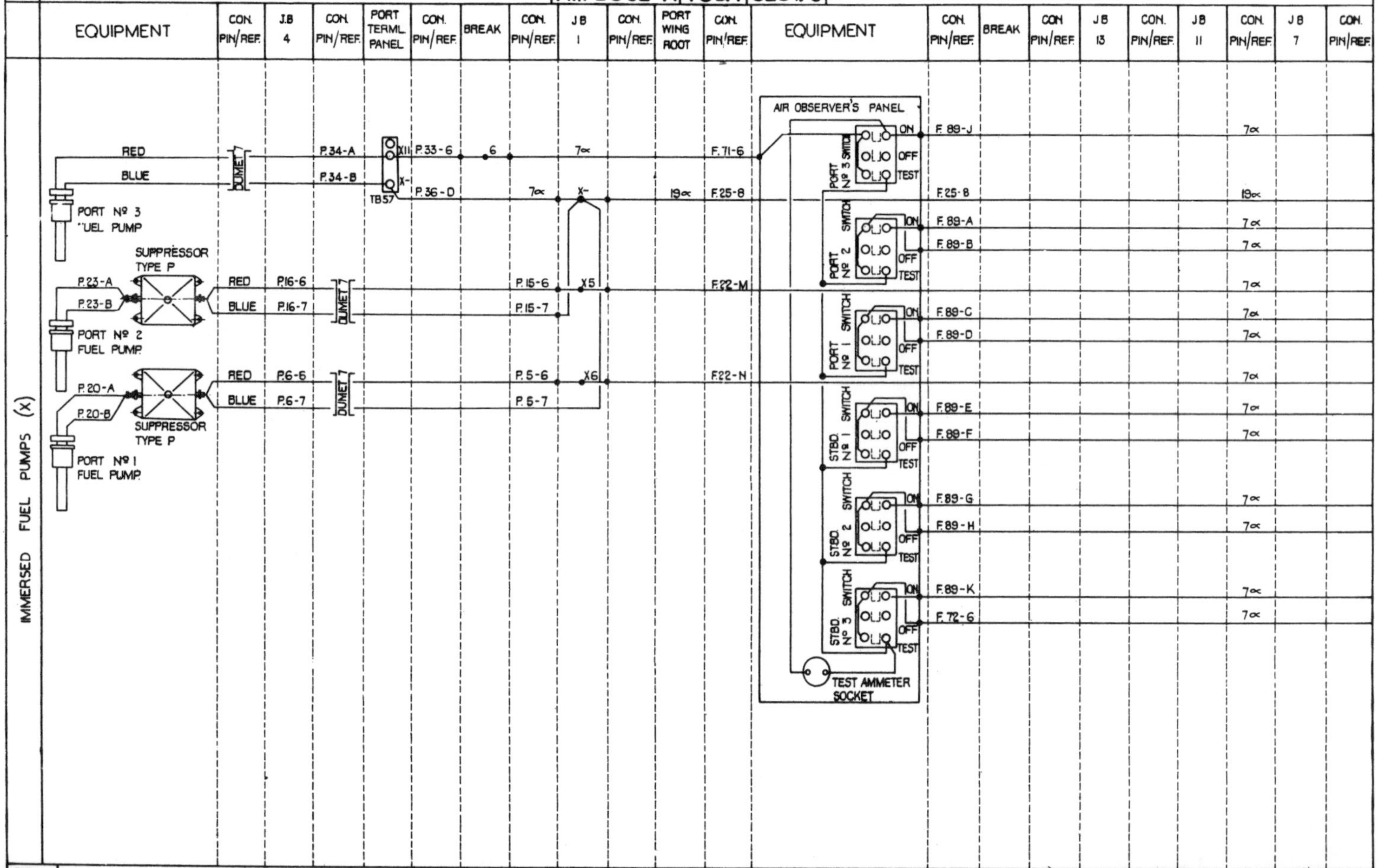

FIG 47 ROUTING CHART

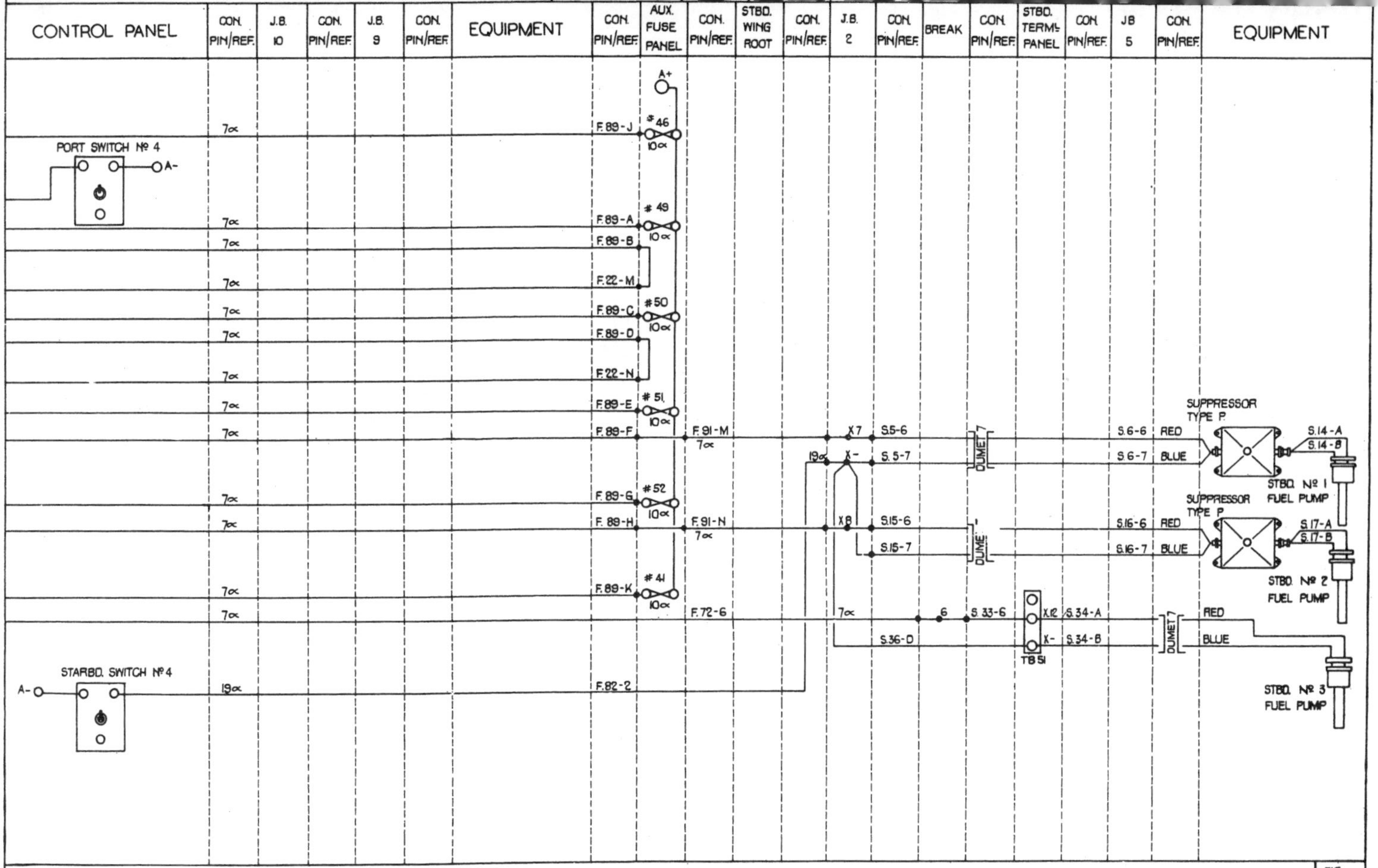

GENERAL SERVICES. SCHEME C & E

FIG. 47

PP2080 M /1095 3/43 3950· C & P Gp. 959 (4)

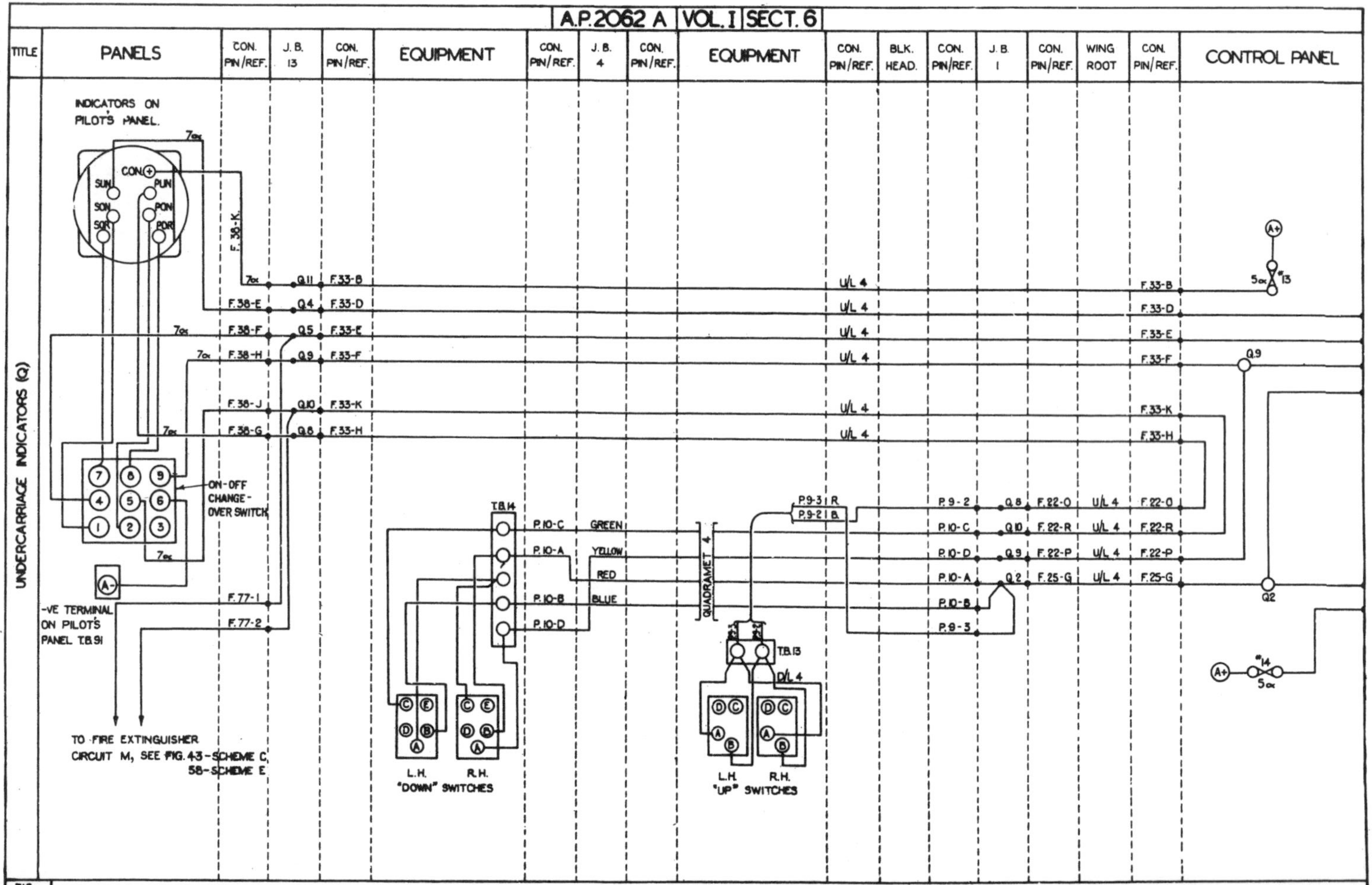

ROUTING CHART

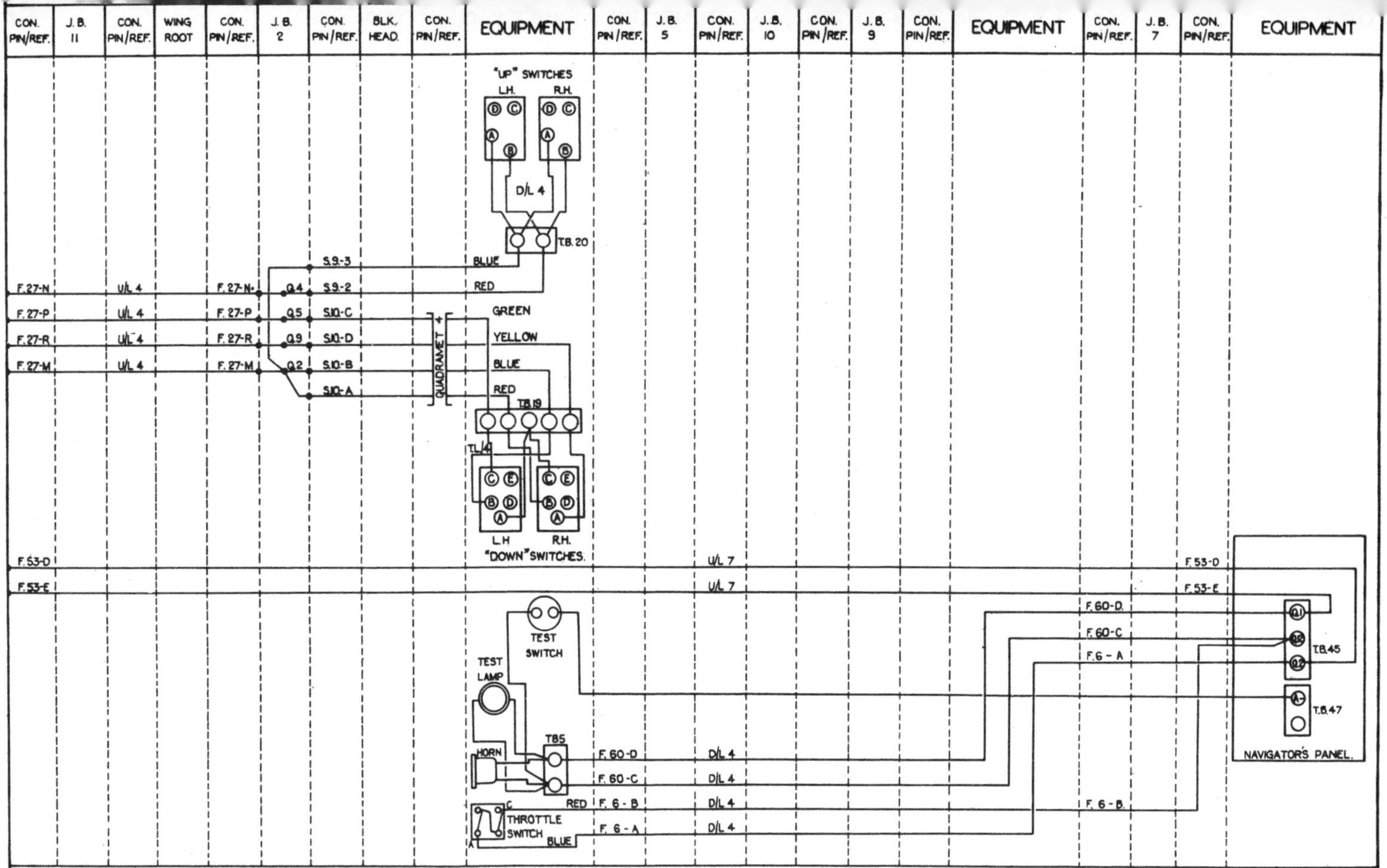

GENERAL SERVICES SCHEME C & E

FIG. 48

PP2080 M /1095 3/43 3950 C & P Gp. 959 (4)

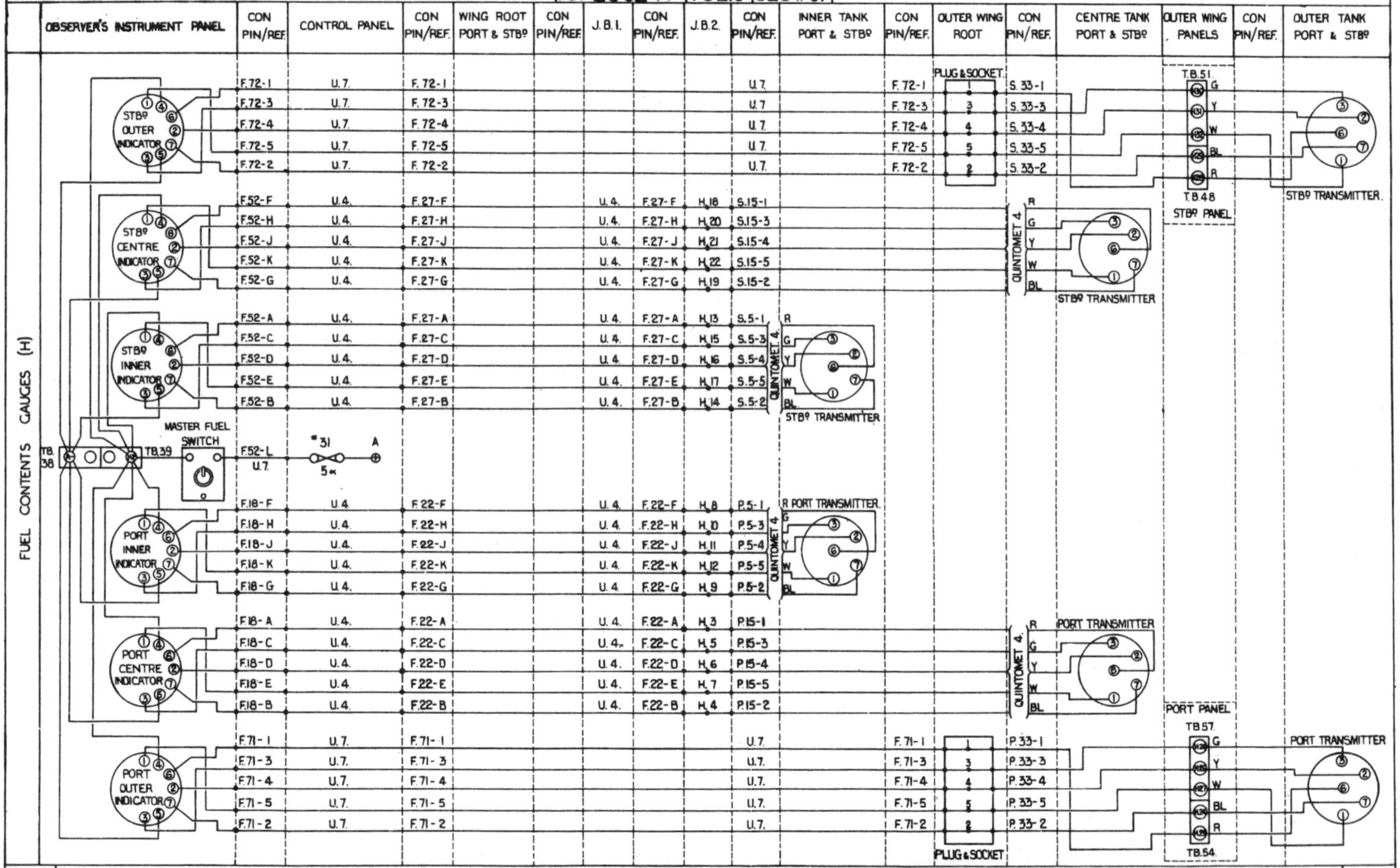

FIG. 49 ROUTING CHART - GENERAL SERVICES - SCHEME C & E

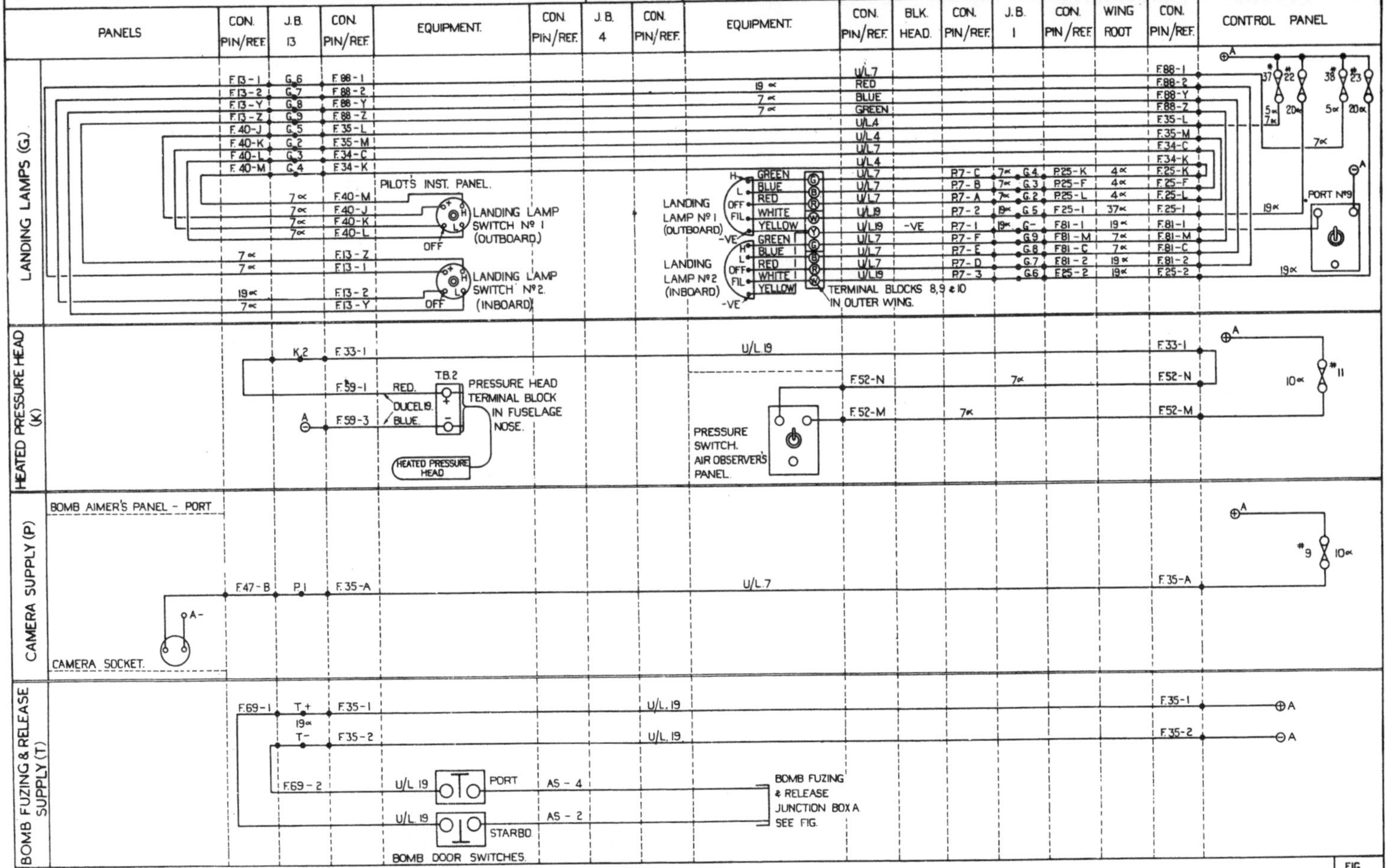

FIG 50

ROUTING CHART—GENERAL SERVICES—SCHEME C & E.

FIG 50

PP2080 M /1095 3/43 3950 C & P Gp. 959 (4)

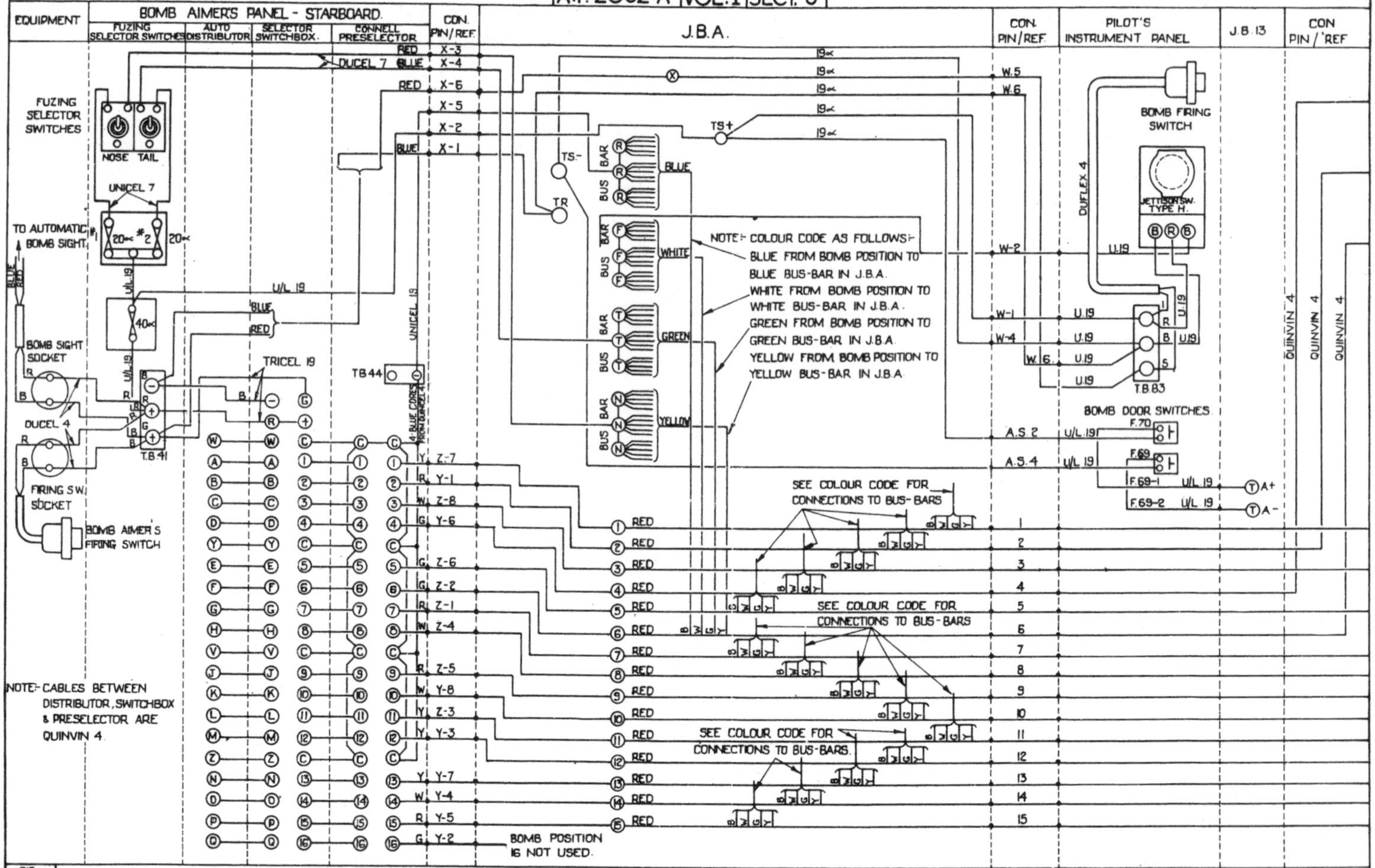

FIG. 51

ROUTING CHART

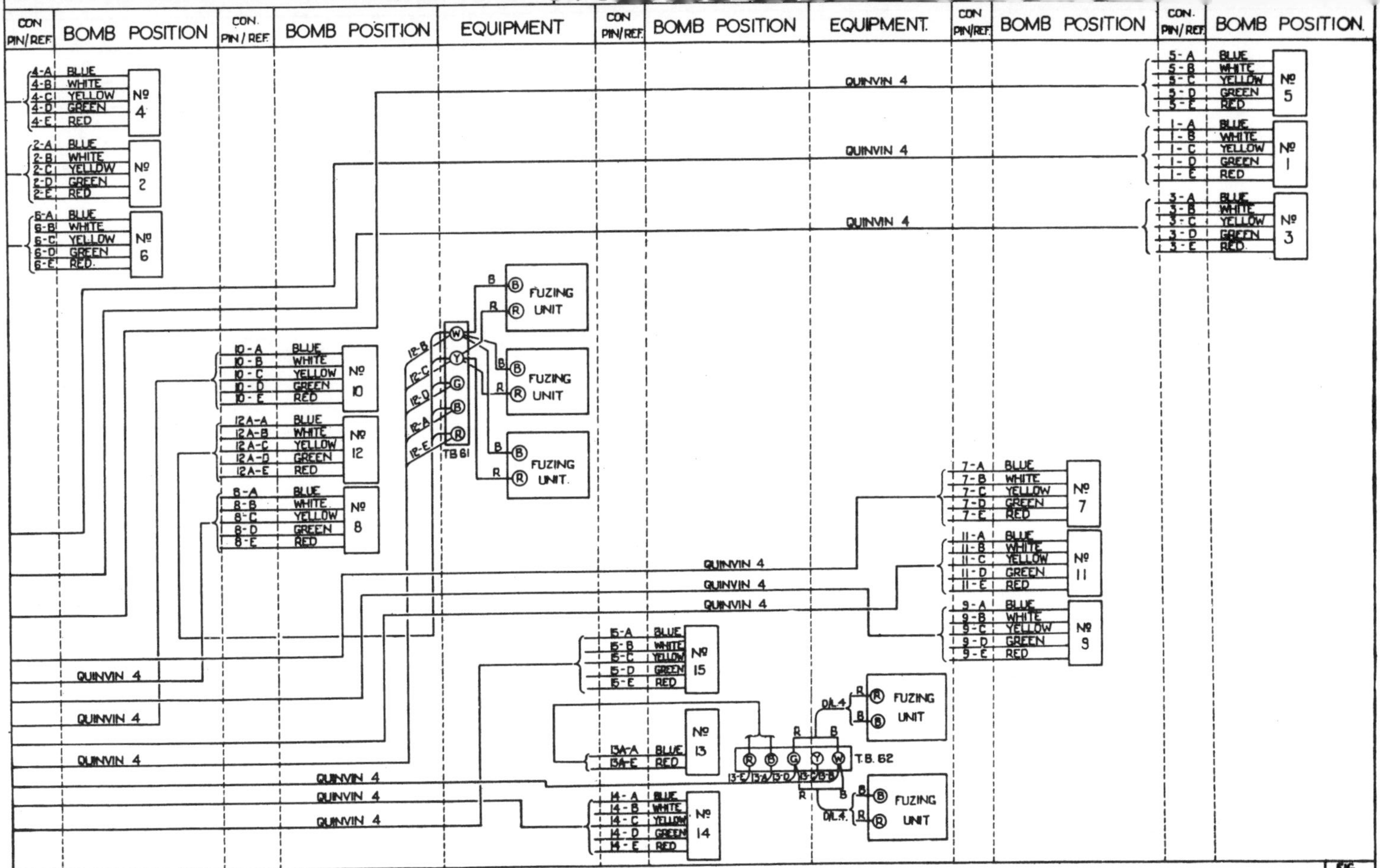

BOMB FUZING & RELEASE – SCHEMES C & E.

FIG 51

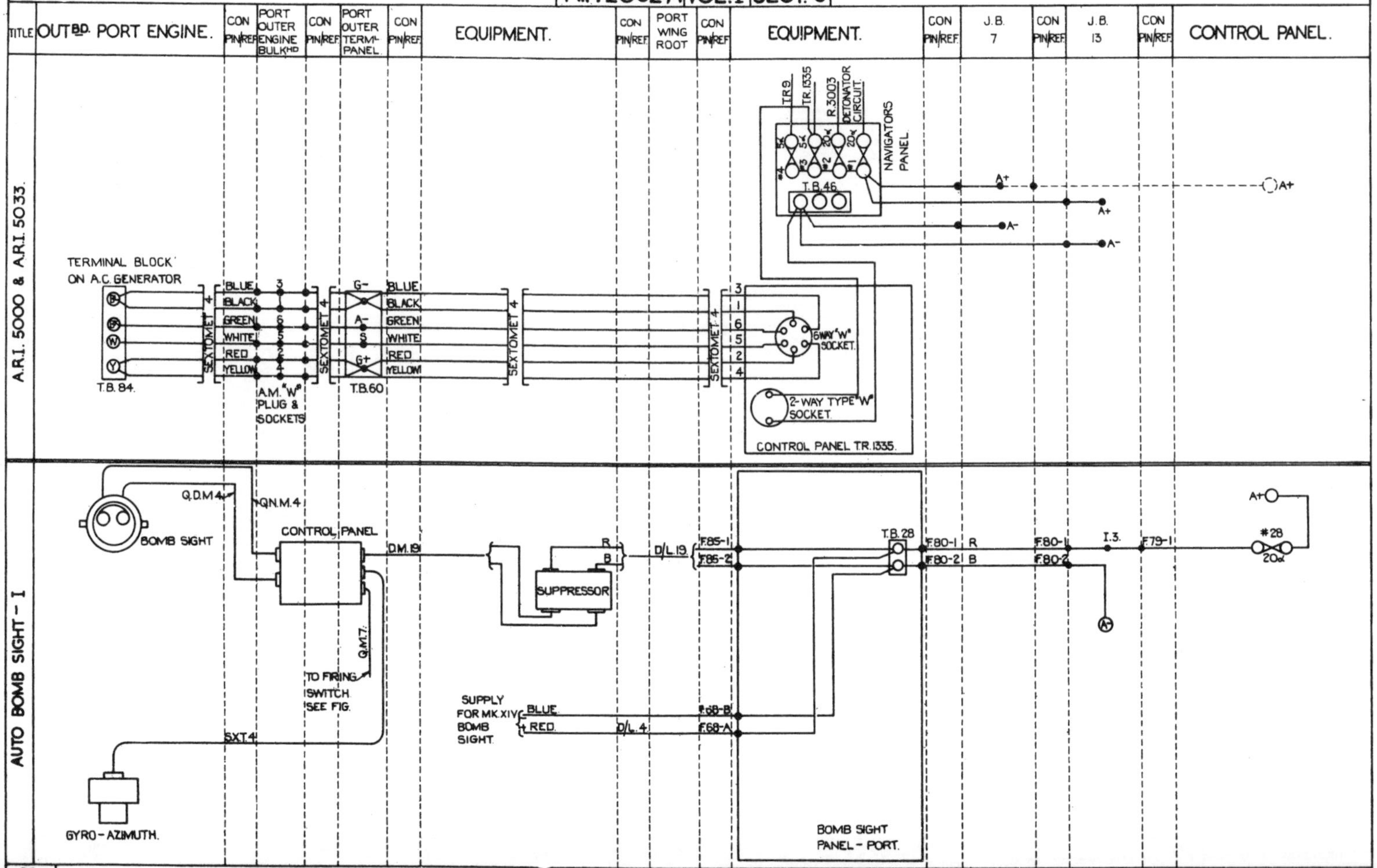
TITLE
OUTBD. PORT ENGINE.
CON PIN/REF
PORT OUTER ENGINE BULKHD
CON PIN/REF
PORT OUTER TERMI-PANEL.
CON PIN/REF
EQUIPMENT.
CON PIN/REF
PORT WING ROOT
CON PIN/REF
EQUIPMENT.
CON PIN/REF
J.B. 7
CON PIN/REF
J.B. 13
CON PIN/REF
CONTROL PANEL.
A.R.I. 5000 & A.R.I. 5033.
TERMINAL BLOCK ON A.C. GENERATOR
T.B. 84.
SEXTOMET 4
BLUE
BLACK
GREEN
WHITE
RED
YELLOW
A.M. "W" PLUG & SOCKETS
G−
A−
G+
T.B.60
6 WAY "W" SOCKET.
2-WAY TYPE "W" SOCKET.
CONTROL PANEL TR.1335.
TR.9
TR.1335
R.3003
DETONATOR CIRCUIT.
NAVIGATORS PANEL
T.B.46
A+
A−
AUTO BOMB SIGHT – I
Q.D.M.4
Q.N.M.4
BOMB SIGHT
CONTROL PANEL
D.M.19
Q.M.7.
TO FIRING SWITCH SEE FIG.
SXT.4
GYRO – AZIMUTH.
SUPPRESSOR
R
B
D/L.19.
F.85-1
F.85-2
SUPPLY FOR MK.XIV BOMB SIGHT
BLUE
RED
D/L.4
F.68-B
F.68-A
T.B.28
BOMB SIGHT PANEL – PORT.
F.80-1 R
F.80-2 B
F.80-1
F.80-2
I.3.
F.79-1
#28
20α
A+

FIG.

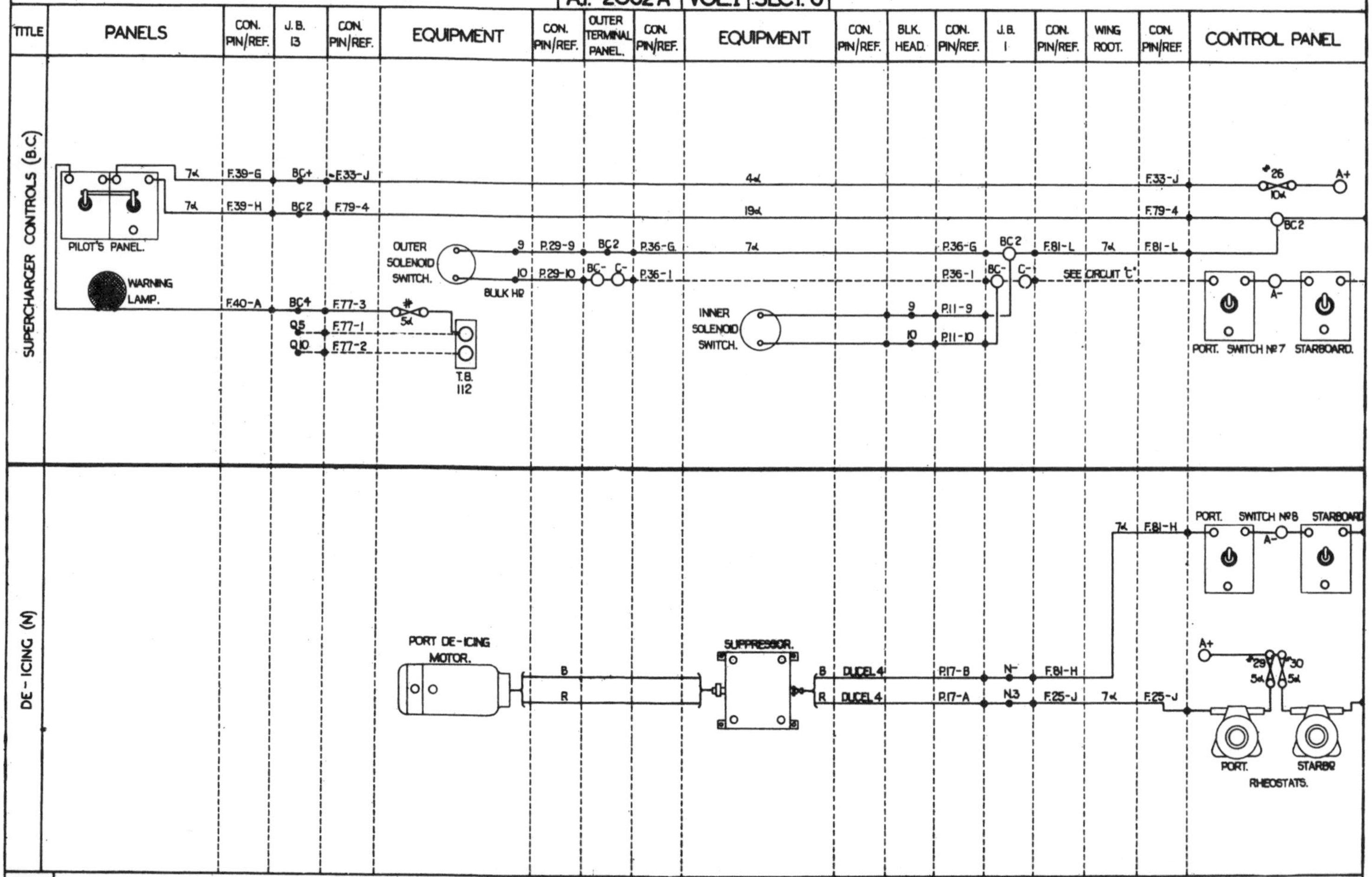
TITLE
PANELS
CON. PIN/REF.
J.B. 13
CON. PIN/REF.
EQUIPMENT
CON. PIN/REF.
OUTER TERMINAL PANEL.
CON. PIN/REF.
EQUIPMENT
CON. PIN/REF.
BLK. HEAD.
CON. PIN/REF.
J.B. 1
CON. PIN/REF.
WING ROOT.
CON. PIN/REF.
CONTROL PANEL
SUPERCHARGER CONTROLS (B.C)
PILOT'S PANEL.
WARNING LAMP.
7∢
F.39-G
BC+
F.33-J
4∢
F.33-J
#26
10∢
A+
7∢
F.39-H
BC2
F.79-4
19∢
F.79-4
BC2
OUTER SOLENOID SWITCH.
9
P.29-9
BC2
P.36-G.
7∢
P.36-G
BC2
F.81-L
7∢
F.81-L
10
P.29-10
BC-
C-
P.36-1
P.36-1
BC-
C-
SEE CIRCUIT 'C'
BULK HD
F.40-A
BC4
F.77-3
#
5∢
Q5
F.77-1
Q10
F.77-2
T.B. 112
INNER SOLENOID SWITCH.
9
P.11-9
10
P.11-10
A-
PORT. SWITCH No 7 STARBOARD.
DE - ICING (N)
PORT. SWITCH No 8 STARBOARD
7∢
F.81-H
A-
PORT DE-ICING MOTOR.
B
R
SUPPRESSOR.
B
DUCEL 4
P.17-B
N-
F.81-H
R
DUCEL 4
P.17-A
N3
F.25-J
7∢
F.25-J
A+
#29
#30
5∢
5∢
PORT.
STARBD
RHEOSTATS.

FIG. 53

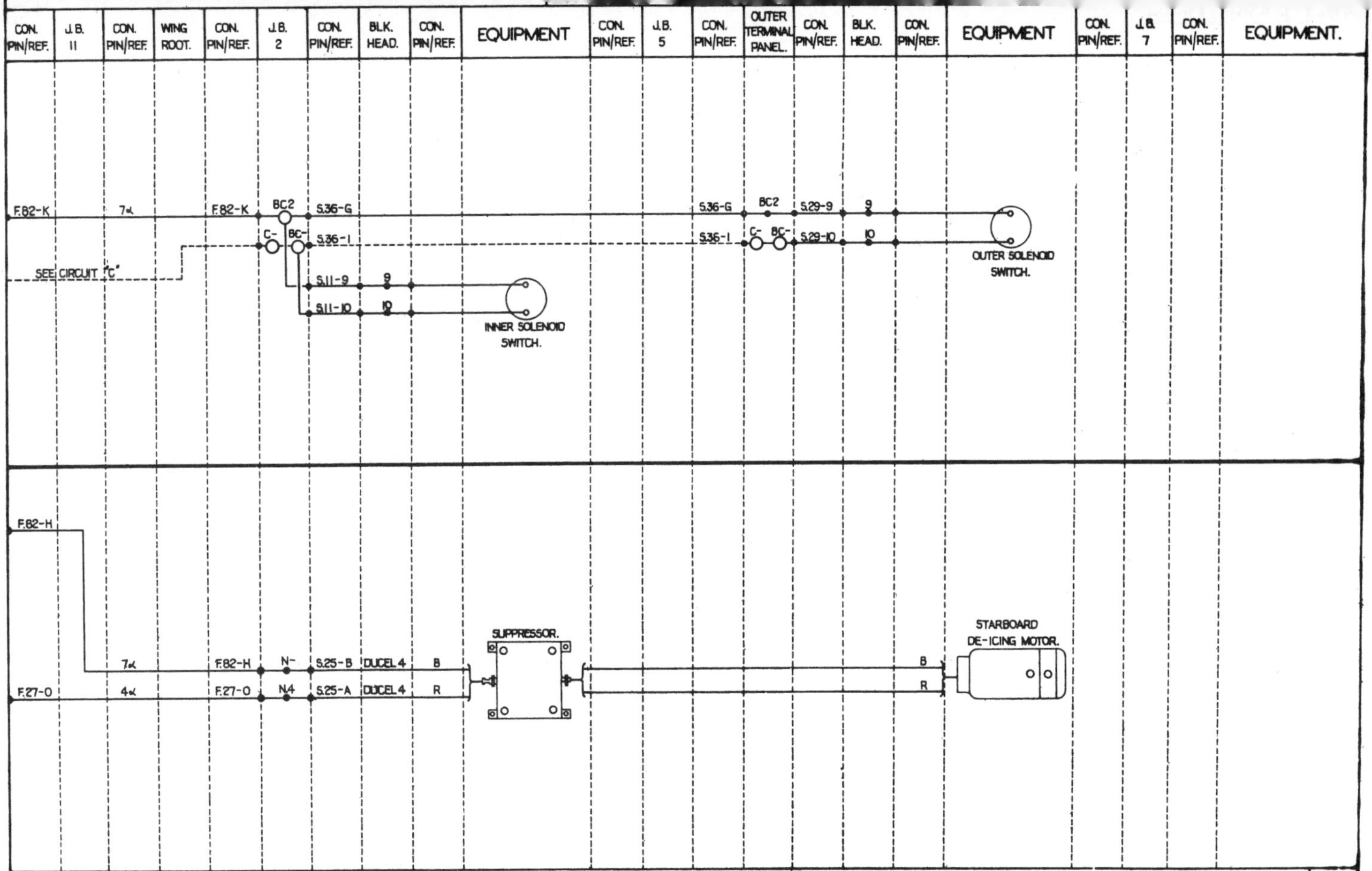

GENERAL SERVICES SCHEME C & E

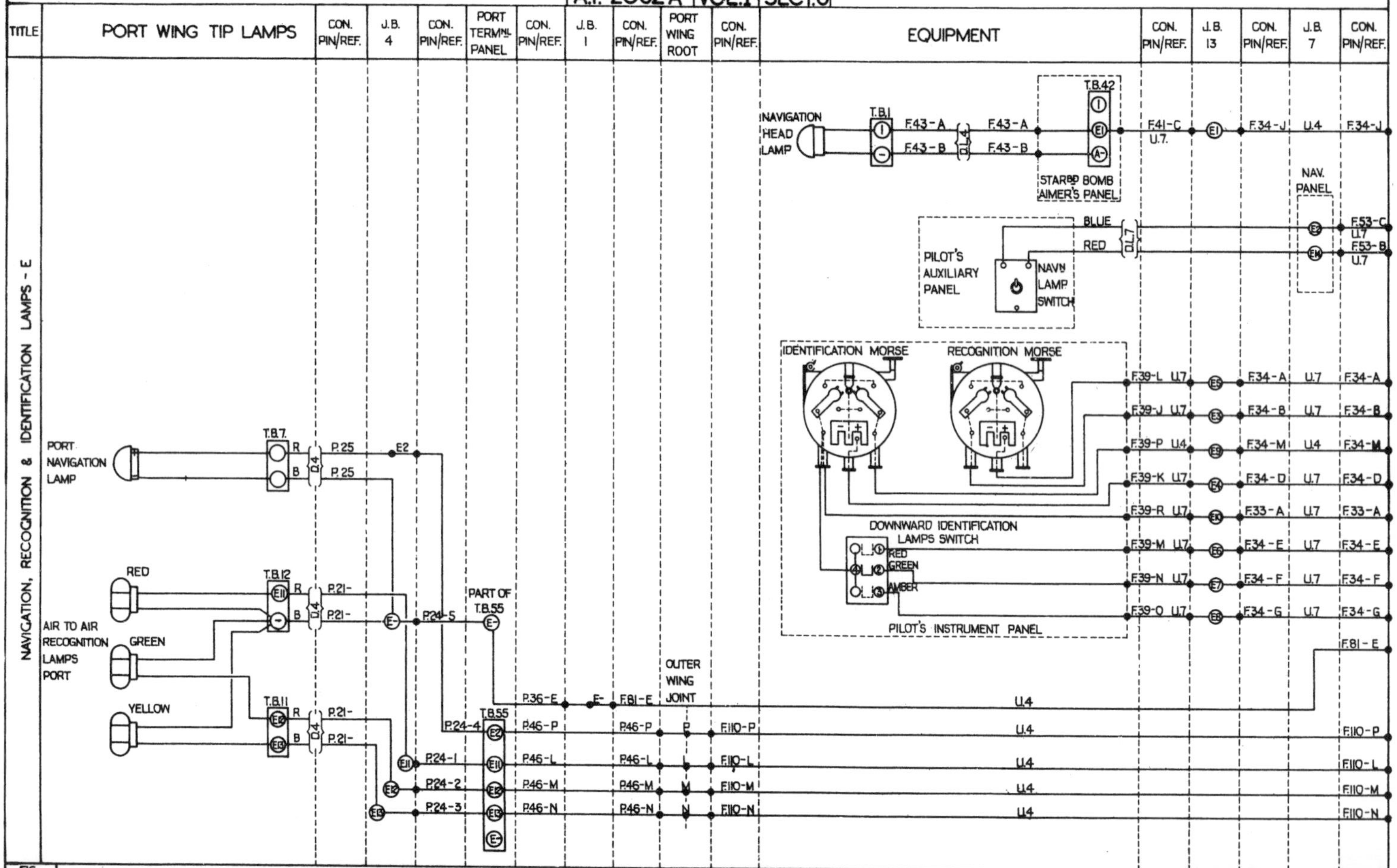

FIG. 55

ROUTING CHART

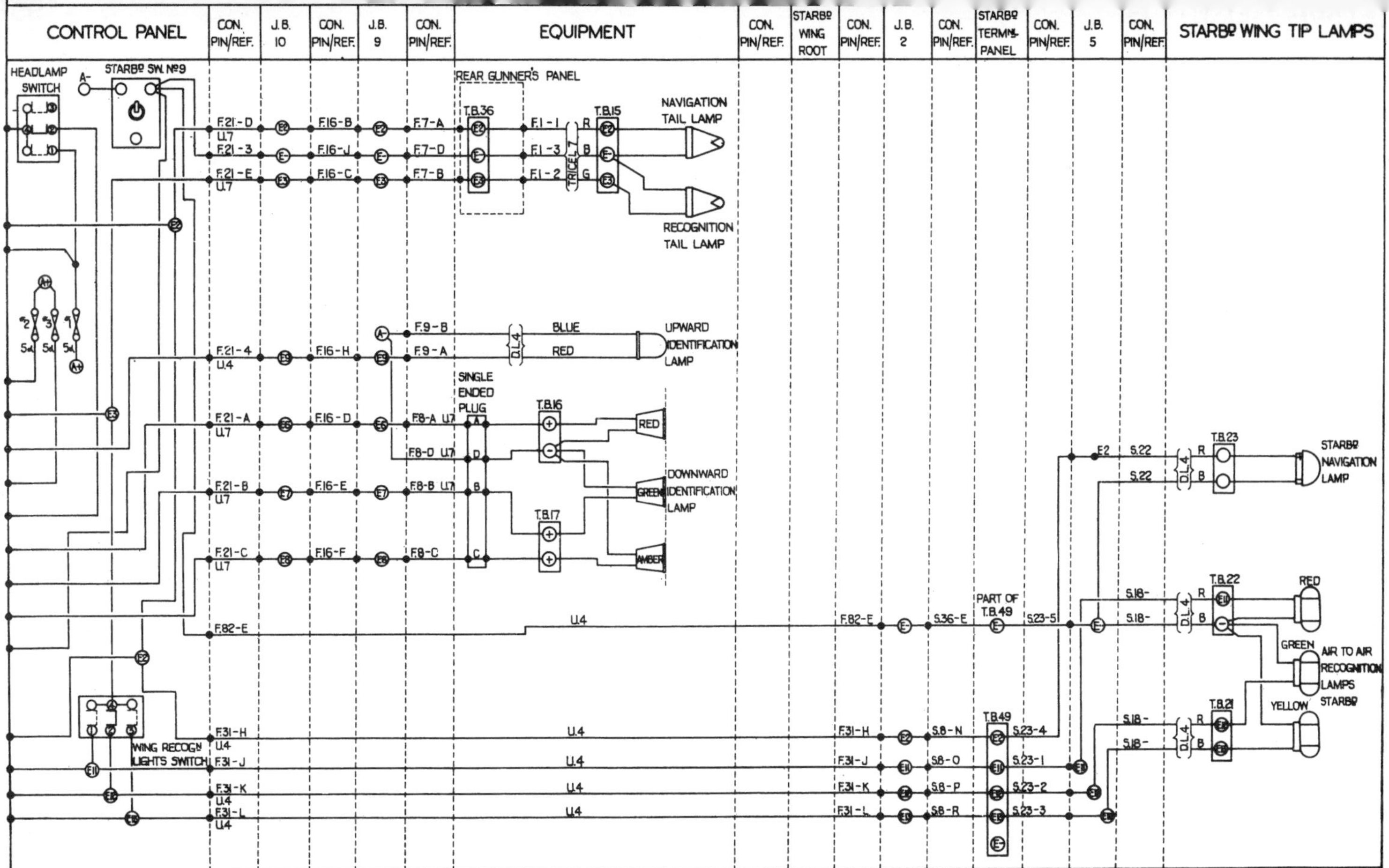

GENERAL SERVICES – SCHEME 'E'

FIG. 55

PP2080 M /1095 3/43 3950 C & P Gp. 959 (4)

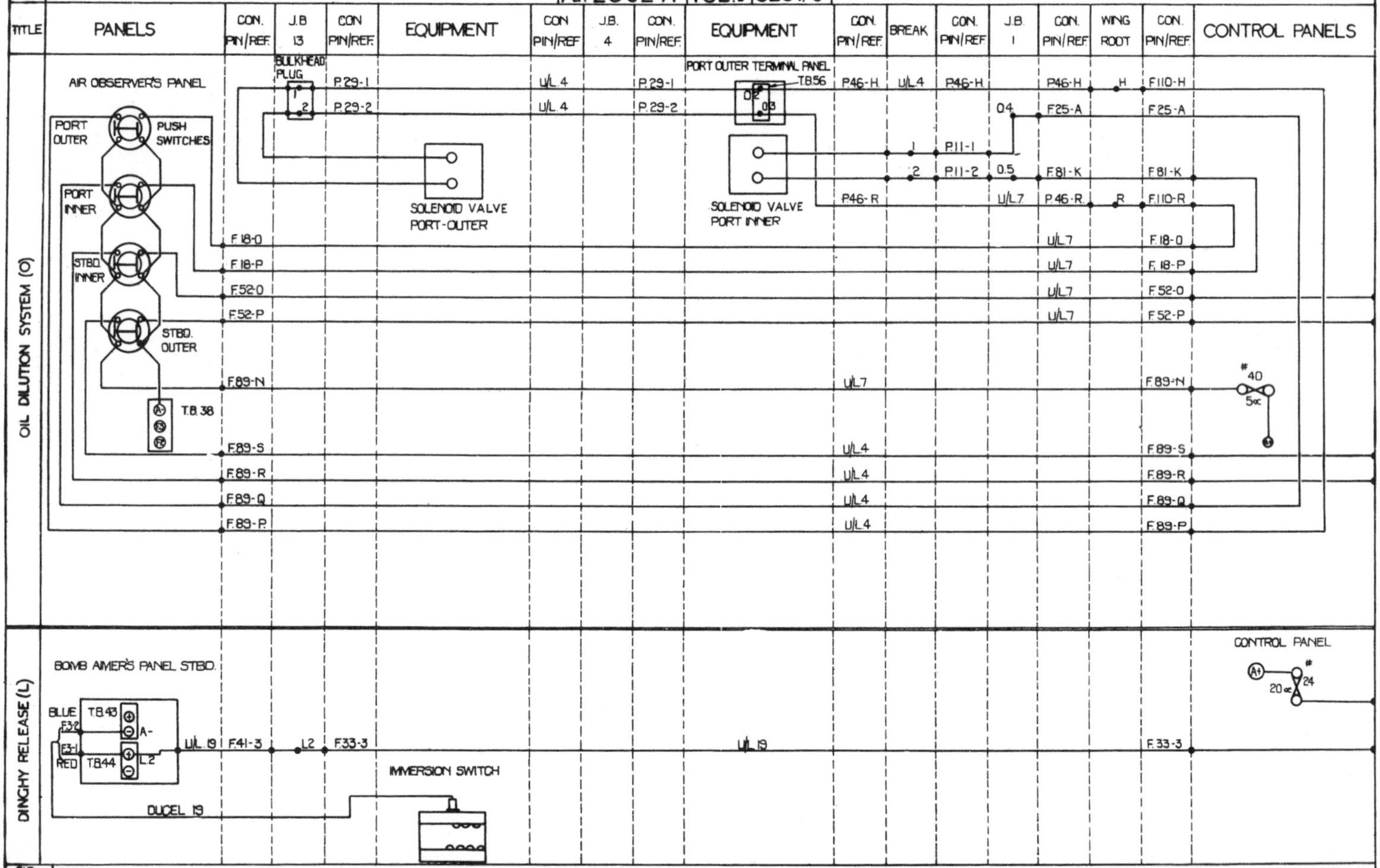

FIG 56 ROUTING CHART

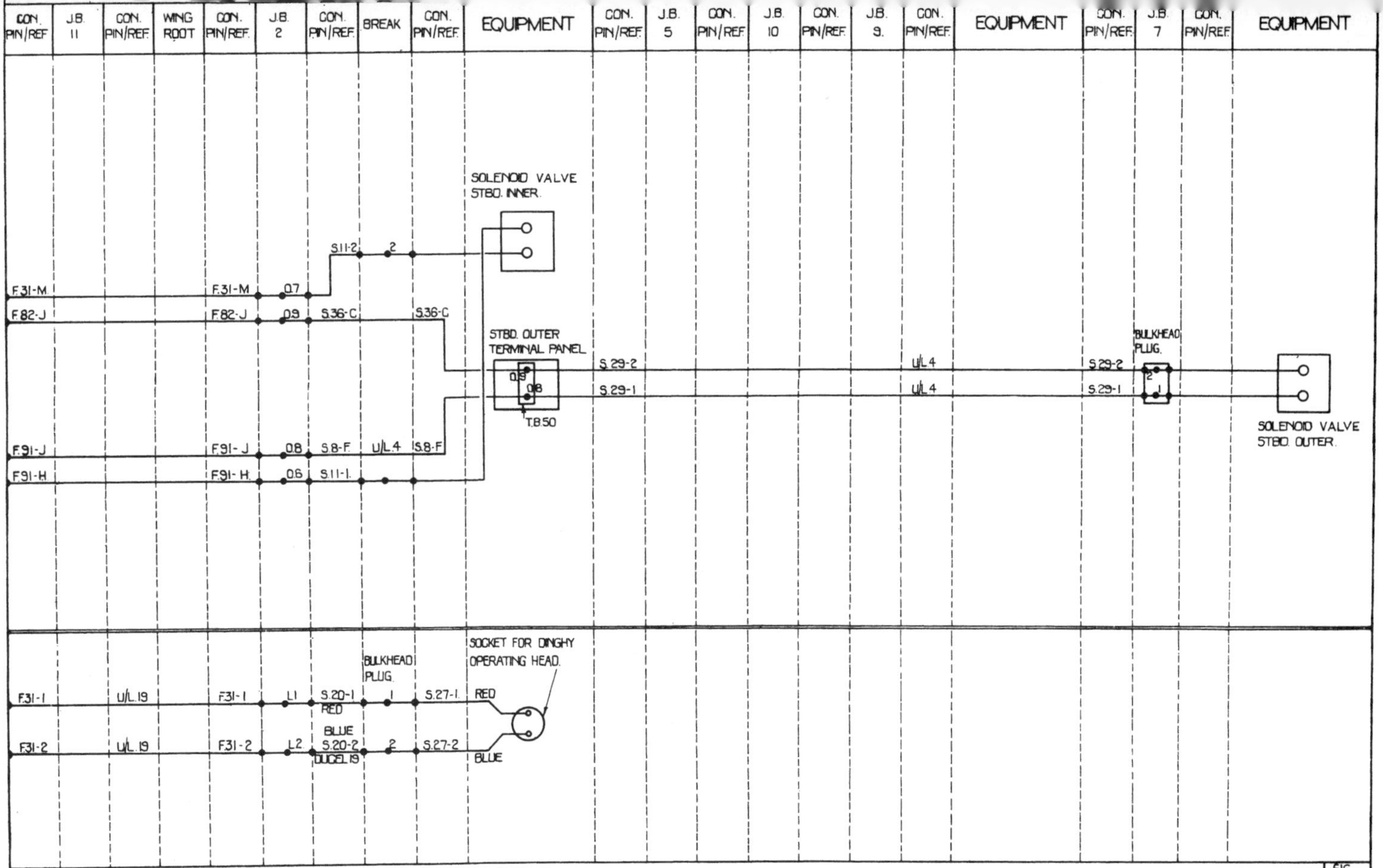

GENERAL SERVICES - SCHEME E.

FIG. 56

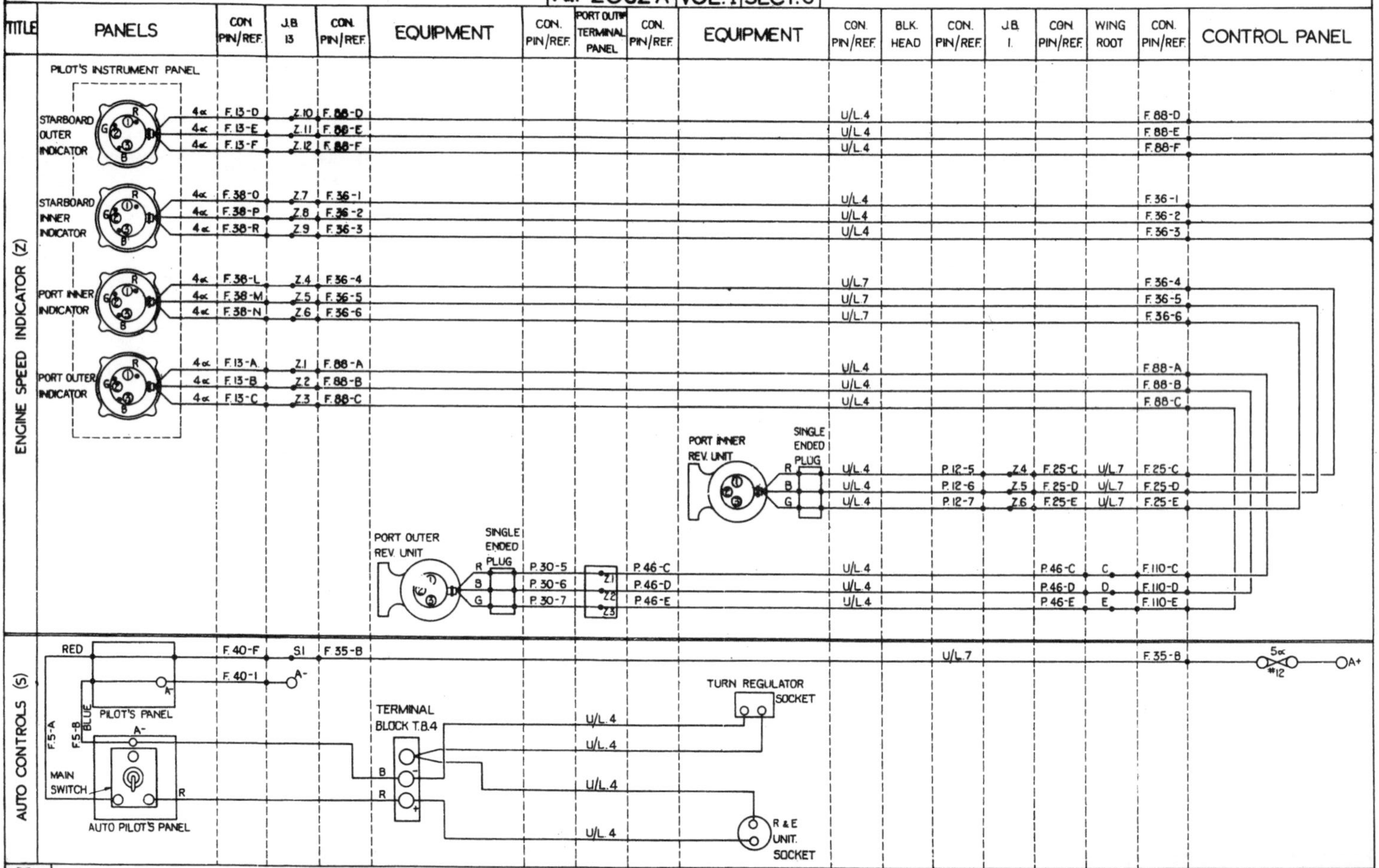

FIG. 57 ROUTING CHART

GENERAL SERVICES. SCHEME E.

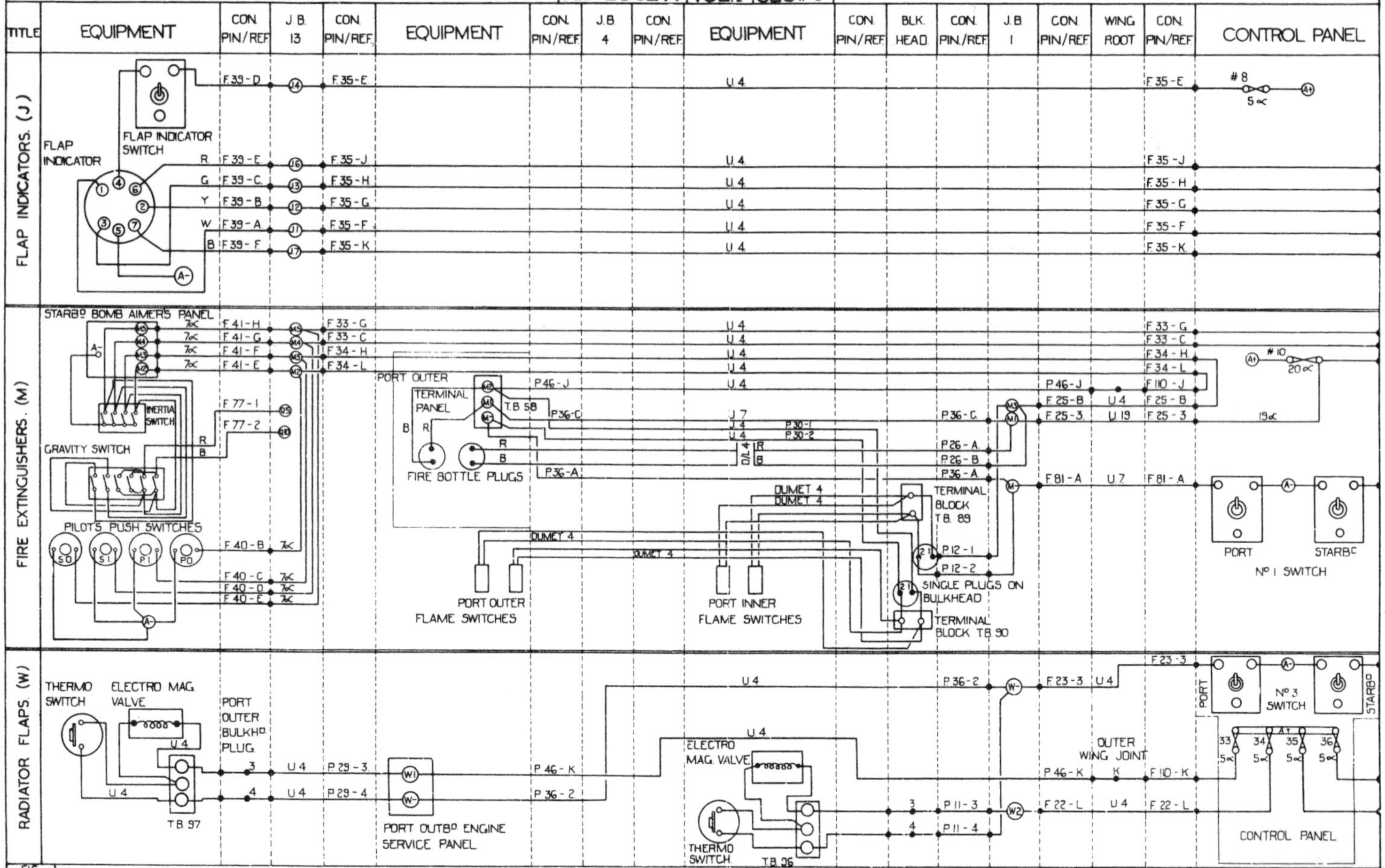

FIG. 58 ROUTING CHART

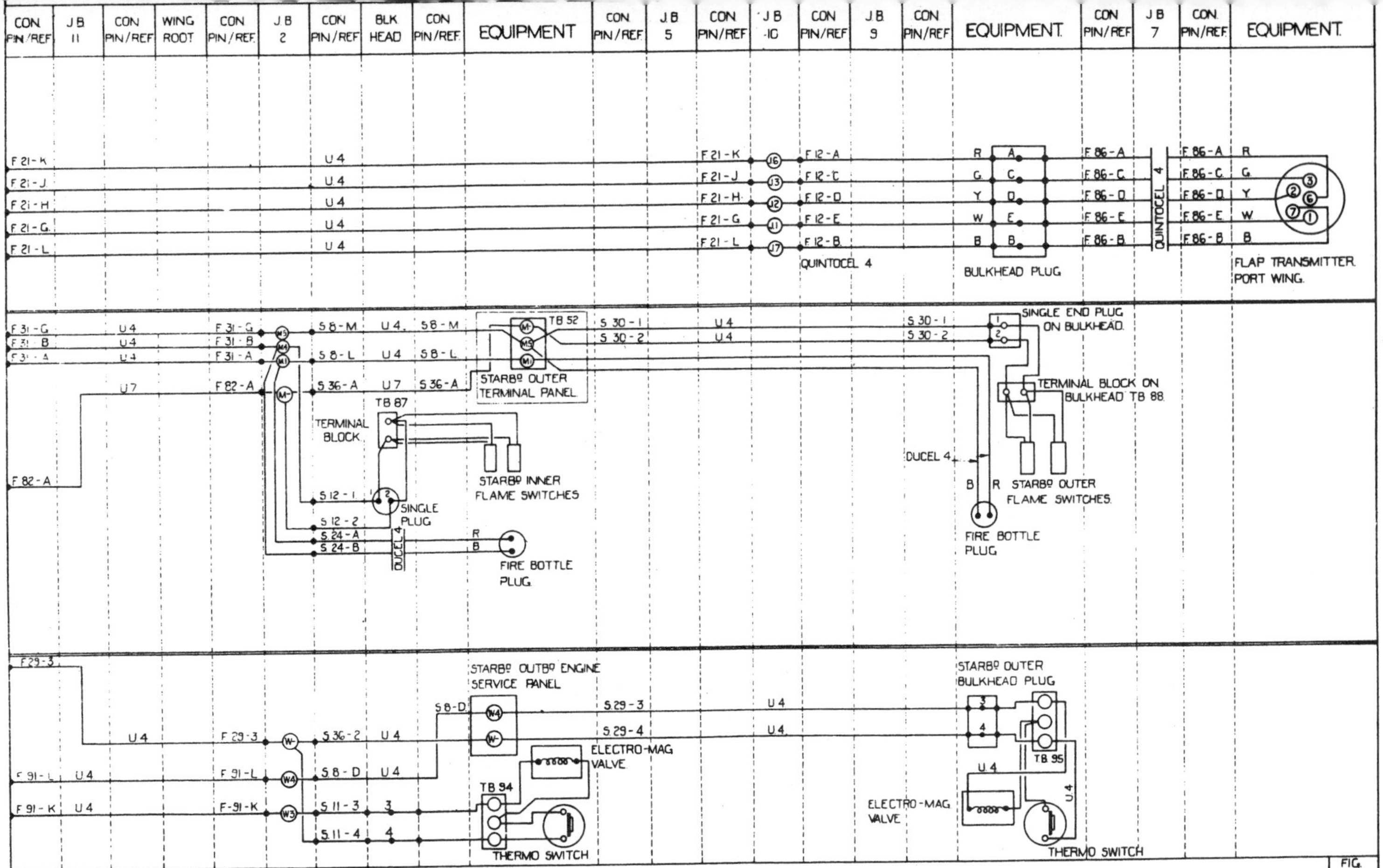

GENERAL SERVICES — SCHEME "E"	FIG. 58

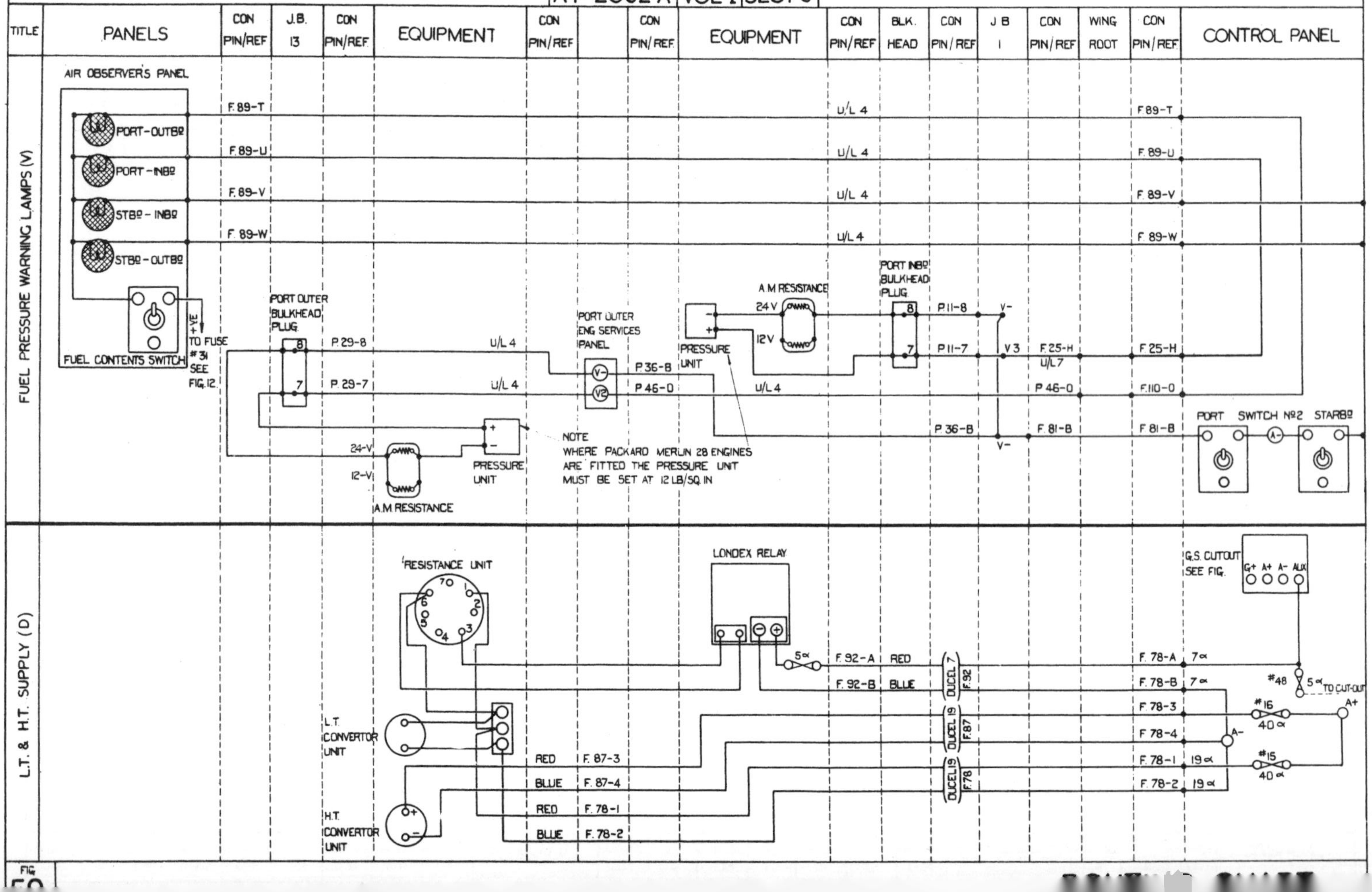

TITLE
PANELS
CON PIN/REF
J.B. 13
EQUIPMENT
BLK. HEAD
J B 1
WING ROOT
CONTROL PANEL
FUEL PRESSURE WARNING LAMPS (V)
AIR OBSERVER'S PANEL
PORT-OUTBº
PORT-INBº
STBº-INBº
STBº-OUTBº
FUEL CONTENTS SWITCH
+VE TO FUSE #31 SEE FIG.12.
F. 89-T
F. 89-U
F. 89-V
F. 89-W
PORT OUTER BULKHEAD PLUG
P. 29-8
P. 29-7
U/L 4
24-V
12-V
A.M. RESISTANCE
PRESSURE UNIT
PORT OUTER ENG SERVICES PANEL
P. 36-B
P. 46-O
NOTE
WHERE PACKARD MERLIN 28 ENGINES ARE FITTED THE PRESSURE UNIT MUST BE SET AT 12 LB/SQ.IN
A.M. RESISTANCE
24 V
12 V
PORT INBº BULKHEAD PLUG
P. 11-8
P. 11-7
V-
V 3
F. 25-H U/L 7
P. 46-O
F. 81-B
F. 25-H
F. 110-O
PORT SWITCH Nº2 STARBº
L.T. & H.T. SUPPLY (D)
RESISTANCE UNIT
L.T. CONVERTOR UNIT
H.T. CONVERTOR UNIT
RED
BLUE
F. 87-3
F. 87-4
F. 78-1
F. 78-2
LONDEX RELAY
5∝
F. 92-A
F. 92-B
DUCEL 7 F.92
DUCEL 19 F.87
DUCEL 19 F.78
F. 78-A
F. 78-B
F. 78-3
F. 78-4
7∝
19∝
G.S. CUTOUT SEE FIG.
G+ A+ A- AUX
#48
5∝ TO CUT-OUT
#16
40∝
#15
A+
A-
FIG

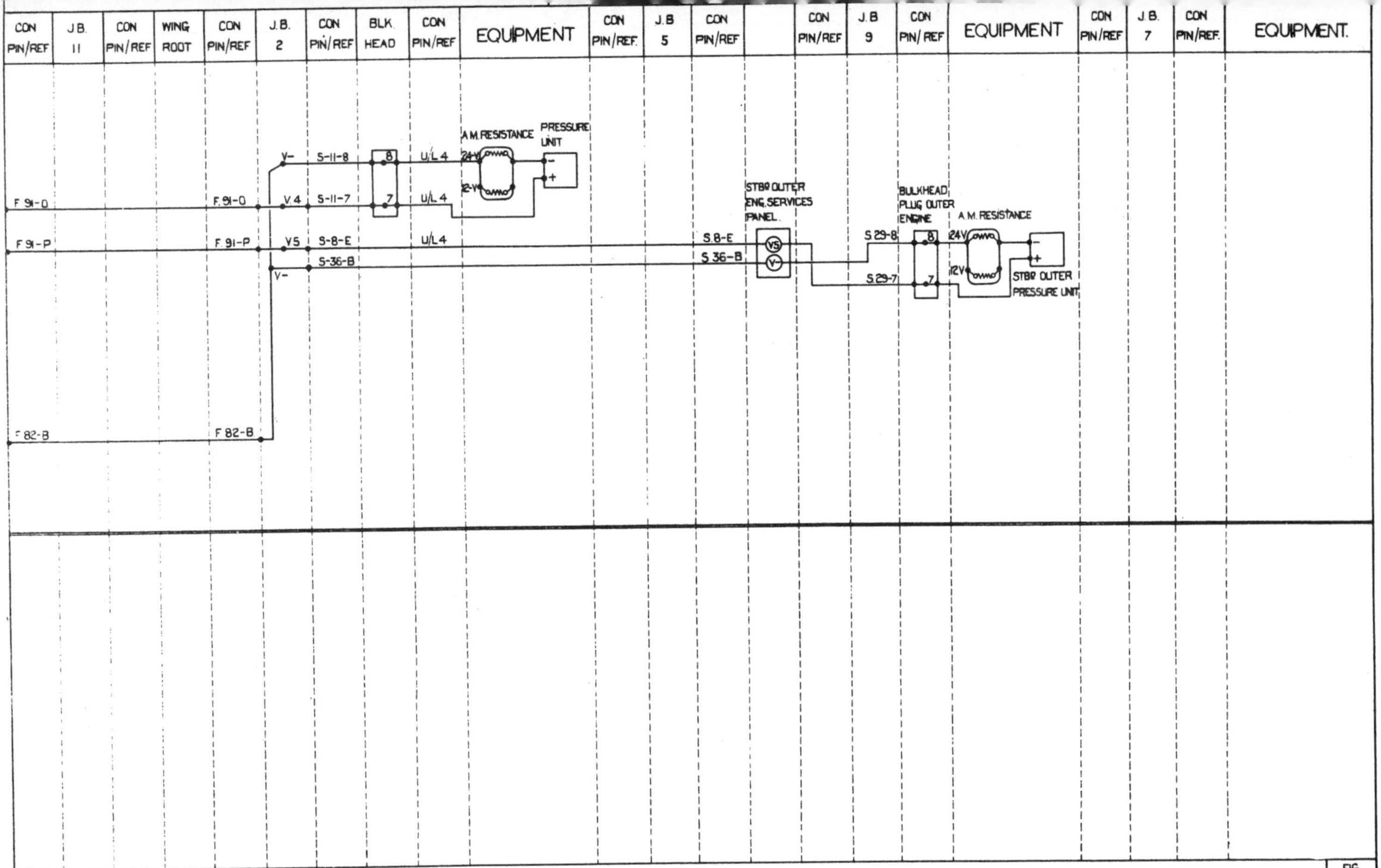

GENERAL SERVICES - SCHEME E

FIG. 59

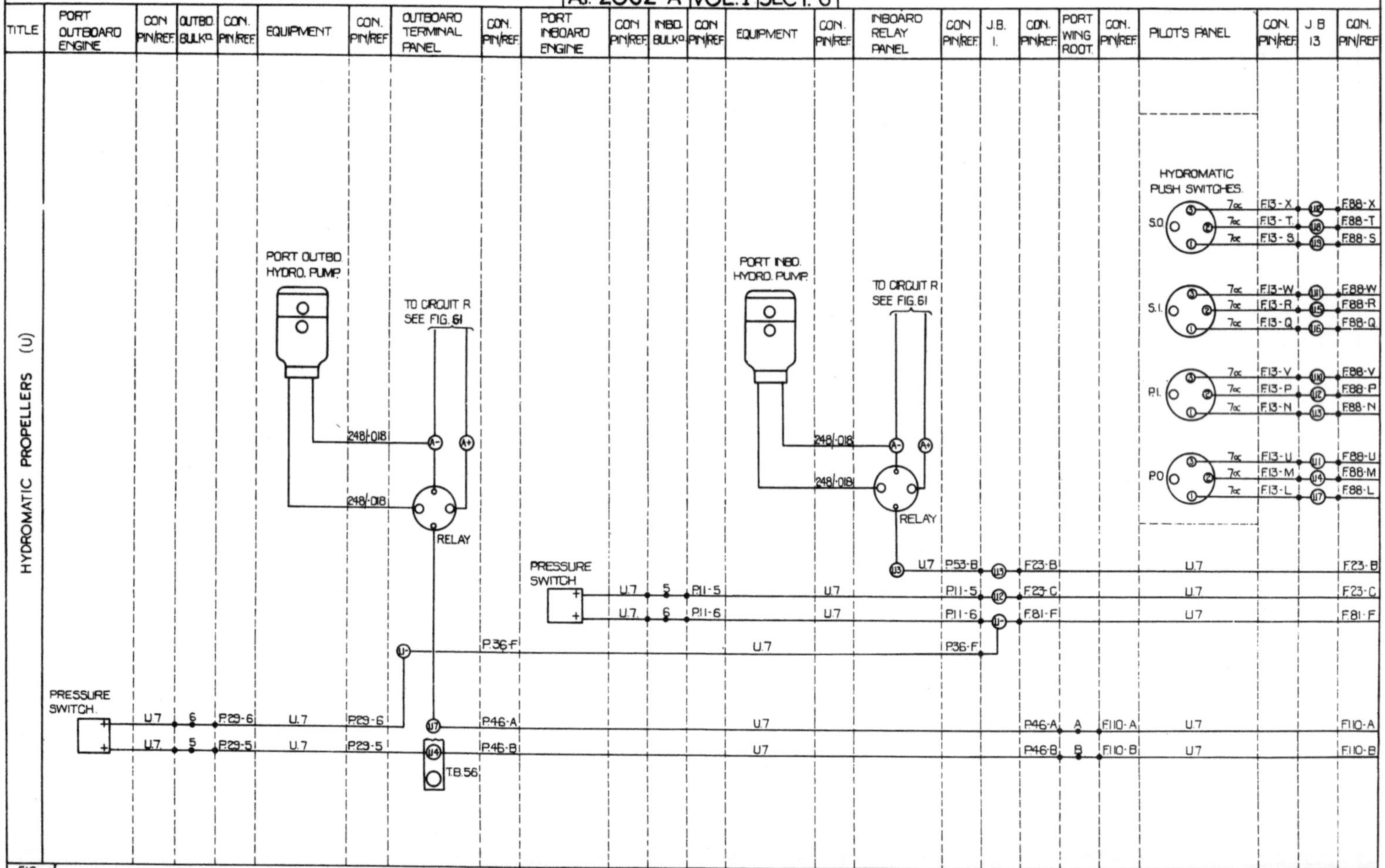
TITLE
PORT OUTBOARD ENGINE
CON PIN/REF
OUTBD. BULKD.
CON. PIN/REF
EQUIPMENT
CON. PIN/REF
OUTBOARD TERMINAL PANEL
CON. PIN/REF
PORT INBOARD ENGINE
CON PIN/REF
INBD. BULKD.
CON PIN/REF
EQUIPMENT
CON. PIN/REF
INBOARD RELAY PANEL
CON PIN/REF
J.B. 1.
CON. PIN/REF
PORT WING ROOT
CON. PIN/REF
PILOT'S PANEL
CON. PIN/REF
J B 13
CON. PIN/REF
HYDROMATIC PROPELLERS (U)
HYDROMATIC PUSH SWITCHES.
S.O.
S.I.
P.I.
P.O.
F.13-X
F.13-T
F.13-S
F.13-W
F.13-R
F.13-Q
F.13-V
F.13-P
F.13-N
F.13-U
F.13-M
F.13-L
F.88-X
F.88-T
F.88-S
F.88-W
F.88-R
F.88-Q
F.88-V
F.88-P
F.88-N
F.88-U
F.88-M
F.88-L
PORT OUTBD. HYDRO. PUMP.
PORT INBD. HYDRO. PUMP.
TO CIRCUIT R SEE FIG. 61
RELAY
248/-018
PRESSURE SWITCH
PRESSURE SWITCH.
U.7
P.53-B
F.23-B
P.11-5
F.23-C
P.11-6
F.81-F
P.36-F
P.29-6
P.29-5
P.46-A
P.46-B
F.110-A
F.110-B
T.B.56
A
B
5
6

FIG. 60

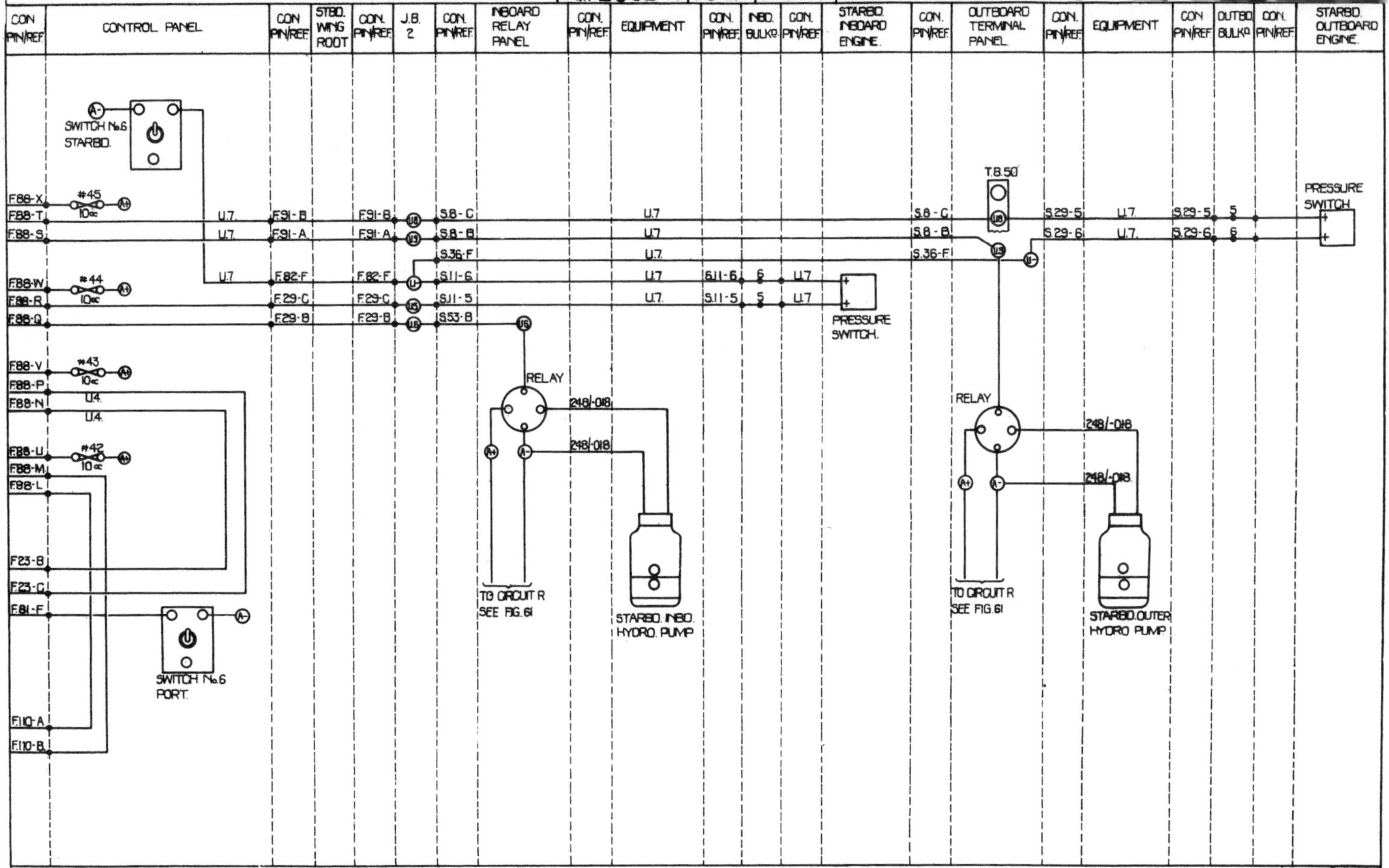

GENERAL SERVICES - SCHEME E

FIG. 60

PP2080 M /1113 3/43 3950 C & P Gp. 959 (4)

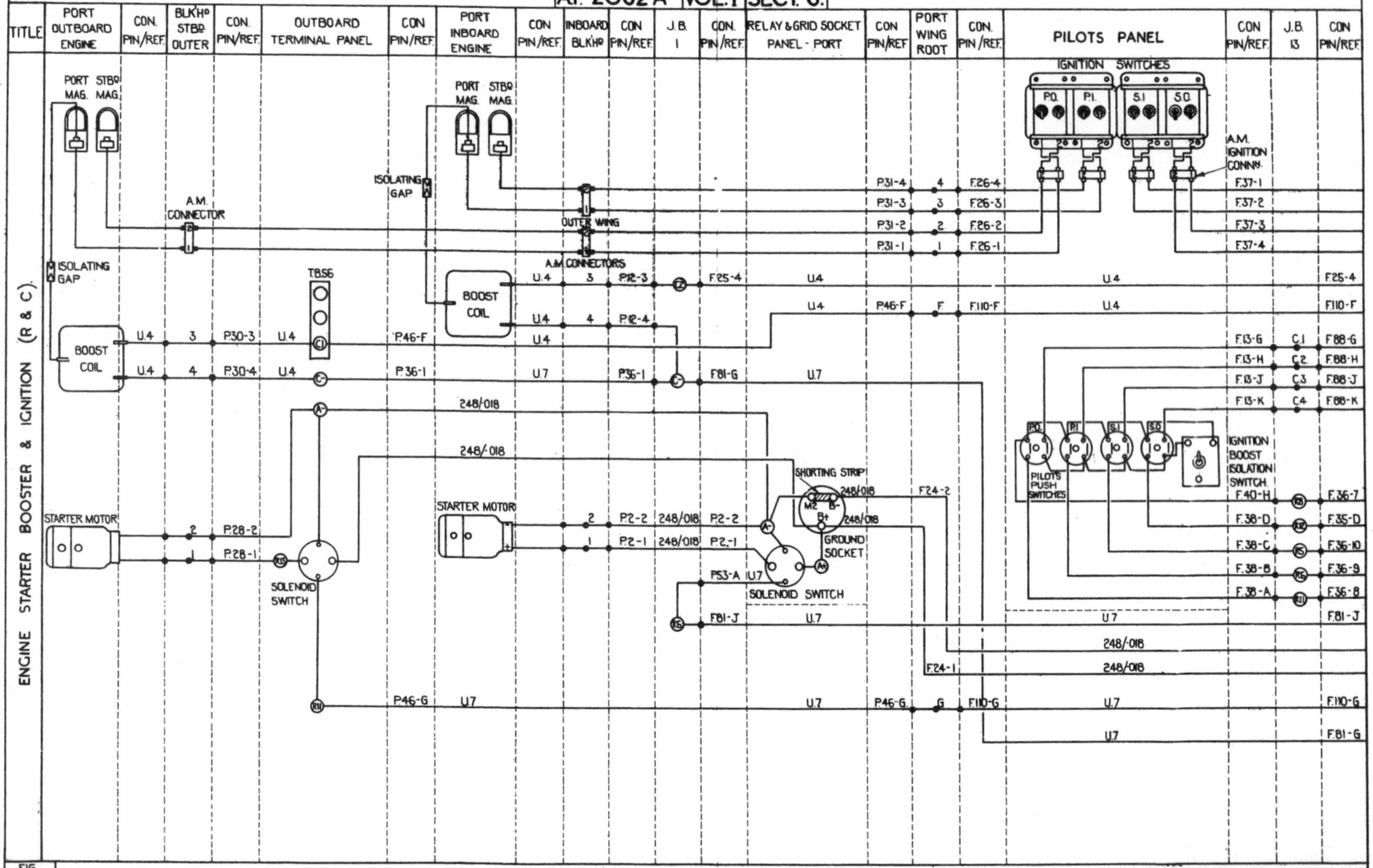

FIG. 61 — ENGINE STARTER BOOSTER & IGNITION (R & C) — ROUTING CHART

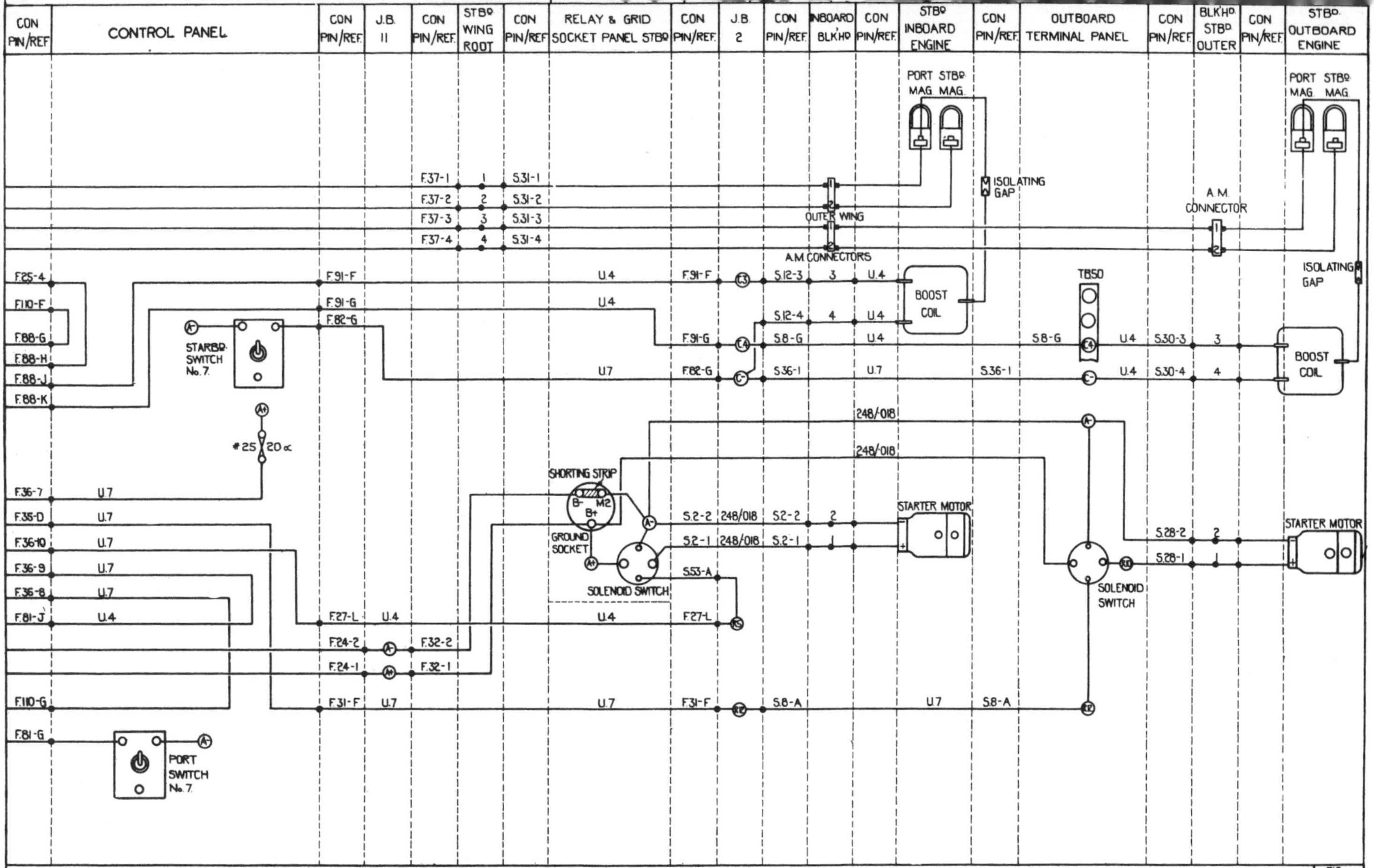

GENERAL SERVICES - SCHEME 'E'

FIG. 61

THIS PAGE ISSUED WITH A.L.10, JUNE, 1943

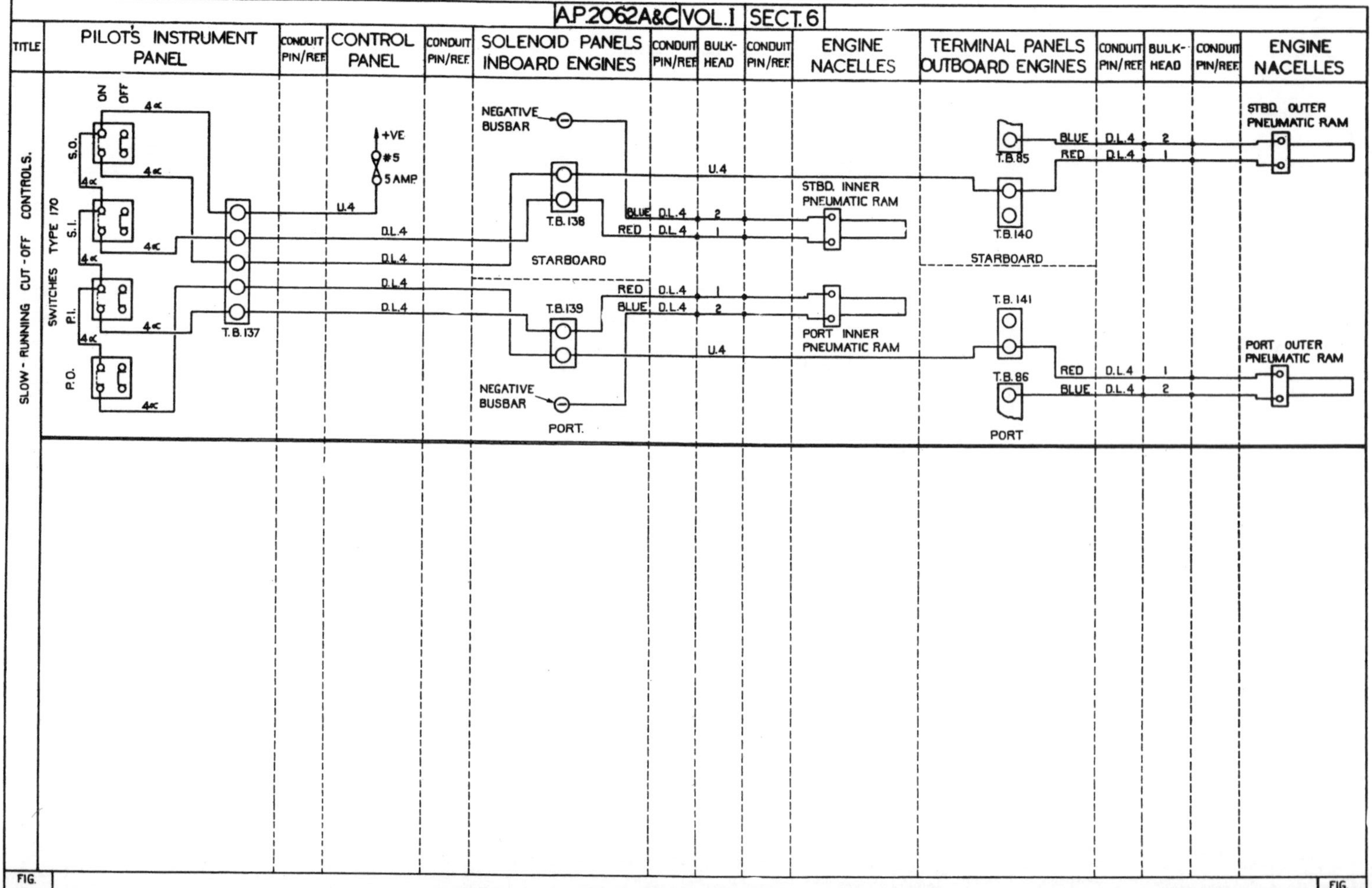

ROUTING CHART GENERAL SERVICES

Section 7:
Design and construction of airframe.

May, 1942
Issued with A.L.6

A.P.2062A, VOL. I

SECTION 7—DESIGN AND CONSTRUCTION OF AIRFRAME

CHAPTER 1—FUSELAGE

LIST OF CONTENTS

	Para.
General	1
Construction	2
Nose	4
Front centre portion	5
Intermediate centre portion	9
Rear centre portion	12
Rear fuselage	16
Bomb doors	17
Canopy	18
Seats	
First pilot's seat	19
Second pilot's seat	20
Navigator's seat	21
Radio operator's seat	22
Rest seat	23
Navigator's table	24

LIST OF ILLUSTRATIONS

	Fig.
Typical fuselage joints	1
Front turret mounting	2
Upper mid turret mounting	3
Lower mid turret mounting	4
Rear turret mounting	5
Bomb door construction	6
Floor construction—Intermediate centre portion	7
Details of canopy construction	8
Tail wheel mounting in fuselage	9
First pilot's seat	10
Second pilot's seat	11

F.S./1
A

A.P.2062A, VOL. I, SECT. 7

CHAPTER 1—FUSELAGE

General

1. The fuselage is divided into five sections viz:—nose, front centre portion, intermediate centre portion, rear centre portion and rear fuselage, for transport purposes only four sections are used; the nose and front centre portion being bolted together to form the front end. The nose houses the front gun turret and bomb aiming station and the front centre portion contains the pilots', observer's, navigator's and radio operator's stations. The intermediate centre portion serves as a rest compartment and the rear centre portion houses the operational equipment and mid turrets. The rear fuselage carries the tail unit and the rear turret.

Construction

2. The fuselage is of light alloy monocoque construction, built up with transverse channel-section formers stiffened by fore-and-aft angle stringers. The framework is covered with light-alloy sheet riveted to the formers and stringers with countersunk-head rivets. The stringers are secured to the formers by small attachment brackets, the formers being cut away to allow the stringers to pass through (see fig. 1). Between formers E and 22, i.e. the length of the bomb compartment, the fuselage section excluding the bomb doors is constant, from former 22 aft, the fuselage tapers slightly in plan and elevation.

3. The fuselage formers (see Sect. 4, Chap. 3, fig. 15) are numbered 1 to 41 proceeding aft from the first complete former in the front centre portion, and lettered A to K, (excluding letter I) proceeding forward from that point. Along the sides of the bomb compartment, formers 1, 6, 9, 12 and 18 are of pressed steel.

Nose

4. In nose of the aeroplane the formers at the rear of the section are complete, but at the front, the tops of the formers are cut away to receive the front gun turret mounting ring (see fig. 2). Brackets riveted on these formers carry the ring which is also supported by a channel member running across the fuselage. Between this member and former (G) is a draughtscreen which is curved to suit the gun turret contour. The hemi-spherical transparent nose is mounted on brackets secured to the front former (K), rubber pads being fitted between the brackets and the transparent material. In the floor of the nose, channel-section intercostals form the opening for the parachute exit door which consists of a wooden framework covered top and bottom with light alloy sheet. It has mounted on it the bomb aimer's kneeling cushions and is located in the floor structure by two pegs at the rear end and a spring loaded bolt at the front end. This bolt is operated by a pull on a ring to which it is connected by a cable. The ring is located beneath the cushions which lift up for this purpose. Two rectangular windows in the fuselage are provided at the bomb aiming station. On the port side of the floor at the rear of the nose portion is a circular window for vertical photography.

Front centre portion

5. The front centre portion is the portion of the fuselage between the front spar and former E. An extruded member runs the full length of the section on each side and carries the transverse channel section floor members, which, with

A.P.2062A, Vol. I, Sect. 7, Chap. 1

the channel section intercostals, form the framework of the floor. The covering of the floor is light alloy sheet, on the top side only. The floor cross members coincide with the fuselage formers (see fig. 7) to which they are attached; below the floor, the formers together with an extruded channel-section, form the sides of the bomb compartment to which the bomb doors are hinged. The formers above the floor form the main cabin, and are hoop shaped except where they are cut away over the pilot's cockpit (see para. 18). Along the top of the latter formers on each side runs the cockpit rail, an inverted U member (see fig. 1). Formers 1, 2, 3 and 4 have steel plates fitted to the top on the port side to give additional protection to the pilot.

6. The extreme front and rear formers of the front centre portion E and 6 respectively, are angle members which form the joints to the other sections, and a bulkhead below the floor level at former E acts as the forward end of the bomb compartment.

7. Three bomb gear housings are fitted between bomb beams B and C, and three between beams 3 and 4, in the main floor. Each of these latter beams is supported for the carriage of heavy bombs by a vertical tie-rod, bolted at the lower end to the beam, near the centre line of the fuselage, and at the upper end to the top of the fuselage former, which is locally reinforced. Cross channels are fitted between the bomb beams and are braced together by light alloy intercostals. In early aeroplanes floor beam 5A is not fitted, but beams 2 and 5 are reinforced.

8. The pilot's floor is a raised platform on the port side in the front of the cockpit, built of fore and aft channel members with intercostals between, and covered with light alloy sheet on both upper and lower surfaces. On the port side it is attached to the formers and on the starboard side it is supported from the main floor on a braced frame of channel members.

Intermediate centre portion

9. The intermediate portion of the fuselage is built on the front and rear spars of the main plane. The section is uniform throughout and of similar construction to the front centre portion except that the floor is deeper and the construction of the front and rear formers is different. These formers are constructed of two angles riveted to an extension of the spar web to form a channel section (see fig. 7). An emergency exit is fitted in the centre of the roof and windows are provided in the sides.

10. At former 7 an armoured bulkhead is provided, consisting of a frame and two doors hung on a central post. This post also serves the purpose of a tie rod supporting the main floor in the vicinity of the bomb gear housings. Plywood panels fill the gap below the armour in order to enclose the heated front cabin.

11. The floor is fitted with three bomb gear housings between bomb beams 8 and 9, the two outer housings are the standard type to carry 500 lb. bombs whilst the centre housing contains an R.A.E. heavy bomb slip unit to carry a 4,000 lb. bomb. In early aeroplanes a top-hat section stiffener is fitted above the floor at floor beam 11, but in later aeroplanes this is replaced by an additional floor beam 11A.

Rear centre portion

12. The rear centre portion comprises that portion of the fuselage aft of the rear spar and up to former 27. The bomb compartment ends at former 22

F.S./2

A.P.2062A, Vol. I, Sect. 7, Chap. 1

and aft of this the fuselage tapers in plan and elevation. The construction up to former 22 is similar to that of the front centre portion. The section of former 22 below the main floor is formed into a bulkhead for the end of the bomb compartment.

13. Six bomb gear housings are fitted into the floor, three between bomb beams 13 and 14, and three between beams 18 and 19. The three housings between beams 13 and 14 are strengthened in a similar manner to those between beams 3 and 4 in the front centre portion (see para. 7).

14. In the top of the fuselage the upper mid turret is mounted (see fig. 3) in a support ring between formers 24 and 26. Formers 24, 25 and 26 are cut away at the supporting frame, further details of which are given in Sect. 11. Detachable fairings are mounted forward and aft of the turret. The lower mid turret is mounted in a wooden support ring (see fig. 4) between formers 24 and 27, formers 25 and 26 being cut away at the support ring. Further details of the mounting are given in Sect. 11.

15. An emergency exit is fitted in the roof above the end of the main floor and seven windows are fitted in each side of the fuselage. The reconnaissance flare chute is mounted on the centre line of the aeroplane immediately aft of the bomb compartment and the removable flare chute extension is stowed on the starboard side, forward of the ammunition ducts and boxes.

Rear fuselage

16. The rear fuselage, which is the portion aft of former 27, is constructed in a similar manner to the rear end of the rear centre portion. The fuselage ends at former 41, and from this a tubular framework projects to support the rear gun turret mounting ring (see fig. 5). A detachable fairing fits under this framework and forms the tail of the fuselage below the turret. Where the tail plane enters the section between formers 35 and 38, the skin, formers, and stringers are cut away. Below this in the centre of the floor is fitted the tail wheel mounting beam, which is a built up structure and houses the tail wheel shock absorber strut (see fig. 9). Between formers 29 and 31 on the starboard side is placed the main entrance door, hinged on the leading edge and opening inwards, and built up from wooden members covered on both sides with plywood. A rubber retaining spring is provided to hold the door open. A wooden walkway is provided over the tail plane and down to the rear turret, which is separated from the main cabin by a pair of wooden draught-proof doors. Four windows are fitted in the rear fuselage, three on the port side and one on the starboard side. Provision is made at the bottom of former 41 for the attachment of a target towing gear bracket.

Bomb doors

17. The bomb doors (see fig. 6), one on each side of the fuselage, enclose the bomb compartment and form the lower surface of the fuselage between formers E and 22. They are of light alloy construction built up from a central spar, with nose and main ribs tapering in each direction, and with special hinge and edge extruded channels. The spar is made up with T-section extruded flanges connected by a sheet web having flanged lightening holes. The main ribs, nose ribs and the special end ribs, are pressings, flanged for the attachment of the inner and outer skins of light alloy sheet. The hydraulic jack attachment at each end consists of a trunnion mounted in ball bearings between the two

special end ribs. Each door has seven ball bearing hinges; one central datum hinge, four intermediate hinges, and two end hinges, all attached to the hinge beam at the bottom of the sides of the bomb compartment. Between the hinges a curved sealing strip, which maintains the seal as the doors move; to seal the joint between the doors when closed, a spruce strip is attached to the projecting flange on the edge channel of the port door, and a brush sealing strip similarly attached to the starboard door. Aft of the bomb doors a wood-framed fairing of light alloy sheet is attached below the fuselage to complete the contour. Openings for the flare chutes are provided in this fairing.

Canopy

18. Above the cut away portion of the front centre portion, and over almost all the roof, is a transparent canopy. The support for this comprises a die cast windscreen frame, to which is bolted a welded steel tubular structure (see fig. 8) extending aft to former 1. The remaining portion of the frame is built up of spruce and fairs into a hemi-spherical dome just forward of the end of the section. An inward opening direct vision window is fitted in each side of the windscreen, and in each side of the canopy at the forward end is a sliding window. In the panel forward of former 1 is an observation dome.

Seats

19. *First pilot's seat.*—This is a box type seat (see fig. 10) with a back built up from channel members. It is mounted in a tubular underframe, and is adjustable in height. The adjustment is made by means of a lever at the pilot's left-hand side, which turns the short levers on the ends of which the seat is mounted. A stud on the handlever engages with a notched quadrant on the underframe and locks the seat in the required position. The stud can be released by pressing a spring-loaded button on the end of the lever. Armour plating is fitted on the back of the seat, and above the seat behind the pilot's head. This latter plate is hinged to allow it to be folded down behind the seat.

20. *Second pilot's seat.*—The second pilot's seat is a folding structure supported on the starboard side of the fuselage. The seat itself is built on a plywood base padded with sponge rubber. The base is stiffened by two inverted U-section members on to which two bearer tubes are welded. A support frame at the outer edge of the seat holds the seat in a horizontal position and when the seat is folded vertically upwards this frame slides in a slot in the seat support members. The back rest for the seat is a strap of canvas webbing, bolted to an eyebolt on the cockpit rail and to the first pilot's seat. The attachment at the first pilot's seat is detachable so that when the seat is in the stowed position the back rest can be folded down the back of the seat. A tubular footrest is fitted in sliding bearings on the underside of the pilot's floor, and when not in use can be slid beneath the pilot's floor.

21. *Navigator's seat.*—The navigator's seat is supported on a pivoted arm of welded tubes, mounted on the aft leg of the table; it can also revolve on its attachment to the arm. The pivoted arm can be locked in any position by means of a hand screw which tightens the upper collar. When not in use the seat is turned under the table. Its movement is limited by a check cable, attached to the floor by a quick release catch to facilitate access to the radio power units.

22. *Radio operator's seat.*—The radio operator's seat is mounted at the front of the front spar cover. It is a box type seat built up with light-alloy

F.S./3

flanged U-section stiffeners and skin. The seat is supported on a frame of welded mild steel tubes bolted to the main floor.

23. *Rest seat.*—The rest seat is formed by the top of the oxygen bottle crate and a backrest mounted on the rear spar. The base of the seat forms a lid on the oxygen crate to which it is attached by six hinges. Check cables prevent the lid from opening too far. The back rest is built up on a spruce frame with a plywood base. It is secured to the top of the rear spar by two hinge brackets and is supported by a centre tube clamped to a cross tube bolted between former 12 and the floor support tube at that point. Adjustment to the backrest is possible by releasing the clamp on the cross tube, the centre support tube being then free to slide through the clamp.

Navigator's table

24. The navigator's table is attached to formers A, 1, 2, 3 and 4, on the port side, the inner edge being supported on two tubular stays. The top is of plywood, with an upper surface of Langite, and is strengthened by two wooden stiffeners and two radio crate bearer rails. A large drawer with a let down front is fitted into the side of the table. The aft end of the table which carries the radio apparatus projects, and is supported from the top of former 3 by tubular members. At this end of the table is a hinged flap which can be folded to gain access to a second drawer in the end. Below the table a crate is provided for the accumulators, supported in runners. A curtain is provided for fixing at the forward end of the table in order to prevent glare in the cockpit. It is attached to the edge of the table and to former 1 by "lift-the-dot" fasteners, and when not in use is rolled up and stowed in the tube below the forward edge of the table.

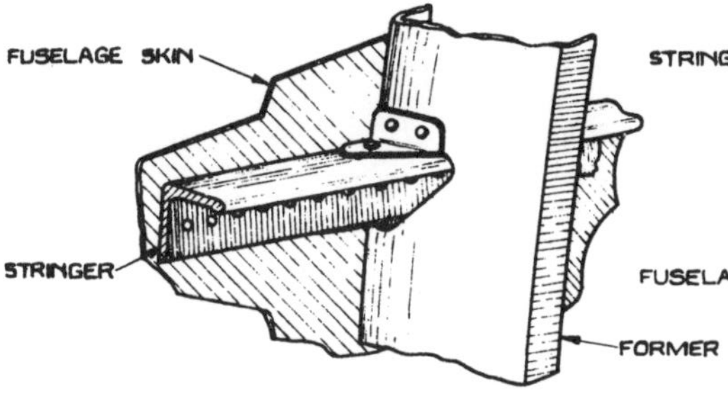

A.P. 2062 A | VOL. I | SECT. 7 | CHAP. I

STRINGER TO FORMER, NOSE AND REAR FUSELAGE.

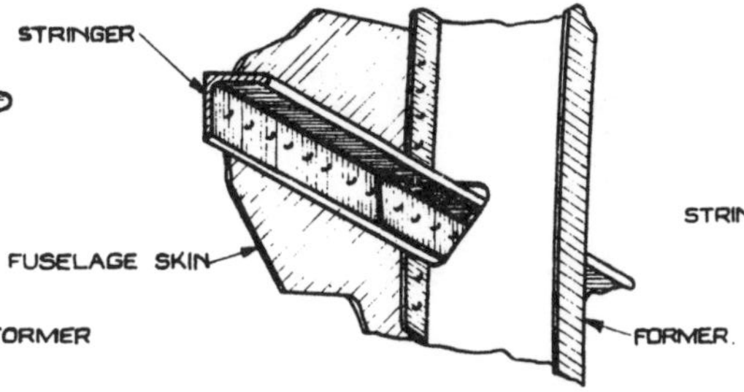

STRINGER TO FORMER, FRONT, CENTRE AND REAR CENTRE PORTION

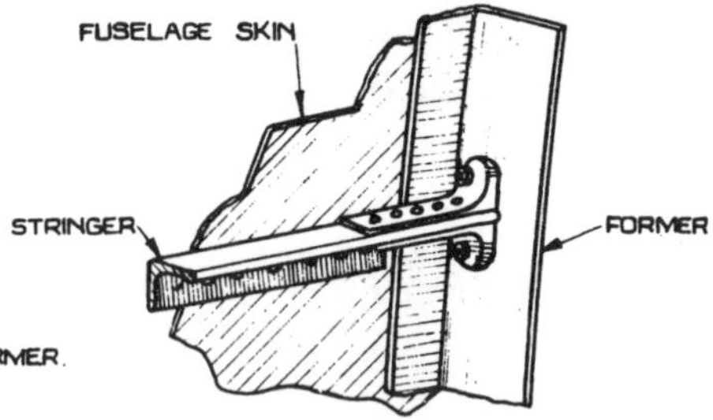

STRINGER TO FORMER AT TRANSPORT JOINTS.

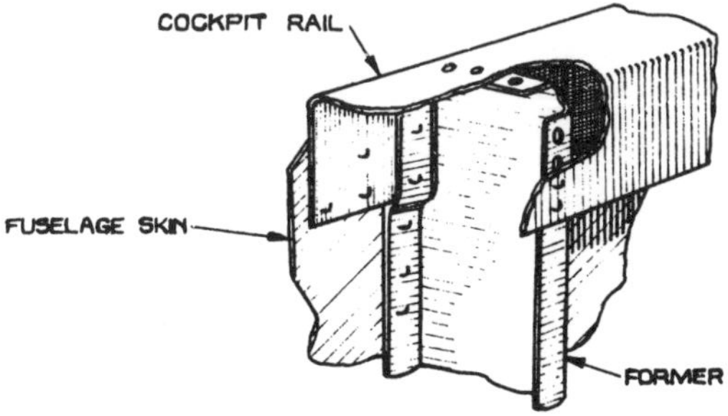

COCKPIT RAIL TO FORMERS A TO E.

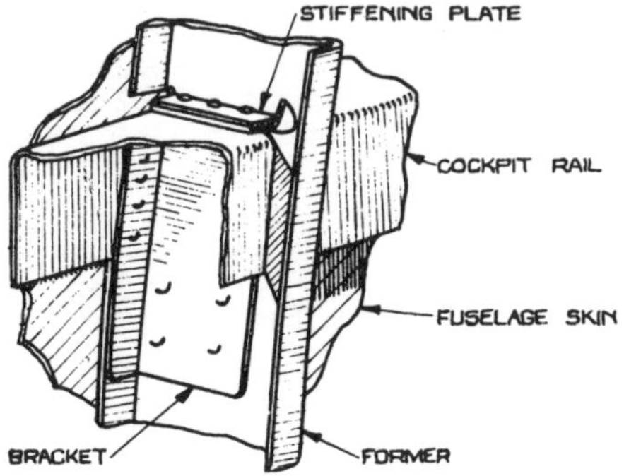

COCKPIT RAIL TO FORMERS 1 AND 2

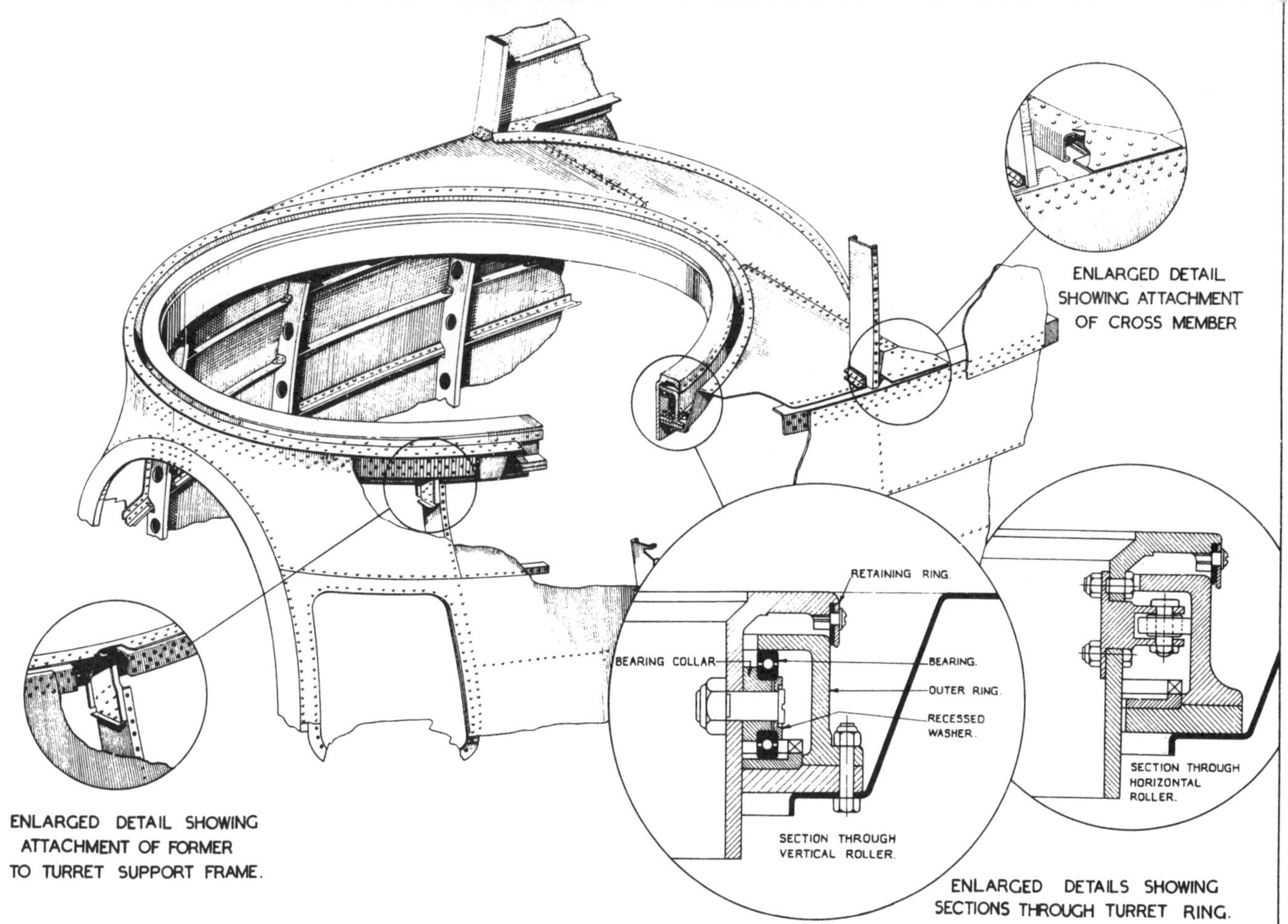

FRONT TURRET MOUNTING.

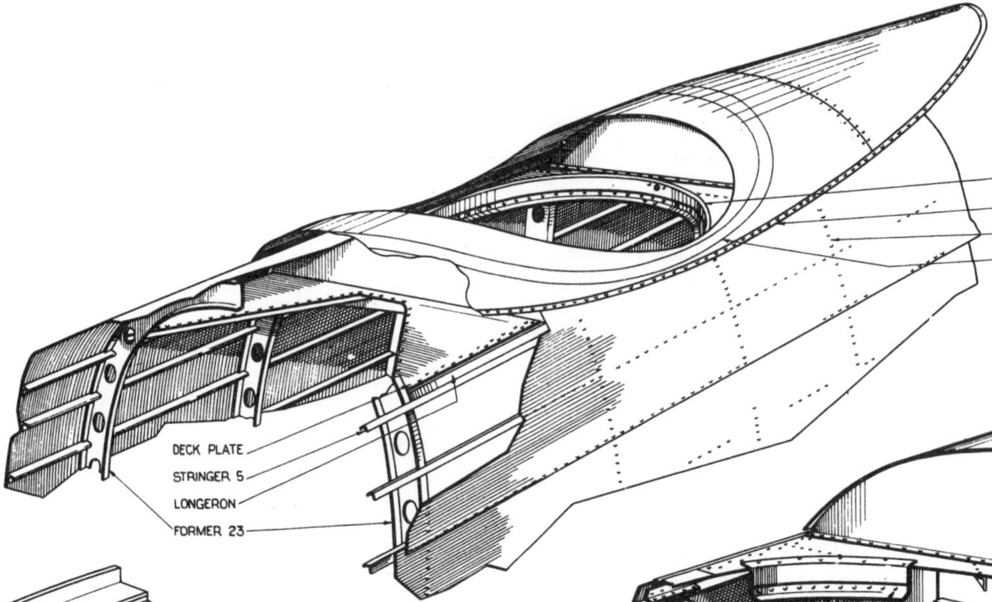

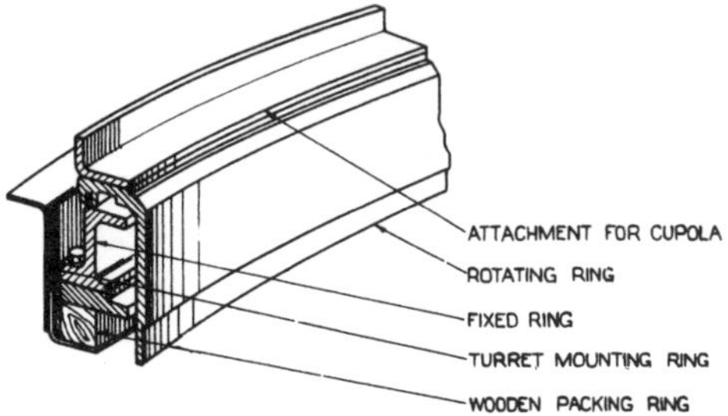

AP 2062 A | VOL.I | SECT.7 | CHAP.I

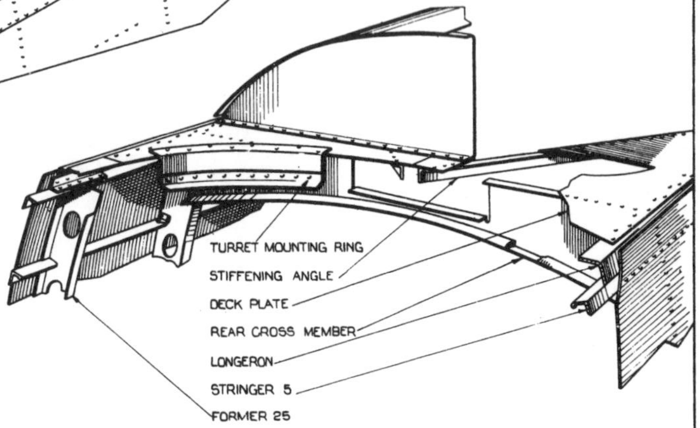

UPPER MID TURRET MOUNTING

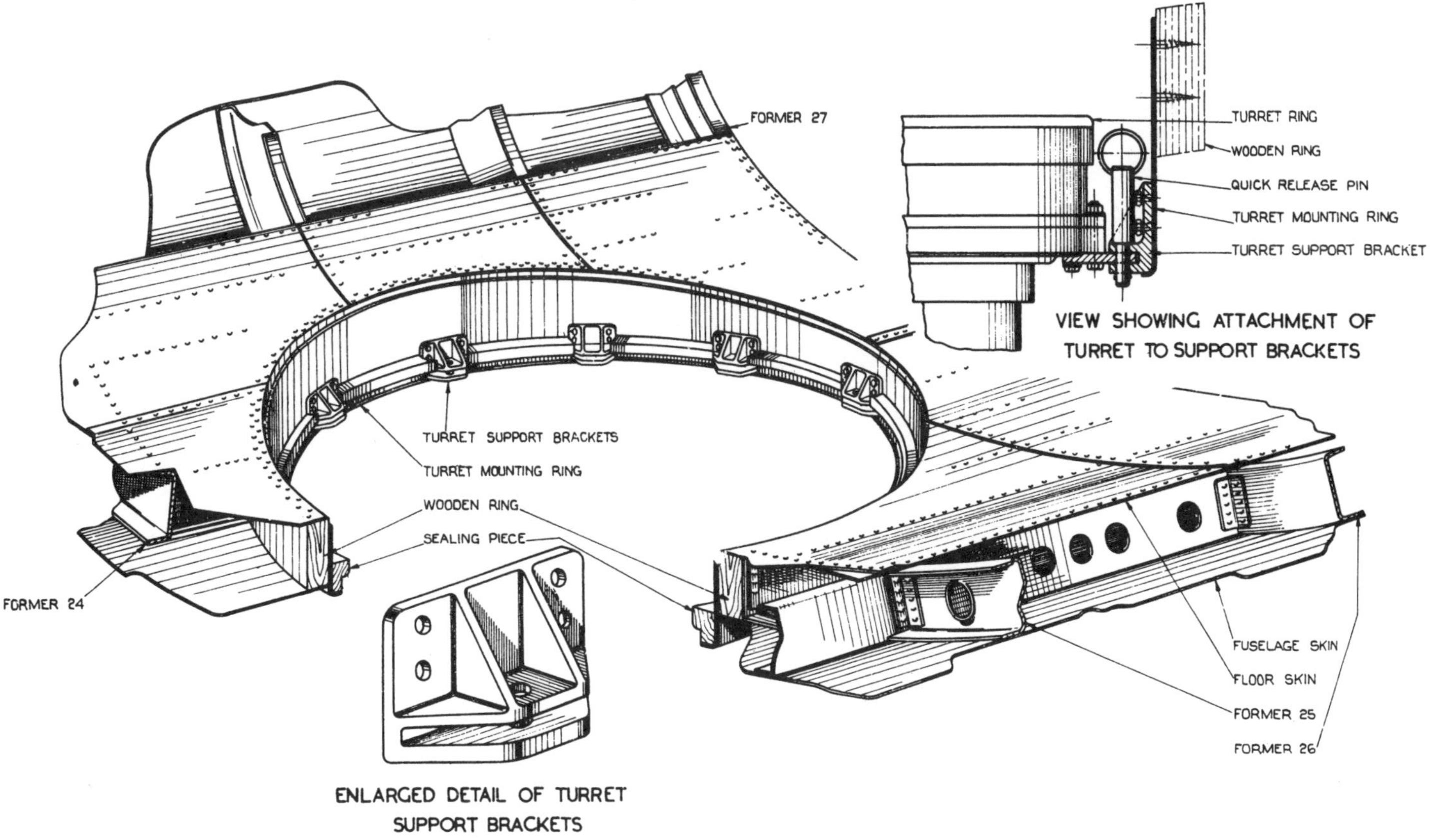

A.P.2062A VOL.I SECT.7 CHAP.1

FIG. 4

TURRET RING
WOODEN RING
QUICK RELEASE PIN
TURRET MOUNTING RING
TURRET SUPPORT BRACKET

VIEW SHOWING ATTACHMENT OF TURRET TO SUPPORT BRACKETS

FUSELAGE SKIN
FLOOR SKIN
FORMER 25
FORMER 26

FORMER 27

TURRET SUPPORT BRACKETS
TURRET MOUNTING RING
WOODEN RING
SEALING PIECE

FORMER 24

ENLARGED DETAIL OF TURRET SUPPORT BRACKETS

LOWER MID TURRET MOUNTING

FIG. 4

AP 2062 A | VOL. I | SECT. 7 | CHAP. I

JUNCTION OF STIFFENERS ON UNDER FAIRING

INSPECTION DOOR

SUPPORT FOR WALKWAY

FORMER 41

ATTACHED AT FORMER 39

CENTRE ATTACHMENT PORT

"A" SHOWS REVOLVING RING IN POSITION ON FIXED RING

DETAIL SHOWING REVOLVING RING IN POSITION

FIXED RING

SECTION THRO' FIXED & REVOLVING RINGS

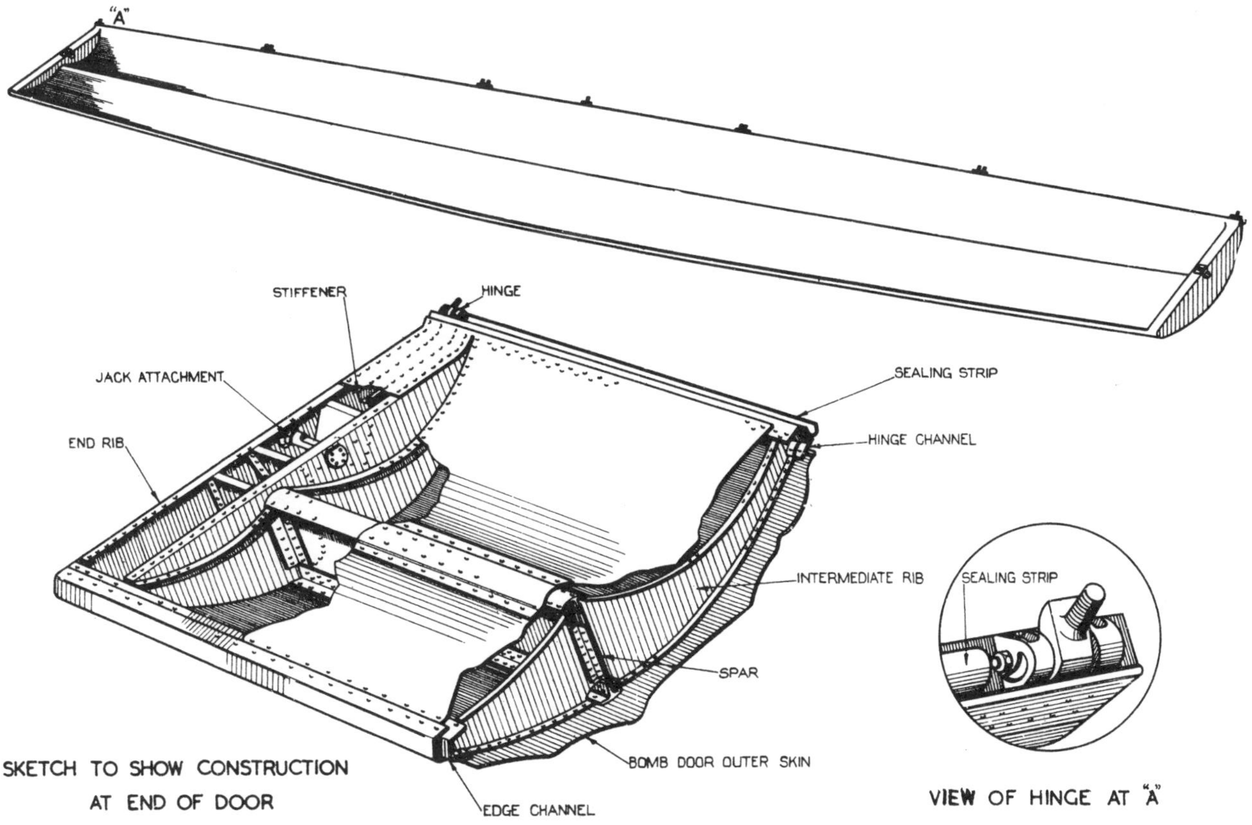

A.P. 2062 A|VOL. I|SECT. 7|CHAP. 1

FIG. 6

BOMB DOOR CONSTRUCTION

SKETCH TO SHOW CONSTRUCTION AT END OF DOOR

VIEW OF HINGE AT "A"

SEALING STRIP
HINGE CHANNEL
INTERMEDIATE RIB
SPAR
BOMB DOOR OUTER SKIN
EDGE CHANNEL
HINGE
STIFFENER
JACK ATTACHMENT
END RIB
SEALING STRIP

FLOOR CONSTRUCTION - INTERMEDIATE CENTRE PORTION

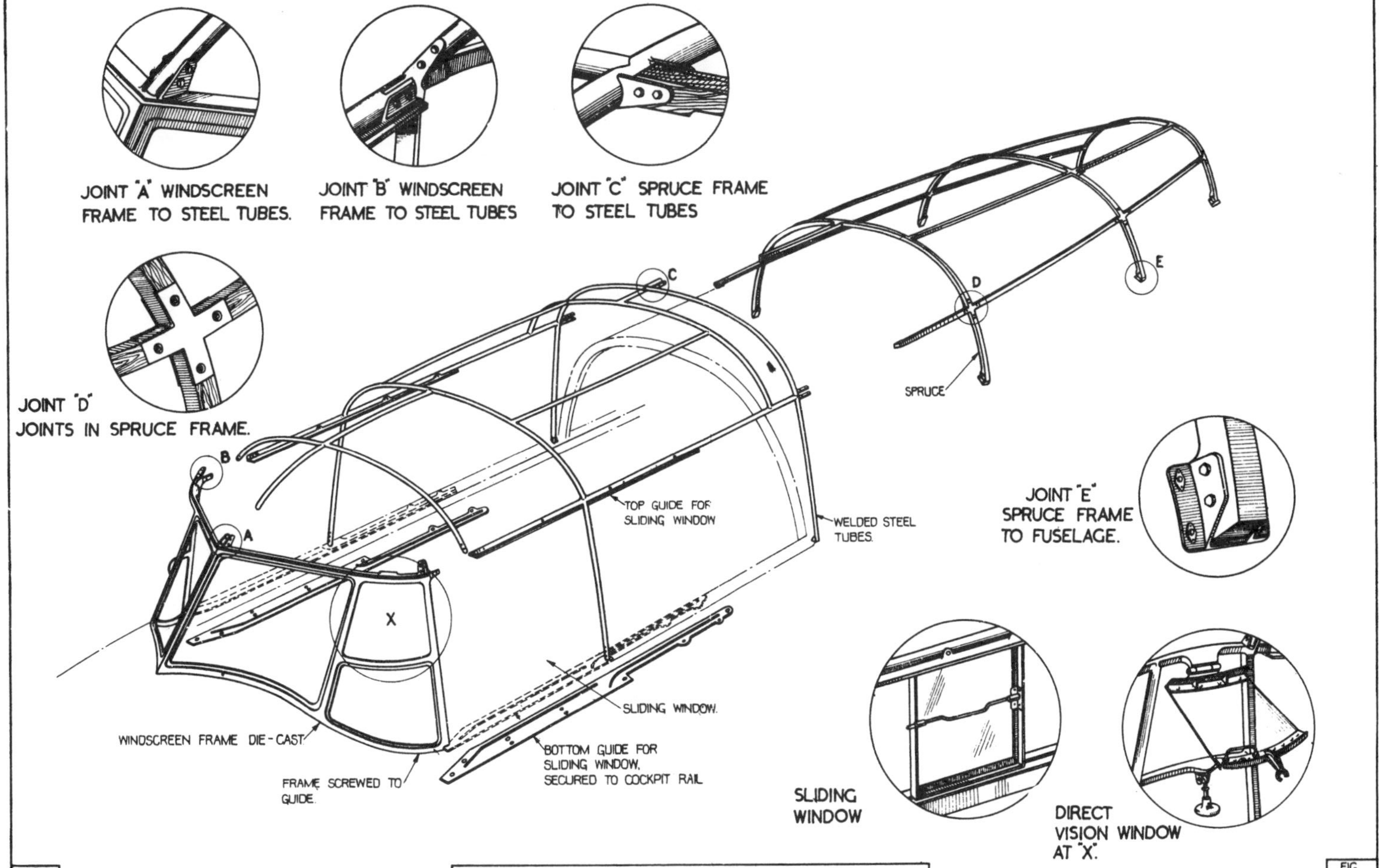

DETAILS OF CANOPY CONSTRUCTION

FIG 8

- JOINT "A" WINDSCREEN FRAME TO STEEL TUBES.
- JOINT "B" WINDSCREEN FRAME TO STEEL TUBES
- JOINT "C" SPRUCE FRAME TO STEEL TUBES
- JOINT "D" JOINTS IN SPRUCE FRAME.
- JOINT "E" SPRUCE FRAME TO FUSELAGE.
- DIRECT VISION WINDOW AT "X".
- SLIDING WINDOW

SPRUCE
WELDED STEEL TUBES
TOP GUIDE FOR SLIDING WINDOW
SLIDING WINDOW.
BOTTOM GUIDE FOR SLIDING WINDOW, SECURED TO COCKPIT RAIL
FRAME SCREWED TO GUIDE.
WINDSCREEN FRAME DIE-CAST

TAIL WHEEL MOUNTING IN FUSELAGE

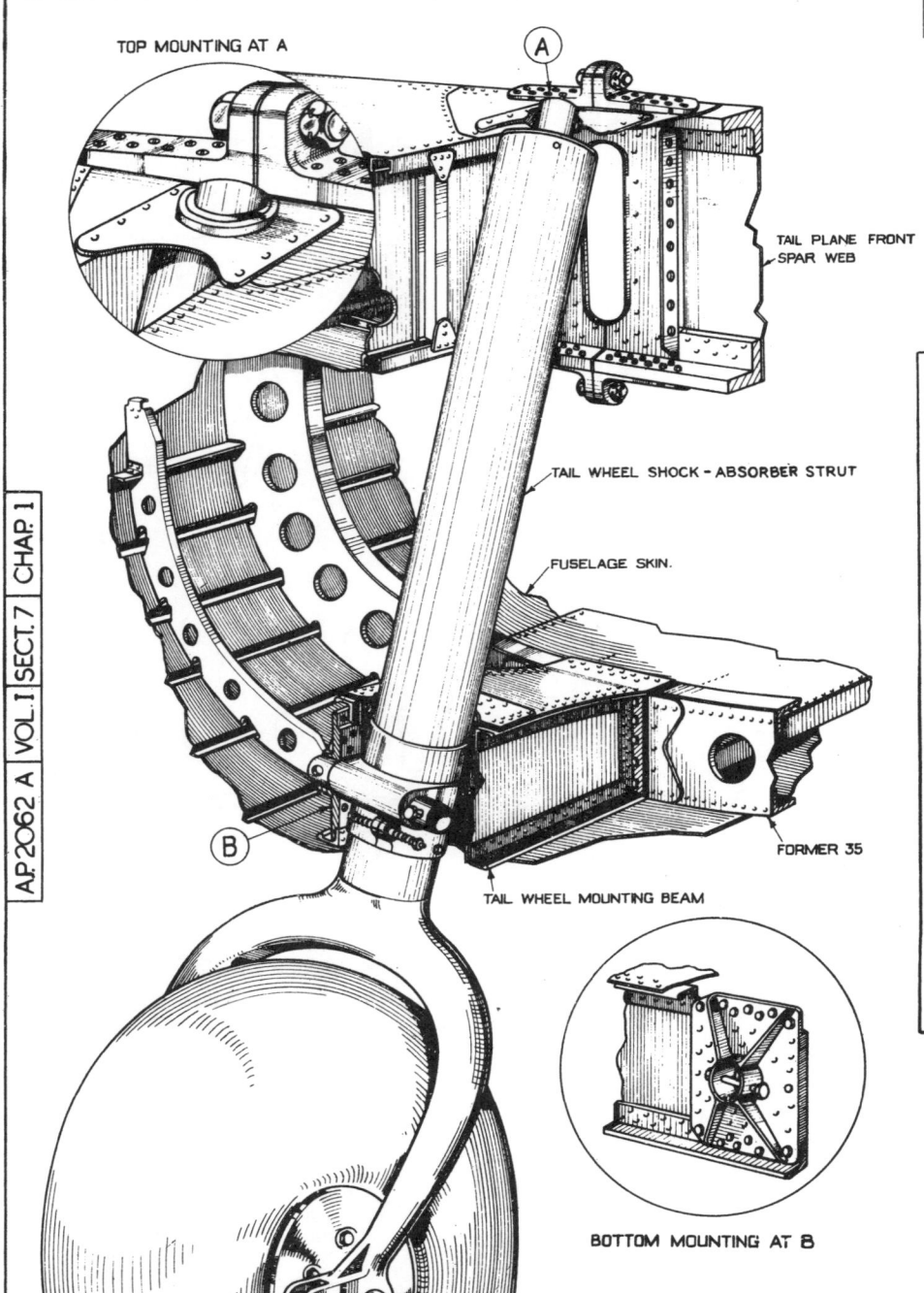

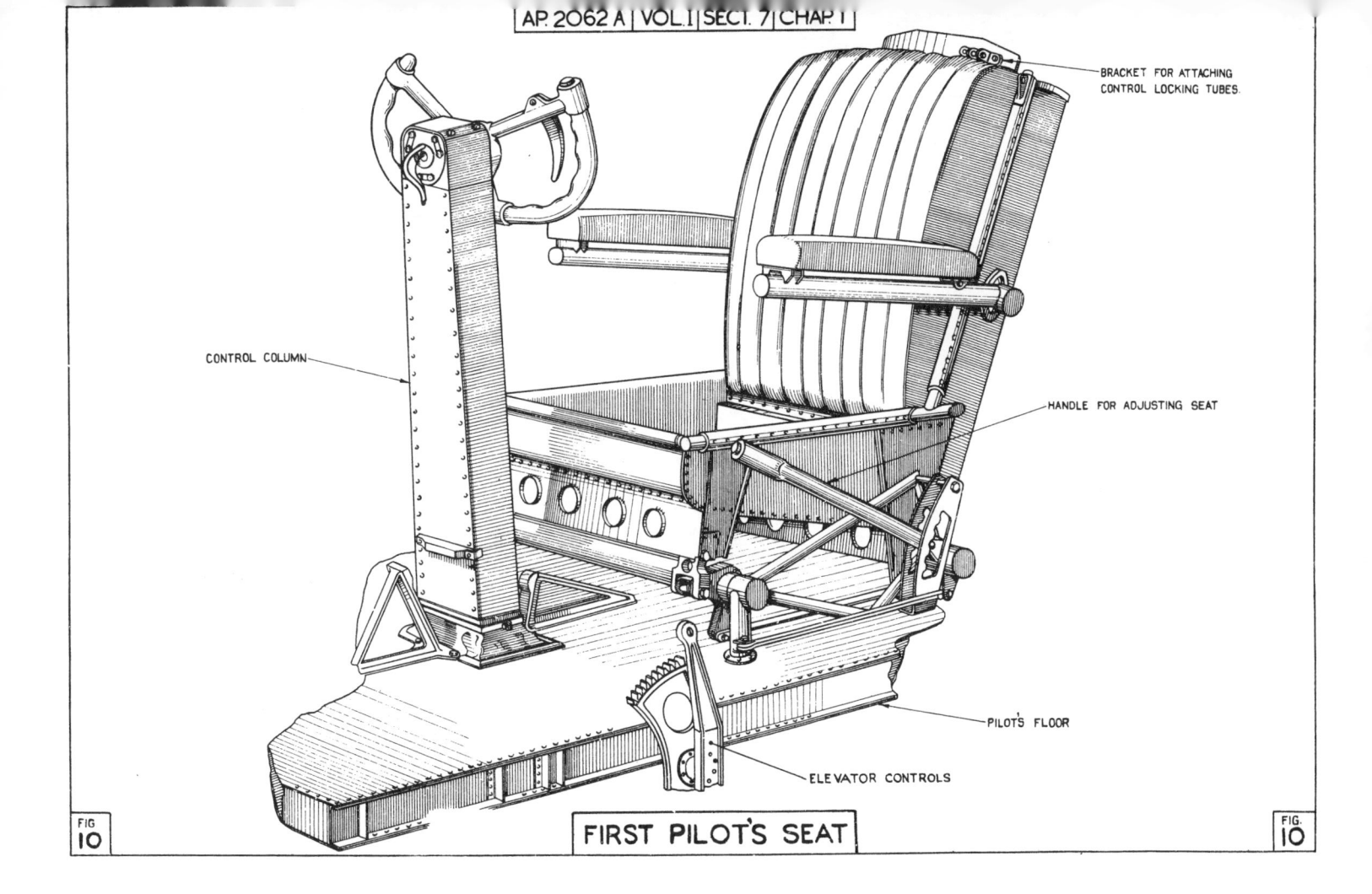

FIRST PILOT'S SEAT

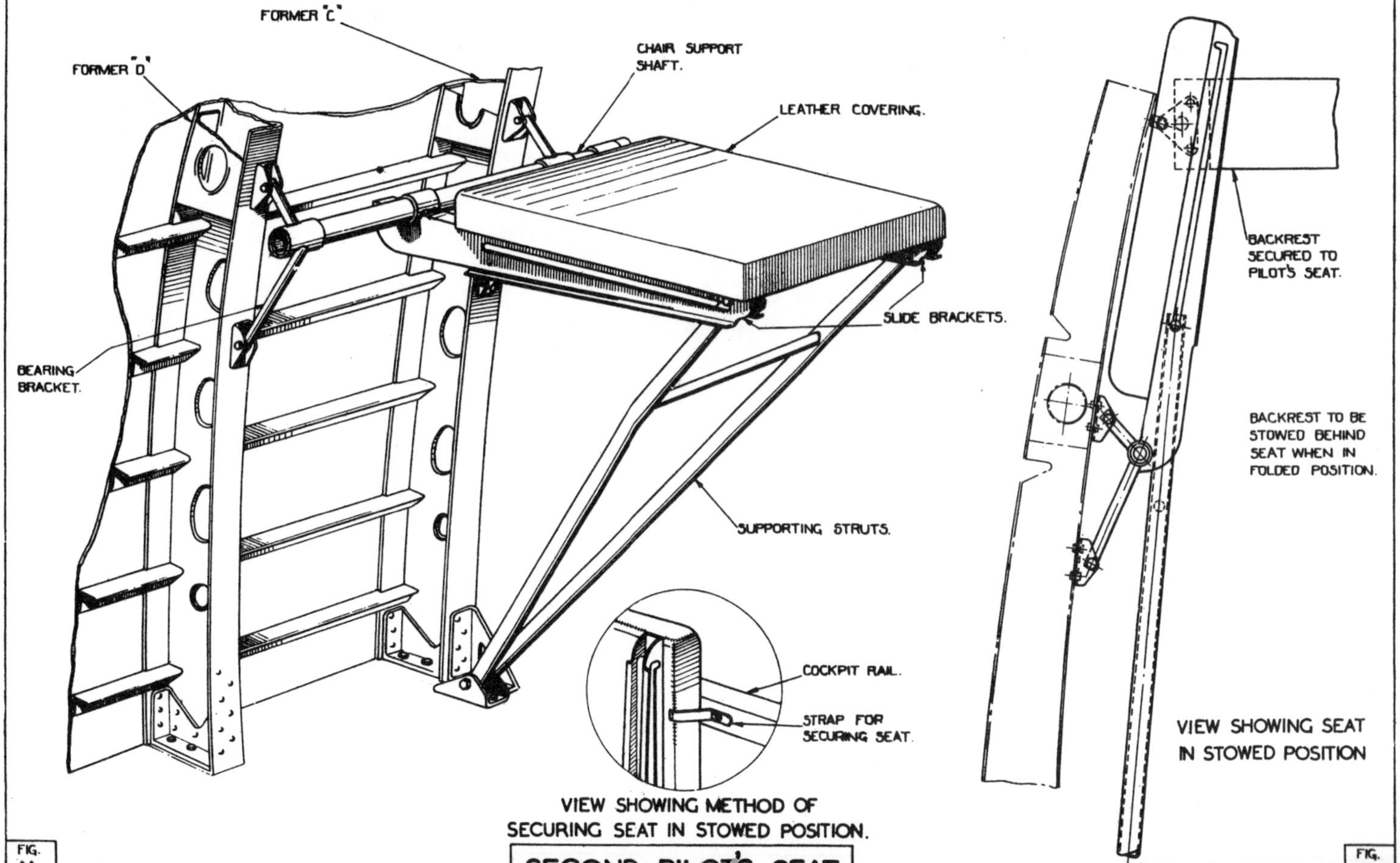

A.P.2062 A. VOL.I SECT.7 CHAP.I

BACKREST SECURED TO PILOT'S SEAT.

BACKREST TO BE STOWED BEHIND SEAT WHEN IN FOLDED POSITION.

VIEW SHOWING SEAT IN STOWED POSITION

SLIDE BRACKETS.

LEATHER COVERING.

SUPPORTING STRUTS.

CHAIR SUPPORT SHAFT.

COCKPIT RAIL.

STRAP FOR SECURING SEAT.

VIEW SHOWING METHOD OF SECURING SEAT IN STOWED POSITION.

FORMER "C"

FORMER "D"

BEARING BRACKET.

SECOND PILOT'S SEAT

May, 1942
Issued with A.L. 6

A.P.2062A, VOL. I

SECTION 7—DESIGN AND CONSTRUCTION OF AIRFRAME

CHAPTER 2—MAIN PLANE

LIST OF CONTENTS

	Para.
General	1
Spars	3
Ribs	4
Centre plane	5
Outer plane	8
Front portion	9
Trailing edge	10
Wing tip	11
Ailerons	12
Trimming tab	13
Balance tabs	14
Flaps	15

LIST OF ILLUSTRATIONS

	Fig.
Typical main plane section	1
Front spar joints	2
Rear spar joints	3
Flap construction	4
Aileron construction	5
Wing tip construction	6
Fuel tank mounting—Inboard	7
Fuel tank mounting—Outboard	8

F.S./1

A.P.2062A, VOL. I, SECT. 7

CHAPTER 2—MAIN PLANE

General

1. The main plane is a cantilever monoplane structure with a uniform horizontal centre section and a tapered outer plane having a dihedral of 70° ± 15'. The incidence of the main plane is constant throughout at 4° on the chord line. To facilitate transport the main plane is constructed in the following separate units:—

    (i)   Centre plane.
   (ii)   Trailing edge, centre plane, port and starboard.
  (iii)   Outer plane, port and starboard.
  (iv)   Trailing edge, outer plane, port and starboard.
   (v)   Wing tip, port and starboard.
  (vi)   Ailerons, port and starboard.
 (vii)   Flaps, two port and two starboard.
(viii)   Centre plane hinged leading edge, port and starboard.

2. The front and rear spars are continuous across the centre plane from rib 22 on one side to rib 22 on the other, and along the outer plane from rib 22 to rib 5, the wing tip from rib 5 outboard being separate structures bolted on. Hydraulically operated split-trailing-edge flaps are fitted to the centre section trailing edge and to the inboard end of the outer plane trailing edge. The ailerons are mounted on the outer end of the outer plane and project into the wing tip. The fuel tanks are housed between the spars in the centre section and in the outer planes. Balloon barrage protection reinforcing plates and cable cutters are fitted in the leading edge.

Spars

3. The front and rear spars are built up in three sections from hiduminium extruded top and bottom booms and alclad sheet webs; vertical top hat stiffeners are riveted on to the webs. The centre section spars pass through the fuselage, the booms being left solid at the fuselage transport joints at the engine ribs and at the outer plane joint, but milled out for lightening purposes elsewhere along their length. The centre and outer planes are interconnected by forged shackles on the spar top and bottom booms secured by bolts which pass right through the booms (see figs. 2 and 3), and by joint plates bolted to each side of the spar web. From these joints the spar booms are tapered to form an angle section which extends to rib 5. Outboard from rib 5 the spars are built integrally with the wing tip (see para. 11).

Ribs

4. The ribs are formed in three sections separated by the spars. Except for some special ribs they are built up from light-alloy sheet, flanged at the top and bottom edges. Vertical top-hat-section stiffeners are riveted at intervals along the web and lightening holes are situated between the bays formed by these stiffeners. A light-alloy channel-section boom is riveted along the top and bottom of the centre and rear sections of the ribs to stiffen the boom where

the cut-outs occur for stringers, the stringers being attached by small brackets riveted to the ribs. The rib sections are attached to the spar web by extruded angle brackets riveted to the rib web (see fig. 1). The middle sections of the ribs are also secured to the spar booms by means of light alloy brackets bolted to the rib boom.

Centre plane

5. This section of the main plane is built integral with the fuselage centre portion. Between the spars, on each side of the fuselage is housed a detachable fuel tank, secured by straps in five bearer ribs. These ribs are built up from flanged pressings, having a double web with diagonal stiffening channels between, and a reinforcing strip at the lower flanges, which follow the upper contour of the tank. The front ends of the ribs are shaped to receive the nose of the tank, the rear end being cut away to allow the tank to be lowered when the straps supporting it are released (see fig. 7). The ribs are cut out for the top-hat-section stringers which strengthen the skin above the tank. A large assembly door, stiffened with top hat section stiffeners, is fitted in the bottom surface of the centre plane to enable the tank to be removed.

6. Outboard of each fuel tank is the engine nacelle which also houses the undercarriage main wheel units when retracted. The undercarriage support beams are bolted to the front spar, which is braced to the rear spar, at this point, by two engine mounting ribs. These ribs are constructed of light-alloy channels, with upper and lower booms, vertical and diagonal bracing members, and front and rear vertical end channels.

7. The ribs are attached to the spars by forged nickel chrome steel attachment brackets bolted into the ends of the booms. The top skin over the undercarriage housing between the spars is supported by two intermediate ribs, braced by transverse stringers. Attachment brackets for the stringers are fitted at the cut-outs. The trailing edge section of the centre plane aft of the rear spar is detachable, and carries the inner trailing edge flaps. In the starboard trailing edge is provided a reinforced compartment for the dinghy. The trailing edge portions of ribs 23 and 32 are built up from a T-section top boom and an angle section bottom boom. The rear end of the rib has a web of light alloy skin with a bearing for the flap operating tube mounted on, whilst the front end is of open construction with a diagonal bracing member.

Outer planes

8. Each outer plane is constructed in three parts, the front portion (forward of the rear spar), the trailing edge portion (which carries the flaps and ailerons) and the wing tip.

9. *Front portion.*—The front portion of the outer plane extends from rib 22 to rib 5 on to which the wing tip is bolted. Forward of the front spar intermediate nose ribs are interposed between the main nose ribs, and at ribs 6 and 20 picketing shackles are fitted between the nose ribs on the front spar. Between the spars the outer and intermediate tanks are mounted in special tank ribs. The outboard tank is mounted between ribs 11 and 14, in bearer ribs 12 and 13, whilst the intermediate tank is mounted between ribs 18 and 22, in bearer ribs 19, 20 and 21. These bearer ribs are of similar construction to the centre plane tank ribs, as also are the stringers above the tank compartment and the tank access door below. An illustration of the outboard tank mounting appears in

F.S./2

fig. 8, the mounting of the intermediate tank being similar, with the exception of an additional tank rib. Rib 22 is of open construction, having a channel-section top and bottom booms braced with channel-section diagonal struts. The joints are formed by gusset plates riveted to both sides of the channel. The remainder of the ribs are similar to those described in para. 4. Two landing lamps are mounted in the under surface of the port outer plane aft of the front spar, one on each side of rib 10. The outboard engine sub-frame is attached to the lower ends of two mounting channels on the front spar between ribs 14 and 17, and to a single mounting channel on the rear spar between ribs 15 and 16. Springs for Dzus fasteners are fitted in the undersurface for the attachment of the rear portion of the nacelle, which when removed exposes an access panel. Below the leading edge an access panel for the engine controls and services extends from the outer plane transport joint to the outboard nacelle.

10. *Trailing edge.*—The trailing edge is constructed from the rear portions of the main ribs mounted on an auxiliary spar. This spar consists of an extruded angle-section top and bottom booms braced with vertical angle stiffeners. The ribs are mounted in a similar manner to the main ribs, and are of similar construction to those described in para. 4. Ribs 5, 8 and 11 have additional reinforcement for the attachment of the aileron hinges. The trailing edge is attached to the main rear spar by stud bolts, and assembly panels are pop riveted on the underside to provide access to these studs.

11. *Wing tip.*—The wing tip (see fig. 6) is built on channel-section spars which form the continuation of the main outer plane spars. There are six ribs, braced by stringers and intercostals, the intermediate ribs being divided into three sections by the spars. The ribs and intercostals are pressed channel members, except for the inboard end rib of which the flanges are separate angle extrusions. The webs of the ribs and intercostals are slotted and fit together at the intersecting joints, where both members are continuous. The extreme tip of the wing is formed by an endsweep of laminated mahogany, which is cut away towards the end for the navigation lamp in the leading edge and the air-to-air recognition lamps in the trailing edge. Transparent mouldings are fitted over the lamps. The skin covering is of light alloy sheet, and includes an access door in the undersurface adjacent to the transport joint.

Ailerons

12. The aileron spar is of channel section riveted to a sheet nose and stiffened by nose riblets which are riveted to the nose and spar (see fig. 5). The trailing edge, formed from alclad rolled section, is riveted to the end of each rib. The ribs aft of the spar are of alclad sheet, flanged along the top and bottom edges. The aileron is fabric covered and is hinged to the main plane by three brackets, and by an end bearing secured to the rib at the inner end of the aileron gap. Mass balancing is by a lead weight ($11\frac{5}{8}$ lb. $\pm \frac{1}{8}$ lb.) mounted in the nose of the aileron at the outboard end.

13. *Trimming tab.*—A trimming tab is fitted to the inboard end of the starboard aileron and is made up of a spruce framework completely covered with three-ply. It is attached to the aileron by a piano type hinge and is adjusted from the pilot's cockpit by means of a handwheel on the trimming tab control box.

14. *Balance tab.*—On each aileron is fitted a balance tab, constructed and attached to the aileron in a similar manner to the trimming tab. It is operated

This leaf issued with A.L. No. 51   A.P.2062A and C, Vol. I, Sect. 7, Chap. 2
November, 1944

by a connecting rod between an eyebolt on one of the hinge brackets and a lever on the tab (*see* fig. 5). Six holes (two in aircraft not incorporating Mod. No. 1272) are provided in the lever to allow for adjustment as described in the setting instructions in Sect. 4, Chap. 3.

Flaps

15. The split-trailing-edge type flaps (*see* fig. 4) are built up in two sections, the inner flaps being located in the centre plane, and the outer flaps at the inner end of the outer plane. They are operated by tubes and links, the outer flap tube being connected to the inner tube by a ball joint. The spars are formed from an inverted U-section, flanged outwards at the bottom and riveted to the skin. The leading edge is a channel-section member, and the trailing edge is made from extruded bar. Ribs flanged top and bottom run between these two members, and the whole is covered with sheet strengthened by corrugated sheets. The trailing edges of the ribs are stiffened by a light alloy strip riveted to the rib flange. The eyebolts in the spar which engage the connecting rods from the flap operating tube in the main plane, comprise eight in the inner flap and six in the outer, and are made from high tensile steel bar. Piano-type hinges are riveted to the flap leading edge, and to the dummy spar in the main plane trailing edge.

F.S./3

A.P. 2062 A | VOL. 1 | SECT. 7 | CHAP. 2

ATTACHMENT OF RIB TO SPAR.

SPAR.
RIB.

AILERON RIB.
REAR SPAR.
FRONT SPAR

ATTACHMENT OF STRINGER TO RIB

STRINGER
RIB.

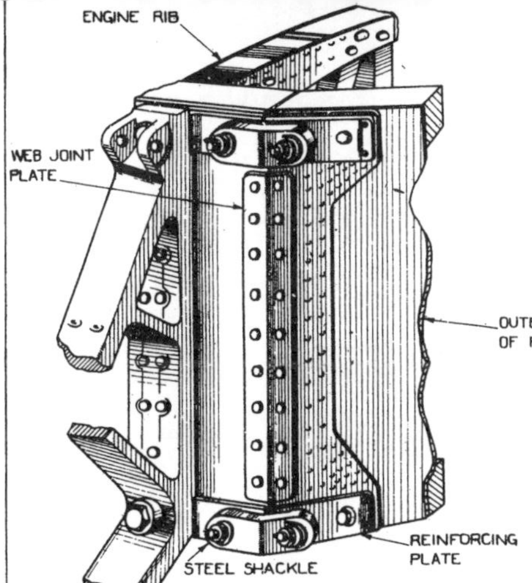

FRONT SPAR JOINTS

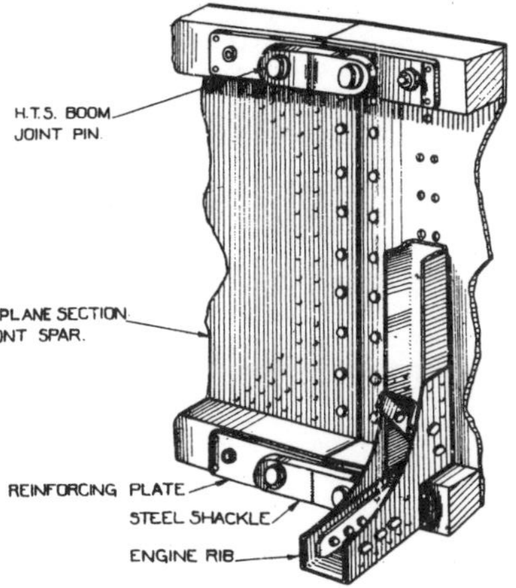

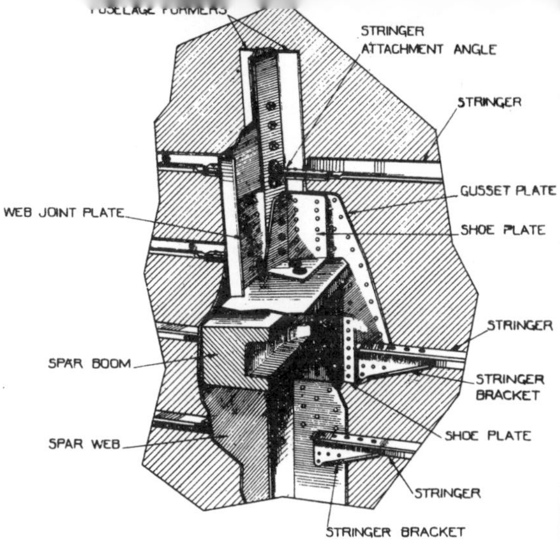

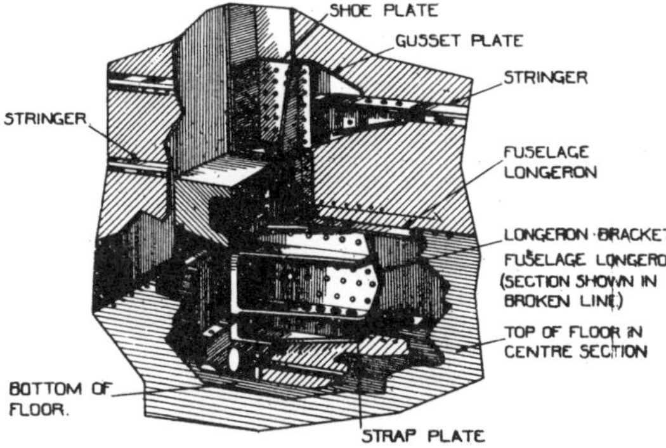

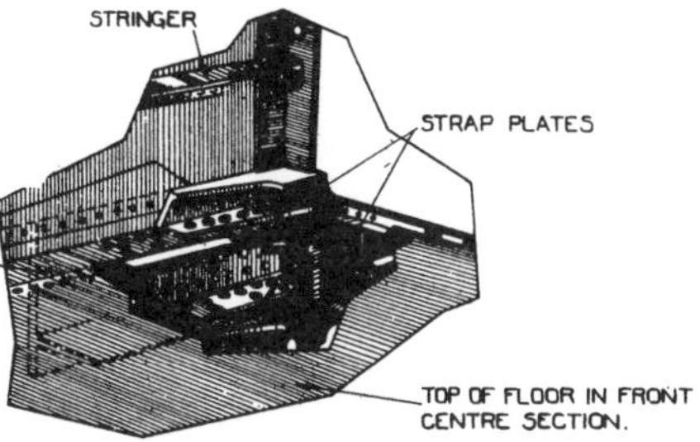

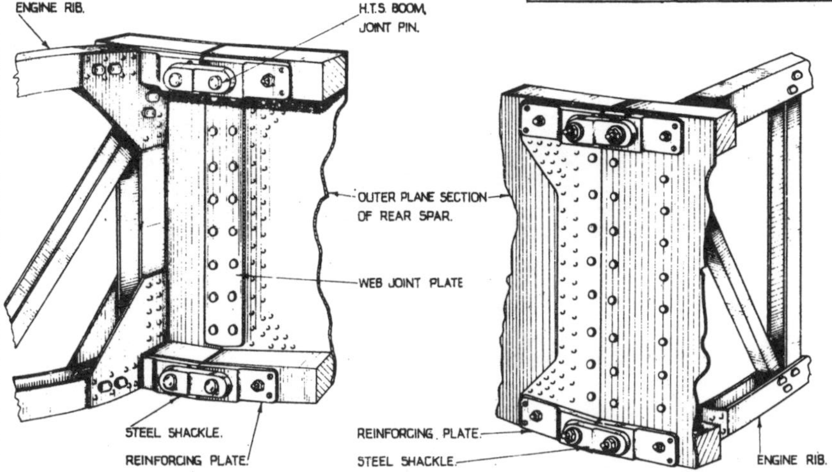

LOOKING AFT.

LOOKING FORWARD.

DETAILS OF REAR SPAR TRANSPORT JOINT - CENTRE SECTION AND OUTER PLANE.

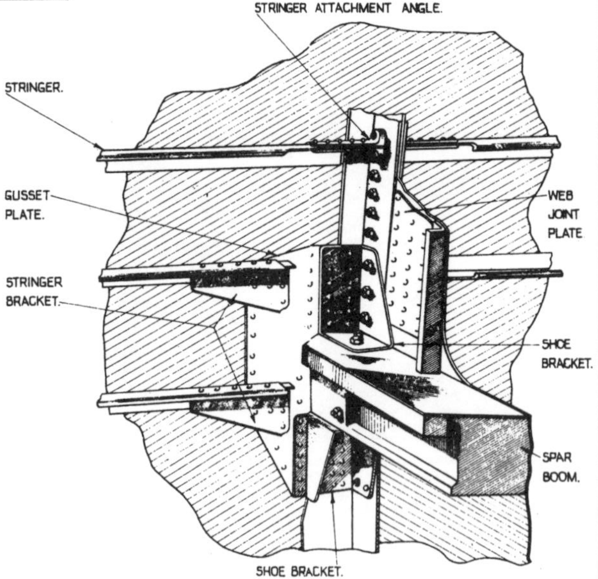

TRANSPORT JOINT - TOP BOOM TO FUSELAGE.

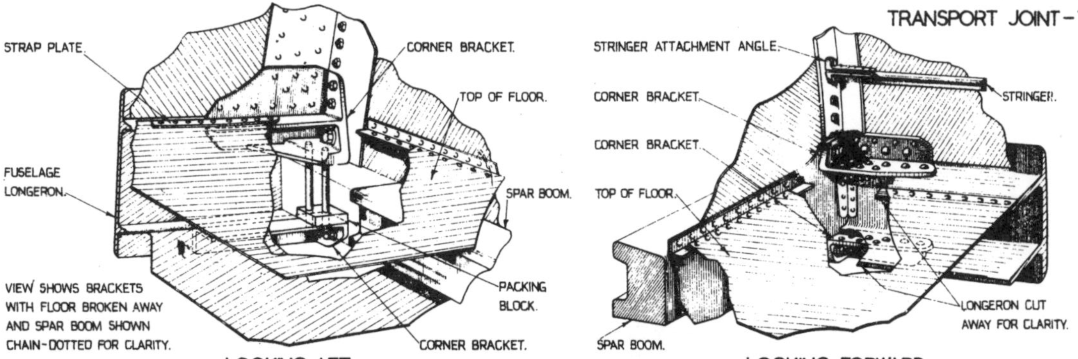

LOOKING AFT

LOOKING FORWARD.

TRANSPORT JOINT - BOTTOM BOOM TO FUSELAGE.

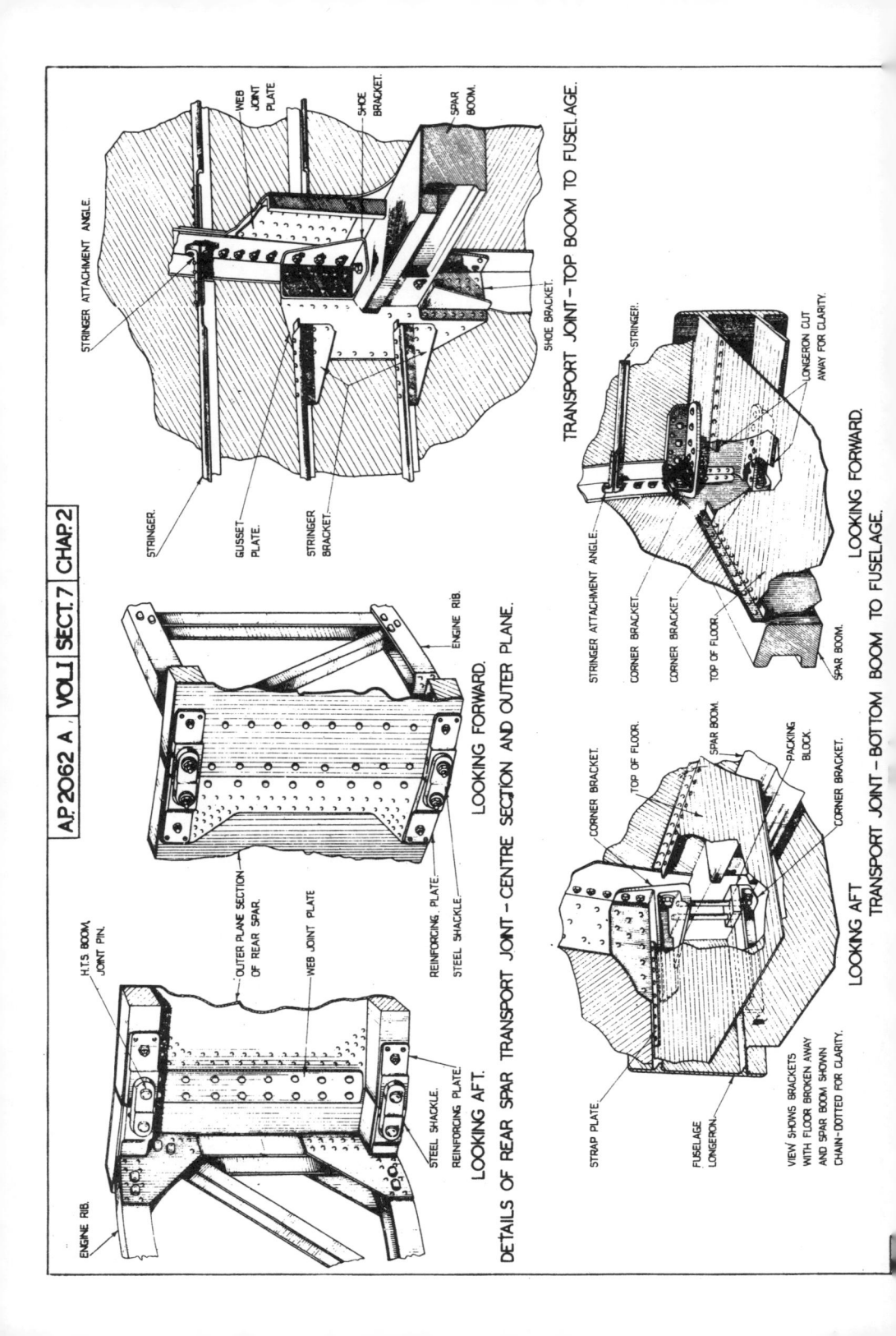

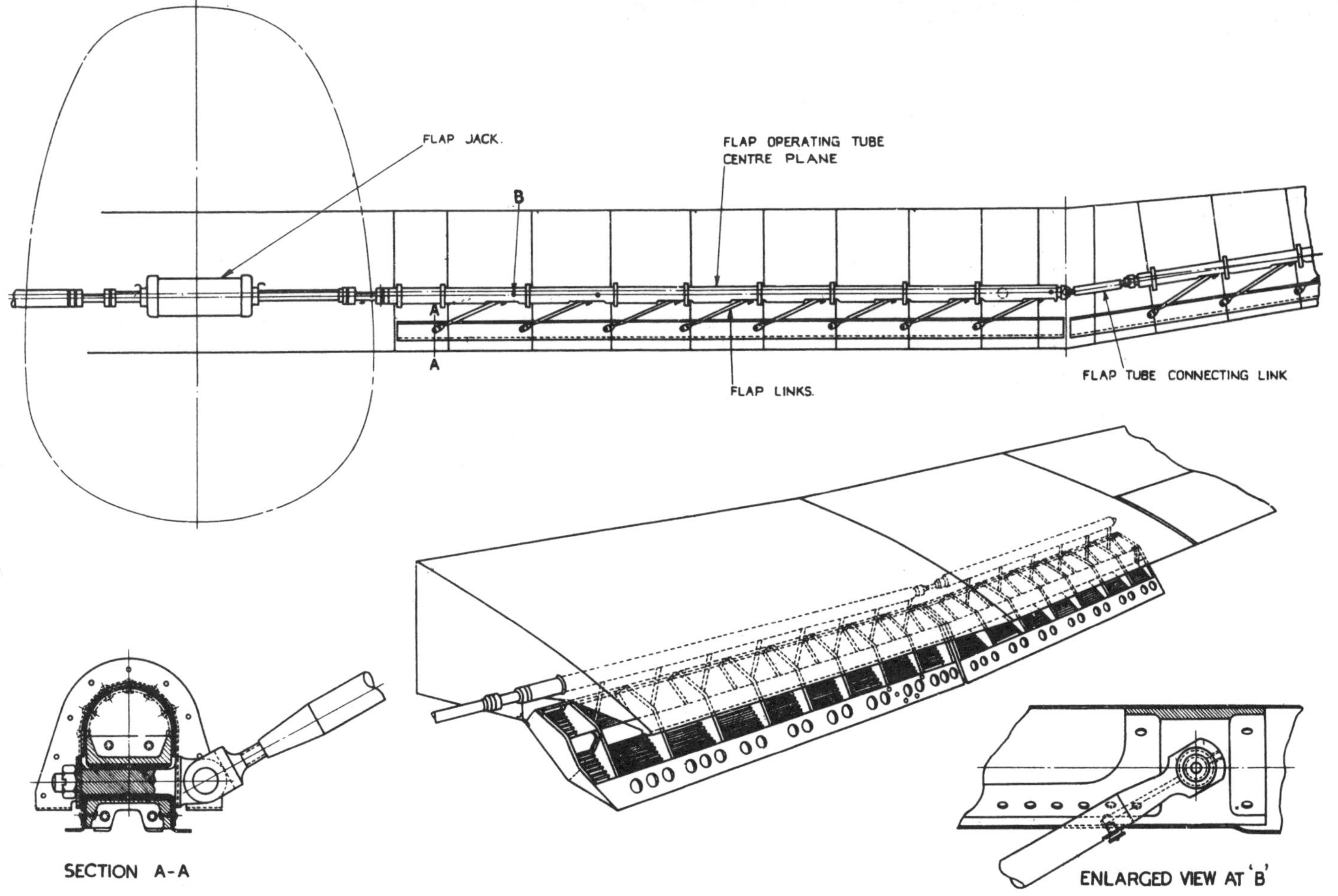

FLAP CONSTRUCTION

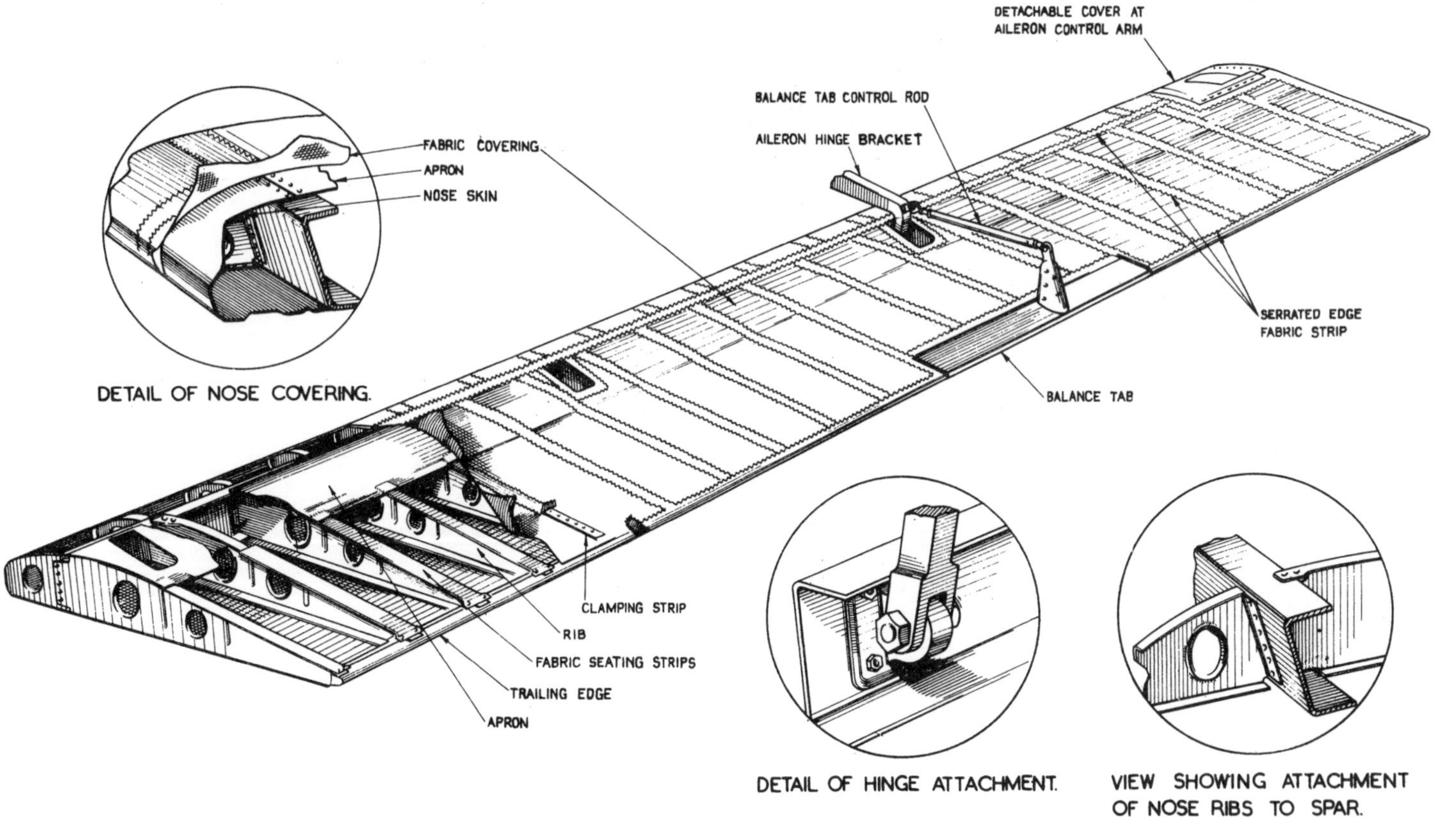

A.P. 2062.A. VOL.I SECT. 7 CHAP. 2

FIG. 5

AILERON CONSTRUCTION.

DETAIL OF NOSE COVERING.

DETAIL OF HINGE ATTACHMENT.

VIEW SHOWING ATTACHMENT OF NOSE RIBS TO SPAR.

FIG. 5

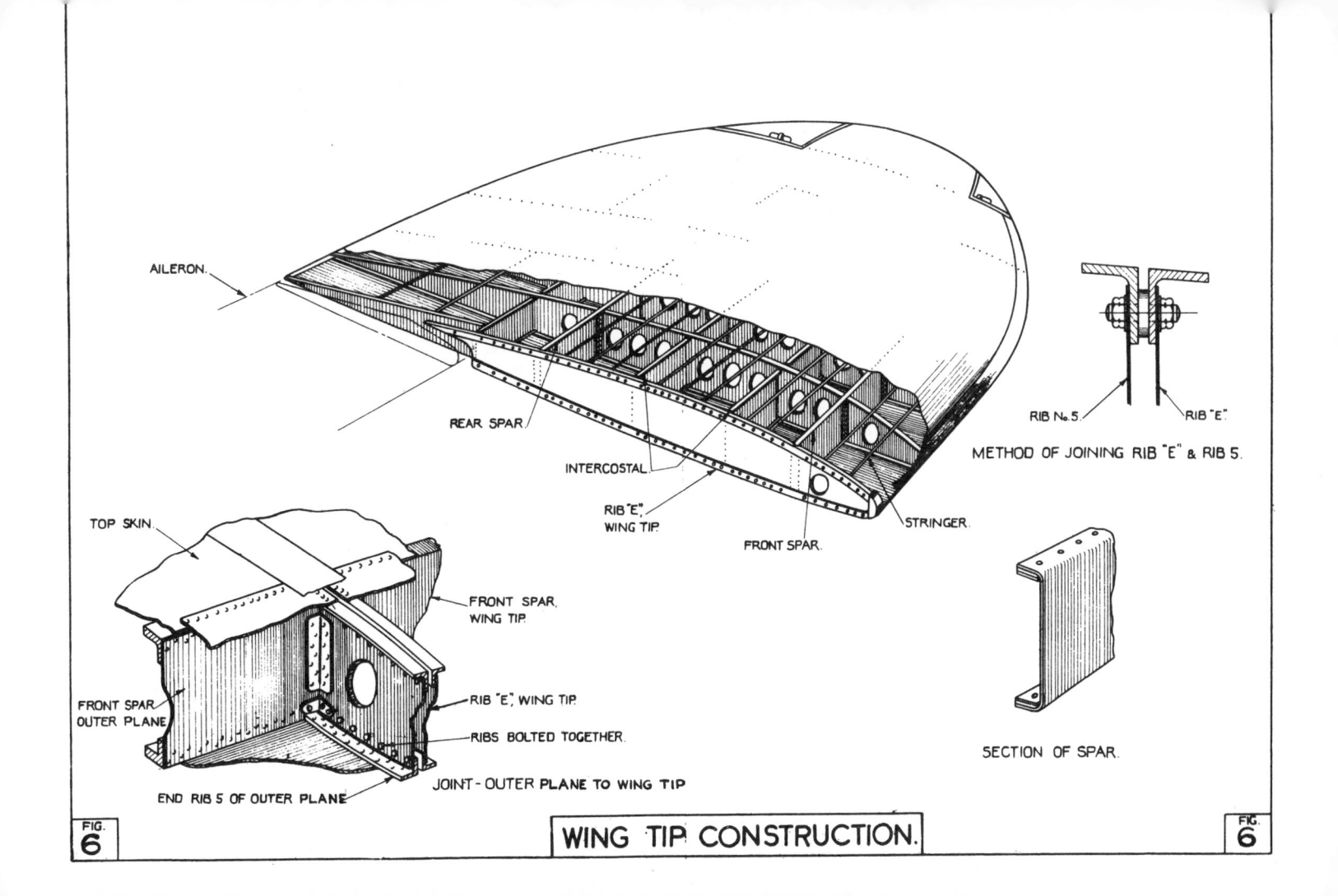

WING TIP CONSTRUCTION.

FIG. 6

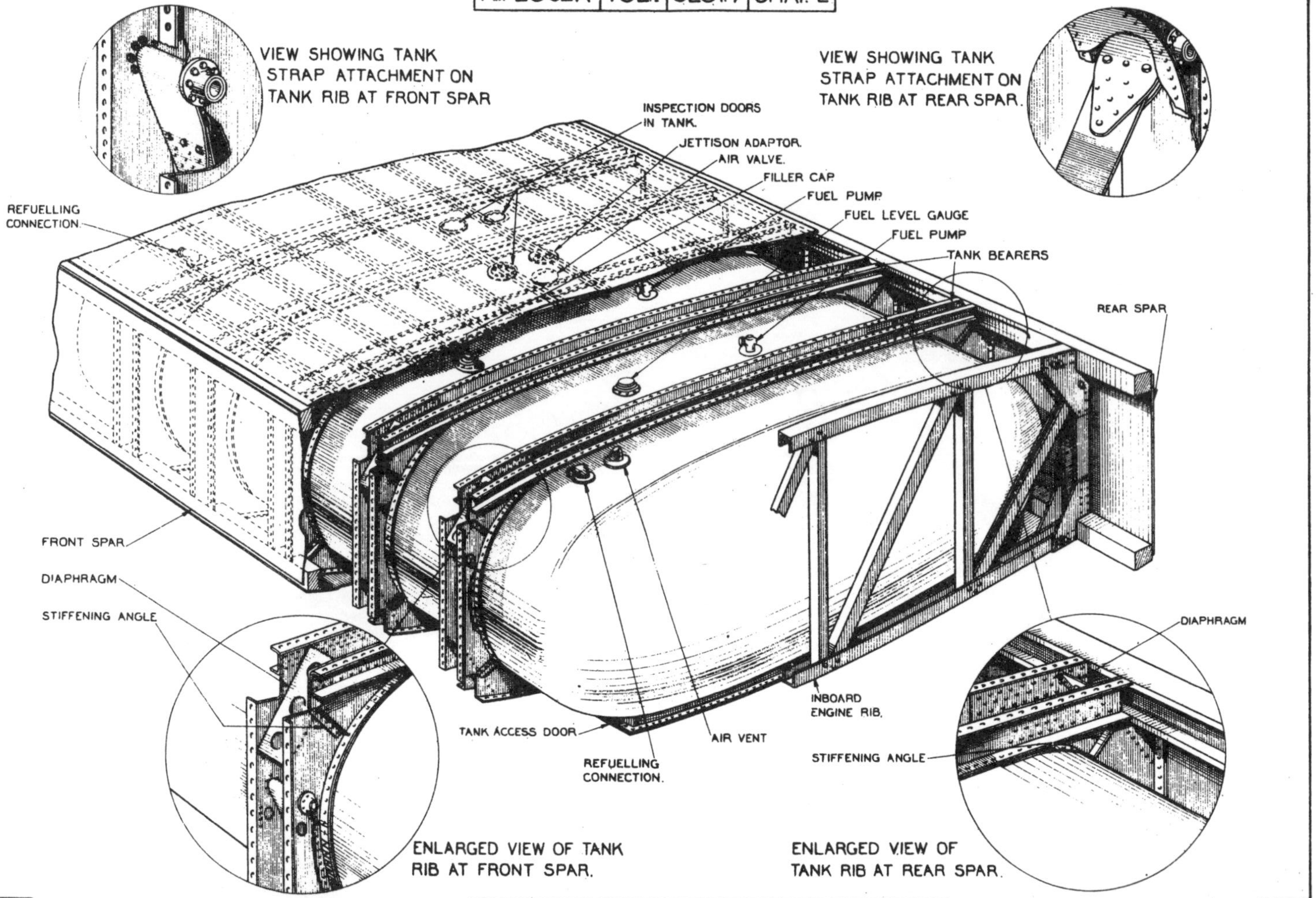

A.P.2062A | VOL.1 | SECT.7 | CHAP.2

VIEW SHOWING TANK
STRAP ATTACHMENT ON
TANK RIB AT REAR SPAR.

REAR SPAR

DIAPHRAGM

TANK BEARERS

INSPECTION DOORS IN TANK.

JETTISON ADAPTOR.
AIR VALVE.
FILLER CAP
FUEL PUMP
FUEL LEVEL GAUGE
FUEL PUMP

INBOARD ENGINE RIB.

STIFFENING ANGLE

ENLARGED VIEW OF
TANK RIB AT REAR SPAR.

AIR VENT

REFUELLING CONNECTION.

TANK ACCESS DOOR

ENLARGED VIEW OF TANK RIB AT FRONT SPAR.

VIEW SHOWING TANK
STRAP ATTACHMENT ON
TANK RIB AT FRONT SPAR

REFUELLING CONNECTION

FRONT SPAR
DIAPHRAGM
STIFFENING ANGLE

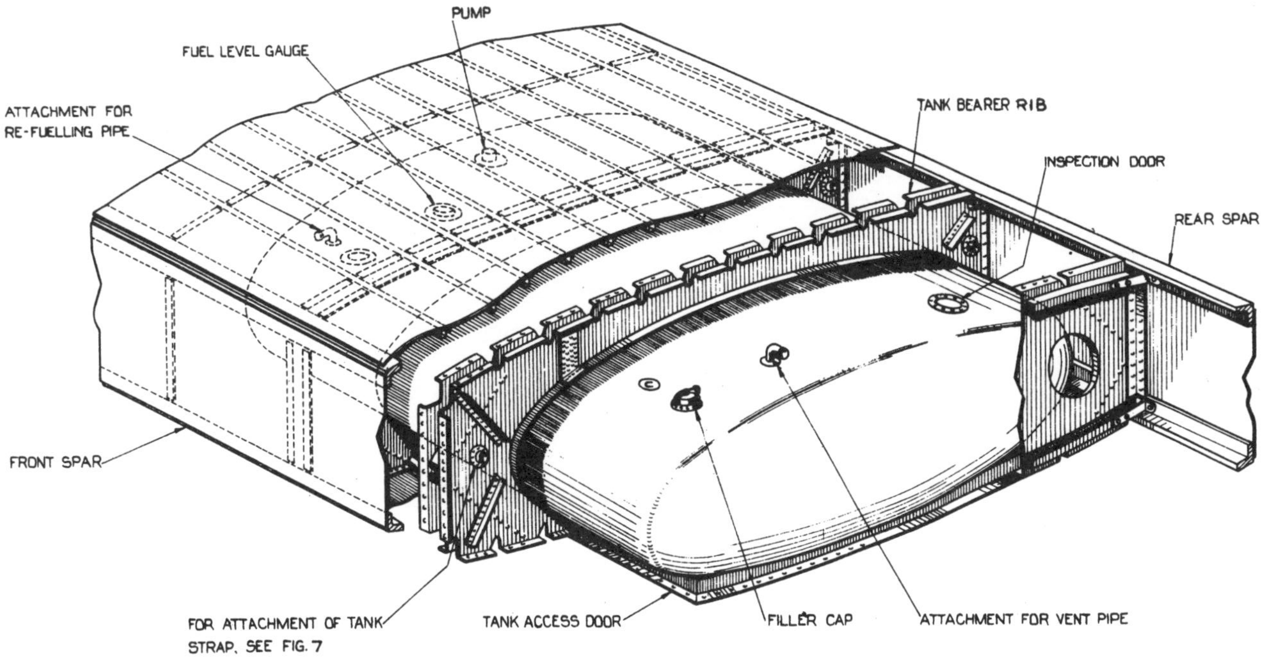

FUEL TANK MOUNTING – OUTBOARD

May, 1942
Issued with A.L. 6

A.P.2062A, VOL. I

SECTION 7—DESIGN AND CONSTRUCTION OF AIRFRAME

CHAPTER 3—TAIL UNIT

LIST OF CONTENTS

	Para.
General	1
Tail plane	2
Elevators	3
Trimming tab	4
Balance tab	5
Fins	6
Rudders	7
Trimming tab	8

LIST OF ILLUSTRATIONS

	Fig.
Tail plane spar joints	1
Tail plane construction	2
Fin and rudder construction	3
Joint of tail plane and fin	4
Elevator construction	5
Elevator balance tab	6
Elevator torque tube	7

F.S./1.

This page amended by A.L. No. 32
November, 1943

A.P.2062A, VOL. I, SECT. 7

CHAPTER 3—TAIL UNIT

General

1. The tail unit consists of a tail plane with fins and rudders at the extreme outboard ends, and a port and starboard elevator. Trimming tabs are fitted in the trailing edges of the rudders whilst the elevators have trimming and balance tabs fitted in the trailing edges. The tail plane is constructed in halves, the inboard ends between the spars being secured in the rear end of the fuselage to formers 35 and 38. The two sections of the tail plane are bolted together at the centre of the fuselage, laminum shims being fitted as necessary (see fig. 1). The fins are mounted on the outboard ends of the tail plane spars, which extend beyond the end ribs (see fig. 4). Both tail plane and elevator taper in plan and elevation from the fuselage to the tip.

Tail plane

2. The tail plane (see fig. 2) consists of port and starboard sections, each built up of a front and rear spar, sixteen ribs braced by transverse stringers, with a light-alloy skin riveted to the ribs and stringers. The leading edge of the tail plane is stiffened by intermediate nose riblets riveted to the front spar. The spars consist of top and bottom extruded angles with a web riveted between them. The ribs are made up in two sections, the nose fitted forward of the front spar, and the centre portion fitted between the spars. These sections are formed from sheet, flanged at the upper and lower edges, and having flanged lightening holes. The webs of the centre portions are also strengthened with vertical top-hat section stiffeners, except rib 14 which has angle stiffeners. At the intersection of the ribs and stringers, the ribs are cut away and secured to the stringers by small attachment brackets. The centre portions of the ribs, i.e. between the spars, are also cut away and fitted with attachment brackets at the spar booms. Three hinge brackets for each elevator are bolted to the rear spar and are of light-alloy; laminum washers are fitted as necessary between the spar and the brackets to ensure the position of the hinge-line. The inner hinge on each side is the datum hinge and is secured in its housing by circlips. The elevator does not extend the full length of the tail plane, as a small detachable trailing edge portion is fitted to the rear spar of the tail plane at the outer end and is cut away to allow for the movement of the rudder.

Elevators

3. The port and starboard elevators (see fig. 5) are connected inside the fuselage by means of a steel torque tube, which is fastened to steel liners in the inboard ends of the elevator spars by means of couplings fitted with spring steel shims (see fig. 7). Each elevator is a welded structure built up on a steel tubular spar, in which openings are cut for the three hinges. Sixteen braced ribs of welded steel tube, with diagonal bracing members between the inboard end ribs, form the contour. A light-alloy nose fairing is riveted to lugs welded on to the ribs, and the surface is covered with doped fabric. The elevator is mass balanced by means of a weighted tube mounted in the leading edge. With lead weights, only the centre tube extending between the inboard and centre hinges is used; with cast-iron weights the outer two tubes also are used. These weights are fixed during assembly and must not be altered. The eyebolts which form the hinges are fitted with ball races and secured in bushes through the steel hinge boxes welded into the elevator spar.

P3349 M   /1257 11/43 3950 C & P   Gp. 1

4. *Trimming tab.*—The trimming tabs at the inner end of the trailing edges of the elevators are built up from a spruce framework and covered with plywood, with serrated fabric tape at the edges. The tabs are mounted on piano type hinges and are operated from the cockpit through a screwed socket in the elevator spars.

5. *Balance tab.*—An additional tab is fitted outboard of the trimming tab, and is operated by means of a connecting rod between a lever on the tab and an arm on the elevator hinge bracket (see fig. 6). The loads on the moving elevator are thus balanced by the movement of the tab. A small mass-balance weight is attached to the balance tab.

Fins

6. The fins are built up from front, rear and intermediate fin posts with vertical stringers and intercostals, and ten horizontal ribs. The structure is covered with light-alloy sheets (see fig. 3). The fin posts are of channel section and are suitably stiffened by means of steel liners riveted inside the channel-section. The rear fin post has also additional stiffeners to take the rudder hinge brackets, which are bolted on to the rear face. The ribs are flanged at the edges and cut away for the stringers and intercostals which are attached to the ribs at these points by small brackets. Flanged lightening holes give additional stiffness to the rib web. The leading edge is of laminated mahogany, the skin being attached by means of countersunk head woodscrews. An aerial attachment is fitted in the top of the fin, with an access door in the outboard skin. Detachable panels are provided in the skin to give access to the rudder trimming tab controls.

Rudders

7. The rudders are of similar construction to the fins (see fig. 3), and are attached to the fins by three ball race hinges which are bolted to the front face of the post. The skin covering is of light-alloy sheet with detachable panels to give access to the rudder trimming tab controls. At the front of the rudder post is a shroud which is cut away for the hinges, cuffs being fitted round these after assembly. The trailing edge is a light-alloy extruded section. Two mass balances are fitted, the upper balance consisting of two weights supported by tubular arms projecting forward, one on each side of the rudder, and the lower balance consisting of a cylindrical lead weight bolted between rudder ribs 9 and 10.

8. *Trimming tab.*—The rudder trimming tabs are hinged into the trailing edge of the rudder and are constructed from light-alloy stiffeners and end blocks completely covered with light-alloy sheet. The trailing edge of the tab is stiffened by a strip riveted between the two skins. A double-armed actuating lever is fixed near the bottom of the tab and two spherical steel mass balance weights are supported on brackets which project forward, one on each side of the tab.

F.S./2

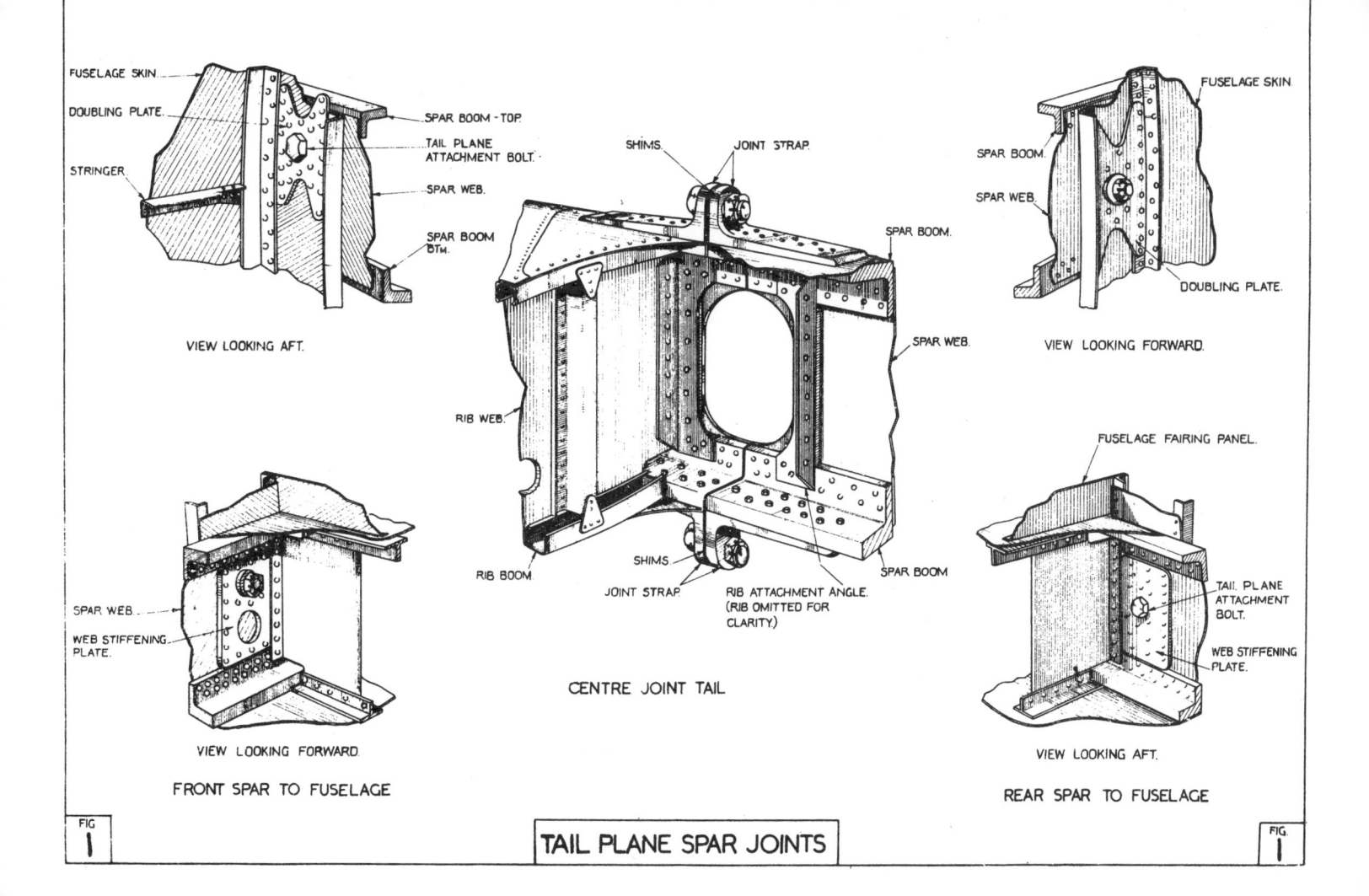

TAIL PLANE SPAR JOINTS

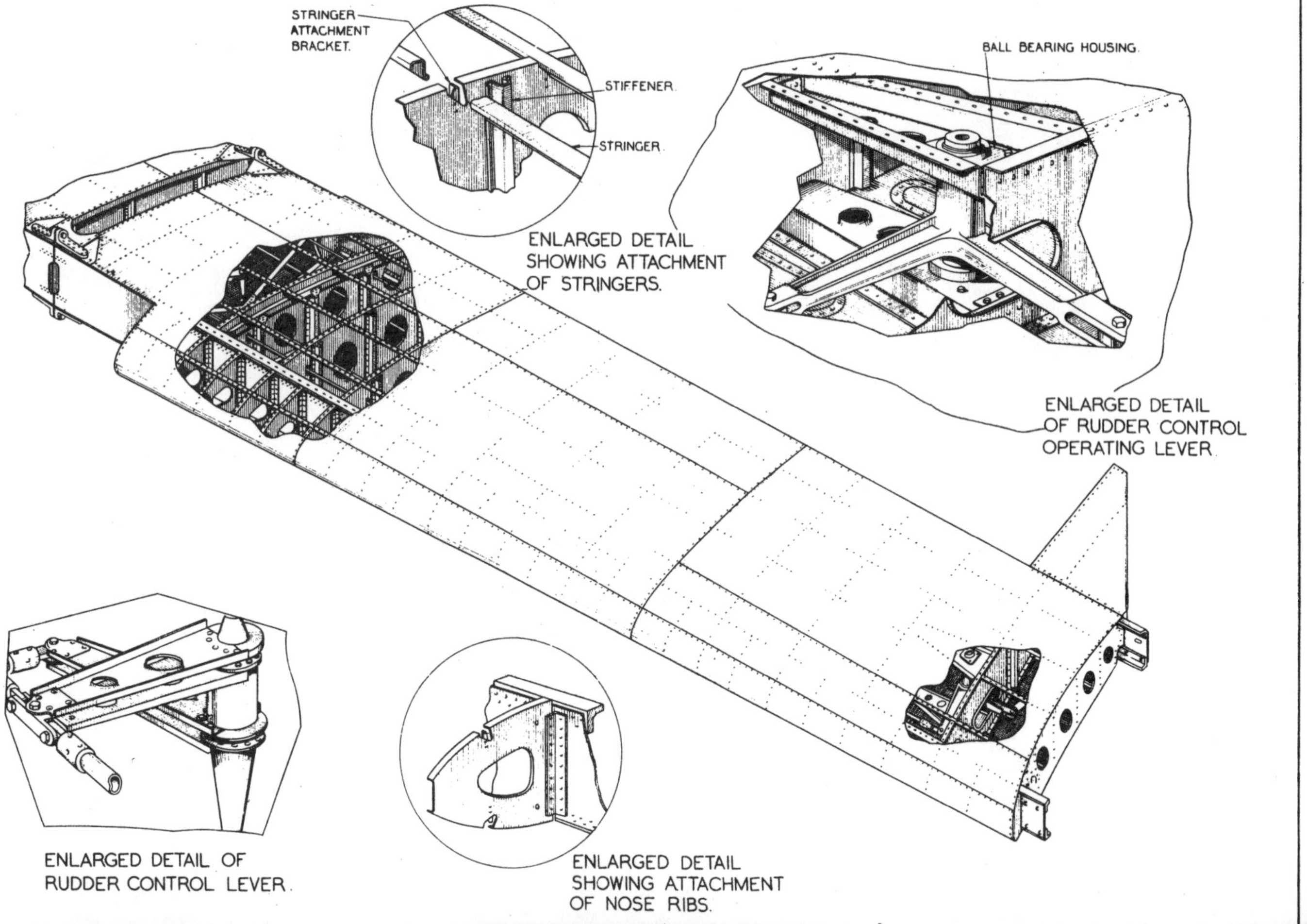

A.P.2062A | VOL.I | SECT.7 | CHAP.3

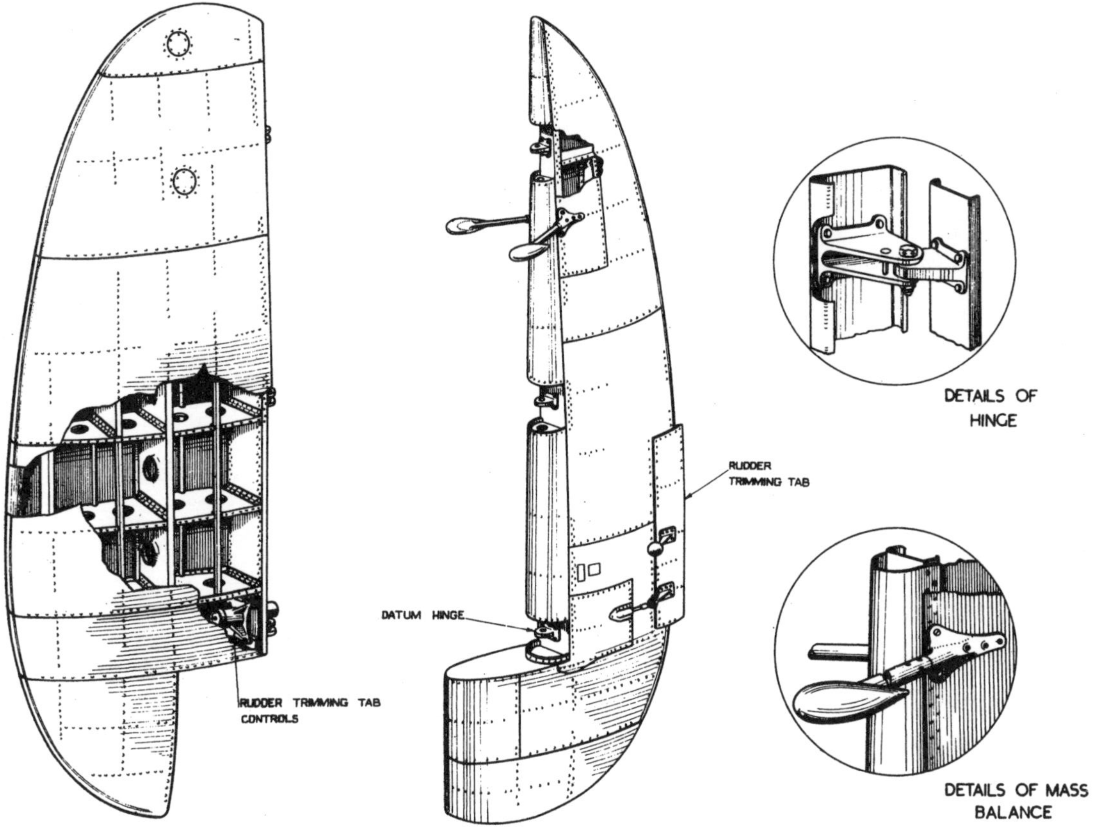

DETAILS OF HINGE

DETAILS OF MASS BALANCE

RUDDER TRIMMING TAB

DATUM HINGE

RUDDER TRIMMING TAB CONTROLS

FIN AND RUDDER CONSTRUCTION

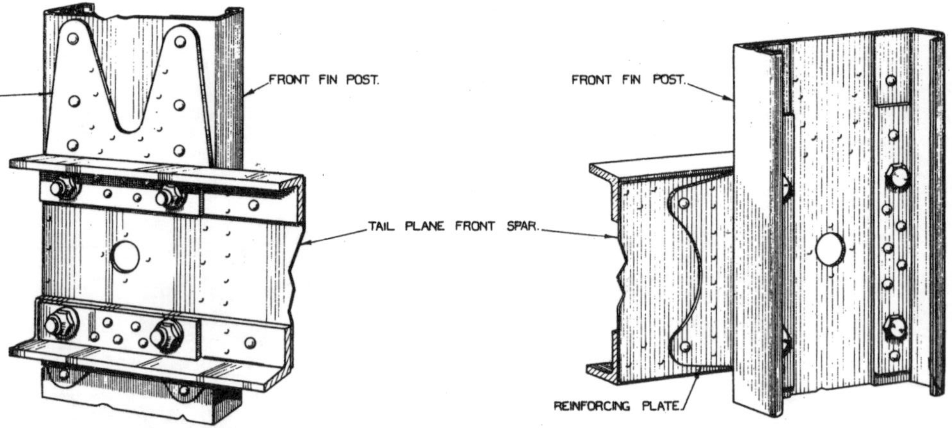

FRONT SPAR TO FRONT FIN POST.

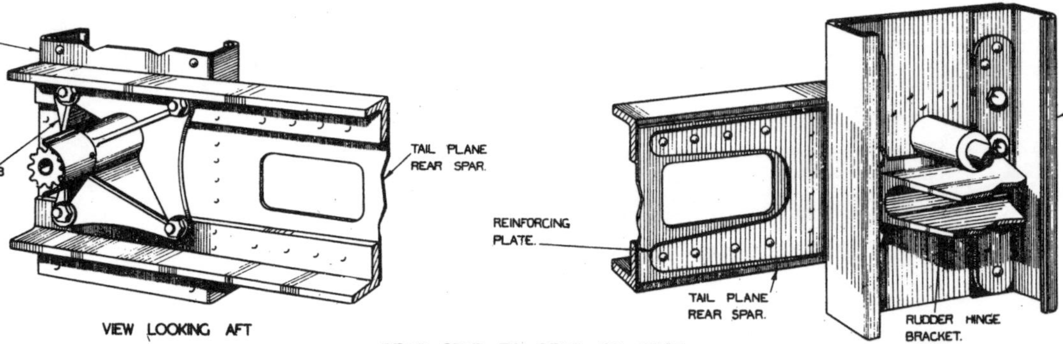

REAR SPAR TO REAR FIN POST

FIG. 4

JOINT OF TAIL PLANE AND FIN

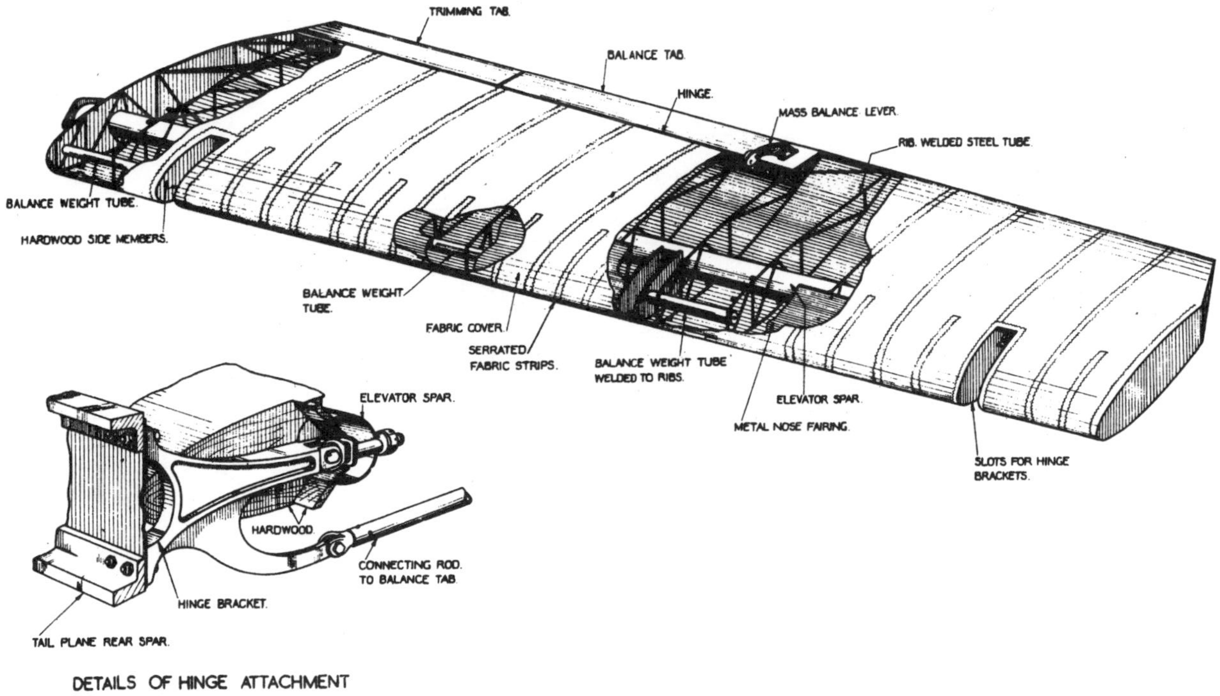

ELEVATOR CONSTRUCTION

DETAILS OF HINGE ATTACHMENT

A.P.2062 A&C | VOL.I | SECT.7 | CHAP.3

ELEVATOR UP, TAB DOWN

BALANCE TAB
HINGE
CONNECTING ROD
ELEVATOR SPAR
ELEVATOR
ELEVATOR HINGE BRACKET
TAIL PLANE REAR SPAR

ELEVATOR IN NORMAL POSITION

ELEVATOR DOWN, TAB UP

ELEVATOR TORQUE TUBE.

May, 1942
Issued with A.L. 6

A.P.2062A, VOL. I

SECTION 7—DESIGN AND CONSTRUCTION OF AIRFRAME

CHAPTER 4—FLYING CONTROLS

LIST OF CONTENTS

	Para.
General	1
Control column	2
Rudder pedals	3
Aileron controls	4
Elevator controls	5
Rudder controls	6
Trimming tab control gearbox	7
Elevator tab controls—	
Trimming tab	8
Balance tab	9
Rudder trimming tab controls	10
Aileron tab controls—	
Trimming tab	11
Balance tab	12

LIST OF ILLUSTRATIONS

	Fig.
Arrangement of flying controls	1
Diagram of aileron controls	2
Diagram of elevator controls	3
Diagram of rudder controls	4
Diagram of elevator trimming tab controls	5
Diagram of rudder trimming tab controls	6
Diagram of aileron trimming tab controls	7
Control column	8
Rudder pedals	9
Trimming tab control gearbox	10

F.S./1
B

A.P.2062A, VOL. I, SECT. 7

CHAPTER 4—FLYING CONTROLS

General

1. Normally single control is fitted with the Mk. IV three-axis automatic controls. A collapsible seat is provided for a second pilot on the starboard side of the cockpit. The ailerons are controlled by the rotation of the hand wheel on the control column, and the elevators are controlled by the fore-and-aft movement of the control column. The rudders are controlled from the U-shaped rudder pedals which are pivoted at the top and are mounted behind the pilot's instrument panel. The rudder, elevator and aileron trimming tabs are operated from a control box mounted on the pilot's floor on the starboard side of the seat. The arrangement of the flying controls is shown in fig. 1.

Control column

2. The control column (see fig. 8) is built up into a box section from light-alloy sheets riveted together. The centre panel at the front is detachable, being secured by screws and Simmonds nuts, to allow for easy access to the control chains and cables. In the top of the control column is the handwheel spindle and bearings and the sprocket for the aileron controls. The base of the control column is bolted to a cross shaft mounted on the underside of the pilot's floor. The handwheel incorporates a wheelbrake lever.

Rudder pedals

3. The rudder is controlled by means of conventional type U-shaped pedals pivoted on torque shafts behind the pilot's instrument panel (see fig. 9). The shafts are interconnected by means of spur gears causing them to rotate in opposite directions. To limit the movement of the pedals a stop bracket is fitted at the forward end of the pilot's floor. The pedals themselves are of tubular construction and can be adjusted by means of a spring-loaded ratchet (see Sect. 1).

Aileron controls

4. The ailerons are controlled by the rotation of the pilot's hand wheel, then by means of chains and sprockets to a torque shaft mounted on the main floor beneath the pilot's floor (see fig. 2). The control from this point is by means of chains, sprockets, tie rods and cables running along the port side of the fuselage to a double armed lever on the rear face of the rear spar. The lever is a light-alloy forging, mounted on an extruded channel section, a stop bracket being provided to limit the movement. A jointed light-alloy push-pull control tube, attached to the top arm of the lever and supported by Tufnol bearings mounted on the ribs, extends to another lever mounted on the fore-and-aft torque shaft in the trailing edge of the main plane at the inner end of the aileron. At the transport joint a double ended adjustment screw, with left- and right-hand threads, is screwed into the end sockets of the tubes and is locked with bolts after the initial setting. An access door is fitted in the upper joint cover. At the rear end of the torque shaft is mounted a rocking lever which actuates the aileron operating fork. The operating fork is secured by a centre pin through a bracket riveted to the inner end of the aileron spar, the aileron inner hinge being mounted at the end of this bracket. The lever on the torque shaft and the aileron operating

This leaf issued with A.L. No. 51   A.P.2062A and C, Vol. I, Sect. 7, Chap. 4
November, 1944

fork are both light-alloy forgings with ball races at all bearing points. A self-aligning bearing is used where the rocking lever connects with the aileron operating fork.

Elevator controls

5. To the lower end of the control column, on the underside of the pilot's floor, is attached a cross shaft mounted on two ball-race bearings. This shaft consists of a forging, bolted to the base of the control column and a transmission tube of non-magnetic steel on the port end of which is mounted a lever for the elevator push-pull tube and a sprocket quadrant for the automatic controls chain. Both the lever and the quadrant are light-alloy forgings. Stop brackets are fitted on to the pilot's floor to limit the fore-and-aft movement of the control column. From the elevator lever a jointed push-pull control tube supported by spherical bearings runs aft through the spars and formers along the port side of the fuselage (*see* fig. 3). The aft section of the control tube is of square-section and supported in square bearings of mild steel in formers 33 and 34. From a bracket on the square rod, a connecting rod extends aft to a lever on the underside of the elevator spar torque shaft (*see* Chap. 3, fig. 7).

Rudder controls

6. The rudder control push-pull rods (*see* fig. 4) are similar to those for the elevator running from a bracket on the port rudder pedal (*see* fig. 9) to a square section rod at formers 32 and 33, from which a connecting rod operates a lever between the tail plane spars. This lever is mounted on a vertical spindle which revolves in ball bearings, the bearing housing being attached to the top and bottom booms of rib No. 1. Attached to this lever is a second lever which is interconnected by means of push-pull rods to one arm of the L-shaped lever at each end of the tail plane. The outer levers are light-alloy forgings and are mounted in a similar manner to the centre lever. The second arm of the outer lever is interconnected with the actuating lever on the rudder by means of an adjustable connecting rod which has a ball race fitted at each end.

Trimming tab control gearbox

7. The control box (*see* fig. 10) is a light-alloy casting bolted to the pilot's floor, the end plates being detachable to allow easy access to the bevel gears which operate the various controls. These gears run in oilite bearings fitted in bosses formed in the casting. Each control has an independent indicator inset in the top of the box.

Elevator trimming tab controls

8. *Trimming tabs.*—The elevator trimming tabs (*see* fig. 5) are operated from a handwheel on the control gearbox, from which cables run downward to the main floor and then through the intercostals to pulley brackets on the port side of the main floor and on former C. From here the cables run aft along the port side of the fuselage, through fairleads on the formers in the bomb compartment to a pulley bracket on former 39. From here the cables pass up into the tail plane round a further pulley and then outboard in each direction along the tail plane. Chains attached to the ends of the cables pass round sprockets in bearings passing through the elevator spar. Each sprocket is screwed internally and has an eyebolt screwed into it which picks up a connecting rod, the other

F.S./2

end of which is attached to the operating lever on the tab. Rotation of the socket moves the connecting rod and thus the tab.

9. *Balance tab.*—The balance tabs on the elevators are interconnected to an arm on the elevator hinge bracket by a rod attached to a lever on the lower surface of the tab. When the elevator is moved the tab is automatically moved in the opposite direction.

Rudder trimming tab controls

10. The rudder trimming tab (*see* fig. 6) is operated from a handwheel on the control gearbox, from which cables run downwards to the main floor and then through the intercostals to pulley brackets on the port side of the main floor. From here the cables run aft along the port side of the fuselage, through fairleads on the formers in the bomb compartment to pulley brackets mounted aft of former 37. From here the cables pass up to a pulley bracket in the tail plane and then outboard in each direction along the tail plane. Chains attached to the ends of the cables pass round sprockets in bearing housings on the forward faces of the rear fin posts and are themselves connected together by a balance cable along the tail plane. The sprockets are attached to shafts which incorporate universal joints at the rudder hinge lines. Aft of this joint the shaft has a turnbuckle action and adjusts a connecting rod which actuates a short lever on the rudder trimming tab.

Aileron tab controls

11. *Trimming tab.*—The trimming tab is on the inboard end of the starboard aileron only and is controlled from a handwheel on the control gearbox. Cables pass from this control box to three double pulleys under the floor members at formers C and D, and then aft along the starboard side of the fuselage through fairleads on the formers in the bomb compartment to a double pulley at former 16. From here the cables pass up through the floor, round a further pulley, and through the fuselage skin into the trailing edge portion of the main plane. The cables are carried in fairleads in the main plane ribs and pass into the aileron to the trimming tab control gear (*see* fig. 7). This gear consists of a cable bobbin on a screwed spindle, operating a threaded sleeve on the end of a control rod connected to the tab. The bobbin is supported on the spar by a ball end which fits into a socket formed on the head of a special bolt in the aileron control forging, a retaining nut being screwed finger tight and secured by a locking plate.

12. *Balance tab.*—A balance tab is fitted to each aileron (see Chap. 2, fig. 5) and is connected to an eyebolt on the aileron hinge arm by a rod attached to a lever on the upper surface of the tab. Six holes (two in aircraft not incorporating Mod. No. 1272) are provided in the lever to allow for adjustment as described in the setting instructions in Sect. 4, Chap. 3.

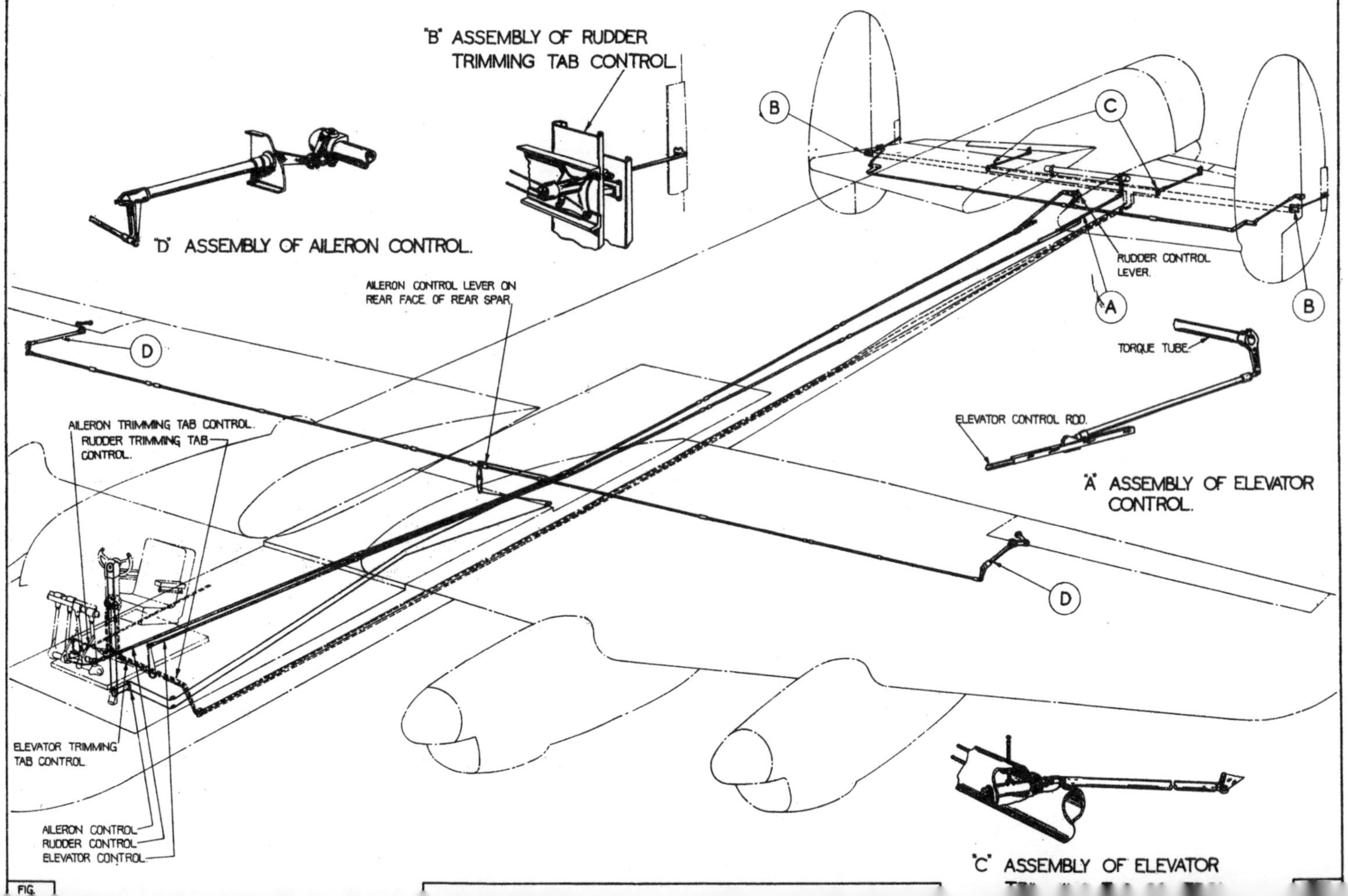

A.P. 2062 A | VOL.I | SECT.7 | CHAP.4

"B" ASSEMBLY OF RUDDER TRIMMING TAB CONTROL.

"A" ASSEMBLY OF ELEVATOR CONTROL.

TORQUE TUBE

ELEVATOR CONTROL ROD

RUDDER CONTROL LEVER.

"C" ASSEMBLY OF ELEVATOR

"D" ASSEMBLY OF AILERON CONTROL.

AILERON CONTROL LEVER ON REAR FACE OF REAR SPAR.

AILERON TRIMMING TAB CONTROL.
RUDDER TRIMMING TAB CONTROL.
ELEVATOR TRIMMING TAB CONTROL.
AILERON CONTROL.
RUDDER CONTROL.
ELEVATOR CONTROL.

FIG.

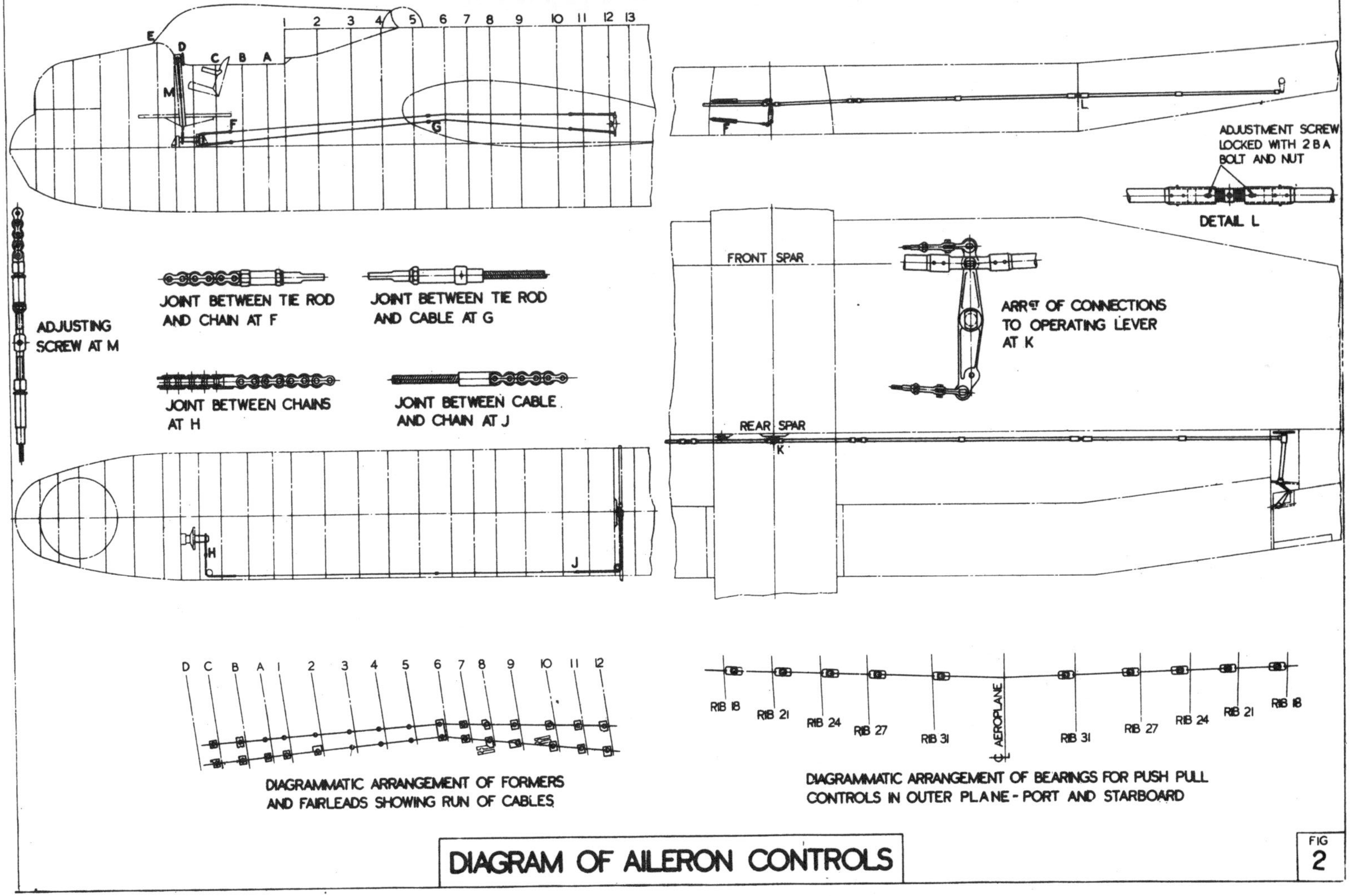

DIAGRAM OF AILERON CONTROLS

FIG 2

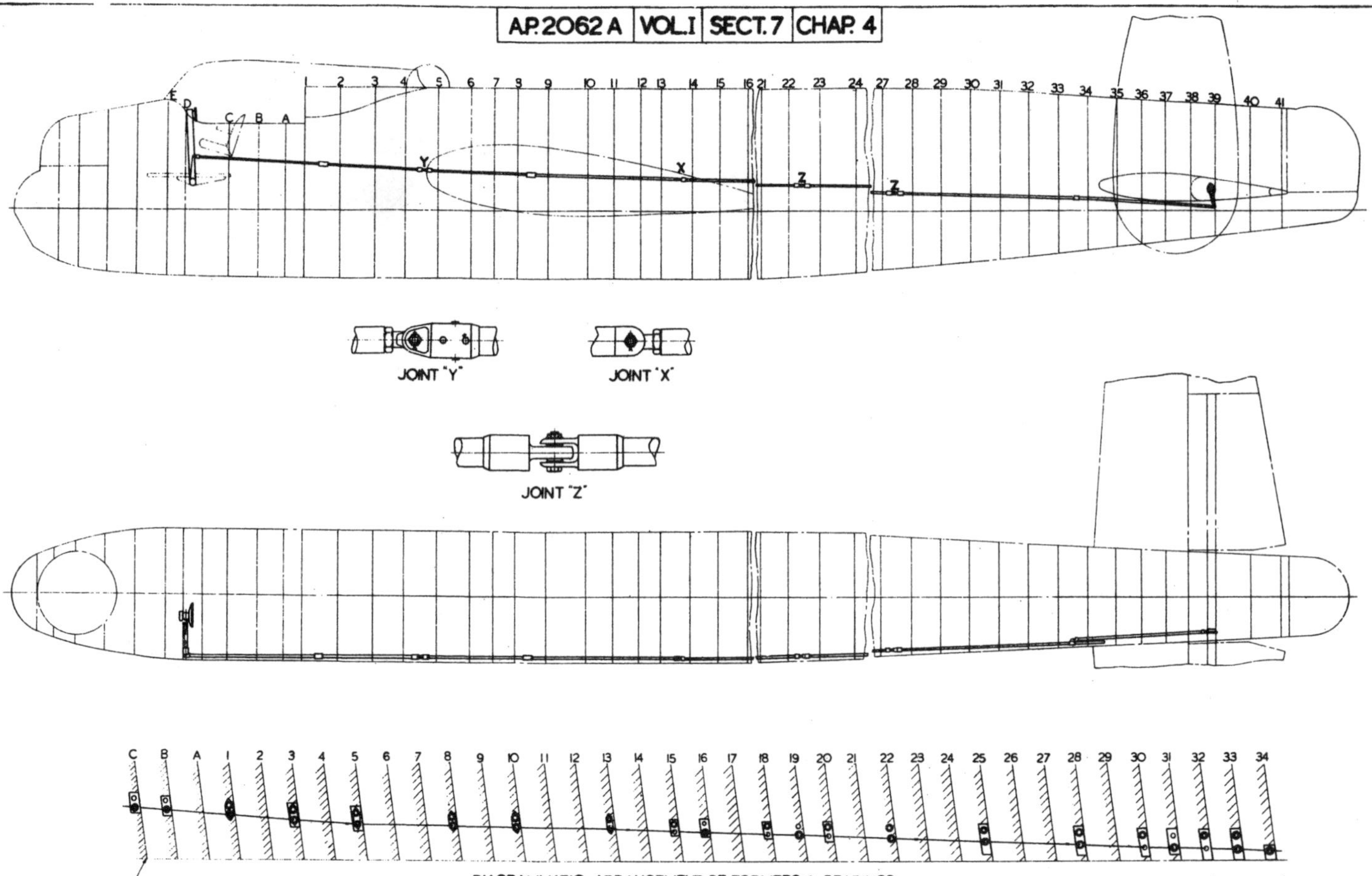

DIAGRAM OF ELEVATOR CONTROLS

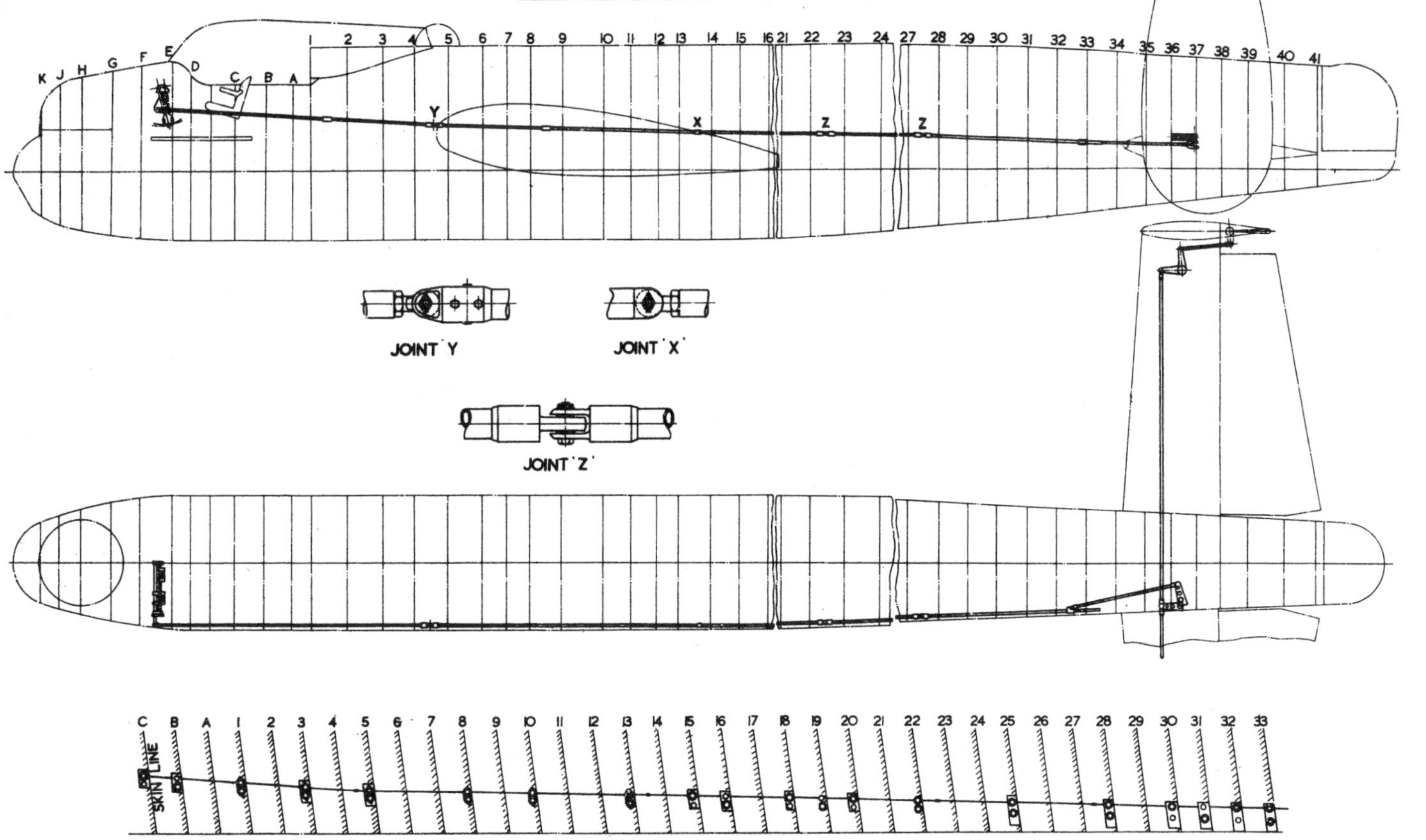

DIAGRAM OF RUDDER CONTROLS

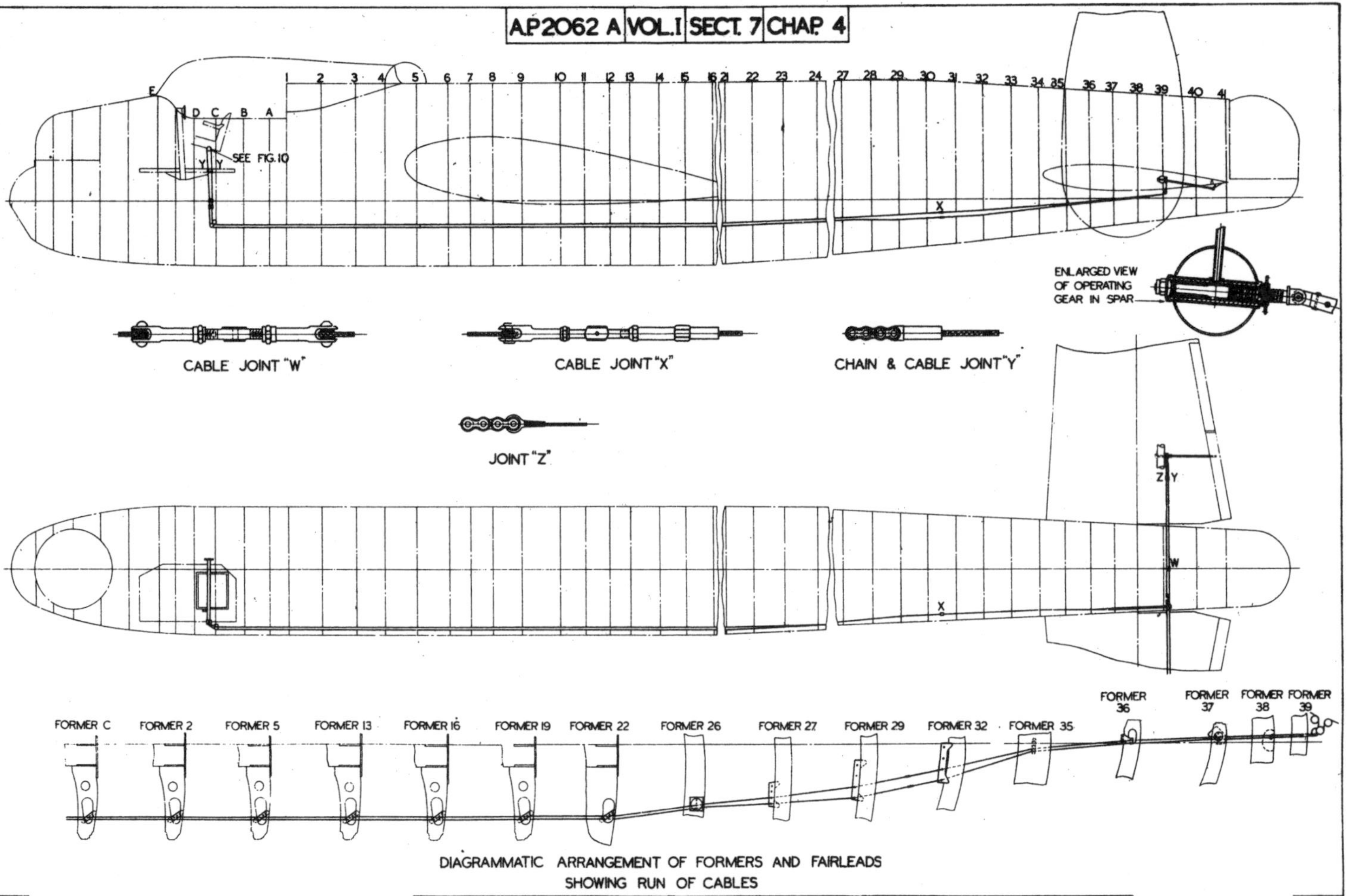

FIG 5

DIAGRAM OF ELEVATOR TRIMMING TAB CONTROLS

FIG. 5

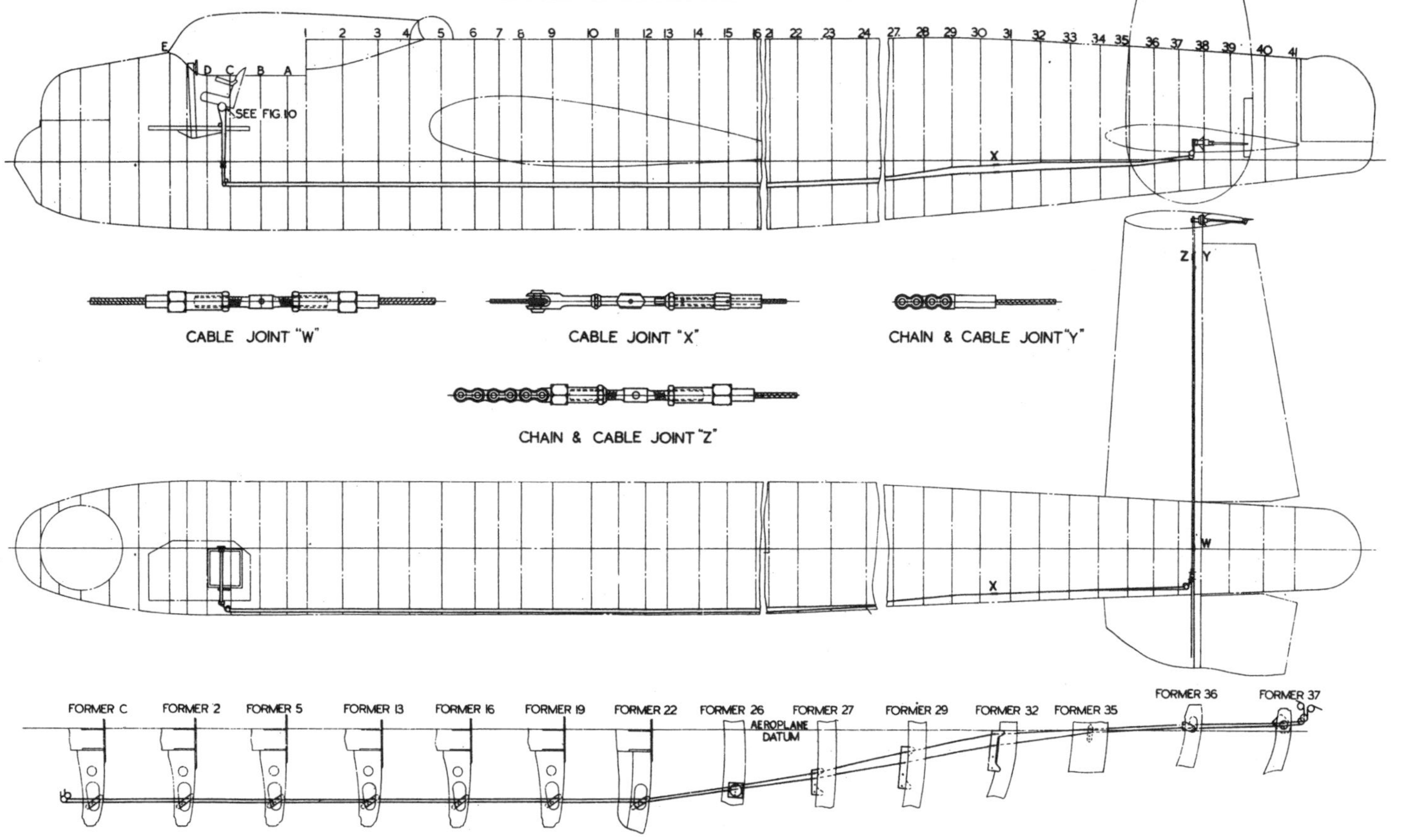

FIG. 6

DIAGRAM OF RUDDER TRIMMING TAB CONTROLS

FIG. 6

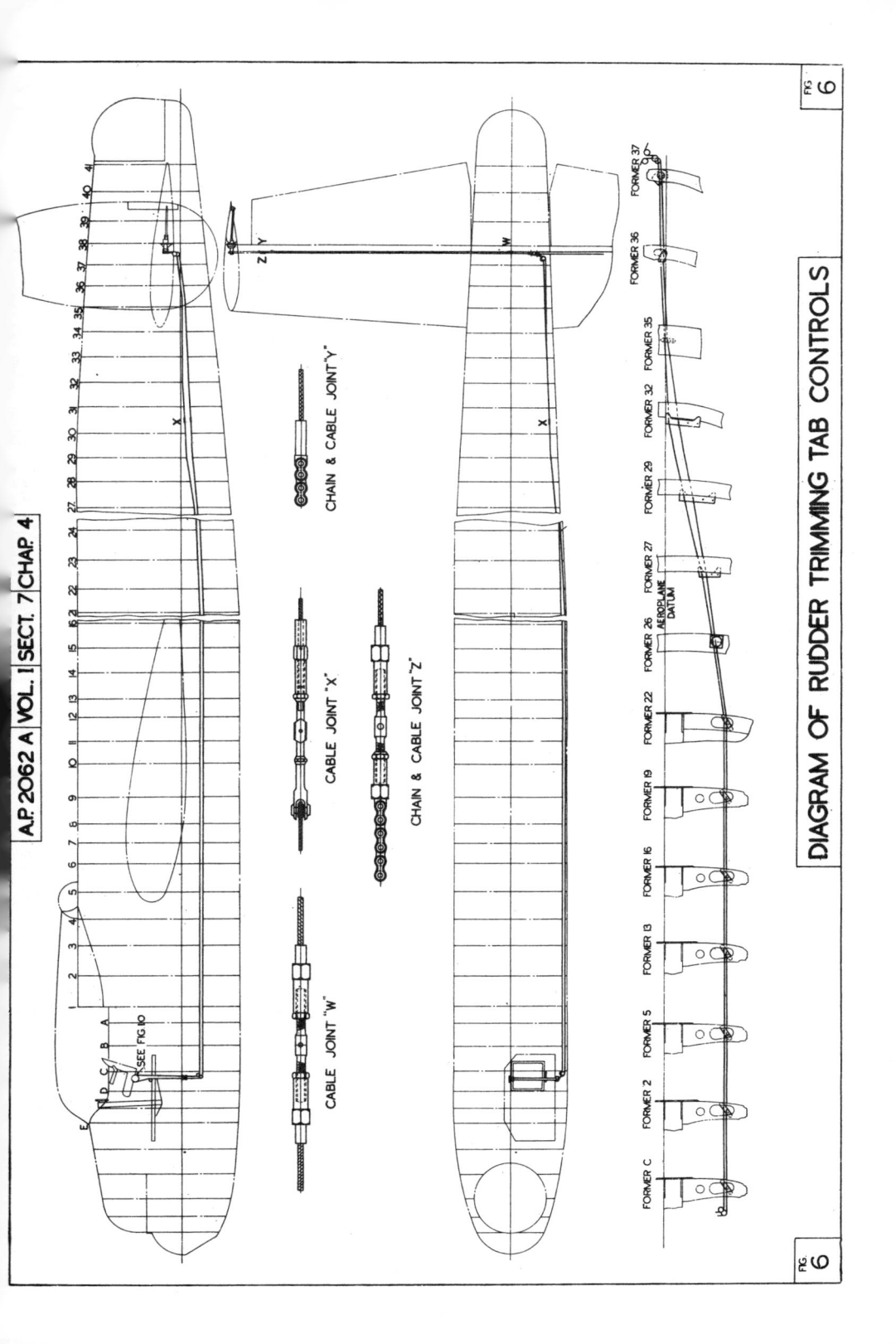

TRIMMING TAB CABLE & TURNBUCKLE JOINT AT 'A'

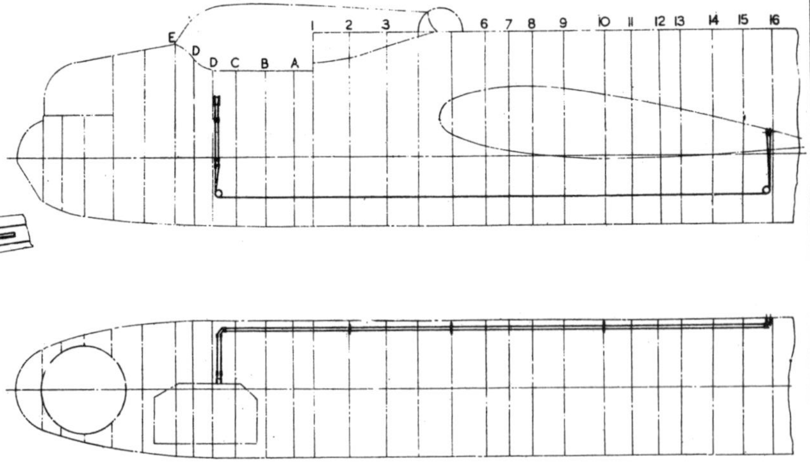

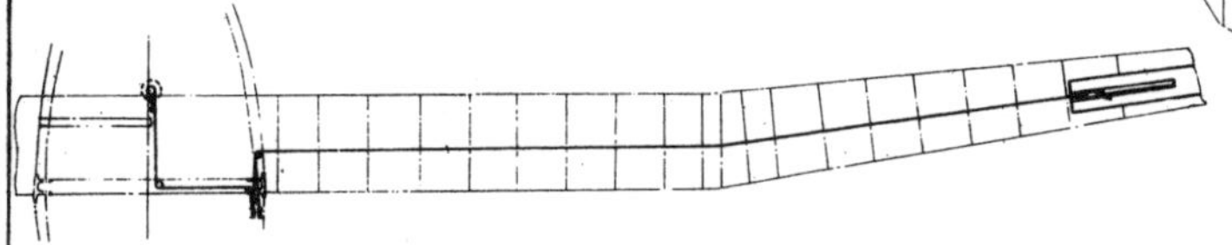

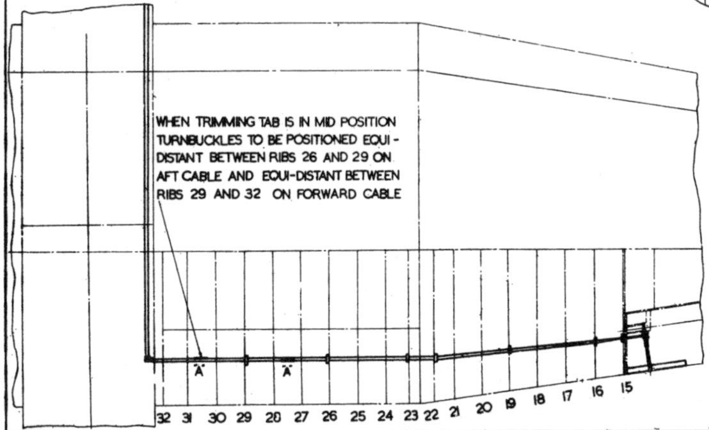

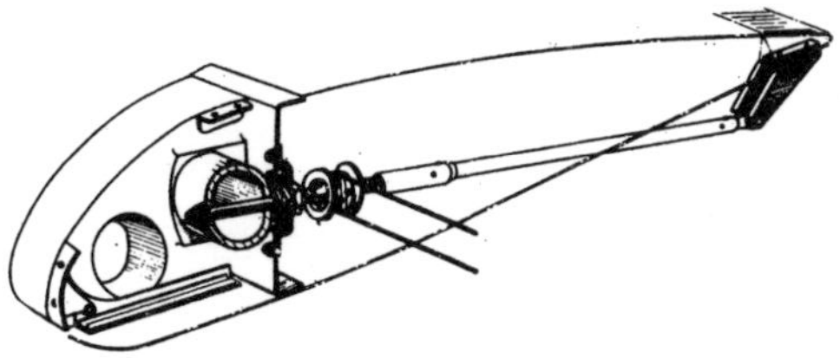

TRIMMING TAB CONTROL GEAR

FIG. 7

DIAGRAM OF AILERON TRIMMING TAB CONTROLS

FIG. 7

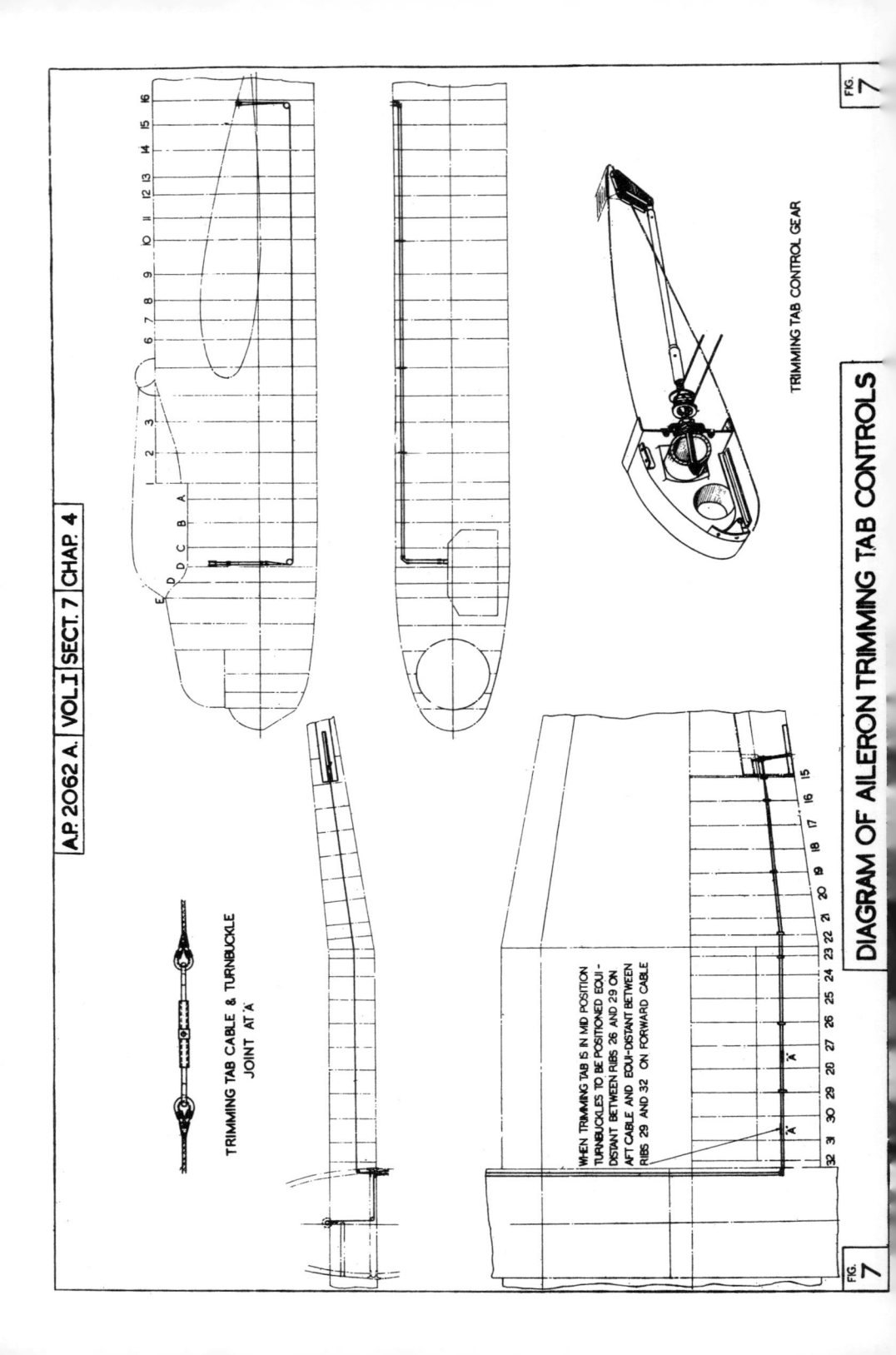

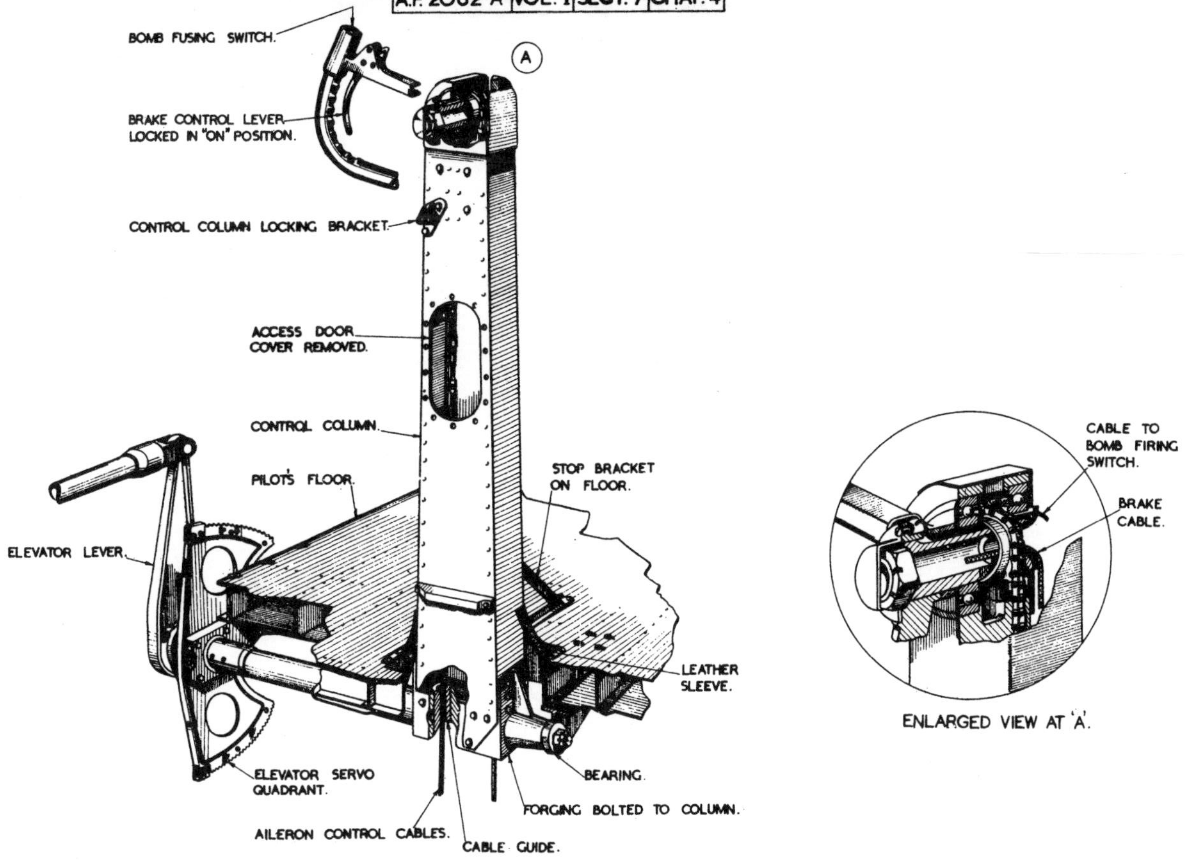

FIG. 8

CONTROL COLUMN.

FIG. 8

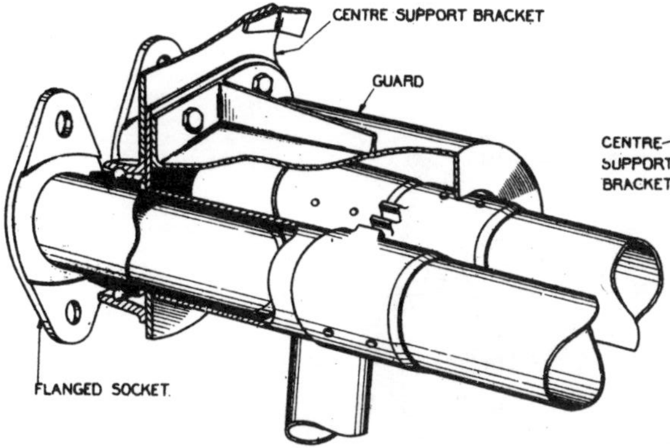

SECTIONAL VIEW OF CENTRE MOUNTING AT A.

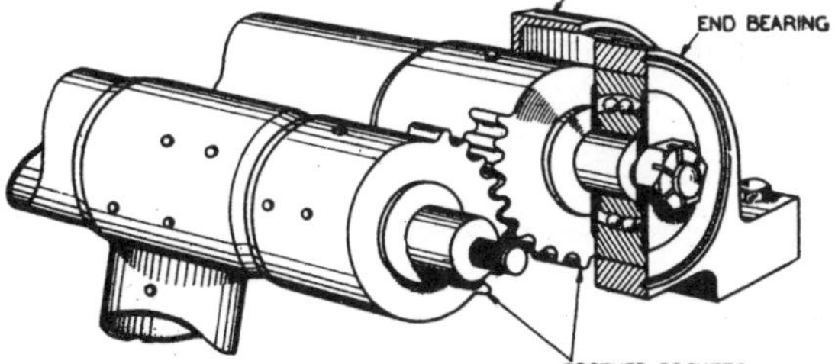

SECTIONAL VIEW OF END MOUNTING AT B.

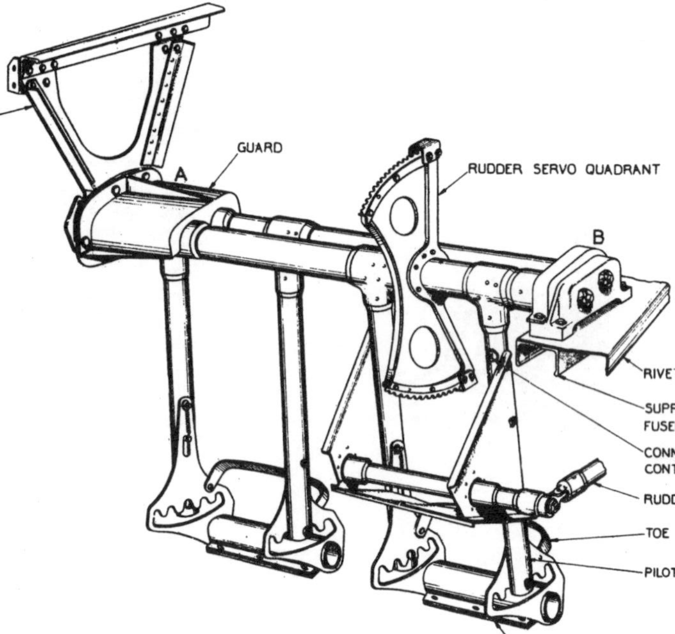

VIEW OF RUDDER PEDALS LOOKING AFT.

FIG. 9

RUDDER PEDALS

FIG. 9

A.P. 2062A | VOL.I | SECT.7 | CHAP.4

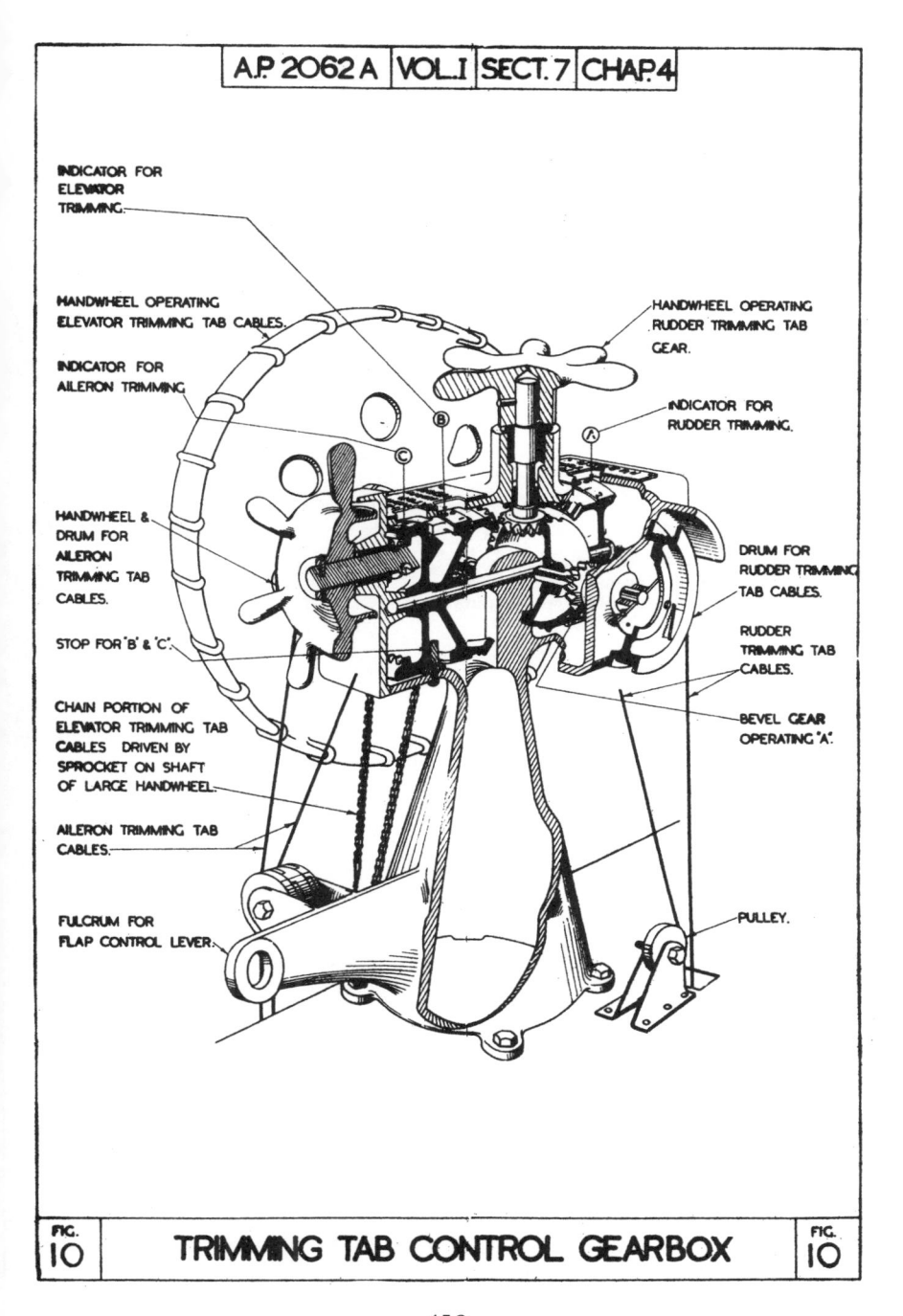

TRIMMING TAB CONTROL GEARBOX

FIG. 10

May. 1942
Issued with A.L. 6

A.P.2062A, VOL. I

SECTION 7—DESIGN AND CONSTRUCTION OF AIRFRAME

CHAPTER 5—UNDERCARRIAGE

LIST OF CONTENTS

	Para.
Main wheel units—	
General	1
Shock-absorber struts	4
Retracting strut and latches	6
Tail wheel unit—	
General	11
Shock absorber strut	12

LIST OF ILLUSTRATIONS

	Fig.
Main wheel unit	1
Main wheel unit shock-absorber struts	2
Retracting strut locking mechanism	3
Rear spar attachments—Main wheel units	4
Tail wheel shock-absorber unit	5

F.S./1

A.P.2062A, VOL. I, SECT. 7

CHAPTER 5—UNDERCARRIAGE

Main wheel units

1. *General.*—Each main wheel unit (see fig. 1) consists principally of two identical shock-absorber struts (see fig. 2) held rigidly together by bracing tubes and carrying a wheel between them. At the top of each strut is fitted an eye end which forms the attachment to the engine sub frame whilst at the lower end is mounted the wheel axle. The construction of the lower end allows easy removal of the wheel and axle. Brake torque load is transmitted to the shock-absorbers through links connected between the lower end fitting of each strut and the brake drum.

2. At the lower end of each shock-absorber strut is an attachment for the jointed retracting strut, the other end of which hinges in a bracket mounted on the bottom boom of the rear spar of the main plane. At the joint in the retracting strut is the locking mechanism (see fig. 3) which secures the unit in its UP or DOWN position. The piston rod of the retracting jack is also attached at this joint and the cylinder of the jack is hinged about a hollow shaft mounted in bearings on the top boom of the rear spar of the aeroplane, and through which hydraulic fluid is supplied to the jacks. Each pair of jacks is connected by bracing struts at the lower ends of the piston rods and a conduit stay at the tops of the cylinders. This conduit also supports an emergency air non-return valve through which fluid (or air in case of emergency) is passed to the jacks. The fitting of a balance pipe between the two shock-absorber struts ensures that the air pressure is the same in both of them and that their action is synchronised.

3. When the jacks are brought into operation to raise the units the initial inward movement of the piston rods releases the DOWN latches and further compression results in the "breaking" of the retracting strut and the complete retraction of the unit, at the end of which the UP latch engages a pin on the ribs at the top of the compartment to lock the unit in the retracted position (see Sect. 4, Chap. 3, fig. 31). When the UP or DOWN latches are operated an electrical circuit is closed and causes an indicator in the cockpit to indicate the position of the unit.

4. *Shock-absorber struts.*—The oleo pneumatic shock-absorber struts (see fig. 2) consist of an upper tube (A), attached to the aeroplane by socket (G), and a lower tube (M) which slides in tube (A) and on which the axle is mounted by means of the fitting (N1). The shock-absorbing action is effected by an assembly in the upper tube, consisting of an upper cylinder (H) containing compressed air, and a lower cylinder (K1) containing oil. As the cylinder (K1) is supported by the rubber rings (J1) the assembly is subjected only to end loads. When the strut is operated, cylinder (K1) slides up over cylinder (H) and oil is forced through the damping valve (H1) and enters the cylinder (H), where it further compresses the air. At the same time the piston (X) is driven up inside the air cylinder (H) by the piston rod (Y1).

5. Upon the load being relieved the damping valve closes and oil expelled from the air chamber by the air pressure is confined to passing through a small hole in the valve. Simultaneously the piston (X) is drawn down the air cylinder and the oil trapped between it and the damping valve can only escape through

This leaf issued with A.L. No. 46   *A.P.2062A & C, Vol. I, Sect. 7, Chap. 5*
September, 1944

the small hole in the damping valve and the two small holes in the piston, thus further retarding the recoil of the strut. To ensure equal pressure in each shock-absorber a balance pipe (F) is fitted.

6. *Retracting struts and latches.*—There are two retracting struts to each main wheel unit. Each one is in two sections, knuckle-jointed together, the lower end being attached to the shock-absorber unit and the upper end hinged to a bracket attached to the rear spar of the centre section. At the knuckle joint, and attached to the upper section of the retracting strut are the UP and DOWN latches which lock the unit in position.

7. The arrangement of the knuckle joint and latch assembly is shown in fig. 3. The DOWN latches (E) engage a pin (B) carried on the lever (K) and the side stays (C) attached to the lugs (D) on the lower section of the retracting strut. The lower end of the lever (K) is hinged on a pin (L) in the fork on the upper section of the strut. The pin (L) also carries the levers (S), which rotate with the lever (K). The UP latch (J) and the DOWN latches (E) are hinged on a bolt (F) in the lugs (G), both the lugs and catches being slotted to receive the restraining bolt (H) to which is connected the jack piston rod. Each latch is also slotted to receive the attachment pin (T) of the spring casing (Q), the spring plunger (R) being secured in the fork end of the lever (S). When the latches snap home they are held in position by these springs on both sides of the strut. The stop (M) which fits into a recess on the underside of lever (K) serves to keep the two sections of the retracting strut in line during the final movement of the down latches.

8. When the unit commences to retract the initial movement of the jack piston rod pulls the down latches off the pin (B), until the limit of the slots is reached, when further movement "folds" the strut and raises the unit. Lever (K) and pin (B) are at the same time pulled round in an arc, away from the latches, by the two stays (C). The UP latch is now free to drop back on to pin (T), which is then moving towards the end of the slots in the two DOWN latches under the action of levers (S). With pin (T) at the end of the slots, the levers then depress the plungers (R) against the springs (P). Near the end of the retracting movement the UP latch is opposed by a pin, (*see* Sect. 4, Chap. 3, fig. 31), attached to a bracket between the engine mounting rib and the intermediate rib, which forces it back and further compresses the springs (P). As the retracting movement is completed, these springs force the catch over the pin, locking the unit in the UP position.

9. When the unit is lowered, the initial movement of the piston rod disengages the UP latch (J) from its pin. With this latch fully off, the unit drops under its own weight, after which full extension of the piston rod completes the straightening of the retracting strut and the lowering of the unit. During this operation lever (K) and pin (B) are returned in an arc towards the latches. The consequent movement of the levers (S) first withdraws the plungers (R) from the spring casings (Q), thus relieving the internal springs (P). The pin (T) is then drawn to the end of the slots in the latches which are pulled forward until restrained by the bolts (H). In the final stages of lowering, the pin (B) strikes the curved heads of the DOWN latches (E), which are forced back against the springs (O) in the casings (Q). As the movement is completed the springs (O) pull the latches (E) home over the pin (B), locking the unit DOWN.

10. The position of the unit is indicated electrically in the cockpit. When retracting the unit the final movement of the UP latch operates a micro switch,

F.S./2

indicating that the unit is locked in the UP position. Similarly the final movement of the down latches depresses a plunger on the micro switch (U), showing that the unit is locked DOWN.

Tail wheel unit

11. *General.*—The tail wheel unit (see fig. 5) is a fixed oleo-pneumatic self-centring type, secured to the rear fuselage by means of plug (A) and sleeve (N). The top of plug (A) fits into a socket behind the centre joint of the tail plane front spar upper boom and the sleeve (N) is secured to the tail wheel mounting beam (*see* Sect. 7, Chap. 1, fig. 9). At the bottom of this sleeve are a friction clip (O) and a bearing bush (F1). The wheel fork is fitted into the lower end of the sliding tube (U) and the axle is prevented from turning by the blocks (Q) which are held in position by bolts (R). The two lugs (G1) are for attaching a steering handle or towing bar.

12. *Shock-absorber strut.*—The case is formed from the lower outer tube (U) and the top outer tube (B1) in which the tube (U) slides. The internal cylinder (F) is attached to the end plug (A), and slides in gland (H). On the outside of the cylinder (F), at the lower end, is attached a self-centring bush (M) which, when the unit is fully extended, bears on another self-centring bush (Z) housed in the tube (U). The self-centring bush (Z) is prevented from turning by two keys which fit into keyways in the tube (U).

13. The cylinder (F) contains compressed air, and the lower tube (U) is filled with fluid. The inflation valve (E1) is screwed into the top of the tube (B1), and is the means by which fluid or air is fed via the standpipe (E) into the cylinder (F). When load is applied at the wheel the tube (U) slides over the cylinder (F) and fluid is forced through the holes in the diaphragm (X), lifting the damping valve (Y) and further compressing the air in the cylinder (F). When the load is relieved the damping valve (Y) closes and the fluid, which is now expelled by the air pressure, can return to the lower cylinder only through the restriction holes in the filter (A1) and in the diaphragm (X), thus providing a recoil damping action. The self-centring bushes (E) and (F) turn the wheel, so that when there is no load on the unit the wheel is in line with the centre line of the aircraft.

P5536 M   /G2058 10/44 3950 C & P **Gp. 1**

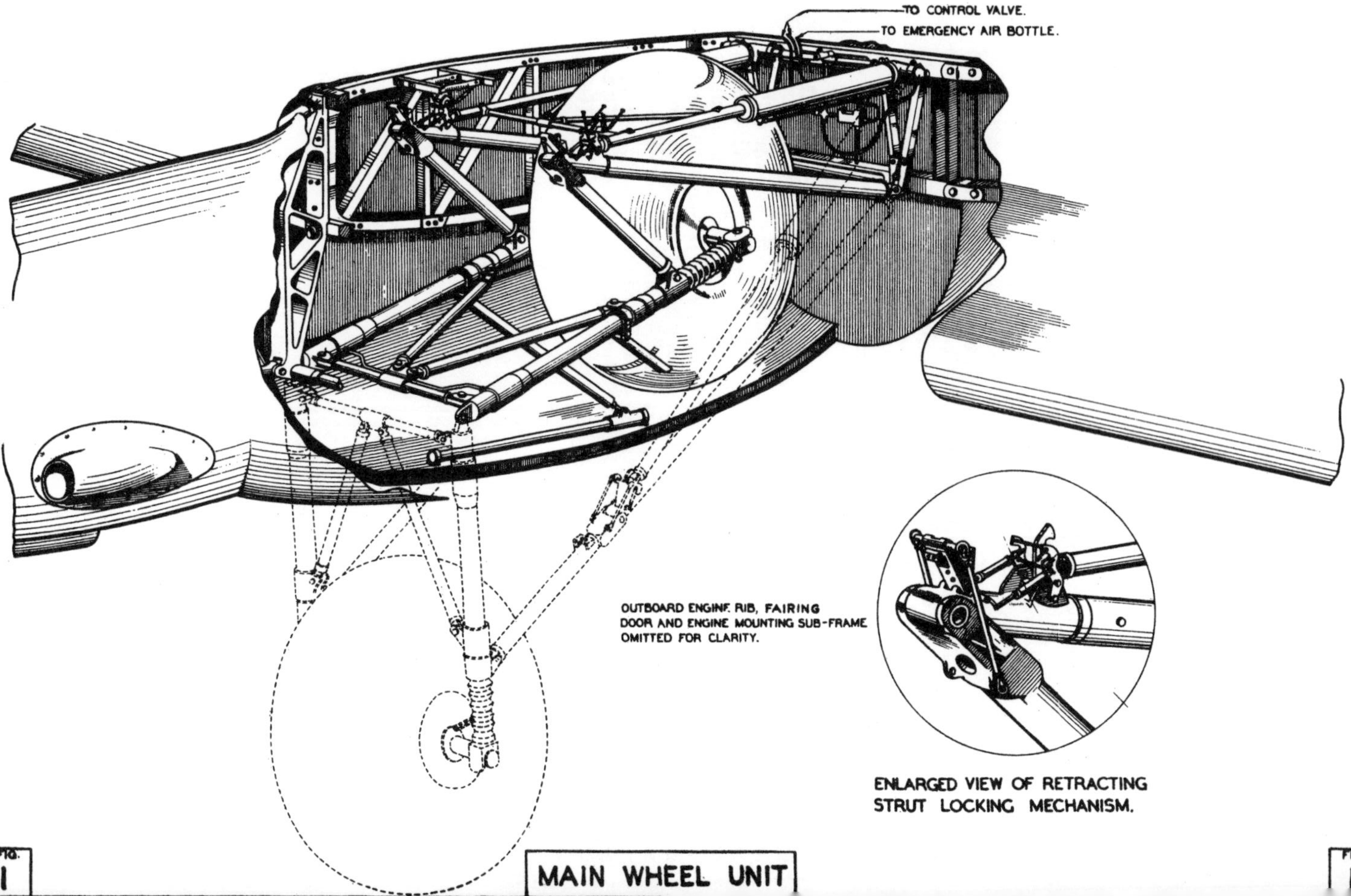

A.P.2062A VOL.I SECT.7 CHAP.5

TO CONTROL VALVE.
TO EMERGENCY AIR BOTTLE.

OUTBOARD ENGINE RIB, FAIRING DOOR AND ENGINE MOUNTING SUB-FRAME OMITTED FOR CLARITY.

ENLARGED VIEW OF RETRACTING STRUT LOCKING MECHANISM.

MAIN WHEEL UNIT

FIG. 1

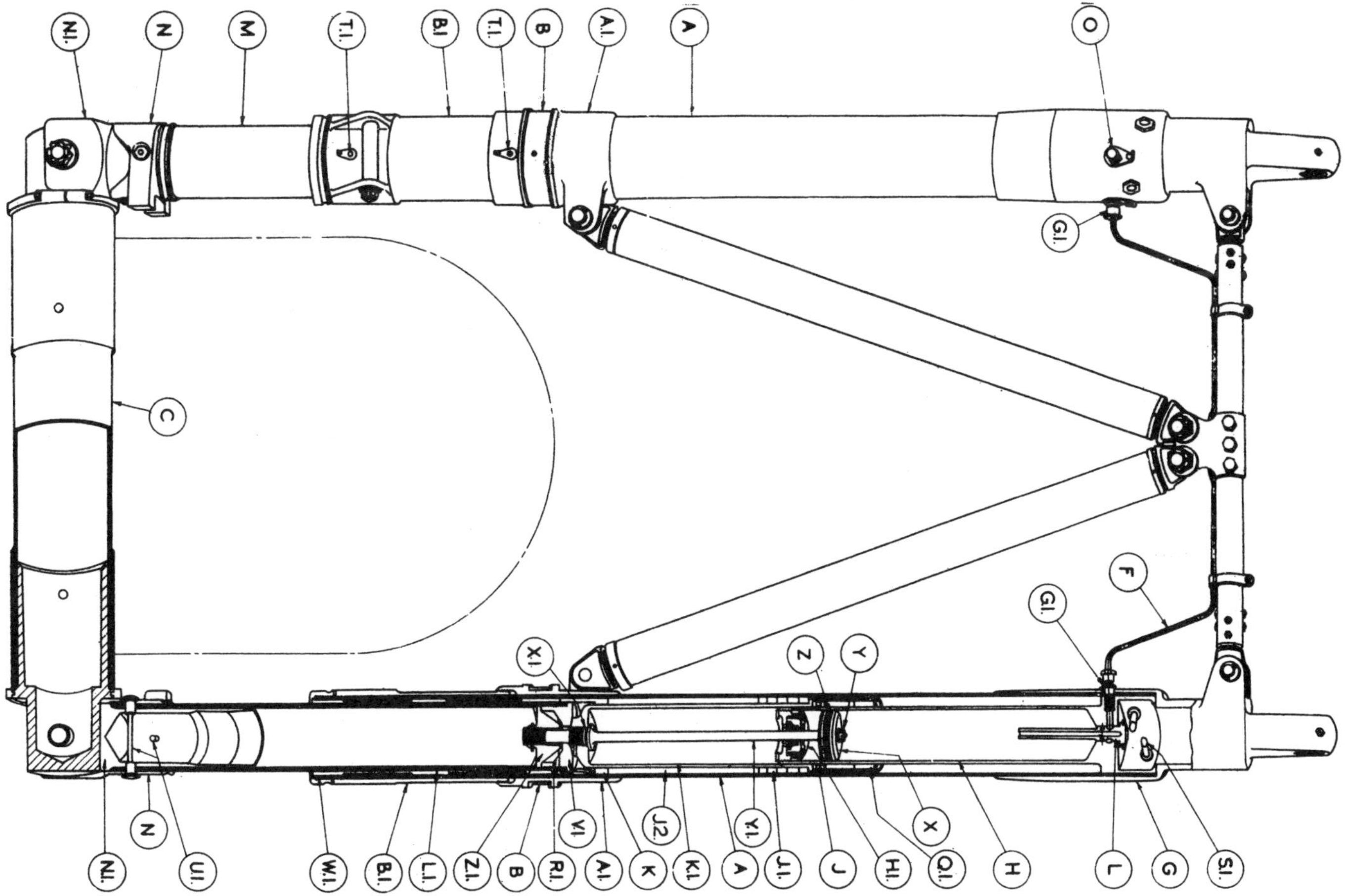

FIG. 2

MAIN WHEEL UNIT SHOCK-ABSORBER STRUTS

FIG. 2

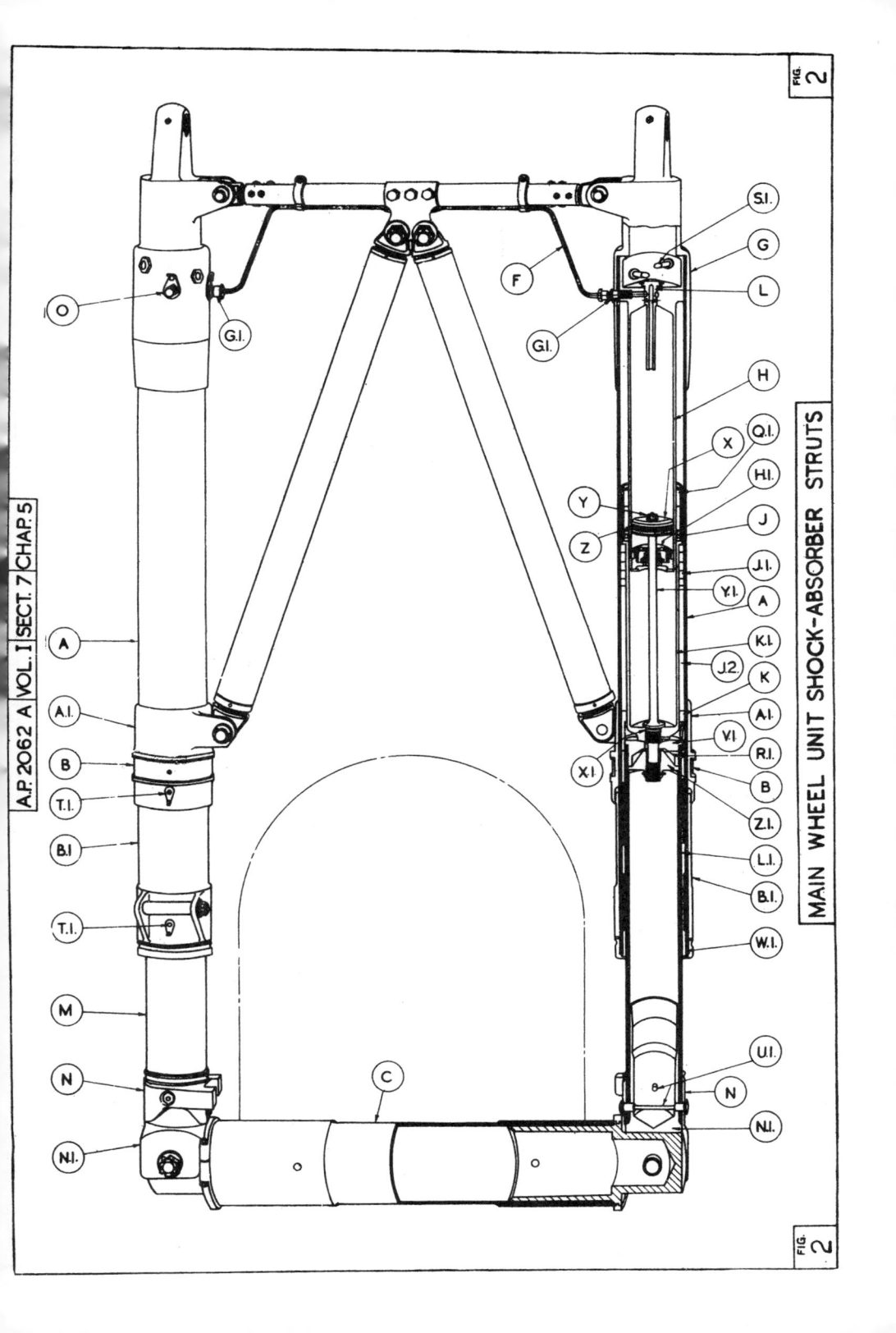

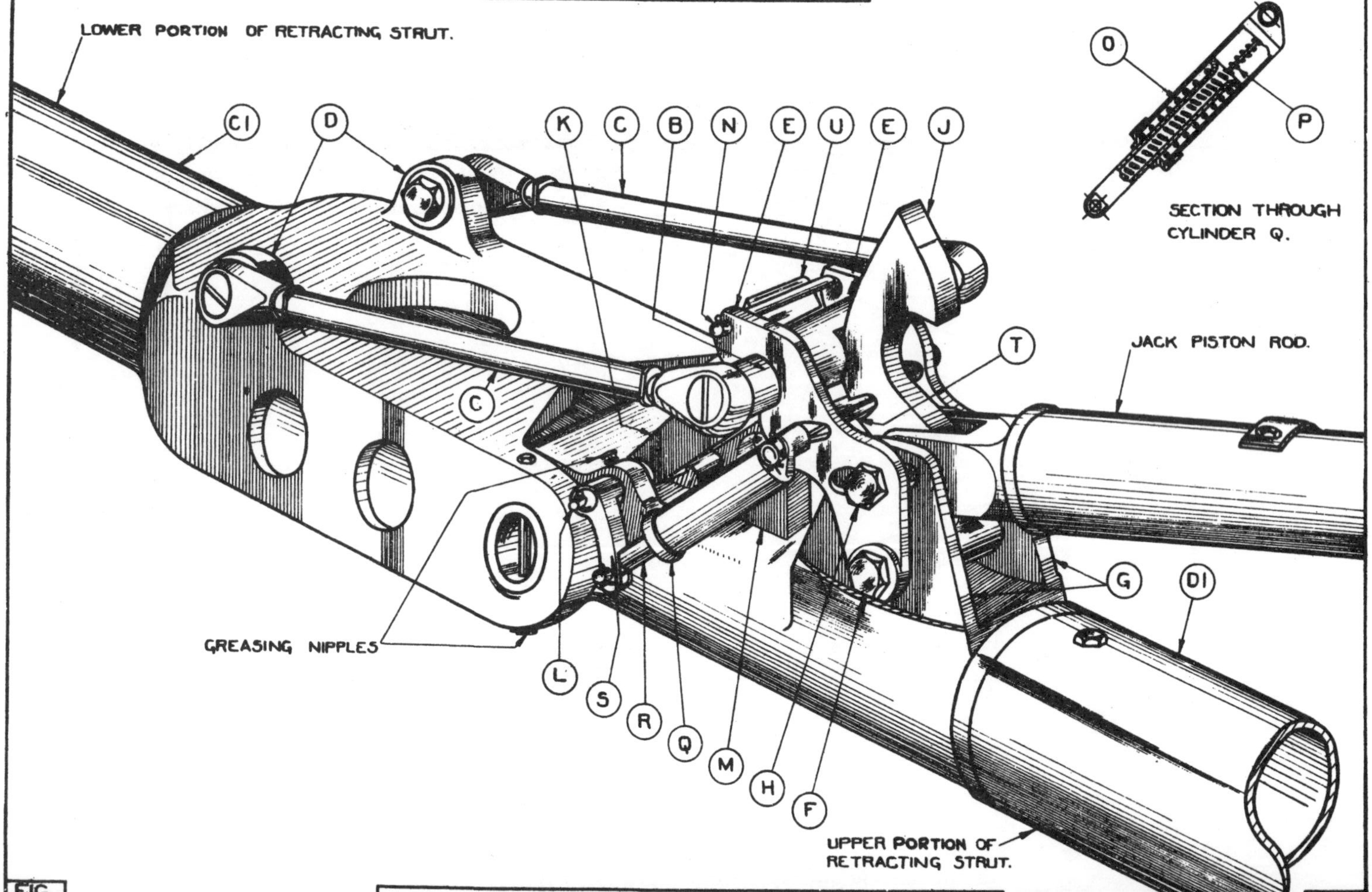

A.P. 2062A VOL. I SECT. 7 CHAP. 5

SECTION THROUGH CYLINDER Q.

JACK PISTON ROD.

UPPER PORTION OF RETRACTING STRUT.

LOWER PORTION OF RETRACTING STRUT.

GREASING NIPPLES

FIG.

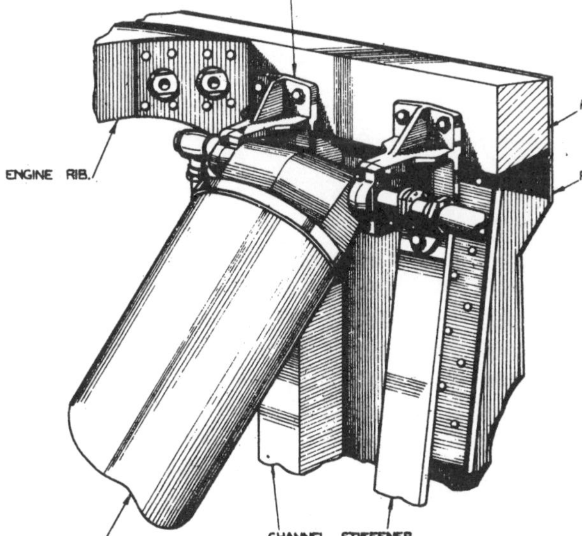

ATTACHMENT OF
JACK TO REAR SPAR.

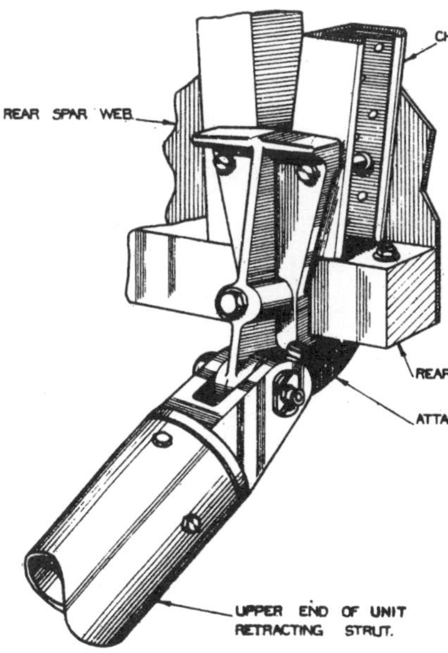

ATTACHMENT OF
RETRACTING STRUT TO REAR SPAR.

FIG. 4

REAR SPAR ATTACHMENTS - MAIN WHEEL UNITS

FIG. 4

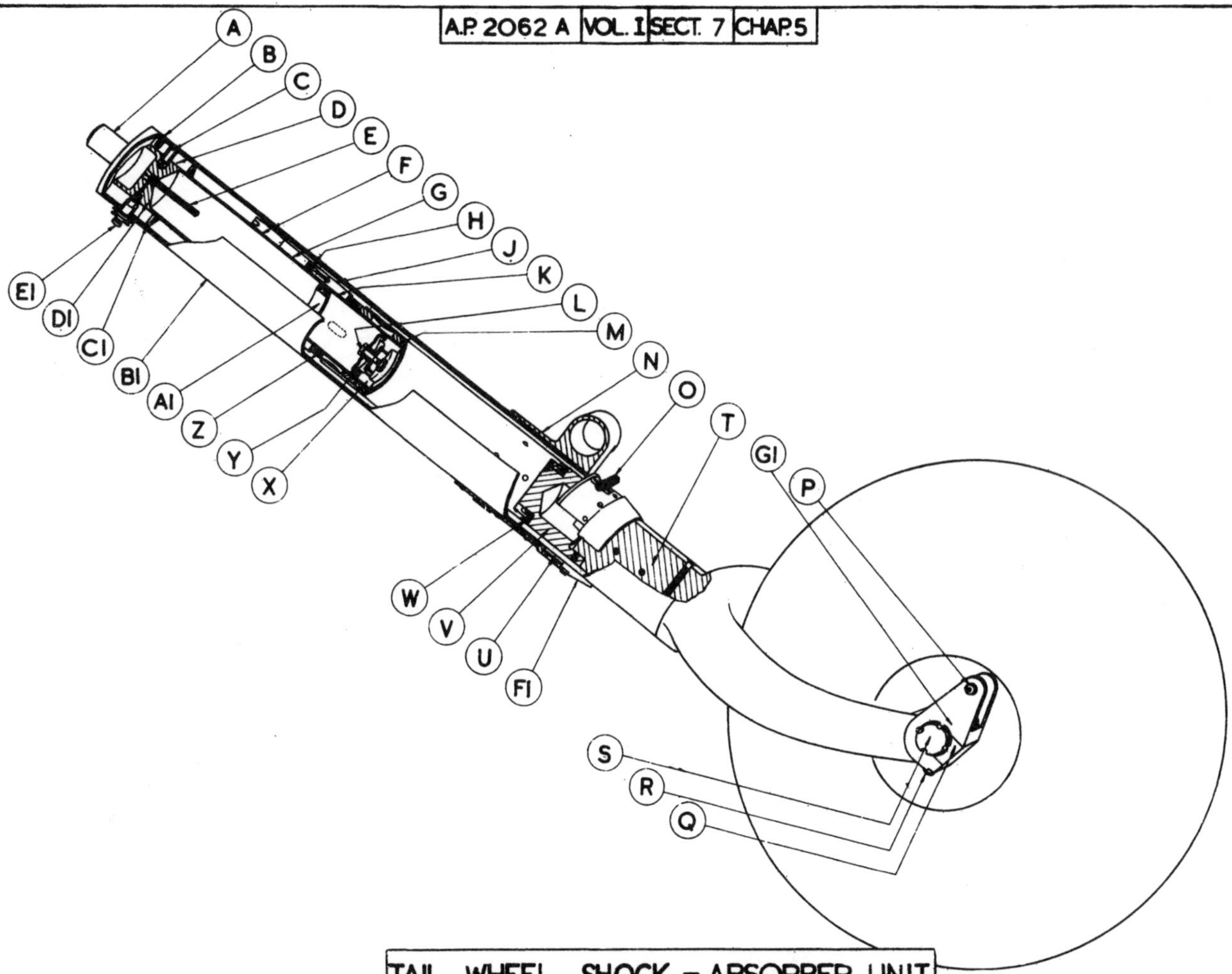

A.P. 2062 A VOL. I SECT. 7 CHAP. 5

FIG. 5

TAIL WHEEL SHOCK – ABSORBER UNIT

Section 8:
Engine installation.

This page amended by A.L. No. 29
July, 1943

A.P.2062A and C, Vol. I

SECTION 8—ENGINE INSTALLATION

LIST OF CONTENTS

	Para.
Introduction	1
Fuel system—	
General	2
Fuel tanks	3
Electric fuel pumps and suction by-pass	8
Fuel jettison system	9
Fuel cocks and controls	10
Vapour vent system	12
Refuelling valve	13
Priming pump (induction)	14
Boost	15
Oil system—	
General	16
Oil tanks	18
Oil filter	22
Engine controls	23
Hot and cold air intakes	27
Cooling system	28
Engine nacelle cowling and fairings	30
Engine cowling forward of bulkhead	31
Fairings aft of bulkhead (inboard nacelle)	32
Fairings aft of bulkhead (outboard nacelle)	33
Main wheel unit doors and valance	34
Nacelle trailing edge fairings	35
Main wheel unit support beams	36
Engine sub-frames	37
Fireproof bulkhead	38
Armour plating	39

LIST OF ILLUSTRATIONS

	Fig.
Engine and secondary controls—fuselage	1
Engine and secondary controls—main plane	2
Engine control details—Cockpit	3
Engine control details—Fuselage	4
Engine control details—Fuselage (contd.)	5
Engine control details—Main plane	6
Engine control details—Countershaft	7
Engine sub-frames	8
Fuel system—Aircraft L.7527 to L.7532	9
Fuel system—Aircraft L.7533 and subsequent	10
Fuel system—Pulsometer F.B. Mk. I pumps	10A
Oil system—one engine unit	11
Slow running cut-out control	12

F.S./1

This page amended by A.L. No. 29
July, 1943

A.P.2062A and C, Vol. I

SECTION 8—ENGINE INSTALLATION

Introduction

1. The power plant installation of Lancaster I and Lancaster III aircraft incorporate Merlin XX and Merlin 28 or 38 engines, respectively, with de-Havilland or Nash-Kelvinator hydromatic constant-speed propellers, and two-speed superchargers. They are pressure cooled, with radiators and oil cooler mounted beneath the engine. The Merlin XX and Merlin 28 or 38 engines are generally similar except that the latter are equipped with Stromberg injection carburettors requiring a vapour vent system, and electro-pneumatically operated slow-running cut-out controls, and do not have the cylinder heads integral with the cylinder blocks. A sub-frame of tubular construction attached to the main plane front spar supports the engine mounting frame and fireproof bulkhead in each engine nacelle. The cowling and fairings are made up of quickly detachable panels. The fuel tanks are mounted in the main plane, and the oil tanks in the engine sub-frame.

FUEL SYSTEM

2. *General.*—The fuel system (*see* fig. 9, 10 and 10A, and Sect. 4, Chap. 3, fig. 10 and 10A) consists of separate port and starboard systems connected by a cross-feed pipe. On each side of the fuselage three fuel tanks are fitted in the main plane (two only in Aircraft No. L.7527 to L.7532) and numbered 1, 2 and 3 outboard from the fuselage. On aircraft not incorporating Mod. 539 each tank has an immersed electric fuel pump and a suction by-pass. Aircraft incorporating this Mod. have Pulsometer F.B. Mk. I pumps instead of immersed pumps. Fuel is drawn by the engine or electric pumps, from No. 1 or No. 2 tanks through the suction by-pass to the tank selector cocks, from which a separate supply is run to each engine carburettor, through the master engine cock, fuel filter and engine driven fuel pump. The No. 3 tanks are arranged to re-fuel the No. 2 tanks only. In each inboard nacelle is an induction priming pump connected to the two engines on the same side. A fuel jettison system is fitted in each No. 1 tank. Boost gauges, electrical fuel contents gauges, fuel pressure warning lamps, and switches for the electric pumps are provided in the cockpit. Flexible self-sealing fuel pipes are used except in aircraft not incorporating Mod. No. 531, which are fitted with Superflexit pipes, and a stainless steel engine supply pipe in the outer main plane leading edge.

2A. The fuel systems of Mk. I and III aircraft differ in that the Stromberg carburettors of the Merlin 28 or 38 engines are provided with a vapour vent system feeding back to the No. 2 fuel tanks, and operated at a higher fuel pressure. The pressure warning lamps are set to 10 lb./sq.in. instead of the 6 lb./sq. in. of Merlin XX engines. A pressure reducing valve between the engine fuel pump and the carburettor is fitted on the Merlin XX engines only.

3. *Fuel tanks.*—The six tanks are secured by steel straps in special bearer ribs extending between the main plane spars. The port and starboard No. 1 tanks, each of 580 gallons capacity, are fitted one on each side of the fuselage in five bearer ribs. The No. 2 and No. 3 tanks are mounted in the outer main plane, on either side of the outboard engine nacelle, and are of 383 and 114 gallons capacity respectively. Three bearer ribs (the centre portions of ribs 19, 20 and 21) support the No. 2 tank, and two ribs (the centre portions of ribs 12 and 13) support the No. 3 tank.

This page amended by A.L. No. 29
July, 1943
A.P.2062A and C, Vol. I, Sect. 8

4. In the six aircraft fitted with four tanks only, the No. 3 tanks were omitted, and the No. 2 tanks were of 275 gallons capacity, the No. 1 tanks being 580 gallons capacity as for the six-tank aircraft.

5. The No. 2 and No. 3 tanks are positioned by end supporting brackets on the ribs at the inboard ends. The tanks are fitted or removed through openings in the under surface of the main plane, a single detachable access panel being provided below each tank. The projection of the sump and Pulsometer pump, when fitted, is accommodated by a blister which also forms an access door. Doors also give access to the strap adjusters for No. 2 and No. 3 tanks, and hinged doors for the jettison pipes are formed in the panels below the No. 1 tanks. In the upper surface of the main plane, doors secured by Dzus fasteners are fitted above the fuel tank filler caps, and inspection doors above the electrical service and pipe connections to the tanks.

6. All the tanks are of, generally, similar construction. The shell is of light-alloy sheet with welded joints, and is stiffened by top-hat-section stringers spot welded to the shell, and by baffles which are bolted to the stringers. The baffles, which are flanged, have additional angles spot welded to the upper and lower edges, vertical top-hat-section stiffeners, and flanged lightening holes in the web. Each tank has a filler cap, an electrical fuel gauge transmitter connected to a gauge on the air observer's instrument panel, and, in aircraft incorporating Mod. No. 539, a sump to which a Pulsometer electric pump type F.B. Mk. I is attached. In earlier aircraft an immersed electric pump type E.P.1 Mk. II is fitted vertically between the top of the tank and a small sump and filter in the bottom. To ensure an accurate reading in the No. 1 tanks a small sump is also provided to receive the float of the fuel gauge. Dipsticks for ground use are stowed on the port side of the fuselage just aft of the main entrance door. Access doors are provided in the top of No. 1 and No. 3 tanks, and a single large access door in the bottom of No. 2 tank. Access to the interior of No. 1 tank may also be obtained by the removal of the jettison valve.

7. A self-sealing protective covering is cemented on over the whole surface of the tanks. The edges are secured with flanged clamping rings where the covering is broken for fittings, except at the access doors which are covered by doped-on rip patches. A separate vent pipe is provided for each tank, (except in the four-tank aircraft—*see* fig. 9) and is taken down to the undersurface of the main plane near the rear outboard corner of the tank. When Pulsometer pumps are fitted, fuel is delivered from the tank through a strainer fitted with a vortex eliminator. The strainer is mounted inside the tank immediately above the sump, and the tank shell is stiffened locally to support these fittings.

8. *Electric fuel pumps and suction by-pass.*—The electric fuel pumps, which are controlled by switches on the air observer's panel, are used for carburettor priming, and for supplementing the engine fuel pumps during take-off, at high altitudes and when cross-feeding from one fuel tank to the engines on the opposite side. The suction by-pass allows fuel to be drawn from the tanks by the engine pumps when the electric pumps are not in use.

8A.* In aircraft equipped with Pulsometer pumps, a projecting sump is attached beneath each fuel tank. The sump is provided with three outlets, of

F.S./2

This page amended by A.L. No. 29
July, 1943

which one in the bottom is closed by a drain plug, while the pump is attached to the rear outlet. At No. 3 tank the forward outlet is blanked off, and the delivery pipe from the sump is led to No. 2 tank (*see* fig. 10A). A non-return valve is fitted to the forward outlet at No. 1 and No. 2 tanks, and the main fuel delivery pipe is connected to the valve. The delivery pipe from the pump enters the main delivery pipe at a connection on the outlet side of the non-return valve, which prevents fuel flowing back through the sump when the pump is in operation. The valve is a floating plate type offering a minimum of resistance to the flow when the engine pumps are drawing fuel through the by-pass.

8B. In aircraft equipped with immersed pumps and a separate suction by-pass the arrangement of the system is different but the operation is the same. Two delivery pipes lead from each No. 1 and No. 2 tank, one from the pump outlet in the top, and one for the suction by-pass from a sump in the bottom. A junction between the two pipes from each tank is formed by a Y-piece, where a non-return valve is fitted in the suction by-pass line to prevent fuel flowing back to the tank when the electric pump is switched on. The Y-piece for No. 1 tank delivery is attached to the tank selector cock, while that for No. 2 tank is mounted on rib 22 aft of the front spar and is connected by a delivery pipe to the tank selector cock.

9. *Fuel jettison system.*—The jettison system (*see* Sect. 4, Chap. 3, fig. 21) provides for the speedy release of the fuel in the No. 1 tanks only. In each No. 1 tank are fitted a jettison valve and an air inlet valve which are hydraulically operated by a control valve handle on the port side of the pilot's floor. Attached to the jettison valve is a double-walled stocking, the lower end of which rests on the hinged door in the No. 1 tank access panel. This door is normally secured by a retaining washer and shear collar on the end of a spindle projecting from the centre of the valve. When the valve is opened to jettison the fuel the spindle is withdrawn, the washer broken and the door released. The stocking pipe then extends to a length of approximately 4 ft. 6 in. and the walls fill with fuel, holding it semi-rigid to carry the escaping fuel clear of the main plane. For details of the hydraulic operation of the system, *see* Sect. 9.

10. *Fuel cocks and controls.*—The fuel cocks and controls of the port and starboard sections of the fuel system are arranged similarly. On each side fuel from the No. 1 and No. 2 tanks is delivered through separate pipes to a tank selector cock on the front face of the front spar between the inboard nacelle and the fuselage. By means of this cock either the No. 1 or No. 2 tanks can be selected to feed both engines on that side. Fuel cannot be supplied from both these tanks at once. The tank selector cock has also an OFF position. The No. 3 tank is controlled only by its electric pump, by means of which the fuel is transferred to the No. 2 tank. A transfer safety valve is fitted at the union on the latter, to prevent fuel syphoning from the No. 3 tank.

11. Fuel passes from the tank selector cock to the cross feed pipe and to the master engine cocks which give individual control of the supplies to the engines. The master cock for the inboard engine is incorporated with the tank selector cock, but the master cock for the outboard engine is a separate unit. The master cock control levers are mounted on each side of the pilot's control quadrant in the cockpit, and the selector cock controls projects through the observer's panel. The controls are connected by means of rods, chains and sprockets with the fuel cocks (*see* fig. 1 and 2). The stop cock in the cross-feed

This page amended by A.L. No. 29   A.P.2062A and C, Vol. I, Sect. 8
July, 1943

pipe is located at the centre of the fuselage in front of the front spar, and is operated through a hole below the step on the front spar cover. This cock is normally kept shut.

12. *Vapour vent system.*—The vapour vent system is fitted to all Lancaster aircraft incorporating Mod. No. 710, but is only connected when Merlin 28 or 38 engines are installed (Mk. III aircraft). Independent systems are provided for the port and starboard engines. The carburettor vent pipe leads from the port side of each fireproof bulkhead to a non-return valve mounted on the sub-frame, and continues along the front spar between the inboard and outboard engines to a T-piece opposite the outer end of No. 2 fuel tank. A connection from the T-piece passes through the spar web to a union on the top of the fuel tank. Up to 7 gallons of fuel per hour may be returned to the tank by each engine through the vent system (approximately two quarts per hour only from early Merlin 28 engines), and No. 2 tanks should, therefore, always be used for take-off in order to avoid the return of fuel to a tank already full.

13. *Re-fuelling valve.*—In early aircraft having a pressure re-fuelling system the re-fuelling valve is mounted in the inboard nacelle on a bracket below the front spar. A re-fuelling pipe for connection to the external supply is attached to the valve, the free end when not in use being secured to a plug on the diagonal strut between the main wheel unit support beams. The valve has four positions: OFF, and a position for supply to each of the three tanks, and is fitted with a spring catch which locks the control lever in any of the positions, and which must be released by lifting the knob before the lever can be moved.

14. *Priming pump (induction).*—A Ki-gass, type B, priming pump serving two engines is mounted on the accessories panel attached to the undercarriage support beams in each inboard nacelle. Fuel is drawn from the sump of No. 1 tank and is pumped to the engine induction pipes, a separate stop cock and delivery pipe being provided between the pump and each engine. When the engine starts the stop cock must be shut and kept shut.

14A. Provision is also made by the introduction of Mod. No. 662, for induction priming with high volatility fuel instead of using fuel drawn from the tanks. A short pipe which projects below the accessories panel is connected to a 3-way cock in the supply line from the tank. A container filled with high volatility fuel is offered up to the pipe, and the 3-way cock operated to close the main supply and allow fuel to be drawn from the external supply.

15. *Boost.*—The boost gauges are mounted on the pilot's instrument panel, and are connected to the engines by pipes which run down the starboard side of the fuselage, and outboard in each direction along the front spar to the fuel traps on the fireproof bulkheads. The boost cut-out control lever is on the extreme left of the pilot's engine control pedestal.

OIL SYSTEM

16. *General.*—An independent oil system is provided for each engine. The oil tank is mounted in the engine sub-frame, and the oil cooler on the starboard side of the coolant radiators below the front of the engine. The main feed pipe is taken from the filter in the tank and passes forward through a fairlead in the

F.S./3

*This page amended by A.L. No. 29
July, 1943*

fireproof bulkhead to the engine oil pump. The oil is returned via the oil cooler to the top of the partial circulation compartment in the tank (*see* fig. 11 and Sect. 4, Chap. 3, fig. 11 and 12). The vent pipe is taken from the top of the oil tank to a connection on the engine. The pipes are of copper with flexible joints, and with the exception of the main feed pipe are supported at the fireproof bulkhead by flanged unions secured by bolts. The propeller feathering pump is mounted in the sub-frame, and is fed by a pipe from the bottom of the oil tank. The oil is led forward from the pump by a flexible pipe and is connected at the bulkhead to the engine pipe.

17. The oil temperature and oil pressure gauges are mounted on the air observer's panel. Provision is made for oil dilution to assist engine starting at low temperatures (*see* Sect. 4, Chap. 2), by means of a solenoid operated valve on the starboard side of the engine mounting. The valve is arranged to pass fuel from the fuel pump outlet to the oil feed pipe when the pushbutton on the air observer's panel is pressed. For further information on the oil system in the engine, *see* A.P.1590G and N, Vol. I.

18. *Oil tanks.*—The inboard and outboard oil tanks differ in shape, but are of the same capacity. Each tank carries $37\frac{1}{2}$ gallons of oil including two gallons for the operation of the hydromatic propeller, and an air space of $4\frac{1}{2}$ gallons. The tanks are constructed of light-alloy sheet with welded joints. The partial circulation compartment is circular in plan and of the full depth of the tank, and the top is formed by a circular de-aerating ramp to which is fitted a diffusing ring. The return oil passes through a nozzle into the ring, and is spread over the ramp as it flows into the compartment which is of 2 gallons capacity. Vent holes are formed in the top of the ramp, which is attached to the tank shell by special bolts. The bottom of the compartment is formed by a separate ring into which the upper portion fits, leaving an annular space between. The upper edge of this ring governs the hydromatic oil reserve level, below which oil cannot enter the filter. The two sections are riveted together but the gap is maintained by distance tubes. The bottom ring and the oil filter are attached to the tank shell by studs.

19. The oil filler cap, which is attached to a hinged arm, is on the port side of the tank, and in the tail down position the oil level corresponds with the bottom edge of the filler opening. A hinged door is provided on the port side of the nacelle fairing to give access to the filler, and a drain plug is provided in the bottom of each tank. Inspection doors are located on the front of the outboard tanks and on the starboard end of the inboard tanks.

20. Semape self-sealing covering is applied to the whole external surface of the tanks, including the inspection doors. Where the covering is broken for fittings and connections these are attached to the tank by studs which project beyond the covering and secure the flanged clamping rings which seal the edges. Canvas reinforcing strips are provided on the surface of the covering in way of the securing straps.

21. The outboard tanks are each supported on two light-alloy bearers which extend aft from the fireproof bulkhead, and are attached to the cross members of the engine sub-frame by bolts and clips. The tank bearers are of box-section, being formed from two side plates with channels between, and are connected at each end by a tubular stay, to which are fixed the tank straps. The inboard tanks are mounted in straps in the engine sub-frame between the main wheel

This page amended by A.L. No. 29   *A.P.2062A and C, Vol. I, Sect. 8*
July, 1943

unit support beams and the fireproof bulkhead. The straps are carried on two cross-tubes attached by means of bolts, brackets and clips to the struts of the sub-frame and to the support beams.

22. *Oil filters.*—An oil filter from which the engine feed is taken is fitted into the bottom of each tank and projects below the surface. The casing is a light-alloy casting. The inlet ports are raised above the tank bottom, and are surrounded by a baffle ring under which the oil passes. Above the ports a piston is normally held in position by prongs projecting from the filter element below. When the element is withdrawn for cleaning a spring forces the piston down and the ports are sealed. The filter element is secured to the lower end of the outer casing by means of a handscrew in a special nut fitting. This nut has two arms which are inserted in a groove in the base of the casing, turned through 90 deg. and locked with wire. The handscrew also is locked with wire after tightening.

ENGINE CONTROLS

23. The control levers for the throttle, propeller and boost cut-out, together with the engine fuel cock controls described in para. 11, are mounted on a quadrant below the pilot's instrument panel (*see* fig. 1 and 2). Chains and tie-rods connect the control levers to the engine control boxes behind the engines, the inboard engine boxes being mounted on the front spar, and the outboard engine boxes on brackets on the front spar. The boost cut-out control is cable operated in the main plane. From the control pedestal the connections are carried down to three telescopic countershafts mounted on the front end of the main floor. These separate the controls into three groups which run aft between the floor intercostals to countershafts at the front spar, the lower connections of the port side group being raised by jockey sprockets at each end to avoid the bomb gear. The controls are then carried up to sprocket boxes on the front face of the front spar along which they run outboard in each direction to the engine control boxes. In the main plane centre section the controls are carried in fairleads in front of the spar. The outboard engine controls pass through a jockey sprocket box on the front spar, a layshaft on the main wheel unit outboard support beam, and through fairleads in the outer plane leading edge to the engine control box. Levers on the engine control box are connected by means of rods to the corresponding levers on the countershaft on the front face of the fireproof bulkhead, from which rods are connected to the engine. A cover is fitted to the centre part of the countershaft assembly and shields the opening through which the connecting rods pass.

24. The supercharger controls are normally electro-pneumatically operated by switches on the pilot's instrument panel, using compressed air from the brakes pneumatic system (*see* Sect. 9). In aircraft retaining mixture and manually operated supercharger controls, these levers also are on the pilot's control quadrant. The controls are divided on each side to serve the inboard and outboard engines (*see* fig. 2), and differential links are fitted at the points of division to ensure that both inboard and outboard controls are brought up to their respective stops. The throttle and mixture levers are interlocked, the mixture lever, if in the WEAK position, automatically returning to the NORMAL position when the throttle is closed for slow running. The boost cut-out control only is cable operated from the port rear countershaft in the main

F.S./4

*This page amended by A.L. No. 29
July, 1943*

floor, through a spring-loaded crank lever on thé jockey sprocket box on the front spar in the inboard nacelle. From the crank lever one cable is led directly to the inboard engine, while the other follows the other controls to the outboard engine.

25. If the main wheels are in any position except locked DOWN when the throttle is less than one-third open a warning horn is automatically sounded. The switch controlling this horn is mounted inside the pilot's control pedestal.

26. The slow-running cut-out controls of Mk. I aircraft are interconnected by means of Teleflex controls with the master engine cock controls (*see* fig. 12) and operate when the cocks are turned off. A joint is provided in the Teleflex control immediately aft of each fireproof bulkhead. In Mk. III aircraft the Teleflex controls are installed as far as these joints and are sealed off just forward of the bulkheads. The control is therefore available in the event of Merlin XX engines being substituted at any time. The slow-running cut-outs of the Merlin 28 or 38 engines of Mk. III aircraft are electro-pneumatically operated by switches on the pilot's instrument panel, using compressed air from the brakes pneumatic system (*see* Sect. 9). For further details of this and other controls forward of the fireproof bulkhead *see* A.P.2140B, C and D, Vol. I.

HOT AND COLD AIR INTAKES

27. The shutters of the hot and cold air intakes for each engine are operated by means of a small hydraulic jack mounted in the engine sub-frame. The jack piston rod passes through a hole in the fireproof bulkhead and operates the shutters. In the outboard sub-frame the jack is mounted on a bracket below the starboard oil tank bearer; in the inboard nacelles it is attached to a bracket on the fireproof bulkhead and to a short stay. The control valve is mounted under the fuselage main floor beneath the forward end of the navigator's table, and is operated by a connecting rod from a handle on the port side of the pilot's floor. For the hydraulic operation of the circuit, *see* Sect. 9, and for details of the hot and cold air intakes, *see* A.P.2140B, C and D, Vol. I.

COOLING SYSTEM

28. The cooling system of each engine (*see* Sect. 4, Chap. 3, fig. 13) comprises a header tank mounted behind the front cowling diaphragm, two radiators attached below the engine in a duct at the front end of the engine cowling, and a thermostat. The system operates under pressure, which is controlled by a thermostatic relief valve in the header tank. The temperature of the coolant is controlled by the thermostat, and the air flow through the radiators is controlled by a flap which is operated by a thermostatically controlled electro-pneumatic ram. For details of the pneumatic system, *see* Sect. 9, and for further information on the cooling system, *see* A.P.2140B, C and D, Vol. I. The coolant consists of 30% by volume of ethylene-glycol (D.T.D.344A) and 70% distilled water.

29. The inboard engine cooling systems are each connected to one of the cabin heating radiators, which are mounted on the front face of the front spar between the inboard nacelles and the fuselage (*see* Sect. 11, fig. 5). The flow pipe to the cabin heating radiator is taken from an outlet at the top of the engine, and the return is connected to the return pipe from the main radiators to the engine. The pipes are provided with Avimo couplings at the bulkheads, and are lead through the engine sub-frame and the main plane leading edge

This page amended by A.L. No. 29   *A.P.2062A and C, Vol. I, Sect. 8*
July, 1943

to connections below the cabin heater. Pet cocks are fitted in the top of the cabin heating radiator and at the highest point of the return pipe, and a drain plug is fitted in the bottom of the radiator. When the air inlet valve to the cabin is closed, the air flow through the radiator continues through a by-pass which opens automatically.

ENGINE NACELLE COWLING AND FAIRINGS

30. The inboard engine nacelle comprises the engine cowling forward of the fireproof bulkhead, the fairing panels aft of the bulkhead, the main wheel unit doors and valance and the fairings under the trailing edge of the main plane. The outboard nacelle comprises the engine cowling, fairing panels aft of the bulkhead, and an end fairing enclosing the rear portion of the engine sub-frame.

31. *Engine cowling forward of bulkhead.*—The engine cowlings consist of the following quickly detachable panels, secured by Dzus fasteners:—top panel, two side panels, main bottom panel (to which are attached the carburettor cold air intake fairings) and the front bottom scoop. For the description of the cowling, including the radiator and oil cooler ducts, the radiator flap, and the hot and cold air intakes, see A.P.2140B, C and D, Vol. I.

32. *Fairings aft of bulkhead (inboard nacelle).*—The nacelle fairings enclosing the engine sub-frame consist of four detachable panels, top, bottom and two side, and one rear hinged fairing at the top. The fairings are formed from light-alloy sheet, the detachable panels having angle stiffeners at the edges and top-hat section intermediate stiffeners. The rear hinged panel is formed with channel section stiffeners, hinge beam and front edge stiffener, and is hinged to the top of the front spar. When closed the panel is supported by the nose ribs on each side of the nacelle, and is secured to clips on the sub-frame struts by means of two Oddie fasteners fitted on brackets at the front edge of the panel. The rear edge of the top detachable panel overlaps the hinged panel and is attached to it. A channel section fairing rail is provided on each side between the fireproof bulkhead and the main wheel unit support beam. The edges of the panels are secured by Dzus fasteners, except the rear edge of the bottom panel, which has no attachment, but is stiffened with a channel member to which is fitted a sealing strip for the main wheel unit doors. An access door is provided in the port side panel for the oil tank filler cap.

Note.—A few early aircraft were fitted with a fixed panel in place of the rear hinged panel.

33. *Fairings aft of bulkhead (outboard nacelle).*—The fairings aft of the fireproof bulkhead consist of four detachable panels, top, bottom and two side, and a detachable rear fairing which is fixed to the undersurface of the outer plane and extends aft to the rear spar. A hinged access door for the oil filler cap is provided in the port side panel. The fairings are formed of light-alloy sheet, and are stiffened by angles at the edges and by top-hat section intermediate stiffeners, while the rear section fairing is built up with a light frame of spruce stringers and plywood formers with laminated spruce flanges. The extreme rear end is a separate pressing which is attached to the rear former, and the upper edges of the fairing are formed of tapering curved fillets which fair off into the undersurface of the main plane, to which they are attached by Dzus

F.S./4A

This page amended by A.L. No. 29
July, 1943

fasteners. Two detachable channel section fairing rails are bolted to brackets on the fireproof bulkhead and the front former of the rear section fairing. The former is clipped to the engine sub-frame. The fairing panels are secured by Dzus fasteners at the edges.

34. *Main wheel unit doors and valance.*—The valance is built up with channel-section formers and stringers which are riveted to the attachment channels at the top and to the channel-section hinge beam at the bottom. The doors, which are attached by means of piano type hinges, are built up with channel-section hinge beams and lower edge members, intercostals and L-section stringers. Both the valance and door skin coverings are of light-alloy sheet. Each door is operated by a connecting link, having one end hinged to a sleeve on the shock-absorber strut, and the other attached to an eye bolt mounted in ball bearings at the lower edge of the door.

(Continued on next page)

A.P.2062A, Vol. I, Sect. 8

35. *Nacelle trailing edge fairings.*—The section of the nacelle attached to the underside of the trailing edge of the main plane, is formed in two separate portions of which the rear portion is attached to the main plane flap and hinges into the forward portion when the flaps are lowered. A bulkhead at the front former of the fairing forms the rear end of the main wheel unit compartment. The fairings are constructed of channel-section formers and L-section stringers covered with light-alloy sheet.

MAIN WHEEL UNIT SUPPORT BEAMS

36. These beams (*see* fig. 8) are bolted to the front spar and the engine ribs in the inboard nacelle. Two beams braced together support each main wheel unit and inboard engine sub frame. The beams are light-alloy castings, with lugs for the attachment of the engine sub-frame and the diagonal tubular strut between the beams. At the lower end of each beam is a fork for the attachment of the shock-absorber strut. The bolt on which the strut pivots also screws into a socket in the end of the strut between the lower ends of the beams. Pads are fitted to the tops of the beams to allow the engine changing gantry attachment sockets to be fitted on the top of the hinged fairing panel above.

ENGINE SUB-FRAMES

37. The inboard and outboard engine sub-frames are tubular structures with welded joints. Each sub-frame carries an engine mounting frame, fireproof bulkhead and oil tank. Two diagonal struts in the bottom of the outboard sub-frames are detachable for the fitting or removal of the oil tanks. Four lugs project at the front joints to pick up the engine mounting frame. The outboard sub-frame, which is mounted below the outer main plane, is bolted to reinforced steel mounting channels on the front spar between nose ribs 14A and 16A, and tapers to a single attachment at the mounting channel on the rear spar. The inboard sub-frame is bolted to lugs at the top and bottom ends of the main wheel unit support beams.

FIREPROOF BULKHEAD

38. A fireproof bulkhead of tinned sheet steel is mounted on the front of each engine sub-frame, and is made up of three plates, of which the bottom plate in the outboard bulkhead is in two sections. The centre and bottom plates are bolted together, but at the other joints the sub-frame members separate the plates, and the joints also form the attachment of the bulkhead to the sub-frame. The joint is formed by a plate which fits round the back of the sub-frame strut, and by semi-circular clips at the front. Sealing plates with asbestos packing are fitted where the sub-frame struts pass through the bulkhead, except in the bottom plate of the inboard bulkhead where flanged attachment plates are bolted round the struts. Light-alloy angles, to which are fitted the Dzus fastener springs for attachment of the engine cowling and fairing panels, are riveted round the edges on both the front and rear face of the bulkhead. The bulkhead is also strengthened by channel section stiffeners and by a flange on the lower edge of the centre plate. Stabilising struts are fitted between the top plate and the sub-frame struts. The bottom plate of the outboard bulkhead is set forward at an angle to the upper portion and contains an access door for the carburettor, while on the lower front face of the inboard bulkhead is mounted a small cylindrical drain tank to which the inboard engine drains are connected.

F.S./5

ARMOUR PLATING

39. Armour plating is provided in the outboard nacelle at the bottom of the fireproof bulkhead, and at the bottom of the front end of the rear fairing. The plating on the bulkhead is bolted to the rear face, from which it is separated by distance pieces. The plating in the rear fairing is attached behind the front former by distance studs and is bolted to clips on the sub-frame struts.

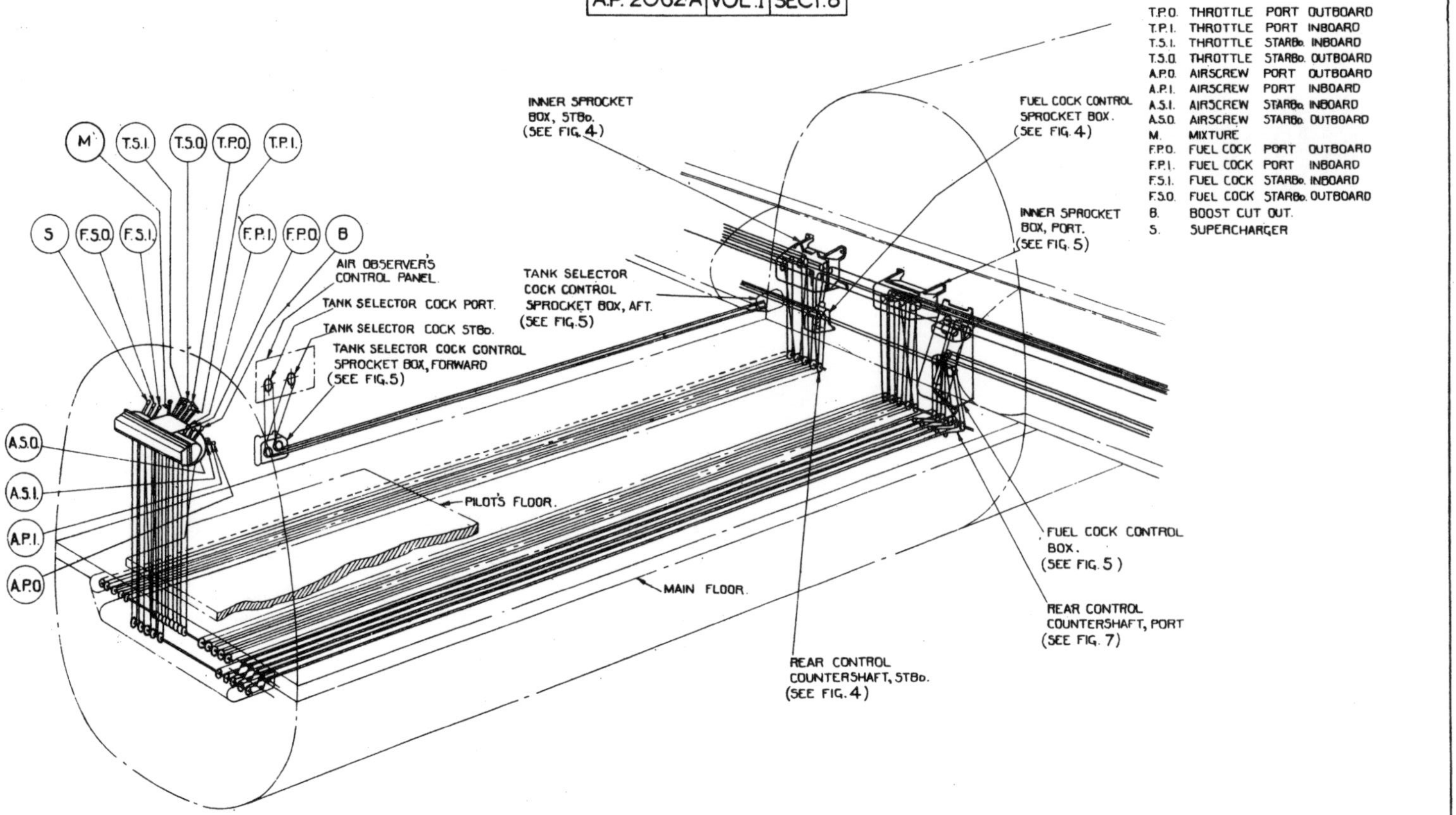

FIG. 1

ENGINE & SECONDARY CONTROLS - FUSELAGE

FIG. 1

T.S.I.	THROTTLE STARBD. INBOARD
A.S.I.	AIRSCREW STARBD. INBOARD.
T.S.O.	THROTTLE STARBD. OUTBOARD.
A.S.O.	AIRSCREW STARBD. OUTBOARD.
M.	MIXTURE.
S.	SUPERCHARGER.

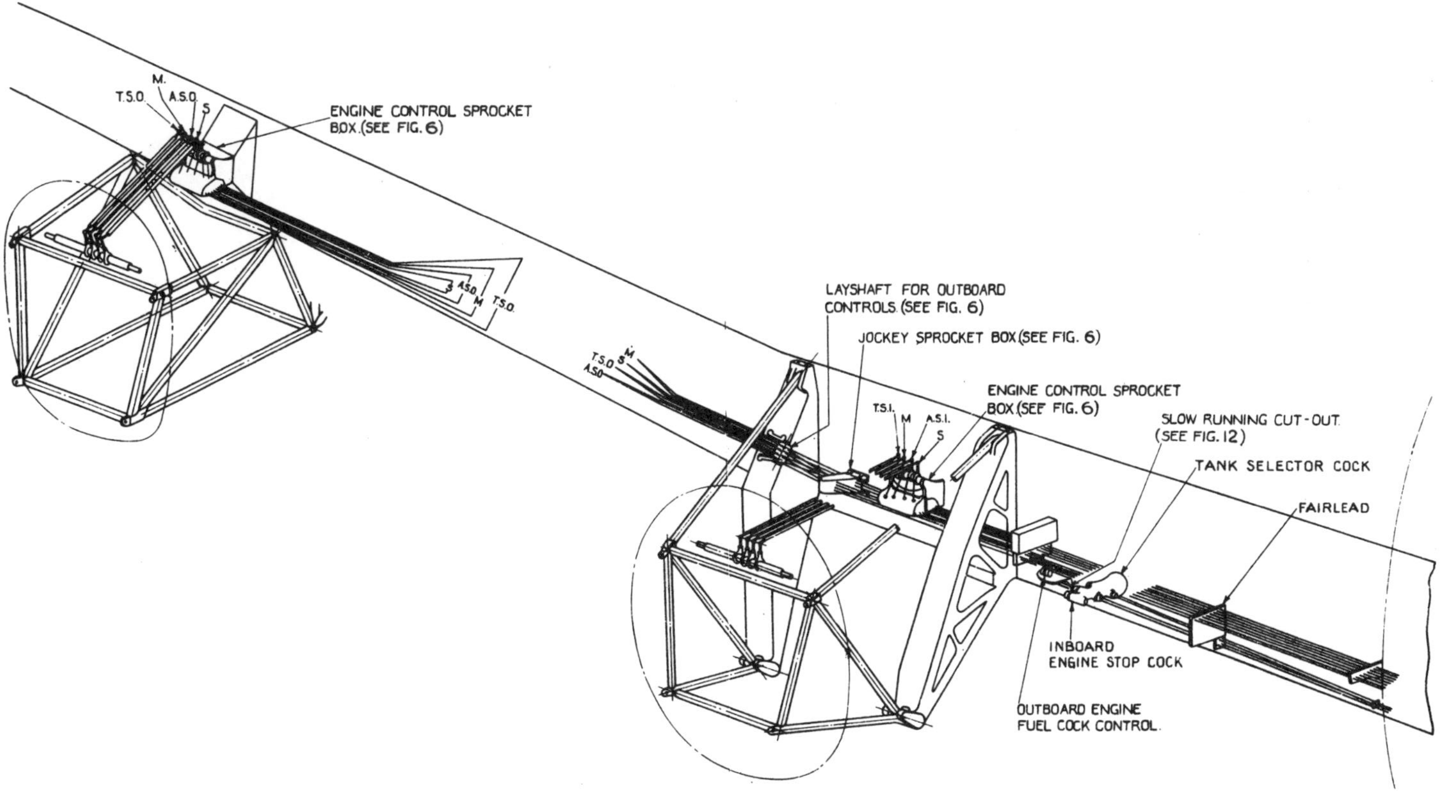

FIG. 2

ENGINE & SECONDARY CONTROLS - MAIN PLANE

FIG 2

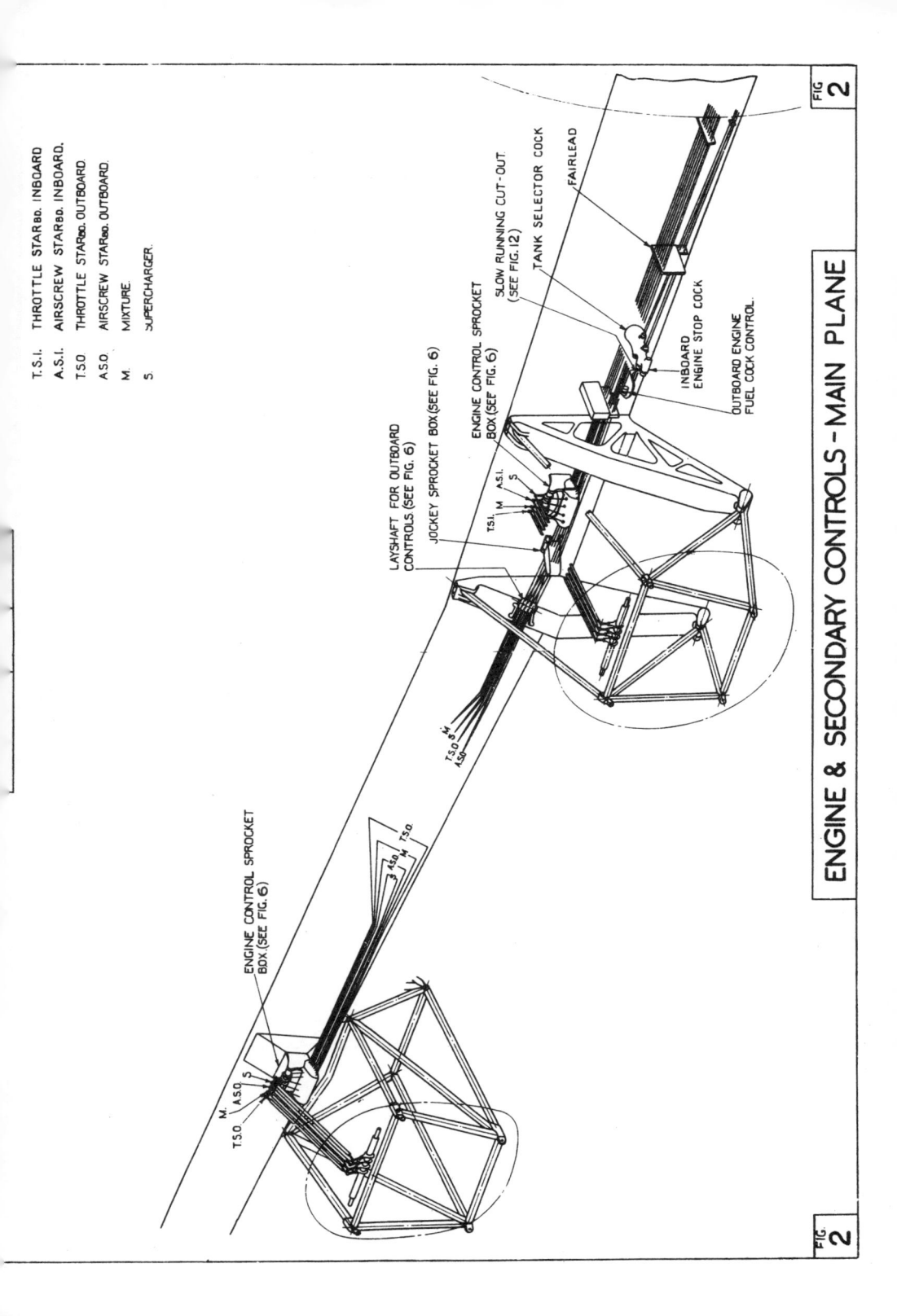

ENGINE CONTROL DETAILS — COCKPIT

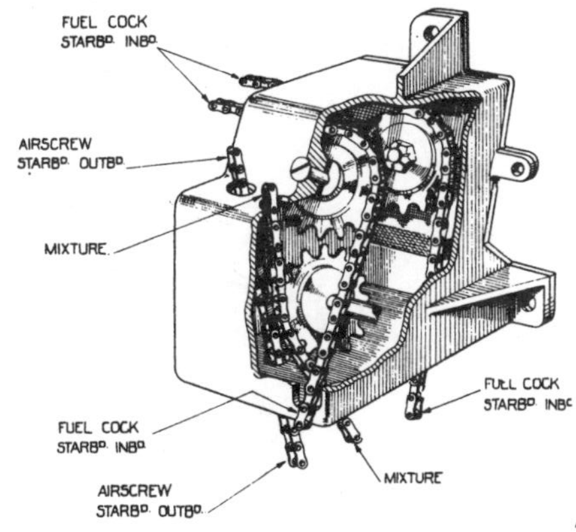

SPROCKET BOX FOR
FUEL COCK CONTROLS.

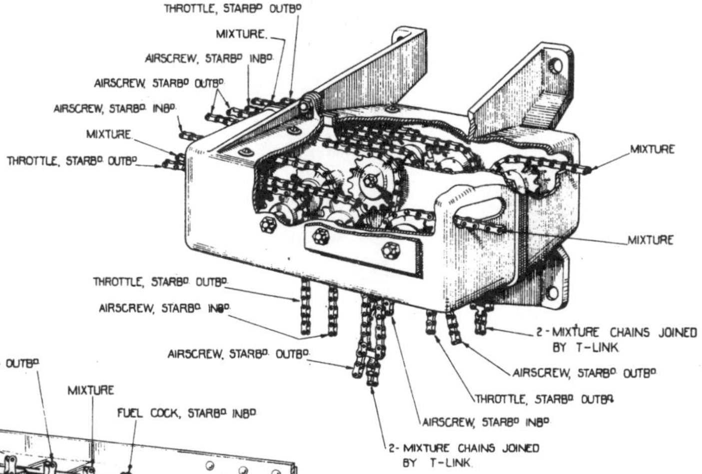

INNER SPROCKET BOX.
STARBOARD.

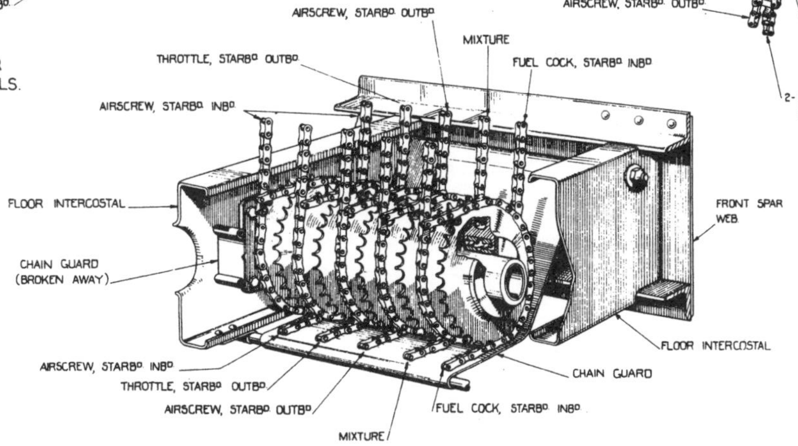

REAR CONTROL COUNTERSHAFT, STARBOARD SIDE, FUSELAGE.

FIG. 4

ENGINE CONTROL DETAILS – FUSELAGE

FIG. 4

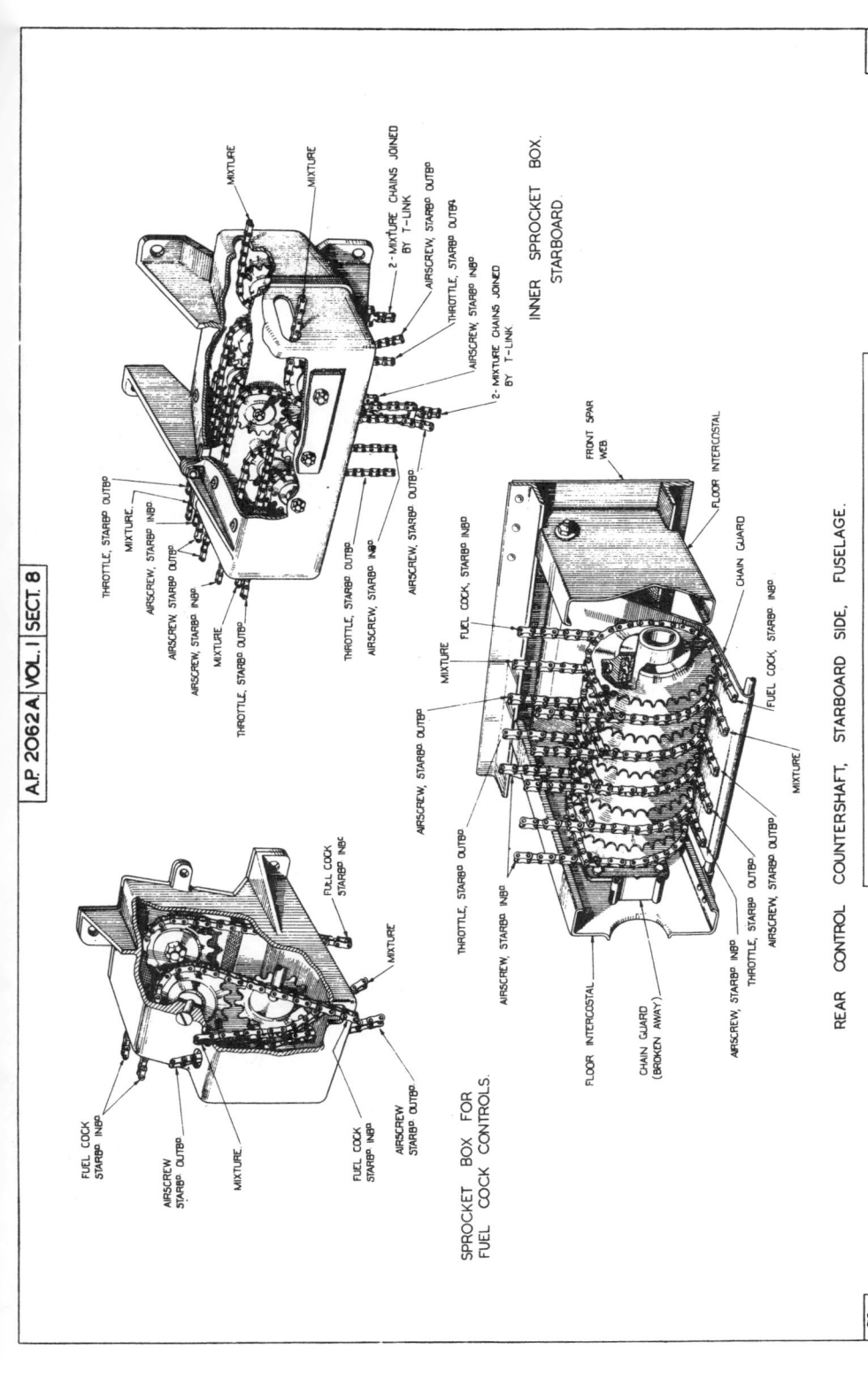

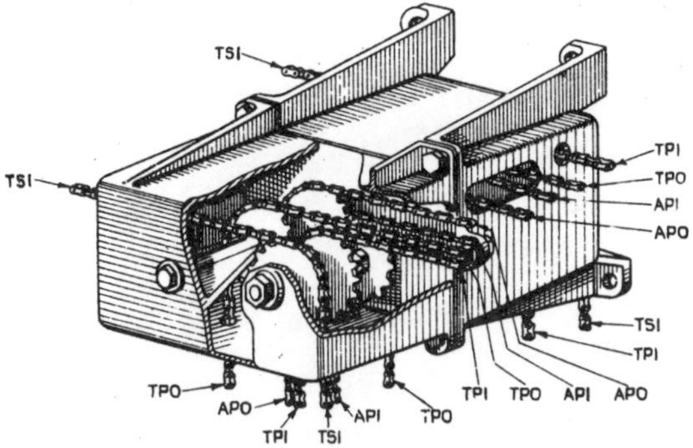

INNER PORT SPROCKET BOX.

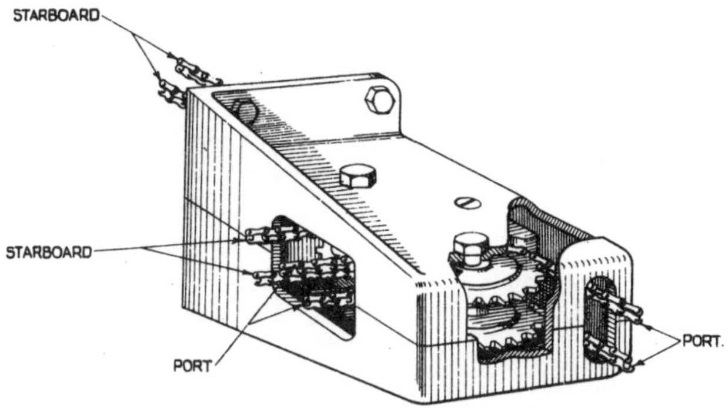

TANK SELECTOR COCK CONTROL SPROCKET BOX, AFT.

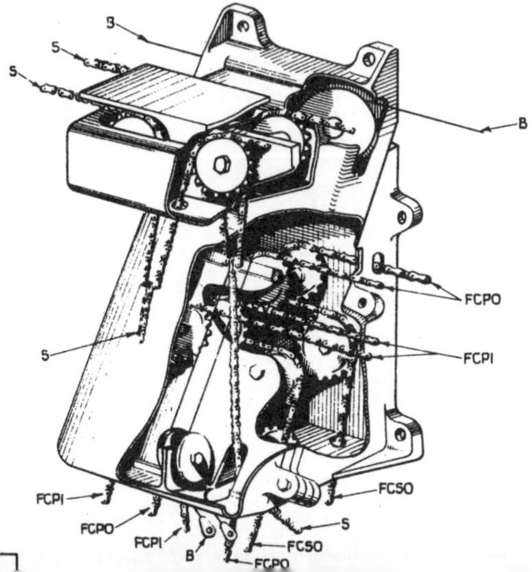

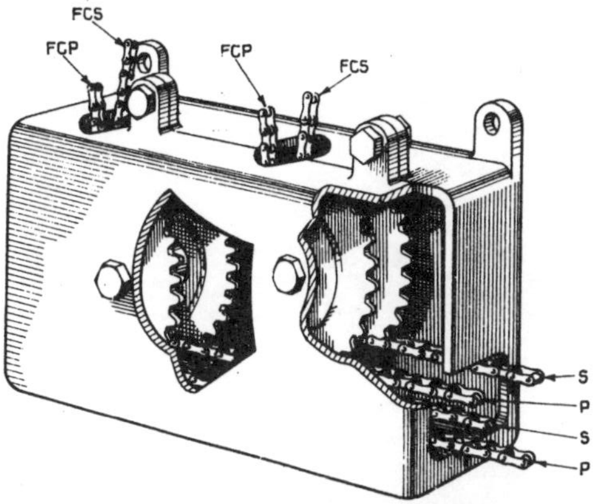

TANK SELECTOR COCK CONTROL SPROCKET BOX, FORWARD.

F.C.P.O.	FUEL COCK PORT OUTBOARD.
F.C.P.I.	FUEL COCK PORT INBOARD.
F.C.S.O.	FUEL COCK STBD OUTBOARD.
B.	BOOST.
S.	SUPERCHARGER.
T.S.I.	THROTTLE STBD INBOARD.
T.P.O.	THROTTLE PORT OUTBOARD.
T.P.I.	THROTTLE PORT INBOARD.
A.P.O.	AIRSCREW PORT OUTBOARD.
A.P.I.	AIRSCREW PORT INBOARD.

FIG.

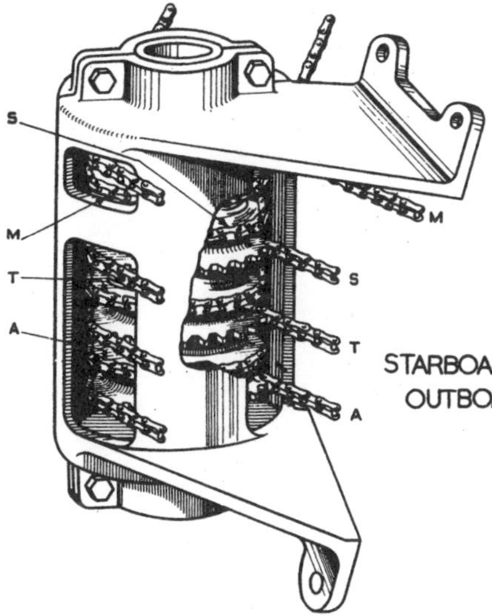

STARBOARD LAYSHAFT FOR OUTBOARD CONTROLS.

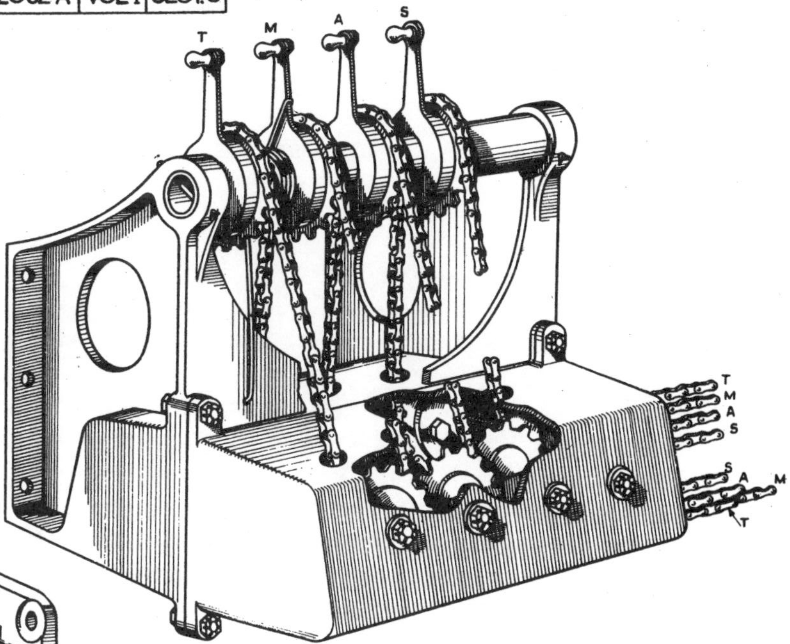

ENGINE CONTROL SPROCKET BOX-STARBOARD INBOARD.

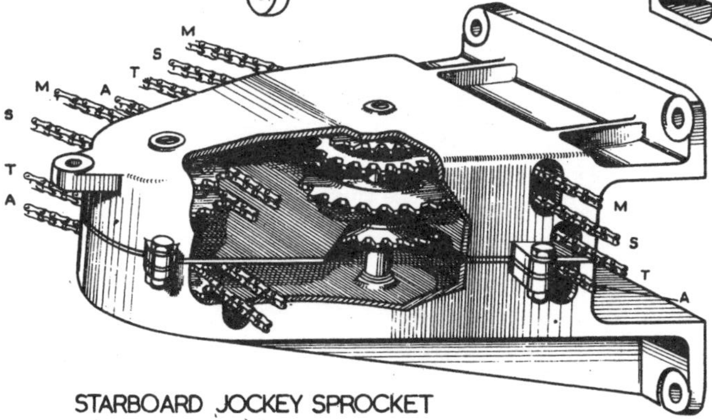

STARBOARD JOCKEY SPROCKET BOX FOR OUTBOARD CONTROLS.

A..................AIRSCREW
M..................MIXTURE
S..................SUPERCHARGER
T..................THROTTLE.

FIG. 6

ENGINE CONTROL DETAILS – MAIN PLANE

FIG. 6

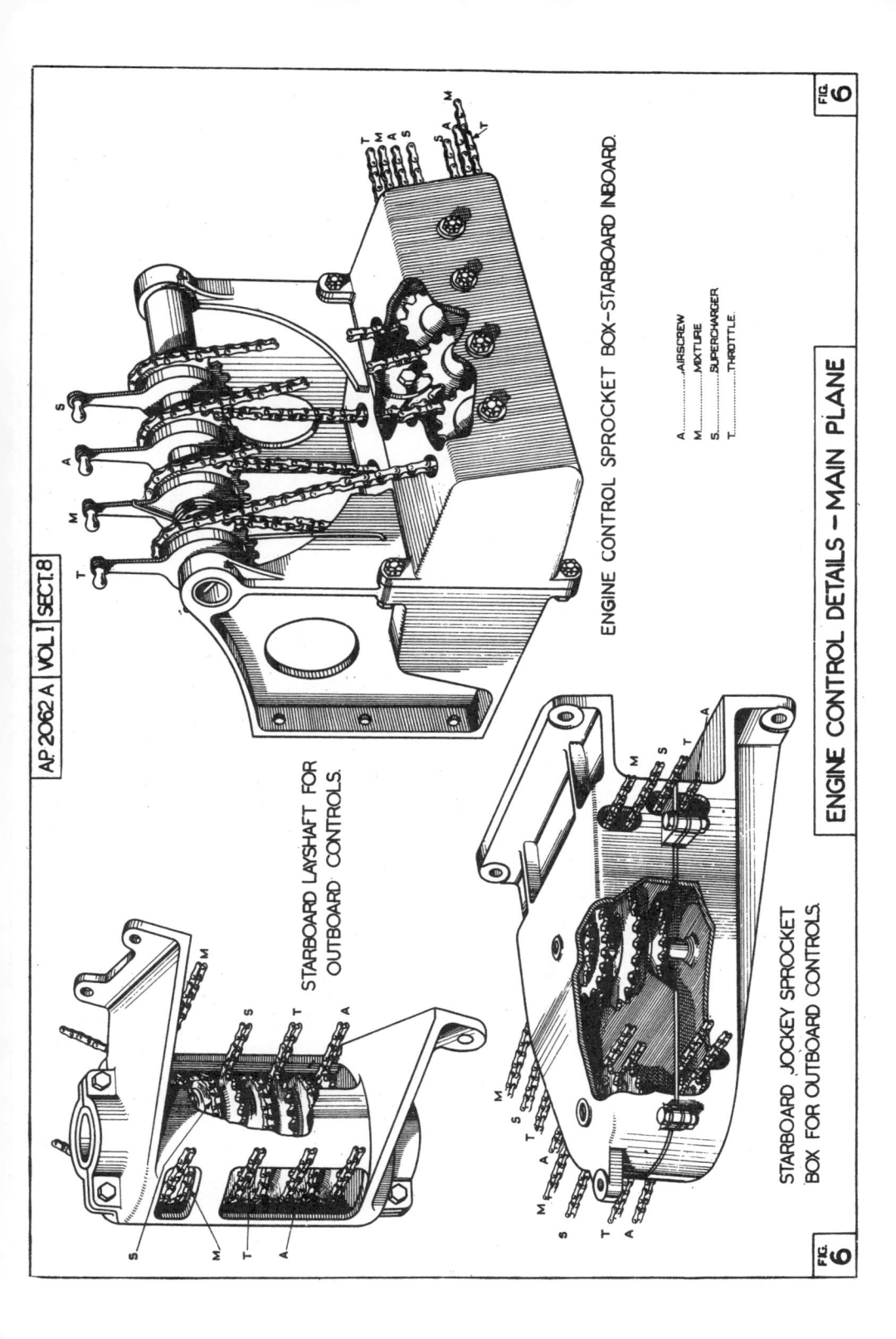

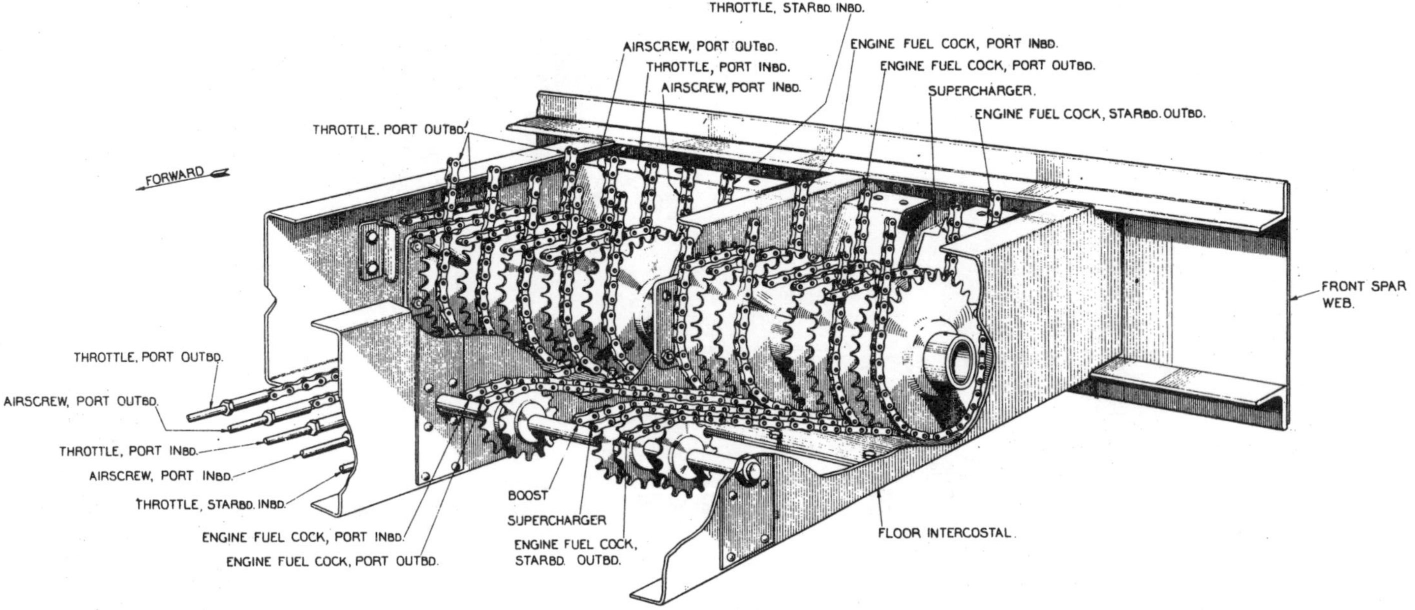

A.P. 2062A | VOL.I | SECT.8

FIG. 7

ENGINE CONTROL DETAILS – COUNTERSHAFT

REAR CONTROL COUNTERSHAFT, PORT SIDE FUSELAGE.

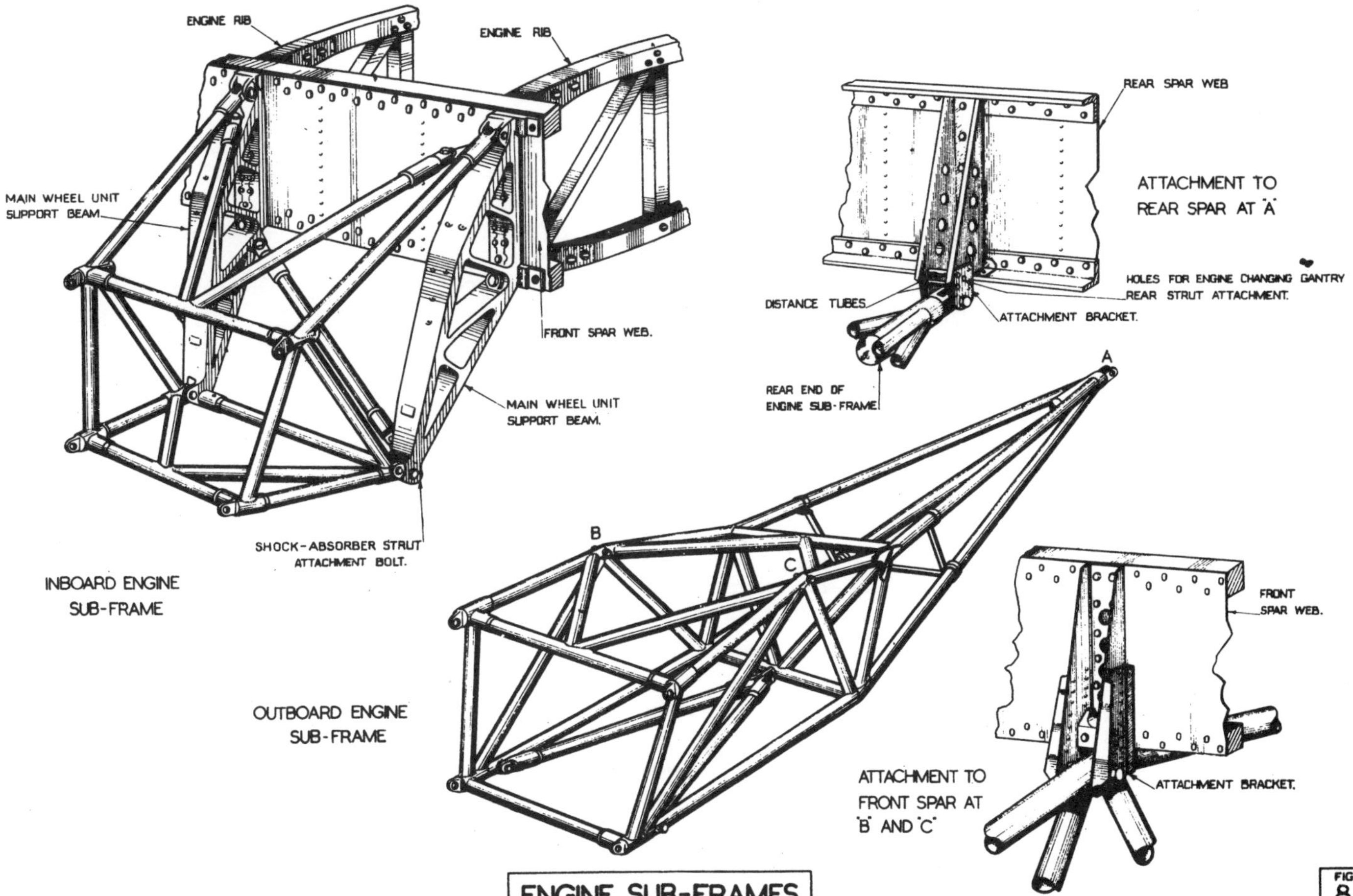

ENGINE SUB-FRAMES.

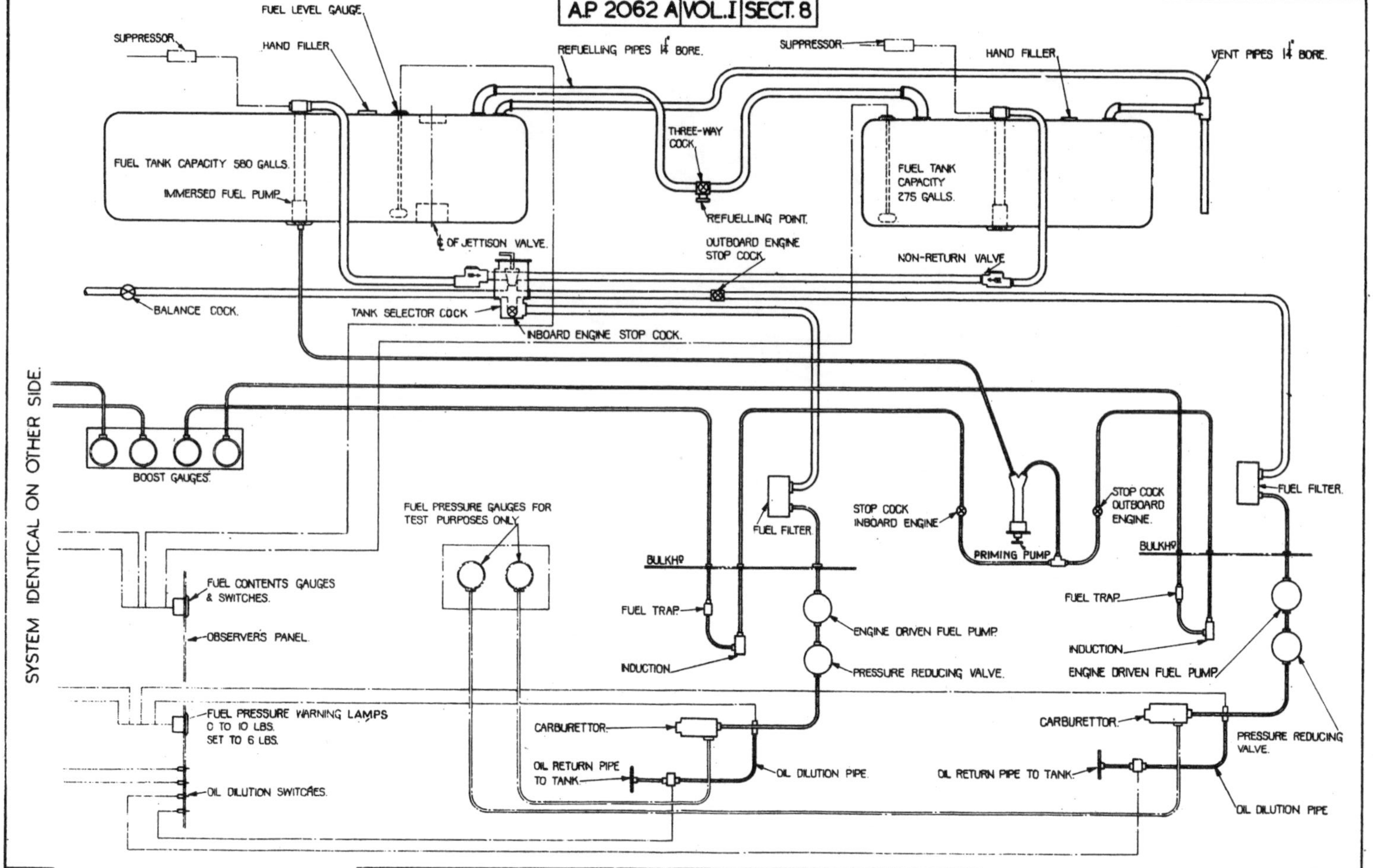

FUEL SYSTEM – AEROPLANES L.7527 TO L.7532

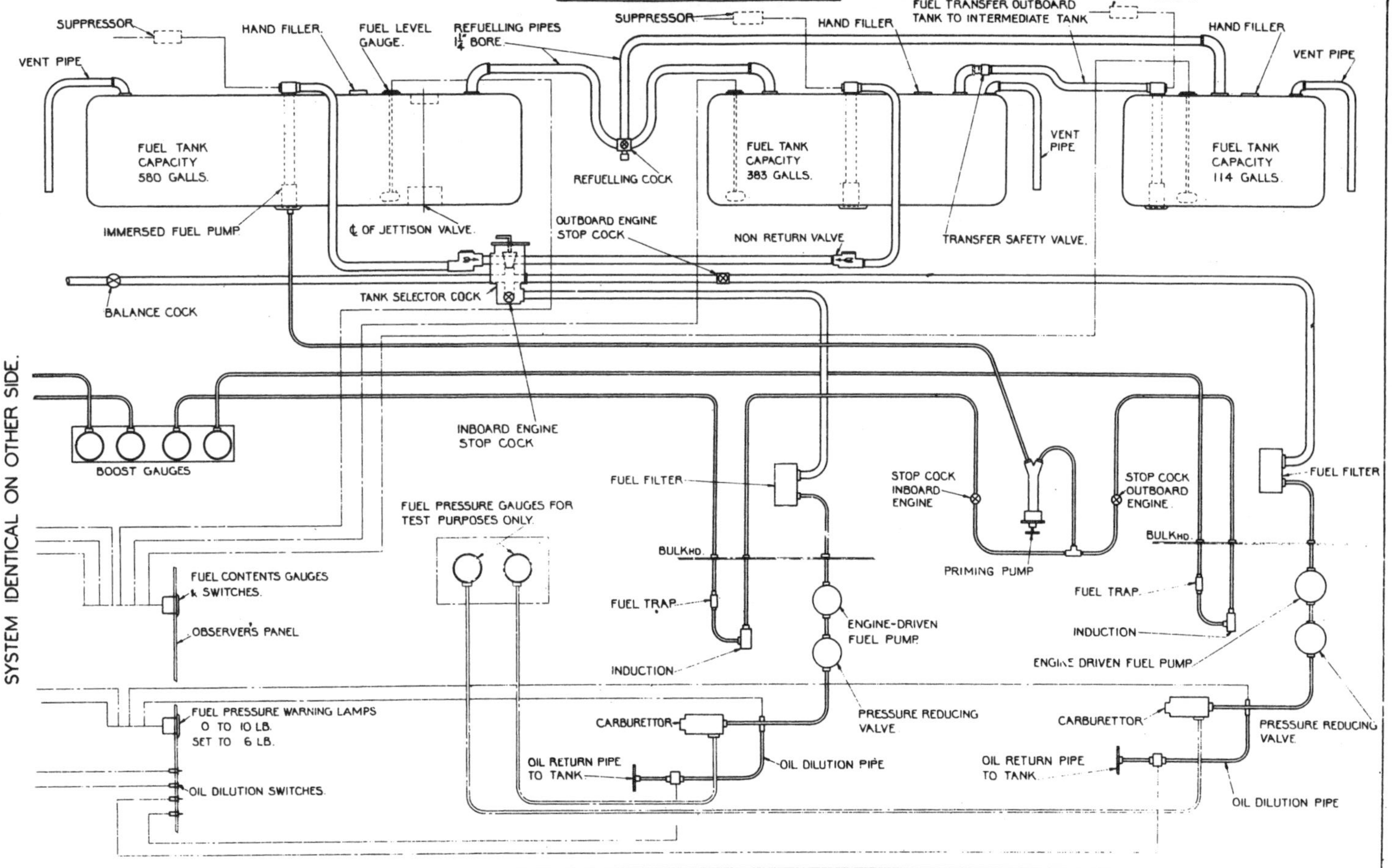

FIG. 10

FUEL SYSTEM - AEROPLANES L.7533 AND SUBSEQUENT

FIG. 10

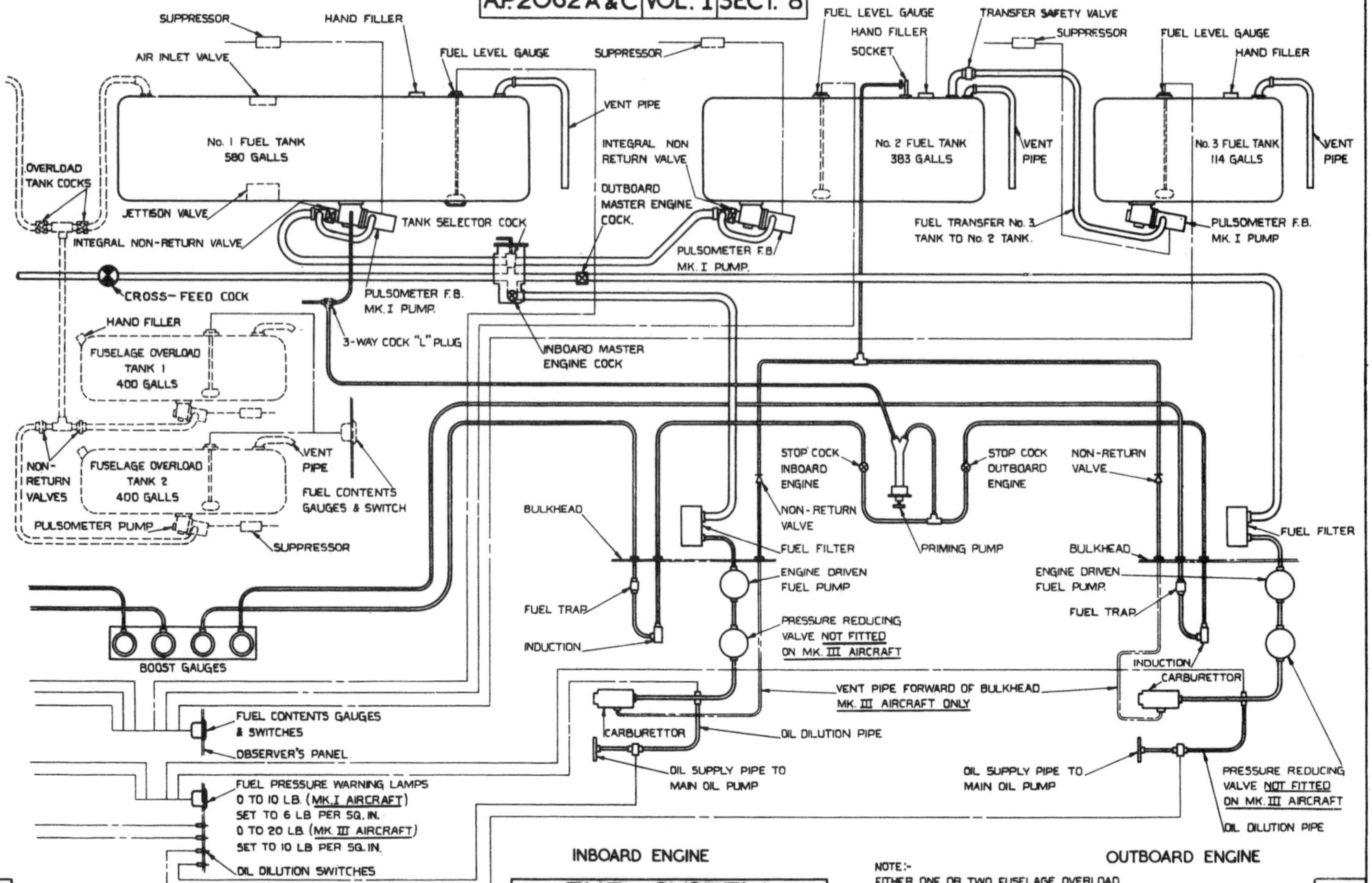

NOTE:-
EITHER ONE OR TWO FUSELAGE OVERLOAD TANKS CAN BE FITTED TO AIRCRAFT INCORPORATING MOD. Nos. 802 AND 803

FIG. 10A

FUEL SYSTEM
WITH PULSOMETER F.B. MK. I PUMPS

FIG. 10A

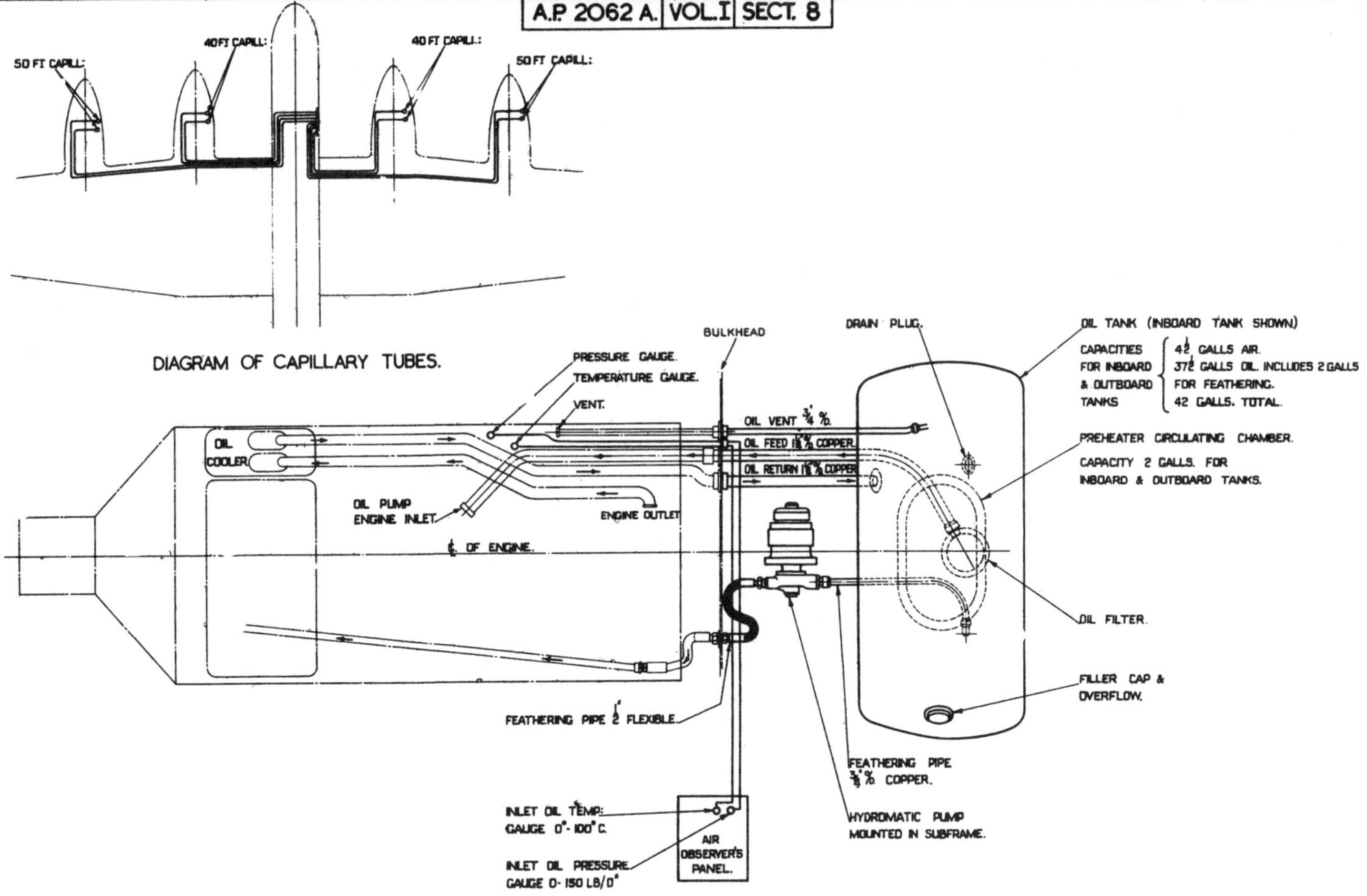

FIG. 11

OIL SYSTEM - ONE ENGINE UNIT.

FIG. 11

PP2096 M27625/2387 3/43 3000 C & P Gp. 959(4)

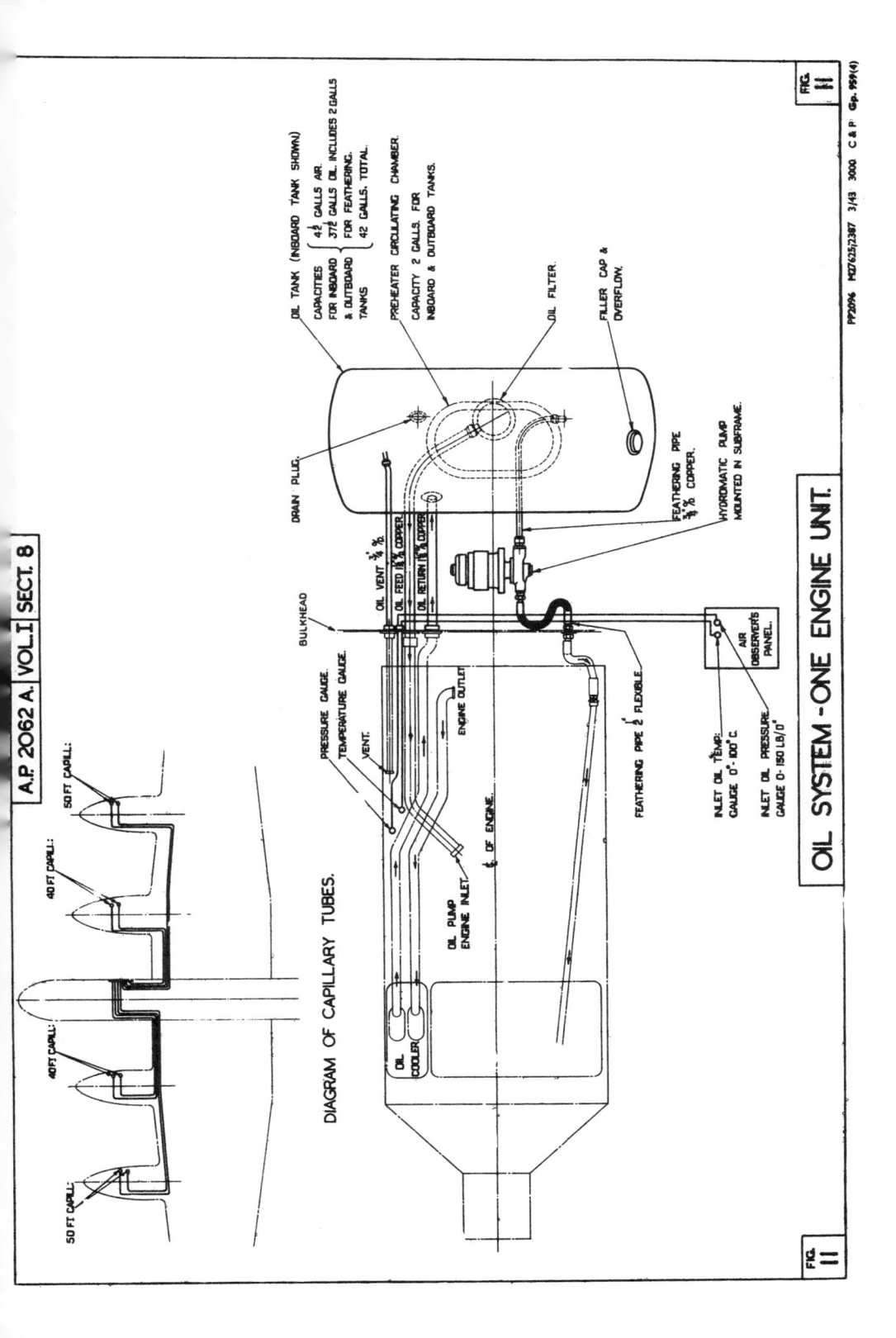

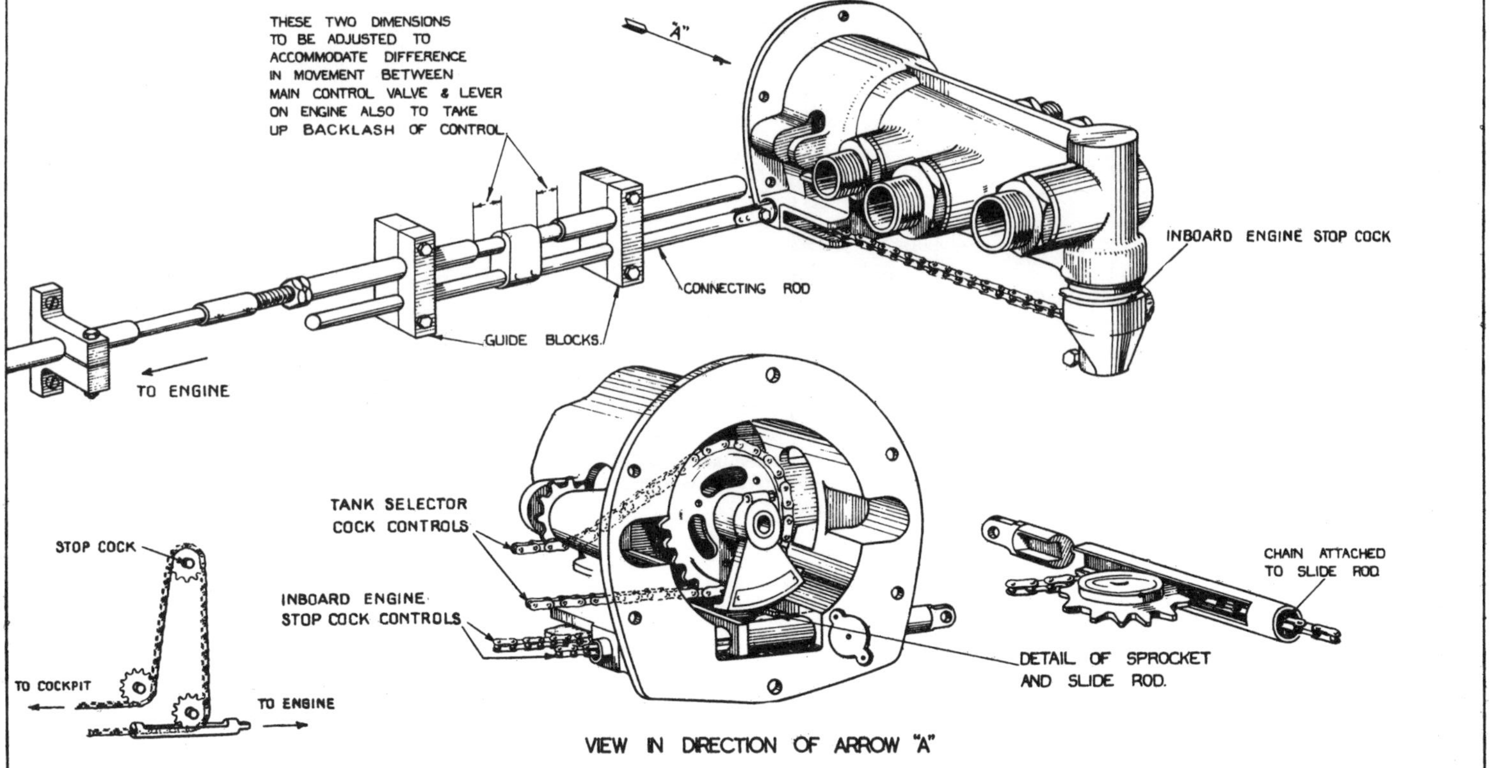

FIG. 12

SLOW RUNNING CUT-OUT CONTROL.

FIG. 12

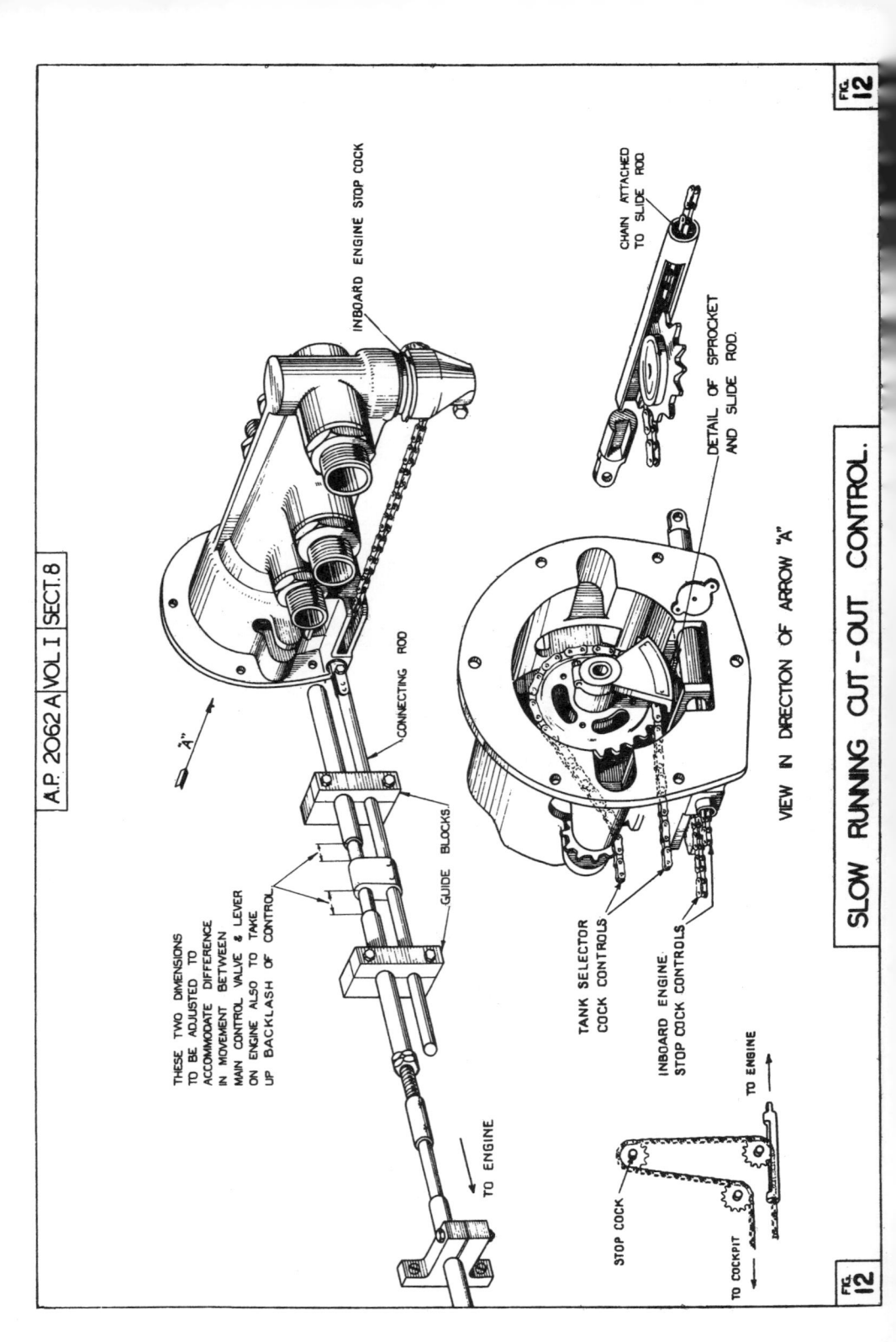

Section 9:
Hydraulic and pneumatic systems.

This page amended by A.L. No. 29
July, 1943

A.P.2062A and C, Vol. I

SECTION 9—HYDRAULIC AND PNEUMATIC SYSTEMS

LIST OF CONTENTS

Hydraulic system—general services

	Para.
General	1
Supply circuit	2
Main wheels circuit	5
Flaps circuit	7
Flaps and main wheels emergency system	9
Bomb door circuit	12
Emergency opening of bomb doors	14
Air-intake shutter circuit	15
Emergency operation of air-intake shutters	18
Fuel jettison system	19
Emergency operation of jettison system	23

Hydraulic system—turrets

General	24

Pneumatic system

General	27
Brakes system	29
Radiator flap system	30
Supercharger controls	31
Slow-running cut-out controls (Mk. III aircraft only)	32
Air charging	33

LIST OF ILLUSTRATIONS

	Fig.
Hydraulic circuit—diagram	1
Turret circuit diagram	2
Diagram of pneumatic system	3

F.S./1

A.P.2062A, VOL. I

SECTION 9—HYDRAULIC AND PNEUMATIC SYSTEMS

Hydraulic System—General services

General

1. The hydraulic system operates the main wheel units, bomb doors, main plane flaps, air-intake shutters and the fuel jettisoning system. The system is operated by two engine-driven pumps, one mounted on each inboard engine, and controlled by levers or handles in the cockpit (*see* Sect. 1). A hand pump is included in the system and mounted on the port side of the fuselage between the armoured bulkhead and the front spar, but is only used to operate the air-intake jacks or the jettison system, in emergency. It is possible to lower the bomb doors by means of the hand pump, but it takes approximately 15 minutes of pumping. Due to the capacities of the jacks it is not normally possible to operate the main wheel units or flaps by hand pump. While none of the units is in operation, the engine pumps are idling and the fluid is circulating at low pressure from the pumps through a filter and an automatic cut-out valve to the reservoir. A circuit diagram of the whole system is shown in fig. 1. The layout of the piping and components of each circuit, are illustrated in Sect. 4, Chap. 3, and the components themselves are described in A.P.1803, Vol. I.

Supply circuit

2. The supply from each pump passes through an external supply valve and a non-return valve, the former being fitted for ground test purposes only. When the ground test rig is connected, the feed from the rig is admitted through the supply valve to the aeroplane circuit by means of an adaptor which screws into one end of the valve and simultaneously blanks off the normal engine supply line. Similarly, a return valve for the rig is fitted in the return line to the engine-driven pump. The non-return valve in each pump supply line prevents the reaction of one engine-driven pump upon the other.

3. When any circuit is operated, power is initially supplied by an accumulator, the main purpose of which is described in para. 15. When the accumulator pressure falls to the cut-in setting of the automatic cut-out valve, the latter directs the fluid delivered by the engine-driven pumps to the circuit being operated at the conclusion of the operation, the pumps continue to deliver fluid to re-charge the accumulator, until the cut-out pressure is reached, when the automatic cut-out valve diverts the delivery of the pumps to the reservoir.

4. For the lowering of the main wheels and flaps in the event of the failure of the hydraulic system, a cylinder of compressed air is provided, from which air can be directed to the DOWN side of the main wheel unit and flap jacks. In later aeroplanes two oxygen-type bottles are used in place of the cylinder.

Main wheels circuit

5. The raising and lowering of the main wheels are governed by the hand operation of a selector valve on the right of the pilot's seat. This is always in either the UP or DOWN position; there is no neutral. When the selector lever is moved to the UP position, fluid is delivered through the non-return valve and selector valve to the underside of the jack pistons, and raises the main wheel units.

This leaf issued with A.L. No. 45 *A.P.2062A and C, Vol. I, Sect. 9*
September, 1944

6. When the selector lever is moved to the DOWN position, the above sequence of operations is repeated, except that this time the fluid is fed to the top side of the jack pistons, via an emergency air transfer valve carried on a stay between each pair of jacks.

Flaps circuit

7. The lowering and raising of the flaps are governed by a control unit mounted below the pilot's floor and controlled by a handle to the right of the pilot's seat. The unit has a neutral position in which the handle is normally set. Fluid is admitted to the control unit through a non-return valve. When the control unit is moved to the DOWN position, fluid is delivered through the non-return valve and the control unit to the DOWN connection on the flap jack. Fluid on the other side of the piston is exhausted through the control unit and return circuit until the jack has completed its stroke and the flaps are lowered. For partial operation of the flaps the control handle should be returned to the neutral position when the desired setting has been obtained.

8. When the control handle is pulled to the UP position, the above sequence of operations is repeated except that fluid is supplied to the UP side of the flap jack and exhausted from the DOWN side.

Flaps and main wheels emergency system

9. In the event of the failure of the engine driven pumps or the main wheels circuit, the main wheels and flaps can be lowered by means of compressed air. In early aircraft the air is stored in a cylinder, and in later aircraft in two oxygen type bottles mounted behind the front spar. The system is operated by turning ON a cock on the starboard side of the fuselage just aft of the front spar (except in aircraft No. L.7527–L.7532, in which a remote control is provided just forward of the observer's instrument panel). When the system is operated the main wheels are lowered at once, but the flap control handle has to be operated in the normal manner. The air is admitted to the DOWN side of the main wheel jacks through a non-return valve, near the cylinder, and through an emergency air valve and a transfer valve to each pair of jacks.

10. The non-return valve serves as a lock for the air once the main wheels have been lowered. The emergency air valves pass the air to the transfer valves and allow the fluid on the underside of the jack pistons to discharge to the atmosphere. The transfer valves blank off the normal fluid supply line and admit air to the jacks.

11. The air is supplied to the flap control unit by a separate pipe-line, but from there to the jacks the air passes through the hydraulic pipe-lines. Two non-return valves are fitted, one to prevent the normal fluid supply from entering the air line, and the other to prevent the emergency air from passing into the fluid line. To lower the flaps when the emergency air cock has been operated, the control must be moved to the DOWN position in order that the air may pass through the control unit to the jack, and the fluid from the jack pass through the control unit back to the reservoir.

Bomb door circuit

12. The opening and closing of the bomb doors are governed by the operation by hand of a selector valve on the left of the pilot's seat. This valve is similar to the main wheel selector valve, having only UP and DOWN positions and no

F.S./2

neutral. When the selector lever is moved to the DOWN position, fluid is delivered through the non-return valve and the selector valve to the piston head side of the bomb door jacks, which extend to open the bomb doors.

13. When the control lever is moved to the UP position the sequence of operations is repeated, except that the fluid is fed to the piston rod side of the jacks.

14. *Emergency opening of bomb doors.*—The bomb doors may be opened if the engine-driven pumps or bomb door circuit fail, by moving the control to the DOWN position, when the doors will fall open under their own weight.

Air-intake shutter circuit

15. A hydraulic accumulator is fitted on the delivery side of the automatic cut-out valve, to overcome the effect of a sudden rise in pressure due to the small diameter of the pipes to the air-intake jacks. This rise in pressure would otherwise cause intermittent delivery through the cut-out valve and consequently a hesitant operation of the jacks.

16. Operation of the shutters is governed by a rotary control valve, mounted in the main floor below the forward end of the navigator's table and operated by a connecting rod from a handle projecting through the port side of the pilot's floor. Positions for HOT AIR and COLD AIR only are provided, as the neutral position is not required.

17. When the valve is set in the HOT AIR position, fluid is delivered through the control valve to the top side of the jack piston, while fluid on the other side of the jack piston is exhausted through the return line.

18. *Emergency operation of air-intake shutters.*—In the event of a failure of the engine-driven pumps, these jacks can be operated by the hand pump on the port side of the fuselage.

Fuel jettison system

19. This system provides for jettisoning the contents of the two inboard fuel tanks. The operation of the circuit opens a jettison valve in the bottom of each tank, through which the fuel is discharged, and also a valve in the top of the tank which admits air.

20. The opening of the jettison valve breaks a small retaining washer and allows a door in the underside of the plane to fall open and release a double walled stocking incorporated in the jettison valve.

21. The operation of the fuel jettison system is governed by a control valve operated from a handle on the port side of the pilot's floor. The handle has two positions, NORMAL or JETTISON. When the control valve is moved to JETTISON, pressure from the hydraulic accumulator delivers fluid through the control valve to the jettison and air inlet valves. The pressure in the accumulator must exceed 650 lb. per sq. in. to ensure efficient operation of the system. The pressure drop will not be sufficient to actuate the automatic cut-out and, if it is necessary to build up the pressure in the accumulator, one of the main hydraulic services (e.g. bomb doors) should be operated momentarily to cut-in the pumps.

22. When the control handle is moved to the NORMAL position, the pressure in the supply line to the jettison and air inlet valves, which are returned by springs, is released, and the fluid flows back through the control valve from which it is exhausted to the atmosphere. No return line to the reservoir is provided in the jettison system.

This leaf issued with A.L. No. 45
September, 1944
A.P.2062A and C, Vol. I, Sect. 9

23. *Emergency operation of jettison system.*—In the event of the failure of the hydraulic feed system the jettison system can be operated from the hydraulic accumulator provided that the pressure available exceeds 650 lb. per sq. in.

Hydraulic System—Turrets

General

24. Four hydraulically-operated rotating gun turrets are fitted:—one in the nose (type F.N.5), one in the top of the fuselage rear centre portion (type F.N.50), one in the bottom of the fuselage rear centre portion (type F.N.64) and one in the rear end of the fuselage (type F.N.20). A turret pump is mounted on each of the four engines, the port inboard and outboard pumps supplying the lower mid and rear turrets respectively, and the starboard inboard and outboard pumps supplying the front and upper mid turrets respectively. The circuits are illustrated in fig. 2 and in Sect. 4, Chap. 3.

25. Each circuit is fitted with a high pressure relief valve on the rear face of the fireproof bulkhead, and with a recuperator and an oil filter in the fuselage. The oil pressure is controlled by the recuperator, which acts also as a reservoir. A low pressure relief valve is also incorporated in the rear turret circuit just forward of the turret, and an external rotation valve, connected to the turret by separate pipes, is fitted just forward of the tail plane front spar. The filter and recuperator for the front turret are mounted on the starboard side of the fuselage nose, for the upper mid turret on the starboard side at the flare station and for the lower mid turret and rear turret on the port side at the flare station. Pressure gauge test couplings are fitted in each circuit near the turret. For details of the recuperators and turrets, *see* A.P.1659A.

26. When the lower mid turret is not fitted the ends of the hydraulic pipes are connected together by a return pipe at the Avery couplings above the turret.

Pneumatic system

General

27. The pneumatic system (*see* fig. 3) operates the Dunlop-type wheel brakes, the thermostatically controlled electro-pneumatic rams of the radiator flaps, and the electro-pneumatic rams for the supercharger controls and, in Mk. III aircraft only, the slow-running cut-out controls also. Compressed air is supplied from a container which is kept charged to 300 lb./sq. in. by a Heywood compressor mounted on the starboard inboard engine. A pressure maintaining valve, set to 100–110 lb./sq. in., is fitted in the supply line to all the services except the brakes to ensure that sufficient pressure is always reserved for brake operation by cutting off the other services if the pressure falls to the set figure. The working pressure of the wheel brakes is 80 lb./sq. in., so that in the event of the compression failing it is possible to obtain several applications of the brakes from the container.

28. A pipe-line from the compressor runs to the pressure regulating valve on the rear face of the fireproof bulkhead through an oil and water trap on the auxiliaries panel between the undercarriage support beams. The pipe is then continued inboard along the front spar and forward on the starboard side of the

F.S./3

fuselage to the air container mounted just aft of the front turret. From the container the air is delivered through a filter on the port side to the various services. The installation of the system is illustrated in Sect. 4, Chap. 3.

Brakes system

29. The brakes are applied by operating the lever on the pilot's handwheel, and differential action is obtained by means of a Dunlop relay valve mounted on fuselage former F, and connected to the port rudder pedal arm by a rod. Air is delivered through the filter to the differential relay valve. Two pipes run aft from the relay valve to the front spar, and outboard to the port and starboard wheel brake units. A triple pressure gauge on the pilot's instrument panel connected to each of these lines and to the delivery to the relay valve indicates the pressure in the container and in each of the brake supply pipes. The description, operation and maintenance of the units included in the brake system will be found in A.P.1519, Vol. I and A.P.2337, Vol. I.

Radiator flap system

30. The pneumatic rams operating the radiator flaps are supplied by a pipe-line which is connected to the supply to the brakes system differential valve. The pipe line leads to a pressure maintaining valve (*see* para. 27) on the port side of the fuselage nose adjacent to the filter, and thence aft on the port side of the bomb compartment and outboard in each direction along the front spar. For details of the operation and thermostatic control of the pneumatic rams, *see* A.P.2140B, C and D, Vol. I.

Supercharger controls

31. The two-speed supercharger control of each engine is operated by an electro-pneumatic ram for which the air supply is taken from the radiator flap system at a connection on the fireproof bulkhead. For the electrical installation, *see* Sect. 6 and Sect. 10, and for details of the control, *see* A.P.2140B, C and D, Vol. I.

Slow-running cut-out controls (Mk. III aircraft only)

32. The slow-running cut-out controls of Merlin 28 or 38 engines are also electro-pneumatically operated. The air supply is taken from a T-piece in the pipe line of the two-speed supercharger control. For the electrical installation, *see* Sect. 6 and Sect. 10, and for details of the control, *see* A.P.2140B, C and D, Vol. I.

Air charging

33. The charging of the cylinder is controlled by the pressure-regulating valve. When the pressure reaches 300–320 lb./sq. in. the back pressure opens and retains open, a valve, which releases the air in the delivery line, allowing the compressor to idle. When the pressure in the container falls to 270–280 lb./sq. in. the valve closes and charging recommences. The container may also be charged from an external supply, through a charging connection on the auxiliaries panel in the starboard inboard nacelle.

HYDRAULIC CIRCUIT DIAGRAM

A.P.2062A|VOL.I|SECT.9

Interpretation of diagram

1. Where a number of symbols is enclosed in a dotted frame, the components represented by the symbols are actually built in one unit.
2. Where a number of components are connected in parallel, only one is drawn but the number off is indicated.
3. Single arrows on pipe lines indicate the direction of flow, but do not mean that flow is always taking place. Double arrows pointing in the same direction indicate that fluid is always flowing when the engine-driven pump is working. Two arrows pointing in opposite directions indicate that flow takes place in both directions. Arrows are not drawn inside a frame enclosing a number of symbols.

Key

- Hand pump
- Non-return valve
- Relief valve
- Transfer valve
- Filter
- Rotary control valve

Components labelled in diagram: Reservoir; Emergency air container; Emergency control; Distributor block; Two pairs external supply valves; Hand pump; Pressure relief valve 850 ± 25 lb/sq.in.; Two engine-driven pumps; Automatic cut-out valve; 2 Off; Non-return valve; Accumulator; Selector valve; Flap control unit; Selector valve; *2 Off; Two emergency air valves; Four undercarriage jacks; One flap jack; Four bomb door jacks; Four carburettor air intake jacks; Vent to atmosphere; Jettison valve; Air valve; Two fuel tanks.

Cut-out pressure 800 lb/sq.in.
Cut-in pressure 180 lb/sq.in.

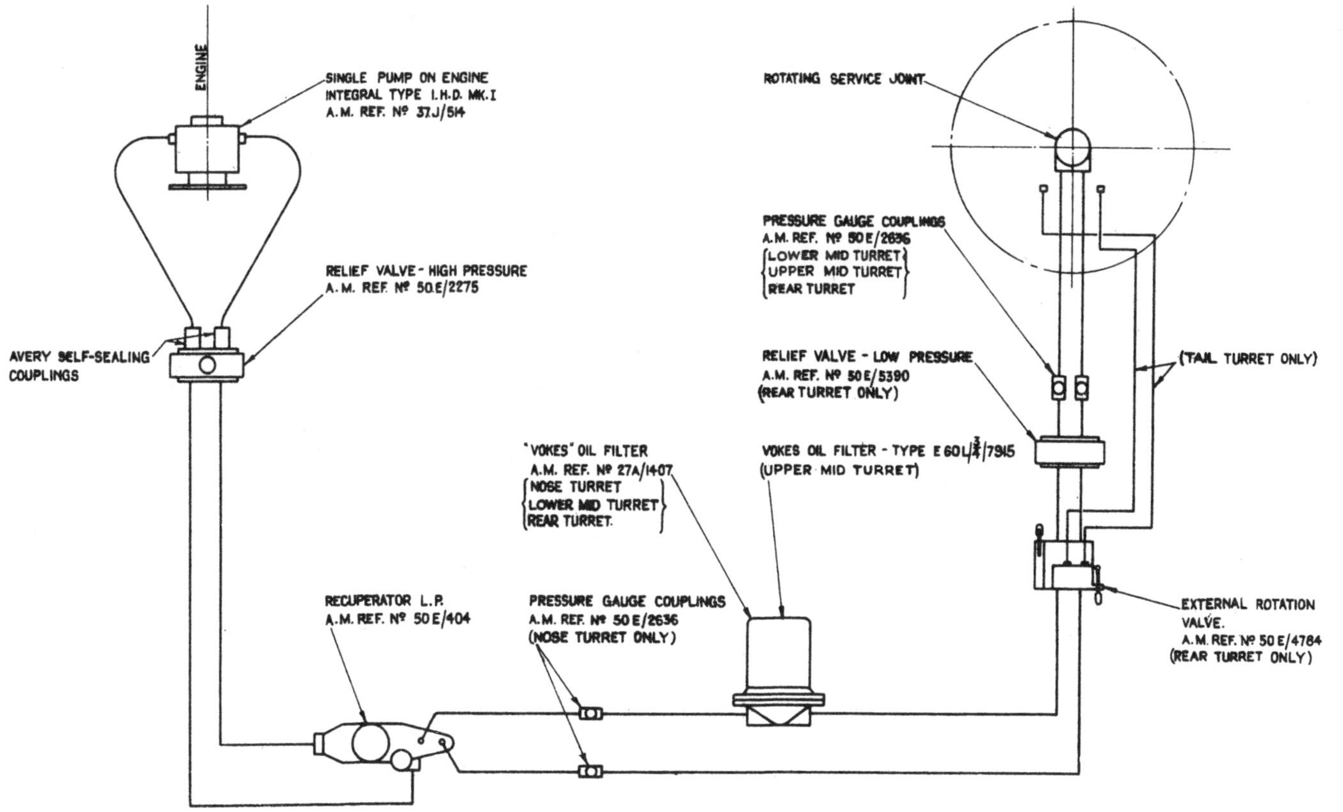

TURRET CIRCUIT DIAGRAM

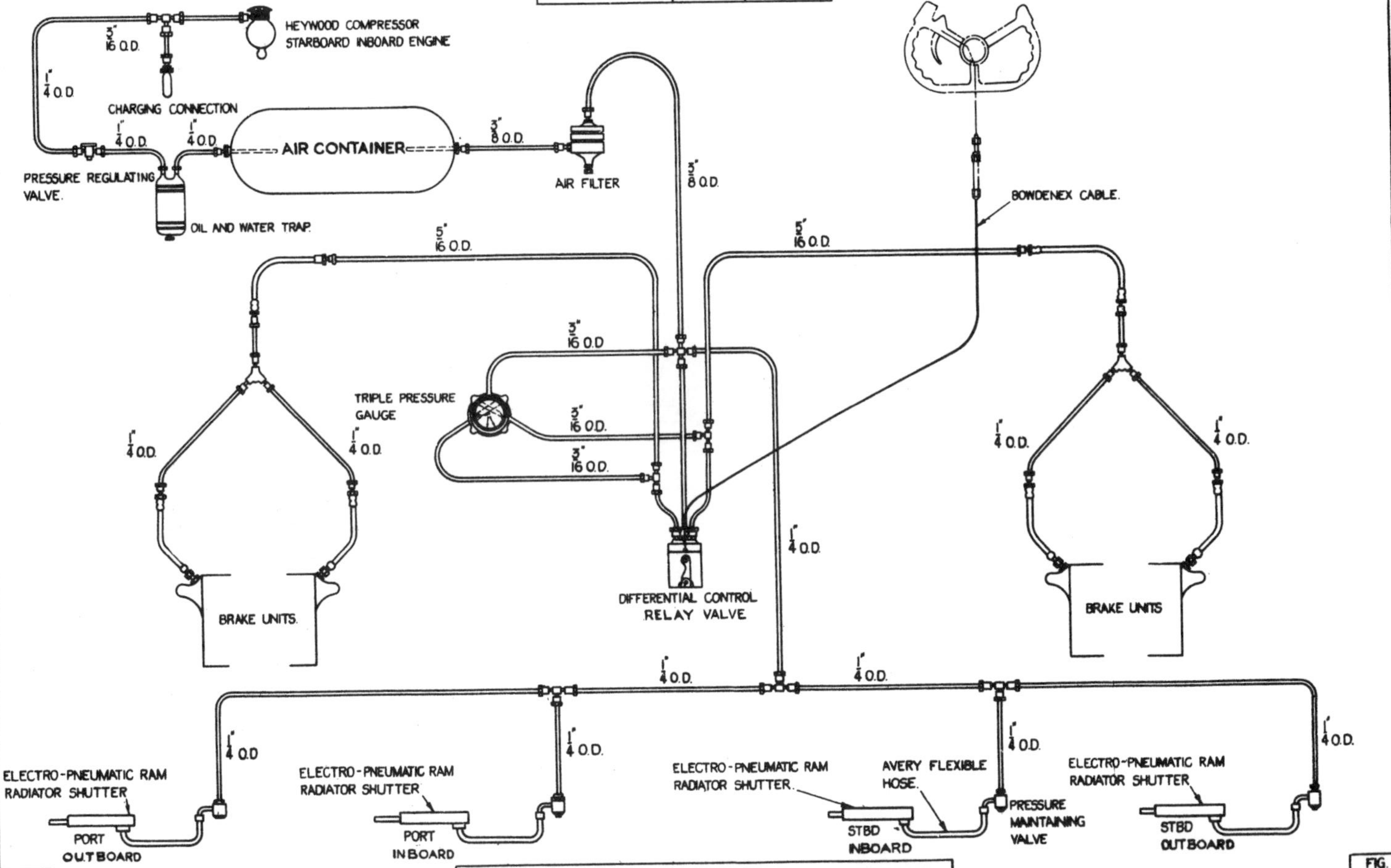

DIAGRAM OF PNEUMATIC SYSTEM

AP 2062 A/VOL I/SECT 9

FIG. 3

Section 10:
Electrical and radio installations - Description.

Issued with A.L. No. 10
June, 1942
This page amended by A.L. No. 28
June, 1943

A.P.2062A and C, Vol. I

SECTION 10

ELECTRICAL AND RADIO INSTALLATIONS—DESCRIPTION

LIST OF CONTENTS

	Para.
General	1
Electrical services panel	3
Junction boxes	4
Circuits—	
Charging and distribution	5
Engine starting and ignition	6
Propeller feathering	8
Flap indicator	11
Fire extinguishers	12
Undercarriage indicators	13
General lighting and turret supplies	15
Navigation lamps	16
Headlamp	17
Identification lamps	18
Recognition lamps	19
Intercommunication call lamps	20
Heated gloves	22
Camera heating	23
Heated bomb gear	24
Landing lamps	25
Pressure head	26
Automatic controls supply	27
Engine-speed indicators	28
Fuel contents gauges	29
Oil dilution	30
Dinghy inflation	31
Fuel pressure warning lamps	32
Automatic bomb sights	33
D.R. compass	34
Camera	35
Bomb fuzing and release	36
Immersed fuel pumps	39
Propeller de-icing	40
Radiator flaps	41
Radiator shutter control switches	41A
Two-speed supercharger controls	41B
Slow-running cut-out controls	41C
Undercarriage indicator	42
Warning horn	43
Undercarriage indicator switch	46
Radio—	
Intercommunication	47
T.1154-R.1155 installation	49
T.R.9F	51
Beam approach installation	52
A.R.I.5033	53
A.R.I.5000	55

F.S./1

A.P.2062A and C, Vol. I

SECTION 10

ELECTRICAL AND RADIO INSTALLATIONS—DESCRIPTION

General

1. This Section gives a description of the electrical installation together with the position in the aircraft of the main components. Wiring and theoretical diagrams, notes on access to components, and maintenance notes on those items peculiar to this aircraft, are given in Sect. 6. Components which are described in other publications are only referred to in this Section. For the bonding of the system, reference should be made to Sect. 6.

2. The installation consists of two supply units, connected in parallel, and the various circuits. A 24-volt generator charging two 12-volt accumulators connected in series through a voltage regulator and a cut-out, form each supply unit.

Electrical services panel

3. This panel is mounted on the starboard side of the fuselage just forward of the front spar. The interior of the panel is used as a junction box, and contains four rows of eight fuses, numbered 1 to 32. This panel also contains the electrical services instruments consisting of two ammeters, one voltmeter, two cut-outs and two main 60 amp. fuses, two switches for the generator fields and a switch for the headlamp.

Junction boxes

4. There are nine junction boxes numbered JB.1 to JB.13, omitting Nos. 3, 6, 8 and 12. They are positioned as follows:—

JB.1. On the front spar adjacent to the centre-line of the port inboard engine.

JB.2. On the front spar adjacent to the centre-line of the starboard inboard engine.

JB.4. On the front spar in the port wing tip, at rib 4.

JB.5. On the front spar in the starboard wing tip, at rib 4.

JB.7. On the starboard side of the fuselage just forward of the electrical services panel.

JB.9. Just aft of the upper mid turret on the port side of the fuselage roof.

JB.10. Just aft of the emergency exit in the centre section roof.

JB.11. On the front spar web at the centre-line of the aircraft.

JB.13. On the starboard side of the cockpit aft of the pilot's instrument panel.

Circuits

5. *Charging and distribution.*—The power for the electrical services is supplied by two 24-volt, 1,000 watt, engine-driven D.C. generators, type K, mounted one on each inboard engine. Suppressors, type O, are mounted on the inboard engine fireproof bulkheads, and voltage regulators, type A, are located just below the electrical services panel. The outputs are fed through

cut-outs, type F, in the panel and two 60-amp. fuses to two 50–0–50 ammeters in circuit with the accumulators. The latter comprise two 24-volt 40 Ah. accumulators (each 2—12-volt 40 Ah. connected in series) connected in parallel and carried in trays on the starboard side of the main floor, just aft of the front spar. For full details of items of equipment used in this circuit reference should be made to A.P.1095.

6. *Engine-starting and ignition.*—The starter motors (C.A.4750) are located on the starboard side of the engines, below the hand-turning gear, and are controlled by push-switches on the pilot's instrument panel, through relays fitted on a ground starter socket and relay panel situated at the bottom of the spar at the inboard engine nacelles. Both booster coils, one mounted on the front face of each fireproof bulkhead, near the top, are connected through an isolating spark gap mounted on the engine and are only in circuit during the starting operation.

7. The engine ignition switches are mounted near the centre of the pilot's instrument panel, to the right of the undercarriage indicator switch (*see* also para. 13). Two magnetos are provided at the front end of each engine, of which only the starting magneto is boosted. For further details of components used in this circuit reference should be made to A.P.1181 and A.P.2140A.

8. *Propeller feathering.*—The four cockpit switches are mounted on the right-hand side of the pilot's instrument panel, relays are incorporated in the ground starter and relay panel, and a pressure switch is fitted on the starboard side of the engine, near the front. The feathering pumps are mounted in the engine sub-frames.

9. When the cockpit switches are depressed they are retained in position by the solenoid coils, the negative returns of which are taken through the pressure switches. The operation of the push-switch closes the relay which controls the feathering pump. When the feathering action is completed the rising oil pressure opens the pressure switch, thus allowing the push-switch and consequently the relay, to return to their normal positions. When it is required to unfeather the propeller, the feathering push-switch must be held in the depressed position in order to allow the pump to build up the greater pressure required for this operation.

10. This circuit can be tested by connecting an external supply to the ground supply socket provided for starting. Tests must always be made with a fully charged accumulator, or damage to the solenoid switches will result. For further details of equipment used in this circuit reference should be made to A.P.2140A.

11. *Flap indicator.*—The flap indicator (Smith's code 26 F.L.) is mounted on the pilot's instrument panel, and above the indicator is an ON-OFF switch. A transmitter (Smith's code 27 F.L.) is fitted to a bracket below rib 31 in the trailing edge of the port centre section main plane, and is connected to the flap by an arm which incorporates an adjusting screw.

12. *Fire extinguishers.*—The fire extinguishing system for the engines consists of an electrically-operated extinguisher cylinder, Mk. IIA, mounted behind the front spar in each inboard nacelle and on the sub-frame in each outboard nacelle, and controlled by either the four push-switches on the pilot's instrument panel, the two flame switches on each fireproof bulkhead, the gravity switch or the impact switch. The two latter switches are located on the star-

board side of the fuselage nose, on formers H and J, respectively. The negative return from the gravity switch is taken through the "locked DOWN" side of the undercarriage indicator DOWN switches, so that the gravity switch is rendered inoperative when the undercarriage is locked up. For further details of this circuit, reference should be made to A.P.1464B.

13. *Undercarriage indicator.*—The undercarriage indicator (Dowty No. 6153) is mounted on the pilot's instrument panel, and gives the following indications for the various positions of the undercarriage:—

    Undercarriage locked UP   ...   No lights
    Undercarriage unlocked   ...   Red lights
    Undercarriage locked DOWN   ...   Green lights

A master switch is mounted adjacent to the ignition switches, and fitted with a bar which prevents the ignition being switched ON until the undercarriage indicator has been switched ON. Conversely, the latter cannot be switched OFF before the ignition. Below the master switch is a changeover switch provided to bring into operation a reserve set of green lamps should the normal set fail. An additional set of red lamps is wired in parallel with the primary set and lights with them.

14. The indicator is operated by the undercarriage UP and DOWN switches (Pye Universal 83460-2). The two UP switches on the UP catches in each nacelle, which are used as ON-OFF switches, are connected in parallel, and remain in the ON position until the undercarriage is locked UP. Red lights will therefore show until both latches on each undercarriage unit have been locked. The two DOWN switches which are fitted in the locking mechanism, are used as two-way switches, and are connected in series, ensuring that the green lights for each undercarriage unit cannot indicate until both switches have been operated. The negative return of the green lamps is connected through one side of the DOWN switches, and that of the red lamps through the UP switches and the other side of the DOWN switches. A warning horn, which is mounted below the port cockpit rail, is connected in series with a throttle switch in the engine control pedestal and the red lamp side of the DOWN switches. The throttle switch closes if the throttle is less than one-third open, and if the undercarriage is in any position except locked DOWN the circuit will be completed through the DOWN switches and the warning horn will sound. A test lamp and test push-switch for the horn are mounted on the port cockpit rail.

15. *General lighting and turret supplies.*—The general lighting services are fed from one fuse, with the exceptions mentioned below, and the following lamps are fitted. Two floodlamps, type B, are provided for the pilot (one on a separate fuse), and single floodlamps for the wireless operator's station, for the D.F. loop and for the electrical services panel. A cabin lamp is fitted on the port side of the nose, at the wireless operator's station, at the rest station, just aft of the rear spar, at the flare station, on the port side just forward of the main door, and just forward of the draughtproof doors. A switch at the main door controls the lamp on the opposite side. Two cockpit lamps, Mk. II, are fitted to the front former for the bomb aimer, and a cockpit lamp is provided on each of the following panels:—Bomb aimer's port and starboard panels, air observer's panel (connected to the pilot's separate floodlamp fuse) and navigator's panel. An angle poise chartboard lamp (Terry type L.315) is provided for the navigator's table.

16. *Navigation lamps.*—The navigation lamps, type A, in the tail and wing tips are connected in parallel and are controlled by a switch, type B, on the port side of the pilot's auxiliary panel.

17. *Headlamp.*—The headlamp, type B, is mounted in the nose on the front former, and is controlled by a three-way switch on the electrical services panel, which enables it to be switched in parallel with either the navigation or the downward identification lamps.

18. *Identification lamps.*—A single upward and three downward identification lamps, type C, are located above and below the forward end of the rear section of the fuselage respectively, and are controlled by an identification switchbox, No. 2, Mk. III, on the right-hand side of the pilot's instrument panel. The three downward lamps can be controlled independently, by the three-unit switchbox, Type B, above the identification switchbox on the left-hand side of the instrument panel. The upward and downward lamps may be used singly or together through the key or on STEADY.

19. *Recognition lamps.*—The three recognition lamps at each wing tip and the lamp at the rear end of the fuselage are controlled by an identification switchbox, No. 2, Mk. III, on the pilot's instrument panel immediately in front of the control column. Only the downward side of the switchbox is connected. The colour of the wing tip recognition lamps, red, green or yellow, must be selected before flight by a three-way switch, type A, fitted on the electrical services panel.

20. *Intercommunication call lamps.*—Call lamp switchboxes are provided at the following positions:—in the front turret, on the port side of the fuselage nose near the bomb aimer's panel, on the pilot's panel (port side), on the navigator's instrument panel, adjacent to the window at the wireless operator's station, at the rest station (port side) on former 10, at the flare station on the forward face of the A.R.I.5000 bracket, in the upper mid turret, for the lower turret between formers 25 and 26, and in the rear turret.

21. The call lamp switchboxes each contain a switch in series with a lamp, and are interconnected so that when any switch is pressed all lamps will light. The switches are connected in parallel between a positive supply and a connection to which the lamps also are wired in parallel, and which provides a positive supply to all the lamps when any switch is pressed. All the lamps are also connected in parallel to negative. In the front and rear turrets the supply is derived from the general turret supply, and in the remainder of the system from the rear gunner's panel. For further details, *see* A.P.1095.

22. *Heated gloves.*—The heated glove sockets are connected to terminal blocks at the following positions:—for the bomb aimer, on the panel on the port side of the nose between formers H and J, just forward of the ON-OFF switch controlling the system; for the first pilot, on the port side below the cockpit rail between formers D and E; for the second pilot and air observer, at the rear inner corner of the pilot's floor; for the navigator, below the edge of the table near the seat pivot tube; and for the wireless operator on the face of former 5 to the left of his seat. Only the red, green and blue terminals of the sockets are used. For further details, *see* A.P.1095.

23. *Camera heating.*—Two sockets for camera heating are provided on a panel between formers G and H, below the port instrument panel in the nose. The plugs are connected to the supply for the heated gloves circuit.

F.S./3

24. *Heated bomb gear.*—Heating is provided for the centre bomb gear housing in the intermediate centre portion of the fuselage. This housing is arranged to carry large sectional bombs. An ON-OFF switch controlling the heating circuit is mounted above the rear end of the bomb aimer's starboard panel.

25. *Landing lamps.*—Two 240-watt, type J, landing lamps are fitted in the port outer main plane. The lamps are retracted and extended electrically by means of 2 two-way and OFF switches on the pilot's instrument panel. A high or low position depending on what the lamp is to be used for, may be selected by means of the two-way and OFF switch. To prevent the lamp being extended when the aeroplane is travelling at high speeds and consequent damage to the wing, a clutch which slips at a speed of 150 miles an hour has been included in the gearing.

26. *Pressure head.*—The pressure head, Mk. VIIID, is located on the port side of the nose, and the switch, type B, controlling the heating circuit is mounted on the air observer's instrument panel. For further information, *see* A.P.1275.

27. *Automatic controls supply.*—The supply to the automatic controls is taken through a switch, type B, on the pilot's port auxiliary panel. For further information, *see* A.P.1469A.

28. *Engine-speed indicators.*—The engine-speed indicators are mounted in the centre of the pilot's instrument panel, and the generators are mounted at the top of each fireproof bulkhead on the port side. Each indicator and appropriate generator form a closed independent circuit in which current flows only when the generator is turned by the engine. For further information, *see* A.P.1275.

29. *Fuel contents gauges.*—Six fuel contents gauges, type 100, are fitted on the air observer's instrument panel, together with a switch which must be switched ON when a reading is required. A transmitter is fitted in each fuel tank. For further information, *see* A.P.1275.

30. *Oil dilution.*—This installation consists of a solenoid-operated valve, type C, for each engine, mounted on the engine. The valves are operated by pushbutton switches on the air observer's instrument panel. For further information, *see* A.P.2140A.

31. *Dinghy inflation.*—An operating head, type H, is provided in the dinghy stowage in the starboard trailing edge of the centre section main plane, and an immersion switch near the floor on the starboard side of former G in the fuselage nose. The immersion switch completes the circuit to the operating head when its plates are immersed in water. For further details, *see* A.P.1464B.

32. *Fuel pressure warning lamps.*—Four fuel pressure warning lamps, Mk. IA, are mounted on the air observer's panel, and are connected through resistances fitted on the port side of the engine struts to pressure-operated switches in the main fuel systems. The pressure-switch unit is operated by the pressure of the fuel on a diaphragm which holds open a pair of contacts. When the fuel pressure drops below 6 lb./sq. in. the contacts close and complete the lamp circuit. The system is fed from the switch controlling the fuel contents gauges system, and this switch must be ON if warning of a drop in fuel pressure is to be given. For further details, *see* A.P.1275.

A.P.2062A and C, Vol. I, Sect. 10

33. *Automatic bomb sight.*—A mounting is provided in the front of the fuselage nose for either an automatic bomb sight, Mk. II, or a course-setting bomb sight, Mk. IX.A. An azimuth bracket, Mk. I is located just below and aft of the bomb sight, and between the azimuth bracket and the port side are mounted a two-way push-switch and an ON-OFF switch for the steering indicator. Below these switches is a control panel. Also mounted on the port side of the nose are an azimuth gyro, Mk. II, and a suppressor, type B. The steering indicator Mk. I.N.A. is fitted near the centre of the pilot's instrument panel.

34. *D.R. compass.*—The master compass, Mk. I, is mounted on the starboard side of the fuselage just forward of the main entrance door, and is plugged into the compass junction box on the aft side of the transport joint at former 27. The transport joints of the cables are formed by double-ended plugs at formers 6 and 12, and at the nose former E. The supply from the electrical services panel is fed through a suppressor, type B, to a distributor box, type D, both mounted forward of the panel. The variation setting corrector, Mk. I is located in the fuselage roof at the navigator's station, between formers 2 and 3. The navigator's repeater is mounted on the navigator's instrument panel. The pilot's repeater is mounted above, and the control panel at the bottom left-hand side of the pilot's instrument panel. A three-way junction box, type A, in the cable to the pilot's repeater, is mounted on the starboard side of the fuselage, near the forward end of the main floor, and from this and the main distributor box connections are run to a 5-way junction box, type A, below the bomber's port instrument panel, making provision for the course-setting bomb sight attachment.

35. *Camera.*—The camera, type F.24 is mounted at the rear of the nose portion of the fuselage on the port side and the motor unit, type B, at the top of the bulkhead behind the camera to which it is connected by a flexible drive. The control panel, type 35, is mounted on the bomber's port instrument panel, and the pilot's push-switch remote control is on the starboard cockpit rail. For further details *see* A.P.1355.

36. *Bomb fuzing and release.*—The following units are fitted on the bomber's starboard panel:—automatic distributor, type VI, selector switchbox, type F, fuzing selector switchbox, type C, a preselector switch unit, 16-point, and two firing switch sockets for plugs on the automatic bomb sight and the bomber's firing switch. A firing switch is also incorporated in the left side of the pilot's hand-wheel. A jettison switch, type H, and the jettison "pull" handle for operating the selector switchbox jettison bars are mounted together on the right-hand side of the pilot's instrument panel.

37. The junction boxes for the bomb fuzing and release gear are referenced with a series of letters and are positioned as follows below the main floor:—

    JB.A   At the front end of the bomb compartment.
    JB.B   Just forward of the front spar.
    JB.C   Just aft of the rear spar.
    JB.D   Between the floor cross-members at formers 1 and 2.
    JB.E   Between the floor cross-members at formers 4 and 5.
    JB.F   Between the floor cross-members at formers 10 and 11.
    JB.G   Between the floor cross-members at formers 15 and 16.
    JB.H   At the rear end of the bomb compartment.

F.S./4

This page amended by A.L. No. 28
June, 1943

38. The release positive terminals in all the junction boxes are referenced by the number of the bomb positions to which they apply. It should be noted that these numbers refer to the selector switches, and coincide with the sequence of numbers by which the bomb gear housings are referenced. In the fuse box JB.A three fuzes are provided in the release negatives and three in the fuzing negatives. In order to prevent the release of bombs when the bomb doors are closed, safety switches are provided in the positive and negative supplies. The switches are mounted on the rear face of the bulkhead at the front end of the bomb compartment, and remain in the OFF position while the doors are closed. For further details, *see* A.P.1095.

39. *Immersed fuel pumps.*—These are fitted to each tank and with the exception of the outer tanks, are wired through a suppressor mounted in the nacelle. They are controlled by separate switches mounted on the observer's panel. A socket into which an ammeter may be plugged for testing purposes is mounted adjacent to the switches.

40. *Propeller de-icing.*—The electrical equipment for de-icing the propellers consists of a combined pump and motor fitted on the rear face of the front spar behind the port and starboard inboard engines, from which run the fluid feed lines for inboard and outboard engines. Fitted adjacent to and in circuit with each pump and motor is a suppressor, type B. The pump and motor circuits are controlled through two rheostats and switches, situated in the fuselage centre-section, behind the front spar on the starboard side.

41. *Radiator flaps.*—The flaps are thermo-electrically controlled by an electro-magnetic valve and a thermo-switch fitted at each engine, which ensure that the radiator flaps are automatically opened and closed.

41A. *Radiator shutter control switches.*—These switches enable the radiator shutter to be opened before the engines are warm enough to being the automatic control into operation. They are mounted on the starboard cockpit rail just aft of the pilot's instrument panel.

41B. *Two-speed supercharger controls.*—The control is operated by an electro-pneumatic ram on each engine (*see* Sect. 9 for pneumatic system). The electro-magnetic valves are operated by a switch on the pilot's instrument panel. Another switch is side by side with the first and is connected to it by a link so that both switches operate together. A red warning lamp, adjacent to the switches and controlled by the second switch, is connected through the fire extinguisher circuit, of which the negative return is made through the "locked DOWN" side of the undercarriage indicator DOWN switches. The lamp is wired so as to light if the F.S. position is selected on the switches, when the main wheels are down, i.e. when the aircraft is on the ground.

41C. *Slow-running cut-out controls.*—Electro-pneumatically operated slow-running cut-out controls are provided on Mk. III aircraft only and are operated by four switches mounted on the pilot's instrument panel just above the engine starter switches. The switches are protected by a metal bar which prevents accidental operation. The wiring for these controls is also included in later Mk. I aircraft, but in these, a terminal block is provided on the panel in place of the operating switches. For notes on the pneumatic system, *see* Sect. 9.

This page issued with A.L. No. 28   A.P.2062A and C, Vol. I, Sect. 10
June, 1943

42. *Undercarriage indicator.*—The indicator is illustrated in Sect. 6, fig. 32. The terminal cover (A) at the rear is attached to the terminal block (B) by four captive screws (P), and is detachable to give access to the cable connections in block (B). The latter is permanently wired to the spring plunger assembly (C), and these two parts are secured to the instrument case (D) by the two retaining screws (E). The removable lamp mounting (H) carries lamps (G), so disposed that their centre contacts and the common contact stud (W) press against the spring plunger contacts (F). The dial assembly unit (J) has permanently attached to it the spider (K), the webs of which locate in the recesses in the lamp mounting (H), forming light-tight cells. A dimming screen (N) which can be partially rotated by the pilot by a knob (V), is provided in the dial assembly, and is pierced in the same way as the dial. The screen can be turned to the DAY position, in which the apertures in the dial and the screen coincide, permitting the full light intensity of the lamps to illuminate the colour screens (L), or to the NIGHT position, in which the dial apertures are covered by the dimming screen, thus reducing the illumination. The lamp mounting (H) and dial and spider assembly (J) and (K) are retained in position by the bezel ring (O) which is screwed on to the front of the case.

43. *Warning horn.*—This unit, which is incorporated in the undercarriage indicator system, is illustrated in Sect. 6, fig. 32, and comprises two assemblies, namely:—

    (i) The unit proper, and
    (ii) A moulded housing.

Sound is emitted by a vibrating plunger striking a steel diaphragm. The unit proper comprises a main assembly plate (B) to the front of which the diaphragm

(Continued on next leaf)

F.S./4A

is rigidly attached. The main assembly carries also the magnet winding, through the centre of which passes the vibrating plunger. An armature and plunger (H) are carried on a flexible spring assembly. When the bobbin winding is energised the armature is attracted towards it, causing the plunger to strike the diaphragm, and also operating a conventional type of make-and-break device. The breaking of the circuit allows the armature to return to its original position when the contacts again close and the cycle is repeated. The plunger and the make-and-break can be adjusted to obtain the optimum output of sound, which largely depends on the rapidity of the vibration and the force with which the plunger strikes the diaphragm.

44. The magnet winding is centrally located on the main assembly plate. Two drag punched arms carry the flat spring and armature assembly, and, above the flat springs, a resistance wound on a mica former and held in position by the contact studs (L). The object of the resistance, which is connected in shunt across the make-and-break contacts, is to obviate sparking. The make-and-break device is built of alternate metal and insulating parts held in position by the two studs (M), and is adjusted by means of the screw (A).

45. Two connecting wires are attached to two terminals on the unit proper and to two shrouded terminals at the rear of the moulded case. The terminals are carried in an integrally moulded housing with a detachable moulded cover (F). The cover, which is secured by three captive screws (G), clamps the cable in position. A large aperture in the back of the case is provided to relieve the internal air pressure set up by the vibration of the diaphragm. The aperture is protected by safety wire gauze which also guards against the ignition of explosive vapours. The unit proper is secured in the case by two studs (J) and locknuts (D). The polarity of the connections is immaterial.

46. *Undercarriage indicator switch.*—This switch comprises two independently operated sections in one housing, namely, a single-pole double-throw ON-OFF section which controls the supply to the indicating system, and a double-pole double-throw section connected to the duplicated lamps illuminating the green apertures of the indicator. The latter is used to bring spare lamps into circuit when required (*see* Sect. 6, fig. 33). The sliding bar (N) is operated by the ON-OFF section lever, and interferes with the ignition switches in a way that ensures that the undercarriage indicator system is always operative whilst the aeroplane may be flown (*see* para. 15). Both sections of the switch are of the positive slow make-and-break type and the contacts (O) are silver plated. Tension springs (J) hold the levers in one position or the other, but failure of these springs will not render the switch inoperative. The cable connections are made to terminals (G) at the rear, the terminals being provided with a moulded shroud (F) and cover (E).

Radio

47. *Intercommunication.*—This system is operated in conjunction with the amplifier A.1134, on the rear face of the wireless operator's panel, and the T.R.9F on the floor below the navigator's table. Tel-mic sockets are provided at the following positions:—

Bomb aimer	Port side of the fuselage nose.
Front gunner	In turret.
First pilot	At the front edge of the seat.

Second pilot	Below the starboard cockpit rail, forward of the observer's instrument panel.
Air observer-navigator	Above the table on the port side of the fuselage roof.
Wireless operator	On the wireless operator's table.
Rest station	Between formers 9 and 10 on the port side of the fuselage roof.
Flare station	On former 22 on the port side.
Upper mid turret	In the turret.
Lower mid turret	On the cross-member below the upper turret.
Rear gunner	In the turret.

48. The intercommunication junction boxes are referenced and positioned as follows:—

JB.WA	In the fuselage nose below the bomb aimer's port instrument panel
JB.WB	On the port side of the fuselage roof just forward of the front spar.
JB.WC	Below the starboard cockpit rail, forward of the observer's instrument panel.
JB.WD	On the port side of the fuselage roof above the rear end of the main floor.
JB.WE	On the main floor below the pilot's floor.
JB.WF	Above the navigator's table on the port side of the fuselage roof, between formers 1 and 2.
JB.WG	Port fuselage roof between formers 9 and 10.

49. *T.1154–R.1155 installation.*—The wireless operator's transmitter and receiver are mounted on the rear face of the radio panel, which is fitted transversely across the table facing the wireless operator. The sets may be connected to either the main fixed aerial on the starboard side or to the trailing aerial, by means of the aerial plug board or aerial switch. The winch for the trailing aerial, together with a spare reel, is located on the port side below the table, just forward of the wireless operator's seat. An H.T. power unit, type 33A, an L.T. power unit, type 35A, and a relay, type 220, are mounted on a stool on the main floor, centrally, beneath the table.

50. The navigator's R.1155 is mounted on the forward side of the radio panel and is connected directly to the D.F. loop, or to the rear section of the port fixed aerial. Two visual indicators are provided in conjunction with this installation, one for the navigator mounted on the radio panel immediately above the R.1155, and one for the pilot above his main instrument panel on the same mounting as the D.R. repeater. A switch is provided on each side of the radio panel, enabling the navigator or the wireless operator to switch this receiver through to the latter. The electrical supply is from the H.T. and L.T. power units referred to in para. 49.

51. *T.R.9F.*—The T.R.9F is mounted on a stool on the floor below the table, near the forward end and adjacent to the fuselage side. It is connected to the forward section of the port fixed aerial. The H.T. supply may be provided by a battery stowed internally, or by a power unit, type 173, similarly stowed. A switch on the navigator's panel and a connection are provided for fitting a

A.P.2062A, Vol. I, Sect. 10

power unit when desired. The L.T. supply is from a 2-volt accumulator which is stowed, with a spare accumulator, in a crate beneath the table. In the same stowage are two 2-volt accumulators (one a spare) and an H.T. battery for use with the amplifier and crystal monitor, which are fitted on the left-hand side of the rear face of the radio installation panel. The remote control unit is mounted on the canopy structure immediately above the pilot, and the NORMAL—SPECIAL switch is on the pilot's port auxiliary instrument panel.

52. *Beam approach installation.*—This equipment is installed in the rear centre portion of the fuselage at the flare station, and is mounted on a platform between the flare chute and the bulkhead at former 22. The main receiver, type R.1124A, is on the port side, the signal receiver, type R.1125A, on the starboard side, and the power unit, type 12, between them. The main junction box, type 7, is mounted above the signal receiver. The wave change remote control is fitted on the A.R.I. 5000 bracket on the port side above the rear end of the main floor, and the control box (without the wave change control) and mixer box, on the pilot's port auxiliary instrument panel. A whip aerial for the main receiver projects below the fuselage just forward of the flare chute, and the dipole aerial for the signal receiver is fitted on the port side below the front end of the rear fuselage.

53. *A.R.I. 5033.*—This installation is mounted at the forward end of the navigator's table. Unit "A" is mounted above the table, the receiver below the table, and the control panel below the receiver. The H.T. supply is provided by an 80-volt, 500-watt A.C. generator, type R, mounted on the port outboard engine. The L.T. supply for the generator, A.R.I 5033, and for the detonator circuit is taken from a fuse box on the navigator's panel, which is connected in duplicate to the general services supply, at JB.7 and JB.11. A whip aerial is fitted, projecting through the canopy just aft of the D.F. loop.

54. The detonator circuit is interconnected with that for A.R.I. 5033 and can be operated by pushbuttons on the navigator's panel, on the table at the wireless operator's station, and on the right-hand side of the pilot's main instrument panel. An impact switch, mounted on the starboard side of the former J in the fuselage nose, also controls the detonator circuits, provided the isolating switch on the navigator's panel is turned to LIVE. Two warning lamps, connected in parallel, are fitted on the navigator's panel, and will light if the impact switch should accidentally be operated while the isolating switch is at SAFE. The pushbutton switches are not affected by the isolating switch.

55. *A.R.I. 5000.*—The receiver is mounted on the port side of the fuselage just aft of the bomb compartment, and the aerials extend on each side from former 27 to the outboard ends of the tail plane. The control unit is also on the port side, above the end of the table at the wireless operator's station, and the pilot's switch is on the right-hand side of his main instrument panel. The detonator circuit is interconnected with that of the A.R.I 5033 and is operated by the same impact switch and push buttons (*see* para. 54).

F.S./6

Section 11:
Armament and general equipment.

May, 1942
Issued with A.L. 8

A.P.2062A, VOL. I

SECTION 11—ARMAMENT AND GENERAL EQUIPMENT

LIST OF CONTENTS

	Para.
Gun turret mountings—	
Front turret ...	1
Upper mid turret	2
Lower mid turret	5
Rear turret ...	8
Ammunition ducts	9
Flare tube and extension ...	12
Photographic equipment ...	16
Positions of F.24 camera	19
Dinghy installation ...	20
Fire extinguisher system ...	23
Airscrew de-icing ...	27
Window de-icing ...	30
Cabin heating ...	33
Oxygen equipment ...	36
B.B.P. equipment ...	39

LIST OF ILLUSTRATIONS

	Fig.
Ammunition ducts ...	1
Photographic equipment ...	2
Dinghy installation ...	3
Fire extinguisher system ...	4
Airscrew de-icing ...	5
Window de-icing ...	6
Cabin heating system ...	7
Oxygen supply system ...	8
B.B.P. equipment ...	9

F.S./1

A.P.2062A, VOL. I

SECTION 11—ARMAMENT AND GENERAL EQUIPMENT

Gun turret mountings

1. *Front turret.*—The front turret, type F.N.5, is mounted on a support ring (see Sect. 7, Chap. 1, fig. 2), and forms the upper part of the nose of the fuselage. Fuselage formers H and J stop at the ring to which they are secured by means of brackets; a transverse channel member carries the rear edge of the ring, and a supporting angle passing round the ring extends aft to former E. The opening between the support ring and the channel member is covered by a draughtproof bulkhead with water-tight joints. Above this bulkhead and behind the turret is a concave panel forming a draughtscreen in the upper part of former G. From the angle between these two panels a drain pipe leads to the turret mounting ring from which a second drain is taken to a vent on the port side. The hydraulic service pipes enter the turret from above, in the centre, and are covered by a fairing.

2. *Upper mid turret.*—The upper mid turret, type F.N.50, is mounted in the top of the fuselage rear centre portion between formers 24 and 26 (see Sect. 7, Chap. 1, fig. 3). The support ring is carried by two angle section longerons, which extend between formers 23 and 27 and are attached to the tops of the intermediate formers, and by two channel section transverse members at formers 24 and 26. The skin and stringers of the fuselage top, and the ends of the fairing plate round the turret, are supported by special formers 24A and 26A. These are fitted between the longerons, forward and aft of formers 24 and 26 respectively, and are of channel section with a horizontal lower flange and a top flange curved to the fuselage contour. The spaces between the turret ring and the angles of the supporting frame are sealed by horizontal deck plates, which act also as stiffeners. Drain outlets are provided at the rear of the deck plates, and a drain pipe leads from the rear of the support ring to an outlet on the starboard side.

3. The services to the turret all run from the starboard side of the fuselage, leaving the gangway clear on the port side. A tube fitted transversely across the fuselage at former 25, supports the hydraulic pipes and electrical wiring for the turret. A mounting step on a pivoted tubular frame and supported by a cable, is also fitted on the starboard side between formers 24 and 25, and when not in use is turned up against the fuselage side and secured by a catch.

4. On the top outer surface of the fuselage, round the turret, is a combined fairing and gun taboo track, extending from former 23 to 29, and supported on a wooden ring. The fairing is in two portions with the joints at former 27 for transport purposes. At this joint is fitted an additional channel section former.

5. *Lower mid turret.*—The lower mid turret, type F.N.64, is mounted in the rear centre portion of the fuselage between formers 24 and 27 (see Sect. 7, Chap. 1, fig. 4), where a ring of laminated ash is mounted in the floor of the fuselage attached to formers 25 and 26 and to the floor intercostals.

6. A flanged turret mounting ring is secured to the inside of the ring by woodscrews. Twelve support brackets are bolted to the inside of the turret mounting ring, and to these the turret is secured by four quick-release pins, equally spaced. Wooden sealing pieces are fitted between each pair of support brackets.

A.P.2062A, Vol. I, Sect. 11

7. The hydraulic feed and return pipes lead from the recuperator fitted on the starboard side of the fuselage between formers 23 and 24, to an Avery self-sealing coupling mounted on the transverse support tube below the upper mid turret. From this coupling flexible feed and return pipes are connected to the lower mid turret.

8. *Rear turret.*—The rear turret, type F.N.20, which forms the extreme rear end of the fuselage, is mounted on a support ring aft of the end former 41 (see Sect. 7, Chap. 1, fig. 5). The ring is carried by an angle-section member passing round the end of the fuselage and extending forward to former 39, being riveted to the skin and to brackets on the formers. A semi-circular angle-section member carries the forward portion of the ring, and tubular struts from formers 39 and 41 support it at each side and the front. Below the turret is the end fairing of the fuselage in which is fitted an inspection cover, immediately beneath the centre of the turret, giving access to the hydraulic pipe connections.

9. *Ammunition ducts.*—The rear turret has servo feed and is supplied with ammunition by means of four ammunition boxes and ducts (see fig. 1.). On each side of the fuselage two boxes are attached to the floor by means of brackets bolted to the floor members and to formers 20, 21 and 22. The boxes are of light alloy sheet with channel-section ends and bottoms, the side panels being strengthened by top-hat section stiffeners. From each box a duct is led aft, the inner duct on either side dropping below and turning under the outer duct. The ducts curve down, bringing those on the starboard side below the door step, and continue along the fuselage to a position below the turret. Covers, secured by spring clips, are fitted to the ducts aft of former 38.

10. Standard ammunition ducts are used and they are supported in brackets bolted to the formers. The sections are jointed by means of end brackets pinned together, the pins being removable and secured by a short chain to one of the brackets.

11. Each box holds 1,900 rounds, and each duct 600 rounds, i.e. 2,500 rounds for each of the four guns.

Flare tube and extension

12. The reconnaissance flare chute (see Sect. 4, Chap. 2, fig. 13) is located at the rear end of the main floor and is supported at each side by a tubular strut. The extension tube is a separate light alloy tube which is inserted into the top of the main tube and pushed down until the flange formed by an angle riveted on the extension tube rests on the top plate of the main tube. Two locating pegs below the flange fit into slots in the top plate of the main tube to ensure correct positioning.

13. Above the flange are two small brackets, facing aft, and above the brackets the extension tube is cut away for the remainder of its length forming an open channel. The brackets carry the flare release mechanism, which consists of a release trigger bracket on which are pivoted two parallel catch plates, connected by a distance tube at their upper ends. This distance tube forms the stop on which the flare is supported. The catch plates are locked by a spring-loaded slide which fits into slots in the release trigger bracket, but when raised allows the catch to be pulled back, thus releasing the flare.

14. The fuze reel is mounted on a spindle in a bracket riveted to the top of the extension tube, a cable being wound on this reel and hooked to the top

F.S./2

of the flare. The cable is covered by a drum cover, and by a guard. The reel is held in contact with a friction washer by means of a spring, and should revolve under a load of 2 lb. $\pm$ 1 lb. applied at the cable.

15. The extension tube is stowed on two hinged brackets on the starboard side of the fuselage at formers 17 and 19, and is secured in them by straps, a quick release strap being fitted at former 19. When not in use these brackets can be folded back against the fuselage, where they are retained by spring catches.

Photographic equipment

16. The F.24 camera is mounted in the nose of the aeroplane on the port side, in front of the bulkhead at former E (see fig. 2). The camera rails fit into two brackets, in which they can slide horizontally at right-angles to the centre-line of the fuselage. The brackets slide vertically on mounting tubes, which are braced to the bulkhead by tubular struts. Six holes are drilled in the mounting tubes to receive screw pins for locking the camera at different heights. The camera is mounted so that the optical axis is normal to the line of flight.

17. An electric motor, mounted at the top of the bulkhead, operates the camera by means of a flexible drive and is controlled from a unit on the bomb-aimer's panel. A socket is fitted on this panel for the electric supply. The pilot's pushbutton control for the camera is mounted on the starboard cockpit rail. The camera heating muff and lens cover are plugged into the sockets on the camera heating panel, fitted below the bomb aimer's panel.

18. A circular window is provided directly under the camera. For further information on photographic equipment, see A.P.1355.

19. *Positions of F.24 camera.*—The camera may be set in any of the following four positions, which are indicated by numbered holes in the tubes:—

    5 in. lens   position No. 6
    8 in. lens   position No. 5
    14 in. lens   position No. 1
    20 in. telephoto lens   position No. 1

Dinghy installation

20. The dinghy stowage (see fig. 3) consists of a box between ribs 29 and 31 in the starboard trailing edge of the centre section main plane, the webs of the ribs forming the sides, and the ends being light-alloy panels with top-hat section stiffeners. The bottom is formed from a flat panel, strengthened by a corrugated panel beneath. The lid, which contains an inspection window over the operating head, is secured by a rubber angle strip, fitting into a built-up channel on the edge, permitting it to be forced off by the expansion of the dinghy when inflated.

21. Carbon dioxide for inflation is contained in a bottle attached to the dinghy, but supported on two cradles whilst in the stowage. The operating head is controlled automatically or by hand. An immersion switch on the starboard side inside the nose of the fuselage at former G automatically releases the dinghy on contact with water. Hand release is by a cord, supported in separate lengths of tube between formers 13 and 35, and operated by pulling down a loop between any two tubes or by an external loop at former 34.

22. The dinghy is connected to the outboard cradle by 30 ft. of cord attached by a clove hitch to the dinghy handline. A hand pump for completing inflation is stowed in the dinghy. A valise which is stowed in the dinghy box contains the following:—

>Six tins of tomato juice
>Six ration tins (Bovril chocolate)
>Six sea markers
>One first-aid outfit
>Three distress signals
>Three hand shields
>Two dinghy paddles

Fire extinguisher system

23. The fire extinguisher system (see fig. 4) consists of an automatic and electrically controlled system in the engine nacelles, and of six portable extinguishers in the fuselage. For further information on fire extinguishers, see A.P.1464B.

24. A Graviner extinguisher is mounted in each engine nacelle, those for the inboard engines on the rear face of the front spar, in the main wheel compartment, and those for the outboard engines attached to the sub-frame. A flexible pipe is lead through the fireproof bulkhead to a union at the rear of each engine, from which branches lead to the air intake and to perforated pipes on the engine. For further details of the power plant installation, see A.P. 2140A.

25. Four methods of operation are provided, all electrical, as follows:—

(i) Two flame switches, mounted on each fireproof bulkhead, operate the extinguisher if the engine catches fire.

(ii) A gravity switch is mounted on former H on the starboard side, in the nose of the fuselage. This comes into circuit when the main wheel units are lowered, and automatically switches on the extinguishers if the machine should turn over on to its back when landing.

(iii) An inertia switch is mounted on former J, above the bomb aimer's panel, and will operate under impact in the event of a crash.

(iv) The pilot can switch on any extinguisher from his instrument panel.

26. Six portable extinguishers are provided in the fuselage, stowed in the following positions:—

(i) In the nose on the port side, between formers G and H.

(ii) On the port cockpit rail, forward of former B.

(iii) On the forward face of a panel on the forward end of the navigator's table.

(iv) In the centre portion on the starboard side, aft of the electrical services panel.

(v) On the starboard side, between formers 27 and 28.

(vi) On the port side, between formers 40 and 41.

Airscrew de-icing

27. The airscrew de-icing system (see fig. 5) is arranged to pump a supply of de-icing fluid to the airscrews and spread it along the blades.

28. A supply tank of 5⅞ gallons capacity is mounted in each inboard nacelle behind the front spar and between the intermediate engine ribs. The tank is formed of welded aluminium sheet, and is strapped into mountings riveted to the skin, in which an access hole is provided for refilling. A dipstick is attached to the filler cap . The tap in the bottom surface is locked in the open position.

29. A pipe is led from each tank to a Dunlop electric pump on the rear face of the front spar behind the inboard engine. The two pumps are separately controlled by rheostats on a small panel in the fuselage intermediate centre portion. The delivery pipe passes through the front spar web and divides, one branch leading directly to the inboard engine, and the other running outboard through the leading edge of the outer plane to the outboard engine. On each engine the pipe runs forward on the starboard side to the jet and slinger ring.

Window de-icing

30. De-icing by means of a glycol spray is provided for the pilot's windscreen and the bomb aimer's window (see fig. 6). The system comprises a supply tank, two Rotax force feed hand pumps, and small diameter delivery pipes. Standard de-icing fluid is used, D.T.D.406A, Stores Ref. 33C/621.

31. A tank of welded aluminium sheet of approximately four gallons capacity is mounted in the fuselage nose on the starboard side of the floor. It is also used as a step when passing from the nose into the pilot's cockpit. The pilot's pump is mounted on a wooden ring bolted to the pilot's floor on the port side and that for the bomb aimer on the port side of the fuselage nose. The pump is operated by pressing down the handle, which is returned by a spring at a varying rate according to the setting of the needle valve at the outlet. A setting of 1⅜ turns is recommended. When operated once a minute the pump delivers fluid at the rate of two pints an hour. When not in use the pump handle is held down by a stirrup catch, and its action begins when the catch is released.

32. At the bomb aimer's window a perforated pipe is fitted round the upper part of the frame and spreads the fluid over the whole external surface. The pipe for the windscreen divides and forms two nozzles above the upper skin of the fuselage nose, arranged to direct the spray on to the windscreen. No jet is formed, but the fluid is dribbled from the nozzle and flung on to the windscreen by the air stream.

Cabin heating

38. The cabin is heated by hot air from two radiators mounted on the front spar between the inboard engine nacelles and the fuselage, and connected with the inboard engine cooling systems by flow and return pipes which are lagged with asbestos cord (see fig. 7). For details of the coolant connections, see Section 8. On each side, air enters a nostril which, with the short duct attached, is integral with the main plane hinged leading edge, and when the latter is closed the flanged end of the inlet duct makes contact with the sponge rubber seal at the end of the outboard duct which leads to the radiator. The outboard duct is mounted on the radiator and one of the front spar brackets; the inboard duct extends from the radiator to the control valve box, to which it is bolted.

34. The control valve box, which is a light alloy casting and is bolted to the fuselage side, has two outlets, one at the inboard end to supply hot air through an opening in the fuselage skin, the other at the bottom connected to the by-pass duct, by which the hot air can be discharged through a louvre below the main plane leading edge. The valve consists of a shutter, operated by a worm gear control from a knob adjacent to the inlet in the cabin, and arranged to close the inlet as the by-pass is opened. The passage of air through the radiator is therefore uninterrupted. Felt strips are fitted to the side edges of the shutter, and felt packing in the top of the casting, to form a seal. The by-pass duct is formed of upper and lower light-alloy castings, the upper casting being bolted to the valve box, and the lower, together with the exit louvre, attached to the bottom of the hinged leading edge. A sponge rubber seal forms the joint between the two castings.

35. Baffles are fitted over the inlets in the cabin in order to diffuse the hot air. The rear of the fuselage is not heated, the armour plate bulkhead at former 8 being completed at the bottom with plywood panels in order to retain the heated air in the front cabin. Extractor louvres, incorporating a sliding door by which the air flow can be controlled, are fitted one on each side of the fuselage nose.

Oxygen equipment

36. The oxygen equipment consists of fifteen bottles connected by a high pressure pipe to a regulator on the pilot's instrument panel, and then by medium pressure pipes to four manifolds. From these manifolds low pressure pipes carry the oxygen to the economisers at the various crew stations (see fig. 8).

37. The bottles are mounted in a crate in the fuselage centre portion, the top of which forms the rest couch. A charging connection mounted in the bomb compartment is connected to a pipe feeding all the bottles and thus enables the bottles to be charged without removal. A stop valve is mounted on the oxygen crate from which a high pressure pipe passes oxygen at a pressure of 1,800 lb./sq. in. to the master control on the pilot's instrument panel. Oxygen leaving this regulator at a reduced pressure, passes through light alloy pipes to four manifolds. From here the pressure is further reduced and passes through aluminium pipes to the economisers. From each economiser a flexible pipe connects the supply to the oxygen socket. When the oxygen is not being used the sockets are stowed in special cut-off clips. The operation of these clips is such that when the socket is inserted a small plunger is depressed, and this ensures that the oxygen supply is cut off. Cut off valves are interposed in the low pressure supply to the turrets.

38. Eight portable oxygen bottles are stowed in wire mesh containers in the following positions:—

    (i) In the fuselage nose on bulkhead E.

    (ii) On the starboard side of the fuselage aft of the second pilot's seat.

    (iii) On the navigator's chair support.

    (iv) On the starboard side of the fuselage just aft of the front spar.

    (v) On the starboard side of the fuselage just forward of the rear spar.

    (vi) On the starboard side of the fuselage just forward of the end of the main floor.

(vii) On the starboard side of the fuselage adjacent to the lower mid turret
(viii) On the starboard side of the fuselage just aft of the draughtproof doors at the tail plane.

B.B.P. equipment

39. The equipment for the balloon barrage protection consists of steel plates riveted along the leading edge of the main plane (see fig. 9), in which are mounted steel containers for the cable cutters. There are eight cutters on each side of the fuselage, one double at the root end and seven singly. When the covers are not in use they are covered by caps secured with spring fasteners.

40. The steel reinforcing plates are secured to the leading edge by light alloy rivets passing through the two foremost stringers in the nose. They extend the whole length of the centre and outer planes part of the wing tip. At several points along their length the plates are jointed, the joint being cut in the form of an arc to prevent the cables from fouling.

41. The containers into which the cutters are fitted consist of a mild steel body with an attachment flange welded at one end and a dished end cover at the other. The end cover is fitted with a special retaining nut which is brazed on. The containers are secured to the reinforcing plates by countersunk head screws and anchor nuts riveted to the flange in the containers. Details of the cutters and their operation and loading, are contained in A.P.2051A, Vol. I.

A.P.2062A VOL.I SECTION II

VIEW SHOWING SECTION THROUGH AMMUNITION CHUTE.

DETAIL OF ATTACHMENT OF AMMUNITION CHUTE AT FORMERS 28, 30, 31, 32, 33, 34, 35, 36 & 40.

DETAIL OF ATTACHMENT OF AMMUNITION CHUTE AT FORMER 23.

DETAIL OF ATTACHMENT OF AMMUNITION CHUTE AT FORMER 22.

AMMUNITION CHUTES CUT-AWAY FOR CLARITY

FORMER.

AMMUNITION BOXES.

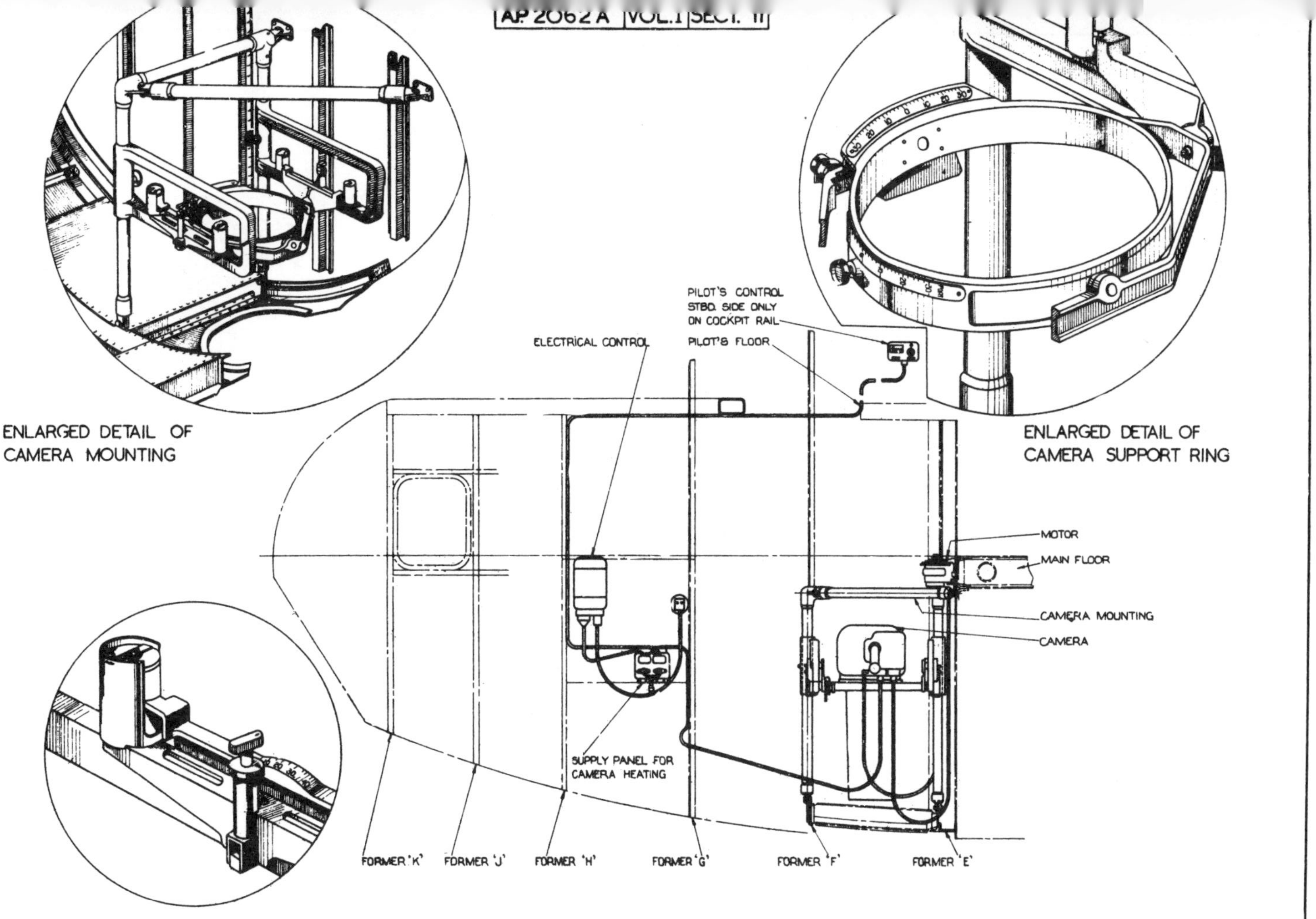

ENLARGED DETAIL OF
CAMERA SUPPORT RING

ENLARGED DETAIL OF
CAMERA MOUNTING

PHOTOGRAPHIC EQUIPMENT

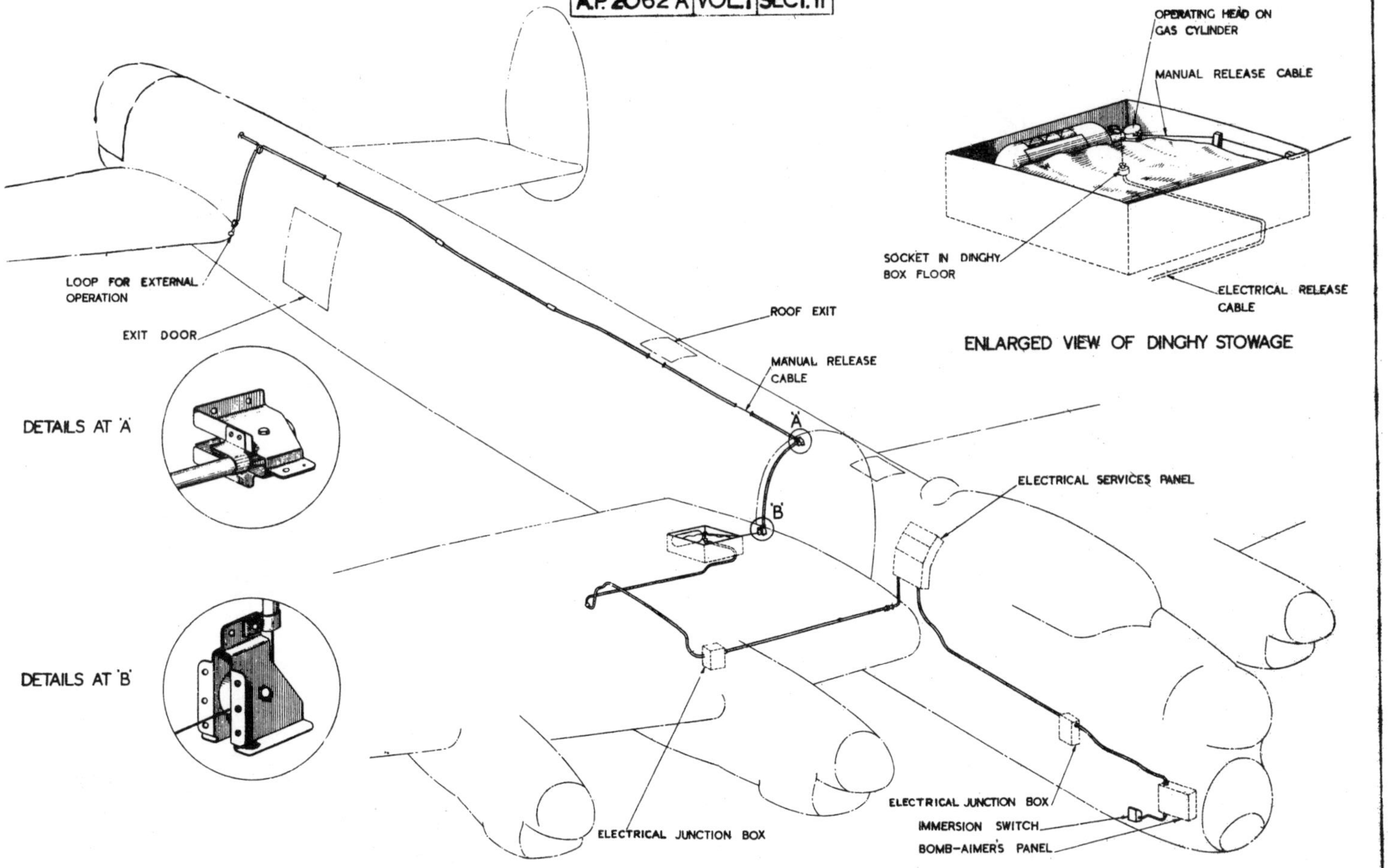

DINGHY INSTALLATION

AP.2062A VOL.I SECT.II

FIG. 3

ENLARGED VIEW OF DINGHY STOWAGE
- OPERATING HEAD ON GAS CYLINDER
- MANUAL RELEASE CABLE
- ELECTRICAL RELEASE CABLE
- SOCKET IN DINGHY BOX FLOOR

- ROOF EXIT
- MANUAL RELEASE CABLE
- ELECTRICAL SERVICES PANEL
- ELECTRICAL JUNCTION BOX
- IMMERSION SWITCH
- BOMB-AIMER'S PANEL
- ELECTRICAL JUNCTION BOX
- EXIT DOOR
- LOOP FOR EXTERNAL OPERATION

DETAILS AT 'A'

DETAILS AT 'B'

FIG. 3

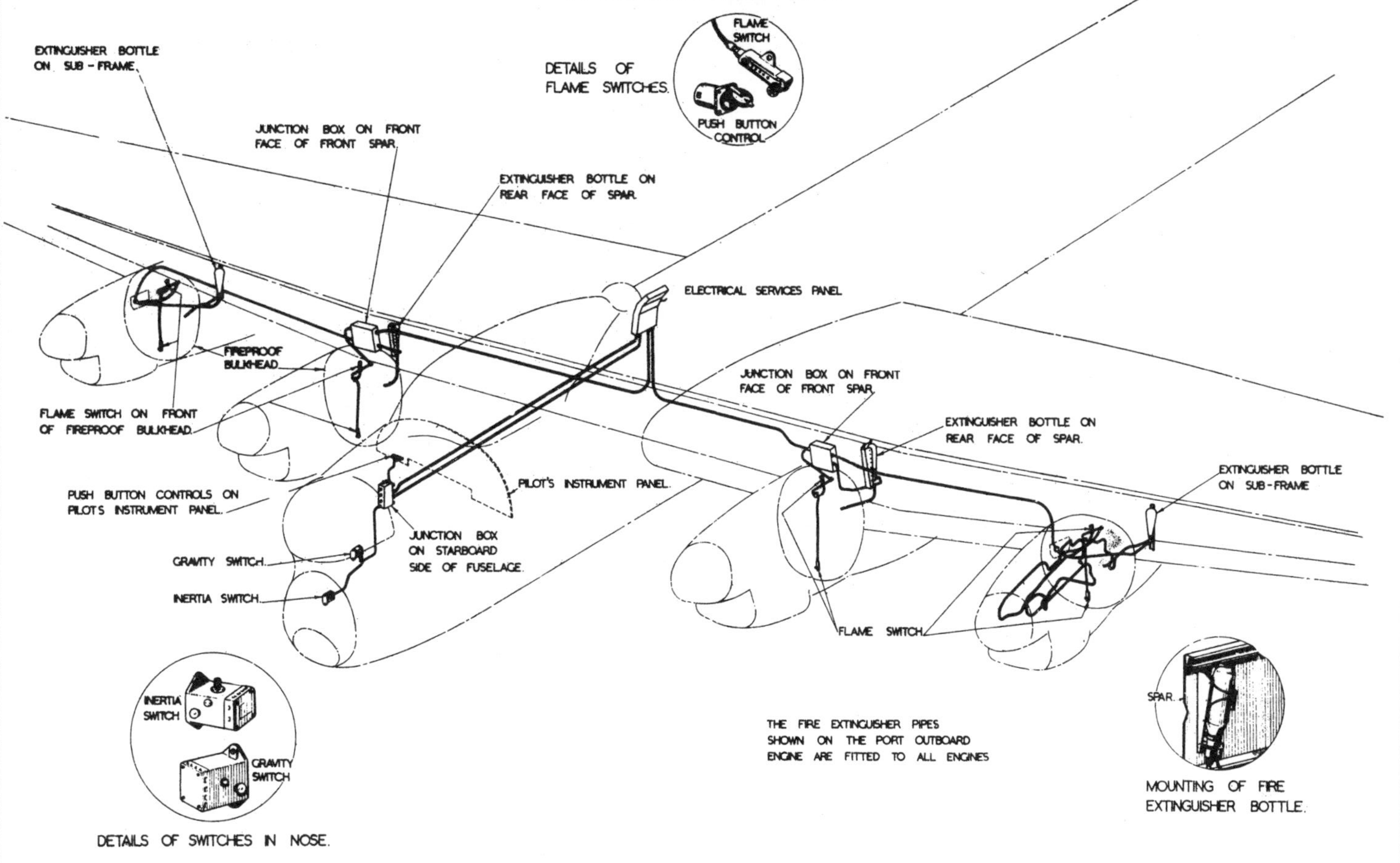

A.P. 2062A | VOL.I | SECT.II

DETAILS OF FLAME SWITCHES.

EXTINGUISHER BOTTLE ON REAR FACE OF SPAR.

EXTINGUISHER BOTTLE ON SUB-FRAME.

EXTINGUISHER BOTTLE ON SUB-FRAME.

EXTINGUISHER BOTTLE ON REAR FACE OF SPAR.

MOUNTING OF FIRE EXTINGUISHER BOTTLE.

SPAR.

JUNCTION BOX ON FRONT FACE OF FRONT SPAR.

ELECTRICAL SERVICES PANEL.

FLAME SWITCH

THE FIRE EXTINGUISHER PIPES SHOWN ON THE PORT OUTBOARD ENGINE ARE FITTED TO ALL ENGINES

JUNCTION BOX ON FRONT FACE OF FRONT SPAR.

PILOT'S INSTRUMENT PANEL.

JUNCTION BOX ON STARBOARD SIDE OF FUSELAGE

FIREPROOF BULKHEAD.

FLAME SWITCH ON FRONT OF FIREPROOF BULKHEAD.

PUSH BUTTON CONTROLS ON PILOT'S INSTRUMENT PANEL.

GRAVITY SWITCH.

INERTIA SWITCH.

INERTIA SWITCH

GRAVITY SWITCH

DETAILS OF SWITCHES IN NOSE.

FIRE EXTINGUISHER SYSTEM.

FIG. 4

IDENTIFICATION MARKINGS.

1 - NARROW YELLOW BAND
1 - BROAD WHITE BAND
1 - NARROW YELLOW BAND

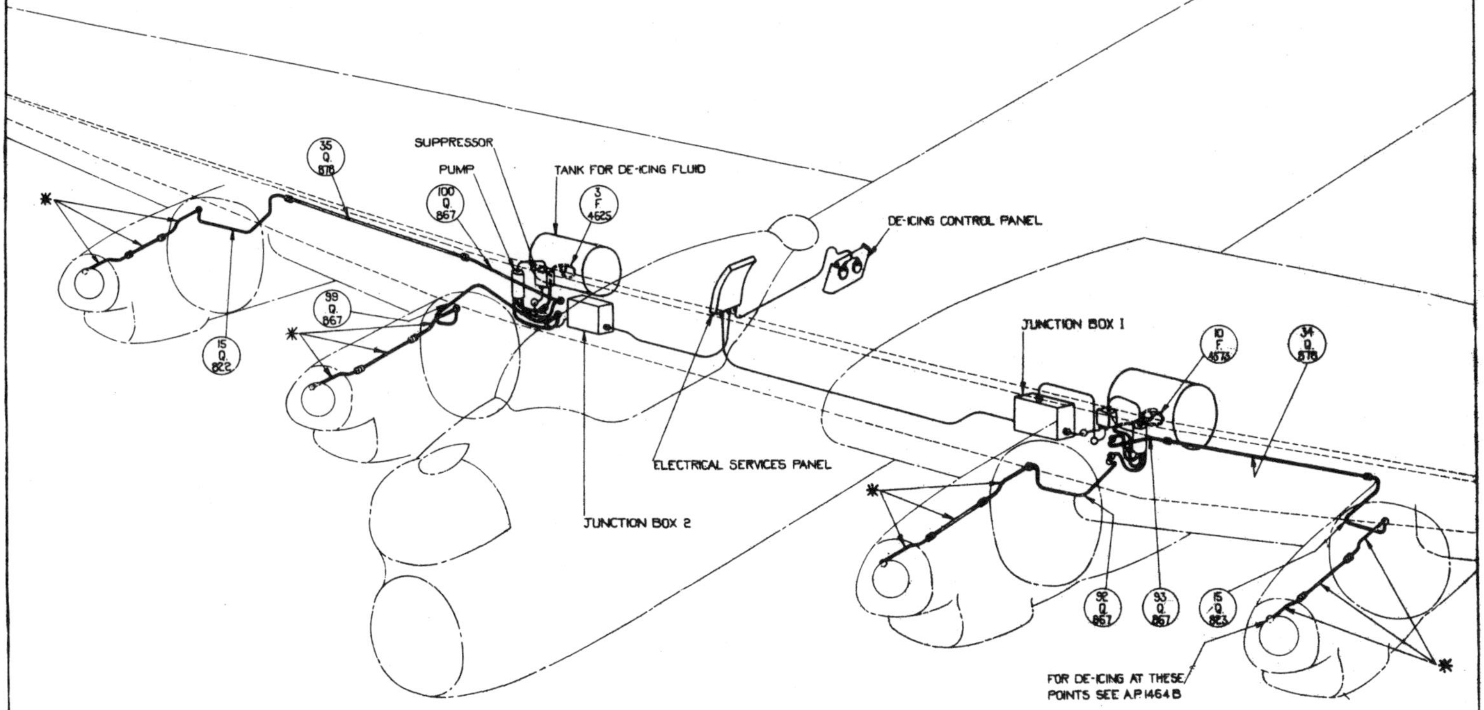

* THESE PIPES ARE SUPPLIED WITH POWER PLANT.

FIG. 5

AIRSCREW DE-ICING.

FIG. 5

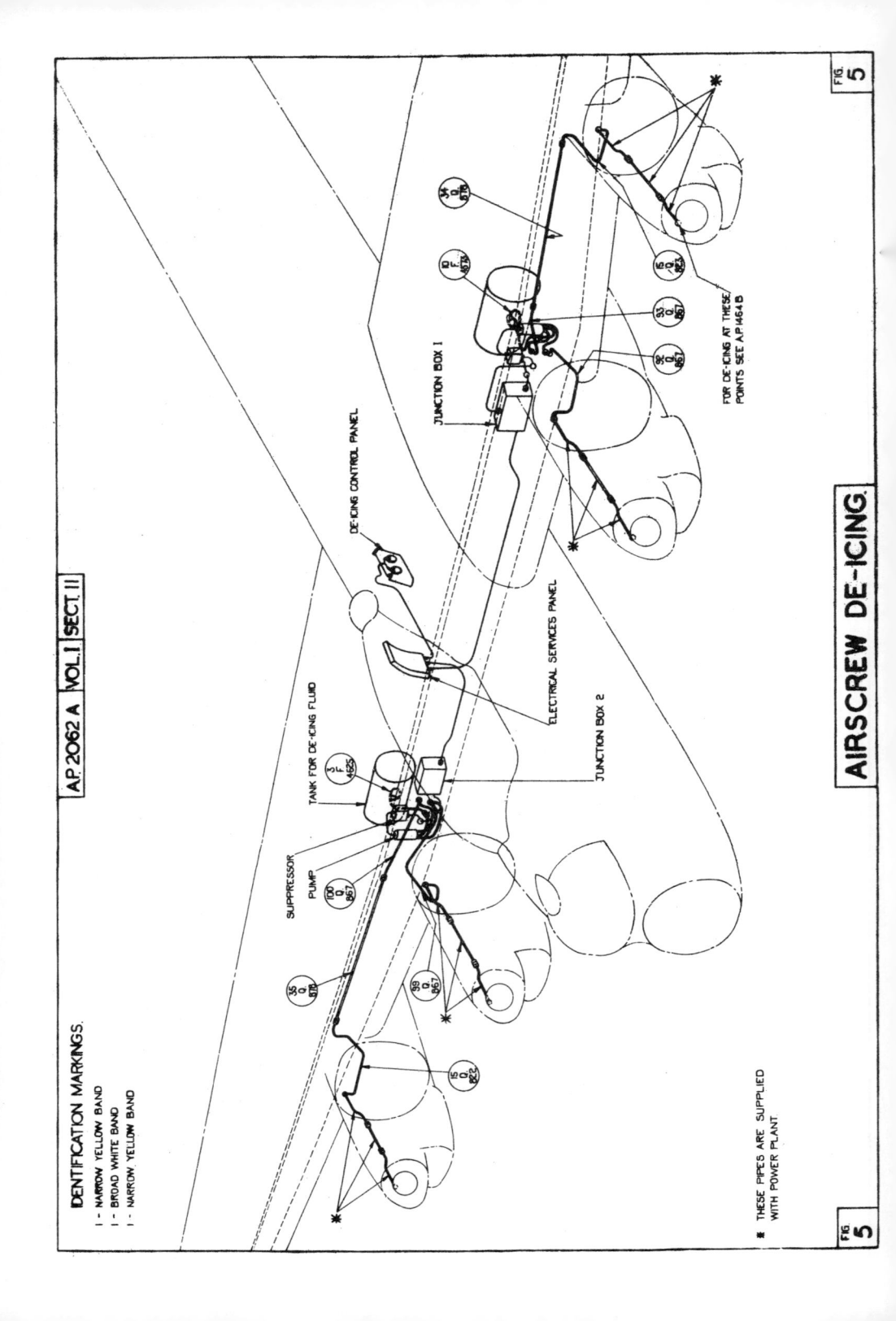

IDENTIFICATION MARKINGS.

1 - NARROW BROWN BAND.
1 - BROAD WHITE BAND.
1 - NARROW BROWN BAND.

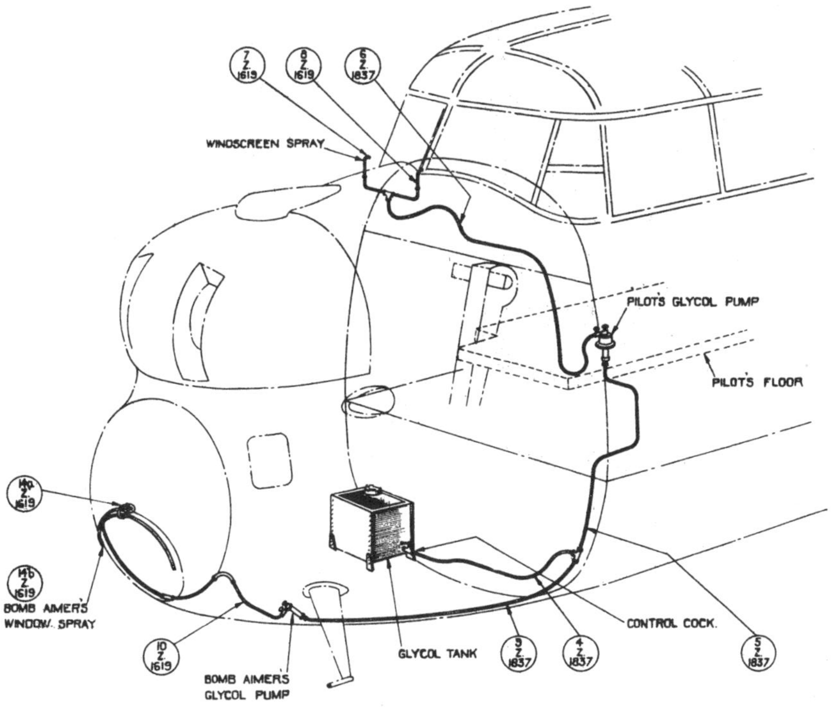

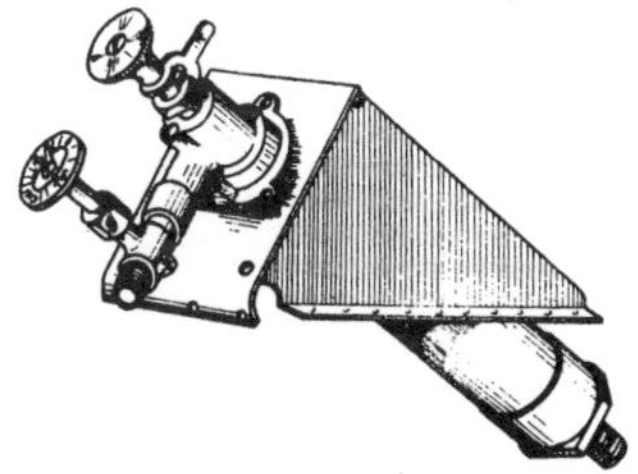

ARRANGEMENT OF BOMB AIMER'S GLYCOL PUMP.

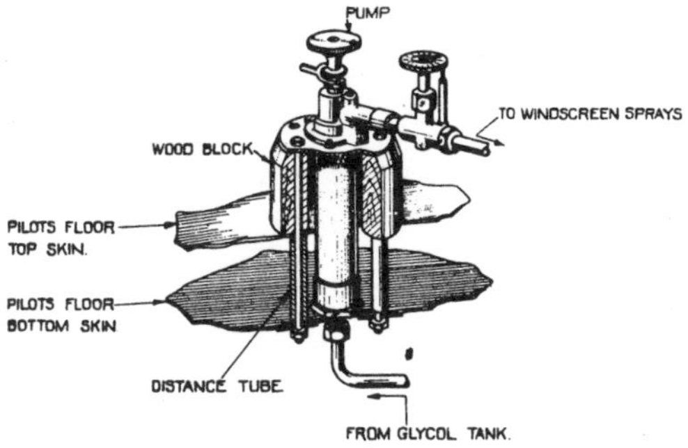

ARRANGEMENT OF PILOT'S GLYCOL PUMP

FIG. 6

WINDOW DE-ICING

FIG. 6

IDENTIFICATION MARKINGS.
1 - BROAD BLUE BAND.

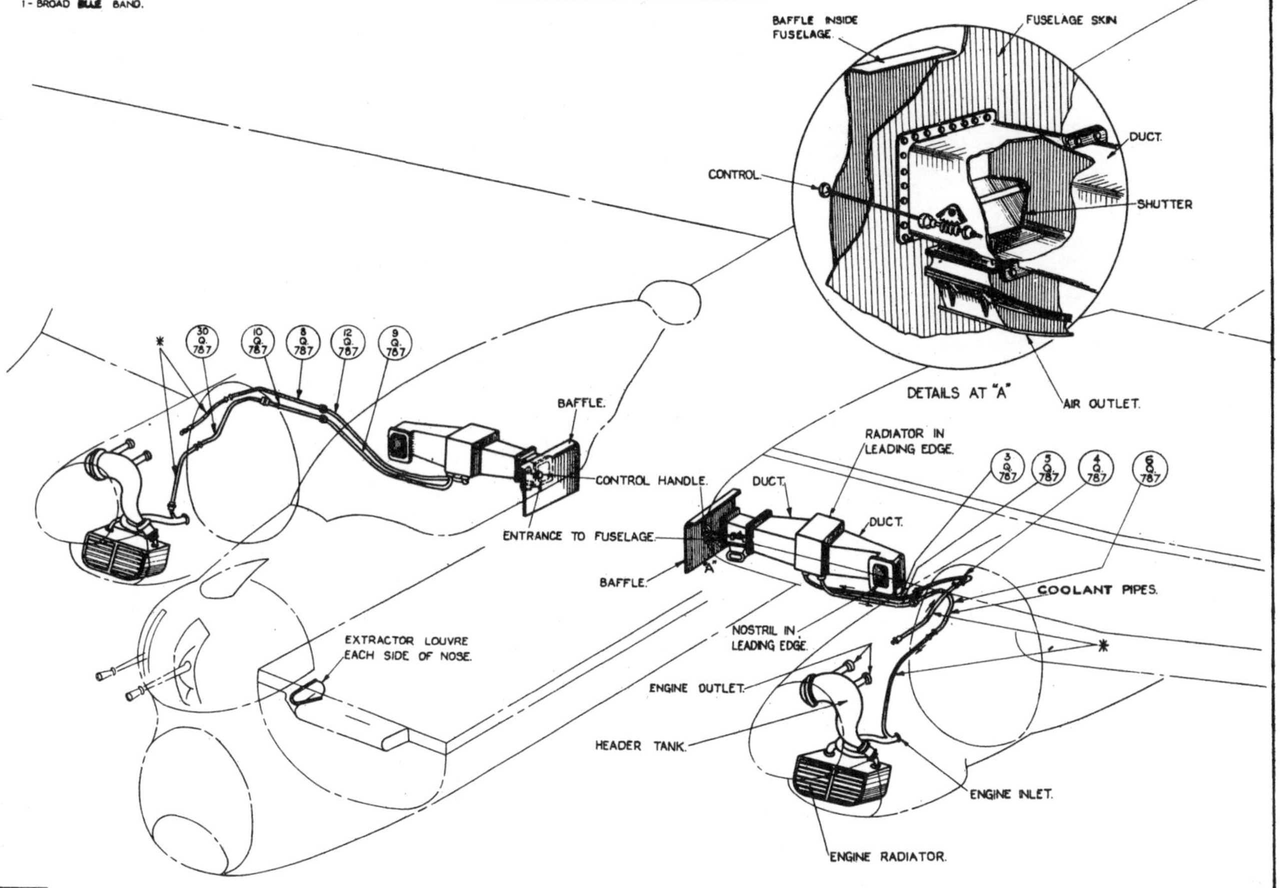

FIG. 7

CABIN HEATING SYSTEM.

* PIPES FORWARD OF FIREPROOF BULKHEAD ARE SUPPLIED WITH POWER PLANT

FIG. 7

PP2096 M27625/2387 3/43 3000 C & P Gp. 959(4)

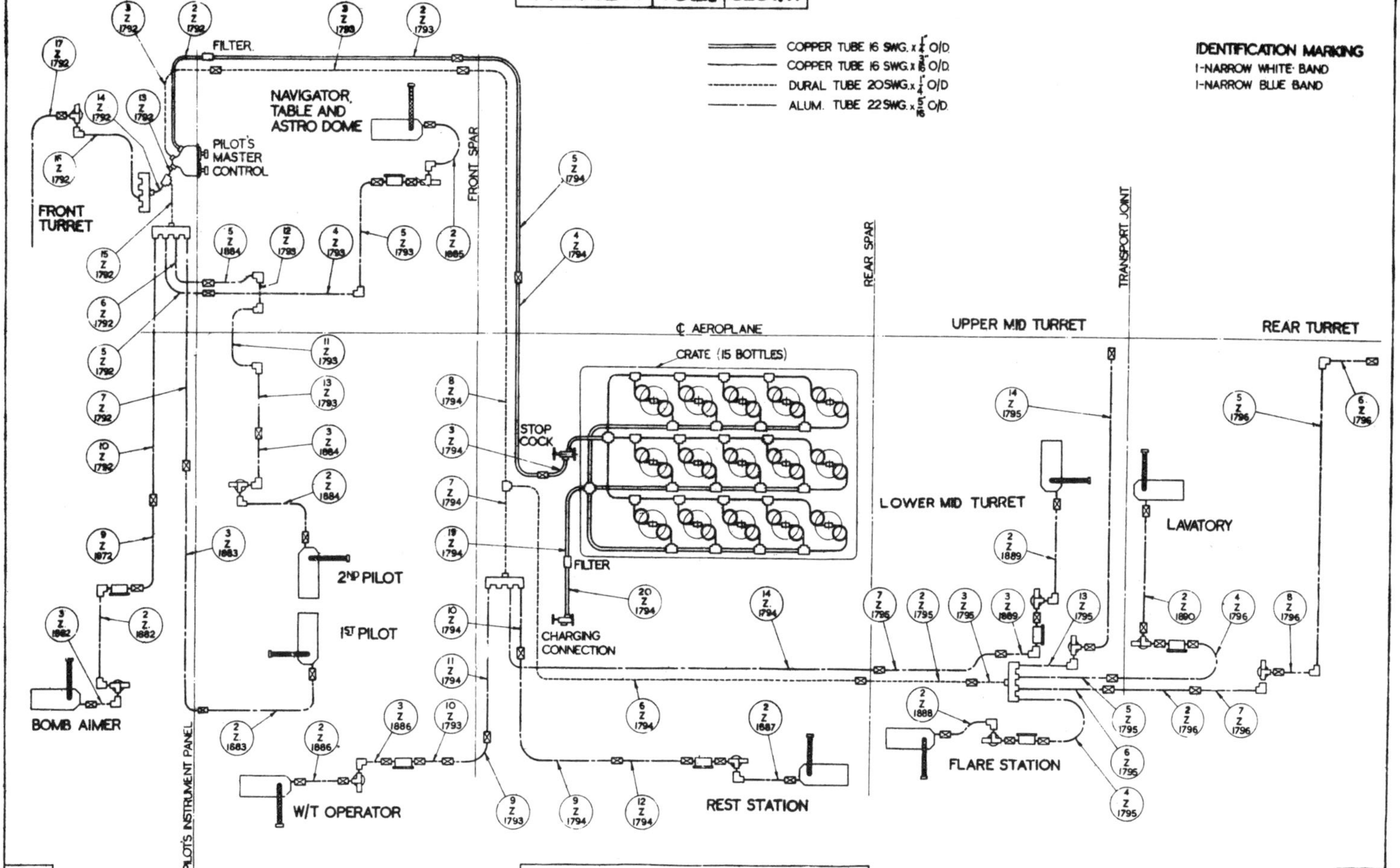

OXYGEN SUPPLY SYSTEM

FIG 8

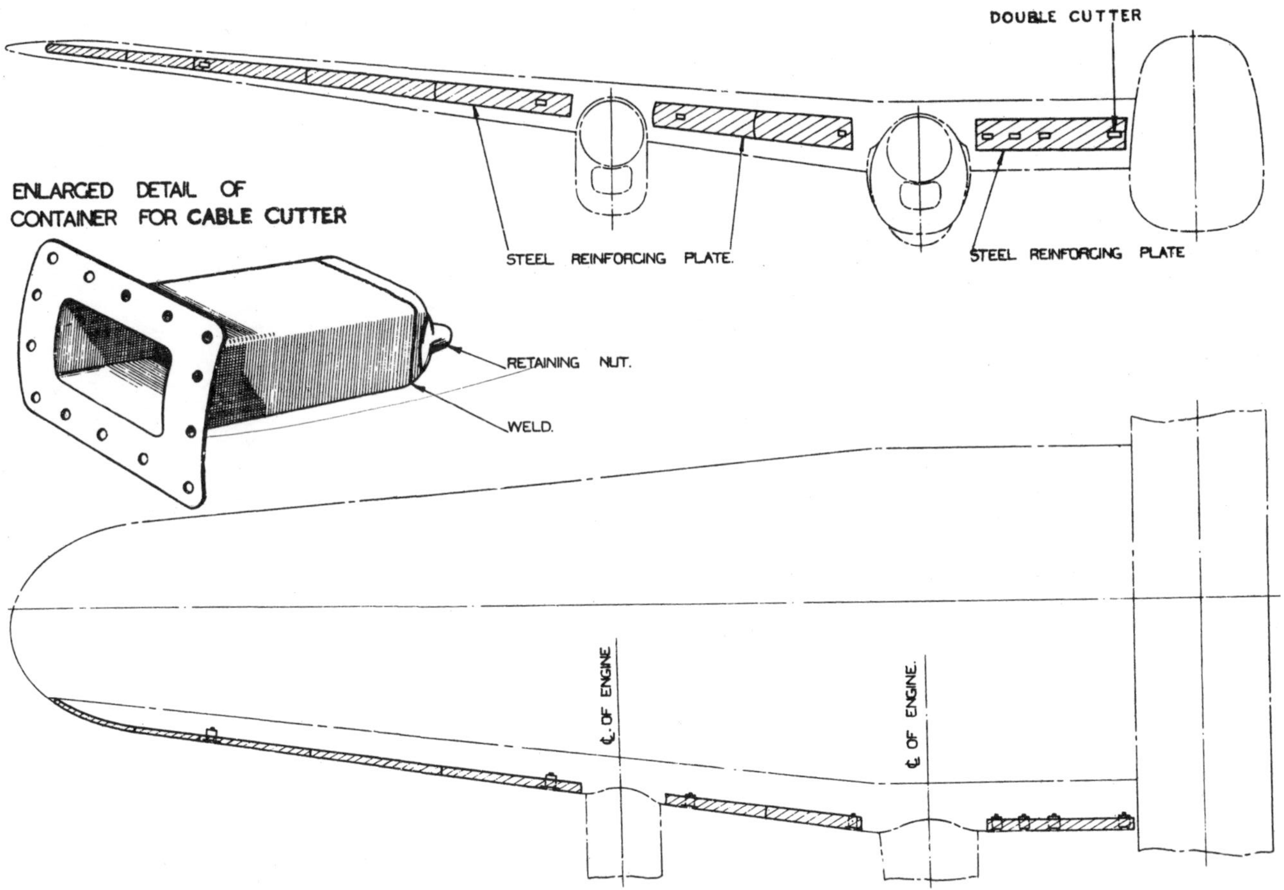

FIG. 9

A.P. 2062 A | VOL. I | SECT. II

DOUBLE CUTTER

STEEL REINFORCING PLATE

STEEL REINFORCING PLATE.

RETAINING NUT.

WELD.

ENLARGED DETAIL OF
CONTAINER FOR CABLE CUTTER

C. OF ENGINE

C. OF ENGINE

B.B.P. EQUIPMENT

FIG. 9